# Changes and Continuities in Chinese Communism

## Volume II: The Economy, Society, and Technology

Published in cooperation with the
Institute of International Relations,
Taipei, Taiwan,
Republic of China

# PART FIVE

# Economy

# 22

# Urban Economic Reform and the Shenzhen Special Economic Zone

*David Wen-wei Chang*

Chinese revolutionary leaders from 1911 to 1949, whether democratic or socialist in persuasion, wanted to build a modern and powerful industrial state in East Asia. On the one hand, the success of Japanese modernization provided the inspiration, and the United States provided the ideal democracy for Sun Yat-sen. On the other, communist victory in Russia after 1917 offered a new revolutionary alternative to Mao Zedong and his idealistic predecessors. Both Sun and Mao not only once cooperated but also agreed to make China strong enough to be treated with equality in the international community. Sun did not know the Western nations were not prepared to aid him, and circumstances forced him to accept assistance from Lenin in 1923. Mao, likewise, failed to realize until 1960 that Stalin was not prepared to help the People's Republic of China (PRC) become a strong partner. A new Sino-Soviet conflict eventually compelled him to reconcile with the United States in the 1970s. All of these twists of history help illustrate clearly one of the many Chinese genuine expectations, to build China into a strong industrial state capable of self-defense and with a higher living standard. The May Fourth movement in 1919 further demonstrated how young intellectuals were devoted to the same purpose through science and democracy.

Sun Yat-sen proposed an "industrialization plan" using Western capital and technology to convert China into an industrial state. Deng Xiaoping today is doing almost exactly what Sun wrote about some seventy years ago. However, Deng calls it Four Modernizations—in defense, science and technology, industry, and agriculture. Urban industrial development was also the central emphasis of Mao's revolution in order to speed up progress to catch up with Great Britain and Japan, for example. However, Mao again failed miserably. It has been Deng's task to revise Mao's timetable to achieve

A different version of this chapter appears as Chapter 6 of David Chang, *China Under Deng Xiaoping*, published in 1988 by St. Martin's Press and The Macmillan Press Ltd.

the success of modernization by the end of this century to give the nation a "socialist economy with Chinese characteristics." Deng has seen in his lifetime the failures of Sun and Mao, who both idealistically insisted on following either the U.S. or the Soviet model. Deng, on the other hand, wants to experiment in China his own way. His strategy of success follows two basic paths: enliven the economy at home and keep the nation open to the outside world.

## Introduction: Mao's Economic Failure and Deng's Innovations

When Taiwan and Hong Kong prospered economically, and when Mao's China in the 1970s was suffering from economic decline, reform became really a matter of survival for Marxism and the Communist Party in China. Intellectuals and youth were faced with a crisis of confidence in Marxism and the party. Deng in the 1970s, as he had done during 1961–1963, had to restore and reform in response to a new crisis for the party's survival. In three years, reform in rural China had succeeded, and experiments for urban economic reform were under way in 1984. Confidence slowly came back. Living conditions were so improved that Deng was ready to launch a greater urban economic reform plan.

The Soviet economic model had to give way. It did not effectively provide the incentive to work in China. Chinese people work harder only when working for themselves. Mao's policy after the First Five-Year Plan (1952–1956) further disrupted the normal inefficiency of the Soviet model. He made his worst mistake in communizing land in the late 1950s, contrary to the wishes of the party and his defense minister, Peng Dehuai, who begged him to discontinue the communes. A short-term policy revision soon followed to restore the economy between 1961 and 1963. When Mao got restless again three years later, he launched a new revolution to replace his loyal followers, to further radicalize the economic and political system. During the next decade, 1966–1976, he did not trust anyone except Lin Biao, his wife Jiang Qing, and a few others. He put up Dachai as a rural production model and Daching as an urban production model. Both models survived only two years under his hand-picked premier, Hua Guofeng, who had his own "little leap forward" during 1976–1978 and failed also. The nation was eager for a new economic model. And peasants themselves began to dismantle the commune system. Hua soon lost majority support in the Political Bureau of the party, and by 1978 he was on his way out as Mao's successor.

Deng's urban economic reform followed his success in rural reform. He had allowed a larger plot of land to each farmer, encouraged more sideline private production, permitted rural free marketing, improved individual income, and stimulated light industrial growth throughout rural China. In strategy, Deng made rural economic stimulation the cornerstone of urban industrial development.[1] After several years of new policy in economic

# Changes and Continuities in Chinese Communism

## Volume II: The Economy, Society, and Technology

EDITED BY

## Yu-ming Shaw

Westview Press
BOULDER & LONDON

*Westview Special Studies on China and East Asia*

This Westview softcover edition is printed on acid-free paper and bound in softcovers that carry the highest rating of the National Association of State Textbook Administrators, in consultation with the Association of American Publishers and the Book Manufacturers' Institute.

Published in 1988 in the United States of America by Westview Press, Inc., 5500 Central Avenue, Boulder, Colorado 80301

Library of Congress Cataloging-in-Publication Data
Changes and Continuities in Chinese communism.
    Contents: v. 1. Ideology, politics, and foreign
policy—v. 2. The economy, society, and technology.
    1. Communism—China—History.  2. China—Politics
and government—1949–    .  3. China—Social
conditions—1976–    .  I. Shaw, Yu-ming.
HX418.5.C473  1988      951.05      87-15928
ISBN 0-8133-7411-1 (v. 1)
ISBN 0-8133-7423-5 (v. 2)

Printed and bound in the United States of America

⊗  The paper used in this publication meets the requirements of the American National
    Standard for Permanence of Paper for Printed Library Materials Z39.48-1984.

6    5    4    3    2    1

# Contents

Parts One through Four (Chapters One through Twenty-one), covering the areas of ideology, politics, and foreign policy in Chinese communism, appear in Volume I, also available from Westview Press.

readjustment, restructuring, consolidation, and improvement, China seemed to have blazed a new trail in socialist development. Although full of theoretical contradictions within Marxist ideology, what Deng has done is what the Chinese people want as an alternative to Mao's failure in improving the people's living standards.

Deng launched his new urban economic reform because it was the main public sector of the economy. Forty thousand major enterprises under public ownership did not function effectively. The party's strong hand of interference in factory production, rigid administrative domination, and lack of purpose in enterprise initiative for production in the past 30 years had destroyed the real economic opportunities for growth at a satisfactory pace. Deng's Four Modernizations were in serious jeopardy unless the urban economy was stimulated. Maximum efficiency of enterprise production, individual enthusiasm for work, correct leadership in management, enterprise responsibility for planning in production and in marketing of goods, and desire for better income of all were all in need of drastic reform for a new trail of economic growth. Under Mao, "Politics took command." Under Deng, "Economics takes command." Under Mao the "Red expert" planned the microdetails for economic progress. Under Deng the "economic expert" is allowed to exercise greater leadership. After several years of unpublicized enterprise-reform experiments, the government in October 1984 declared its grand scheme of urban economic reform to be carried out in three years.[2]

Growth and expansion in industrialization are the key to transforming the economy. Western technology and science, capital investment, and management skill are among China's strategic needs. Therefore, one of Deng's long-term policies is to keep China open to the outside world. Chinese imports and exports will play a major part in the decades to come. The Special Economic Zones in the coastal areas will be the middle ground to bind China to the rest of the world. Among the four Special Economic Zones, Shenzhen is of greatest importance because of a variety of unique factors. First, Shenzhen is near Hong Kong, which is a part of the free world economy and which will be a part of China in 1997. Second, together with Zhuhai, Macao, and Hong Kong, Shenzhen will play a major role in the economic and technological development of the greater Pearl River Delta, scheduled for rapid industrialization when the oil of the South China Sea has been further explored and refined. Shenzhen represents a Chinese multiple-purpose innovation that will enjoy the easiest access to the outside world by air and by sea, while at the same time acting as a transmission belt for technology in the development of China's hinterland.

## Thirty Years of Unstable Political Economy in China

In a socialist state, politics and economics are much more combined as an integrated whole than they are elsewhere. Politics and policy from the political arena dominate economic development not by the science of economics but by the dogma of Marx, Engels, and Lenin. Records show that all communist states are doing worse than noncommunist states in economic growth. Political economy in the communist world has an entirely different emphasis, such as the law of value. Thus the operational, organizational, and structural aspects of the economy are sacrificed to ideological preeminence. As a result, political rulers remain powerful as decision makers and the citizens are powerless victims without opportunities to take initiative to maximize their own private income potential. Thus, the Soviet economic model has failed in the Soviet Union, East Europe, North Korea, and a few other socialist states as well. In the capitalist countries, greater productivity brings about a greater enjoyment of material life by all citizens, who have a far better material life than citizens in most of the socialist states. Politicians and policymakers in a capitalist state are much less able to dominate production and competition among the common citizens, who are able also to reduce inequality between rich and the poor in the necessities of material life. China has learned about economic wastefulness and the disadvantages of the Soviet model of socialism. China has also learned from its Russian big brother the painful experience of the Soviet economic aid cutoff in 1960 and the withdrawal of the 1,000 technicians, aid materials, and project blueprints. In short, as a loyal socialist member in the Soviet orbit, China paid dearly since 1949, especially in its sacrifices during the Korean War years. Chinese leaders found, to their surprise, that the Soviet leadership never intended to treat China as an equal partner or with trust and confidence. This fact led to mutual distrust between them in late 1950s and was a critical factor in Mao's radical economic policy. Mao was a restless person eager for quick results. Moderate and more rational colleagues failed to restrain Mao from his radical leftist policies because they, too, were shocked by their treatment at Soviet hands, whether under Stalin or Khrushchev. These reasons were part of the basic background of China's thirty years of instability in both politics and economics. The painful experience resulted in its backwardness behind Taiwan, South Korea, Hong Kong, Malaysia, and Singapore in economic development.

Deng had to reform the economic system. It could not be done, however, without some fundamental reorientation, first of all, in the political system and a new relation with economic development. To get a better perspective, it is worthwhile to quickly summarize the past thirty years of political and economic instability. This sequence of instability and changes can be divided into stages as follows: period of rehabilitation, 1949–1952; efficient growth with popular support, 1953–1956; Mao's economic disaster, 1958–1961; corrective adjustment, 1961–1966; political chaos and economic decline, 1966–1976; failure of Hua's "little leap forward," 1976–1978; and Deng's readjustment and reform, 1979 to the present. During all these years, the emphasis was on urban economic development or reform in order to quickly build a modern industrial state. The facts in the following pages will best illustrate the past instability and failure as well as significant achievements made in some areas under the communist regime.

In 1949 the communists inherited, of course, a bankrupt economy which did not have a large segment of modern industry. According to Beijing's statistics, production of grain (−25 percent), cotton (−48 percent), and peanuts (−60 percent), for example, were all below the production levels of 1937 by substantial percentages. China's production of steel, electricity, and coal were less than 1 or 2 percent of the world's total in 1949.[3] Upon achieving power, the communist government confiscated all segments of modern industries owned by former government officials and foreigners. All enterprises handed in their revenues to the government for unified control of expenditure. The state became responsible for allocating grain, cotton, and all industrial equipment. Such complete control reduced the need for currency and market exchange. By 1952, rehabilitation of war damage was largely completed. Production of steel and pig iron, for example, registered large increases. From 1952 forward, economic transformation accelerated during the next four years. The "state economy" owned by the whole people became the leading economic force. It consisted of enterprises taken over from the Nationalist government and new enterprises created after 1949. "Cooperative economy" was owned by the working people. And "individual economy" owned by the people privately still constituted a relatively free segment of the economy. These three segments coexisted in early 1950s. By 1955–1956, agriculture was transformed into rural cooperatives and production mutual aid teams.[4]

The worst crisis in politics and economics occurred in the late 1950s when Mao's leftist mistakes damaged the economy gravely. He was not satisfied with the speed of transformation into a socialist economy, including the handicraft industry, which still counted for nearly 8 million full-time craftsmen and women in 1955, and small businesses of traders and street peddlers, who supported nearly 3 million households in 1956. Between 1952 and 1967, strong emphasis was placed on economic growth in heavy industry at the expense of the living standard of the people. The rural population suffered most, while industrial workers were relatively better off. Grave imbalance was imposed on the people because of the concentration on capital accumulation and negligence of daily consumption. Therefore, growth achievements were made in spite of management and leftist mistakes, as shown in Table 22.1.

A defense industry was built up from nothing at all. The many new industries that were built in China's hinterland accounted for 36 percent of annual industrial output. In agriculture, large-scale irrigation projects were undertaken to make it possible to put 20 million more hectares of land under irrigation. Flood control measures were undertaken to improve water flow in the Yangtze River, Yellow River, Huaihe, and Pearl River regions. Grain output by 1980 reached 318,200,000 tons, which was almost double the production figure in 1952. In rural China, means of production were drastically improved, as shown in Table 22.2.

Although the nation's population nearly doubled between 1949 and 1982, China is today able to feed and clothe its people. The progress in education and road construction in rural China must be counted as a major achievement that has overcome some of the physical isolation in the countryside and

TABLE 22.1
Rise in the Output of Major Industrial Products, 1952–1980

|  | 1980 Output | Increase over 1952 |
|---|---|---|
| Cotton yarn | 2,930,000 tons | 4.5 times |
| Coal | 620,000,000 tons | 9.5 times |
| Electricity | 300 billion kilowatt-hours | 41.0 times |
| Crude oil | 105,950,000 tons | 241.0 times |
| Steel | 37,120,000 tons | 27.0 times |
| Machinery | 127 billion yuan in value | 54.0 times |
| Metal-cutting tools | 134,000 units | 9.8 times |

*Source:* China Handbook Editorial Committee, *Economy* (Beijing: Foreign Language Press, 1984), p. 40.

TABLE 22.2
Means of Production Improvement in Rural China Between 1952 and 1980

|  | 1980 Figure | Increase over 1952 |
|---|---|---|
| Tractors of all sizes | 745,000 | 570 times |
| Pumping equipment | 74,645,000 horsepower | 583 times |
| Farm trucks | 135,000 | 474 times |

*Source:* China Handbook Editorial Committee, *Economy* (Beijing: Foreign Language Press, 1984), p. 42.

illiteracy among rural people. However, progress would have been far more impressive if China had not gone through phases of economic disaster and political upheaval. By far, the disproportionate allocation of resources between heavy industry on the one hand, and agriculture and light consumer goods on the other, the blind following of the Soviet economic organizational model, and the ignorance shown in the search for faster industrial growth were all man-made policy mistakes. Several times economic readjustments were made to correct the government's own mistakes, especially during 1961–1963, 1976–1978, and 1979–1981, before the current long-term new policy of readjustment, restructuring, consolidation, and improvement during the Sixth Five-Year Plan (1981–1985). This zigzagging economic instability was caused by political instability, which itself was caused by blindly following the alien, inapplicable ideology of Marxism and the Soviet model of economic structure. Much time in the last thirty years was also wasted in political campaigns and mass mobilizations. A period of ten years was given to futile ideological battle among Communist Party members and factions during the Cultural Revolution. Everything suffered setbacks, including human sacrifice, educational neglect, and economic decline.

Hua Guofeng did not have anything new to offer to the nation, although he was eager to correct some of the political and economic mistakes of the previous decade. He did not make any changes at all on the ideological front. On the contrary, he depended on Mao's old prestige and political legacy to govern post-Mao China. He deliberately tried to imitate Mao's personal appearance to create his own legitimacy for succession. Hua failed to join hands with the Dengist reformers who had basic differences over Mao's personality cult, leftist ideology, class struggle, and so on. Therefore, a new round of political instability occurred during the policy struggle from Deng's return to power in 1977 until Hua's departure in 1981. Even after Hua's departure, antireform conservative senior leaders still remained within the party hierarchy. A retirement system had to be implemented after the party's Twelfth Congress to formally, or legally, separate them from the policymaking function. Nevertheless, they still interfere indirectly in political and economic policies. In short, political compromise and concern, or potential for instability, has always been a major factor since the communist takeover in 1949. Some purged party leaders whom Deng has rehabilitated refuse to relinquish their executive power in the economic sphere. They have been quite reluctant to accept fundamental but peaceful reform in recent years.

The urban economy has been placed at the core of Deng's reform in order to stimulate the economy at home and open the country to foreign technology and trade. The early measures of readjustment between 1979 and 1981 can be summarized as follows:

First, the relation between capital accumulation and consumer spending has been readjusted in a number of ways. Deng's policy included the raising of government purchase prices for grains and other sideline rural products and the lowering of taxes or exemption from taxes for all poor communes. Government-paid prices to farmers have been made even higher than the free-market prices for grain, cotton, and other products to stimulate the rural economy. The government buying prices, for example, rose 22.1 percent higher in 1979 than in the previous year and another 7.1 percent in 1980. In two years, the government spent 48 billion yuan in higher-price purchasing. Furthermore, farmers are allowed to grow anything they see as profitable in order to increase production. On average, a peasant gained 89 yuan during 1979–1981. Farmers were encouraged to exercise greater production initiative. They could do anything they wished after the government's quota purchase was fulfilled. With extra income, peasants have begun, among other things, to build additional housing units and to buy sewing machines, radios, watches, and other goods. In urban areas, 26 million people found new jobs during 1979–1981. Wages and bonuses for industrial workers in 1981 were increased by some 25 percent on the average, from 614 yuan in 1978 to 772 yuan in 1981. As in rural areas, more housing construction took place during 1979–1981, from 30 million square meters per year previously to 220 million square meters of housing for the three-year period. National income distribution between capital accumulation and consumption is shown for a four-year comparison in Table 22.3. In socialist countries, the living standard is controlled by government allocation. China after 1949 never placed people above heavy industry and capital construction.

TABLE 22.3
Accumulation Versus Consumption in National Income Distribution, 1978–1981 (percentages in 1981 prices)

|      | Accumulation | Consumption |
|------|--------------|-------------|
| 1978 | 36.5         | 63.5        |
| 1979 | 34.6         | 65.4        |
| 1980 | 32.4         | 67.6        |
| 1981 | 30           | 70          |

*Source:* China Handbook Editorial Committee, *Economy* (Beijing: Foreign Language Press, 1984), p. 52. See also *Beijing Review*, no. 5, February 1985, p. 4.

Second, a new policy of faster growth of agriculture and light industry has increased and enriched the supply of consumer goods in rural areas, reversing the practice of the previous thirty years. The implementation measures were as follows: (1) ensuring the policy independence of rural communes, production brigades, and teams in their production decisions through a system of contractual obligations for the duration of long-term contracts; (2) diversification of production specialization and sideline production through encouragement of the rural free market for commercial exchange; and (3) subsidies to rural sideline production through price supports. These policies induced more peasant enthusiasm to produce for their own assured greater income. For example, grain production reached an all-time high of 332,120,000 tons in 1979. Even terrible floods and droughts in both north and south China did not prevent grain production from reaching 318,220,000 tons in 1980, the second highest since 1949. The value of gross agricultural output was augmented by an average of 5.5 percent during 1979–1981. The same high rate of growth was true for cotton, oil-bearing crops, forestry, animal husbandry, and fishery. Light industry in the 1979–1981 period received larger sums of government loans for expansion. For the first time since 1949, light industry grew faster than heavy industry. Thus market commodity supplies suddenly increased. Annual retail sales jumped up by several times in 1979, unique in comparison to any single previous year and more than the entire decade of 1960s. Heavy industry was purposely reduced in growth rate through control of resource allocations. A comparison between them is shown in Table 22.4. During 1979–1980, because policy emphasis was on improving living conditions, tax exemptions and financial subsidies reduced government revenues. Because of the practical difficulties of slowing down capital construction and other government administrative costs, a huge deficit occurred for both 1979 and 1980 for a combined total of nearly 30 billion yuan. This deficit in turn caused inflation and price hikes, which were controlled effectively in the following year through budget revision to assure needed economic and political stability.

Third, greater effort than originally expected was needed to readjust the economy after 1981. A new policy was adopted to continue the readjustment

TABLE 22.4
Proportion of Light and Heavy Industry in Gross National Output Value, 1978–1981
(in percentages)

|      | Light Industry | Heavy Industry |
|------|----------------|----------------|
| 1978 | 42.7 | 57.3 |
| 1979 | 43.1 | 56.9 |
| 1980 | 46.9 | 53.1 |
| 1981 | 51.4 | 48.6 |

*Source:* China Handbook Editorial Committee, *Economy* (Beijing: Foreign Language Press, 1984), p. 54.

for five more years during the Sixth Five-Year Plan (1981–1985) and even beyond. Drastic economic changes through policy guidelines and specific steps finally came in October 1984 when massive urban economic reform measures were announced. The reform thrust called for changes in the following specific areas:

1. Creation of a dynamic socialist economy in China;
2. Invigoration of policy as the key to restructuring the national economy;
3. Creation of a planning system to foster development of a socialist commodity economy;
4. Reform in price system and utilization of all economic levers for competition in production and management efficiency;
5. Separation of government from enterprise in the latter's internal decision making and operation through "enterprise autonomy and internal collective decision making";
6. Institutionalization of responsibility and accountability through wage differentials and salary reward;
7. Development of diverse economic forms in both domestic and foreign economic exchanges;
8. Training of "a new generation of cadres" and managerial personnel for the new socialist economy; and
9. Strengthening the party leadership "to ensure the success of reform."[5]

The Sixth Five-Year Plan has been completed (1981–1985). And the Seventh Five-Year Plan was offered to the party conference of September 1985. For future rapid growth, emphasis is given to coordinating the three segments of the economy: the public command economy, the collective economy owned by groups, and the individual economy. Creation of a price system and a wage system in relation to enterprise reform, capital accumulation, and consumption is being pushed forward meticulously. Faster economic growth is cautiously expected during the seventh plan, 1986–1990. But rapid growth, or even a real takeoff in economic production, is confidently expected during the 1990s. Even then, however, the living standard in China is not expected to go beyond a per capita annual average income of US$1,000 by A.D. 2000. Without doubt it looks as if China's gross industrial and agricultural output value will be quadrupled over its 1980 level. There seems to be an enormous self-confidence on the part of the Chinese leaders in the "inherent superiority" of the socialist system and the control of its productive potential. The command sector of the economy, fully subject to national planning, is looked upon as the socialist weapon to prevent the rise of "economic anarchism" which disrupts the "unregulated free enterprises" of the West. This is the Chinese rational and theoretical claim. Of course, the truth is that there is today no such "anarchist economy" in any of the capitalist states of the West, including even Japan in Asia, a close neighbor of China.

The most difficult part of the reform seems to be the government's ability to create a workable and more efficient economic management institution consisting of good banking, a credit system, inflation control, wage and price relations, and the like. Will China eventually have a market economy under socialist planning? Or will it remain a socialist economy with a less regulated but insignificant rural consumer-oriented "free market"? Much depends on the political leadership beyond Deng and his immediate followers. The Chinese leadership attempts to combine the virtues of both the socialist and the capitalist economic systems. Can they be combined without contradictions in ideological inconsistency? Such a combination was predicted by Chen Yun at the Eighth Party Congress in 1956:

> As regards planning, the bulk of the industrial and agricultural output of the country will be produced according to plan; but, at the same, a certain amount of production will be carried on freely, with the changing conditions of the market as its guide and within the scope prescribed by the state plan. . . . This kind of market under a socialist economy is in no way a capitalist free market, but a unified socialist market. In the unified socialist market, the state market is the mainstay and attached to it is a free market of certain proportions under the guidance of the state that supplements the state market.[6]

It remains to be tested in China's future economy whether Chen Yun's theoretical prescription is possible or not in actual practice. In fact, China tried in 1958 to decentralize a number of centrally operated enterprises and place them under local government management. The practice did not seem to produce positive results. In short, the Chinese economy before 1979 had revealed similar defects in common socialist practices. These defects relate to whether the central government directly manages certain enterprises or puts them under local control while it remains in command of unified planning itself. In the case of Chinese past economic failures more specifically, the defects were overcentralization, extreme egalitarianism, and bureaucratic inefficiency.

In the current economic reform of the managerial system, the government has been very cautious. It began with limited "enterprise decision-making autonomy" in 1978 in six enterprises in Sichuan province. The number was increased to 106 in 1979. Eighty-four of them were state-owned enterprises, and the other twenty-two were under direct management of the central government. The general stipulations in those experiments were indicative of still strong control by central directives or planning. An enterprise could not market its products in the free market, for example, until it had fulfilled the planned quota first.[7] Profit for the enterprise was possible only after other costs, such as depreciation, were first taken care of. The enterprise was allowed to hire only "the middle-level leaders without permission from their leading bodies."

In 1979, some 4,000 enterprises took part in some phase of autonomous management experiments. In the following year, more than 6,600 enterprises were in these experiments. They made up only 16 percent of some 42,000 large enterprises that were required by law to hand in their annual profit to the government. However, these 6,600 enterprises accounted for more than 60 percent of the value of industrial output and 70 percent of expected profits for the government. So the experiment was a quiet but significant undertaking. The result was obviously a success. For example, the eighty-four Sichuan local enterprises increased their annual output value by 14.9 percent over the previous year, and their profits by 33 percent, of which 24.2 percent was turned over to the government. However, small enterprises, which did not take part in the experiments, made even larger increases— 25 percent in output value, 120 percent in profits, and 100 percent in profits turned over to the state. Upon further analysis of 5,422 enterprises that participated in the experiments, decision-making decentralization did not have a significant impact on production.[8]

Another experiment in enterprise production and profit making was tried out in 1980 in Shanghai, Sichuan, and Guangxi. This time the experiment was the introduction of an income tax to replace profit to be delivered to the government. The enterprise was made solely responsible for either profits or losses. The State Economic Commission asked every province to select an enterprise for the experiment with the new tax approach in place of profits, to take place in 1980. In total, 191 enterprises throughout the country participated in this experiment. Toward the end of the year, the State Council issued "ten provisional" regulations to promote and protect socialist competition throughout the nation against local barriers. In short, urban economic reform had five years of quiet experiments throughout the country before its official formal inauguration in October 1984.

Among recent reform experiments was the government's effort to recreate an individual economy of craftsmanship, for example. As the reader may recall, the government in 1955 compelled all peddlers and owners of small craft shops to join cooperatives. More than 96 percent of them did, except those in far remote areas of the country. In 1962 there were still 2 million individual handicrafts people and traders within the cooperatives. By 1978 only 150,000 were left. However, between 1978 and 1980, under a new policy of rehabilitation and freer expansion, the number grew to 810,000. More jobs and competition will likely develop as individual economy is encouraged by the state. In short, competition and growth are related closely to the expansion of the free market. The reform policy is using the market mechanism as an auxiliary regulator of the economy, which is basically controlled by the state planners. Today in China consumer goods through market channels, as opposed to those handled by the government, account for 20 percent of industrial production and 25 percent of total retail sales. And one-third of total rural produce is being purchased by the government. The prospect appears that more market economy in China is most likely. Rural population will revolve around this freer sector of the economy.

Proper handling of the relations between government planning and market mechanism will always be crucial to managerial reform. The free market as a supplementary regulator of the socialist economy has alerted experts to call for "four different forms of management":

1. "Production carried out under mandatory state plans": This category applies to key enterprises and major products that are most vital to the people and the economy. Their output value "accounts for the greater part of the gross national product, although the types of goods are limited in number.
2. "Production based on changes in market demands, but limited to the specified categories in the state plan": This type of production includes a great variety of small commodities that are made by a large number of small enterprises and individual producers, but their total output value constitutes only a small part of the gross national product.
3. "Goods produced largely according to state plan but a small part of them are made by enterprises or individuals on their own": These goods are close to those of the first category.
4. "Goods made according to changes in the market demand, and only a small part of them are made under the state plan": These goods are close to those in the second category.[9]

Such a managerial and production structure is intended to integrate state guidance with the initiative of the enterprises. This pattern may be what Deng calls "socialism with Chinese characteristics." It will clearly be different from the rigid Soviet economic model, on the one hand, and also unlike the market economy of free capitalism. It will be a planned economy with a market stimulator. Whatever the reform result, planning and reforming in China is a difficult task, to say the least. With a large population and uneven economic development in a huge country handicapped by lack of transportation and technology, it is, indeed, a difficult if not impossible, task to attempt to ensure the end products of any intelligent planning exercise. However, the wishes of the people and their desire to improve their own living standards must be considered the best guides to planners. They cannot be ignored anymore.

In conclusion, political upheavals of the first thirty years under Mao's policy caused economic setbacks. In addition, the lack of market knowledge

TABLE 22.5
Composition of National Income in 1966 and 1976 (in percent)

|  | 1966 | 1976 |
|---|---|---|
| Total national income: | 100.0 | 100.0 |
| Industry | 38.2 | 43.3 |
| Agriculture | 43.6 | 41.0 |
| Building | 3.7 | 4.9 |
| Transport | 4.2 | 3.8 |
| Commerce | 10.3 | 7.0 |
| Proportion in net industrial output value: |  |  |
| Light industry | 47.2 | 40.4 |
| Heavy industry | 52.8 | 59.6 |

*Source:* Yu Kuangyuan, ed., *China's Socialist Modernization* (Beijing: Foreign Language Press, 1956), vol. 2, p. 8.

on economic competition and its proper growth aggravated political and policy debate between Mao, who wanted faster growth and a concentration on heavy industry at the expense of raising living standards, and the moderates, who failed to resist Mao's economic policy or to prevent class struggle. The people paid a heavy price for mistakes of the Communist Party leadership in the economic area, especially in the imbalance of economic growth and national income during the Cultural Revolution, as shown in Table 22.5.

Such officially imposed imbalance in national income composition naturally created general distress over per capita real income for each citizen. The management of economy simply violated the natural forces of supply and demand and the experience of growth success of the non-communist countries, and thus created economic problems unnecessarily. People can suffer for a while, in the interest of their nation. They can not forever make sacrifice after sacrifice for unnecessary revolutionary radicalism and egalitarian utopianism. Deng tried to correct the situation during 1974–1976. He was soon dismissed by Mao for political reasons in 1976. After Mao's death Premier Hua tried to correct some of Mao's mistakes. But he made other grave mistakes of his own, because he, in fact, did not have a new economic and political orientation of his own different from Mao's wrong economic approach and political dictatorship. The need for economic adjustment and reform during 1977 and 1978 was inevitably delayed pending the outcome of the leadership conflict between Hua and Deng in the early 1980s. Thus it is only fair to conclude that political instability and economic disaster from the 1950s to the 1970s were aggravated by repetitious conflicts between politics and economics caused by contradictions in Mao's own thinking.

From December 1978 to the present, Deng's economic reform has emphasized the following: increase of people's living standards, greater rural freedom for production and profit making, increase of light industry over heavy industry, reforms in the price and wage system, and import of foreign technology and capital investment. In short, Deng's reform has been to continue to stimulate domestic economic development and to bring China into closer contact with the rest of the world. Shenzhen and other special economic zones are the transmission belts in China's economic development through foreign investment, technology, and world trade. China has become an integrative experimental model of both socialism and capitalism, with practical emphasis on Chinese indigenous characteristics.

## The Case of Shenzhen as a Capital-Technology Transmission Belt in Chinese Economic Stimulation

In January 1984, Deng Xiaoping and his entourage came to the Shenzhen Special Economic Zone for an inspection, or study tour, in order to assess a policy decision on its future. Some members on this tour have been known to be very critical of this nonsocialist experiment. Rumors had it that many anti-Shenzhen senior leaders and generals had come to Shenzhen before and wept on sight. They felt Mao's cause of socialist revolution had been eliminated totally in Shenzhen. Special economic zones are "danger signals" against socialist revolution for the rest of the country. If such a sentiment was and still is that strong for some leaders, it is easy to realize how significant was Deng's tour in his later economic policy decision. At the end of his inspection on January 26, Deng wrote a one-sentence souvenir statement: "Shenzhen's development and experience has proved our policy as correct in the creation of such economic special zones." How relevant his tour was to the October 20, 1984, party decision on urban economic reform will be of interest for researchers to discover. In the short run, his tour convinced him and other "doubtful colleagues" to end their dialogue over Shenzhen itself.

Whether Shenzhen signals a conversion from socialism to capitalism will be speculated about later. My interview-study tour to Shenzhen in July 1985 made many things clear to me as far as this experiment itself is concerned. I shall first of all introduce certain relevant information about this experiment. Discussion will take place on laws and regulations concerning foreign capital and technology to be attracted to Shenzhen and on the profits made by foreign investors. There are a number of serious questions I raised in my interviews with many individuals, especially with the vice-president of Shenzhen University, Fang Sheng, who is an economist himself and who has traveled abroad and answered many questions similar to those I raised during the interview.

### Introduction to the Shenzhen Experiment

In the interest of international economic cooperation and technological exchange to advance socialist modernization in China, the Standing Committee of the National People's Congress in 1981 formally declared Shenzhen, Chuhai, Shantou, and Xiamen as four Special Economic Development Zones. Shenzhen is the largest of the four. It emphasizes industrial development, commerce, agriculture, and tourism. Shenzhen Special Economic Zone (SSEZ) is a part of Shenzhen Municipality along the seacoast and is closest to Hong Kong. It has a total size of 327.5 square kilometers and is already one of China's largest import-export centers. Whatever Hong Kong represents as a present and future economic advantage for China, Shenzhen is the direct transit port for this advantage. After 1997, Shenzhen and Hong Kong will easily produce joint prosperity because Shenzhen can bring all the available Chinese resources to assure its future expansion and act as a hinterland for Hong Kong. In the far distant future Hong Kong and Shenzhen may simply become one single commercial-industrial center for southeastern China. According to its current development blueprint, its population will grow from 250,000 in 1985, to 400,000 by 1990, and 800,000 in the year 2000. Since its start in 1981, Shenzhen has developed faster than expected. It is now the best known foreign investment center in China. As one rides through Shenzhen, he is easily overwhelmed by the number of high-rise buildings under construction vis-à-vis other buildings already in use by commerce and industry or as tourist hotels. There seem to be more buildings under construction than those already in use. Construction workers have actually come from all parts of China in addition to Guangdong Province. They have come through competition to claim their share of the profit in Shenzhen's fast development. So also have the many commercial firms here representing all twenty-eight other provinces and municipalities in China. It looks like an emerging twin city of Hong Kong or its suburb, only more sparsely occupied in population density. Of its 327.5 square kilometers in size, only 17.4 are in use. Some 310 square kilometers in the suburbs are still reserved for future development. Land development in Shenzhen began in 1979, and by 1983 it had cost US$824 million. In the Shekou industrial area of Shenzhen, transportation, the electricity supply, the water system, postal services, and telecommunications have been more fully completed (the industrial sector of Shekou is only 1.3 square kilometers). A larger area of 20 square kilometers, in addition to the presently used 17.4 square kilometers, is being rapidly developed as the site of a future industrial-commercial complex. Chinese industrial and construction workers in Shenzhen's development today are the best prepared or trained human resources. The city of Shenzhen (which is next to the Shenzhen economic zone) itself has a working force of 100,000. The other 100,000 selected workers came from other parts of the country. These 200,000 construction people have generally completed their high school education. In addition, they now receive on-the-job training for occupational specialization provided by various factories. For technologically advanced future development in human resources, in 1982 the central government in Beijing approved the establishment of Shenzhen University, which is totally financed by Shenzhen itself and is providing students with a curriculum that is Western in content and in depth (more to be said later). The university promotes basic research in Shenzhen's future technological development. Another major undertaking is the construction of a nuclear power station to supply electricity fully for all expected future industrial and commercial uses.

Both the land and water transportation systems between Shenzhen and the rest of the country and the world at large are being improved. The special zone will be fully linked with the national network of railroads and highways. Future harbor development for world trade and for South China Sea oil exploration is also under way. At present, 3,000-ton ships are navigating between Hong Kong and Shekou. Future harbors are planned to handle 10,000- and 100,000-ton ships for an annual total weight of 20 million tons of business. This will be especially useful to oil refining for crude oil from the South China Sea. The Shenzhen Navigation Company is presently in charge of water transport with most major cities reachable by water in heavy-tonnage ships.

In just four years from the start in 1981, Shenzhen became an attractive center to people of many interests—tourists, merchants, industrialists, academic experts, China specialists, and economists in particular. They have come to Shenzhen from all over the world to learn about recent Chinese economic development through the example in Shenzhen. For example, for economic investment reasons many foreign banks from Japan, North America, Europe, Hong Kong, and Southeast Asia have recently opened branch offices here at Shenzhen.

At present, there are eleven different laws and regulations that govern the economic activities in Shenzhen. Other laws are being proposed to deal with growing complexities. On the whole, foreign investors or Chinese from abroad can gain comparatively better profit and enjoy many extra privileges also. In enterprise management, foreign investors can operate independently or enter joint ventures with Chinese partners. They can invite in foreign workers, overseas Chinese, or Chinese experts from Hong Kong as technology or management advisers. If Chinese workers are preferred, the Shenzhen Worker's Bureau may take charge of the recruitment. Every enterprise can hire independently on its own to select the best workers through specific tests administered to job seekers. Both sides can negotiate wage contracts. Violations by Chinese workers of the contract may receive either a warning, mild penalty, wage reduction, or dismissal. According to the nature of the enterprise, wages may be determined by day, hour, or work piece accomplished.

Free of import duties, an enterprise may import equipment for production, repair or replacement parts, raw material, transport equipment, and other production material. Other useful daily articles may also be duty free, or as determined by contract, except whiskey and cigarettes at half of the lowest such duty charge. Products or semi-products made in Shenzhen are duty free for export. Income tax on enterprises is 15 percent. However, on investment amounts larger than US$5 million, or in advanced stages of new technology, or on investments of long-term duration, there will be tax reductions between 25 and 50 percent, or even total tax exemption for one to three years. Foreign investor's profit may be exempted from profit tax entirely or reduced if such profits are reinvested in Shenzhen for a new period of more than five years.

On investor's land use, the Special Zone Authority can satisfy needs on a variety of land uses as follows: industrial use for thirty years, commercial and residential for fifty years, school-medical for fifty, tourist for thirty, and agricultural-dairy for twenty. After the completion of a contracted period, new contractual extension is possible. Rates of charge on land use vary according to types of usage, location, and duration of contract per square meter per year. At present users will pay as follows in Chinese yuan (US$1 = 2.7 yuan): industrial, 10 to 30; commercial and residential, 30 to 60; tourist, 60 to 100, and agricultural-dairy, subject to contract negotiation. Enterprises that entered contracts on land use prior to 1985 have built into their contracts a reduction of fee in land use by 30 to 50 percent because of previous inadequate development in land quality or incompleteness in land development itself. Those enterprises having undeveloped land, slope, hills, or swamp area for varied purposes may receive a fee reduction for from one to five years at the initial stage. However, the land usage fee is subject to readjustment every three years to future users. But such fee readjustment each time will not be more than 30 percent of the existing amount. With regard to investment in the fields of education, cultural affairs, science-technology, medicine-health, and other social welfare, fees for land use will be substantially reduced. Any investment in the most advanced technology and in nonprofit fields will pay no fees for land use.

On the control of foreign exchange, all foreign enterprises must open their accounts with the Bank of China in the special zone or with such other foreign banks as approved and certified to do business by the Chinese authority. Foreign investors and businessmen, workers, or Chinese from Hong Kong and Macao may remit their properly earned profits after having paid their income taxes. Such remittances must be handled by the Bank of China or such other designated foreign banks in the special zone. Foreign enterprises seeking terminations of their business before normal expiration of the contracted period may transfer their capital to other companies, or remit it abroad after having applied for termination as regulated and having paid all financial debts.

On sales of products manufactured in the special zone, Chinese law requires such products to be exported unless otherwise entered into the contract in advance. If such manufactured articles are those which China imports, they are permitted to enter the Chinese domestic market on a fixed ratio as determined by domestic demands. On the whole, in any dispute or misunderstanding arising from the contract in a joint venture between the guest investor and the Chinese investor, both sides may negotiate for a solution on the basis of equality and mutual benefit. After failing in doing so, such disputes may then be submitted to the Chinese arbitration authority for mediation and arbitration. And finally, for the convenience of entry to and exit from Shenzhen Special Economic Zone by all foreign investors and those having residence in Shenzhen as merchants or alien residents, the Shenzhen authority provides them with special permits issued by the Shenzhen Special Economic Zone Development Company, or other permits with multiple-entry and multiple-exit privileges upon application by the foreign users.

In short, because of these privileges and protections as granted by the Chinese authority, foreign investment is increasing rapidly. Those coming for inquiry or contract negotiation are from various parts of the world, including the United States, Britain, Japan, France, West Germany, Norway, Sweden, Ireland, Australia, the Philippines, Singapore, Hong Kong, and Macao. Those who came earlier were from small companies. Many of them today represent large corporations, big financial combines, and multinational corporations. Enterprises that came earlier were generally interested in assembly work of imported parts by Chinese laborers. Today, joint ventures in investment or independent foreign investment have undertaken diversified production of heavy articles. Investment companies in production of a single article have varied in size from a few dozens of thousands of Hong Kong dollars to now tens of billions of Hong Kong dollars. During the first two and half years ending in June 1983, contracts with guest investors reached 2,300 in number and the total amount reached 1.2 billion Hong Kong dollars. Many investors have already gained big profits from some 120 kinds of products. U.S. Coca-Cola export from Shenzhen to Hong Kong and Southeast Asia is today making a considerable profit. Joint ventures between China and foreign investors in agriculture (chicken and pig breeding, etc.) are so successful that supply cannot meet demand at the present. In short, investment in Shenzhen seems to have little or no danger at all. Profit making is inevitable because the Chinese want this experiment to be a success. They will be able to regulate the development for mutual benefit as the Chinese government may see fit from time to time as provided by law.

One of the Chinese companies in Shenzhen, in particular, provides varied services to foreign investors. It is a multipurpose enterprise itself and the largest in the zone. This firm is the Shenzhen Economic Zone Development Company. It undertakes the task of attracting foreign investments and Chinese enterprises to the zone. Its specific functions include negotiations for foreign investment, cooperation among domestic enterprises, investment by foreign-Chinese joint ventures or foreign independent enterprises to develop land use, expansion of industry and commerce, building transportation and tourism, management of real estate, collection of land use fees, and promotion of export. This company helped negotiate and sign some sixty-six major foreign contracts before the end of 1983 for a total investment of 9.2 billion Hong Kong dollars. The company itself was divided into thirty-three specialized branches to pursue their separate divisions of labor. It will likely subdivide into more functional specializations according to future demands, as Chen told me during my interview with him on July 14, 1985. For example, some of the branch companies of the Shenzhen Economic Zone Development Company are doing the following:

1. Managing real-estate services together with guest investors to build a hundred or more offices or residential buildings no less than eighteen stories high and several hundred luxurious villas;

2. Developing and managing Wen Jin Du Industrial District's and Houhai Bay New District's cultural, residential, and preparatory tasks to create an Asian University in this new district;
3. Improving and developing the old city of Huacheng into a new commercial and tourist city with Chinese cultural-national characteristics;
4. Developing and managing Futian New Town, which is 30 square kilometers in size;
5. Developing a cement enterprise through a joint venture with Japanese investors to reach 200,000 tons of annual production in cement;
6. Developing and managing Honey Lake Holiday Resort;
7. Developing a science and technology exchange center; and
8. Other similar developments for a total of some thirty-three projects under thirty-three subsidiary companies of the Shenzhen Special Economic Zone Development Company.[10]

In short, this special zone development company is the official vehicle for both the Guangdong provincial government and the Beijing government to devise, develop, and coordinate many services in competition with other nonofficial companies. The creation of some thirty-three subsidiary companies is clearly for the purpose of avoiding a mushrooming growth of the head company's bureaucracy. As subunits, each branch company is competitively responsible for its own separate finance and accountability. Many of the Beijing government policy guidelines are transmitted directly or indirectly through the head office of this giant semi-independent company. The company itself is producing many advanced technology-intensive articles, such as satellite ground stations for television reception and microcomputers, together with the expansion of South China Sea oil exploration. Shenzhen is to be one of the unavoidable future oil refining and distributing centers. Petrochemical industrial development will be another potential in Shenzhen's future. At the present, a few of the major steps in contract negotiation required to invest in Shenzhen are as follows:

1. All prospective foreign investors must contact and negotiate with the foreign investment negotiation department or its branch offices in Hong Kong or with the Hong Kong office of Shekou Industrial Zone. Prospective foreign investors must submit the application forms and an investment proposal indicating purpose, list of products, size of capital, land to be used, methods of investment (independent, joint or cooperative in nature), justification for investment success, and a list of needs to be provided by the Chinese side.
2. The prospective guest investor will inevitably get a reply on whether the proposal is acceptable. If it is acceptable, there is an accompanying invitation for further discussion.
3. When agreement on the investment is achieved, the contract will soon be formally signed and delivered to the Shenzhen People's City Government for formal approval before it takes legal effect.

4. When approval is given, both sides then work out a list of articles or equipment to be imported from abroad for submission to the Shenzhen city government for approval. After that, the investor begins to arrange with Chinese customs authorities on materials to be imported.

5. Before the investment enterprise formally starts, registration with and certification from the Shenzhen Industrial-Commercial Administrative Commission are required. All the documents of approval, the enterprise charter, the names of the board of directors, and a copy of the registration certificate must be submitted.

6. Finally, later-stage activities can be performed by the special zone development company's trade service division on behalf of the foreign investors. The company's trade service division also may act on behalf of the Shenzhen city government on such matters as real estate transfer and land development fees.

### China Merchants and the Shekou Industrial Zone

At the western end of Shenzhen Special Economic Zone is a uniquely developed subunit all by itself. My visit to the area and interview with its deputy director, Chen, can be summarized succinctly on its specific differences from that of Shenzhen.[11]

The primary initiative of Shekou Industrial Zone came originally from China Merchants Steam Navigation Company, Ltd. (CMSN), which was established in 1872. In 1978, more than a hundred years later, it received approval from the Beijing government to expand and diversify its business beyond just shipping. As a government-owned corporation headquartered in Hong Kong, it applied for and in 1979 received authority from the State Council to build the Shekou Industrial Zone (SKIZ). This bold action of both CMSN and the State Council opened up a new chapter in CMSN's history. During its first six busy years, CMSN has brought to SKIZ advanced technology, foreign capital, and management experience from Hong Kong, Macao, and foreign states. Shekou is a small industrial port. It has finished its first stage of development. Its total area is 10 square kilometers, of which half is now usable land. SKIZ is administered by CMSN, which has converted a "desolate beach and barren hills" into a small port city. As a matter of fact, SKIZ is only one of many subsidiary operations and subcompanies built up in recent years by CMSN, which has total capital amounting to 8 billion Hong Kong dollars. Although it is a government agency under the Ministry of Communication, with its board of directors sitting in Beijing, CMSN operates out of its Hong Kong head office relatively free of any interference from the central government. Its business expertise is far advanced beyond the government's ability to participate effectively or constructively. In the development of SKIZ, CMSN has been singly able to bring to Shekou many foreign investors in a variety of fields through its Planning and Development Division. The SKIZ's success under CMSN is surely a matter of pride for the Chinese. This success has brought Deng Xiaoping (1984),

Hu Yaobang (1983), Zhao Ziyang (1981), and Ye Jianying (1980) to SKIZ to observe its progress.

In July 1984, the People's Guangdong Provincial Government ratified a plan to establish the Administrative Bureau of Shekou District. Although it is legally under the Shenzhen people's government, the bureau exercises its functions quite autonomously as a local administrative body in charge of SKIZ, Chiwan Bay, and Shekou town, a total land area of 14 square kilometers. The Shenzhen people's government has relinquished a large number of rights to the Shekou bureau, including rights to ratify investment agreements and contracts, import of materials, application for household registration by aliens and by overseas Chinese, and the right to set up its own public security, tax units, and postal services. Under the Administration Committee, SKIZ is governed directly by many subunits as functional service branches. SKIZ also has an Oil Service Office to act as a liaison organ to provide logistic services for oil exploration in the South China Sea and to "render consulting service to oil companies and contractors." Like Shenzhen special zone, SKIZ has a large volume of joint ventures and sole foreign investment ventures, or other cooperative enterprises. Forty-five percent of joint ventures involve investment of 21 percent from the United States, 17 percent from Thailand, 6 percent from Japan, 5.4 percent from West Europe, and 4 percent from Singapore. The categories of investment are as follows: industry, 77.5 percent; real estate and construction, 10 percent; commerce and service, 8.2 percent; tourism, 2.2 percent; and communication and transport, 1.6 percent.[12]

SKIZ had a population of 12,000 in 1985, and it was projected to reach 100,000 in the year 1990. Its future seems closely related to the development of transport for the oil resources of the Pearl River Delta and the South China Sea. Since 1983, the China National Off-shore Oil Corporation has concluded eighteen contracts with foreign oil companies, of which twelve are related to the Shekou basin. The second feature of Shekou is its emphasis on industrial production as opposed to the multiplicity of investments in Shenzhen or Chuhai.[13] The third feature of Shekou is the fact that it is being developed by a Chinese company without any sharing of authority with other domestic or foreign agencies, unlike the situation in Shenzhen. It is quite possible that Shekou will always be more efficient in management and more easily adaptable to domestic and international market realities or changes. The economic and managerial resources and experience of CMSN are totally behind the development in Shekou in competition with other economic zones, which are larger but less efficient.

## Special Economic Zones, Educational Reform, and the Prospect for Capitalism

One of the most outstanding features in Shenzhen's development is its newly founded Shenzhen University. It began to operate on September 27, 1983, when Beijing gave its approval to create experimentally a "new and comprehensive university." It is new also in educational methods, unique curriculum, and its mission of serving Shenzhen's future development. Under president Zhang Wei, there are four vice-presidents. I had the privilege of interviewing vice-president Fang Sheng, who is also an economist and has traveled abroad to observe economic development in several nonsocialist states. Incidentally, Vice-President Fang attended National Taiwan University before 1949. When I mentioned my university education in Taiwan, he assumed that I was from his alma mater and showed a special intimacy toward me. When I identified myself as not one of his fellow alumni, he quickly stopped talking about how well he was received abroad by graduates of National Taiwan University. He seemed disappointed not to be able to continue a sentimental conversation to express his friendship as host to an alumnus from Taiwan. He is a very thoughtful scholar and fundamental thinker on the most basic economic issues of socialism and capitalism.

Shenzhen University is situated at Yue Hai Men (Gate of the South China Sea) near the coast of Houhai Bay. It has a 250-acre campus. By the fall of 1984, the first phase of construction had been completed, consisting of a modern classroom building, an experimental factory, several student dormitories, and living quarters for the faculty. After the completion of the second phase of construction, which started at the beginning of 1985, there will be a total of 138,000 square meters of buildings of all kinds in use. To meet the needs of Shenzhen's long-term development, the university offers various practical specialties. Ten academic departments were in operation at the time of my interview: departments of Chinese language, foreign languages, economics, economic management, law, architecture, electronic engineering, applied mathematics and physics, structural and municipal engineering, and precision machinery and instruments. Other departments were being organized, including chemistry and chemical engineering, industrial arts and crafts, statistics, and tourism. The university at present is divided into four colleges: arts, law, natural sciences, and engineering and economic management. Students are trained with practical knowledge and ability to solve problems under varied conditions. Computers and foreign languages are especially emphasized. All students must spend five years for a B.A. degree. There are only about 1,000 full-time students at the present and some 300 cadres attending various special courses. Some 400 adults are studying on a part-time basis. In two years the university offered a variety of short-course training classes to 5,000 people. Graduates are likely to work in the coastal provinces of Guangdong, Fujian, Chejiang, and Jiangsu and the three metropolitan regions of Beijing, Shanghai, and Tianjin, because they have been recruited from these areas. Only Shenzhen students are admitted as part-time students for short courses.

Unlike other universities in China, Shenzhen University follows a Western credit system to allow students the latitude to select their courses in nonrequired areas. They can graduate early or late. Less capable students can thus stay on for extra time for their graduation. They can also change their major or minor fields. Some 40 percent of students receive scholarships. Student loans are also available for those from poor family background. All graduates will work in Shenzhen immediately after graduation. The government does not find jobs for them. Upon graduation, they must find positions for themselves and work in Shenzhen before later transferring to other locations. This is a new experience in China: Graduates will no longer be assigned to places with no regard for individual preferences, as China has done for the last thirty-five years. Another feature of Shenzhen University is its support for students to take part-time jobs while still in school: "running shops, restaurants, guest houses or small factories, selling books, magazines and newspapers, operating postal agency, cleaning grounds around the campus, working as assistants in the university's administrative departments and research centers."[14] The emphasis is on the student's self-management, self-discipline, self-dependence, and self-support to face the real world. Eventually the university will grow into a research institution to meet Shenzhen's development needs. There are several research institutes already in existence, including the institutes of special zone economic study, classical Chinese literature, comparative literature, structural engineering, new energy sources, Hong Kong and Taiwan literature, and biochemical experiments. The university is already moving toward graduate studies in such fields as industrial management and special zone economy. In short, the university is staffed with an imaginative and creative administrative leadership that is training a new generation of young people capable of meeting new economic growth demand in Shenzhen and other special economic zones and major coastal cities. Fourteen such cities were recently declared open to the outside world for investment, trade, and other activities.

As an economist, Vice-President Fang Sheng expressed his various conclusions concerning Shenzhen's economic future. In the lead article of the inaugural issue of the *Journal of Shenzhen University*, he said essentially that China's special zone economic development is intended to expand state capital under socialist guidance. It is an economy that is multifaceted in nature, allowing several sectors to coexist, with the "state sector playing the leading role and state capitalism enjoying priority."[15] He also predicted in the same article that "it is beyond doubt that there will be an ever broadening range of economic relation and collaboration between continuous economic prosperity, mutual promotion and mutual complementing, and work division."[16]

In my interview with him, he provided an historical interpretation of China's failure to meet foreign economic challenges since the nineteenth century: "From self-reliance and self-sufficiency, economic isolation, foreign economic imperialism, and finally, to certain historical limiting conditions since 1949, Chinese handling of foreign relations, in general, has been too narrow-minded until 1979." For a long time under socialism, China "had little or no knowledge in handling her economic relations with foreign countries," no experience to appreciate advanced foreign technology and foreign economic management skill. Poverty in China was aggravated further by "leftist ideology" and thus created a new isolationist policy after 1949. The Cultural Revolution made the situation worse. Vice-President Fang happily asserted that international economic-technological exchange and mutual dependence in recent decades has been a correct historic trend, according to the Marxist point of view. China should join it and promote the trend further. China's recent economic policy since 1979, has been, in fact, a real awakening to this trend. This new lesson is the fundamental reason for China's long-term opening of the nation to the outside world. The special zone is the focus of this intensified opening to the outside world, such as tax exemption, high profit percentage, and other favorable concessions in order to bring in foreign technology and management science. Chinese special economic zones are more than an effort to build up a processing industry for exporting goods; the most important point, he asserted, is to "open up a window to the outside world—a window of technology, a window of knowledge and a window of management." Chinese economic structural experimentation in the special zone is an experiment to train new people, to extend, if successful, to the rest of the nation this advanced new success. Many new experiments are "carried out without any prior knowledge." The main message, from the Marxist theoretical point of view, is to override the frozen concept that "individual economy" is inferior to "collective economy" and "collective economy" is inferior to "an economy owned by the whole nation." In the special zone all sectors coexist among enterprises owned by the nation (banks, postal service, etc.), cooperative enterprises, domestic joint ventures, joint Chinese-foreign ventures, enterprises owned wholly by foreigners, and others owned by private individuals. This "structurally unique" economy is so far obviously succeeding. All sectors are mutually dependent, mutually influencing, and competing, and each is full of vitality. The socialist sector, which includes energy supply, transportation, public utilities, and currency management, is controlled by the government. The sector of the joint venture consists of both socialist shares and foreign capitalist shares. So Shenzhen is a "mixed enterprise" or "mixed economy." Many of "our socialist laws and regulations" are applied to capitalist joint ventures. Thus such foreign-Chinese joint ventures become partially "a state capitalism." The wholly foreign-owned enterprises enjoy even more management autonomy in a socialist state. Except for taxes and expenses, all the profits belong to the entrepreneurs. However, such wholly foreign-owned autonomous enterprises are being guided, supervised, and licensed by a socialist state. In the final analysis, "Without socialistic national capitalism, there cannot be a special economic zone."

Furthermore, the vice-president added, the special zone economic "management structure" is basically "a combination of planning adjustment and market adjustment." The zonal economic structure itself and its management structure are part and parcel of an overall national plan. For example, zonal commodity production, marketing, transportation, and the like are basically under Chinese national planning. How to properly manage the planning adjustment and market adjustment is itself a planning problem—a theoretical problem to stimulate the Chinese economy at home. In the past, Chinese Marxist theorists perceived "socialist planned economy" and "Market adjustment" as mutually exclusive or "unmixable." Certain Marxist theorists denied market adjustment as functionally useful. They thus planted the seeds of China's economic failure in the past thirty years. Since 1978, China has begun to realize the utility of commodity production and the changes in the law of value. We learn to prevent blind economic development and, at the same time, not to neglect the usefulness of market adjustment.

China's special zone economy is an "advanced commodity economy." It grows in close relation with the future international commodity market. This fact will soon bring more understanding to Chinese policymakers to realize the inevitable commodity competition in the international market and China's need to respond to the international market challenge.

Vice-president Fang emphasized especially the need to dispose of one critical question: Is the special economic zone a capitalist development? He said that he had been repeatedly asked to respond during his travel to the United States. He kindly gave me a copy of his recently composed essay to reply to this question directly. We discussed some of the main points of this essay during the interview. He emphatically admitted that special zone development is in the interests of socialist China. It is a method to demonstrate the "superiority of socialism by learning the best of capitalism." In the special zone, China invites foreign investors to make a profit, which is a form of exploitation. However, the exploitation is in China's own best interest: to acquire foreign technology and to benefit foreign investors in order to advance China's Four Modernizations. This foreign exploitation takes place within certain limits, such as income tax and reinvestment. In practice, China makes the special zone economy serve the socialist economy in general, not the other way around.[17]

## Special Zones Benefit Both China and Foreign Investors

Many major questions can be raised about this new adventure undertaken by China since 1981. In fact, this scheme to stabilize long-term economic relations between a socialist state and all or any capitalist investors has never been attempted before by a socialist state. Why does China have to choose this path? Is this a stopgap approach or a serious experiment on China's part? What effects will it have politically if it fails? How well have the experiments been truly accepted by the leftist elements in the Communist Party? How can this experiment be related to democratization in China and the government's goal of quadrupling the national income by the year 2000? Special zone experiments conform to Deng's two revolutionary goals: (1) to keep China open to the outside world and (2) to stimulate the economy for growth. The pledge to these twin goals since 1979 has been so strong and so well accepted that it seems impossible for any future leadership to abandon it without unpredictable consequences. Even if setbacks and corruption should occur in the special zones, they would not likely reverse China's policy to remain open to the outside world. On the other hand, foreign investors have made long-term investment decisions when they came to invest in China. They are not able to withdraw easily under any adverse changes in Chinese politics. After a closer observation of this economic experiment one can easily relate the special zones to four long-term benefits: (1) foreign investment security and guaranteed profits; (2) assurance that foreign capital can be retrieved; (3) a gateway for technology and capital inflow; and (4) the internal need for continuity. These four "preliminary observations" are based on a long-term assumption that China needs a constant inflow of foreign technology and capital. It must allow greater investment competition for both profits and security to foreign investors. If one examines Chinese laws and regulations on the special zone experiment, he will find the above four observations are quite well supported. A simple explanation for each is suggested in the following sections.

### Foreign Investment Security and Guaranteed Profit

There are now some twenty-two separate pieces of regulation and legislation promulgated by both the National People's Congress and the provincial governments in Guangdong and Fujian. For example, the more important ones are the Law of the People's Republic of China on Chinese-Foreign Joint Ventures, Procedures of the People's Republic of China for the Regulation and Administration of Chinese-Foreign Joint Ventures, Interim Procedures for the Handling of Loans by the Bank of China to Chinese-Foreign Joint Ventures, the Income Tax Law of the People's Republic of China Concerning Chinese-Foreign Joint Ventures, and the Rule for the Implementation of the Individual Income Tax Law of the People's Republic of China. Other regulations may concern such matters as foreign exchange control over enterprises or individual income and profit, resident foreigners and foreign company representatives, export-import licensing, and foreign enterprise registration. These laws and regulations or procedures are fair, well intended, and so far well administered. The percentage of tax on profit is low and outflow of profit is quite easy. Joint ventures between Chinese and foreigners "to organize company, enterprise or other economic organizations" are to take place "in accordance with the principle of equality and mutual benefit and subject to approval by the Chinese Government."[18] Article 2 of the first piece of legislation passed by the National People's Congress (NPC) on foreign investment, in July 1979, declares, "The Chinese Government protects the investment of joint ventures, the profits due them and their other lawful rights and interests in a joint venture." The law carefully sets up the agency and investment commission to handle applications for such joint ventures. Foreign investors do not have to contribute more than 25 percent of the total capital to a joint venture. Such 25 percent of capital investment does not have to be in cash and can be in the form of "advanced technology and equipment that actually suit our country's needs."[19] All enterprises, whether joint ventures or not, must be governed by a board of directors agreed upon among the investors. The chairman of the board must be a Chinese and the rest can all be foreigners. The board "decides on all major problems" of the venture. The "net profit" is defined as that portion left after the enterprise has paid its income tax and set aside a reserve fund, a bonus and welfare fund for staff and workers, and the enterprise's expansion fund. This net profit shall be distributed among investors according to their share of contribution to the capital of the enterprise. The law encourages import of "advanced technology by world stand" by any joint venture through "reduction or exemption of income tax for the first two or three profit-making years." As a second attraction, the law stipulates that "a foreign joint venturer that reinvests in China his share of the net profit may apply for refund of a part of the income tax already paid." The Bank of China or its approved foreign banks in the special zone shall have rights as protected by law to take care of the financial transactions of all joint ventures. But enterprise insurance shall be provided by Chinese insurance companies, a protected right to earn premiums but also an obligation to compensate for any big loss. This itself is evidence of the sincerity of the undertaking and also an expression of self-confidence in providing security to all joint ventures. "A joint venture is encouraged to market its products outside China," and they "may also be distributed in the Chinese market." Finally, the same NPC law declares the methods of settling disputes between partners of joint ventures (1) by the board of directors or (2) through mediation or arbitration by a Chinese agency or any other arbitration agency mutually agreed upon among partners to the joint venture.[20]

According to the "Interim Procedures" of the State Council of March 13, 1981, the Bank of China shall handle a variety of loans to joint ventures, including (1) working capital loans on revolving funds for deficits; (2) loans for settlement of accounts when their production fund is tied up in goods; and (3) fixed asset loans when the joint venture needs to expand its business or to make more fixed-asset investments. Details on loans convince an observer that the Chinese government is very seriously involved in the irreversible success or failure of the special economic zones in which China cannot unilaterally change conditions to exploit foreign investors or joint venturers.

On income tax, the NPC promulgated its law on September 10, 1980. The law is quite similar to that of the United States. Taxable income is defined as the amount after all "deductible costs, expenses and losses." The rate of tax on joint ventures is 30 percent and a local income tax, 10 percent. Thus the total is 40 percent. When profit itself obtained from investment is remitted abroad, an additional tax of 10 percent is levied on the profit. The law exempts income tax or reduces it by 50 percent if a joint venture starts with a pledge "to operate for a period of ten years or more." In such cases, the enterprise must apply for its tax exemption or 50 percent deduction for the first three years. If investment is made in a low-profit region, it may gain an additional tax deduction of 15 to 30 percent for a period of 10 years after the first three years of tax exemption.[21] These are enough examples to illustrate how China is eager to have joint ventures with foreign investment partners even if its share is only 25 percent, and its taxes easily reduced or exempted. In short, because of its interest in acquiring advanced technology and exporting manufactured goods, China has established this unique special economic zone to benefit both sides fairly. Investment security and guaranteed profits are assured both in the existing law and also by contracts.

## Assurance of Capital Retrieval

Investment laws very specifically spell out the procedure for the retrieval from China of the original capital, profits made from such investment, and wages of foreign staff members and workers. All of these incomes can be remitted out of China as described by the laws. The best details in each case come technically from the contract itself of each joint venture, which can include any detailed conditions during the negotiation. The Chinese tax system is clearly designed to induce foreign investors to reinvest their net profits in more profitable new ventures. For a longer period of investment commitment, more tax benefit is still available. In short, China is prepared to tie down as much capital as it can get for as long as possible. If such a successful trend continues, foreign capital, equipment, and national gross income will increase with accelerating speed. Domestic employment, internal market development, foreign trade expansion, and new technological gains will be such that China will eventually be deeply dependent on the international economic network and trade transactions. On the other hand, without such unique special economic zones and investment tax benefits under law, foreigners would not be so easily attracted to China. And its Four Modernizations would not be able to count confidently on such foreign participation. Given all these factors and their critical consequences, it is easy to appreciate why China is institutionalizing in the direction of a long-term opening of the country toward the outside world. To provide strong confidence to foreign investors, China must allow easy retrieval of capital from the country by any investor.

## A Gateway for Technology and Capital Inflow

Any developing country has to be fairly successful in such things as economic growth, political stability, positive social trends, good internal transportation and communications, an ample power supply, a good human resource supply, and a better domestic consumption market before any foreign investor is attracted for fixed capital investment in the country. For example, Singapore and Malaysia are often considered safe and good places for foreign investment, but not the Philippines or Communist Vietnam and Communist North Korea. How could China attract many foreign investors soon after the death of Mao and when the country was still in political turmoil until Deng's resumption of leadership? Yet China must have foreign investment to finance its Four Modernizations. Foreign investment and modernization are inseparable for China to catch up with the rest of the world. Foreign capital and technology are critically needed to build up adequate transportation, energy supply, and the educational standard. There has been, until recently, little domestic market consumption to convince foreigners to invest in China. Deng Xiaoping's leadership skillfully thought out such a special economic zone scheme to provide foreign potential investors with a very attractive offer in exchange for advanced technology and cash in foreign exchange, or foreign exchange cash earned by China in the special economic zones. Furthermore, the joint venture itself may manufacture articles and heavy machines in the special zone for China's expanding domestic market for industrial equipment and consumer goods.

## The Internal Need for Continuity

Any visitor traveling in China knows it is a nation on the move. The Chinese people in both rural and urban regions demand a higher standard of living. Many Communists themselves are embarrassed that China's living standard remains too far behind Hong Kong, Taiwan, South Korea, Malaysia, and Singapore. Thirty years of communist misrule has been long enough to learn the lesson that the ideological leftist crisis of the Communist Party, especially during Mao's last ten years, has been responsible for the embarrassing economic consequences. Vice-Premier Deng Xiaoping during 1974–1975 had proposed his Four Modernizations even before Mao's death. Since 1977 he has naturally remained eager to again pursue his Four Modernizations. The people are eager to support rapid economic development and a higher living standard. Deng's leadership seems universally praised everywhere in China for (1) his dismantling of the commune system and his policy of allowing the peasants to help themselves economically; (2) his emphasis on economic stimulation to quadruple the national income by the year 2000; (3) his decision to reform the urban economic structure; and (4) the opening of the country to the outside world. The Chinese people expect more material improvement. More emphasis is naturally devoted to the success of light industrial progress to meet popular demands. This very fact will likely prevent any future successor to Deng from turning the clock backward. Therefore, the special economic zones, as a symbol of commitment and a vehicle to accelerate modernization, could only be abandoned with revolutionary adverse consequences for any future regime. There is today a "new revolution of rising expectations" in China.

Finally, this chapter has avoided a survey of economic difficulties and new crises resulting from rapid growth. Such a survey would require another long engagement. For example, China today is still unable yet to manage fast growth and inflation, the wage system and price stability, economic crime, and bureaucratic inefficiency. Above all, many experts at home and abroad are seriously concerned about future political stability after Deng's death and possible reemergence of factional leadership struggles within the Communist Party itself. Economic planning is currently under serious trial in terms of scope and depth. Competition between the relatively free market sector of the economy and the planned command sector is an ever-growing threat to the established guidelines of socialist development. Even if all proceeds as expected, it may require a decade or so for the socialist planners to build a coherent and integrated infrastructure of a new and experimental economic system. This new system is, indeed, a new model of its own, which Deng calls "socialism with Chinese characteristics." To this writer, it looks like a "halfway mixed economy" between socialism and capitalism.

## Notes

The author appreciates partial funding from the Pacific Cultural Foundation, Taipei, Taiwan.

1. See Ma Hong, *New Strategy for China's Economy,* especially chapter 2, "Toward a Rational Economic Structure," pp. 31–82 (Beijing: New Word Press, Foreign Language Printing House, 1983).

2. Xue Muqiao, *China's Socialist Economy,* chapter 9, "Socialist Modernization of the National Economy," pp. 234–265 (Beijing: Foreign Language Press, 1981). See also *Beijing Review,* no. 14, p. 8, April 1985.

3. The China Handbook Editorial Committee, *Economy* (Beijing: Foreign Language Press, 1984) (translated into English by Hu Gengkang, Liu Bingwen, and others), p. 3.

4. The number of peasant households absorbed into mutual aid teams or early private cooperatives by annual growth percentages between 1950 and 1956 were as follows: 1950 (10.7), 1951 (19.2), 1952 (40.0), 1953 (39.5), 1954 (60.3), 1955 (64.9), and 1956 (77.2). See China Handbook Editorial Committee, *Economy,* p. 19, 1984.

5. *Decision of the Central Committee of the Communist Party of China on Reform of the Economic Structure,* adopted by the Twelfth Central Committee of the CPC at its Third Plenum on October 20, 1984 (Beijing: Foreign Language Press, 1984).

6. *The Eighth National Congress of the Communist Party of China* (Beijing: Foreign Language Press, 1956), vol. 2, pp. 175–176.

7. Yu Kuangyuan, ed., *China's Socialist Modernization* (Beijing: Foreign Language Press, 1956), vol. 2.

8. Ibid., p. 48.

9. China Handbook Editorial Committee, *Economy,* pp. 68–69.

10. The thirty-three subsidiary branches represent the long-term development of the greater Shenzhen Special Zone. These thirty-three branch companies are Nan Shan Development Company; Zhan Hua Construction Material Company, Ltd.; Honey Lake Country Club; Shenzhen Golf Club Company, Ltd.; Su Fa Union Company; Tutian New Town Development Company, Ltd.; Hong Kong Restaurant; Shenzhen Railway Station Development Company, Ltd.; Head Company of Shenzhen Special Economic Zone Development Company; Shenzhen Classic Project Design and Decoration Company; Real Estate and Properties Company; Shenzhen International Arcade; Regal Freight Service Company; Shenzhen Lian Cheng (Wen Jin Du) Joint Development, Ltd.; Sang Hing Hong Filling Station, Ltd.; Shen Xi Building Decoration Company; Machinery Installation Division of Shenzhen Properties and Estate Company; Shenzhen Lian Hua Industry and Trade Company; Duacheng Development Company; Zhen-tung Air-Conditioning and Engineering Company; Xiao Meisha Beach Vacation Camp Development; Shenzhen Properties Management Company; Hua Hui Aluminum Fabricating and Engineering Company; Shui Bei Industrial District; China-Japan Automobile Engineering Company; Sanho Limited; Xin Fa Enterprise Company, Ltd.; Wan Lai Renovation and Furniture Company; Oriental Pearl Cooperation Development Company, Ltd.; Shenzhen Chia Tai Conti, Ltd.; Texaco Petroleum Products Distributor, Ltd.; and Shenzhen Cement Enterprise Company, Ltd.

11. My interview with the deputy director of the Shekou Industrial Zone took place on July 13, 1985, at his office. Chen himself was instrumental in Shekou's development. I am grateful to him. Some of the statistical figures and quotations in the next several pages have been taken directly from my taped interview.

12. *Shekou Investment Guide*, 1984, p. 18.

13. *Beijing Review*, no. 13, p. 23, March 1985, reviews the Chuhai development at the western end of the Pearl River Delta. Chuhai and Shantou are the other two special economic zones in Guangdong Province, while Xiamen, the fourth special economic zone, is located in Fujian Province.

14. *Shenzhen University*, a university publication, April 1985, p. 8.

15. Fang Sheng, "My View on Some Economic Problems in Special Zones," *Journal of Shenzhen University*, vol. 1, no. 1, 1984, pp. 3–7.

16. Ibid., p. 7.

17. Fang Sheng, "Is Chinese Special Economic Zone a Capitalist Development?—Answer to the Question of a Foreign Friend," p. 7. This was given to me to read during the interview. I am not aware of its publication outside of China anywhere yet.

18. *China's Foreign Economic Legislation (CFEL)*, vol. 1, no. 1 (Beijing: Foreign Language Press, 1982; second printing, 1984). It includes some twenty-two different laws, regulations, and procedures governing foreigners, their investment, income, and profit, whether in joint ventures or individually.

19. *CFEL*, vol. 1, no. 1, p. 2, Articles 3 and 4.

20. Ibid., p. 7.

21. Ibid., pp. 36–37.

# 23

# Economic Reform in Mainland China: Consequences and Prospects

*Chu-yuan Cheng*

## Introduction

More than eight years have elapsed since Beijing's leaders launched the reform in economic structure. Starting with the changes in farming systems in the rural areas, experimental reforms in planning and management in industry were also introduced between 1979 and 1983. In October 1984, bolstered by the initial success of rural reform, the Third Plenary Session of the Twelfth Central Committee of the Chinese Communist Party (CCP) adopted the "Decision on Reform of the Urban Economy." The overall program involves revamping the planning system, price, the function of the state organization, and the labor and wage system. The officially proclaimed goal of the reform was to move away from the highly centralized, excessively rigid, and grossly irrational system transplanted from the Soviet Union in the early 1950s and to establish in the People's Republic of China (PRC) "a socialist planned commodity economy with distinct Chinese characteristics."[1]

While the reform has generated short-run positive effects in the agricultural sector, it failed to invigorate the urban economy. Between 1984 and 1986, the laxity of macroeconomic control led to overexpansion in consumption and investment resulting in rampant inflation and budget deficit. The reforms have also bred corruption, large-scale fraud, and considerable uncertainty among segments of the population. Factional jousting in the party hierarchy has intensified as the schism between the conservatives and the reformists concerning the current program and the future course of the reform grows wider. Faced with the mounting social tension, the reformists have since 1986 slowed down the pace of transformation and reexamined the entire program.

The purpose of this chapter is to assess the consequences of the reform program on three major aspects: the macroeconomic effects, the microeconomic effects, and the social-political effects. It will also examine the fundamental problems confronting the reform program and probe the future path the reformists may have to travel.

## The Reform Programs

In the thirty years between 1949 and 1978, the economic system in Mainland China was a duplicate of the Soviet model. The entire economy was guided by a uniform national plan. The planning authority was concentrated at the top and imposed rigid norms and regulations on various regions and industrial enterprises. The state not only set detailed production plans, supplied materials, and marketed the products, but also took away most of the enterprises' profits and made up their losses.

Under this system, the whole nation was treated as a large corporation. All decision-making power was in the hands of government departments. The enterprises had no authority to run their own business and became mere appendages to the governmental organs. There was virtually no linkage between an enterprise's performance and its workers' and employees' remunerations. No one cared for the economic results of the enterprises. Having no voice in management, enterprise managers lacked the motivation to improve performance. As a result, by 1978, a quarter of the state enterprises had suffered chronic losses.

In resource allocation, capital goods were totally excluded from circulation and were directly allocated according to state plan. The bulk of consumer goods were strictly controlled by state commercial departments. Since the circulation of a commodity was organized along the lines of administrative division, people were restricted to carrying out business within the boundaries of their administrative areas. There were too many links in the chain, causing circuitous transport, excessive overhead expenses, and slow turnover. Moreover, since producers and distributors were out of touch with end users of the products, useless goods piled up in warehouses at the government's expenses. By the end of June 1978, official statistics showed that unsold products stockpiled in warehouses amounted to 200 billion yuan in value, equal to half of the annual industrial output value of the country.

The labor employment system was also irrational. Workers were arbitrarily assigned work by labor departments. Neither the enterprise nor the individual worker had any freedom of choice. The result was a mismatch of training and employment. Furthermore, those employed could not be fired. People metaphorically described the system as owning an "iron rice bowl." This system encouraged indolence and stifled the industrious. The result was overstaffing and low labor productivity.

In agriculture, after 1958, the 170 million peasant households were organized into 54,000 communes, each of which on the average consisted of thirteen production brigades, 108 production teams, 3,400 households, and 16,000 people. The communes, brigades, and teams were assigned plans for cropping as well as yield and delivery quotas for sale to the state. Similar to industrial setups, the peasants' rewards did not correspond to their work performance. The communes had apportioned income largely on a per capita basis, with work points accounting for only 10 percent of the calculations. This egalitarian policy weakened peasant motivation.

Under the commune system, China's agriculture remained stagnant. By 1978, twenty years after the communization, food-grain output per capita was only 318 kilograms, slightly higher than in 1957, yet it did not reach the prewar level of 330 kilograms in 1936. Per capita grain consumption was much smaller than per capita production. The average per capita food grain ration during 1976–1978 for the rural population was even lower than that in 1956 and 1957, right before the communization.[2]

In view of these problems, the Third Plenary Session of the Eleventh CCP Central Committee in December 1978 decided on the reform of the existing planning and management system in industry and agriculture. In the urban economy the mainstay of the reform was the devolution of greater authority to individual enterprises, in order to transform an enterprise into a relatively independent economic unit accounting for its own successes and failures. The experiment was first introduced among 100 industrial and transportational enterprises in 1979. By June 1980, the program involved more than 7,000 major enterprises, accounting for 60 percent of the gross value of the output and 70 percent of the profits of all state-owned enterprises. Under the new system, each enterprise could draw 15 to 25 percent of the profit made from production above its state quotas. The retained profit could be used to expand production, improve workers' welfare, and pay bonuses to the workers and employees. The firms could also engage directly in exports of their products and could retain a share of the foreign exchange for the import of new technology, raw materials, and key equipment. Moreover, the firms now had the right to recruit or dismiss their own workers, thus breaking the traditional "iron rice bowl system" of permanent employment.[3]

While reforms in the urban area were cautious and slow, the reform in the rural area was rapid. Beginning from the latter part of 1978, with the initiation of peasants, the "contract responsibility system" was introduced to gradually replace collective farming. While the land remains collectively owned, plots of land are now contracted to individual farm households for cultivation. There are two forms of the contract system:

1. *Baochan-daohu,* or contracting output quotas to individual households, with the production team conducting unified accounting. In this form, the production team contracts the collectively owned farmland to individual households for separate cultivation. The contracts signed between the households and the teams define the peasants' responsibilities, with the quota output surrendered to the production team for unified distribution among team members. This quota output is either shared between the team and the contractor or goes entirely to the contractor as a bonus.

2. *Baogan daohu,* or contracting output quotas to individual households without the team conducting unified accounting. This arrangement

has a pronounced character of individual family operation. The production team divides the collectively owned land and small farm tools among individual households. By contract, the household has to surrender to the team specific crops in specified amounts as payment of agricultural taxes and as contributions to the team's public accumulation and welfare funds. Apart from this, the household may grow any crop and treat the above-quota output as its own possession. In effect, under this system, the relationship between the production team and the farm household is not very different from the landlord-tenant relationship in traditional China.[4]

The contract system has quickly become the major form of organization in the countryside. By October 1981, 97.8 percent of the 6 million production teams had established some form of contract responsibilities system.

Compared with the previous system, the new farming system displays several significant improvements:

1. It changes unified management dominated by a few cadres to household management, each responsible for its own profit and loss.
2. Since the tax and procurement obligations for each household are fixed at the time of signing the contract, peasants are now in control of their own income. The more a farmer produces, the more he or she can retain for individual consumption. A linkage between reward and effort has been established, thus breaking the egalitarianism which stifled the peasants' enthusiasm and initiative for more than two decades.
3. The new system gives each household some flexibility in allocating its own time and resources and thus is more agreeable with local conditions.[5]

The implementation of the contract responsibility system activated peasant incentive and generated a positive effect on agricultural production. Between 1979 and 1982, the growth rate of agricultural output was 5.5 percent per annum, double that of the preceeding twenty years. In early 1983, the CCP Central Committee issued a new document entitled "Some Questions Concerning the Current Rural Economic Policies." The document reaffirms the superiority of the new system. For further consolidation and expansion of the system a new fourteen-point guideline was announced.

The most significant new reform is the separation of local administration from the commune management and the eventual abolition of the commune and the production brigade. Since 1958, the communes had performed the dual function of local government and agriculture management. In October 1983, the CCP Central Committee and the state council jointly issued a notice that stipulated that the basic administrative organizations in the rural area were to be separated from the communes to become township governments and villagers' committees. It also stipulated that the name "people's commune" be abandoned by the end of 1984, thus ensuring the demise of the ill-conceived system.

The party's new guidelines also encouraged peasant households to purchase machinery, small tractors, and small motorboats as means of production and transportation, to exchange labor between peasant households, to hire casual laborers and seasonal laborers, to run processing businesses relating to their products, and to develop into specialized households concentrating in certain kinds of production. By 1983 about 2 percent of the farm households had become specialized households.

In January 1984 and in 1985 the CCP issued two additional documents that put individual households instead of collectives at the center of rural economy and granted the peasants all kinds of freedom never before enjoyed since the start of the collectivization in 1953.

First, the duration of the contract, originally set at one to three years, has now been extended to fifteen years. The duration of contract for work in the mountainous and lake areas has now been extended to thirty to fifty years. Moreover, plants and forests thus contracted for can be passed down to descendants or transferred to others.

Second, peasants are allowed to transfer contracted land to other skilled farmers, build houses on contracted land, operate transportation services, and undertake construction projects.

Third, the contract responsibility system will be extended to state farms, with the final objectives of transforming the state farms into family farm cooperatives.

The advent of the contract responsibility system heralds significant change in agricultural operation. As peasants now have freedom to allot their time, they seize new opportunities to engage in processing specific products or in nonfarming activities. Some talented households sign contracts with the collective for a certain area of farmland, forest, orchard, fish pond, pastureland, or a processing workshop and engage in poultry and fish breeding, sideline-product processing, and small industrial undertakings. As prohibitions on business activities have been progressively lifted, peasants can acquire vehicles and boats to transport goods locally and even nationally, and they can set up business in town or in the rural areas. By early 1985, 4 million households, and 2.4 percent of all rural households, had become specialized households who no longer tie up their labor in farming. They are now viewed by the Chinese communist government as models for other peasants. Policymakers view them as a "new productive force" and the "key to rural modernization."[6]

In the urban economy, however, the initial reform failed to touch several fundamental problems of the urban economy. Among other things, the reform did not correct the irrational price system that failed to reflect production costs and market conditions. Generally speaking, prices of mineral products, raw materials, and energy are too low; state procurement prices of agricutural products since 1979 have been higher than their market prices, and prices of many products do not reflect their quality. The irrational price system has created numerous difficulties, including the following:

1. Because an enterprise's bonuses and benefits are now linked directly to profits, which are affected by the prices of their products, the reform is bestowing the fattest profits on those enterprises that enjoy arbitrarily high fixed prices, such as consumer appliances and many processing industries. However, the reform inadvertently punishes those industries whose product prices are deliberately set at very low levels, such as energy, transportation, raw materials, and mineral products.
2. Because state procurement prices of major farm products exceed their retail prices (under the state rationing system) the differences have to be subsidized by the state budget. The subsidies have soared every year since 1979 and reached 35 billion yuan in 1984, constituting an unbearable financial burden on the state.
3. Since there is no price differentiation for diverse quality, supply of high-quality products falls short of demand, and their output cannot be expanded. On the other hand, inferior products that are unsalable and overstocked flood the market, resulting in tremendous waste.[7]

To deal with these problems, the Third Plenary Session of the Twelfth Central Committee of the CCP in October 1984 adopted the "Decision on Reform of the Economic Structure," launching a sweeping reform of the urban economy. Key aspects of the decision cover the following four points:

1. *Reducing the scope of mandatory planning.* Under the new reform, the state will issue a plan for the production of major products affecting the national economy and the lives of the population. In 1985 the state economic commission decided to cut the number of industrial products under its mandatory plan from 120 to sixty and agricultural and sideline products from twenty-nine to ten. The number of goods and materials directly allocated by the state will be reduced from 256 to sixty. Besides the state-controlled products, there will be a guiding plan for a vast number of goods and services. Guidance on their production will be exerted through economic levers such as prices, taxes, credit, and other economic means.
2. *Delegating more decision-making power to the enterprises.* While continuing to work under the state plan, the enterprises will have the power to decide their form of management and to arrange their own production and sales. After paying taxes, they will have the right to keep the rest of their profit and use it as they wish. They are entitled to choose their own workers, decide wage and bonus systems, and set the prices of their products within the state guideline.
3. *To strengthen the function of enterprises, separation of governmental departments and enterprises.* In the past, governmental administrative organs always directly controlled enterprises, rendering enterprises powerless. The new reform guideline stipulates that from now on, governmental departments at various levels will, in principle, not manage or operate enterprises directly. Their function should be

concentrated in the formulation of strategy, plans, principles, and
policies in general economic and social development.

4. *Reforming the irrational price system.* In 1985, the first year of the price
reform, the basic policy was to relax price controls while readjusting
some prices. The reform will be primarily carried out in the following
manner: (a) The state monopoly on grain purchasing will be abolished
and replaced by contract purchasing. The purchasing prices of rice,
wheat, and corn within the quotas set by the contracts will be fixed
according to a 3:7 ratio, namely 30 percent will be bought at the
original state price and the remaining 70 percent will be bought at a
higher price. Grain not purchased by the state can be sold freely on
the market. (b) Fees for short-distance railway passengers and freight
transport will be raised. (c) The practice of fixing higher prices for
better-quality products and low prices for poor-quality products was
to be implemented in 1985. In general, the price reform is rather
limited because of the rising inflationary pressure on the commodity
market.[8]

## The Macroeconomic Effects

The economic reforms that started in 1978 produced mixed economic
results. While the contract responsibility systems in rural areas generated
a short-run positive production effect, reforms in enterprises failed to achieve
the proclaimed goals.

### The Production Effect in Agriculture

In response to the higher procurement price and the new contract system,
peasants in China rapidly expanded their cash crop production and achieved
notable results. Grain output rose from 304.8 million tons in 1978 to 407
million tons in 1984, for an annual growth of 4.9 percent, more than double
the growth rate achieved between 1957 and 1978. Output of cotton jumped
from 2.167 million tons in 1984, more than doubling.[9] The rapid growth
of the cash crop was partly due to the rise of the procurement price in
1979, but the freedom given to peasant households to dispose of above-
quota products also provided incentives to expand output.

Profound changes are also taking place in rural labor distribution. In the
last few years, about 100 million peasants have switched from grain production
to other lines of production such as poultry and fish breeding, sideline
products, processing, small industrial undertakings, transportation, and commerce. Among these, approximately 30 million peasants, or 10 percent of
the total labor force in the rural areas, are employed in small factories and
enterprises. About 17.6 million peasant households, or 10 percent of the
total number of peasant households, have switched from crop planting to
animal husbandry, flower planting, fish breeding, or other specialized undertakings. About 1.27 million peasant households are engaged in private
commerce. The institution of the contract responsibility system apparently

expedited the diversification. It has brought about sizable increases in the peasants' income. The average annual income for the peasants rose from 133.6 yuan in 1978 to 309.8 yuan in 1983, increasing 131 percent. The incentive effect of the contract responsibility system is quite evident.[10]

The new policy, however, also brought about many "hidden dangers," as the party document described—rapid decline of farmland per capita, excessive felling of trees, fragmentation of farmlands, and the deterioration of agricultural infrastructure.

Under the contract system, the land is assigned to peasant households according to the family size. A large family is considered superior to a small one in manpower supply and multiple cropping as well as in sideline operations. This situation rekindles the traditions of early marriage and a large family in the rural areas. The natural growth rate of population was 14.55 per thousand in 1981 and 14.49 per thousand in 1982, up from 10.7 per thousand in 1980. At this rate of growth, the total population would top the 1.3 billion mark by the end of this century, 100 million higher than the official target.

The new agricultural system also prompts a boom in housing construction. Official statistics showed that between 1978 and 1983, total floor space of new housing in rural area added up to 2.8 billion square meters.[11] Most of the new houses are built on good farmland. Between 1949 and 1979, because of capital construction and the alkalization of farm land, cultivated acreage in China had been reduced by 12 percent. Per capita land acreage in 1980 amounted to only half that in 1949. The recent house-construction surge further reduced farmland for cultivation. In Zhejiang Province of East China where the farmland per capita is only 0.7 mu (0.115 acres), the decreased farmland area in 1984 is equivalent to the total decrease of the previous three years; the farmland in Henan Province in Central China decreased by 1.5 million mu (247,000 acres) in 1984, 43 percent more than the average decrease of the previous 28 years, while the farmland in Shandong Province decreased by 730,000 mu (120,230 acres) the same year, 70 percent more than the previous year's decrease. In 1983 and 1984 farmland in the country as a whole has decreased by about 20 million mu (3.29 million acres) annually, equivalent to the area of farmland in Fujian Province. If no emergency measures are taken to halt the diminution, it is bound to pose a serious threat to agricultural development.[12]

The continued expansion of the rural population also increases demand for fuel, most of which comes from direct burning of stalks, wood, and animal manure. The supply of noncommercial fuel, however, is far below the growing demand. Some 30 percent of the rural households face a chronic shortage of fuel. To make up the deficiency, peasants collect whatever they can gather. There is a widespread felling of trees throughout the whole country. As a result of large-scale destruction of forests, huge mountain areas in northeast and southwest China have been denuded of vegetation. Each year erosion has stripped away topsoil and dumped millions of tons of silt into the rivers. An official survey indicates that in recent years, about

5 billion tons of topsoil have been washed away each year, and the loss of fertility through erosion is equivalent to the annual output of the chemical fertilizer produced in the country. Although the situation has existed for quite some time, the recent house-construction zeal has greatly increased the demand for lumber and thus accelerated illegal forest cutting. This produces a disastrous effect on the ecological environment and raises the potential for floods and other calamities.

Utilization of farmland also suffers from the fragmentation of land under the new system. Since the quantity and location of each piece of land are different, the contract system demands that each household be allocated not one piece of land but many small land parcels of different quality. On average, each household has contracted about ten pieces of land, thus making it extremely difficult to fully utilize them.[13]

Before 1984, land was contracted to each household for a period of three years. After three years, the contracted land could be slated for reallocation. The short tenure discouraged peasants from making long-term plans. Many have resorted to exploitative methods to reap maximum short-term gains by neglecting the preservation of soil fertility. Moreover, most of the rural infrastructures were collectively owned and managed. Decollectivization made repair and maintenance extremely difficult. Since 1978, the state investment in agriculture has declined by about half. Most peasants have spent their increased income primarily on housing improvements and consumer appliances rather than on production investment. In 1985 the sale of chemical fertilizer registered a 20 percent decline, and the application of organic fertilizer dropped by more than 50 percent. The lack of proper maintenance caused the rapid deterioration of dams, ditches, and reservoirs.

In view of these detrimental effects, the upsurge of agricultural output in the 1979–1984 period may prove to be a short-run phenomenon. As cultivated land continues to shrink and public and private investment fails to increase, agricultural output begins to take its toll. Food grain output in 1985 fell 7 percent, and cotton output declined by 33.7 percent, the sharpest drop in six years. Grain output for 1986 showed only slight improvement over 1985.[14] The earlier optimism that a responsibility system could solve the agricultural problem appears to be illusory.

## The Effects on Capital Investment

The delegation of greater discretionary authority to enterprises and local government causes a drastic curtailment of state revenue, which in turn has had serious consequences on the structure of Mainland China's investment program. State revenue as percentage of national income dropped from 37.2 percent in 1978, to 27.4 percent in 1981, and to only 25.5 percent in 1982. The reduction of state revenue and the mounting rise of state subsidies for agricultural products resulted in a huge state deficit. By the end of 1984, the accumulated deficit reached 45 billion yuan. To finance the deficit, the state has issued bonds of 17.5 billion yuan and incurred foreign debts by

TABLE 23.1
Capital Investment Within and Outside the State Budget, 1978–1984

| | Amount (billion yuan) | | | Percent (total = 100) | |
| | Total | Investment Within Budget | Investment Outside Budget | Investment Within Budget | Investment Outside Budget |
| --- | --- | --- | --- | --- | --- |
| 1978 | 50.1 | 41.7 | 8.4 | 83.3 | 16.7 |
| 1979 | 52.4 | 41.9 | 10.5 | 80.0 | 20.0 |
| 1980 | 55.9 | 34.9 | 21.0 | 62.5 | 37.5 |
| 1981 | 44.3 | 25.2 | 19.1 | 56.8 | 43.2 |
| 1982 | 55.6 | 27.7 | 27.9 | 49.8 | 50.2 |
| 1983 | 59.4 | 34.6 | 24.8 | 58.2 | 41.8 |
| 1984 | 74.3 | 40.4 | 33.4 | 54.4 | 45.6 |

Source: State Statistical Bureau, China Statistical Yearbook, 1985 (Beijing, 1986), p. 420.

more than 20 billion yuan. All these developments signify the loss of control by the central government over the country's financial resources.

The laxity of macromanagement led to the shift of capital investment from central control to local control. During the 1978–1984 period, capital investment outside the state budget grew from 16.7 percent of the total investment to 45.6 percent (see Table 23.1).

The dispersion of the capital fund has caused an overextension of the scale of capital investment. In 1981, the first year of decentralization, some 71,000 construction projects were started, 11,000 more than in the previous year. Of these 34,000 are duplicate projects. In 1982 capital investment rose by 25 percent, resulting in a critical shortage of construction material. In 1984 capital investment rose another 23.8 percent, far exceeding the state target.

The scale of investment was out of control in 1985, when it rose 42.8 percent over the preceding year, the highest since the Great Leap Forward (1958–1960). Many Chinese economists termed the phenomenon "the hunger for investment."[15] This blind expansion of capital investment has inflicted severe damage on the Chinese economy.

Most investment made by enterprises and localities has been concentralized in ordinary processing production capacity. Many of these investments are duplicates and wasteful, and they have been made by those seeking only quick profits. These duplicates compete with large enterprises for energy and raw materials. To support those newly built plants, many local departments have withheld raw materials for local enterprises. They even took measures to restrict or ban the movements of productive materials outside their territories. The newly created barriers constitute an antithesis to the economic reform, which aims at the removal of these barriers.[16]

Of the total capital investment, the share of nonproductive investment grew very rapidly. During the 1978–1985 period, while total investment rose 9.9 percent per year, nonproductive investment went up 15.3 percent per annum and productive investment rose only 6.6 percent. The bulk of the nonproductive investment was for residential housing construction. A survey of nineteen major cities reveals that during the 1983–1985 period, nonproductive investment accounted for 60 percent of the total investment, of which 70 percent was for the construction of residential houses. Many enterprises and localities used funds earmarked for technical transformation to build houses. The sharp decline of investment for productive uses is bound to have an adverse effect on future economic growth.[17]

Although energy and transportation are two bottlenecks of the Chinese economy, investment in these two sectors was crowded out by general investment. During the first half of 1985, when investment zeal was at the peak, investment for energy dropped from the 23.3 percent of total invested in 1984 to only 19.7 percent, and investment for transportation fell from 15.1 to only 13.9 percent.[18] The distortion effect on capital allocation is bound to hamper future economic growth.

The dispersion of investment also reduced the size of projects and thus the scale of operation. Statistics of ten major cities indicate that more than half of the construction projects in recent years have been very small, investing less than a half million yuan per project. Most of the plants built are suboptimal. For instance, the minimum scale of operation for a washer plant is 200,000 units per year. Yet of the 110 plants manufacturing washers in China in 1984, only nine reached this scale. The average annual output per firm was only 4,600 units. There are now more than 100 auto makers in China. The average annual output per plant was only 2,000 cars.[19] The minuscule scale of operations not only raises the production costs but also hinders technical innovation.

The ill effect of the current reform on capital investment was summarized by Zhao Ziyang in his report to the Fourth Session of the Sixth National People's Congress (NPC) in March 1986:

> Currently, not only the scale of investment tends to be excessive, the investment structure is also irrational, as manifested mainly in the low proportion of energy, transport, communications, raw materials, and other infrastructure, as well as the investment in basic industry. Other manifestations include a high proportion of investment in the ordinary processing industry and construction of a non-productive nature; as well as the fact that investments for renovation and remodeling activities are insufficient, with a considerable portion of such investments being used for capital construction. Failure to change such an irrational investment structure will result in either an uncontrollable general scale of investments, or the lack of sustaining power to develop the economy.[20]

## The Effects on Growth and Stability

The most crucial test of the current reform must be gauged by the records of the overall economic growth and stability.

Official statements in recent years tend to emphasize the reform's stimulating effect on economic growth. According to Zhao Ziyang, the average annual growth rate of the total output value of industry and agriculture

TABLE 23.2
Growth Rates of Agriculture, Industry, Total Product of the Society, and National Income,
1978–1986

| | 1978 | 1979 | 1980 | 1981 | 1982 | 1983 | 1984 | 1985 | 1986ᵃ | 1978– 1984 | 1952– 1978 |
|---|---|---|---|---|---|---|---|---|---|---|---|
| Total product of the society | 13.1 | 8.5 | 7.9 | 4.7 | 9.0 | 10.0 | 12.0 | 16.2 | 9.1 | 8.8 | 7.9 |
| Total output value of industry and agriculture | 12.3 | 8.5 | 7.5 | 4.6 | 8.7 | 10.2 | 14.2 | 16.4 | 9.3 | 8.0 | 8.2 |
| Agriculture output value | 9.0 | 8.4 | 3.9 | 6.6 | 11.0 | 9.5 | 9.9 | 13.0 | 3.5 | 8.2 | 3.2 |
| Industrial output value | 13.5 | 8.5 | 8.8 | 4.1 | 7.7 | 10.5 | 15.9 | 18.0 | 11.1 | 9.2 | 11.2 |
| Light industry | 10.8 | 9.6 | 18.4 | 14.1 | 5.7 | 8.7 | 13.9 | 18.1 | 12.7 | 11.7 | 7.8 |
| Heavy industry | 15.6 | 7.7 | 1.4 | -4.7 | 9.9 | 12.4 | 14.1 | 17.9 | 9.6 | 6.6 | 13.6 |
| National income | 12.3 | 7.0 | 6.1 | 4.8 | 7.4 | 9.0 | 12.0 | 12.3 | 7.4 | 8.0 | 6.0 |

*Sources:* State Statistical Bureau, *Statistical Yearbook, 1984* and "Communiqué of 1985 Economic Plan"; 1986 figures from State Statistical Bureau, "Communiqué of 1986 Economic Plan," *Ren min Ribao* (People's Daily), February 20, 1987, p. 2.

ᵃ1986 figures are planned.

during 1981–1985 was 11 percent, substantially higher than the 8.2 percent achieved between 1952 and 1978.[21] The official claim, however, requires closer scrutiny.

From Table 23.2, it is evident that, with the exception of 1985 when the economy was out of control, the growth rate from 1978 to 1984 was not much different from that for the years 1952–1978. The 1984 growth rate was quite similar to 1978, the year before the reform. In 1986, since the policymakers decided to curb the excessive growth, the growth rates of agriculture and industry are quite in line with 1980, the year of adjustment. These comparisons would suggest that the growth pattern is basically a function of investment, independent of the institutional reform, although agriculture has been affected by the responsibility systems during the 1982–1984 period.

Moreover, the high rate of economic growth in 1984 and 1985, apart from being affected by the exceedingly high rate of investment, also stems from several other factors. First, since the worker's bonuses are tied to output, enterprises tend to exaggerate their production performance. Fabrications of statistics by local management has become a common practice. Second, for the sake of obtaining a higher reward, many enterprises have turned out large quantities of substandard products to fulfill or exceed the state quotas. These malpractices have helped to inflate the growth rates in recent years.

Furthermore, the rapid growth in 1984 and 1985 has been fueled by an excessive expansion of aggregate demand through three channels: the expansion of the consumption fund by raising wages and bonuses, the expansion of capital investment as discussed in preceding sections, and the expansion of banking credit. In the second half of 1984, the government stipulated that the amount of credit funds that could be independently and freely used by various specialized banks (the Industrial and Commercial Bank, the Agricultural Bank, the Construction Bank, and the Bank of China) would be fixed on the basis of the actual amounts of loans they had extended to peasants, individual business units, and state enterprises in 1984. The total amount of wages for each enterprise would also be fixed on the basis of the wage bill in 1984. In order to enlarge their base, banking units resorted to offering loans to customers, and the enterprises rushed to raise wages and bonuses indiscriminately to everybody. Consequently, the economy was fueled by inflated wages, huge loanable funds, and excessive bank notes. Total expenditures on wages and bonuses in 1984 rose 22.3 percent over those of 1983, and capital investment rose by 24.5 percent, all surpassing the 12 percent growth of national income. In 1985 expenditures on wages, bonuses, and capital investment increased 25 percent over 1984.[22] The result was a demand-pull inflation. The official retail price index for large cities went up 12.2 percent in 1985, but many Chinese economists challenged this figure. They believe that the inflation rate must be in the neighborhood of 25 to 30 percent.[23] The high rate of economic growth during 1984–1985 was thus achieved at the expense of stability.

## The Microeconomic Effects

The goal in microeconomic reform is to promote efficiency, invigorate state enterprises, and redress the distorted price system. Up to the end of 1985, very little had been achieved.

### Effects on Efficiency

Low efficiency has been a chronic flaw for all central-planning economies. The condition in Mainland China has been especially bleak. The backwardness of the economy, the lack of initiative and incentive of workers and managers, and the overstaffing and underequipment all have contributed to low efficiency. Reforms since 1979 have failed to turn the country around.

One major concern of the reformists has been that the number of state enterprises operating at a loss remains very high. Not only did large numbers of industrial firms suffer losses, but many enterprises in commerce and foreign trade did as well. Between 1983 and 1985, although the number of industrial firms incurring losses show signs of decline, the number of firms in trade that suffered losses registered a large increase. According to official statistics, state industrial enterprises operating at a loss constituted 23.7 percent of the total in 1979, 23.3 percent in 1980, and 27.1 percent in 1981, and the figure reached 30 percent in 1982. The situation improved in 1983 and 1984 but resumed its upward trend in 1985. In 1983 state subsidies for the loss in industry, transport, commerce, food, agriculture, and construction exceeded 20 billion yuan, and became an unbearable burden on the state budget.[24]

Other indications of low efficiency include the following:

1. Profit per 100 yuan of fixed assets in the state industrial enterprises dropped from 19 yuan in 1952, to 15.7 yuan in 1980, to only 13.4 yuan in 1983, the last year official statistics on losses were available.
2. Output per 100 yuan of fixed asset in the state industrial enterprises dropped from 134 yuan in 1952 to only 95.1 yuan in 1983.
3. Profit and tax revenue per 100 yuan of capital dropped from 25.5 yuan in 1952 to 23.3 yuan in 1983.[25]
4. The percentage of capital construction projects that was put into operation decreased from 53.2 percent in 1983 to 48 percent in 1984.[26]
5. Of the total production costs in industry, 80 to 90 percent were material consumption. Only 10 percent were wages and bonuses, compared to 40 to 50 percent in advanced countries.[27]

In 1985 many enterprises expanded production blindly and suffered losses either from the shortage of raw materials and energy or from the stockpiling of large quantities of substandard and unsold products. The upward adjustment of raw materials and intermediate goods increased the cost and thus the number of firms suffering losses.

*Effects on Management*

The failure of microeconomic reform has also been reflected in the sluggish performance of the key enterprises that constitute the backbone of the nation's industrial production.

A recent survey of the state Economic Commission shows that of the 1,300 key state enterprises only 195, or 15 percent of the total, have benefited from the current reform by upgrading their products, carrying out technological transformation, and yielding positive results in management. The overwhelming majority of state key enterprises, accounting for 65 percent of the total, so far have spawned little improvement in their management. The remaining 20 percent are plagued with a variety of structural problems and have been unable to turn even a small profit. Many have incurred substantial losses.[28]

According to Lu Dong, chairman of the State Planning Commission, the conspicuous problems of these key enterprises stem from the backwardness of their products, technology, and management. The machine-building industry, which provides equipment for the economy, continues to turn out outdated machinery. Only 20 percent of the machinery products are up to the international standards of the 1970s and early 1980s. The 156 key enterprises constructed with Soviet aid during the 1953–1957 period have become obsolete. Without a thorough technical revamping, there will be no significant improvement in efficiency.[29] The causes of the poor performance, according to Lu Dong are (1) the lack of decision-making power in production and management, (2) the excessive tax burden, and (3) the low depreciation rate. Despite the purported goal of delegating decision-making power to enterprises, the policy has not been effectively implemented. Profits retained by enterprises are rather slim. Average profit retention amounted to only 460 yuan ($150) per worker and employee. The lion's share of the retained profit was used for various compulsory obligations including the purchase of state bonds, contributions to energy and transportation surcharges, payment of workers' bonuses, and numerous contributions to the local community. The part used for technical transformation is negligible. The rate of depreciation, even after recent adjustments, still stands at only 5 percent. Most enterprises lack the ability to renovate their equipment.[30] How to invigorate these key enterprises will be the crucial test of the urban reform.

## Effects on the Price System

In the October 1984 decision on economic reform, redress of the irrational price system was considered a key to the institutional transformation. Beijing took several measures in 1985. The state monopoly on the purchase and marketing of food grains, cotton, and edible oils was replaced by a purchase contract system. Price controls on meat, vegetables, and other perishable foods were lifted, and free markets for these goods were allowed. Prices of small products for daily use were decontrolled and fees for short-distance trains were increased.

In industrial products, raw materials, and intermediate goods, the irrational price system remains basically intact. Prices for coal, petroleum, iron ore, and many mineral products are far below their production costs, while prices for processed products are very high, generating extremely high profits for the producers. The irrational pricing system hampers the development of energy industries, encourages the waste of energy and raw materials, and creates artificial disparities in profit distribution among and within industries, hampering the reform in management.

At present, the state planned price of coal stands at around 26 yuan per ton on average, or about one fifth of the international price. In many cases, production costs exceeded the selling price by as much as 10 yuan per ton. In 1983, 63 percent of the country's ninety-six major coal-mining enterprises were operating at a loss.[31] The lack of profits inhibits efforts to seek greater mechanization, better equipment, and safer working conditions. It also dampens the attempts to raise the resource-recovery rate.

Low coal prices also discourage energy conservation. The fuel efficiency rate for mainland China by the early 1980s was under 25 percent, compared to 57 percent for Japan, 51 percent for the United States, and 40 percent for the European Community countries.[32]

Moreover, the low price of coal acts as an indirect subsidy to inefficient enterprises such as small chemical-fertilizer plants and small building-material plants. Their continued existence not only constitutes a great waste in energy, but also hampers the general effort to cut deadwood and improve efficiency.

To redress this situation, the Chinese communist government has implemented since 1983 a three-tier price system for most industrial intermediate goods: a state planned price for material allocation within the state plan, negotiated prices which are well above the planned prices, and a market price determined by demand and supply. The existence of a planned price and a negotiated price, while providing some incentive for the producer, has created numerous new problems: (1) The multilevel system leads to unjustified disparities in competitive power. Firms that can obtain raw materials and fuel at a state planned price can achieve profit rates several times higher than firms that have to secure their supply at negotiated or market price. (2) Firms that produce products that can be sold at negotiated or market price will reap a much higher profit than firms that cannot. Since the profit rate of a firm has little relationship with its management performance but is the result of the irrational price system, no one cares for the improvement of efficiency. Instead, they have been concentrating their efforts on securing low-cost materials and increasing the number of products that are allowed to be sold at negotiated prices. The overall effect of the price reform in recent years was a steep rise of nonstaple food prices and a general rise in the price of coal and other raw materials. This in turn has triggered a chain reaction, touching off a series of price hikes throughout the industrial sector and an inflationary pressure on the economy as a whole. The high rate of inflation in 1985 sparked widespread speculation and complaints among urban residents, forcing the Chinese communist leadership to halt a new major price reform for 1986.[33]

## The Social-Political Effects

Since the reform touches almost every fabric of the society, its impact cannot be confined to the economic sphere. In certain aspects, the effects in social and political life are at least as profound as in economic affairs. The most notable consequences are the emergence of a privileged new class, the spread of the so-called "unhealthy tendencies," and the increase of social tension.

### The Rise of a New Class

The existence of a new class in a self-proclaimed "classless society" is not a new discovery. In 1956, in his diagnosis of the Yugoslavia system, Milovan Djilas first pointed out this phenomenon. Thirty years later, Tatyana Zaslavskaya, a leading Soviet economist, published an article asserting how economic opportunity in the Soviet Union is still determined, to a large extent, by a person's social status, connections, and geographic location. The Soviet system, according to Zaslavskaya, favors the children of well-connected government officials in Moscow by giving them the opportunity to attend the best schools and to have access to the best jobs.[34] The observations of these two communist theoreticians are fully applicable to the PRC.

For more than thirty years, the CCP has created an image as the paragon of an egalitarian society not only for equality in income distribution but also for opportunities in education and employment. This image has now disappeared. The creation of a new elite class has been proceeding apace since the commencement of the new reform.

The most notable change has come in the educational system. Under Mao's rule, for quite a long period, those selected for college enrollment were mostly the children of workers and peasants. Since 1977 the old system of elite education has been restored. Survey samples indicate that of the students enrolled in colleges in recent years, most come from cadre and intellectual families. Particularly, after the CCP decided to dispatch large numbers of students to study in Western countries, the great majority of students selected are offspring of the influential ranking officials. To date, about 14,000 students from mainland China are studying in the United States. According to Western diplomats, more than 150 are the children of "readily recognizable officials." Many more are children of officials who are not as well known. At one time, as many as six of the CCP's twenty Politburo members had children studying in the United States.[35]

Higher education leads to high party and government positions. When the CCP reshuffled its party and government organizations in 1985, large numbers of children and relatives of influential families were promoted to key positions. Of nine new cabinet ministers appointed in June 1985, at least three were relatives of leading officers.[36] The rapid rise of high officers' children in the political scene has earned them the rubric of the "Crown Prince Party" (Taizi Dong).

In rural areas, the emergence of the 10,000-yuan family also created a new elite class. The new policy that encouraged those specialized households to use their surplus capital to acquire more extensive land holdings, to set up transport companies, and to invest in local enterprise has also steadily enhanced their social and political power. Official reports reveal that some individual enterprises now each employ 500 or even 1,000 people.[37] A new rich peasant class has quickly taken shape.

## The Spread of Unhealthy Tendencies

Taking advantage of current reform, the majority of the party and government bureaucracy have engaged in some sort of "malpractice" enriching themselves at the expense of public interest.

Official documents and government reports disclose that party and government organs and cadres exploit loopholes in the reform to grab illegal wealth. Some set up branch companies to enable the cadres, staff, and relatives to become shareholders and enjoy dividends by using the funds, facilities, and personnel of the parent state companies. Many party and government organs and cadres form speculating companies buying up vehicles, steel products, imported consumer appliances, and all kinds of materials urgently needed by the society and resell them at high profits. In one famous case, the local officials of Hainan Island abused the autonomy granted them by the central government. They engaged in collective smuggling, spending more than $1.5 billion to import 80,000 automobiles and more than 2 million color television sets, as well as tape recorders and motorcycles. They then resold these goods at considerable profits in other parts of the country.[38] Chen Yun, chairman of the party's Central Disciplinary Inspection Commission, summarized the situation in his speech on September 24, 1985:

> Whenever we talk about the policy of opening to the world and invigorating the domestic economy, some party, government and military institutions, party and administrative cadres and their children swarm forward to do business. According to surveys in a dozen provinces and cities, since the last quarter of 1984, some 20,000 various companies have sprung up, a considerable number of which collaborate with law-breakers and unscrupulous foreign businessmen. Taking advantage of reforms, these new companies have been involved in all sorts of criminal activities, including speculating on the rise and fall of prices, engaging in illegal trade, offering or taking bribes and trafficking in smuggled goods. They also have resorted to deception, extortion, evading customs duties and selling counterfeit medicine and liquor, which are lethal to human lives, just for ill-gotten gains.[39]

In Jinjiang, Fujian Province, a dozen local plants engaged in producing counterfeit medicine for more than three years with the local party secretary's support. Their products sold in the whole country.

Other types of "unhealthy tendencies" involve embezzlement, bribery, tax evasion, and swindling. According to a report by the Supreme People's Procuratorate, its local organs investigated 28,000 economic crimes in 1985, almost 30 percent more than 1984. More than 260 million yuan ($81 million) were recovered for the state. The number of major crimes has soared in recent years. In Hebei, for instance, the provincial procuratorate handled more than 400 major crimes in 1985, more than triple the number of the year before. In Henan the provincial procuratorate discovered eighty-four important cases, fifty-three of them involving more than 100,000 yuan, and six involved a million yuan or more.[40]

The "unhealthy tendencies" became so prevalent that people in various localities, trades, and professions used whatever means they had to enhance their personal welfare at the expense of the state. The situation was so severe that in early 1986 the CCP Central Committee launched a national campaign to crack down on crime but found their orders mostly unheeded.

The root of this unhealthy trend stems from the fact that after thirty-five years in power, the "new class" in China has become powerful and corrupt. Economic reform without democraticization in a political system can only create new opportunities for the privileged class. In many cases, teenagers with parents or relatives in authority have gotten away with robbery, violent attacks, or rape, because their important connections protected them. A society without the force of checks and balances is bound to be corrupt and power abusing.

*The Intensification of Social Tensions*

The emergence of a privileged class and the widespread corruption and abuse of power have created high social tensions that may become a time bomb in the society.

The popular indignation was captured by Hu Qili, a member of the CCP Politburo: "In general, reforms in the past few years have promoted the development of production and have enabled urban and rural people to increase their income and improve their livelihood. . . . However, some people are still discontented with the situation. Their attitude can be described with the saying 'Holding up the bowl to eat meat, and putting down the chopsticks to shout abuses.'"[41]

Hu identified the "unhealthy tendencies" as the main source of people's discontent. "Some cadres, especially some leading cadres, have definitely abused their power by taking graft and bribes and engaging in other malpractices. This has aroused the resentment of the masses."[42]

Another source of social tension has been the polarization of income. Over the past few years, the rapid expansion of individual economy in the cities and the rise of specialized peasant households in the villages has substantially widened the income gap among various segments of the population and caused mounting social conflicts. A recent official survey reveals that the income of individual businessmen is much higher than workers and employees and sometimes several times that of the intellectuals, who receive no bonuses. While a professor in a college earned 150 yuan, or $50 a month, a man who runs a market stall may make 500 to 1,000 yuan a month. Many consider the situation unjust and irritating.[43]

To display their resentment, students in several major cities have staged large-scale demonstrations, partly to address their disapproval over the CCP's political and economic concessions toward Japan and partly to protest their poor living conditions. Workers with fixed income also expressed their deep discontent. In November and December 1985, bus drivers of the Beijing Public Transit System staged a protest by deliberately missing their bus schedule during the rush hours on winter mornings. The concerted action dramatized their bitterness toward the income gap between public bus drivers and private taxi drivers. More than 10,000 of them openly requested job transfers. Toward the end of 1985, several thousand workers in the Loyang Tractor Plant, the nation's leading tractor producer, staged a sit-in strike to protest the high rate of inflation and the discriminatory treatment of wages and bonuses among different enterprises.

Intentional acts of sabotage also occurred in the railroad systems when workers damaged tens of thousands of refrigerators and television sets that they could not afford to purchase.

Without proper action to deal with these expressions of popular resentment, the reform may lead to large-scale social disturbances as exemplified by Poland in the early 1980s.

## Problems and Prospects

During their beginning, the reform programs, while generating some initial stimulating effects on agriculture, have confronted numerous problems. Some problems have arisen from the programs themselves; many stem from human factors.

### The Lack of an Overall Blueprint

Economic reform is a complicated and intricate process. It requires a well-conceived blueprint to establish the goal of the reform, outline the concrete measures to achieve the goal, and set up a timetable for its progress. When Hungary and Czechoslovakia embarked on their reforms in the 1960s, they recruited a large number of experts in various fields to study problems involved in the original system and to formulate policies and measures to overcome these problems. Economic reform in mainland China was carried out immediately after the fall of the "Gang of Four" without a period of deliberation. From the very beginning, the programs have been carried out on a trial-and-error basis. The whole program was described by Tian Jiyun, a deputy premier of the state council, as "like wading a river by groping stone by stone for a solid footing on the riverbed." The lack of a well-defined, well-designed, comprehensive plan has undermined the confidence of cadres and people. No one knows what the next step will be. As a result, everyone tends to pursue only immediate gains. In the rural areas peasants adopt exploitative methods to maximize their current output, ignoring long-term investment. In the urban areas, the managers issue bonuses indiscriminately to every worker, because they consider the reform just a transitional action that may soon be rescinded whenever the political climate changes.

The lack of a comprehensive plan also inhibits the coordination of all programs. The reforms in wages, prices, bonuses, profits, taxes, and credit were carried out separately without a coordinated plan. Consequently, they cannot be brought into full play to support the macroeconomic adjustments.

### The Lack of Consensus

In Eastern Europe, economic reforms are partially motivated by a strong sentiment to resist Soviet suppression and exploitation. A general consensus exists in the ruling hierarchy. No such consensus has developed in the PRC. At the initial stage, strong resistance came from the radicals, who condemned the reform as betraying Mao's socialist ethics of egalitarianism, job security, and the doctrine of proletarian dictatorship. In recent years, a schism has formed between the reformists and the conservatives who consider the 1950s as China's golden age and want everything to return to the old days. They have drawn attention to the increasing income disparities among the population, the widespread speculating and profiteering, and other social evils and attributed the blame for these vices to the economic reform.

The lack of consensus surfaced in September 1985 when Deng Xiaoping and Chen Yun aired their contradictory views in the party's delegation congress. The open split between these two top leaders further aroused skepticism among party members and common people. A recent article in a government journal lists a series of questions: "Is socialist China undergoing a crisis of values? Have the economic reforms set off a general scramble for money and material things above all else? Has China's policy of opening to the outside world allowed decadent ideas and habits to creep in?"[44] The raising of these soul-searching questions signifies the loss of confidence among the population.

## The Absence of a Legal Framework

For almost thirty years, mainland China was a land without civil law. The reform introduces many new changes in the way of conducting business. Administrative controls are supposed to be replaced by economic levers. The relationship between enterprises and the relationship between enterprises and government agents will also be shifted from vertical to horizontal relations. Many of their transactions will be carried out by bilateral contracts. In rural areas, the contract system replaces unified purchases. A legal framework becomes indispensable for the functioning of these new setups.

Yet, the people of mainland China not only lack a legal system but also demonstrate general absence of a law-abiding mentality. Lawbreaking has become the symbol of power. Many "unhealthy tendencies" spring from the weakness of the legal system. The situation has essentially not changed during the years since reform began. Bo Yibo, vice-chairman of the party's central advisory committee, recently lamented that "a current rather outstanding problem has been the replacing of law by the individual and by power. Many problems in party style and social mood are closely related to the slackness in discipline and law." Bo appealed to the party's leading cadres "to acquire knowledge of law, to study constitution and all kinds of laws, and to act according to law."[45] Bo's statement bespeaks the fundamental flaw of the economic reform.

## The Influence of the Old Ideas and Old System

The current reform is being carried out in a transitional period when many elements of the old system coexist with the new ones and the old ideas still prevail in the society.

Among the deep-seated old systems, the system of "eating from the same big pot" (egalitarianism) still dominates Chinese thinking and behavior. For instance, the bonus system, originally intended to provide material incentive for industrious workers, has now been used as subsidies for all workers in the same unit regardless of individual contribution. Its stimulating function is totally lost. Today, the entire Chinese industrial system is still operating according to the old doctrine. The profitable enterprises have to pay exceedingly high taxes in order to keep the inefficient enterprises alive. In recent years, because of the income discrepancy between peasants engaging in rural industries and those engaging in farming, the government has introduced a new policy of collecting high taxes from industry to subsidize the peasants, a de facto revival of the "big pot" policy. The result is the depression of rural industrialists without any discernible improvement in farmer's productivity.[46]

Another deep-seated barrier, the barrier between different departments and between different localities, has also continued to the detriment of the development of a nationwide market. Despite numerous regulations, the old structure that separates economic activities in one locality or department from another has not changed. Many mandatory plans have continued to be carried out through the original channels in various departments and localities. Decision-making powers still remain concentrated either in local authorities or in monopoly companies. To increase their tax base, each locality in recent years took measures to protect its own interests by restricting or banning movement of production materials and consumer goods from its own territory to other territories. Some have even set up checkpoints along the borders to collect duties for goods delivered to other localities.[47]

The root of this kind of mentality and behavior lies in the fact that the poor and the weak in Chinese society have relied on public support for thirty-five years. They are accustomed to the "big pot." At the same time, those in power tend to view a department or a locality as their own kingdom and refuse to share their power with other units.

## The Low Quality of Personnel

Any successful reform, in the final analysis, can only be achieved through the devoted efforts of large numbers of energetic, well-educated, and well-intentioned people. Of the 46 million party members and 20 million government bureaucrats (many of them overlap), few are of this caliber. Although many top leaders see the reform as the only hope for China, many middle-echelon bureaucrats view the reform as a direct threat to their authority and privilege and seek to create trouble to stall the program. These vested interest groups form all sorts of protection nets to sabotage the reform. In some units where the reformists are a minority, the interest groups will lay out all kinds of schemes to bring them down. In recent months, the government news media have carried many stories to report how the reformists have been "shot off from the horse."[48]

Among the reformists, many are incompetent and lacking in willpower to persevere in the reform. Others cannot carry out the policies. The shortage of qualified personnel has been identified by Deng Xiaoping as the most critical problem. In a recent interview with some well-known Hong Kong capitalists, Deng concluded that "our weaknesses and difficulties in carrying out the Four Modernizations are mainly the lack of knowledge and qualified personnel. But sufficient knowledge and qualified personnel could not be obtained overnight."[49]

In view of these problems, the reform has since 1986 lost its momentum. In his report on the draft of the Seventh Five-Year Plan (1986–1990) to the

National People's Congress on March 25, 1986, Zhao Ziyang highlighted the following features of the reform for the five-year period:

1. Turning a great majority of enterprises into relatively independent entities fully responsible for their own profits and losses;
2. Promoting economic ties among enterprises and gradually establishing groups of enterprises in different forms;
3. Developing a socialist commodity market by reducing the varieties and quantities of products under state allocation and distribution;
4. Developing interregional and interdepartmental commodity circulation;
5. Expanding the markets for consumer goods and capital goods; and
6. Establishing a new system by which the state will gradually change from direct to indirect control in its management of enterprises.[50]

In short, mainland China will basically follow a path similar to the market socialism of Hungary and Yugoslavia. Experience in Eastern Europe shows that the programs outlined by Zhao are easy to formulate but difficult to execute.

First, to invigorate the 400,000 state enterprises, the inefficient units must be shut down. In a competitive system, a company that continues to suffer a loss must be closed. But in the PRC, an enterprise is the basic social provider. It provides not only jobs but also health care and pensions to its employees. If it is forced to fail, where will the safety net come from? If 30,000 inefficient plants have to shut down, how could the 15 million unemployed be accommodated?

Second, experience in Hungary shows that public ownership of the means of production is the root of inefficiency. When assets of an enterprise are publicly owned, no one actually contributes to its initial capital, and as a result, no one feels responsible for its utilization and maintenance. As all means of production are publicly owned, there is no genuine competition. Firms losing money can receive government subsidies to avoid bankruptcy. The system continues to protect the laggards and hampers the drive to introduce innovation. Unless private ownership of means of production is restored, no effective reform can be successful.

Third, combining a central plan with the market mechanism is also an extremely difficult task. The plan requires a command structure, while the market relies on spontaneous forces. In order for the plan goals to be realized, production units must comply with the plan directives issued from the top. But for products to match with consumer desires, consumer sovereignty is indispensable. There is no operational formula for a proper reconciliation of these two requirements.

Facing these dilemmas, the prospect of the reform appears to be rather bleak. After the setbacks in 1985, the CCP Central Committee has in 1986 put forth a new guideline of "consolidation, digestion, retrenchment, and improvement." The new tone is cautious and defensive. Many people in the PRC view the new guideline as a sign of retrogression. Some even openly express their desire to abolish some of the reform measures.[51] The social mood in recent months clearly reflects that the reform has encountered growing resistance. Its fate in the near future is far from certain.

## Notes

1. "Decision of the Central Committee of the Communist Party of China on Reform of the Economic Structure," *Beijing Review*, no. 44 (October 29, 1984), pp. I–XV.

2. Liu Baifu, "The Way of Agriculture," *Beijing Review*, no. 4 (January 24, 1983), pp. 14–17.

3. Huan Xiang, "On Reform of Chinese Economic Structure," *Beijing Review*, no. 20 (May 20, 1985), pp. 15–19.

4. Jan S. Prybyla, "*Baogan Daohu:* The Other Side," paper presented to the Fourteenth Sino-American Conference on Mainland China, Ohio State University, June 10–14, 1985, p. 14.

5. Ibid.

6. Thomas P. Berstein, "Reforming Chinese Agriculture," *Chinese Business Review*, March–April 1985, pp. 45–46.

7. Tian Jiyun, "Actively and Steadily Carry Out Reform of the Pricing Systems," *Renmin Ribao* (People's Daily), January 8, 1985, pp. 1–2.

8. Ibid.

9. State Statistical Bureau, "Communiqué on National Economic and Social Development in 1984," *Renmin Ribao*, March 9, 1985.

10. Ibid.

11. *Hongqi* (Red Flag), no. 20 (October 21, 1984), p. 25.

12. Xinhua (New China News Agency)–Beijing, April 2, 1986.

13. "Fragmentation of Contracted Land Is Disadvantageous to Production," *Renmin Ribao*, November 3, 1983, p. 5.

14. *China Daily News* (New York), April 18, 1986, p. 4.

15. Fang Gongwen, "Correctly Evaluate the 1985 Reform of the Economic Structure," *Guangming Ribao*, Beijing, March 22, 1986, p. 3.

16. *Renmin Ribao*, April 7, 1986, p. 2.

17. *Jingji Yanjiu* (Economic Research), Beijing, no. 11, 1985.

18. Ibid.

19. Ibid.

20. *Renmin Ribao*, March 26, 1986.

21. Ibid.

22. Hu Ji, "Carrying Out the Reform with Coordinated Policy and Keeping the Appropriate Growth," *Jingji Yanjiu*, no. 1, 1986, p. 5.

23. Qian Jiaju, a renowned Chinese economist has criticized the official price indices as understatement of the real inflation rate. See Qian's remarks in the fourth session of the Sixth Central Committee of the CCP, *China Daily News*, New York, April 14, 1986.

24. Wang Bingqian, Minister of Finance, "The New Subject of Public Finance," *Hongqi*, no. 7, 1984.

25. Yan Kalin, "On Bankruptcy of an Enterprise," *Jingji Wenti Tansuo* (Inquiry into Economic Problems), no. 12, 1985, p. 11.

26. State Statistical Bureau, "1984 Statistical Communiqué."

27. *Hongqi*, no. 21, 1985, p. 5.

28. *Beijing Review,* no. 48, December 2, 1985, p. 4.

29. Lu Dong, "Further Enliven Our Key Enterprises," *Hongqi,* no. 21, 1985, pp. 3–5.

30. Ibid.

31. Mei Jingyan, "Problems in Coal Prices and Suggestions on Their Reform," *Gongye Jingji Ganli Congkan* (Industrial and Economic Management Annals), November 1984, pp. 25–26.

32. Zhang Chunyin, "The Urgency and Complexity of the Coal Price Reform," *Caimao Jingji* (Finance and Trade Economics), June 1985, p. 48.

33. *Beijing Review,* no. 11 (March 17, 1986), p. 4.

34. *New York Times,* January 27, 1986, p. 4.

35. *Wall Street Journal,* October 29, 1985, p. 26.

36. They are Ding Henggao, minister in charge of the Commission of Science, Technology, and Industry of National Defense, who is the son-in-law of Nie Rongzhen, a retired Politburo member; Li Tieying, minister of electronics, who is the son of a Communist Party Central Committee member; and Zou Jiahua, minister of ordnance industry, who is the son-in-law of Ye Jianying, a retired member of the Politburo standing committee and the former chairman of the NPC.

37. *Wenzhai Bao,* Beijing, March 30, 1986.

38. *China Reconstructs,* no. 5, May 1986, p. 28.

39. *Beijing Review,* no. 41 (October 14, 1985), pp. 15–16.

40. *China Daily,* Beijing, March 8, 1986, p. 1.

41. *Zhongguo Xinwen She,* Beijing, April 17, 1986.

42. Ibid.

43. *New York Times,* August 22, 1985, p. 29.

44. Yi Xu, "Corruption: Why It Occurs, What's Being Done?" *China Reconstructs,* May 1986, p. 26.

45. Foreign Broadcast Information Service (FBIS), April 4, 1986, pp. K15–16.

46. Commentator's article, *Renmin Ribao,* March 1, 1986, p. 1.

47. *Renmin Ribao,* April 7, 1986, p. 2.

48. *Zhongguo Xinwen She,* Beijing, April 9, 1986; and FBIS, April 30, 1986, pp. K1–K2.

49. *Ta Kung Pao,* Hong Kong, April 20, 1986, p. 1.

50. *Beijing Review,* no. 13 (March 31, 1986) pp. 5–6.

51. Commentator's article, *Chongqing Ribao* (Daily News), Chongqing, April 20, 1986, p. 1.

# 24

## Foreign Capital in Mainland China

### Teh-pei Yu

Since the Third Plenary Session of the Chinese Communist Party's Eleventh Central Committee in late December 1978, the decision of the People's Republic of China (PRC) to undertake economic reform and economic development has been regarded as being of the topmost priority in the overall program of national reconstruction. Given that the amount of capital needed is too large and the level of technology required is too complicated to achieve China's target of quadrupling the 1980 level of industrial and agricultural production by the year 2000 on its own, the introduction of capital from abroad, together with technology, has become one of mainland China's main policies since the opening of its doors to the rest of the world.[1] As a consequence, the attraction of foreign capital and technology has played a very important role in China's economic development since the late 1970s.

In order to attract foreign capital, the PRC, like other developing countries, has adopted both fiscal and nonfiscal incentives. The fiscal incentives include tax deductions and exemptions in the industries that need to be encouraged. The nonfiscal incentives include the limited decentralization of foreign exchange control, a greater degree of autonomy with respect to investment decision making at the local level, and the expansion of financial operations associated with the foreign banking sector.

To that end, the PRC began by improving its legal system, and an example of this improvement is the Law on Joint Chinese-Foreign ventures, which was promulgated in July 1979. In accordance with this law, the Foreign Investment Commission and the Export and Import Commission were established. The former was to be responsible for examining and approving the contracts of Chinese-Foreign joint ventures, and the latter was to be in charge of the management of the export and import business. In March 1982, the two commissions were merged and put under the auspices of the Ministry of Foreign Economic Relations and Trade (MOFERT).

Subsequently, over the next few years, various laws and regulations relating to the inflow of foreign capital were announced from time to time, with the intention of attracting foreign investors. Such announcements included the Income Tax Law on Joint Chinese-Foreign Ventures and the

Tax Reductions and Exemptions for Special Economic Zones and the Fourteen Coastal Cities, among others.[2] More recently, in April 1986, the Law on All-Foreign Enterprises, in which special emphasis was laid on encouraging the development of wholly foreign-owned enterprises, was passed during the fourth session of the Sixth National People's Congress.[3]

After several years of making such efforts, the PRC has been successful to some extent in attracting capital from foreign countries as well as international organizations. However, at the same time, a number of unresolved problems and difficulties associated with the introduction of foreign capital have come to the surface, drawing the attention of the rest of the world.

Given the fact that the period of time that has lapsed since the introduction of foreign capital into the PRC is not really very long, and in view of the very limited and incomplete statistical records that have been published, we are not yet able to conduct a systematic and thorough analysis of the effects of the foreign capital inflow on the PRC's economy that is based on a theoretical framework. Therefore, the main thrust of this chapter is to emphasize the following: (1) the policies and plans regarding foreign capital recently adopted by the PRC; (2) the actual introduction of foreign capital; (3) the kinds of difficulties and problems faced by foreign investors doing business with mainland China; and (4) the prospects regarding the inflow of foreign capital in the near future.

## Policies and Plans Regarding the Introduction of Foreign Capital

### Development of Foreign Capital Policy

*Objectives, Strategies, and Principles.* Although the introduction of foreign capital has been emphasized since the Third Plenary Session of the CCP's Eleventh Central Committee in late December 1978, no definite and concrete policy description has yet been given. Looking at the law as the last legitimate part of the policymaking process, we can make an attempt to outline the PRC's policies regarding the introduction of foreign capital since 1979 by examining the relevant laws and regulations that have been announced in recent years.[4]

The objectives and strategies of the PRC's policies on foreign capital can be discerned mainly from the Law on Chinese-Foreign Joint Ventures and the Law on All Foreign-Owned Enterprises, as well as from various supplementary rules and regulations. It is obvious that, like other developing countries, the major objective of the PRC is to accelerate its economic development by promoting international economic cooperation and the exchange of technology, which will mainly come as a result of the inflow of foreign capital.[5]

The strategies adopted by the PRC for utilizing foreign capital have been multiple since 1979. First, foreign capital should be used to improve local technology and management expertise.[6] Second, because of the stipulation that joint ventures must export 70 to 80 percent of their products, the introduction of foreign capital plays the role of expanding the export market.[7] Third, by limiting foreign enterprises or joint ventures to buying insurance from the local Chinese market, the PRC has seen that foreign capital serves to stimulate the development of service industries, starting with the insurance industry.[8] Fourth, foreign capital has been used to assist in the exploitation of natural resources that are quite capital-intensive, especially oil and coal.[9] Fifth, with the intention of improving the investment climate, the inflow of foreign capital into the basic infrastructure, including the transportation and communication systems, has been encouraged.[10]

According to statements made by the PRC itself, the major principles associated with the policies adopted by mainland China since 1978 to attract foreign capital may be summarized as follows:

1. The principle of self-reliance is still uppermost in the minds of the Chinese, with foreign capital playing only a supplementary role. As a consequence, in the Sixth Five-Year Plan, the proportion of foreign capital in basic construction investment planned by the PRC was about 11.35 percent, which is still quite small.

2. The second principle concerns mutual benefit and guarantee of rights based on equal opportunities. To make this a reality, mainland China has attempted to promulgate a number of laws and regulations to improve the investment climate. The economic implication of such improvements is to help direct the new investors who are interested in investing in mainland China, whereas the legal implication is to protect the rights and advantages of the foreign enterprises that have already established operations in mainland China.

In recent years, foreign capital has been brought into mainland China in the following two ways.[11] The first is by means of foreign borrowing, which includes borrowing from foreign and international financial organizations as well as from the private sector in the form of commercial credit, export credit, and bond issues. The second way is by encouraging foreign direct investment, including joint ventures, joint cooperation, the joint cooperative exploitation of natural resources, wholly foreign management, compensation trade, and assembling and processing.

*Recent Policy Changes.* The introduction of foreign capital took firm root during the Twelfth National Congress of the Communist Party in September 1982, and the subsequent fifth session of the Fifth National People's Congress in late 1982 shifted China's emphasis on foreign capital inflow toward foreign direct investment in joint ventures and other undertakings from medium- and long-term low-interest loans.[12] At the National People's Congress session in late 1982, Premier Zhao Ziyang reconfirmed the importance of the PRC's economic relations with the rest of the world, and foreign direct investment was mentioned as being a major way of expanding the economic relations between the PRC and the rest of the world. Moreover, at a nationwide conference on the promotion of foreign capital held by the State Council in July 1983, even greater importance was attached to foreign indirect investment. Meanwhile, it was proposed that there should be a deemphasis on borrowing by means of short-term credit.

Among the many forms of foreign direct investment that have taken place, the joint venture has been encouraged most of all by the PRC by means of special incentives. A likely explanation for this emphasis may be expressed as follows. From a long-term point of view, joint ventures will bring in a stable supply of foreign capital along with advanced technology and management expertise that will be favorable to the technological reconstruction required in industrial development, especially for items that need a huge amount of investment or complicated technology or items that have the potential for export expansion. Therefore, a series of laws and regulations related to the management of joint ventures, taxation, and foreign exchange control designed to provide more incentives have been promulgated since 1979 in order to encourage the development of joint ventures.

However, the importance of attracting loans from the World Bank, foreign governments, and the private sector was mentioned in October 1985.[13] The foreign borrowing was encouraged with the proviso that the foreign loans had to be used in such a way as to bring in foreign exchange equal to 10 to 15 percent of the amount borrowed. In April 1986, during the fourth session of the Sixth National People's Congress, the Law on All-Foreign Enterprises was passed, implying that the wholly foreign-owned enterprises would become another important source of foreign direct investment encouraged by the PRC, in addition to the joint ventures in the near future.

### Plans Regarding the Introduction of Foreign Capital

As to the plans that the PRC has had in mind with regard to foreign capital, the Sixth and Seventh Five-Year Plans provide us with a simple basis for understanding the PRC's utilization of foreign capital.

It is estimated that the amount of capital needed in Mainland China's Four Modernizations program during the period between 1978 and 1985 is in the region of US$600 or US$700 billion. Details as to how much of this should be foreign capital are not explicitly given by the PRC. However, in the Sixth Five-Year Plan, mainland China planned to attract foreign capital amounting to US$20 billion, this sum being mostly concentrated in the years 1983 to 1985. As to the sources of foreign capital, US$14 billion was to be in the form of loans from the rest of the world and international financial organizations, and the remaining US$6 billion was to take the form of foreign direct investment.[14]

As regards the allocation of the foreign capital, US$15 billion was mainly to be used in developing the following items:[15]

1. the exploitation of natural resources, including petroleum, coal, and electricity;

2. basic construction, in the form of railroads, harbors, telecommunications facilities and industrial parks;
3. light industries, textiles, petrochemicals, metallurgy, machinery, electronics, construction materials, and tourism;
4. projects delayed or stopped because of the shortage of financial capital, such as Paoshan Steel.

The other US$5 billion was to be used to assist in technological reconstruction, particularly in replacing equipment in old enterprises and factories.

According to the Seventh Five-Year Plan (1986–1990), the PRC plans to absorb US$30 billion, this amount being some 50 percent higher than that proposed in the Sixth Five-Year Plan. Of this total, from US$5 to US$7 billion will be devoted to foreign direct investment, and the remaining US$23 to US$25 billion will consist of foreign borrowing.[16] In other words, although the PRC's leaders claimed in 1983 that they were going to shift the emphasis from foreign borrowing to foreign direct investment, in the Seventh Five-Year Plan foreign loans still account for the major proportion. The top priority with respect to foreign capital utilization will be the exploitation of energy and the improvement of transportation and communications.[17]

From the contents of the Sixth and Seventh Five-Year Plans, it appears that the PRC has tended to utilize foreign capital with the following objectives in view:

1. to improve the basic infrastructure in such a way that the investment environment can be improved;
2. to assist in the development of labor-intensive industries (over which mainland China has comparative advantages for export), such as textiles, electronics, and machinery;
3. to help the development of natural resources, especially oil and coal, in view of slackening production in existing offshore oil fields.

## The Introduction of Foreign Capital

*Main Incentive Measures Adopted*

Before the open-door policy was adopted in 1979, to a large extent the PRC's investment decisions had been formulated by the State Planning Commission and implemented by local government at different levels. Therefore, it was not considered necessary to provide incentive measures for domestic investments. However, since the economy was opened up to the outside world in 1979, the PRC's dependency on foreign capital as a basis for its economic development has forced it to adopt incentive programs to induce foreign investors to engage in business in mainland China.

Given that foreign investors have always been used to protecting their interests in business activities through the legal systems in their home countries, the first pressing need faced by the PRC in attracting foreign investment was to create an investment environment with a minimum of laws and regulations. With this objective in mind, a number of economic laws and regulations relating to foreign investments have been announced by the PRC since 1979 to legitimize the interests of foreign investors and the repatriation of profits with the hope of attracting a massive influx of foreign capital.

From these promulgated economic laws and regulations related to foreign investment and other steps adopted by the PRC, we can summarize the incentive measures as follows.

*Tax Incentive Measures.* Tax incentive measures, including tax reductions and exemptions include the following:[18]

Income tax: (1) Joint ventures with a contracted period of over 10 years will be exempted from income tax for the first two years after they start making profits. During the following three years, the normal income tax levy will be halved.[19] (2) Joint ventures in the agricultural sector or those located in underdeveloped areas usually make low profits compared with those in the manufacturing sector or more developed areas. They will be exempted from income tax for the first five years, and in the following ten years the normal rate of income tax will be reduced by 15 to 30 percent.

Provision for income tax: (1) Research and development expenditures related to agricultural production or scientific studies, and expenses related to the transfer of technology in energy exploitation, energy saving, transportation development, pollution prevention, and so on can be exempted from income tax, and the income tax rate is 10 percent in this case. However, if the technology transfer is significant with preferential terms, the related expenses can be exempted completely.

Unified industry and commerce tax: (1) An industry and commerce tax system similar to the one for ordinary domestic enterprises is adopted for Chinese-foreign joint ventures or foreign enterprises in the PRC. If joint ventures manufacturing products for export suffer deficits under ordinary operations, the amount of industry and commerce tax levied on them will be reduced to an appropriate level. (2) Neither import tariffs nor industry and commerce taxes will be imposed on machinery and equipment imported by foreign enterprises as contracted plant investment or by joint ventures utilizing their own capital. Moreover, neither foreign enterprises nor joint ventures will be charged on other necessary goods and raw materials that cannot be domestically supplied and that are imported by enterprises as extra investment.

Real estate tax: (1) Joint ventures or comanagement enterprises that regularly pay rent for land they use in mainland China will be exempted from real estate tax.

Personal income tax: (1) The professionals, experts, and civil servants sent by foreign governments or the private sector to assist in the PRC's development will get subsidies or allowances, and such income will be exempted from personal income tax.

*Greater Autonomy on Approval of Foreign Investment at the Local Level.* Although the open-door policy and the introduction of foreign capital have been emphasized since 1979, the work of screening and approving foreign investment contracts was still controlled by the State Council or institutions assigned by the State Council. In 1983, in order to induce the inflow of foreign capital by means of an increase in administrative efficiency regarding examining foreign investment contracts, the PRC started to increase the degree of autonomy with respect to the foreign investment decision-making process at the provincial and municipal levels.[20]

Under the new revised approach to screening and approving foreign investment, the provincial or municipal governments report the estimated amount of foreign capital they are going to use to the State Planning Commission, which has the right to examine and approve such an amount. However, with respect to those applications of joint ventures or foreign enterprises where there is already self-sufficiency in capital, energy, transportation, and raw materials needed in the production process, the provincial, directly governed municipality, and autonomous region authorities, as well as the agencies related to the State Council, are permitted to approve the establishment of foreign enterprises or joint ventures if the amount of investment falls within certain limits. The limits vary from place to place and can be broken down as follows: no more than US$10 million in Liaoning and Beijing; and no more than US$5 million in Wuchang, Hankou, Chengdu and other provinces and autonomous regions.

The fourteen coastal cities and harbors have even greater autonomy with regard to approving the establishment of foreign enterprises or joint ventures than do the other areas in mainland China. The municipal authorities of the fourteen coastal cities and harbors have autonomy within a certain range with respect to approving the establishment of foreign investment if those joint ventures or foreign enterprises are characterized by the following:[21] (1) Items produced are for a material-producing purpose; (2) the supply and demand of these items are not to be balanced by the central planning authorities; (3) the sales of products are not necessarily guaranteed by the state; (4) the exports of these items do not fall within the export quota; and (5) they can finance the overall production process themselves. The amounts of foreign investment these municipal authorities in coastal areas can approve vary from city to city. For example, the Tianjin and Shanghai municipal authorities are allowed to approve the establishment of foreign investment that satisfies the given conditions provided it does not exceed US$30 million; for Guangzhou and Dalian the amount is not more than US$10 million; and for other cities in the coastal area, not more than US$5 million.

*Loosening of Restrictions in Foreign Banking Operations.* In order to match the economic activities that foreign investors carry out in Mainland China, the PRC has shown a strong intention to moderate the restrictions on foreign

TABLE 24.1
Foreign Capital Pledged in the PRC, 1979–1985 (in US$100 million)

|                                        | 1979–1982 | 1983  | 1984  | 1985  | 1979–1985 |
|----------------------------------------|-----------|-------|-------|-------|-----------|
| Total foreign capital pledged (A)      | 201.72    | 34.2  | 47.91 | 97.4  | 381.23    |
| Foreign borrowing pledged (B)          |           |       |       |       |           |
| Amount                                 | 152.14    | 15.1  | 19.16 | 38.9  | 225.30    |
| Ratio of B/A                           | 75.42     | 44.15 | 39.99 | 39.94 | 59.10     |
| Foreign direct investment pledged (C)  |           |       |       |       |           |
| Amount                                 | 49.58     | 19.1  | 28.75 | 58.5  | 155.93    |
| Ratio of C/A                           | 24.58     | 55.85 | 60.01 | 60.06 | 40.90     |

*Sources:* The statistics for 1979–1982 came from *Guide to China's Foreign Economic Relations and Trade*, 1983, p. 106. Data for 1983 and 1984 were quoted from *Almanac of China's Foreign Economic Relations and Trade* (Beijing: The Editorial Board of the Almanac of China's Foreign Economic Relations and Trade), 1984, p. 1092; 1985, p. 1066. The statistics for 1985 were from *Ta Kun Pao* (Hong Kong: Ta-Kung-Pao Company Limited), January 30, 1986, p. 1.

banking operations. This became evident in 1984 when the PRC permitted foreign banks in Shanghai, including the Standard Chartered Bank, the Hong Kong and Shanghai Commercial Banking Corporation, the Bank of East Asia Ltd., and Overseas Chinese Banking Corporation, to establish foreign currency deposits and loans.[22] By enlarging the range of services offered by foreign banks in mainland China, the PRC intends to attract more capital from abroad, especially loans from international financial organizations. Furthermore, the expansion of the foreign banks' operations in mainland China will bring in advanced financial management and technology from the rest of the world, which will consequently improve the quality of service offered by the PRC's local banking sector. To obtain more loans with low interest rate terms, since 1984 the PRC has begun to be very active in the international financial market, showing a special interest in obtaining loans from the World Bank.[23]

## The Actual Introduction of Foreign Capital

*Foreign Capital Approved and Realized.* As indicated in Table 24.1, in mainland China from 1979 to 1985 the pledged capital inflow from the rest of the world amounted to US$38.12 billion. Of this amount, foreign borrowings pledged in the form of loans from international financial organizations and foreign governments and private commercial institutions came to US$22.53 billion, accounting for 59.1 percent of the total foreign capital pledged, while foreign direct investment pledged was US$15.59 billion, explaining 40.9 percent of the total foreign capital approved.[24] However, the actual capital inflow into the PRC during the same period under consideration, as shown in Table 24.2, was US$21.63 billion, about 56.72 percent of the total amount of foreign capital pledged by the rest of the world.

A decomposition of the foreign capital actually attracted by the PRC from 1979 to 1985 indicates that the realized amount of foreign borrowing

TABLE 24.2
Foreign Capital Actually Utilized in the PRC, 1979–1985 (in US$100 million)

| | 1979–1981 | 1982 | 1983 | 1984 | 1985 | 1979–1985 |
|---|---|---|---|---|---|---|
| Amount of foreign capital actually utilized (A) | 120.08 | 24.32 | 19.81 | 27.04 | 43.00 | 216.25 |
| Foreign borrowing actually utilized (B) | | | | | | |
| Amount | 90.88 | 17.83 | 10.65 | 12.86 | 27.30 | 159.52 |
| Ratio of B/A | 89.03 | 73.31 | 53.76 | 47.56 | 63.49 | 73.77 |
| Foreign direct investment actually utilized (C) | | | | | | |
| Amount | 11.20 | 6.49 | 9.16 | 14.18 | 15.70 | 56.73 |
| Ratio of C/A | 10.97 | 26.69 | 46.24 | 52.44 | 36.51 | 26.23 |

*Sources:* Same as Table 24.1.

from the rest of the world came to US$15.95 billion, or 70.8 percent of the foreign borrowing pledged, while the realized foreign direct investment was US$5.67 billion, only 36.4 percent of the foreign direct investment pledged. In brief, the proportion of realized foreign borrowing out of pledged foreign borrowing is much higher than that of realized foreign direct investment out of pledged foreign direct investment in mainland China. This situation has arisen because the major part of the PRC's foreign borrowing consisted of intergovernmental loans or loans from international financial organizations that have a shorter time lag between the pledge and realization than do the foreign direct investments, which have been mainly undertaken by the private sector.

Because of the scarcity of statistics, a more detailed analysis of the PRC's foreign capital can only be made based on available data for the period from 1979 to 1984. As shown in Table 24.3, during the period under consideration, mainland China had attracted pledged foreign capital up to US$26.28 billion and approved 4,735 contracts with the rest of the world. Loans from foreign governments and international financial organizations registered an amount of US$15.95 billion, with 117 contracts being made. The amount of foreign direct investment was US$10.33 billion, and 4,618 contracts were negotiated between the PRC and foreign investors. Among the many forms of foreign direct investment, comanagement topped the list both in terms of the number of contracts and the amount of investment.

However, the actually utilized foreign capital in mainland China during the period between 1979 and 1984 was US$17.33 billion, of which foreign borrowing amounted to US$13.22 billion, or 76.31 percent of the realized amount of foreign borrowing, and foreign direct investment was US$4.195 billion, accounting for 23.6 percent of the total actual foreign capital inflow (see Table 24.4). In other words, the ratio of actually realized foreign direct investment to the total of actually realized foreign capital is much lower than that ratio calculated on the basis of approved foreign direct investment

68

TABLE 24.3
Number of Contracts and the Amount of Foreign Capital Pledged in the PRC, 1979–1984

|  | Number of Contracts Pledged | Amount of Foreign Capital Pledged (US$100 million) |
|---|---|---|
| Foreign borrowing | 117 | 159.51 |
| Loans from foreign governments | 96 | 38.42 |
| Loans from international financial organizations | 21 | 29.28 |
| Other | — | 91.82 |
| Foreign direct investment | 4,618 | 103.28 |
| Joint ventures | 931 | 13.82 |
| Comanagement | 2,212 | 47.14 |
| Cooperative exploration (offshore oil exploration) | 31 | 24.23 |
| Wholly foreign-owned management | 74 | 4.71 |
| Compensation trade | 1,370 | 9.93 |
| Other | — | 3.44 |
| Total | 4,375 | 262.79 |

*Sources: Almanac of China's Economic Relations and Trade* (Beijing: The Editorial Board of the Almanac of China's Foreign Economic Relations and Trade), 1984, p. 1092; 1985, p. 1066.

TABLE 24.4
Foreign Capital Actually Utilized in the PRC, 1979–1984

|  | Amount Actually Utilized (US$100 million) | Ratio of Utilized to Pledged Amount (%) |
|---|---|---|
| Foreign borrowing | 132.24 | 82.29 |
| Loans from foreign governments | 29.17 | 75.92 |
| Loans from international financial organizations | 11.91 | — |
| Buyers credit | 6.34 | — |
| Loans on convertible currency through the Bank of China | 75.60 | — |
| Other | 9.21 | — |
| Foreign direct investment | 41.95 | 39.75 |
| Joint venture | 4.28 | 30.97 |
| Comanagement | 12.23 | 25.94 |
| Cooperative exploration (offshore oil exploration) | 13.11 | 54.11 |
| Wholly foreign-owned management | 0.98 | 20.81 |
| Compensation trade | 7.00 | 70.49 |
| Other | 3.44 | — |
| Total | 173.29 | 65.94 |

*Sources:* Same as Table 24.3.

TABLE 24.5
Chinese-Foreign Joint Ventures Classified According to Country of Origin, 1979–1984[a]
(in US$10 thousands)

| | Total | Foreign Borrowing | Foreign Direct Investment |
|---|---|---|---|
| Hong Kong, Macao | 663,123 | 13,659 | 649,464 |
| Japan | 496,109 | 380,314 | 115,795 |
| United States | 125,810 | 23,311 | 102,499 |
| United Kingdom | 60,903 | 27,510 | 33,402 |
| France | 43,757 | 22,502 | 21,255 |
| West Germany | 41,399 | 27,218 | 14,181 |
| Italy | 22,669 | 11,371 | 11,298 |
| Australia | 15,340 | 6,223 | 9,117 |
| Kuwait | 15,200 | 15,200 | — |
| Belgium | 11,977 | 6,966 | 5,011 |
| Singapore | 11,703 | — | 11,703 |
| Canada | 9,862 | 3,302 | 6,560 |

*Sources: Almanac of China's Foreign Economic Relations and Trade* (Beijing: The Editorial Board of the Almanac of China's Foreign Economic Relations and Trade), 1984, p. 1093; 1985, p. 1067.

[a]Because this table lists only major countries, the total amount of foreign capital here will not equal the total amount shown in Table 24.4.

and pledged total foreign capital (39.3 percent). This difference indicates that in mainland China capital inflow in the form of foreign direct investment is not as large as that in the form of foreign borrowings that the PRC has planned to introduce.

## Sources of Foreign Capital

*Country of Origin.* If the foreign capital in mainland China is classified according to the country of origin, Japan, the United States, Hong Kong, and Macao are shown to have provided the most capital. Table 24.5 lists the sources of the capital the PRC has attracted from the rest of the world during the period from 1979 to 1984. Considering that Hong Kong and Macao are geographically close to mainland China, especially to the four special economic zones in Guangdong and Fujian provinces, they have comparative advantages over the investors in other countries in making foreign direct investment in mainland China. In addition, speculation regarding Hong Kong's future after 1997 has since 1982 induced part of Hong Kong's capital flow into the special economic zones in mainland China. It is not surprising therefore, to find that Hong Kong is one of the major suppliers of foreign capital to the PRC, with a special interest in foreign direct investment.

Japan is the PRC's number-one foreign capital supplier, the capital mainly taking the form of loans with a proviso for specific usage. Prior to 1979,

Japanese businessmen began to carry on direct investment in the PRC. However, Japanese businessmen hesitated to expand their direct investment in mainland China, for fear that a successful transfer of technology or technological cooperation between Japan and the PRC would make mainland China a potential competitor of Japan in the world export market. Besides, many Japanese businessmen are not satisfied with the investment environment in mainland China.[25] Consequently, the growth of Japanese direct investment in the PRC has been very limited in recent years.

The United States, on the contrary, has experienced rapid growth in direct investment in mainland China since 1984 when the Reagan administration and the Coordinating Committee for Exports to Communist Countries (COCOM) decided to moderate the restrictions on the export of technology to the PRC. Since then, U.S. computer, automobile, and nuclear electricity industries have carried out large direct investment in mainland China at a rather fast pace.[26] As far as the supply of U.S. loans to the PRC is concerned, owing to the restriction imposed by U.S. domestic laws, during the period from 1979 to 1984, the ratio of U.S. loans to mainland China to the total supply of capital from the U.S. to mainland China was about 18.52 percent.

*Forms Introduced.* Loans that the PRC has received from foreign governments and international financial organizations are listed in Table 24.6. As far as loans from foreign governments are concerned, Japan was the most important foreign loan supplier to mainland China and accounted for more than 90 percent of total foreign loans. The possible reasons for the PRC's high concentration of loans from Japan can be stated as follows: (1) Both geographically and economically the PRC and Japan are complementary to each other; (2) Japan is one of the countries that have huge trade surpluses and hence the capacity to lend abroad; and (3) historically, Japanese economic and political interests have strong links with mainland China.

As for loans from international financial organizations, the PRC has so far been the World Bank's third biggest borrower. The PRC has taken advantage of the regulation of the World Bank that loans made to low-income and overpopulated countries would be preferentially considered. The loans from the World Bank were allocated to energy exploration, agricultural development, the promotion of education, and so on.

With respect to foreign direct investment, as mentioned earlier, joint ventures have been the major form of direct investment that the PRC has encouraged by means of different incentive measures. In terms of the data concerning 931 joint venture enterprises approved prior to the end of 1984, 80 percent of investors in joint ventures came from Hong Kong (as referred to in Table 24.7, and their investment accounted for about 57.8 percent of the foreign direct investment in joint ventures in mainland China. If one takes the amount of investment in joint ventures as an indicator of the size of foreign business in mainland China, it becomes clear that the United States, Japan, West Germany, Belgium, and Singapore are ranked after Hong Kong.

TABLE 24.6
China's Borrowing from Foreign Government and International Organizations, 1979–1984

| | Unit | 1979–1984 |
|---|---|---|
| Loans from Japan Overseas Economic Assistance Fund | 100 million yen | 3,715 |
| Itemized loan | 100 million yen | 2,415 |
| Commodity loan | 100 million yen | 1,300 |
| Energy loan from Japan Export and Import Bank | 100 million yen | 3,416 |
| Loan from Belgian government | Belgian francs (100 million) | 15 |
| Mixed loans from Danish government | Danish krone (10 thousand) | 42,050 |
| Government loan | Danish krone (10 thousand) | 27,500 |
| Export credit | Danish krone (10 thousand) | 14,550 |
| Mixed loan from Australian government | Australian dollars (10 thousand) | 4,753 |
| Government grants | Australian dollars (10 thousand) | 1,160 |
| Export credit | Australian dollars (10 thousand) | 3,593 |
| Loan from Swedish government | Swedish krone (10 thousand) | 595 |
| Loan from Kuwaiti government | Kuwaiti dinar (10 thousand) | 4,360 |
| Loans from World Bank | US dollars (10 thousand) | 193,390 |
| International Bank of Reconstruction and Development (IBRD) | US dollars (10 thousand) | 122,000 |
| International Development Association | Special Drawing US dollars (10 thousand) | 63,000 |
| International Fund of Agricultural Development (IFAD) | US dollars (10 thousand) | 5,160 |

*Sources:* Economic Research Center of State Council, People's Republic of China and State Statistical Bureau, *Almanac of China's Economy* (Hong Kong: The Almanac of China's Economy Company Limited), 1983, p. IV-130; 1984, p. V-200; 1985, p. V-207.

## The Utilization of Foreign Capital

Loans from foreign governments and international financial organizations with low interest rates were by and large used in the following kinds of circumstances: (1) The amount of investment involved was massive and beyond the capability of individuals or the local governments to finance on their own; (2) the construction period was very long and the rate of return on investment was low; or (3) the projects had to import huge amounts of

TABLE 24.7
Chinese-Foreign Joint Ventures Classified According to Country of Origin, 1979–1984

| Country of Origin | Number of Joint Ventures Approved | Foreign Capital Inflow | |
|---|---|---|---|
| | | US$10,000 | Percentage |
| Hong Kong | 741 | 79,768 | 57.72 |
| Japan | 57 | 12,119 | 8.77 |
| Singapore | 15 | 4,396 | 3.18 |
| Thailand | 9 | 2,272 | 1.64 |
| Philippines | 5 | 211 | 0.15 |
| Malaysia | 1 | 14 | 0.01 |
| Lebanon | 1 | 24 | 0.02 |
| Jordan | 1 | 1,925 | 1.39 |
| United Kingdom | 8 | 4,622 | 3.34 |
| Italy | 7 | 601 | 0.43 |
| West Germany | 5 | 10,441 | 7.56 |
| Belgium | 3 | 4,761 | 3.45 |
| France | 3 | 291 | 0.21 |
| Denmark | 2 | 367 | 0.27 |
| Norway | 2 | 146 | 0.11 |
| Switzerland | 2 | 418 | 0.30 |
| Finland | 1 | 521 | 0.38 |
| Sweden | 1 | 600 | 0.43 |
| United States | 61 | 13,352 | 9.66 |
| Australia | 4 | 424 | 0.31 |
| New Zealand | 1 | 40 | 0.03 |
| Libya | 1 | 885 | 0.64 |
| Total | 931 | 138,198 | 100.00 |

*Source:* Economic Research Center of State Council, People's Republic of China and State Statistical Bureau, *Almanac of China's Economy* (Hong Kong: The Almanac of China's Economy Company Limited), 1985, p. V-208.

raw materials and pieces of equipment when the foreign exchange was not available. According to these criteria, foreign borrowings in the PRC since 1979 have been utilized in the construction or improvement of harbors, railroad networks, telecommunications facilities, rural irrigation systems, electricity stations, education, and so on. However, the details of actual allocation of foreign borrowings in various industries in mainland China are not available.

As to foreign direct investment, in order both to meet the PRC's demand and to satisfy foreign investors' interests, most of it was used in projects where the expected rate of return on investment was high, where there was a rapid return on investment, or where foreign exchange could be earned. In general, foreign direct investment concentrated on such areas as offshore oil exploration, coal mining machinery and electronics, petroleum chemicals, and tourism services, among others.

Because of the shortage as well as the limitations of statistical data, we cannot analyze the actual distribution of foreign direct investment among

TABLE 24.8
Chinese-Foreign Joint Ventures Classified by Industry, 1979–1984

| Industry | Number of Approved Joint Ventures | Foreign Capital Inflow Millions of U.S. Dollars | Percentage |
|---|---|---|---|
| Communications and telecommunications | 58 | 10,088 | 7.3 |
| Machinery and electronics | 192 | 25,152 | 18.2 |
| Metal | 13 | 1,658 | 1.2 |
| Petroleum chemicals | 44 | 3,593 | 2.6 |
| Textiles | 190 | 11,194 | 8.1 |
| Construction and construction materials | 92 | 9,950 | 7.2 |
| Food and drugs | 47 | 8,845 | 6.4 |
| Agriculture, husbandry, and fishery | 57 | 1,797 | 1.3 |
| Tourism services | 73 | 50,857 | 36.8 |
| Commerce | 113 | 7,048 | 5.1 |
| Real estate and others | 52 | 8,015 | 5.8 |
| Total | 931 | 138,198 | 100.0 |

*Source:* Economic Research Center of State Council, People's Republic of China and State Statistical Bureau, *Almanac of China's Economy* (Hong Kong: The Almanac of China's Economy Company Limited), 1985, p. V-207.

various industries in the PRC. However, if we take the 931 joint-venture enterprises approved between 1979 and 1984, the statistics listed in Table 24.8 show the planned allocation of foreign direct investment in Chinese-foreign joint ventures to be as follows: tourism (36.8 percent), machinery and electronics (18.2 percent), light industries and textiles (8.1 percent), transportation and electricity (7.3 percent), and construction and construction materials (7.2 percent).

This allocation of foreign direct investment in joint ventures by industry suggests that the actual priorities regarding the utilization of foreign capital that were actually determined by both demand and supply forces are quite different from what the PRC had planned before. That is, a higher priority has been put on the exploitation of natural resources (with special emphasis on oil and coal), the improvement of the investment environment, and the development of labor-intensive industries.

## Problems Associated with the Introduction of Foreign Capital

Although many incentive measures have been adopted by the PRC since 1979 and a massive amount of foreign capital has been flowing into mainland China, there are still some difficulties and unresolved problems associated with the introduction of foreign capital, in particular with foreign direct investment. Such problems arise mainly because of the incongruity between a market economy and a predominantly planned economy and the lack of information and experience shared by both the foreign investors and the PRC. In addition, the poor investment environment is regarded as another major problem. These problems can be briefly summarized as follows:

## Inadequate Infrastructure

The energy supply and the transportation network are the key bottlenecks in the PRC's economic development over the past few years. Even prior to 1979, the supply of the major means of transportation—railroads—could only meet 70 to 80 percent of the domestic demand in mainland China. Given that the target rate of transportation growth in the Sixth Five-Year Plan was lower than the rapid rate of actual economic growth, there is no doubt that the rapid economic growth during the period covered by the Sixth Five-Year Plan and possibly that of the subsequent Seventh Five-Year Plan has been increasing the gap between supply and demand for transportation in mainland China.

As to the supply of energy, the shortage of energy during 1981 and 1983 led about 20 percent of manufacturing factories to cease production operations, and the lost production as a consequence of the energy shortage was estimated to amount to 70 billion RMB dollars per annum. (RMB is the PRC's local currency unit. Currently, one US dollar is approximately equal to 2.7 RMB dollars.) Although Chinese-foreign joint ventures and foreign enterprises in special economic zones were given priority with regard to the use of energy (mainly electricity), they suffered nevertheless because of the lost production resulting from the inadequate supply of public utilities.[27]

In addition, because of the congestion in harbors along the coastal areas, many raw materials and pieces of equipment imported by Chinese-foreign joint ventures or foreign enterprises have been forced to stay outside the harbors for one or two months while all imported goods are unloaded. This inefficiency in harbor facilities has cost foreign investors a great deal in terms of the timing of production and hence the sales of their products in the market. It is very clear that foreign investors will be reluctant to invest their money if they must make additional investments in infrastructure.

## A Shortage of Factors of Production

In general, joint ventures or foreign enterprises are guaranteed access to necessary raw materials at the appropriate times in their production process. However, if the raw materials needed by joint ventures are not included in the plans of their local suppliers in advance, these joint ventures are still confronted with a shortage of raw materials just as the local enterprises or factories are.[28]

With respect to the supply of labor in the PRC, a generally prevailing impression is that the PRC has a comparative advantage in labor costs because of its abundant labor force. However, if the nominal wage rate in mainland China is deflated by average labor productivity (which takes into account the quality and the experience of labor), surprisingly, the actual unit labor cost is higher than that in Japan, Hong Kong, and Singapore.[29] As the degree of openness in mainland China increases, unless labor productivity in mainland China can be improved, the dissemination of information regarding the true cost of labor in the PRC will become an unfavorable factor with respect to attracting foreign capital in the near future.

## Loopholes in the Legal System

Though a series of laws and regulations relating to the inflow of foreign capital have been proclaimed now and then since 1979 to protect foreign investors' interests in mainland China, some foreign businesses still feel that the contents of these existing laws and regulations associated with foreign direct investment in mainland China are very vague and incomplete as far as the protection of their interests and the introduction of advanced technology into the PRC are concerned. Moreover, the necessary revisions to the contracts of joint ventures resulting from the continuous announcement of new laws and regulations tend to increase the adjustment cost to foreign investors in the PRC. According to the bylaw on joint ventures, the duration of the joint ventures should be from ten to thirty years. This stipulation, though it may be extended up to fifty years through negotiations, discourages foreign investors from introducing new technology and making additional investments. This bylaw will lead to a curb in the scope of development possibilities regarding foreign capital.

## Bureaucracy

As a consequence of the open-door policy, the local authorities have also been given some power of approval over foreign capital inflow since the beginning of the 1980s. Considering that the economic system is to a large extent centrally planned in nature even though it regards itself as a combination of central planning and the market mechanism, the rigidities and inefficiency prevailing in the PRC's bureaucratic system will of course be a barrier to the introduction of further foreign capital. For example, in any joint-venture project, it takes three months for foreign businesses to negotiate with the PRC and another three months for the PRC to give its approval.[30] Given the fact that the nature of the current political system will not change very much in the foreseeable future, the degree of bureaucracy will not be expected to be reduced, significantly, and the bureaucracy will probably remain as one of the major barriers to foreign investors.

## Restrictions on the Sale of Products

The regulation that joint ventures or foreign enterprises are obliged to bear a heavy export burden (70 to 80 percent) makes it very difficult for foreign concerns to invest in internationally competitive fields and discourages the foreign investors who are interested in mainland China as a potential market. The PRC eased export obligations in October 1983 by allowing some products manufactured by joint ventures to be sold in local markets. The products involved are those urgently needed or those that would otherwise have to be imported by the PRC. However, from the point of view of the foreign investors, it remains uncertain which products are "urgently needed," and this problem in turn will introduce a new uncertainty for foreign businesses with respect to production and marketing plans.[31]

## The Prospects of Foreign Capital in Mainland China

In order to quadruple its 1980 level of industrial and agricultural production by the year 2000, the PRC has since 1979 laid a great deal of emphasis on an open-door policy, and consequently, the introduction of foreign capital and technology has been playing an important role in the Four Modernizations. Officially, the PRC has repeatedly announced that there will be no changes in the open-door policy and that the introduction of foreign capital will continue to be stressed in the future. To this end, a number of incentive measures have been adopted by the PRC with the intention of expressing its determination to undertake this policy and to protect the foreign investors' interests.

It is evident that the actual capital inflow from the rest of the world between 1979 and 1985 came to US$21.63 billion, which exceeded the US$20 billion target set in the Sixth Five-Year Plan. Hence, in view of the current volatile economic situation and the unresolved problems associated with the introduction of foreign capital in mainland China, the prospects of foreign capital in mainland China can be briefly summarized as follows:

First, the PRC has maintained a very conservative attitude toward the introduction of foreign capital. In terms of the target that the PRC set to introduce foreign capital during the period of the Sixth Five-Year Plan, the average amount of capital the PRC planned to attract ranged from US$4 to 6 billion per year. Since this is not a significantly large amount in the international financial market, and since the PRC has a good reputation in repaying foreign debts incurred in previous years, it should not be very difficult for the PRC to attract foreign capital in the near future as rapidly as it did in the past if China is politically and economically stable domestically.

Second, foreign borrowing will continue to be the major way of inducing foreign capital to come into the PRC, even in view of the fact that in recent years mainland China has consistently stressed on various occasions that the emphasis has shifted from foreign borrowings to foreign direct investment. The investment environment in mainland China either with respect to infrastructure or to the legal system cannot be improved significantly in the near future, so that the environment is in all probability not as attractive as that of other developing countries.

Third, loans from international financial organizations, especially from the World Bank, have been one of the major sources of the supply of foreign capital to the PRC over the past few years. However, according to a statement made by the World Bank, loans made to the PRC with preferential terms during the latter half of the 1980s will be limited to a maximum amount of US$600 million annually.[32] In other words, the supply of loans from the World Bank to the PRC will be limited in the near future. Given such a situation, it appears very likely that loans from foreign governments and the private sector will become an alternative means for the PRC to attract loans from the international financial market. As far as loans from foreign governments are concerned, Japan has been the biggest supplier of inter-governmental loans to the PRC since 1979 and will be expected to continue to play a similar role in the foreseeable future.

Fourth, in terms of the country of origin, the foreign capital that flowed into mainland China came mainly from Hong Kong, Macao, Japan, and the United States during the period from 1979 to 1984. The movement of capital from Hong Kong and Macao to mainland China will continue, but at a slackening pace, because the outflow of capital from Hong Kong and Macao, especially that which has flowed into mainland China, has passed its peak level. Given the economic as well as the political interests of both the United States and Japan in mainland China, these two countries are going to be the major suppliers of capital to the PRC in the future.

## Notes

Special thanks go to Jen-jen Hou for helping me collect data.

1. According to the PRC's own estimation, the amount of foreign capital needed for the Four Modernizations during the period from 1978 to 1985 will be about RMB$1,000 billion (or US$630 billion). This figure was mentioned by Li Xian-nian in September 1978 when he visited Japan and by Deng Xiao-ping in February 1979 when he was in Tokyo. For details, please refer to Chu-yuan Cheng, "The Concepts and Reality of the PRC's Four Modernizations," *Chung Kung Ching Chi De Chen Tuan* (Taipei: Lien Ching, 1983).

2. The economic laws and regulations promulgated by the PRC since 1979 can be found in *Ching Chi Fa Kuai Hsüan Pien*, edited by Hei Lung Chiang Fa Hsueh Yen Chiu Suo; *Almanac of China's Economy*, 1984 and 1985.

3. See the PRC's *People's Daily*, April 18, 1986, p. 2.

4. In general, the laws and regulations relating to the introduction of foreign capital in the PRC can reflect its policy on foreign capital to a large extent. However, it should be kept in mind that if one tries to derive the PRC's policy with regard to foreign capital on the basis of the relevant laws and regulations, one may take the risk of missing some of the foreign capital policy that did not take legal form.

5. The objectives of foreign capital policy can be understood from Article 1 of the Law on Chinese-Foreign Joint Ventures, *Ching Chi Fa Kuai Hsuan Pien*, pp. 541–544; and also Article 1 of the Law on All-Foreign Enterprises, which can be found in the *People's Daily*, April 18, 1986, p. 2.

6. Foreign capital should be introduced into the PRC along with foreign technology and management. This intention can be found in Chapter 6 of the Regulations for the Implementation of the Law on Chinese-Foreign Joint Ventures and Article 3 of the Law on All-Foreign Enterprises.

7. As to the restrictions on the sales of the products of joint ventures or foreign enterprises in mainland China, please see Article 3 of the Law on All-Foreign Enterprises and Chapter 8 of the Regulations for the Implementation of the Law on Chinese-Foreign Joint Ventures.

8. The PRC intended to introduce foreign capital as a protection measure to help the development of its local service industries, starting with the insurance industry. This can be found in Article 16 of the Law on All-Foreign Enterprises.

9. Refer to Article 15 of the Law on All-Foreign Enterprises.

10. Please refer to Chie Ch'ung-wei, "The Conditions and Policies Concerning the Introduction of Foreign Capital in the PRC," no. 1713, April 1, 1981, p. 8; and Wei Yu-ming, "The Policy Concerning the Introduction of Foreign Direct Investment in the PRC," *Ching Chi Tao Pao*, no. 1773, June 14, 1982, p. 18.

11. Please see Chapter 4 of *The Investment Directory in Mainland China* (Hong Kong: Economic Information Agency, 1982).

12. Please refer to the *People's Daily*, July 21, 1983, p. 2.

13. This point was made by the deputy minister of the Ministry of Finance, Ch'i Hai-bin. Please see "Mainland China's Plan to Emphasize the Utilization of Foreign Loans in the Seventh Five-Year Plan," *Chung Kung Tui Wai Ching Mao Yen Chiu*, no. 229, January 16, 1986, p. 44.

14. Wei, "The Policy Concerning the Introduction."

15. Chie, "The Conditions and Policies." Also see Cheng Shou-chen, "The New Direction of the Utilization of Foreign Capital in the PRC," *Fei Ch'ing Yueh Pao*, vol. 26, no. 8, p. 49.

16. Please see "The PRC Plans to Attract US$300 Billion of Foreign Capital in the Seventh Five-Year Plan," *Chung Kung Tui Wai Ching Mao Yen Chiu*, no. 204, January 1, 1985, p. 46.

17. Please refer to "The PRC's Economic Reform Is at a Crossroads," *Chung Kung Tui Wai Ching Mao Yen Chiu*, no. 230, February 1, 1986, p. 16.

18. Please refer to Shui Chung, "Income Tax on Chinese-Foreign Joint Ventures," *Finance*, February 1984, pp. 34–36. Also see Shui Chung, "Income Tax on Industry and Commerce," *Finance*, January 1984, pp. 27–28.

19. The regulation became effective in 1983.

20. See *The Almanac of China's Economy*, 1985, p. X–7.

21. Ibid.

22. Please see "The PRC is Drafting the Seventh Five-Year Plan," *Chung Kung Tui Wai Ching Mao Yen Chiu*, no. 202, December 1, 1984, p. 47.

23. See note 13.

24. The total amount of foreign capital approved and realized between 1979 and 1985 in the PRC as published by the PRC's officials is different from that obtained from other sources. For example, the approved and realized amounts of foreign capital for the same period under consideration are US$30.5 billion and US$21.2 billion, respectively, in the article written by Mary Lee, "New Rules Help, but It's Still a Struggle for Some," *Far Eastern Economic Review*, March 20, 1986.

25. See Satoshi Imai, "Joint Ventures in China and Related Problems," *China Newsletter*, no. 51, January-February, 1984, p. 23.

26. See Fu Wen, "Ba-Li Tong Chou Wei Yuan Hui Fang Kuan Jung Yun Yu Xiang-gang," *Ching Chi Tao Pao*, no. 1943, October 28, 1985, p. 5.

27. Please see "The Barriers to the Introduction of Foreign Capital in the PRC," *Chung Kung Tai Wai Ching Mao Yen Chiu*, no. 232, March 1, 1986.

28. Imai, "Joint Ventures in China."

29. Please see Jung-feng Chang, *A Study on Special Economic Zones in Mainland China*, Taipei: Chung-Hua Institution for Economic Research, economic paper No. 40, September 1983, p. 67.

30. Please see Yuan Liu, "The Introduction of Technology by Domestic and Foreign Concerns Will Be Different," *The Nineties*, July 1985, p. 56.

31. Please see Hiroko Kawai, "Direct Investment in China in 1983," *China Newsletter*, no. 48, July-August 1984, pp. 15–19.

32. Please see "The World Bank Will Set Limits on Loans to the PRC," *Chung Kung Tui Wai Ching Mao Yen Chiu*, no. 228, January 1, 1986, p. 49.

# 25

## China's Development Strategy: Investment Financing Needs and Sources

*Robert F. Dernberger*

Few observers of contemporary developments in China would disagree with the argument that the death of Mao Zedong and ensuing emergence of the leadership of Deng Xiaoping and Zhao Ziyang has involved a dramatic change in economic development strategy. This change has consisted of changes in objectives (sectoral priorities), means (sources of growth), institutional change (reform of the economic system), and even behavioral rules (the use of economic levers). The popular journals have reported sensational anecdotal accounts of the poor peasant who takes over a losing state enterprise and turns it into a profit-making showpiece of capitalist enterprise and other equally dramatic, but equally unique, examples of the changes taking place. Changes are taking place, but much of my own research and writing in the past few years has been devoted to showing that economies and societies such as China may undergo radical change on the surface rather quickly, but there exist many continuities that prove to be rather persistent. Those earlier papers, including one presented to the Thirteenth Sino-American Conference on Mainland China,[1] were largely devoted to showing that despite many changes in economic strategy, policies, and even some institutional change, the economy of the People's Republic of China (PRC) remained a planned and centrally controlled economy and was not an example of market socialism.

I still believe that argument to be true. However, in this chapter I turn from a discussion of economic institutions and policies in general to focus on a single area of economic activity in China's economy that has undergone great changes, yet retains important continuities: the investment sector. Investment is accepted by most observers as the most crucial explanatory variable for China's rapid record of extensive growth in the period before 1980. With the change in development strategy of the new leadership, much greater attention is being given to technological change, increases in factor productivity, incentive mechanisms, and several other sources for intensive—rather than extensive—economic development.[2] Yet, although I believe this simplified analysis does capture a major change in China's development strategy, China is still a developing economy and investment will continue to be an important and necessary source of growth even if emphasis is given to intensive as against extensive development. Thus the level of investment financing will not only remain a constraint on China's economic growth in the future, but will become an even greater constraint because of the economic reforms in the way in which investment is to be financed in the future.

## Investment and China's Economic Growth: The Record of the Past

China's record of economic growth, in terms of the major macroeconomic indicators, was both unique and readily explainable in the three decades after 1949 (see Table 25.1). Although the record varied significantly between time periods and among sectors, few countries, especially those having per capita incomes as low as China, could claim an average annual real rate of growth of 6 percent (4 percent on a per capita basis) over this same period.[3] The explanation of this success lies mainly in the rate of investment, also exceptionally high for countries at similar levels of per capita income[4] (see Table 25.2). Quite simply, soon after the Chinese Communists assumed power on the mainland, they introduced an economic system—the Soviet-type, centrally planned economic system—and a development strategy—the big push or Stalinist development strategy—which led to the mobilization of national income for the purpose of investment in additional productive capacity, that is, extensive development. With abundant natural resources and a surplus labor force, the achievement of these relatively high rates of growth by means of relatively high rates of investments in fixed capital (China's stock of fixed capital was twenty-eight times larger in 1984 than in 1952) is neither puzzling nor unexpected, even though it can be regarded as unique.

In an earlier period in history, the Soviet Union under Stalin had developed the economic system and adopted the development strategy to accomplish these same results. By means of nationalized units of production and administered prices and wages, profits accrue to the state as budget revenue and are determined by the prices and wages set by the state. Agricultural prices and raw material prices are set low, while output prices are set relatively high, especially for consumer goods. The difference between the costs of production and retail prices can be set as a turnover tax, as in the Soviet Union, or merely set as a profit markup to the producer, as in China; the result is the same—indirect taxes that end up in the budget as revenue of the state.

The story of how the socialist countries, such as China, are able to maintain very high rates of investment in fixed capital, however, does not lie solely on the revenue side of the state's budget; although China's budget revenue as a share of national income is exceptionally high (about one third

TABLE 25.1
Chinese Economic Growth, 1953–1985 (annual rates of growth in percent)

|              | Output: National Income | Inputs | | Total Factor Productivity | |
|--------------|-------------------------|--------|--------------|-------|-------|
|              |                         | Labor  | Fixed Capital | (1)   | (2)   |
| 1953–1957    | 8.9                     | 2.8    | 21.7         | -5.2  | -1.5  |
| 1958–1962    | -3.1                    | 1.7    | 17.4         | -14.2 | -11.1 |
| 1963–1965    | 14.7                    | 3.4    | 4.1          | 10.9  | 11.0  |
| 1966–1970    | 8.3                     | 3.7    | 5.9          | 3.3   | 3.7   |
| 1971–1975    | 5.5                     | 2.1    | 9.3          | -0.9  | 0.5   |
| 1976–1980    | 6.0                     | 1.9    | 8.2          | 0.3   | 1.6   |
| 1981–1984    | 8.7                     | 3.2    | 8.3          | 2.4   | 3.5   |
| 1953–1980    | 6.0                     | 2.5    | 11.4         | -1.8  | -0.1  |

*Sources and data:* All rates of growth based on data presented in State Statistical Bureau, PRC, *Statistical Yearbook of China, 1984* and *China: A Statistics Survey in 1985.* National income statistics are presented in "comparable" prices; total labor force is measured in number of individuals, excluding unemployed, students, and those engaged in household chores; and fixed capital refers to total fixed assets in state units only.

*Methodology:* Obviously there are several problems with the adequacy of the data used— national income measured in "comparable" prices, while fixed capital refers to only state units and is estimated by taking the book value of fixed assets in 1952, assuming an annual depreciation rate of 5 percent, and adding each year's annual investment in fixed assets in current prices. The labor input is measured in number of laborers, not in man-years or days. Finally, to estimate total factor productivity, we combine labor and fixed assets according to two sets of weights: 40 percent for labor and 60 percent for capital in (1) and 60 percent for labor and 40 percent for capital in (2). Given the nature of the data and methodology, the effort to convince the skeptics would be useless. Thus, I can merely repeat a quote from Robert Solow's defense of this methodology in his famous article on "Technical Change and the Aggregate Production Function": We make no attempt "to justify what follows by calling on fancy theorems on aggregation and index numbers. Either this kind of aggregate economics appeals or it doesn't." Besides, our use of the data in this table is for the purpose of illustrating a point, not proving it.

of national income, see "Financial Revenue as a Percentage of National Income" in Table 25.2) compared to other countries. The really distinctive feature of China's budget process that explains the very high rates of investment (accumulation amounted to about 30 percent of national income, and investment in fixed capital amounted to about three-fourths of accumulation)[5] in the three decades after 1949 is the extraordinarily high share of these budget revenues that were allocated to investment (approximately two-fifths of budget revenue was allocated to capital construction; see Table 25.2).[6] Finally, the role of the budget process in this program of extensive development is made clear by the fact that capital construction expenditures accounted for the dominant share of investments in capital construction were financed by the state budget (see Table 25.2). In other words, the high growth rate of national income during 1953–1980 in Table 25.1 was a result

TABLE 25.2
Investment in China, 1953–1985 (in percent share; all values are current values)

| | Accumulation as a Percentage of National Income | Financial Revenue as a Percentage of National Income[a] | Appropriations for Capital Construction as a Percentage of Financial Expenditures |
|---|---|---|---|
| 1953–1957 | 24.2 | 33.6 | 37.6 |
| 1958–1962 | 30.8 | 38.6 | 46.0 |
| 1963–1965 | 22.7 | 34.2` | 30.1 |
| 1966–1970 | 26.3 | 31.5 | 38.7 |
| 1971–1975 | 33.0 | 34.4 | 40.2 |
| 1976–1980 | 33.3 | 32.8 | 38.1 |
| 1981–1984 | 29.7 | 26.8 | 28.8 |

| | Investment in Fixed Assets as a Percentage of Accumulation | Capital Construction as a Percentage of Investments in Fixed Assets | State Budget Investment in Capital Construction as Share of Total |
|---|---|---|---|
| 1953–1957 | 62.3 | 96.2 | 90.3 |
| 1958–1962 | 74.8 | 92.3 | 78.3 |
| 1963–1965 | 72.6 | 84.5 | 88.1 |
| 1966–1970 | 67.0 | 80.7 | 89.3 |
| 1971–1975 | 72.7 | 77.5 | 82.5 |
| 1976–1980 | 75.8 | 73.5 | 77.2 |
| 1981–1984 | 66.7 | 64.0 | 54.7 |

| | Investment in Productive Capacity as a Percentage of Total | Investment in Industry as a Share of Total | Foreign Loans as a Share of Financial Revenue |
|---|---|---|---|
| 1953–1957 | 67.0 | 42.5 | 2.7 |
| 1958–1962 | 85.4 | 60.4 | 0.1[b] |
| 1963–1965 | 79.4 | 49.8 | 0 |
| 1966–1970 | 83.8 | 55.5 | 0 |
| 1971–1975 | 82.5 | 55.4 | 0.1[b] |
| 1976–1980 | 73.9 | 52.6 | 1.5 |
| 1981–1984 | 57.6 | 47.1 | 4.7 |

*Sources:* Same publications of the State Statistical Bureau as cited in Table 25.1.

[a]Includes foreign loans.
[b]Greater than zero, but less than 0.1 percent.

TABLE 25.3
Investment in Capital Construction (in percent share)

| | Total | Agriculture | Industry | |
| --- | --- | --- | --- | --- |
| | | | Light | Heavy |
| 1953–1957 | 100 | 7.1 | 6.4 | 36.1 |
| 1958–1962 | 100 | 11.3 | 6.4 | 54.0 |
| 1963–1965 | 100 | 17.7 | 3.9 | 45.9 |
| 1966–1970 | 100 | 10.7 | 4.4 | 51.1 |
| 1971–1975 | 100 | 9.8 | 5.8 | 49.6 |
| 1976–1980 | 100 | 10.5 | 6.7 | 45.9 |
| 1981–1984 | 100 | 5.8 | 7.3 | 39.8 |

| As a Share of Total Investment in Industry | Metallurgy | Energy | Machine Building | Total for These Three Sectors |
| --- | --- | --- | --- | --- |
| 1953–1957 | 18.6 | 28.6 | 15.4 | 62.6 |
| 1958–1962 | 23.2 | 27.5 | 16.0 | 66.7 |
| 1963–1965 | 16.1 | 30.3 | 11.6 | 58.0 |
| 1966–1970 | 18.2 | 28.5 | 13.7 | 60.4 |
| 1971–1975 | 17.7 | 31.6 | 22.2 | 71.5 |
| 1976–1980 | 15.4 | 39.6 | 14.5 | 69.5 |
| 1981–1984[a] | 14.9 | 42.1 | 10.3 | 67.3 |

Sources: Same publications of the State Statistical Bureau as cited in Table 25.1.

[a]1981–1983.

of the rate of growth in fixed assets that was almost twice as high, the latter being made possible by the budget process in China's Soviet-type economy, which mobilized resources for that very purpose.

The allocation of these investments was in the hands of the planners; and the Stalinist development strategy, or the "big push" development strategy, involves not only a high rate of investment being devoted to the expansion of production capacity, but also requires that new productive capacity to be concentrated in industry, especially heavy industry. As the statistics in Table 25.2 show, more than three-fourths of capital construction investment was devoted to the creation of new productive capacity, and more than 50 percent of investment in capital construction was allocated to industry. The further concentration of investment within industry to heavy industry and to the three priority sectors is shown in Table 25.3. Thus, as a result of the mobilization of resources and their allocation to investment in productive capacity, not only did the Chinese economy realize rapid growth over these three decades, but achieved a significantly rapid change in the structure of the economy as well. In 1952 the agricultural sector accounted for 57.7 percent of China's national income, but by 1983 the share had fallen to 44.9 percent; industry's share over the same period increased from 19.5 percent to 41.9 percent, while the service sectors (construction, transport, and commerce) declined from 22.8 percent to only 13.2 percent.[7]

All of these investment statistics merely lay out the quantitative description of a classical big-push development strategy of extensive economic development. In fact, given the low level of economic development from which the Chinese began their efforts at extensive economic development, this statistical picture of rates and allocations of investment represents a rather extreme example of this type of development strategy. In addition, again given the low level of development from which they started, a most unique feature of China's extensive-development strategy over this period was the limited reliance on foreign funds in the mobilization of the financial revenues for carrying out their investment program (see Table 25.2). During the First Five-Year Plan only 2.7 percent of China's financial revenues came from foreign borrowings, and foreign borrowings were insignificant over the next two decades. Imported machinery and equipment was a much larger share of total investments in fixed assets, especially during the 1950s. By definition, as a developing country with a major program of investment, China had to rely on imports of machinery and equipment to realize that investment program. Yet, although imports of machinery and equipment accounted for approximately 40 percent of China's total investment in machinery and equipment in the 1950s, that share had declined to below 10 percent in 1962 through 1973.[8] In other words, China's planners not only implemented a rigorous Stalinist-type, big-push program of extensive economic development, they also sought to achieve that development while pursuing a policy of self-sufficiency.

The preceding discussion clearly indicates the crucial and dominant role played by investment in China's economic growth over these three decades. That China's economic growth was obtained by means of extensive development is borne out by the consequences of that growth (see Table 25.1). As shown in Table 25.1, the increase in output is almost totally explained by the increase in the quantity of inputs, with almost no technological change or increase in total factor productivity in the aggregate production function. If fixed capital is given the weight of 60 percent (labor 40 percent), then total factor productivity declined by almost 2 percent a year from 1953 to 1980; if the larger weight is given to the labor input, it would result in a much smaller annual decline.[9] Even if the calculations are limited to the industrial sector, the leading growth sector, the results are not improved much: 0.6 percent and 1.5 percent growth in total factor productivity for 1952–1982 according to the higher and lower weights for fixed assets, respectively.[10] Finally, submitting the available data for industrial output and inputs to an econometric analysis more sophisticated than the data probably warrants, the results are remarkably consistent and rational: Industrial output did increase proportionately to increases in inputs. In fact, especially relevant to our argument here, that econometric analysis concludes: "Our limited data . . . suggest that industrial output increased in China mainly as a result of the increase in capital assets, rather than of improvement in technology, because a constant production function without incorporating technological change is capable of explaining aggregate output from 1952 to 1981."[11]

True economic growth, as a self-sustaining process to achieve higher standards of living, is quite different from a program of mobilizing resources, labor, and investment on an ever-expanding scale to obtain proportionate increases in output—no matter how great the rate of increase in output. The generation and adaptation of new technology, developing new and better products, reducing costs and relative prices, obtaining steady increases in productivity of both labor and capital—these are the signs of successful economic development, development obtained by means of a program of intensive growth. In the former pattern of economic development, per capita incomes do not increase rapidly and do so by means of changes in the structure of production (a process that cannot continue forever); in the latter pattern of economic development, per capita incomes increase even though there is no change in the structure of production (output per unit of input goes up in all sectors). Per capita incomes did increase in China in the three decades after 1949, but largely because of the changes in the structure of production, and the rate of increase was stagnating over time.

Furthermore, because of human errors introduced into the allocation of resources and management of the economy by policy makers, who had been given extensive control over the economy by the adoption of a Soviet-type, centrally planned economic system, the Chinese economy was becoming increasingly more inefficient owing to bottlenecks, increasing costs, stockpiles of unwanted or below-standard products, failures of the incentive system, and a serious lag in technological improvements.[12] Quite simply, continued growth by means of the traditional means of extensive growth was becoming less and less sustainable. The change in development strategy was brought about by the death of Mao in late 1976 and the emergence of a new, post-Mao leadership over the next few years. This new leadership represented those who had opposed the economic policies of Mao in the past, or who had come to appreciate the extent to which the earlier development strategy had failed to achieve the true objectives of growth—technological change and increases in the real standard of living. That new leadership also has drawn into its ranks at the top a younger generation who are willing and desire to seek a different and more effective solution to China's economic development problems.

## China's New Development Strategy:
## The Role of Investment and Investment Financing

Time and space do not permit a complete and detailed discussion of the new development strategy that has been introduced as a result of the economic reform program that began in 1979. Only those aspects of that new development strategy of greatest relevance to investment and investment financing are included in this discussion. Obviously, inasmuch as investment was a key explanatory variable in the high growth rates achieved in the three decades after 1949, the mobilization of resources for investment and the allocation and financing of that investment also were a major source of the economic problems inherited by the Deng-Zhao-Hu leadership. In other words, the rate of accumulation, the financing of investment, and the allocation of investment have been major targets for the economic reforms that have been introduced since 1979. These reforms in the investment sector also reflect the attempt of the new leadership to shift from a development strategy of extensive growth to one of intensive growth.

## Restructuring Investment

Among the first targets of attack by the new leadership was the excessive rate of accumulation and investment. The workers and peasants had not shared in China's remarkable economic growth, but they had received limited increases in incomes and the standard of living. The high rates of accumulation and investment were assigned a large share of the blame. Rather than growth of material output for its own sake, as in the past, increases in the standard of living were defined to be the ultimate objective of socialist economic development. Based on their newly adopted empiricism, the record of other developing countries was cited to show that an "optimum" rate of accumulation and investment was approximately 25 percent, "optimum" because that rate would produce both aggregate economic growth at an acceptable rate and a sustainable and satisfactory rate of increase in the standard of living as well.[13] Thus, lowering the rate of accumulation and investment to below 30 percent became a policy objective of the new development strategy.[14]

A much more important reform, in terms of long-run growth potential, was the recognition that the allocation of investment was an important determinant of balance between supplies and demands in the economy. Thus a major reform needed to restore equilibrium and remove the serious bottlenecks that were becoming constraints on future growth was a reallocation of investment priorities among the various sectors of the economy.[15] Thus the switch to greater emphasis on consumerism also involved the allocation of a larger share of investment to the light industries and a smaller share to heavy industry.[16] Furthermore, the allocation of investment to heavy industry was to be based on the principle of derived demand: the allocation of investment to the heavy industry sector on the basis of needs of production for final demand—that is, the production of goods needed for consumption, exports, government consumption, and investment projects themselves, not the production of heavy industrial products to achieve a high rate of growth in the sector desired by the planners or the politically powerful heavy-industrial ministries. Although no absolute targets for the relative shares were given—only that the share for light industry was to go up while the share for heavy industry was to go down—a litmus test that seemed to be used by the Chinese was for investment in industry to be allocated so that light industrial output would grow faster than output in the heavy industrial sectors.

Of course, investments in heavy industry in the past had come at the expense of all other sectors, not just light industry, and this neglect of those other sectors was emerging as a serious constraint on future growth in the mid-1970s. For example, more than three-fourths of China's labor force worked in agriculture, and agricultural products constituted a dominant share of consumption, exports, and inputs in light industry. Yet productivity and incomes in the sector were stagnant, while agriculture received only 11 percent of total capital construction in state units between 1953 and 1980, most of that investment going to water conservancy projects. Transport and communications and nonproductive investments—social overhead capital or infrastructure, housing, culture, education, and so on—were being seriously strained and were in short supply owing to previous neglect. They were specifically identified as sectors requiring greater shares of investment than in the past by the new leadership. Several reforms in the planning system, the enterprise management system, the trading system, and the pricing system also were aimed at removing imbalances of supply and demand throughout the economy, but the reallocation of investment among sectors by the planners themselves was intended to help correct for that portion of the problem that was a legacy of the planners of unbalanced investment priorities in the past.

The change in emphasis to consumerism and to a balanced economy in the new leadership's development strategy would be enough to cause these changes in investment priorities in the future, but the most dramatic change in the new leaders' development strategy, as far as the implications for investment are concerned, was the change from extensive to intensive development. Thus not only would the relative shares of investment among the productive sectors be readjusted and the share of investment in fixed assets allocated to nonproduction facilities increase, but the share of investment allocated to "technical updating, transformation, and reconstruction" of existing facilities was to increase significantly as well.[17] As a share of investment in fixed assets, investment in capital construction would decline, while "investment in technical transformation" would increase.

### Control over Investment Decisions

One of the major sources of inefficiency in a Soviet-type, centrally planned economy is the excessive extent to which economic decisions are made by planners at the apex of the economic bureaucracy in the capital. Thus a major feature of the economic reforms introduced by the Deng-Zhao leadership was the attempt to stimulate local initiative and efficiency by decentralizing control over some resources and economic activities. Insofar as investment is concerned, local governments gained additional resources by means of significant increases in revenue sharing rates and by increases in the retained earnings and depreciation funds the enterprises under their control were allowed to keep. In addition, in a desire to increase nonbudget financing for investment projects while creating a better system of monitoring the use of those funds, bank loans were to be made available for preferred sectors and uses—that is, for the expansion of the light and textile industries and for the modernization of existing facilities in those industries. Another reform to make investment activities more efficient was the move to allow competitive bidding by collective construction units for work on investment projects in the belief that this initiative would lower costs, reduce time of completion, and improve the quality of the investment project.

It is most important to note that, despite the decentralization in decision making, management, and financing in the investment sector, investment remains a "commanding height" economic activity—that is, one of the crucial economic activities that must be ultimately "controlled" by the planners. According to the Chinese definition of a socialist economy, it is a planned economy, which means that the allocation of investment is under the direction of the planners. The fine distinction between what is directly planned and what is indirectly controlled by the planners is a difficult one to make, but the Chinese economic reforms center on the attempt to shift from mandatory planning to guidance by the planners, whatever it means.[18] Nonetheless, the principle of the central government retaining control over investment has been made clear even by the most ardent advocates of economic reform among the leadership.

## Financing of Investment

Indeed, much investment is still planned and financed by unilateral grants in the budget, as in the past. Investment projects in this category, of course, will be the ones that are larger and more important—from the standpoint of the planners. There are other investment projects that will be approved by the planners and included in the plan, but unlike such projects in the past, these will be financed by local government units or by the enterprises themselves out of local funds, out of retained earnings, or from bank loans. Then, some investment projects will not be included in the plan, but they must either be below a specific value (depending upon the location and unit of government undertaking the investment) and on the list of projects, or they must be types of investment that have been approved by the central planners. Economic levels also will be used to help influence local investment decisions in the desired direction; that is, bank loans used to finance investment projects will have differential interest rates and repayment schedules favoring the desired uses.[19]

A major new source of investment financing, which is being relied upon for obtaining modern technology as well, is the foreigner. To alleviate the burden on domestic resources, foreign loans—especially cheap, concessionary loans from international financial institutions (the World Bank, International Monetary Fund, etc.)—are being obtained by the central government and included in the budget as revenue for use in investment projects. In addition, foreign investment in joint ventures and even in some wholly-owned foreign enterprises in China are encouraged, especially in activities that bring new and modern technology to China. Finally, the sale of Chinese bonds on foreign money markets has begun on a limited and experimental scale, and foreign banks are being allowed to open branches in China and receive deposits and extend loans.

Here, too, the central government plans to retain control over this new source of investment financing. In order to free up local initiative and facilitate a more rapid transfer of modern technology from abroad, specific regions and cities have been allowed to negotiate foreign loans and investments directly, subject to specific limits on the amount of investment or borrowing involved. Four special economic zones along the coasts and Hainan Island have been given the greatest freedom to deal directly with foreigners, and fourteen cities were declared open to foreigners with only slightly more stringent restrictions.[20] The provinces of Guangzhou and Fujian (where many families have relatives living overseas) also have been given some freedom to deal directly with foreigners for the purpose of stimulating foreign loans to and investment in those provinces. In terms of the constraints on China's future economic growth, the introduction of this new source of investment financing may be very significant, because it is to be directly linked with the acquisition of new and modern technology, especially in the expansion of capacity in China's most serious bottleneck sectors—that is, energy and transportation.

The preceding discussion is only a brief review of the economic reforms introduced that aim to readjust the rate and structure of China's investment, to decentralize decision making in and management of investment projects, and to introduce a much wider variety of sources for funds to finance those investment projects. A richer discussion of the many interesting twists and turns in the introduction of these reforms and greater details of their exact formulation is far beyond the scope or purpose of this paper. For our purpose here, however, two questions must be raised about these reforms. As with all of the reforms that have been introduced by the Deng-Zhao leadership, the preceding discussion may describe the intent of the reforms, but what has been their actual impact on the investment sector? Then, even if effectively implemented so as to achieve a reasonable approximation of their desired purpose, what is the implication of these reforms for the importance of investment in China's future growth? That is, will investment remain the single most important determinant of China's growth?

## Results of the Reforms

In a remark to a visiting foreigner, Deng Xiaoping correctly admonished foreign experts for judging the results of the reform program before it had a chance to be implemented, and we should heed his advice. Yet, in the past few years, rather clear and informative trends have occurred in the investment sector that permit some tentative conclusions. As for the attempt to restructure investment, the efforts thus far have not been very successful in some areas, but very successful in others. Reductions in the rate of investment were achieved by a 40 percent reduction in the level of investment financed by unilateral grants in the state budget between 1979 and 1982, with the rate of accumulation declining from 34.6 to 29.0 percent over the same period.[21] Unfortunately, however, once the output mix of the machine-building and other heavy industries had been readjusted to better meet the needs of other producers, the rate of growth of heavy industry began to increase, as did the level of investment financed by the state budget and the share of that investment going to heavy industry.

Equally troublesome in the attempt to reduce the rate of investment was the rapid growth of investment outside the plan (and outside the state budget) resulting from the reforms that decentralized the management and financing of investment. In 1979 only 20 percent of investment in capital construction was outside the state budget; by 1984 the share was 45.6 percent.[22] Thus, although the state budget allocations for investment in capital construction were no higher in 1984 than in 1979, the level of total investment in the economy was 42 percent higher in 1984 than in 1979, the rate of accumulation only declining from 34.6 percent in 1979 to 31.2 percent in 1984. At the end of 1985, therefore, the state authorities had lost considerable control over the level of investment, and the rate of accumulation was increasing, adding to the inflationary forces being generated by the economic reforms.[23]

As for the attempt to restructure investment within the material producing sectors, the new leadership soon discovered that China's agricultural problem could not be solved in the near future by increased investment—the investment required was well beyond the funds available.[24] The solution to China's agricultural problem was to be found elsewhere; in "correct policies" (the contract responsibility system) and in technological innovation. Whereas investment in agriculture had been 11.1 percent of total investment in 1979, it was only 5 percent in 1984; in fact, the absolute level of investment in agriculture declined by 35 percent during that period.[25] Because of local investment outside of the state budget and central plan, investment in light industry did increase between 1979 and 1984 (by 40 percent), but as a share of total investment it remained relatively stable at about 6 percent.[26] On the other hand, despite their criticism of investments in heavy industry dominating the allocations of investment funds in earlier periods, that sector's share of total investment remained above 40 percent. Quite simply, any major development program in a developing country such as China, even one emphasizing balanced growth, requires significant investments in the producer's goods industry. This statement is even more true of an economy suffering from serious shortages of energy, construction materials, agricultural inputs and machinery, and transportation equipment.

The attempt to restructure the allocation of investments as between the "productive" sectors and the "nonproductive" sectors of the economy and also in favor of improving existing facilities as against creating new facilities was much more successful. In 1979, productive construction accounted for 70 percent of total investment, by 1984, it accounted for 60 percent. In absolute terms, nonproductive investment increased by almost 100 percent between 1979 and 1984; residential housing accounting for about one-half of nonproductive investment during this period.[27] Finally, the attempt to technically improve existing enterprises was responsible for a considerable shift in the mix of investment in new facilities versus investments in existing facilities. In 1979 the former was one-third larger than the latter; in 1984 they were about equal.[28] As for investments in "technical updating and transformation expenditures" as a share of investments on fixed assets in state-owned units, the former made up 25 percent of total investment in fixed assets in 1979, 37 percent of the total in 1984.[29]

The attempt to decentralize the management and financing of investment, in one sense, can be said to have been too successful. Local governments and economic units have used their freedom to invest, but have often done so by creating enterprises that compete with more efficient production facilities operated by the state. These locally owned and operated enterprises would compete for the needed inputs and markets for outputs, forcing the national enterprises to operate at low levels of capacity utilization, that is, very inefficiently. These investment decisions merely emphasized the need for price reform; they certainly did not reflect "national" interests. In addition, the access of local units to new sources of investment funds and their use of those funds led to increases in the money supply (because of excessive bank loans), excess demand, and inflationary pressures. In 1985 these problems of undesirable investment projects (from the central authorities' point of view) and uncontrolled increases in inflationary pressures created a crisis, leading the central authorities to recentralize control over investment decisions and financing.

Unfortunately, statistics to illustrate these changes are available only from 1984, but they do indicate the clear trends that are involved.[30] In 1979 only 20 percent of capital construction investments in state-owned units were outside the state budget; by 1984, 45.6 percent of investments in state-owned enterprises were outside the state budget. Furthermore, by 1984 total investment in state-owned units had declined to less than two-thirds of total investment in fixed assets, while the collective sector accounted for 13 percent of the total and the private sector (mostly house building) accounted for 22.3 percent of the total. In terms of financing, only data for 1983 are available, but already the state budget had decline significantly as a source of investment funds, representing only 40.1 percent of total investment in fixed assets. Domestic loans supplied 14.3 percent and foreign investment 1.7 percent of the investments in fixed assets in that year. Remarkably, the largest source of investment funds was "self-raised funds and other sources" (i.e., local revenues and revenue-sharing funds, depreciation funds, retained earnings, and private savings), accounting for 43.4 percent of total investment in fixed assets.

It is with regard to the change in policy calling for reliance on the foreigner for technology transfer, investment projects, and investment financing that the admonition to wait and see for a few more years before passing judgment is most appropriate. Thus far, most foreign investment has been in the form of money; loan agreements were signed for US$20.3 billion during 1979–1985 ($3.53 billion in 1985 alone), and $15.6 billion had been utilized ($2.43 billion in 1985 alone).[31] Thus, as indicated in Table 25.2, foreign loans accounted for about 5 percent of the state's financial resources in the 1980s. Those loans were largely concessional loans associated with projects approved by international institutions. Commercial credits extended during 1979–1985 amounted to US$1.7 billion, and $1.3 billion had been utilized. If the Chinese were willing to pay commercial rates on loans, of course, they would have access to a much larger flow of funds, but they are well aware of the problem of debt financing being faced by many other developing countries and have been very conservative in this regard.

The major hope in relying on the foreigner to transfer technology and know-how to China and to help finance the transfer of technology was in the area of direct investment, and by the end of 1985 there were 2,300 joint ventures, 3,700 cooperative enterprises, 120 foreign-owned enterprises, and thirty-five offshore oil cooperative exploitation projects. Yet, although the total contract value of direct foreign investment was US$16.2 billion, only $4.6 billion of that amount had actually been used. Furthermore, most of the foreign investment projects were by overseas Chinese businessmen from Hong Kong and Macao and involved processing facilities in which China already had mastered the relevant technology—if not the management techniques. Finally, for those foreign-owned enterprises that did bring new and advanced technology to China, in almost every case, they had invested in China only because they had been granted access to the Chinese domestic market for the distribution of their product (or provided services directly to foreign visitors).

The real test of these reforms in the investment sector, of course, is the extent to which efficiency or factor productivity is improved and the extent to which investment and investment financing are alleviated as a constraint on China's future growth. In their annual statistical reports, the Chinese now include many indicators for measuring improvements in efficiency and productivity in various industries or activities. The interpretation or evaluation of this statistical information is not a simple matter and cannot be undertaken in this paper. Obviously, certain indicators can be cited to show considerable improvement, while others can be cited to show continued inefficiency and poor results. For example, the crude aggregate statistics cited in table 25.1 show a definite turn for the better in terms of total factor productivity in the 1980s, an annual increase in total factor productivity between 2.4 and 3.5 percent a year. Yet, as with most of the statistics that can be cited to show an improvement in efficiency or productivity, one has to be cautious and determine the source of improvement before coming to a definite conclusion.[32]

Thus far our review of results of the economic reforms in the investment sector merely repeats the lessons learned in the results of the economic reform program as a whole: The results are mixed and quick-fix solutions to China's economic problems are unlikely to work; some adjustments or corrections come more easily than others; attempts to decentralize decision making must be accompanied by other reforms if it is to succeed, that is, price reform and realistic economic levers (taxes and interest rates); and so forth.

The remolding of the Chinese economy into an economy in which technological innovation, efficient operations, and growing productivity is a common or typical phenomenon will be a long, slow process. On the other hand, at this point in time anyway, the growing awareness of these lessons has not deterred the Deng-Zhao leadership from pursuing the economic reform program, nor has it generated an unmanageable backlash against the reforms. Our best guess, therefore, is that the leadership will be given more time to continue the economic reforms in the investment sector and, given that time, may be able to achieve their objectives. Whether or not they will, of course, only time can tell.

## Role of Investment

Our purpose in this paper is to determine whether or not investment needs and the sources for financing those investment needs will continue to be a serious constraint on China's future economic growth. In answering this question, we can assume that the likely changes in the efficiency or productivity of capital in the Chinese economy over the next fifteen years will not be dramatic. Even if successful, the economic reform program in the investment sector involves a very marginal portion of the total capital stock or fixed assets. Thus, on the average, the amount of investment required per unit of output will change very slowly. In addition, a change in the rate of savings and investment will also be somewhat small: The major change from excessively high rates to 30 percent and below has already occurred. Given the magnitude of China's development program, a rate of savings and investment below 25 percent is most unlikely.

In the intermediate period (about fifteen years), the rate of savings and capital accumulation are major determinants of growth in any theoretical model of economic growth; but with a very significant distinction—the rate of growth of output adjusts to the rate of growth of the capital stock (in other words, the quantity of fixed assets and their rate of growth remain as one of the single most important determinants of the level and rate of growth of output), while marginal changes in the rate of savings and investment and in the productivity of investment are either one-time changes in conditions that soon lose their impact on the results, or can be incorporated as additional determinants of the rate of increase of output if those changes are continuous. The whole point of our argument here is to say that no matter what the rate of savings and investment or the rate of change in the efficiency of capital, the level and rate of increase in investment are bound to remain a major determinant of China's economic growth. Furthermore, given the high targets for that future growth, investment will remain a constraint on that growth—the same role that investment played in the past.

## Forecast of Investment Needs and
## Sources of Investment Funds

What follows is more for the purpose of illustrating our argument that China's investment needs in the future are likely to be very large and the sources of funding those needs rather limited than for the purpose of presenting any forecast of the future. In addition, these estimates rely exclusively on the work already carried out by others. All other estimates accept the Chinese target of quadrupling gross output between 1980 and the end of the century. Each estimate also implicitly or explicitly accepts investment as the major determinant or constraint on China's economic growth.

The official target implies an average rate of growth in total agricultural and industrial output over the twenty-year period 1980–2000 of 7.2 percent.[33] Total agricultural and industrial output involves much double counting and grows faster than national income; the World Bank estimates that the 7.2 percent growth in total agricultural and industrial output is consistent with a 6.6 percent growth in national income (gross domestic product).[34] To achieve this growth, using a sectoral model with considerable detail and demands on consistency, the World Bank estimates that the Chinese will need to maintain a rate of investment of 30 percent. Chinese estimates have been published, but involve much less rigor in the methodology by which they were obtained. In any event, the Chinese believe the rate of investment will need to be 26 to 29 percent. The difference between the two estimates may well lie in the assumptions about increases in efficiency and total factor productivity in the economy, but the World Bank estimates do assume an increase of total factor productivity of 1.6 percent a year, which accounts for one-fourth of the total growth in output between 1980 and 2000.

Assuming no changes in prices, official statistics for 1980 and the estimates in the previous paragraph indicate that China's national income and investment in the year 2000 will be 1,324 billion yuan and 397.2 billion yuan, respectively. To achieve this target for investment, investment would have to grow by 6.3 percent a year between 1980 and 2000. Of course, not all this investment would go to increase fixed assets. According to World Bank estimates, over the twenty-year period, fixed assets would increase their share of the total capital stock slightly from 65 percent to 67.5 percent, with circulating capital declining from 35 percent to 32.5 percent. More dramatic, however, would be the shift in the sectoral capital stock: The agricultural, light industrial, and services sectors' shares of the capital stock would decline, and heavy industry and infrastructure would increase their share—heavy industry because of the demand for producers' goods in a program of quadrupling output in twenty years, infrastructure because of past neglect.

By the year 2000, therefore, we estimate that the Chinese will require, in constant prices, an amount of investment that is almost 3.5 times the level of total investment in 1980. Time, space, and ability preclude our dissecting this estimate to determine whether or not this large increase in investment over two decades is feasible and consistent in terms of the demand and supply of capital goods. At the macro level, however, the commodity side on the investment sector would not appear to be the bottleneck. If total production increases as targeted, the investment required calls for the rate of accumulation to remain at 29 percent of national income, while total factor productivity increases at 1.9 percent a year—not a terribly high ratio, given the rates achieved for most periods after the post–Great Leap Forward crisis (1958–1962) in Table 25.1. The Chinese development strategy over this period obviously calls for greater reliance on the foreigner— that is, imports of modern technology—than in the past; but the problem there is not the foreigner's ability to supply the desired producers' goods, but in the Chinese ability to pay for them.

The most serious problem with China's future investment program will be on the financing side because of an interesting consequence of the economic reforms. On the commodity side, although the economic reforms are trying to increase factor productivity, remove bottlenecks, eliminate losses, improve product quality, create incentives for innovation, and so on, all of these changes will lead to significant, but marginal, changes in the marginal capital/output ratio. Nevertheless, the level and rate of growth in investment must remain as the single most important determinant of output growth, and the increase in the level of investment needed will be only slightly less than the desired increase in total output, even with the success of the economic reforms. At the same time, the reforms have changed the manner in which investment is to be financed. In the past, the budget was used to mobilize savings and place those savings in the hands of the planners, who allocated investment to desired uses by means of unilateral budget grants. Inasmuch as the unbalanced priorities of the planners created many bottlenecks in the economy and the means by which investment financing was provided—free—involved no incentive to use investment funds efficiently, the economic reforms are trying to change the system by allowing greater decentralization in both the determination of investment projects and their financing. Inasmuch as the investment needs estimated for the year 2000 remain less than 30 percent of national income in that year, the old system should not have been overwhelmed by the problem of raising the necessary funds when it was able to raise more than 30 percent during most years in the past. Now that the means for financing investment have been considerably diversified, however, the financing of investment may well become a serious constraint on China's future growth.

Centrally planned investment projects, financed by means of unilateral budget grants, will continue as in the past; they just will not be the dominant or only source of investment funds. For example, from 1980 to 1984, financial revenue as a percentage of national income declined to about one-fourth from its one-third share typical in the pre-1980 period, while appropriations for capital construction as a percentage of financial expenditure in the budget declined to slightly less than 30 percent in the 1980s from the traditional level of about 40 percent. As a result, state budget investment in capital construction as a share of total capital construction declined to slightly more than 50 percent in the 1980s as compared to its traditional level of more than 80 percent. In short, the central authorities can be expected to retain direct control over at least one-half of investment and should be able to funnel the necessary financial funds for those investment activities through the central budget as unilateral grants as in the past.

Self-raised funds, of course, have been used in the 1980s for financing a large share of investment, and they account for as great a share of the total as unilateral budget grants. The problem, of course, is that the central authorities did not want this source of finance so large a volume of investment and have tried repeatedly to restrict these expenditures without much success. These self-financed investment expenditures have made actual investment exceed planned investment by a large margin, adding to the inflationary problems of the central authorities. Equally important, with the administered price system yet to be reformed to reflect the true values of alternative choices (even if they were to reflect the planners values, not the consumers), decentralized decision making in the investment sector only leads to decisions judged irrational or inappropriate by the central authorities.

In other words, decentralized decision making and financing in the investment sector are quite capable of accounting for a significant share of total investment, but are unlikely to be allowed to do so *until* the proper "economic levels" have been adopted to assure that the level and allocation of that investment is in keeping with "national" interests. Those economic levers do not now exist, and this is a major reason for all the problems being experienced in this sector at the present time. The more serious problem, of course, is that the Chinese leaders have continually postponed introducing the necessary price reform and adoption of the necessary economic levers. Until the necessary changes in prices and economic levers have been made, attempts to rely heavily on "self-raised funds" for investment financing will only generate the problems now being experienced, leading the central authorities to use administrative means to restrict and directly control this source of investment financing.

A much smaller source at the present time, but one that could become the largest source of investment financing, is domestic bank loans borrowed by the enterprise for investment projects and to be repaid at an interest rate. In 1982 and 1983 this source financed about 15 percent of total investment in fixed assets and a slightly larger share of investments in "technical updating and transformation" of existing enterprises.[35] The advantages of this source are that it comes from all savings deposited in the banking system (personal and enterprise, as well as government), that investment allocations can be directly influenced by economic levers (the interest rate), and that required repayments create incentives for the efficient use of the funds. These very merits also cause problems. Investment allocation decisions are turned over to bankers and rely on the initiative of the individual enterprises. In those socialist systems in which this type of investment financing has been tried out, including China, the central authorities end up adopting differential interest rates by broad categories and differential repayment schedules as well; the borrowers end up borrowing money for one type of investment, but somehow using it for another. In addition, the interest rates are all set too low, so that investment fund rationing must be handled by the bankers in another manner, giving the funds to "preferred" customers, such as those with political leverage or those with prior approval of the planners. In addition, the banking personnel in these socialist systems lack the professional training and the political prestige to perform the tasks required of them, that is, to replace the planners as the major source of financing for investment projects in the economy. For all these reasons, I expect that bank loans will remain the source for less than one-third of China's investment financing in the future, restricted to specific purposes or specific industries, rather than become—as they should in a true market socialist economy—the major source of investment financing.

The final new source of investment financing has received the greatest publicity in the West, but has remained less than 2 percent of total investment: foreign investment. Given the very conservative attitude of the central authorities toward ratios of debt servicing to export earnings, foreign sources of investment funds would probably be limited to less than 10 percent of total investment in China by the year 2000. Yet, with the growth of the domestic economy, even these conservative banking practices would allow China's foreign debt to increase rather significantly. In the World Bank estimates relied upon earlier in this chapter, China's foreign debt by the year 2000 would grow to US$56 billion (net of earlier payments of interest and principle), but this still falls well within the limit of 15 percent of export earnings to service the debt. In other words, if they chose to do so, the Chinese could borrow commercial loans abroad and take advantage of concessionary loans from international organizations to finance a small portion of their investment needs, but the use of this source of investment funds will undoubtedly be kept well below the total amount available.

Rather than loans, the Chinese leaders hope, as a result of their open-economy policy, that foreigners will provide investment financing in the form of direct investments, joint ventures and wholly foreign-owned enterprises. There are, however, three major obstacles to achieving this objective: the lack of a well-defined and operational set of regulations and laws that govern these foreign investments so that foreigners can estimate with some degree of certainty the costs and benefits of such an investment; the lack of a guarantee or established method for the repatriation of profits into convertible currency; and—most important of all—the lack of access to the domestic market. Without these, the foreigner will be investing merely for future potential and on blind faith, incentives that will not lure a large flow of foreign investment to China.

The first two problems can be dealt with in due course, and the Chinese have indicated they intend to do so, but the matter of access to the Chinese market is not very promising to the potential foreign investor. The Chinese leaders have made it quite clear, especially in their criticism of the special economic zones, that the foreigner is being invited to China to bring new technology and products to China and to increase China's export earnings, not to compete with domestic producers. If foreign investors were allowed to compete with domestic producers and expatriate their profits, of course, direct foreign investment in China would increase dramatically.

This review of the sources that have been introduced to supplement and replace unilateral budget grants in financing investment has come to a rather clear conclusion. Because of various problems of the economic system and environment that are unlikely to be corrected soon or because of restrictions imposed by the central authorities so as to assure "national interests," unilateral budget grants are likely to remain the dominant form of investment financing in China. In addition, because of the failure of the alternative sources to provide sufficient funds for the investment projects desired by the central authorities, these sources are likely to be further restricted and, therefore, even less likely to provide the share of investment financing they otherwise could provide. As a result, unilateral budget grants, administratively allocated bank loans, and specified or planned uses of retained earnings by local enterprises and units of government are likely to be called upon to finance China's investment program through the remainder of the century.

## Conclusion

This chapter is an attempt to put some thoughts on paper in the midst of a new research project concerned with forecasting and the role of investment and investment financing over the near future in China. Because that project is still under way, many of the arguments presented here are tentative and incomplete. Yet, I believe the major themes or hypothesis that have emerged from that research have been made clear in this chapter. These are as follows:

1. At the macro level of aggregate statistics, China's development experience is a classic case of what has been termed "extensive" development—investment in new production facilities with limited technological change or increase in factor productivity. Some would argue that this process is not representative of true economic development, only of growth in an absolute sense. In any event, the role of investment and investment financing in this process is critical and a major feature of any Soviet-type economy pursuing a Stalinist development strategy.

2. The economic reforms of the Deng-Zhao leadership are said to have changed this development strategy to one seeking "intensive" economic development; growth through technological innovation, increasing factor productivity, better quality of goods and services, and so on. As part of this reform, the investment sector was to undergo fundamental change in

regard to the level of investment (lower rate of accumulation, higher rate of consumption), allocation of investment (redirected to the previously neglected sectors), decentralization in the management of investment projects (including freedom to make investment decisions in certain types of investments), and the development of several new sources of investment financing (bank loans, retained earnings, and foreign investment). These reforms were to make investment more efficient or productive and remove constraints on various types of investment and the financing of investment.

3. The extent to which these reforms have been implemented successfully is relatively uneven. Undoubtedly one can claim they have been partially successful, but one must also list the several problems and failures that have been encountered as well. The major point to be made is that even if these reforms are successful, investment will remain a critical explanatory variable in China's future growth, no less than in the past, and the new sources of financing will not remove investment as a major constraint on China's future growth.

4. An attempt was made to provide a numerical illustration of how and why investment and its financing will continue to be a constraint on China's future growth. To be more useful as an illustration, however, this section of the chapter requires more detailed research. The main point to be made is that the investment sector will remain a dominant sector in China's activity, with producers' goods even increasing their share of investment allocations and share of fixed capital. This statement will be true as long as China pursues an attempt to quadruple output between 1980 and 2000, which calls for rather rapid growth over this period. In any event, this point is consistent with economic theory and historical experience throughout the world; that is, no matter what development strategy is followed, investment is a crucial ingredient of that strategy.

The arguments about sources of investment financing are harder to illustrate without further research and documentation. Yet, the principle is clear. While the desire is to rely on sources outside the budget, the necessary steps to make those sources achieve their potential in ways that are acceptable to the planners have not been taken or cannot be taken because they are unacceptable to the planners. Thus, without these steps being taken, the attempt to rely on these sources will only cause the central authorities to reimpose administrative control in the investment sector and increase their reliance upon funds at their disposal—unilateral budget grants. Yet, the economic reforms have reduced, in a relative sense, the funds available to them to a considerable extent and also have increased the competitive claims upon them. In other words, without true and complete reform, the central authorities who want to retain control over investment will find their attempt at reform to open new sources of investment financing has only reduced their control and the funds available to them, perhaps creating a constraint on their planned growth even greater than was true in the past.

## Notes

1. Robert F. Dernberger, "Mainland China's Economic System: A New Model or Variations on an Old Theme?" Paper presented at Panel 3: The Economy; at Thirteenth Sino-American Conference on Mainland China, "Whither Mainland China: Reforms and Problems," Taipei, Taiwan, June 11–17, 1984. My latest paper on this subject is Robert F. Dernberger, "Economic Policy and Performance," in Joint Economic Committee, U.S. Congress, *The Chinese Economy in The Eighties* (Washington, D.C.: U.S. Government Printing Office, 1986). A complete list of my articles on this topic is included as footnote 1 in that article.

2. Extensive development emphasizes growth of output by increasing the quantity of inputs, including fixed capital; intensive development stresses increases in output per unit of input, even if fixed capital were to remain constant. Technological change and increases in factor productivity are necessary conditions for the latter, but may remain constant in the former.

3. Of the thirty-four countries with per capita GNP below $400 (the low-income economies) in 1982, the highest rate of growth in per capita GNP from 1960 to 1982 (excluding China) was 2.8 percent in Pakistan and Kenya, followed by 2.6 percent in Sri Lanka, then 2.5 percent in Burundi. The average rate of growth in per capita income from 1960 to 1982 for the thirty-eight lower middle-income countries (per capita incomes between $400 and $1,650) was 3.2 percent. For the nineteen industrial market economies, the average rate of growth was 3.3 percent. The World Bank, *World Development Report 1984* (New York: Oxford University Press, 1984), pp. 218–219.

4. According to the World Bank estimates, compared to China's rate of investment of more than 25 percent, gross domestic investment as a share of gross domestic product was 13 percent in the low-income countries (excluding India and China) in 1960 and 1982; 15 and 23 percent in 1960 and 1982, respectively, in the lower middle-income countries; and 21 and 20 percent, respectively, in the industrial market economies (World Bank, pp. 226–227). In terms of international market economies (World Bank, *World Development Report, 1984*, pp. 226–227). In terms of international comparisons, growth rates of per capita income and the rates of investment in China were most similar to those of the twenty-two upper-middle-income countries during the 1960s and 1970s.

5. Accumulation is best defined as everything that is not defined as consumption, that is, national income − consumption = accumulation; but that begs the question. In essence, accumulation refers to that share of national income devoted to increases in fixed capital assets (both productive and non-productive), working capital, and material reserves.

6. Investments in fixed assets consist of two parts: investment in capital construction and investment in technical renovation and transformation. Capital construction covers that part of investment in fixed assets that involves the construction and expansion of facilities and the purchase and installation of equipment, but it excludes that portion of investment in fixed assets that involves technical updating and transformation projects.

7. State Statistical Bureau, *Statistical Yearbook of China, 1984* (Hong Kong: Economic Information & Agency, 1984), p. 31.

8. Robert F. Dernberger, "Economic Development and Modernization in China: The Attempt to Limit Dependence on the Transfer of Modern Industrial Technology

from Abroad and to Control Its Corruption of the Maoist Model," in Frederic J. Fleron, Jr., ed., *Technology and Communist Culture* (New York: Praeger, 1977), p. 238.

9. Without getting involved in a rather complicated debate about statistical methodology, assigning a unit of capital a weight of 60 percent and labor a weight of 40 percent is compatible with the econometric estimates of their relative contributions to output growth, while 40 percent and 60 percent weights on capital and labor are compatible with their share in income distribution. Thus, I would prefer the former set of weights, but others may argue for the latter, so both are included here and in many other analyses of total factor productivity.

10. World Bank, *China: Long-Term Development Issues and Options*, A World Bank Country Economic Report (Baltimore: Johns Hopkins Press, 1985), Table 7.1, p. 111.

11. Gregory C. Chow, *The Chinese Economy* (New York: Harper & Row, 1985), p. 131.

12. For a catalog of the various problems plaguing the Chinese economy in the mid-1970s, see Robert F. Dernberger, "The Chinese Search for the Path of Self-Sustained Growth in the 1980's: An Assessment," in Joint Economic Committee, U.S. Congress, *China Under the Four Modernizations* (Washington, D.C.: U.S. Government Printing Office, 1982), section of paper on "Background," pp. 20–27.

13. In a theoretical model, of course, the "optimum" rate of accumulation or investment would depend on the target year for achieving maximum consumption per capita or the specification of a social rate of interest for discounting all future consumption, all this assuming that the largest consumption per capita is the objective—not the maximum rate of growth. In long-run models of economic growth, the rate of capital accumulation is not a constraint. Rather, in the long run, the rate of growth of the labor force and of technological change are the only constraints on growth; that is, capital is not scarce in the long run with technology and resources fixed.

14. With the lower rate of accumulation and investment, the absolute level of investment will still grow as fast as the growth in national income, once the transition to the lower rate has been achieved. In other words, the change in policy leads to a one-time change in the division of national income between consumption and investment. Furthermore, the rate of 25 percent would still leave China with one of the highest rates of accumulation and investment among the developing countries.

15. Because planners in a Soviet-type, centrally planned economy are continually being faced with scarcities and bottlenecks (these economies often being referred to as economies of shortages), it is rational for the planners to assign the highest priority to producer's goods rather than consumer's goods: Inputs that can be used to produce other goods (i.e., machines, metals, energy) have a greater value than end products that are unusable as far as the planner is concerned. This natural behavioral trait of the planner is just another variation of growth for growth's sake, as against the satisfaction of consumer demand or striving for increases in the standard of living.

16. Inasmuch as investment in heavy industry was about eight times larger than that in light industry, even a major change in priorities to give the former less and the latter more would still leave heavy industry with a dominant share of investment in industry. In fact, that is a major lesson the Chinese have learned in the last few years; because of the dictates of modern technology and the capital intensity of the most modern technology, any major development effort will involve large investments in heavy industry—even when the desired end result is more consumer goods.

17. Initially, the new Chinese leadership relied on imports of complete plants, such as the Baoshan Iron and Steel Complex, but almost immediately realized that carrying out the technological transformation of their economy by means of adding

new facilities on the margin not only would take a very long time, but would be prohibitively costly. In addition, existing production facilities will dominate the Chinese economy for some time to come and, unless renovated with new technology, would continue to operate inefficiently and waste resources.

18. During a visit by U.S. economists at the end of 1984, just after the release of the document on urban and industrial reform that had been adopted by the Third Plenum of the Central Committee of the Twelfth Party Congress, repeated reference was made to the move from mandatory to guidance planning, as called for in the document, by Chinese officials who met with the delegation. Yet, upon questioning, few Chinese could define "guidance" planning very specifically and few agreed on the same definition. See the section "Guidance Planning" in Barry Naughton's "Summary of Findings," *Economic Reform in China*, Report of the American Economists Study Team to the People's Republic of China, National Committee on U.S.-China Relations (New York, no date), pp. 11–14.

19. These reforms, if successful, would considerably reduce the burden on the government's central budget for investment financing and greatly increase the local supervision over and interest in efficient and productive investment projects, while retaining the planners' priorities in the allocation of investment. This does not mean (a qualification that must always be made in regard to economic policies in China) that everyone will abide by the rules and there will be no unplanned, nonapproved investment activity.

20. Because the local officials in these cities reacted aggressively in the attempt to lure foreign investment, promising tax concessions and committing resources for building infrastructure as would any active governor in the United States, the central government soon realized the commitment of Chinese investment funds to develop the urban infrastructure was far beyond the amount of funds available for that purpose. Thus ten of the cities were put on tighter control from the central authorities, although still listed as open cities. The four that remained relatively open, although not quite as open as the special economic zones, were Dalien, Tianjin, Shanghai, and Guangzhou.

21. State Statistical Bureau, PRC, *Statistical Yearbook of China, 1984* (Hong Kong: Economic Information & Agency, 1984), pp. 35 and 301.

22. *Statistical Yearbook of China, 1984*, p. 301.

23. The problem with the official price indices as indicators of inflationary pressures is that these indices include fixed prices and negotiated prices, as well as market prices. According to the official statistics, the general index of retail prices in 1984 stood at 117.7 (1978 = 100). See "Index of Various Commodity Prices," in State Statistical Bureau, PRC, *China: A Statistics Survey in 1985* (Beijing: China Statistical Information and Consultancy Service Center, 1985), p. 93. The complaints in the Chinese press, observations of foreigners, and official recognition of the inflation problem in the speeches by China's political leaders indicate that the relevant increase in uncontrolled prices is many times the officially reported 17 percent increase over the seven years after 1978.

24. See the discussion of this problem in Zhao Ziyang, "The Present Economic Situation and the Principles for Future Economic Construction," *Beijing Review*, vol. 24, no. 51 (21 December 1981).

25. *China: A Statistics Survey in 1985*, pp. 67–68.

26. Ibid.

27. Ibid., p. 69.

28. Ibid.

29. *Statistical Yearbook of China, 1984*, pp. 301 and 333; *China; A Statistics Survey in 1985*, p. 65.

30. Statistics in this paragraph are from *China: A Statistics Survey in 1985,* pp. 65–66; *Statistical Yearbook of China, 1984,* p. 302.

31. Statistics in this and the following paragraph are from "Key Projects Encourage Investment," *Beijing Review,* vol. 29, no. 6 & 7 (February 1986), p. 28.

32. For example, did total factor productivity increase because of increases in the productivity of the individual inputs of labor and capital, or did the overall index increase because of a change in the sectoral employment of those factors? If the industries that were relatively labor intensive accounted for a large share of the rate of growth, while the capital-intensive industries lagged behind, the average capital/output ratio would decline even though the capital/output ratio in each industry stayed the same. From 1979 to 1983, the fastest growing branches of industry were the textile (12.9 percent a year), food (9.3 percent), chemical (9.2 percent), and building materials (8.1 percent) industries; these industries also had the lowest capital/output ratios—1.15, 1.07, 2.16, and 1.87, respectively. On the other hand, the slowest-growing branch of industry was coal and coke (1.9 percent a year), which has the highest capital/output ratio of all branches of industry, 5.83.

33. In a major political speech given by Hu Yaobang to the Twelfth Party Congress (September 1, 1983), obviously intended to rally the party cadres behind the new party leadership, Hu introduced a new slogan: "The general objective of China's economic construction for the two decades between 1981 and the end of the century . . . is to quadruple the gross value of industrial and agricultural production [placing] China in the front ranks of the countries of the world in income." When I expressed my disappointment to several economists in China with this reversion to a crude slogan, compared to the detailed and honest policy discussions and problem-solving analyses that were becoming a trademark of the new leadership, pointing out that Hu's speech had generated all sorts of mechanical or simplistic arguments as to how this or that region or unit would achieve the target of quadrupling everything by the end of the century, I was told that the Chinese were having difficulty in understanding and appreciating the more detailed and frank analyses of their economic problems and worked better with these slogans. In other words, the Chinese need simple quantitative targets and timetables to mobilize their development efforts. On the other hand, other Chinese (as well as outside observers) have accepted "quadrupling" as an operational target and have developed analyses of China's economic problems within that framework. For example, see the twenty-five essays by prominent economists that investigate the various sectoral implications of this target in the volume edited by Liu Guoguang, *Investigation of Problems in China's Economic Development Strategy* (Shanghai: People's Publishers, 1984), in Chinese. This target is also accepted as the Chinese official target by the World Bank in making their estimates of its investment implications in World Bank, *China: Long-Term Development Issues and Options* (Baltimore: Johns Hopkins University Press, 1985). The projections for the investment needs by the end of the century made by the World Bank are those under the projections for the "Quadruple" model and are found on pp. 38–39. The detailed methodology and results of the projections made in the "Quadruple" model are presented in Annex 4 to the main report.

34. This estimate is from p. 36 of the World Bank report cited in note 33, while the estimates in the remainder of the paragraph are from pp. 38–39.

35. *Statistical Yearbook of China, 1984,* pp. 302 and 333.

# 26

## Major Contradictions in Beijing's Economic Reforms

*Edward K. Sah*

Generally speaking, economists in mainland China have classified all socialist economic systems, either historical or existing, into five kinds, namely, the supply system based on military communism; the traditional centralized planning system; the improved centralized planning system; the system that organically combines planned economy with market mechanism; and the system of "market socialism."

Since the establishment of the People's Republic of China (PRC) on October 1, 1949, Beijing has practiced the traditional centralized planning system after the Soviet model; and in recent years Beijing initiated economic reforms in an attempt to effect a transition to a system similar to the system that organically combines planned economy with market mechanism. In this chapter, the writer will analyze some contradictions arising from these reforms.

The many thorny problems Beijing has encountered during its attempt to effect the transition to a comparatively more flexible economic system have been caused or aggravated by five major contradictions, namely, the contradiction between the planned economy and the market economy; the contradiction between macroeconomic control and microeconomic flexibility; the contradiction between the socialist and nonsocialist ownership systems; the contradiction arising from the separation of ownership and management rights; and the contradiction arising from polarization.

### The Contradiction Between the Planned Economy and the Market Economy

Beijing is aware of the importance of developing a commodity economy under socialist conditions and of implementing the law of value. It regards the full development of a commodity economy as "the only way to invigorate its economy and to prompt enterprises to raise their efficiency, carry out flexible operations and promptly adapt themselves to complex and changing social demands, which surely cannot be achieved by relying only on administrative means and mandatory plans." On the other hand, Beijing is afraid that without guidance, regulation, and administrative control through "state" planning, the free development of a commodity economy would probably lead to disorder, causing inappropriate proportions between various sectors of the national economy.[1] Thus mainland economists have formed two different views about the relations between planned control and market regulation.

A group of economists, represented by Beijing's official mouthpiece Hsüeh Mu-ch'iao, said that in a socialist economy, it is necessary to regard planned economy as the key link and market regulation as a supplementary factor.[2] Beijing, which is prudently promoting economic reforms, supports that opinion. The Decision on Reform of the Economic Structure, adopted by the Twelfth Central Committee of the Chinese Communist Party (CCP) at its Third Plenary Session on October 20, 1984, asserted: "Our economy on the whole is a planned economy, that is, a planned commodity economy, not a market economy that is entirely subject to market regulation."[3]

Another group of economists hold the contrary view that market regulation, instead of planned control, should play the guiding role. Chiang Hsüeh-mo, a mainland economist, asserted:

> We should make clear that mandatory planning is only a regulatory means. As it is carried out from the top to the bottom by administrative means, its integration with the nature of the commodity economy and the rights of commodity producers, including the rights of autonomy, competition and equality, is difficult. It is more easily integrated with guidance planning. Therefore, under the conditions of the socialist commodity economy, it can only be regarded as a regulatory means. The factor that plays the guiding role should be market regulation.[4]

The basis of Chiang's argument was that planned control is by nature incompatible with commodity production.

Janos Kornai, a renowned Hungarian economist, judging from Hungary's experience in economic reforms, maintained that Beijing's reform of the economic structure could not rely solely on the operation of market mechanism. He said: "Market mechanism involves many interrelated factors, which should be regarded as a whole set of systems. For instance, when reforming the price system, consideration must also be given to the practice of the system under which enterprises assume sole responsibility for their profits and losses and the abolition of the system under which raw materials are rationed by administrative orders." He concluded that to achieve flexibility in the price system so that prices of various products will be decided by supply-demand relations, mainland China must abolish the raw materials rationing systems and set up a system of material incentives and financial responsibility.[5]

About six months after the adoption by the CCP's Central Committee of the Decision on Reform of the Economic Structure, Chao Tzu-yang, in a speech at the Third Session of the Sixth National People's Congress (NPC) at the end of March 1985, asserted that in previous years small enterprises had been invigorated at the expense of large and medium-sized ones, which had not been given the same decision-making power. He stressed that it was necessary to concentrate efforts on invigorating large and medium-sized enterprises by implementing, in an all-around way, all regulations finalized by the state concerning the extension of the decision-making power of enterprises, and by reducing mandatory planning tasks for large and medium-sized enterprises.[6] On an inspection tour to Wuhan in mid-April the same year, Chao spoke of the economic reforms in cities, describing them as the key link in the economic restructuring of the whole country. He conceded that one of the functions of cities was to promote the development of the socialist planned commodity economy, that invigoration of enterprises was both the starting point and the foundation of reforms in cities, and that enterprises could probably be invigorated only by "opening the door wide" to other places at home and to foreign countries. He emphasized that the state should use more economic levers to guide enterprises, apply more economic laws to strengthen their management, and use fewer administrative means that interfere with their operation.[7] Judging by these remarks, it is very likely that Beijing will gradually adopt a new system with market mechanism as the key link and planned control as a supplementary factor.

Some articles and reports by mainland economists in the second half of 1985 provided similar clues. For instance, in September of that year, at about the same time as the CCP's National Conference of Delegates was held, Wang Chi-yeh, a pro–Teng Hsiao-p'ing economist, published an article on the transition of the economic structure from an old to a new pattern. He asserted:

> To adapt to the transition from the old pattern to the new one, regulatory means must be correspondingly changed. Under the old pattern, we relied mainly on mandatory planning and administrative means to link the macro- and micro-economies. Now we should turn mainly to the use of economic levers, without excluding administrative means. The problem, however, is this: where is their linking point? It seems that the policy readjustment with economic levers as the primary factor may probably be a way out.[8]

Obviously, Wang stood for the principle of "taking market regulation as the key link." The same idea was also clearly stated in a summary of *China in the Year 2000*, a tome containing about 2 million Chinese characters. The summary said that "opening up domestically mainly means expanding the decision-making power of enterprises, forming a socialist unified market, and establishing a market system with commodity production as the key link."[9] This indicated that to guarantee the continuance of his reform plan, Teng Hsiao-p'ing had outlined for Hu Yao-pang and Chao Tzu-yang a long-term orientation for the economic development of the mainland, that is, to build up a more "open" and freer economic system. Teng's stand is very different from Ch'en Yun's assertion in his speech at the CCP's National Conference of Delegates that "in terms of the country as a whole, the planned economy's primacy and the subordinate role of market regulation are still necessary"[10]—a standpoint that is even contradictory to the previously mentioned statements from the Decision on Reform of the Economic Structure.

Teng's plan to use market mechanism to remedy the shortcomings of centralized planned control by absorbing the planned economy into the market economy is difficult to achieve for the following reasons:

1. The planned economy and the market economy have different economic bases. Commodity production emerged on the basis of the system of private ownership. It had experienced many socioeconomic forms and its functions were not fully developed and best manifested until the emergence of a capitalist society. It was in a capitalist society that market mechanism began to show its amazing power. Historically, commodity production exists in the last stage of the primitive commune, the slave society, the feudal society, and the capitalist society, but the economic forms of those four kinds of societies are all based on the system of private ownership. On the other hand, the planned economy is based on the system of public ownership, which is by nature different from the system of private ownership. Any attempt to absorb the market economy into the planned economy will produce an economic form that is neither entirely a planned economy nor entirely a market economy, because the planned economy cannot effectively control the nonsocialist operation tendencies in the market economy; and the market economy, interfered with by the planned economy, will be unable to give full play to its functions of readjusting automatically the circulation and production of commodities. This contradiction is the basic reason why Beijing's reform of the economic structure has long been mired in a dilemma.

In fact, there is no necessary connection between nationalization, state interference, and the socialist system of public ownership. For instance, capitalist countries, including fascist Germany, Britain, Japan, and France, also adopted at different periods a similar policy, that is, nationalizing some sectors or enterprises that have a vital bearing on the national economy and the people's well-being such as banks, railways, posts and communications, subways, and the petroleum industry. Although the state-owned enterprises of capitalist countries are different from those of socialist countries in relation to the system of ownership, they have the same shortcomings, including low efficiency and low quality of service, and are either a profit-making monopoly or an enterprise with constant deficits. It was because of these shortcomings that some capitalist countries that had once practiced a nationalization policy finally restored the nationalized sectors and enterprises to private administration. As the nationalization policy has been proved ineffective even under the system of private ownership, it is certain that the Chinese Communists will encounter many problems in their attempt to develop a market economy on the basis of the system of public ownership.

2. For macroeconomic control, the planned economy relies mainly on mandatory planning and administrative means, but the market economy

depends mainly on economic means. The functions of these means are completely different, thereby triggering many difficult problems.

3. The market economy shows a quick response to changes in the demand of various commodities, but the planned economy does not. Under the market economy system, enterprisers are able to modify promptly their management policies to meet the needs of the market. State enterprises under the system of planned control, however, are often inefficient, unconscious of market information, and slow in responding to market needs. They have lagged far behind when an imbalance between their production plan and market needs is finally discovered. Then, the state has to slow down the speed of development and readjust the economic structure as well as the overall distribution of raw materials.[11] For these reasons, Beijing has repeatedly encountered in its economic reforms such problems as "overexpansion" and the "need to reduce the scope of construction plans."

### The Contradiction Between Macroeconomic Control and Microeconomic Flexibility

In the Decision on Reform of the Economic Structure, Beijing emphasized the need to establish a planning system under which the law of value is consciously applied for developing a socialist economy. The basic principle for establishing such a system is "exercising control over major issues and allowing flexibility in minor ones."[12] This principle, however, is very difficult to carry out.

For instance, most large and medium-sized enterprises in the PRC are key construction projects. They are, of course, put under state-planned control and must perform mandatory planning tasks. The "excessively rigid control" by the state, one of the characteristics of the centralized planning system, has strangled the enthusiasm and creativeness of their personnel. Many of their scientists and technicians have left to work for collective enterprises. According to the current wage reform in enterprises, wages of their personnel are linked with economic performance. If the general profit of an enterprise rises by 1 percent, the total of wages of its personnel may be increased by 0.7 percent. Nevertheless, only 70 percent of the raw and semifinished materials needed by state enterprises for key construction projects is supplied according to state plans, and the rest has to be bought on the market at negotiated prices. State enterprises, though burdened with higher production costs, are not allowed to raise the selling prices of their products. They therefore cannot attain their profit targets and cannot increase the wages of their personnel, inevitably hampering the development of production. Besides, because of their ignorance of the fluctuation trend of negotiated prices, many state enterprises find it difficult to accomplish their predetermined plans.[13] Judging by these observations, in the field of macroeconomy, "control" may be achieved, but "efficiency" and "flexibility" are out of the question. No wonder that large and medium-sized enterprises have asked to be subject to less control and to be given more decision-making power, like small enterprises.

Since Beijing called for expanding the decision-making power of enterprises, the policy has not been satisfactorily implemented. According to an investigation conducted by the CCP's Fukien provincial committee, in the summer of 1985, nearly half of the 205 state-owned enterprises had not really been given decision-making power, and some enterprises that had been given the power were deprived of it soon afterward. The implementation of the policy in other areas in the mainland is more or less the same.[14] So far, only small state enterprises and collective-owned enterprises, as well as about 20 percent of large and medium-sized state enterprises, have been allowed comparatively greater flexibility.[15] In fact, the current problem is that the enterprises are having too little, not too much, decision-making power. Even in this case, the market economy, which is small in quantity but dynamic in maneuverability, has already caused "disorder" in the mainland. Beijing became frightened. Since the second half of 1985, mainland economists have published many articles on the relations between macroeconomic control and microeconomic flexibility. Nearly all of them came to the conclusion that macroeconomic control should be strengthened to guarantee a basic balance between the total demand and the total supply, an appropriate proportion between accumulation and consumption, the stabilization of prices, and the well-being of the people. Judging by the CCP Central Committee's "Proposal for the Seventh Five-Year Plan for National Economic and Social Development" adopted at the party's National Conference of Delegates in September 1985 and the "Explanation of the Proposal for the Seventh Five-Year Plan" presented by Chao Tzu-yang at the same conference, Beijing will continue to regard planned economy as the key link and market economy as a supplementary factor, and, at the same time, will further strengthen macroeconomic control in two major respects.

The first major way in which the PRC government will strengthen its control is by enabling state enterprises to perform the function of "macroeconomic control" well, by enabling state commercial organs to serve as the main channel in commodity circulation, and by allowing state industrial and commercial enterprises to play a leading role in the national economy as a whole. Teng Hsiao-p'ing, Hu Yao-pang, and Chao Tzu-yang have repeated this intention at meetings with foreign guests. For instance, at a reception on September 16, 1985, for a delegation composed of Italian Socialist Party members of parliament, Hu Yao-pang asserted that in economic reforms, Beijing would firmly uphold the absolute dominance of public ownership in the country's economy.[16] In a speech at the CCP's National Conference of Delegates, Teng Hsiao-p'ing said that Beijing's constant adherence to the predominance of the socialist public sector of the economy is a basic guarantee and that the current reform of the economic structure will not change the socialist nature of mainland China.[17] Since the beginning of the reform, the total production value of public ownership enterprises has constantly accounted for more than 98 percent of the gross industrial output value, and the retail sales made by state-owned and collective-owned commercial enterprises have accounted for more than 85 percent of the total

TABLE 26.1
Output Value of Various Economic Forms in the Gross Industrial Output Value (in percent)

| Year[a] | State Ownership | Collective Ownership | Individual Ownership | Others[b] |
|---|---|---|---|---|
| 1980 | 78.7 | 20.7 | | 0.6 |
| 1981 | 78.3 | 21.0 | | 0.6 |
| 1982 | 77.8 | 21.4 | 0.1 | 0.7 |
| 1983 | 77.0 | 22.0 | 0.1 | 0.9 |
| 1984 | 73.6 | 25.0 | 0.2 | 1.2 |

*Sources:* For figures from 1980 to 1983, see State Statistical Bureau, *Chung-kuo t'ung-chi nien-chien 1984* (Statistical Yearbook of China, overseas edition in Chinese (Hong Kong: Economic Information & Agency, 1984), 194. For the 1984 figures, see *Chung-kuo t'ung-chi chai-yao 1985* (Summary of Statistical Records of China) (Beijing: China Statistical Press, 1985), 46.

[a]The 1980 figures were calculated on the basis of 1970 constant prices, and the figures for 1981–1984 on 1980 constant prices.
[b]The category "others" includes enterprises of joint state-collective ownership, those of joint state-private ownership, joint ventures using Chinese and foreign investment, enterprises operated by overseas Chinese or Hong Kong and Macao businessmen, and those operated by foreigners.

TABLE 26.2
Retail Sales of Commodities by Types of Economic Forms (in percent)

| Year | State Ownership[a] | Collective Ownership | Joint Ownership[b] | Individual Ownership | Retail Sales by Peasants to Nonagricultural Residents |
|---|---|---|---|---|---|
| 1980 | 84.0 | 21.1 | | 0.7 | 3.2 |
| 1981 | 80.0 | 14.5 | 0.1 | 1.6 | 3.8 |
| 1982 | 76.6 | 16.1 | 0.1 | 2.9 | 4.3 |
| 1983 | 72.1 | 16.6 | 0.1 | 6.5 | 4.7 |
| 1984 | 45.6 | 39.6 | 0.2 | 9.6 | 5.0 |

*Source:* State Statistical Bureau, *Chung-kuo t'ung-chi chai-yao 1985* (Summary of Statistical Records of China) (Beijing: China Statistical Press, 1985), 83.

[a]The retail sales of supply and marketing cooperatives from 1980 to 1983 were included in the retail sales by state ownership enterprises, but their sales in 1984 were included in those of collective ownership enterprises.
[b]Joint ownership refers to all kinds of jointly operated enterprises and joint ventures using Chinese and foreign investment.

value of retail sales of commodities. This dominance is shown in Tables 26.1 and 26.2.

In its second major method for reinforcing macroeconomic control, Beijing will not revoke the decision-making power that has already been given to enterprises, but will carry out a policy of readjustment with economic levers as the key. According to the CCP Central Committee's proposal for the

Seventh Five-Year Plan, Beijing will gradually reduce state management of enterprises from direct to indirect control, and will supervise and regulate economic activity mainly by economic, statutory, and, if necessary, administrative measures. It is ready to shift the emphasis of planning to exercising indirect but more comprehensive macroeconomic control through various economic policies and measures.[18] It intends to readjust and control the total demands of the people through financial, taxation, and banking measures, to reinforce economic supervision and law enforcement, and to strengthen the industrial and commercial administration, audit, statistical, measurement, and standardization departments.

Beijing presumes that it is able to achieve both macroeconomic control and microeconomic flexibility through the foregoing measures. This belief, however, is wishful thinking because, as Wang Chi-yeh asserted in 1985, the difficult problem in restructuring the planning system is, How is it possible to correctly integrate macroeconomic control and microeconomic flexibility?[19] The most important points of this problem are as follows:

1. The planned economy and the market economy, as already mentioned, are by nature different. They function differently in the field of macroeconomic control. The main regulatory mechanisms of the planned economy are mandatory planning and administrative means, but those of the market economy are economic means. Under the conditions of a commodity economy, economic means can only be operated in a market; that is, production is spontaneously regulated by the market. Beijing's theorists, however, hold that market regulation involves no planning, blindly allowing supply and demand to determine production.[20] In such a case, the strengthening of macroeconomic control will surely lead to the consolidation of the centralized planned economy, and flexibility will be out of the question. On the other hand, the market mechanism, interfered with by planned control, cannot give full play to its spontaneous regulatory function, thereby impairing microeconomic flexibility. Indeed, Beijing's ideal of "achieving flexibility without causing disorder" is difficult to attain.

2. Currently, economic forms that are different by nature are coexisting on the mainland. So far, state enterprises based on ownership by the whole people are not allowed freely to select their production orientation and buyers in accordance with the fluctuation of market prices because market mechanism is unable to regulate the overall economic activity flexibly.[21] The production of the individual economy, on the other hand, is subject to regulation by the supply-demand relations because of full competition. The coexistence of different economic forms has created difficulties in solving the contradiction between macroeconomic control and microeconomic flexibility.

3. Beijing is trying to solve the foregoing difficulties by gradually reducing state management of enterprises from direct to indirect control and by supervising and regulating economic activities mainly through economic, statutory, and administrative means. In a speech at the Third Session of the Sixth NPC in the spring of 1985, Ch'ien Chia-chu, a renowned economist,

asserted that it is impractical to rely on administrative means to stabilize prices. He urged price departments to believe in objective economic laws instead of relying excessively on administrative orders. He said: "We rely on administrative orders to stabilize prices, but prices will rise all the same. This is an objective law unaffected by the subjective will of the people. We should believe that economic laws function all the time but administrative orders can only be temporarily effective."[22] As to statutory means, they can only be effective in countries in which all people are equal before the law. In mainland China where there are many privileged persons and the rule of law is not really in practice, statutory measures can only be used to deal with ordinary people, not high-ranking cadres or their children and other relatives. As to economic measures, they mainly include economic levers such as financial, banking, price, and wage systems. A whole set of reforms in these fields, however, has just been launched and will not be basically realized until about five years later. Besides, the reform of the price system in mid-1985 quickly led to unrestrained inflation, a feeling of insecurity among the people, and social instability. Judging by this, without a fundamental reform of the whole politico-economic system, it will be difficult for Beijing to strengthen macroeconomic control only through the exercise of indirect control.

4. The function of the competition mechanism in eliminating improper enterprises and the regulatory role of various economic levers can only be brought into full play in a free market characterized by keen competition. Beijing, however, wants to set up a socialist unified market guided by "state" policies and plans.[23] In this case, how can it achieve effective macroeconomic control over the market by exercising indirect control?

5. If the state wants to strengthen macroeconomic control by enabling price, banking, and financial policies to give play to their functions, it will have to set up sound supervisory organizations staffed by specialists in industrial and commercial administration, audit, statistics, management, and standardization. There is, however, a serious shortage of such specialists in the PRC. For instance, currently more than 20,000 staffers of Beijing's auditing departments have to supervise more than 800,000 state economic units; and a greater number of enterprises managed by collectives and small towns and villages are not subject to any supervision by auditing units.[24] Under such circumstances, Beijing's plan to shift from direct to indirect macroeconomic control is nothing but an empty ideal.

## The Contradiction Between the Socialist and Nonsocialist Ownership Systems

One of the characteristics of the socialist economy is the system of public ownership of the means of production. Beijing, therefore, began to transform agriculture and private industrial and commercial enterprises into collective ownership and ownership by the whole people (state ownership) immediately after the establishment of the Communist regime in October 1949. However, since it adopted the policy of "invigorating the domestic economy and opening to the outside world," the composition of ownership systems in the economic structure of the PRC has greatly changed. Public ownership, including ownership by the whole people and collective ownership, is no longer the only system in practice. The changes in industry and commerce have been shown in Tables 26.1 and 26.2. As to agriculture, following the implementation of the system of contracting farm production to individual households in rural areas in 1980, farm households that signed various kinds of production contracts increased quickly, for instance, from 78 percent in 1982 to 98.3 percent in 1983.[25] The farm production responsibility system is, in reality, a system of tenant farmers in a disguised form, with the state as the only landowner. Beijing is indulging in self-deception in continuing to regard this kind of agricultural production as a part of collective ownership.

The CCP Central Committee's Decision on Reform of the Economic Structure asserted that the state ownership economy constitutes the leading force in the socialist economy, that the collective economy is an important component of the socialist economy, and that the individual economy and various forms of enterprises using foreign investment are a necessary and beneficial complement to the socialist economy.[26] Facts, however, have proved that the existence and development of nonsocialist ownership systems will inevitably aggravate their contradictions with socialist ownership systems. This contradiction is mainly manifested in three major respects.

First, the nonsocialist economic sector on the mainland will grow much faster than the socialist economic sector. It is commonly acknowledged that whether an economic system is superior depends on whether it can effectively promote productive forces. The system of planned economy is being reformed by all socialist countries exactly because this sort of production relations obstructs and restrains the development of productive forces. Even Teng Hsiao-p'ing frankly admitted this. At a meeting on October 23, 1985, with a delegation of entrepreneurs organized by *Time* magazine, he said: "We used to practice planned economy. Past experience showed that planned economy alone tended to restrain the development of the productive forces, and that a combination of planned economy and market economy could further liberate the productive forces and accelerate their development."[27] In fact, a comparison of the speed of development between the socialist and nonsocialist sectors in the PRC might clearly show that a planned economy is inferior to a free economy.

In 1983 production of the individual economy and the capitalist economy accounted for only 1 percent of the gross value of industrial and agricultural output, but their retail sales reached as high as 11.3 percent of the total retail sales of commodities (see Tables 26.1 and 26.2). Since these two kinds of economy are by nature compatible with commodity production, they have great potential for development under the conditions of the market economy. In 1984, when the economic restructuring with the urban economy as the focus had not yet been launched in an all-around way, the production value of state ownership enterprises rose by 11 percent over 1983, that of

TABLE 26.3
Industrial Output Value by Types of Ownership

|  | 1981 | 1982 | 1983 | 1984 |
|---|---|---|---|---|
| **By types of ownership (in units of 100 million yuan)** | | | | |
| National total | 5,177.67 | 5,577.45 | 6,164.41 | 7,029.90 |
| State-owned industry | 4,054.37 | 4,340.30 | 4,747.78 | 5,171.20 |
| Collective-owned industry | 1,089.27 | 1,192.81 | 1,354.23 | 1,757.80 |
| Commune-run industry | 323.21 | 354.26 | | |
| Village-run industry | | | 413.26 | 538.60 |
| Individual industry | | | 7.50 | 14.80 |
| Others | 34.03 | 44.34 | 54.90 | 86.10 |
| **Growth indexes (output value as percentage of the previous year)** | | | | |
| National total | 104.13 | 107.70 | 110.50 | 114.00 |
| State-owned industry | 102.53 | 107.10 | 109.40 | 111.00 |
| Collective-owned industry | 109.36 | 109.50 | 113.50 | 121.90 |
| Commune-run industry | 110.45 | 109.60 | | |
| Village-run industry | | | 116.70 | 130.30 |
| Individual industry | | | | 197.30 |
| Others | 134.50 | 130.30 | 140.70 | 156.80 |

*Sources:* For figures from 1981 to 1983, see *Chung-kuo t'ung-chi nien-chien* (Statistical Yearbook of China), overseas edition in Chinese (Hong Kong: Economic Information & Agency), 1981, 208; 1983, 222; 1984, 201. For the 1984 figures, see *Chung-kuo t'ung-chi chai-yao 1985* (Summary of Statistical Records of China) (Beijing: China Statistical Press, 1985), 45.

collective ownership enterprises by 21.9 percent, and that of other types of the economy by 56.8 percent (see Table 26.3). The development trend is even more obvious in commerce. In 1984 retail sales by units of collective ownership increased by 182.17 percent over 1983, those by units of joint ownership by 111.11 percent, those by the individual economy by 75.26 percent, and those by peasants to nonagricultural residents by 27.82 percent, but retail sales by units of state ownership decreased to 74.86 percent of the 1983 figure[28] (see Table 26.4). Along with the promotion of urban reforms, the development of tertiary industry, the increase of specialized households in rural areas, and the establishment of small towns (which was referred to by Yu Kuang-yuan, a renowned economist in mainland China, as the "new orientation of rural development after the implementation of the contracted farm production responsibility system"),[29] the individual economy and the capitalist economy are expected to play an increasingly important role in the mainland economy. The proportion of the individual economy in the economic structure, in particular, will increase quickly.

The second major reason why contradictions will be aggravated is that the nonsocialist economic sector is far more vigorous than the socialist

TABLE 26.4
Retail Sales of Commodities by Types of Ownership

|  | 1980 | 1981 | 1982 | 1983 | 1984 |
|---|---|---|---|---|---|
| **By types of ownership (units of 100 million yuan)** | | | | | |
| Total | 2,140.00 | 2,350.00 | 2,570.00 | 2,849.40 | 3,376.40 |
| State-owned units | 1,797.80 | 1,880.60 | 1,968.00 | 2,054.40 | 1,537.90 |
| Collective-owned units | 257.80 | 341.50 | 414.40 | 473.90 | 1,337.20 |
| Units of joint ownership | 0.40 | 1.10 | 1.60 | 3.60 | 7.60 |
| Units of individual ownership | 15.00 | 37.40 | 74.60 | 184.50 | 323.70 |
| Retail sales by peasants to nonagricultural residents | 69.00 | 89.40 | 110.80 | 133.00 | 170.00 |
| **Growth indexes (retail sales as percentage of the previous year)** | | | | | |
| Total |  | 109.81 | 109.36 | 110.87 | 118.50 |
| State-owned units |  | 104.61 | 104.68 | 104.36 | 74.86 |
| Collective-owned units |  | 132.47 | 121.35 | 114.36 | 282.17 |
| Units of joint ownership |  | 275.00 | 145.46 | 225.00 | 211.11 |
| Units of individual ownership |  | 379.00 | 199.47 | 247.65 | 175.26 |
| Retail sales by peasants to nonagricultural residents |  | 129.57 | 123.94 | 120.04 | 127.82 |

*Source: Chung-kuo t'ung-chi chai-yao 1985* (Summary of Statistical Records of China) (Beijing: China Statistical Press, 1985), 83.

*Note:* The retail sales of supply and marketing cooperatives from 1980 to 1983 were included in the retail sales by state-owned units, but their sales in 1984 were included in those of collective-owned units; joint ownership refers to all kinds of jointly operated enterprises and joint ventures using Chinese and foreign investment.

economic sector. This vigor is manifested mainly in the fact that enterprises of the nonsocialist economic sector can better modify their production plans to suit the changes in market needs, can place themselves in a more advantageous position in promoting sales, and can improve their management and operation to achieve higher efficiency and better economic performance. The reasons for these advantages are that enterprises in the nonsocialist sector have more decision-making power than those in the socialist sector, that they are subject to fewer restraints from "state" plans, and that they are able to bring the potential and superiority of commodity production into full play. If the lack of "vigor" is not solved, the socialist economy will collapse before the nonsocialist economy unless strong administrative means are employed. It is for this reason that Beijing's current economic restructuring places special emphasis on invigorating enterprises, especially large and medium-sized state enterprises.

The third major manifestation of the contradictions between the non-socialist and socialist economic sectors occurs in market operation. Since prices were allowed to rise in May 1985, the contradiction has been accentuated and the short supply of nonstaple food and sharp price rises have further aggravated social instability. These events indicate that state-owned industrial and commercial enterprises are unable to ensure normal operation of the national economy as they did in the past and that individual industry and commerce are playing an increasingly important role in the life of town and village residents in the production and service trades. Total sales by the individual commercial units rose quickly from 1.5 billion yuan in 1980 to 32.37 billion yuan in 1984 (see Table 26.4), and the proportion of their retail sales of commodities rose from 0.7 percent in 1980 to 9.6 percent in 1984 (see Table 26.2). According to statistics released by Beijing's State Administration for Industry and Commerce, as of October 1985 there were a total of 11 million licensed individual industrial and commercial units in towns and villages, 3.8 million of them in rural areas; and total sales of individual industrial and commercial units in the first half of 1985 reached 38 billion yuan, exceeding their total sales of 33.85 billion yuan in 1984.[30] Although Beijing has admitted that the existence and development of individual industry and commerce are conducive to solving problems such as "feeding and providing services and transport to the people" in some localities, it is still worrying about the negative influence caused by such a capitalist management style.

After all, capitalism is incompatible with socialism, and the individual economy "engenders capitalism and the bourgeoisie continuously, daily, hourly, spontaneously, and on a mass scale."[31] Therefore, the contradiction between the socialist and nonsocialist systems will erupt sooner or later. Then the Communists will be faced with the problem of how to suppress and eliminate the already developed individual economy. There is, however, no need to discuss this problem at present because, in the current stage, the reformists are advocating that the individual economy should be vigorously developed.[32] For a deep insight into the development of the contradiction between the socialist and nonsocialist ownership systems, it is necessary to examine the socialist practice of separating ownership from management rights.

### The Contradiction Arising from the Separation of Ownership and Management Rights

The separation of ownership and management rights is the theoretical basis for Beijing's policy of expanding the decision-making power of enterprises. To prove that it is possible to expand decision-making power under socialist conditions, mainland theorists often quoted from Karl Marx's *Capital* the following excerpt: "The capitalist mode of production has brought matters to a point where the work of supervision, entirely divorced from the ownership of capital, is always readily obtainable. It has, therefore, come to be useless for the capitalist to perform it himself. An orchestra conductor need not own the instruments of his orchestra."[33] Nevertheless, Beijing did not expect that the separation of ownership and management rights could bring about many new thorny problems.

Let us first examine the situation in rural areas. The first main problem is the contradiction caused by the time limit of cultivation contracts. At present, the responsibility system of contracting farm production to individual households is widely implemented in rural areas. The state is the owner of land and leases it to peasants for cultivation through contracts. In brief, the ownership of land and the right of cultivation are separated, but are then linked by contracts. Since the state may take back the right of cultivation from the peasants when the contracts expire, it grasps the lifeline of the individual economy and can control its development. Under these circumstances, the shorter the time limit of the contracts, the better the state can control the individual economy. On the other hand, long-term contracts are to the advantage of the people engaging in individual economy. Short-term contracts, from which they can obtain only limited profits, cannot really arouse their enthusiasm for production. This statement is especially true for forestry and agriculture, whose production needs a comparatively long period of cultivation.[34] In view of this fact, the Communist regime, which firmly upholds the socialist public ownership system, issued in January 1984 a "No. 1 Document" to extend the time limit of all land-cultivation contracts to fifteen years. However, whether the peasants will return the land to the state on the expiration of these fifteen-year contracts will be a problem. For instance, the Hsinmin Village in suburban Chengtu already extended the time limit of their contracts on land cultivation from twenty to thirty years.[35] The Linyi Area in Shantung Province, in an attempt to restore the forest zone that had been destroyed for grain production, extended the time limit of forestry contracts from thirty to fifty years.[36] Such long-term contracts have not only weakened the direct control of the Communist regime, but have also led to other problems.

The second major problem is that the economic restructuring with the urban economy as the focus in October 1984 and the reform of the price system in May 1985 added new elements to Beijing's practice of separating ownership from management rights. As mentioned before, Beijing links together, by means of contracts, the land ownership and management rights that are originally separated, and at the same time exercises control over the peasants by fixing the time limit of the contracts. This policy, however, must be based on the premise that the peasants are attached to the land they cultivate. It was so in the rural areas before the reform of the economic structure because at that time peasants were actually serfs subordinate to the land. Land was their most important means of production, and they could earn their living through farming, though land belonged to the state. Now, the situation is different. Industrial and sideline production has quickly developed in the suburbs of large and medium-sized cities, leading to an increase in employment opportunities. The peasants' dependence on land has thus been weakened. They not only expect to earn their living through farming, but also to become well off. If they cannot obtain the necessary profits from land, they may grow other things instead of grain (or vegetables), or reduce the area for growing grain (or vegetables), or even abandon their cultivation rights and leave for towns and cities to earn their living. This not only happens in grain- or vegetable-growing areas, but also exists in varying degrees throughout the rural areas in the mainland. Along with the establishment of the "city combinations" with large cities as centers, the readjustment of the rural production structure, the development of town- and village-run enterprises, the growth of the tertiary industry in rural areas, and the rise of small cities and towns, this problem will become increasingly serious.

A third serious problem is that the separation of ownership and man- agement rights provides a material basis for polarization in rural areas. Since the peasants have the land cultivation rights, it is possible that they will invest their funds and labor in the kind of production that yields them the greatest profit. Farm households that have a relatively strong labor force, sufficient funds, or special skills are able to become well off quickly. Clear proof is provided by the emergence of "conspicuous households" and "ten- thousand-yuan households." This has accelerated the polarization trend in rural areas, thereby changing rural class relations after the "land reform," especially those after the cooperativization movement and the establishment of the people's communes.

The fourth main problem is that the peasants desire for a private land ownership system has been accentuated. In reality, the extension of the time limit of contracts for land use to fifteen years and more has already made the land-use right of peasants semipermanent. Some mainland theorists have already admitted this fact. For instance, when questioned on the subject by a Japanese professor, a mainland theorist said: "At present, the land- use right is actually becoming semipermanent. It may probably develop into a substantive private land ownership system in the future. Many peasants have already regarded the current practice as 'land distribution.' I think that in the next fifteen or thirty years, the economy of the mainland, especially the tertiary industry, will show tremendous progress. The crux of the current problem, therefore, is this: If the principle of public ownership is overemphasized, the peasants will lose enthusiasm for production and even resist reforms."[37]

Judging by the current situation, the extension of land-use contracts to fifteen years cannot truly satisfy the peasants for the following reasons:

1. The extension of their land-use rights to fifteen years or more is good, but there is still a time limit. They, of course, prefer owning the land to being granted land-use rights for a limited period.
2. The conclusion of land-use contracts is not a sure guarantee for the peasants. When rural cadres discover that the contractors obtain much profit from contracted items, they often use their power to cancel the contracts, thereby causing much loss to the peasants. In March and April 1984, in Wenteng County in Shantung Province, cadres canceled many contracts, and some specialized households preferred discon- tinuation of their contracts, though they had to pay fines.[38]

In brief, the peasants may probably demand land ownership to ensure that they can own the profit from their long-term investment. Without doubt, their demand for restoration of private ownership will not be accepted. Beijing prefers to keep, at least outwardly, the public ownership system. Long-term contracts have thus been used as a substitute. However, as the investment by the peasants and specialized households continues to increase, the separation of land ownership from land-use rights will accentuate the struggle between the Communist regime and the peasants. Currently, Beijing is encouraging peasants and specialized households to form new "economic combinations" in the hope of diverting the peasants' attention from claiming land ownership and guiding them to a new road of collectivization and socialization.

It should be noted that the separation of land ownership from land-use rights had enabled the peasants to become less dependent on the land. They may decide whether to accept the land-use rights after considering how to use them under the conditions offered by the contracts. Moreover, the rise of small towns and the development of tertiary industry have further enhanced the peasants' initiative in this respect. For instance, in addition to growing grain, the peasants of Changcheng village in the suburbs of Shanghai plant vegetables as their main production item. They have even abandoned the traditional method of contracting farm production to individual households and introduced a method of fixing the output quotas of collective production groups. In 1985 agricultural production accounted for only 30 percent of the total income of the village, and the rest came from light industry and sideline production.[39] This trend in rural areas of expanding nonagricultural income will give rise to a new problem: The country will not be stable without a solid agricultural base.

Now let us review how state enterprises in cities are administered. The large and medium-sized enterprises are under the direct control of factory directors (managers) assigned by the state, as they were before the implementation of economic reforms. However, government administration is now separated from the management of enterprises that enjoy more management rights than before and are granted decision-making power in some fields. Therefore, in large and medium-sized enterprises, ownership and management rights are unified. On the other hand, the "state" has transferred management rights to small enterprises. Factory directors (managers), who are elected or employed, are entrusted to exercise such management rights by the enterprises. The system of contracted economic responsibility is practiced. Therefore, in small "state" enterprises, ownership and management rights are separated, but are again linked together through contracts.

In large and medium-sized "state" enterprises, ownership and management rights are unified on the basis of public ownership. Therefore, it is difficult to rid them of the shortcomings of centralized planned control and to invigorate them. On the other hand, the expansion of the management rights of enterprises provides objective and favorable conditions to factory directors for seeking their private interests. The directors may easily use their power to turn the property of the whole people into the property of the collective, transform production funds into consumption funds, and distribute or use up all the profit. This problem is especially obvious in small enterprises in which the ownership and management rights are completely separated. Since "state" enterprises have the backing of the party as well as wide connections, they are furnished with ample opportunity to commit such crimes as embezzlement, smuggling, and trafficking. According to the China News Service, of the 10,000 smuggling cases investigated by secret service personnel of the customs in 1985, 90 percent involved state enterprises or organizations.[40] Judging by this trend, unification of ownership and management rights is a fundamental guarantee for preserving the socialist development orientation of the socialist economy. It is for this reason that Marxist classics often regard enterprises under the direct management of the state to be "units owned by the whole people." In short, Beijing's current move to separate ownership from management rights and to allow the market economy to function at the same time will lead to many unexpected problems.

Finally, let us observe the development of specialized households and individual industry and commerce. These individual economies often have their own farm tools, tractors, automobiles, machines, and other means of production. Their ownership and management rights are unified on the basis of the private ownership system, not the public ownership system. As owners of their means of production, they are free from the psychological pressure of knowing that their rights of use may expire. Moreover, they have been granted management rights and are not restrained by the planned economy. Therefore, they show the greatest flexibility and vigor.

To invigorate enterprises, Beijing has separated ownership rights from management rights. Thus, in the economic sector of the socialist public ownership, enterprises or units whose ownership and management rights are separated show more vigor; and enterprises and units whose ownership and management rights are unified on the basis of private ownership are the most vigorous (see Tables 26.4 and 26.5). Judging by this comparison, Beijing cannot really develop its economy and invigorate its enterprises unless it abandons the socialist system.

## The Contradiction Arising from Polarization

In the Decision on Reform of the Economic Structure, the Communists stressed the necessity of allowing enterprises to compete with one another, saying the "competition is conducive to improving production technology and management of enterprises because only the best enterprises can survive it." On the other hand, the Communists did not want to be criticized for polarization arising from competition. Therefore, they contended in the same decision that "allowing some people and enterprises to get better off first is the only road to prosperity for the people as a whole." Later, some economists even tried to furnish a theoretical basis for this official viewpoint and described it as "an objective law of socialism."[41]

TABLE 26.5
Industrial Output Value by Size of Enterprises

|  | 1981 | 1982 | 1983 | 1984 |
|---|---|---|---|---|
| National total (in units of 100 million yuan) | 5,177.67 | 5,577.45 | 6,164.41 | 7,029.90 |
| By size of enterprises (in units of 100 million yuan) |  |  |  |  |
| Large | 1,316.59 | 1,456.35 | 1,617.28 | 1,842.20 |
| Medium | 915.81 | 1,027.43 | 1,158.24 | 1,311.00 |
| Small | 2,945.27 | 3,093.67 | 3,388.89 | 3,876.70 |
| Growth indexes (output value as percentage of the previous year) |  |  |  |  |
| Large | 102.93 | 110.60 | 111.10 | 113.90 |
| Medium | 101.82 | 112.20 | 112.70 | 113.20 |
| Small | 105.40 | 105.00 | 109.50 | 114.40 |

*Sources:* See Table 26.3.

The viewpoint that the prosperity of some people will prompt more and more people, one group after another, to take the road to prosperity[42] is not a new theory, but a repetition of S. Kuznets' theory of "first prosperity and then equality" advanced a few decades ago.

Now, let us analyze the situation between cities and the countryside.

The implementation of the contracted responsibility system based on individual households has actually aroused among the peasants enthusiasm for production. Along with the improvement in agricultural productivity, the peasants earn more income. The per capita net income of peasant households rose from 134 yuan in 1978 to 310 yuan in 1983, up 131.34 percent. On the other hand, the average wage of staff and workers in state-owned units rose from 644 yuan in 1978 to 865 yuan in 1983, up only 34.32 percent; and the wage of staff and workers in collective-owned units in cities and towns rose from 505 yuan to 698 yuan, up only 38.22 percent. In 1978 the average wage of staff and workers in state-owned units was 4.8 times the average per capita net income of peasant households, but was reduced to only 2.79 times in 1983; and the wage of staff and workers in collective-owned units in cities and towns was 3.77 times the average per capita net income of peasant households in 1978, but was reduced to only 2.25 times in 1983 (see Tables 26.6 and 26.7). Judging by these figures, since 1978 the difference between cities and countryside has been narrowed to a certain degree. Theoretically, this trend should have been conducive to improving the worker-peasant relations and consolidating the worker-peasant alliance. However, it has accentuated the contradiction between cities and the countryside for the following reasons:

TABLE 26.6
The Increase in Income of Residents in Cities and the Countryside (in yuan)

| | 1978 | 1979 | 1980 | 1981 | 1982 | 1983 | 1984 |
|---|---|---|---|---|---|---|---|
| Average wage of staff and workers | 614 | 668 | 762 | 772 | 798 | 826 | 974 |
| Wage of staff and workers in state-owned units | 644 | 705 | 803 | 812 | 836 | 865 | 1,034 |
| Wage of staff and workers in collective-owned units in cities and towns | 505 | 542 | 624 | 642 | 671 | 698 | 811 |
| Per capita net income of peasant households | 134 | 160 | 191 | 223 | 270 | 310 | 355 |

*Sources: Chung-kuo t'ung-chi nien-chien* (Statistical Yearbook of China), overseas edition in Chinese (Hong Kong: Economic Information & Agency), 1983, 485, 499; 1984, 455, 457, 471; and *Chung-kuo t'ung-chi chai-yao* (Summary of Statistical Records of China) (Beijing: China Statistical Press, 1985), 96, 99.

1. Seeing that some peasants have got rich quickly and are able to own their own cars and housing units in a few years, staff and workers in cities are filled with envy. As early as 1982, when the livelihood of the peasants began to improve, the workers were already dissatisfied. They complained: "Owing to the implementation of the responsibility system in rural areas, the peasants have earned much more. They are not exploited and have the freedom to build their own housing units. However, we workers might not be assigned a room in ten years."[43] Their discontent will grow as the living standard of the peasants is still further improved. In fact, the contradiction between the workers and the peasants, the two components of the worker-peasant alliance, has already forced the Communists to carry out "new economic reforms" in cities. Since 1984, the difference between cities and the countryside has again widened (see Tables 26.6 and 26.7).

2. The wages of staff and workers in cities are relatively fixed. They thus have no opportunity to increase their income on a large scale. On the other hand, the peasants have ample opportunity to become better off because they may plant private plots as well as become members of specialized households. The workers' envy of the peasants will gradually turn into dissatisfaction against the Communist regime.

3. Before the economic reforms, the prices of industrial products were too high, while those of agricultural and sideline products were too low. According to an estimate by a mainland economist, the prices of industrial products in 1979 were 11.8 percent higher than their value; those of agricultural products were 28 percent lower than their value; and the total of the scissors differences between the prices of industrial and agricultural products reached as high as 30.12 billion yuan. Obviously, this situation was disadvantageous to the peasants. However, things have developed differently after the introduction of economic reforms. Prices of agricultural

TABLE 26.7
Increase Indexes of the Income of Residents in Cities and the Countryside

| | 1978 | 1979 | 1980 | 1981 | 1982 | 1983 | 1984 |
|---|---|---|---|---|---|---|---|
| Each year as percentage of 1978 | | | | | | | |
| Average wage of staff and workers | 100.00 | 108.79 | 124.10 | 125.73 | 129.97 | 134.53 | 158.63 |
| Wage of staff and workers in state-owned units | 100.00 | 109.47 | 124.69 | 126.09 | 129.81 | 134.32 | 160.56 |
| Wage of staff and workers in collective-owned units in cities and towns | 100.00 | 107.33 | 123.56 | 127.13 | 132.87 | 138.22 | 160.59 |
| Per capita net income of peasant households | 100.00 | 119.40 | 142.54 | 166.42 | 201.49 | 231.34 | 264.93 |
| Per capita net income of peasant households as percentage of the following: | | | | | | | |
| Wage of staff and workers in state-owned units | 480.60 | 440.62 | 420.42 | 364.13 | 309.63 | 279.03 | 291.27 |
| Wage of staff and workers in collective-owned units in cities and towns | 376.87 | 338.75 | 326.70 | 287.89 | 248.52 | 225.16 | 228.45 |

Sources: See Table 26.6.

and sideline products have been allowed to fluctuate in accordance with the supply-demand relations, thereby leading to sharp price rises. This is advantageous to the peasants who produce and sell agricultural and sideline products, but it is disadvantageous to staff and workers who depend on their fixed wages for their living. At present, rural areas in the PRC are busy with production, but complaints are heard everywhere in cities. Should the problem of prices remain unsolved, the prospects of Beijing's economic reforms will be very doubtful.

Contradictions also exist in rural areas:

1. The system of contracting farm production takes individual households as basic units. The households that have more labor force are allocated more land and are able to earn more income, but the households that have less of a labor force get less land and less income. Thus the difference between the rich and the poor in rural areas has been widened. A report released by the Communists after a close examination admitted that the peasants have become increasingly concerned about the growing difference between the rich and the poor. The report said: "The rich households use their relatively abundant funds and relatively good production technology to encroach on, either directly or indirectly, the interests of the poor households. The situation of equal opportunities for both the rich and the poor has been disrupted. Some poor households have sold their means of production and even their contracted land in a covert manner. The gradual expansion of the difference between the rich and the poor will undermine social stability and development."[44]

2. Various forms of specialized households have developed very quickly in rural areas. At the end of 1983, there were throughout the mainland 24,820,000 specialized households, accounting for 13.6 percent of the peasant households.[45] More than two-thirds of the income of these households came from their specialized items. In 1984 the average annual income of specialized households was 600 to 700 yuan. They earned much more than ordinary peasants.

In rural areas in the mainland, people who do farming are earning less than those who are engaged in industrial production or sideline occupations. The difference between their income is so big that peasants prefer industrial production and sideline occupations to farming. In some places, the peasants even let the land lie waste. In Tungfeng Village in Wuhsi County, Kiangsu Province, an agricultural laborer who cultivated 1.74 mu (one mu is equivalent to one-sixth of an acre) of "responsibility plot" earned on the average a net income of less than 200 yuan a year, but the average income of industrial laborers reached 900 to 1,000 yuan, 4.5 to 6 times that of agricultural laborers. In Hungch'i village in Wuhsi County, an agricultural laborer who cultivated 1.25 mu of "responsibility plot" earned on the average a net income of a little more than 100 yuan, and the average income of industrial workers was 6 to 8 times that of agricultural laborers.[46]

3. The vast mainland is characterized by varying natural conditions. Judging by Beijing's current level of science and technology, it is impossible

to improve in a short period of time the natural conditions of some areas such as soil, climate, and irrigation resources. Therefore, allowing some people to become well off cannot reduce the differences existing in rural areas, and polarization is hard to avoid. In brief, the peasants in the suburbs of big cities, southeastern coastal areas, or areas along big rivers earn much more than those in mountainous, border, and remote areas. Though Beijing might provide the poor households and poor areas with social relief, preferential treatment, and material and technological aid, it is still difficult to realize "common prosperity for all."

Since 1979, Beijing has improved its economic performance by carrying out economic reforms and using economic levers to promote commodity production. However, the reforms of the economic basis must be matched with corresponding reforms in the superstructure; otherwise, the superstructure will soon restrain the development of the productive force. Therefore, Beijing cannot really invigorate its economy unless it abandons the centralized macroeconomic control. Besides, Beijing's policy of relaxing control over the economic sphere but simultaneously maintaining tight political control will not be effective for long. Only through economic liberalization and political democratization can the Chinese people obtain lasting prosperity and happiness.

## Notes

1. "Decision of the CCP Central Committee on Reform of the Economic Structure," *People's Daily*, October 21, 1984, 2.

2. Hsüeh Mu-ch'iao, "Our Socialist Economic Construction: Its Past and Future," *Red Flag*, 1984, no. 18:6.

3. See note 1.

4. Chiang Hsüeh-mo, "On the Planned Commodity Economy Based on the System of Public Ownership," *Hsüeh-shu yueh-k'an* (Academic Monthly) (Shanghai), 1985, no. 1:13–14.

5. Wang Po-ming, "Professor Kornai on Economic Reforms," *Economic Daily* (Beijing), March 28, 1985, 4.

6. Chao Tzu-yang, "The Current Economic Situation and Reform of the Economic Structure," *People's Daily*, April 12, 1985, 2.

7. Chao Tzu-yang, "Give Full Play to the Function of Cities and Promote an All-around Reform of Economic Life," *People's Daily*, April 29, 1985, 1.

8. Wang Chi-yeh, "On the Transition of the Economic Structure from the Old to the New Pattern," *People's Daily*, September 13, 1985, 5.

9. Chang Pan, Wang Hui-chiung, et al., "The General Strategy for Advancing Toward the Year 2000," *Economic Daily*, November 2, 1985, 2.

10. Ch'en Yun, "Speech at the National Conference of Delegates of the Chinese Communist Party," *People's Daily*, September 24, 1985, 2.

11. Wu Yuan-li, "Beijing's Economic Reform Tactics: Development and Difficulties," *Kung-shang shih-pao* (Industrial and Commercial Times) (Taiwan), August 4, 1985, 2.

12. See note 1.

13. Huang Pai-pin, a delegate from Yunnan; Cheng Lin-sun, a delegate from Shanghai; and Wu Chien-sheng, a delegate from Anhwei, all referred to this problem. See *People's Daily*, April 3, 1985, 2.

14. "Commentator" article, "Further Thoroughly Implement the Policy Concerning Autonomy of Enterprises," *People's Daily*, September 28, 1985, 1.

15. Lü Tung, "Further Increase the Vigor of Large and Medium-Sized Enterprises," *Red Flag*, 1985, no. 21:3–4.

16. *People's Daily*, September 16, 1985, 1.

17. Teng Hsiao-p'ing, "Speech at the National Conference of Delegates of the Chinese Communist Party," *People's Daily*, September 24, 1985, 1.

18. "Proposal of the CCP Central Committee for the Seventh Five-Year Plan for National Economic and Social Development," *People's Daily*, September 26, 1985, 3.

19. Wang, "On the Transition of the Economic Structure."

20. Ch'en, Wang, et al., "The General Strategy for Advancing."

21. Wang, "On the Transition of the Economic Structure."

22. "Ch'ien Chia-chu's Speech," *People's Daily*, April 2, 1985, 4.

23. "Proposal for the Seventh Five-Year Plan."

24. Kuo Shu-ch'ing, Liu Chi-jui, and Ch'iu Shu-fang, "On the Question of Shifting from Direct Control to Indirect Control," *People's Daily*, November 22, 1985, 5.

25. Shih I-hsing, "A Comparison Between 'Land to the Tiller' and Beijing's System of Agricultural Production Responsibility," *Fei-ch'ing yueh-pao* (Chinese Communist Affairs Monthly) (Taipei) 26, no. 12 (June 1984):34.

26. "Decision on Reform of the Economic Structure," 3.

27. *People's Daily*, October 23, 1985, 1.

28. These figures are different from those in the State Statistical Bureau's Communiqué on the National Economic and Social Development in 1984. *People's Daily*, March 10, 1985, 2. According to the communiqué, retail sales by units of state ownership increased by 9.7 percent, those by units of collective ownership by 16.4 percent, those by units of joint ownership by 110 percent, those by the individual economy by 76.4 percent, and those by peasants to nonagricultural residents by 27.8 percent.

29. Yu Kuang-yuan, "Reforms During the Period of Socialist Construction as Seen from World and Chinese History," *Chung-kuo she-hui k'e-hsüeh* (China's Social Sciences) (Bimonthly) (Beijing), 1985, no. 1:64.

30. "People Engaging in Individual Industry and Commerce Have Reached 16 Million," *People's Daily*, October 30, 1985, 2.

31. V. I. Lenin, "'Left-Wing' Communism—An Infantile Disorder," in *Collected Works*, vol. 31 (Moscow: Progress Publishers, 1966), 24.

32. "Decision on Reform of the Economic Structure," 3.

33. Karl Marx, *Capital*, vol. 3 (Moscow: Foreign Languages Publishing House, 1962), 379.

34. Li Yung-fa, "The Time Limit for Contracts on the Use of Fish Ponds Should Be Long," *People's Daily*, May 6, 1985, 2.

35. *Economist* (weekly; Tokyo), October 22, 1985, 78.

36. "Cultivation of 500,000 mu of Land Has Stopped for Rebuilding Forests in Linyi Area," *People's Daily*, April 20, 1985, 2.

37. Chao Ch'ien, "Sequelae of Peking's Open-Door and Reform Policy," *Chung-kuo ta-lu yen-chiu* (Mainland China Studies) (Taipei) 28, no. 6 (December 1985):48.

38. Ts'ui Wen-yu and Chang P'ing-li, "How Can Contracts of Production Responsibility Be Canceled at Will?" *People's Daily*, May 4, 1985, 5.

39. Chao, "Sequelae of Peking's Open-Door and Reform Policy," 49.

40. *Hsiang-kang shih-pao* (Hong Kong Times), January 16, 1986, 1.

41. Feng Lan-jui, "'Some People Get Well Off Earlier' Is an Objective Law of Socialism," *Wen Hui Pao* (Shanghai), October 27, 1984, 3.

42. Wu, "Beijing's Economic Reform Tactics."

43. Hsu Tse-min and Huang Lung-hui, "On Rural Modernization and Social Difference," *Ming-pao yueh-k'an* (Ming Pao Monthly) (Hong Kong), no. 230 (February 1985):82.

44. Research Group of Chinese Rural Development, "Some New Questions in Rural Development—An Investigation of the Rural Areas in Ch'u County in Anhwei Province After the Implementation of the Two Forms of Contracting Farm Production to Individual Households," *Chung-kuo she-hui k'e-hsüeh*, 1982, no. 3:99.

45. Yu Kuo-yao, "The Rise of Specialized Households in Chinese Rural Areas," *Ching-chi tao-pao* (Economic Reporter) (Hong Kong), 1984, no. 22:18.

46. T'ien Shan-fu, "Changes in 'Scissors Difference' Between Our Industrial and Agricultural Products in the Past Fifteen Years," *Ts'ai-mao ching-chi* (Finance and Trade Economics) (Monthly) (Beijing), 1985, no. 5:32.

# 27

## Economic Reform in the PRC, Soviet Union, and East Europe: Comparative Themes Toward the Year 2000

*John P. Hardt*

### Centrally Planned Economies in Flux

The question of reform in the planning and management of the centrally planned economies has in recent years captured the attention of most of the world's major socialist nations.[1] By introducing or, at the least, seriously discussing extensive changes in the planning and management of their economies, the centrally planned economy countries hope to succeed in improving the quality and quantity of economic performance:

- The Chinese purport to be developing a new form of socialism—a unique mixture of central planning and market forces, referred to as "a socialist system with Chinese characteristics."
- Mikhail Gorbachev has called for "radical reform" in the Soviet economy based on energizing the economic cadre, mobilizing more effectively the economic resources, "intensifying" the use of energy, metals, labor, and capital, and entering the new technological information revolution.
- East European countries are calling for change in their economic planning and management mechanisms paralleling or exceeding those of the Soviet Union or the People's Republic of China (PRC).

The selective comments that follow may provide some comparative insights on reform in centrally planned economies on the assumption that the economic development of the PRC, the Soviet Union, and East European countries share two important common features: (1) ideology—Marxism-Leninism, and (2) some common heritage from the Soviet development process under Stalin. However, the differences in historical traditions, culture, level of economic development, and scale, all should be kept in mind in judging the relevance of a comparative approach. With all these qualifications in mind, some general observations may be made with a view toward fostering a dialogue among specialists on the economies of the PRC, the Soviet Union, and East Europe.

Reforms in the PRC have received particular attention of late in view of this country's economic performance. Administration and systemic changes are generally taken more seriously in the East and West when economic performance has improved. This has been the case for the PRC, which, under the Four Modernizations and openness policies of the Deng Xiaoping regime, has shown improved performance even though the performance may, in part, represent recovery from the economically disasterous Cultural Revolution under Mao Zedong and his radical followers (the "Gang of Four") and improvements in the abnormally low productivity of China's economic system. In contrast, prospects for change in the Soviet Union and improved performance so far exist primarily in policy statements, while evidence of beneficial results from reform is still lacking. Indeed there is considerable doubt among many Western specialists that the rhetoric of Mikhail Gorbachev will ever be translated into economically productive change.

Despite these differences in progress, three fundamental areas of change proposed or adopted in the PRC, the Soviet Union, and East Europe are of special interest because these reforms—if implemented and effective— would have a potentially significant impact on the traditional systems of planning and management, might lead to substantial improvements in performance, and might be of significant impact on the socialist system of governance.

- *Rural reform is announced or under way in several planned economies:* Rural reform as described in the Soviet CPSU Central Committee resolution of March 29, 1986, is more detailed and apparently as far reaching as that of the Chinese Eleventh Central Committee, Third Plenum communiqué of December 23, 1978, in terms of the incentives provided for incremental output and decentralization of decision-making power to the local farm unit. As in China, changes in the management of agriculture and the rural economy in the Soviet Union and East Europe may be the forerunner of more comprehensive changes in the urban industrial economies and show more early short-term improvements in performance.

    The common concept shared by Chinese rural reform and Gorbachev's agro-industrial proposals is the Leninist concept from the New Economic Policy that agricultural production can be increased by guaranteeing to the peasant freedom to dispose of his surpluses and freedom and security in land tenure, within a centrally planned system.
- *Decentralization of management:* Measures to reduce the managerial powers of the central ministerial economic bureaucracy are proceeding more rapidly in the PRC than in the Soviet Union, providing a basis for decentralized management in the rural and urban economy as a

precondition toward guidance planning or local financial autonomy. This may in part be because Chinese planning was never as comprehensive, detailed, and controlled by a centralized ministerial bureaucracy as in the USSR.

Nonetheless, devolution of managerial rights, responsibilities, and rewards to the local enterprises, reinforced by more centralized control by the top party leadership—Lenin's "commanding heights approach"— is a common course for change. A centerpiece of substantial long-term change will have to include some rational system of pricing. Application of this Leninist approach may lead to further centralization in policy and planning to assure decentralization and further centralization of planning in some key sectors.

- *Reduction of the burden of the party apparatus on economic performance:* The power of the Communist Party through the *nomenklatura* system to control economic cadres, retain privileges not directly related to economic performance, and intervene in the management process has been questioned in differing degrees in the PRC, the Soviet Union, and some East European countries such as Poland. More explicit references to redressing the party role are currently being made in the USSR and East Europe, perhaps with less prospect of success than already has been attained in the PRC.

    Again, what may be involved is a return to the earlier Leninist formulation of democratic centralism that in economic management called for sharing of power by the party with the professional managers and the workers' representatives in policy matters, withdrawal of the party from direct intervention in management, and a stricter code of conduct involving party responsibility and privilege.

Were the changes discussed in these three areas fully implemented and carried through, they might all contribute significantly to the efficiency of the respective economies while having a revolutionary effect on the systems of political-economic governance. Looking toward the year 2000, it is possible that with favorable economic performance, change-oriented leadership, and fortuitous developments external to the contries involved, such major changes might reach fruition.

Beneficial as such economic changes might be, the full costs of attaining the economic reforms involved by the year 2000 might be substantial and might be paralleled by significant ideological, political, and systemic effects:

- The cultural and social impact of increasing inequities and changing social status, resulting from progressively differential incentive systems, may be substantial. The economic restructuring and new reform process may create an upper and an under class in rural and urban settings that could generate social and ideological backlash.
- The creation of a new managerial, scientific, and intellectual elite may not be deemed sufficiently beneficial to justify its full social, cultural

and political costs if the success model of a powerful party member is replaced by that of a technologically successful and economically well-to-do manager of rural and urban enterprises.

• Effective measures to deal with corruption and the establishment of equitable and effective incentive systems will need to be continued to assure the full fruits of modernization. If cynicism of the past is replaced by an effective incentive environment, rising expectations may develop a strong momentum of their own to influence future leadership decisions.

• The changes resulting from accelerated economic growth facilitated by selective reform under Deng Xiaoping and Gorbachev, if adopted and continued, might result in destabilization of the established Communist political economic system, diversification of culture, and opening of the society. Such changes could be no less radical than the political-ideological changes instituted under Mao or Stalin.

Even selected "radical reforms" may not be carried forward in the USSR and East Europe. The respective leaderships may find the ideological, political, and systemic changes too costly to be justified by even optimistic projections in improved economic performance resulting from reforms. However, if they were to be carried foward throughout the centrally planned economies, the ideological, political, and systemic impacts of these economic reforms might require more significant change than the economic reforms themselves.

Soviet political commentator Fedor Burlatsky reporting on an official delegation to the PRC noted that the prospects for economic reform—"building socialism with specific Chinese features"—may have implications for transforming the society and the system. His comparative frames of reference appeared to recognize that significant changes were under way in both Communist giants and that the diversified experience of the past and of smaller East European socialist countries were relevant: "Here we speak of five socialist economic models: 1—'war communism' in the USSR; 2—the Soviet economic system which developed in the thirties; 3—the system evolving in the USSR now under the influence of reforms; 4—the Hungarian model; and 5—the Yugoslav model."[2] Implicit in these alternative models is the assumption that a variety of approaches are possible for modifying a centrally planned socialist system to improve efficiency and modernize. Some Western observers would argue that halfway measures will lead either to an offsetting of benefits or an unstable relationship that generates pressure either toward "marketization and privatization" or a "retrogression toward some form of modernized Stalinist administrative command" system.[3]

### Rural Reform: Problems and Prospects for Improved Performance

Since the introduction of rural reform (1979 to date), improvement in Chinese agricultural performance has been remarkable, especially in comparison to Soviet accomplishments during the same period. Since taking power in March 1985, Gorbachev has introduced new programs for changing the organization of agriculture at the center and providing for some incentives and local autonomy for the peasants at the farm level. Indeed the decentralization and incentive measures issued in March 1986 are initially in some ways more sweeping and detailed than those of the Third Plenum of the Eleventh Central Committee of the People's Republic of China in December 1978.[4] The 1978 decree called for some price incentives and improvement in the commune system; the large-scale adoption of the family responsibility system came several years later. The Soviet resolution on changing the rural management could conceivably take on dynamics of change rivaling the rural reform of the PRC if weather is good, if the leadership follows through on delegating responsibility to the locality, and if the new incentive systems are successful in getting the peasants and collectives to work more efficiently.

In the first year under Gorbachev, the Soviet administrative changes in central planning and management of agriculture, in central investment, and in shifting to local responsibility management were noteworthy:

1. The creation of the State Agro-Industrial Committee established a power base for Gorbachev's lieutenants' control over key policy and planning at the center and to implement decentralization. This ministerial reorganization is the first step in what Gorbachev recognizes as a multistage effort to place agriculture under workable economic norms: "The USSR State Agro-Industrial Committee sets the following task: to transfer in the next 2 years basically all kolkhozes and sovkhozes to complete financial autonomy . . . [and] improve economic management and the efficient utilization of levers like prices, profits, and profitability."

2. Vsevolod Murakhovsky—head of this "superministry" is to implement the concept of Lenin's "food tax" as described at the Party Congress. This would involve giving authority to the local unit (e.g., family) to make planting decisions, control distribution and marketing of part of the harvest, and retain profits resulting from revenue in excess of costs. If the weather is average or good, it might be expected that the "food tax experiment" would be applied most effectively to the south, given the fact that Gorbachev and his lieutenants came from Krasnodar, Stavropol, and environs. Further effective extension of this decentralization over time might eventually involve contracted control of land tenure that would enhance the potential incentive impact of these policy changes.

At the Soviet Party Congress in February and March 1986, Gorbachev and other party leaders referred to the "food tax" (*prodnalog*), a principal tool of the New Economic Policy under Lenin,[5] and other reforms in agriculture accepted by the Politburo in March 1921 as a guide for the greater decentralization of agriculture. Gorbachev has indicated that farm units, including the family, may gain responsibility and have rights to market a substantial share of their output. Under the program introduced by Lenin, rural trade, agricultural control of production and marketing, and land tenure were also raised. However, as 1921 was a year of famine, with the harvest just 43 percent of the 1909–1913 average, and a time of political disruption—the Kronstadt rebellion—the implementation of Lenin's agricultural reform was restrained. Nevertheless, the relevance of the early NEP, and even of the ideological textbook of the time—Nikolai Bukharin's "Economics of Transition" for restructuring of rural economies—is now being formally and informally discussed in Moscow, as well as in Beijing.

In explaning the "significant successes" of Chinese rural reform, the Soviet delegation referred to previously pointed to a number of changes:

> First and foremost—transition to contractual responsibility. Contracts within the framework of the family, cooperative, rural industrial enterprise, or trade association. Second—orientation toward diversified agricultural production, and also expansion of stock raising, vegetable growing, and industrial crops. Third— fast growth of small and medium industrial production in the countryside.
>
> And finally—and this process is only just beginning—utilization of modern scientific achievements, particularly in the sphere of horticulture and fertilizers.[6]

One may wonder if the Soviet proponents of economic reform in agriculture such as Burlatsky and Bogomolov are using both Lenin's NEP policy and Chinese rural reform successes as arguments for implementing the comparable Soviet decrees and resolutions of the Gorbachev era. To be sure, the policy statements have a familiar ring to them. The difference would be in their implementation in letter and spirit.

While in China the decentralization of the rural economy and the establishment of a highly differentiated, market-stimulating reward and family-responsibility system have been adopted in practice, rural reform is only a declared policy in the USSR. In China the "baogan system" of family responsibility for planting and sales has been extended not only to control of the field and rural labor, but also to the farm to market distribution system, to rural industrial enterprises, and to retail sales. The new contract system permits households to raise income through diligent labor, to improve management, and to make better use of appropriate technology. Farmers are also permitted to work in rural towns and invest capital in enterprises outside their collective.[7]

Although the concept of the work-payment system, in which the local unit could negotiate the production and marketing of the harvest and the payment to the higher collective unit, was set out in the 1979 decree, the system was initially implemented in the context of the old commune organization and was not widely applied throughout rural China.[8] The wide-scale adoption of the household–family responsibility system (the *baogan* system) was during the period 1982 to 1984.

So, although Chinese rural reform had less specificity in 1979 than the recent Soviet resolution on changing the agricultural management system, by 1982–1984, the changes in the PRC had gone substantially beyond those proposed in the USSR. It is important to note that 1979–1984 was a period of expanding output in the PRC both for traditional crop production and for rural enterprises. Likewise, the leadership followed through on rural reform and overcame resistance to adoption of new organizational rules and mechanisms set up for the rural economy. Finally, the Chinese peasant responded, apparently enthusiastically, to the opportunities for higher income and increased autonomy. Thus three factors were important to the dynamics of rural reform in China: favorable weather; enforcement by central leadership of the letter and the spirit of the decentralized, family responsibility system; and a very positive response from the peasantry to their new rights and incentives.

With these comparative factors of Chinese rural economic success in mind, it is important to clearly state a number of reservations at this early stage of rural reform in the Soviet Union based on Gorbachev's agricultural resolution.[9]

1. Centralized power in the hands of the State Agriculture Committee (Gosagroprom) must take from the relevant ministries the authority to set basic rural economy policy guidelines, establish the parameters for agricultural planning, and assure that a substantial transfer of managerial rights and responsibilities devolves to the local enterprises. Although some of the formidable central agricultural bureaucracy may have been disbanded with formation of the Gosagroprom, the long-established agricultural ministerial bureaucracies in Moscow, the republics, regions, and oblasts have no counterpart in the PRC.

2. The resolution of March 29 on expanding the autonomy of the local agricultural units will, if carried through, provide significantly increased rights and responsibilities for local units in planting, investment, marketing, and incomes policy. Since a good deal of its real impact depends on the farmers' success in reaching or approaching the Twelfth Five-Year Plan goals (1986–1990) and since much of the local flexibility is tied to control of output *above* the levels of the Eleventh Five-Year Plan, weather and growing conditions must be favorable.

   As Karl Waedekin notes, the decrees have the effect of splitting the market: The required deliveries based on past averages would be at procured prices below costs of production (the difference thus being a form of tax); the sales above the past average levels would bring a profit depending on the margin of harvest above the average.[10] Good weather and good luck, already challenged by the Chernobyl nuclear accident, will be critical for achieving a level of performance that will allow the new measures to work. Without substantially improved performance, the incentive measures designed to generate improved performance will be less influential—this may be a kind of Catch-22.

3. Local units and the peasantry will have to respond to new incentives and local autonomy with increased productivity and effort. The verbiage

of the decrees may be appropriate theoretically to produce improvement, but the Soviet peasants and local units must respond for the measures to be actually effective. Judging by Chinese and selected East European experience, effective local autonomy and incentive systems are usually the factors in improved performance.[11]

Assuming that the Gosagroprom does initiate a centralization of overall policy and planning and decentralization of management; that the revision of the agricultural system provides a significant margin for local autonomy in planting, marketing, investment and income policy; and that the local units are responsive, the specific innovations in the resolutions may be instrumental in improving productivity in Soviet agriculture.

Some highlights of the March 29 resolutions are as follows:

## 1. New Incentives

- Premium payments (increased prices) of up to 100 percent for grains, legumes, and sugar beets;
- Availability of additional equipment (tractors, trucks) based on harvest performance;
- Participation in R&D and construction decisions and credit from Gosbank at favorable long-term interest rates;
- Pension payments of up to 100 percent increase in income to attract older workers to agriculture, reducing peasant labor shortage;
- Variation of plan requests by land fertility, capital and labor force availability;
- Insurance for natural disasters of up to 60 percent of value of shortfall;
- Integration of private-plot output into state marketing and supply systems.

## 2. Local Autonomy: Rights and Responsibilities from Decentralization

- Right to market food, milk, meat, and other production above previous five-year plan levels through markets including family and personal contractual arrangements;
- Payment to collective and state farm workers and directors based on revenue and profits; bonuses also tried to productivity;
- Discretionary use of construction funds from central investment, credit from Gosbank, and retained profits permitted by local units.

Emphasis in the resolutions is placed on the quality and accountability of the local cadre. Indeed, if the party from Gorbachev down stresses reward by performance and an up-or-out cadre policy, the system may be energized. But it must be recognized that we can only speculate at this time, and it will be important to see how the resolutions are interpreted and implemented in practice. The resolutions may represent a new set of "panaceas" if implemented under favorable natural conditions.[12]

Chinese rural reform, once under way and successful, proceeded farther than Soviet proposals, especially in the adoption of the family responsibility system—for example, in land tenure (the fifteen-year family contract), the right to invest earnings from the family plot in rural enterprises outside the collective, and the ability to hire out part of the family labor force to enterprises outside the family plot. These kinds of measures of land tenure and local autonomy were reportedly discussed during Lenin's New Economic Policy but were never adopted in principle in the USSR. In encouraging rural reform, Deng Xiaoping even echoed the famous slogan of Bukharin when he told the Chinese peasants to "enrich themselves." And, indeed, they have. Partly because of this incentive system, the performance of agriculture reported by Chinese officials from 1978 to 1984 represents a "new plateau in agriculture performance," permitting a shift to fodder, meat, and fish in the Chinese food program.[13] When it became an exporter of grain and soybeans to the USSR in 1984, China added further evidence of the success of its rural policy as compared to that of the USSR.

The most notable achievements of Deng's rural modernization to date have followed the introduction of a system of local autonomy providing more incentives to local organizations. The 800 million people in the countryside engaged in agriculture, previously organized in egalitarian communes, were placed under the family responsibility system.[14] Not only did output in grain and basic necessities such as cotton fiber increase as a result, but rural industry burgeoned, representing 10 percent of total industrial output and employing 20 percent of the rural labor force by 1985. The successful expansion of food-production and population-control programs have permitted the world's largest nation to escape the specter of Malthus and become an exporter of food. Personal income and rural output increases during the rural reform period have been impressive:

- Peasant income has doubled in less than a decade; per capita farm income rose from 134 to 310 Yuan during the years 1978–1984. Increased rural income resulted in a sharp rise in peasant consumption and private housing construction. The sharply differentiated incentive system has not only changed land tenure but has begun to change the social structure of rural China.
- From 1978 to 1984, grain production grew 4.9 percent as compared to only 2.1 percent from 1957 to 1978.
- Output of other crops grew still more rapidly as China became a net exporter of coarse grains, soybeans, and raw cotton.

These increases were accomplished without a significant burden on centrally planned investment. While state investment in agriculture decreased, the use of rural credit went up. Moreover, increased output was produced on reduced acreage in cultivated farmland through more efficient use of existing resources—in part a result of increased incentives inherent in the family responsibility system. The national self-sufficiency of China, indeed the development of an agricultural export capability, is a major accomplishment; it is of global importance that the PRC, with one-fifth of the world's population, is no longer a burden on world food resources. While by key per capita income measures China still ranks near the bottom among developing countries, viewed in the historical perspective, China's achievement of a human-to-food-resource balance has been an important part of its development process.

Chinese and Soviet rural reform will likely face both the problem of satisfying rising consumer expectations and the social and ideological problem of land tenure and differentiated incomes. Likewise the policy on investment—local and central—may become crucial to continued improvement in performance if present incentives have their effect primarily in the short run.

As the Chinese economy has grown, so have Chinese consumers' expectations—from the income level typical of a developing country where workers and peasants alike worked to buy bicycles, watches, sewing machines, and radios, to the current expectation of successful peasants and workers for consumer durable goods such as motorcycles, refrigerators, and television sets.

While on the average Soviet peasants are on a higher plane of living, there is nonetheless a common problem of closing the gap between rising incomes and available goods that will satisfy the increasing purchasing power. The Soviet Union also faces the thorny problem of reducing the massive subsidies to agriculture. If they are reduced, as some of Gorbachev's lieutenants suggest, farm income may go down.

The issue of socialist ownership and the possibility of revival of sharp differences in income and wealth are current concerns to the PRC and a potentially contentious issue for the USSR as well. The family responsibility system raised the issue of the differences between private and socialist ownership—specifically, the question of whether under the family responsibility system socialist humanism and lack of alienation could be achieved. An authoritative Chinese response to this question affirmed the consistency of rural reform with Marxist-Leninist-Maoist ideology, but it is not entirely convincing. Still, such a full and balanced discussion of Marxian ideological precepts on socialist and private ownership as that of Hu Quiamu has not appeared in Soviet ideological literature since the 1920s.[15] Overall, one is left with the impression that the ideological basis of Chinese rural reform is not a settled issue and may well be challenged in the PRC, as well as in other Communist countries.[16]

Although in the use of family units for production and contracting sales are limited in the Soviet Union, debate on their existence required a response by the head of Gosagroprom: "It is in no way contrary to our principles. The land belongs to the state, the fertilizer and the machinery belong to the Kolkhoz, but it is the individual or his family that does the actual work."[17]

Burlatsky also notes that family contracts and private holdings in agriculture and trade pose no threat in China to socialist ownership, as he describes the Chinese view:

We have firmly established that the socialized sector will continue to occupy a leading position in our economy. At present, the overwhelming bulk of the entire national product is produced by the socialized sector. The family contract does not affect the relations of ownership, since the land remains, like before, in the hands of collectives, and is allocated for only a limited period of time to use by individual peasant households. The fixed assets of production will remain in the hands of the state and of collectives. As far as private ownership is concerned, it is not developing as fast as it may seem. For example, 80 percent of retail trade is still carried out by state and collective enterprises. A firm commercial foundation has been laid for the socialized sector. Under these conditions, we need not be afraid of the development of individual enterprise, especially in the services sphere, trade, handicrafts, cottage industries, and small enterprises. . . . Out of the three component elements of property rights—ownership, use, and control—the state, while remaining the owner, transfers at least two—use and control—into the hands of enterprises and collectives—on the basis of contract or lease.[18]

The problem of differentiation, leading to widening differences in the countryside and inflation of food prices to urban workers, has in fact become an important issue in the current debate in China, according to Fred Crook.[19] There is a possibility that the new, differentiated system might lead to a new class of owners and tenants. Successful Chinese families may accumulate wealth by acquiring control over the land of less successful families, as well as over transport and other resources, leading to a development of classes of landholders and landless peasant labor. This process of accumulation may have already given rise to the development of "have" and "have-not" groups in rural China and the fear that this trend may lead to the recreation of some aspects of the landlord and tenant system of the past. Although successful peasants are told to "enrich themselves" through merit and superior performance, the introduction of political forces, even corruption, which is already said to be evident in some localities, could bring frictions and dissatisfaction into the rural scene.

Population trends are critical to China's ability to provide an adequate or improving standard of living to the populace and to live up to its social and ideological requirement of full employment—the right to work. In the final analysis, the level of China's overall unemployment and underemployment will depend on the management of the countryside. Closing rural-urban income differentials and maintaining control of urban housing make rural employment levels the key to national full employment. The goal is to increase nonagricultural activities in the rural areas, develop small and medium-sized towns, limit the number of laborers involved in crop cultivation, and, of course, increase productivity.

Both Chinese and Soviet rural productivity improvement will also turn on increased investment from both the center and the locality. Local investment may have to be supplemented by more central investment in the PRC; in the USSR, central investment—currently very large—will need to be supplemented by increased local investment.

In China there are at least two schools of thought on continued potential in the rural economy: (1) *Outside sources of growth:* Improvements in the future must come from outside the rural economy; that is, rural gains have been largely exhausted, and now increased state investment is needed to improve transport marketing networks and other ties to the national economy. (2) *Rural sources of growth:* Improvements in performance are still possible inside the rural economy; financing may come from reinvestment by rural collectives and peasant households. These views are not necessarily mutually exclusive.[20]

Those arguing a greater need for centralized investment in the Chinese rural economy point to the bottlenecks with diminished returns to inputs that are thus slowing real growth.

- Long-term increases in agricultural output and productivity, albeit difficult, may be sustained through continued incentive effects of de-collectivizing land holdings; increased specialization and marketization; continued stimulation from increases in key modern inputs—for example, mineral fertilizer. However, each of these important sources of. past growth in productivity may have diminishing effects in the future. Success in rural production will make more important the necessary improvement in the underdeveloped rural infrastructure and marketing systems. Incentives to facilitate marketing are urgently needed—development of rural infrastructure, inland waterways, water supply, power generation, rural road network, storage, refrigeration, and food processing may all be significant for continued improvement in productivity.
- Effectively joining increased supplies in rich rural provinces with demand in urban and less productive rural provincial areas will be a challenging, complex process of transport development.

A high rate of central investment in the Soviet agricultural sector—28 percent of total investment (possibly rising to one-third, according to Nikolai Ryzhkov's Party Congress speech)—is planned to continue.[21] From this investment, the Soviets expect results to include sharp reductions in harvest losses, improved food processing and better farm-to-market supply. As one example of what can be achieved by investment, Gorbachev stated that the use of the new DON-1500 combine harvester will alone reduce the stock of grain harvesting machines, disengage about 400,000 machine operators, and reduce the losses of grain by millions of metric tons.

Much of the Soviet rural improvement, however, is to come from increased local responsibility, and improved infrastructure—rural housing, transport, roads, and storage—supported by local funds. The local enterprises, collective farms, and family units are expected to use their profits to invest in local improvements. Whether the local authorities will choose the most profitable and effective investments remains to be seen. Polish experience in generating local investment in private agriculture is not impressive. The continued dominance of horses in Poland's farms bears evidence of a persistence of old ways.

## Central Control of Planning and Management

Because Chinese and Western observers alike often refer to reform of planning and management in China in terms of changes from the Soviet pattern or model, one might expect the Chinese system of planning and management to have resembled its Soviet counterpart.[22] It never did, and the current reforms are pushing the two systems even further apart. Whereas Soviet planning and management are comprehensive, detailed, and centralized, and management is controlled by a large ministerial bureaucracy, Chinese economic planning is far less comprehensive, and management decisions seem to emanate largely from the State Economic Commission, rather than a large ministerial bureaucracy. Likewise, management decisions in China have never been controlled as much from the center as in the Soviet Union.

Although highly developed and staffed and fortified by tradition and political power, the governmental economic bureaucracy is precisely what Gorbachev has identified as his major reform target—he seems to be calling for a kind of "euthanasia of the central governmental economic class." In this administrative reform, the task for Gorbachev may be much more difficult than that undertaken by Deng, given the absence in China of a fully developed Soviet-style planning and management system and bureaucracy.

While China's urban reform has proceeded further than the USSR's, Chinese success in this effort will require the resolution of inherent dilemmas:

- Chinese urban reform, with its shift from mandatory to guidance planning, is more complex than rural reform; to the extent that central planning is limited to a restricted number of industrial products and guidance planning is synonymous with production not centrally controlled, decentralization need not occur. Decentralized or better controlled local enterprises are the key to effective decentralization and development of a good profitability measure—for example, one based on prices and costs that reflect relative scarcity and on interest rates and taxes that respond to market forces.
- Continued, even enhanced, centralized, mandatory planning in critical sectors such as energy, transportation, and defense may restrict development of guidance planning.
- Shift of decision-making power from the center to enterprises and from the planning bureaucracy to professional managers may be politically easier now while Deng has broad-based political support for reform, but, without the concomitant development of rational prices, interest rates, and other monetary measures necessary to determine profitability, it will be difficult to evaluate success under guidance planning.

Restructuring of the Chinese urban economy calling for a shift from mandatory to guidance planning and a decentralization of decision making giving more authority and responsibility to the enterprises in industry was set out in the detailed party plenum statements of October 1984, and it is described by the Chinese as a shift away from Soviet-type planning and management. While Soviet planning has been comprehensive, detailed, and centralized with management controlled from the center by a large ministerial bureaucracy, it has been largely supply constrained. We often refer to the Soviet economic planning process as *taut*, that is, targets are set progressively higher, optimally to strain the ability of the enterprises to just meet output targets with available resources or with less than previously planned input-output ratios.

Even though the Chinese describe their old system as Soviet style, it is clear that Chinese planning and management through the State Planning Commission and the State Economic Commission were never as comprehensive as the planning and management of the traditional Soviet process.[23] Although supply constrained, the Chinese planning and management process should not be described as having optional tautness but perhaps optimal slackness. Key parts of priority sectors, to be sure, have been centralized and tightly planned—for example, some defense industries, as well as some parts of key industrial sectors. These priority industries have always been assured needed supplies, but a wide range of Chinese industries and agriculture could never be described as centrally controlled and administered as in the Soviet Union. Consequently, urban reform toward guidance planning represents far less of a change in the PRC than it would in the USSR.

Where the Chinese start institutionally in their reform—the "baseline"[24] for urban reform—is important for judging change and prospects for reform. What is the "baseline" for central planning in the PRC and how must the Chinese change to bring about decentralization of management?

- Only a portion of the economy has ever been effectively under central planning control. Even for key industrial sectors such as steel, coal, and machine building only parts of the industry were controlled.
- Chinese central planning is administered through a negotiation process: (1) Policy-oriented, "suggested" control figures are set down for a few major targets (growth of production, investment, output of coal and steel). (2) After approval by the State Council a preliminary document is sent down to enterprises, and a reaggregation of key control figures takes place. (3) Then the State Planning Commission calls a national planning conference of representatives of relevant agencies above the enterprises. Plans for material supply, investment, production, labor, wages, and commerce are hammered out at these conferences. Only sixty commodity production levels were planned at the 1985 conferences. (4) Local conferences are then held to communicate the decisions on those production areas centrally controlled but—more important—to plan those wide areas of economic activity outside the central plan. "Guidance planning" especially applies to this area of local control outside the purview of the central planners.

- In areas of guidance planning—either in local enterprises outside mandatory planning or decentralized industries—problems of effective pricing, wage, and employment policy and financial planning remain. The "market fringe" where many consumer goods are produced does not reflect full costing, including capital costs. Wages are only reflective of marginal productivity to the extent it can be increased. Full employment and "the right to work" conditions reduce the effectiveness of the theoretical right of managers to hire and fire. Sharply rising incomes tend to widen the gap between purchasing power and value of goods available to absorb purchasing power. Profits, taxes, and enterprises' financial autonomy are closely related but not well developed.[25]

The Soviet delegation to the PRC in 1986 had some reports from the Chinese on urban reform:

> The most important commodities which are in short supply, like steel, copper, and cement, will be distributed by the state like before, even though a certain proportion of them is already available on the market. For example, we distribute centrally 80 percent of steel, but only 20 percent of cement. The ultimate aim is that all materials, including the ones in short supply (with the exception, of course, of the military industry sphere), will be distributed via the market. . . .
>
> The reform now affects basically the medium and small enterprises, which are introducing a system of responsibility in various forms. Furthermore, extensive rights have been given to provinces, districts, and cities. And probably the most important aspect is the fact that we have embarked on the transition from deductions from profits to tax collection. The tax at present is equal to approximately 50 percent of net profits. This means that the remainder of the profit stays with the enterprises which use it for technical reconstruction, wage increases, the building of housing and of children's and cultural institutions, and also as a bonus fund.[26]

In a comparative assessment of the decentralization and use of market forces in planning and management under Gorbachev and Deng, it is also important to consider the historical example of the New Economic Policy with emphasis on the "commanding heights."[27] The Chinese economy with its limited urban-industrial planning and control and with decentralized agriculture has always been closer to the NEP than its Soviet counterpart. Yet, as perceived by the new, younger Soviet leader, Mikhail Gorbachev, the traditional entrenched central planning and management system is the central problem for effective Soviet economic reform. Soon after taking office, in an unprecedented discussion with Soviet industrial and agricultural managers in a Central Committee meeting, Gorbachev criticized detailed centralized planning and management and called for establishment of "the correctly defined rights and obligations of each level of management." Gorbachev further stressed that the Soviets need to reduce the excessive control of the ministries over enterprise management, ". . . the need to remove the fetters of poor and superfluous instructions from them, decisively decreasing accountability of higher organs and freeing ourselves from the paper chase, which will at the same time contribute to a reduction of the management apparatus."[28]

The leading Soviet theoretical economist, Nikolai Federenko, also made a detailed critique of the bureaucratic problems arising from the complexity and size of the economic planning bureaucracy in the Soviet Union. Federenko called attention to the 4,000 major product categories used by the State Planning Commission, the 40,000–50,000 specifications of ministries, and the one million specialized specifications of the State Committee for Supply.[29]

Apparently, a coherent, comprehensive strategy for reforming the Soviet governmental and party economic bureaucracies, one that would provide for both more effective central planning and decentralized management, has not yet been worked out, but Gorbachev's speech at the Party Congress contained many of the code phrases signaling the type of change required and legitimizing the commitment of many in his administration to go forward with reform both over the short and long term:

- Relevance of prices ("Prices are to become an active tool of economic and social policy"). A first step may be physical quotas or rationing of scarce labor and energy inputs and bonuses for output that meets world market standards.[30]
- The right of industrial enterprises to sell many of their own products. ("Enterprises . . . should be given the right to independently market above-plan output, unused raw and manufactured materials and equipment"). This reform parallels the decentralization of agricultural decision making on planting, cultivation, and marketing to the family unit ("Subcontracting and the piece-work system at the team level among work units and families will become more widespread").
- Legalization or cooption of the informal or illegal services sector ("Decisive measures must be adopted to eliminate marked imbalances between demand for services and their supply").

Certainly, many questions remain unresolved. Abel Aganbegyan, a reform-minded economist and leading adviser to Gorbachev, spelled out the gaps in the economic strategy during a postcongress conference: How will retail prices be made more realistic? How will the leadership close or restructure unprofitable enterprises? What will be done with manual workers replaced by machines? He noted, too, that the massive subsidies on bread, meat, and milk must be reduced if retail prices are to be rationalized (according to a precongress Gorbachev speech at Tselinograd, subsidies for meat alone now cost 20 billion rubles per year). Volgograd party official V. I. Kalashnikov called for an increase in food prices to close the subsidy gap in his speech to the congress. But reduction of subsidies would pose a direct challenge to the equally important need to support consumption and increase urban and rural living standards. These dilemmas, among others, will have to be faced if reform proceeds over the long term.

To strengthen the central economic ministries but narrow their focus from "operational management" to long-range structural planning, several superministries have been created—the State Agro-Industrial Committee (Gosagroprom), which merged five agricultural ministries and a committee as discussed in the section on rural reform, a Machine-Building Bureau that spans several industries, and a new energy "superministry" bureau under Boris Shcherbina (whose first major job was to chair the Inquiry Commission at Chernobyl). This centralization of planning involves more horizontal coordination, an emphasis on strategy at a higher political level, and more decentralization of decision making and authority to the regions and individual enterprises. As noted previously, the Gosagroprom seems to be a central body that controls policy and macroeconomic planning, including centralized investment, but leaves most specific production, marketing, and local investment decisions to the local authorities and managers. This policy has not been applied to industry through the bureaus established to date.[31]

Gosagroprom may be the model for industrial reorganization that Gorbachev will use. The creation of the new State Agro-Industrial Committee removed many of the top government agricultural officials of the old regime and established a new team that includes two of Gorbachev's former associates from Stavropol: his longtime Stavropol deputy and successor as kray first secretary, V. S. Murakhovsky, who became chairman and first deputy premier; and Lenin Agricultural Academy President A. A. Nikonov, head of the Stavropol agricultural institute while Gorbachev was kray first secretary, who became a deputy chairman. Another agricultural official from neighboring Krasnodar, G. A. Romanenko, was also made a deputy chairman of the new committee. Romanenko had headed the Krasnodar agricultural institute since his promotion from deputy director in mid-1985. Significantly, the ministry merger in agriculture has not simply combined the bureaucracies into a still larger, more inert bureaucracy, but rather has required a reduction in force, reportedly leading to the temporary unemployment of as many as 3,200 and even the institution of unemployment benefits—an unprecedented occurrence. This reduction in staff has not yet led to a transfer of place of employment from Moscow to localities, which would be a significant step. Whether such a strategy applied throughout the urban-industrial economy would be acceptable and achievable, given the political and social questions it raises, remains to be seen. Moreover, more growth through intensification programs implies central pressure, whereas decentralized decision making would require more flexibility, even slack, in planning. Job security is still considered a right by manager and worker alike, adding further inflexibility.

The initiation of direct two-way communication between the top Soviet leadership and the 2-million-strong brigade leadership is said to be one key to the new Soviet policy of socialist democracy and self-management. Gorbachev's "town meeting" approach to discussion of managerial problems may be a stimulating new departure in the USSR, but it may in the end lead to less decentralization than already exists in China. Instead of a shift of authority to the enterprise and locality Gorbachev's urban reform may indeed be more streamlining of the central apparatus than change in rights and responsibilities.

Though many of these indications of a need for urban-industrial reform in the Soviet Union are largely declarations of intent, it should be noted that Gorbachev has personally associated himself with "radical reform"; this time it is not an Aleksei Kosygin reform (the number-two man) but the general secretary himself who is assuming responsibility. Gorbachev may mean what he says about shifting the rights and responsibilities of management of both the rural and urban economy to the local level.

But, as noted earlier, in the PRC the starting point in planning and management is much more conducive to the development of guidance or decentralized planning than the status quo in the USSR. As Lenin would say, the Chinese do not have to remember the "lessons of the Paris Commune"—that is, the need to eliminate the old institutions and bureaucracy to make changes irreversible.

Why did China not develop the Soviet-style comprehensive, detailed, centralized system of planning and management with its large economic bureaucracy? Looking at the period when Soviet influence was dominant on Chinese economic development from 1949 to 1960, one may hypothesize that new investment planning and industrial administration decisions during the critical and successful First Five-Year Plan (1953–1957) were largely preempted by the massive Soviet aid program obviating the need for a Soviet-style system in Beijing: "The Soviet Union was the chief supplier of complete plants. During the decade, agreements were signed with the U.S.S.R. for the construction of 291 major industrial installations in China. . . . In addition to supplying equipment for these installations, the Soviet Union provided China with valuable technical aid including: (a) blueprints and technical information, (b) some 10,000 Soviet technicians and advisors, and (c) training for 15,000 Chinese technicians and academic students in the U.S.S.R."[32]

The impact of Soviet aid termination in mid-1960 on Chinese industrial output was severe and indicated the control of Soviet decision makers on Chinese economic plans: "In 1961, industrial production fell sharply to a level slightly above that of 1957 but only two-thirds of the peak reached in 1959. After the withdrawal of the Soviet technicians in mid-1960, the Chinese found that they could not operate many of the heavy industrial plants built as Soviet aid projects and they were forced to cut production drastically."[33]

Robert Dernberger made an interesting calculation of how much China would have suffered had Soviet aid not been available indicating the importance of Soviet aid to the fulfillment of Chinese plans. "Elsewhere, using a very simple economic model with fixed coefficients, assuming that domestic production was a perfect substitution for imports and restricting the analysis to the First Five-Year Plan period (1953–57), for which sufficient data is available, I have estimated that the loss China would have suffered if denied these imports of machinery and equipment would have been a

20 to 30 percent reduction in China's estimated rate of growth."[34] Thus, in a sense, one might say that a good deal of the planning of investment in new capacity, as well as the industrial administration and management decision making, during the Chinese economic development in the 1950s was made in Moscow and transferred in a predigested package complete with technicians, blueprints, and detailed management directions to the PRC. In the decade of the 1960s, the attention and energies of Chinese economic decision makers were largely consumed with the problems of recovery from loss of Soviet aid in industrial production, adjustments following the abortive Great Leap. Forward program, and coping with the Cultural Revolution. Agriculture was effectively decentralized during the 1960s. As a result, Soviet-style comprehensive, central planning did not develop with its formidable entrenched bureaucracy in rural China; industry was recouping to the 1957 level. Ironically, then, the Chinese may have been saved from the burden of the Soviet centralized planning system by the control the Soviets exercised over their aid program during the period when they might have emulated the Soviet system. Moreover, the Mao-inspired Great Leap Forward and the Cultural Revolution had the effect of disrupting and weakening the control of the economic and party bureaucracy that was already in place. Even had the direct Soviet influence not been present during the First Five-Year Plan, China might not have followed in substance Soviet planning and management style as the East Europeans did. The Chinese seem to have a tradition of "Sinofying" all foreign systemic imports, even those that appear to be formally adopted.

At the same time, Chinese central planning may need to be further strengthened in the "commanding heights" approach—especially for energy, transportation, and the defense industry. China has experienced energy shortages, though these shortfalls have not been for lack of natural resources. Richly endowed in oil, gas, coal, and hydro, China has the resource capability to provide for its own needs and become a major exporter of energy. Development of nuclear electric power potential may help resolve China's regional electric power supply and demand inequities; but energy output and supply have fallen far short of the needs and potential, making energy the pervasive bottleneck for meeting macro- and microeconomic goals.[35]

The defense sector, like those of energy and transportation, may require a continued, strong role for centralized planning and management in order to establish security priorities and meet long-term development needs. Modernization of the military is under way, but it remains the fourth modernization. The continued low priority of military modernization is in tune with the generally nonmilitary character of the noncommunist Pacific region. Thus "guns" are characteristically submerged to the claims of "growth" and "butter":

- The short-term objectives of defense modernization are aimed at improvement in combat readiness of forces through adaptation of combined arms operations; improvement in the technical, professional skills of officer corps; and creation of monetary incentives keyed to improved professional performance.

- The long-term objectives may be served by improvement in the scientific and technical base making it capable of developing and producing weapons based on modern technology; and by the development and deployment of strategic systems that provide a more credible nuclear deterrent.

PRC military expenditures are exceeded only by those of the United States and USSR, and the Chinese defense industrial base is among the world's largest; nevertheless, the burden of defense has not offset or seriously retarded civilian modernization. Defense allocations have not increased appreciably since 1972, except for a modest increase to fund the Vietnam invasion of 1979. Still, military modernization will in time represent a major overhaul of the defense establishment. Although some external assistance will be needed, the primary objective is to develop a self-sustaining defense infrastructure. The traditional multifunctional role of the armed forces in the Chinese economy and society has been maintained with continuing attention to its symbolism, even when the substance of resources for priority modernization is lacking.[36] Upgraded military modernization always threatens other modernization efforts and would require decision making from the center on resource allocation:

- Growth needs may create hard choices in military modernization, particularly if the external threat increases and the security requirements are upgraded.
- Perceived threats or opportunities in the external environment that may lead Chinese leaders to upgrade military modernization would tend to further generate threats in an escalating process.

An enhanced and expanded military modernization program in the USSR may have a similar effect on further centralization of related aspects of Soviet economic decision making, thereby restricting decentralization of related industrial management.

## Party Role in Management

The Chinese Communist Party (CCP) does not appear to directly and substantively intervene in the day-to-day management of local enterprises and farms. The Chinese government officials, peasants, and workers seem to share power with officials of Chinese counterparts of the Soviet *raikom* and *obkom* (regional and local party committees). This nature of party involvement in Chinese management was suggested by the observations of the American Economists Study Team:

Members were particularly interested in determining whether enterprise-level disputes are typically resolved by recourse to the local-level Party machinery;

i.e., whether a system of Party "prefects" such as that described by Hough exists in China. The answer seemed to be no. Instead, enterprises first carry all problems to their immediate supervisory organs. Minor differences are resolved at this level, while major differences might be referred up the governmental hierarchy. When different industrial systems are involved, problems are in theory to be solved by the Industry-Commerce Management Bureau (*gongshang guanli ju*), but this body was not mentioned in any other accounts of problem solving. In practice, functional industrial problems at the municipal level are mediated by the vice mayor in charge of industrial work, who might be regarded as adjudicator of industrial disputes on that level.[37]

This same limited party role appeared to carry over to the local enterprises in the countryside, "The purpose of the [party] cells is to actively implement party policy and to organize sessions to study major party documents and ideological works."[38]

Under Deng's restructuring of the economy, the economic management role of the CCP has apparently not been expanded. Though the CCP continues to play the central role in establishing the basic direction of economic policy, its role does not appear to carry over to management.[39] This limited party intervention in the economic management process seems to apply especially to the regional and local role of the party. Whereas the oblast party chairman (*obkom*) in the Soviet system, acting through the personnel management control of the *nomenklatura*, governs through appointments, rewards, dismissals, and so on, and is a formidable day-to-day force in the Soviet management system, Chinese party officials in all the localities and enterprises the AEST visited appeared to have a much more modest role. Local government officials—for example, mayors of major cities, such as in Chongqing and Guangzhou—seem currently to have the central role in management policy. Also somewhat surprising to a Soviet–East European specialist is the apparent importance of workers in Chinese management. Indeed, the famous "triangle" of early Soviet NEP experience, composed of the professional managers, the workers, and the party officials seems to have reemerged in China, so that each of the three groups is important in its own right.

In the Soviet Union, a major restructuring of the ministerial system to narrow management at the center and revise the "*nomenklatura* system" that ensures party control of personnel privileges and rewards at all levels of the economy may be essential for successful reform but, some would say, politically impossible.[40] Nevertheless, the role of the party—*nomenklatura*—has been brought into the central discussion of economic change at the Party Congress and by various academicians. Notably, at the Party Congress, Gorbachev's new head of the Moscow party organization, Boris Yeltsin, attacked the party bureaucracy directly, asking, "Why, even now, is the demand for radical changes getting stuck in the inert layers of time-servers who possess party cards?" Questions have also been raised about needs to increase the public responsibility of the party and reduce privileges based primarily on party position.

The reform position on the party role in the Polish economy may provide some indication of the parameters of approved policy by the Soviet Union in East Europe that might eventually be extended to the USSR itself. In Poland the formally approved changes in the party role in the economy go further than elsewhere in developing a policy of laissez-faire—removal of the direct intervention of the party in the day-to-day management of the economy. According to Mario Nuti:

> Last but not least the official reform project which was approved by the IX Extraordinary Congress of the PZPR (Polish Workers Party) and by Parliament made the first attempt on record at providing a clearer definition and reduction of Party influence on economic life, stating that the Party should not interfere with current operational management, with technical choices, and with appointment of managers and officials and assigning a much greater role in policy-making and control over the planning process to Parliament and its Committees. While these provisions have remained dead letter the fact that they are enshrined in a document which is still quoted as the guideline for Polish reform makes easier—though by no means certain—their future restatement, even if one looked pessimistically—as one should—at the prospect of reviving the spirit of Party "odnowa" [renewal] and independent unions.[41]

It is assumed throughout this discussion that reduction of the "burden" of the party apparatus on economic performance is an important part of reform in socialist economies. The power of the Communist Party through the *nomenklatura* system to control economic cadres, retain privileges not directly related to economic performance, and intervene in the management process has been questioned in differing degrees in the PRC, the Soviet Union, and Poland. More explicit reference to redressing the party role is currently being discussed in the USSR and East Europe, perhaps with less prospect of success than that already attained in the PRC.

Again, what may be required is a return to the earlier Leninist formulation of democratic centralism that in economic management called for sharing of power by the party with the professional managers and the workers' representatives in policy matters, withdrawal of the party from direct intervention in management, and a stricter code of conduct involving party responsibility and privilege.

## Economic Change: Not Only Problematic but Costly

If the changes discussed in these three areas—rural reform, central control of planning and management, and the party role in management—were fully implemented and carried through in the PRC, Soviet Union, and East Europe, they might all contribute significantly to the efficiency of the respective economies while having a revolutionary effect on the systems of political-economic governance. Looking toward the year 2000, it is possible that with favorable economic performance, change-oriented leadership, and fortuitous developments external to the countries involved, such major changes might occur.

Beneficial as such economic change might be, the full costs of attaining the economic reforms involved by the year 2000 might be substantial and could require significant ideological, political, and systemic changes:

- The changes resulting from accelerated economic growth facilitated by selective reform under Deng Xiaoping and Gorbachev, if adopted and continued, might result in destabilization of the established communist political economic system, diversification of culture, and opening of the society. Such changes could be no less radical than the political-ideological changes instituted under Mao or Stalin.
- The cultural and social impact of increasing inequities and changing social status, resulting from progressively differential incentive systems, may be substantial. The economic restructuring and new reform process may create an upper and an under class in rural and urban settings that could generate social and ideological backlash.
- The creation of a new managerial, scientific, and intellectual elite may not be deemed sufficiently beneficial to justify its full social, cultural, and political costs if the success model of a powerful party member is replaced by that of a technologically successful and economically well-to-do manager of rural and urban enterprises.
- Effective measures to deal with corruption and the establishment of equitable and effective incentive systems will need to be continued to assure the full fruits of modernization. If cynicism of the past is replaced by an effective incentive environment, rising expectations may develop a strong momentum of their own to influence future leadership decisions.

Even selected "radical" reforms may not be carried forward in the USSR and East Europe. The respective leaderships may find the ideological, political, and systemic changes too costly to be justified by even optimistic projections in economic performance. However, if they were to be carried forward throughout the centrally planned economies, the ideological, political, and systemic impacts of these economic reforms might require more significant change than the economic reforms themselves. If the leadership shares this view of the substantial political and systemic effects of implementation of significant, even effective, economic reform, these changes may be significant costs that outweigh the perceived economic benefits of change.

## Notes

1. This discussion draws heavily on *Highlights, China Looks Toward the Year 2000,* volumes 1 and 2, Joint Economic Committee, U.S. Congress, May 1986, *Economic Reform in China,* Report of the American Economists Study Team to the People's Republic of China, November 29–December 15, 1984 (Abram Bergson, Robert Dernberger, Arthur J. Alexander, John P. Hardt, Ed A. Hewett, Barry Naughton, Susan Shirk, and Janet Cady, editors, National Committee on United States–China

Relations, New York, April 1986, hereafter AEST Report. See also Joint Economic Committee, U.S. Congress, October 1985 and April 1986, *Highlights, East European Economies: Slow Growth in the 1980's*, vols. 1, 2, and 3.

2. Fedor Burlatsky, "Conversations About Economic Reforms in China," *Literaturnaya gazeta*, June 11, 1986, translated in Foreign Broadcast Information Service, USSR International Affairs, June 18, 1986, pp. B1–B9.

3. Jan S. Prybyla, "Mainland China and Hungary: To Market, to Market . . ." (see p. 155 of this volume) and Chu-yuan Cheng, "Economic Reform in Mainland China: Consequences and Prospects" (see p. 34 of this volume), presented at the Fifteenth Sino-American Conference on Mainland China. Dr. Cheng's view is that in spite of some short-term positive economic results, reform has lost its momentum in the PRC and has generated growing resistance from party and populace.

4. A State Agro-Industrial Committee was set up combining five ministries and several committees, *Pravda*, November 23, 1985; party and government resolution "On Further Improving the Economic Management Mechanism in the Country's Agro-Industrial Complex," *Pravda*, March 29, 1986.

5. Particulars of the proceedings in the Politburo, together with the text of Lenin's draft, taken from unpublished party archives, are in V. I. Lenin, *Sochineniya*, xxvi, 651–653, note 2. See Edward Hallett Carr, *A History of Soviet Russia*, vol. 2: *The Bolshevik Revolution, 1917–1923* (New York: Macmillan, 1952), pp. 280–297; Alec Nove, *An Economic History of the U.S.S.R.* (London: Penguin Books, 1982), pp. 83–86. For favorable reference to family responsibility in East European agriculture, see Oleg Bogomolov, "Comparative Agricultural Policies in CMEA Countries and International Comparisons" at Workshop on East-West European Economic Interaction, Session 9: Industrial Policies and Structural Change, Vienna Institute for Comparative Economic Studies, Vienna, December 2–5, 1985.

6. Burlatsky, "Conversations About Economic Reforms in China."

7. Frederick W. Crook, "The Commune System in Transition: China's Search for New Mechanisms to Manage and Control the Rural Economy," in Joint Economic Committee, *China Looks Toward the Year 2000*, May 1986, pp. 354–356.

8. Communiqué of the Third Plenary session of the Eleventh Central Committee of the Communist Party of China, adopted on December 22, 1978, translated in Foreign Broadcast Information Service, PRC, National Affairs, December 26, 1978, pp. E4–13.

9. The CPSU Central Committee and the USSR Council of Ministers adopted a resolution "On Further Improving the Economic Management Mechanism in the Country's Agro-Industrial Complex," *Pravda*, March 29, 1986, translated in Foreign Broadcast Information Service (FBIS), *USSR Agricultural Affairs*, pp. T1–10, April 2, 1986.

10. Karl-Eugen Waedekin, "Agrarian Policy at the Twenty-Seventh CPSU Party Congress," *Radio Liberty Research*, RL 170–86, April 24, 1986.

11. Studies comparing East-East and East-West agricultural performance indicate that the way in which agriculture is structured and managed is a critical factor in performance. Specifically smaller, more autonomous units of private farms were more productive than larger, less autonomous units—for example, comparing FRG and GDR, Polish and Belorussian farms; Karl-Eugen Waedekin, *Agriculture in Inter-System Comparison: Communist and Non Communist Cases* (Berlin: Duncker & Humbolt, 1985).

12. Alain Giroux, "Gorbatchev et l'agriculture—Cinq ans pour convaincre" (Gorbachev and Agriculture: Five Years to Convince), *Le courrier des pays de l'est*, no. 305, April 1986, pp. 3–21.

13. See Nicholas Lardy, "Overview: Agricultural Reform and the Rural Economy," in Joint Economic Committee, *China Looks Toward the Year 2000*, vol. 1, pp. 330–335.

14. Crook, "The Commune System in Transition," pp. 361–364.

15. Hu Quiamu speech "On Humanism and Alienation" in Central Party School, January 3, 1984, published in Beijing, *Renmin Ribao* in Chinese, January 27, 1984, pp. 1–5, translated in full in FBIS, *China PRC National Affairs*, February 7, 1984, pp. K1–33.

16. A debate in the Polish press on private family farming is also interesting. In 1983 a constitutional amendment guaranteed the permanence of individual family farms in Poland. Nonetheless, a debate ensued on whether private farming is compatible with socialism. Ryszard Manteuffel in *Politika*, August 25, 1984, maintained that private Polish farmers should not be considered capitalist as long as they did not exploit anyone. Makolaj Waleszko in *Politika*, October 29, 1984, argued that private Polish farming was neither socialized nor efficient. Polish government approval of the Vatican-based fund to aid private agriculture also would seem to add fuel to this debate.

17. In an interview of Murakhovsky in *Lituraturnaya gazeta*, no. 4, 1986, p. 2, quoted by Waedekin, "Agrarian Policy."

18. Burlatsky, "Conversations About Economic Reforms in China," pp. B–6, B–8.

19. Crook, "The Commune System in Transition," pp. 372f.

20. Lardy, "Overview," p. 335.

21. Speech of Nikolai Ryzhkov at the Twenty-seventh CPSU Party Congress, *Pravda*, March 4, 1986, translated in FBIS, *USSR National Affairs*, March 5, 1986, pp. 8–28.

22. Chinese urban reform was the focus of the American Economists Study Team report. Comments in this section draw from our interviews and especially from the Summary report by Barry Naughton, AEST Report, pp. 6–25.

23. Barry Naughton noted that in our discussions Chinese planners confirmed the crudeness of central planning in China, "Actually, we never succeeded in putting the entire economy under central planning." We were told, moreover, that not even all of the critical ferrous metals industry was under mandatory planning. AEST Report, p. 8.

24. See Ed A. Hewett, AEST Report, pp. 35f.

25. Naughton, AEST Report, passim.

26. Burlatsky, "Conversations About Economic Reforms in China," p. B–6.

27. Y. Ambartsumov, *Voprosi istorii* (Problems of History), no. 4, 1984.

28. See *Pravda*, April 12, 1985; cf. Rodolfo Brancoli, "Mikhail Gorbachev's Secret Report," *La Repubblica* (Rome), March 27, 1985, translated in FBIS *Soviet Union Daily Report*, March 28, 1985, pp. R1–4.

29. In the Novosibirsk publication, *Ekonomika: Organizatitsya Promyshlennogo Proizvodstva* (EKO), no. 12, 1984, pp. 7–8.

30. M. S. Gorbachev in plenum speech, June 16, 1986, seemed to echo comments of GDR leaders in their "Intensification Program" in the early 1980s in calling for more output at levels of world technology and use of Western analogues for inputs—for example, increased quantity and quality of output without more labor, energy, or metal. In fact, the specific comments on successful Soviet enterprises such as Sumy seemed to echo German praise of their successful *kombinats; Pravda*, June 17, 1986.

31. See Philip Hanson, "Super Ministries: The State of Play," *Radio Liberty Research*, RL 167–86, April 21, 1986.

32. R. Michael Field, in, Joint Economic Committee, *An Economic Profile of Mainland China*, vol. 1, February 1967, pp. 276–277; A. Usack and R. E. Batsavage, "The International Trade of the People's Republic of China," in Joint Economic Committee, *People's Republic of China: An Economic Assessment*, (Washington, D.C.: Government Printing Office, 1972), p. 344.

33. R. Michael Field, "Chinese Industrial Development, 1949–1970, in Joint Economic Committee, *People's Republic of China, An Economic Assessment*, p. 64.

34. Robert F. Dernberger, "The Foreign Trade and Capital Movements of Communist China" (Ph.D. dissertation, Harvard University, 1965); Alexander Eckstein, *Communist China's Growth and Foreign Trade* (New York: McGraw-Hill, 1966), pp. 123–124. Quoted in Robert Dernberger, "Economic Development and Modernization in Contemporary China: The Attempt to Limit Dependence on the Transfer of Modern Industrial Technology from Abroad and to Control Its Corruption of the Maoist Social Revolution," in Fred Fleron (editor), *Technology and Communist Culture: The Socio-Cultural Impact of Technology under Socialism* (New York: Praeger, 1977), pp. 261–262.

35. Tom Fingar, "Overview: Energy in China," in Joint Economic Committee, *China Looks Toward the Year 2000*, vol. 2, pp. 1–21.

36. Paul Godwin, "Overview: China's Defense Modernization," and June Teufel Dreyer, "The Role of the Military in the Chinese Economy," in Joint Economic Committee, *China Looks Toward the Year 2000*, vol. 2, pp. 133–147, 186–198.

37. Naughton, AEST Report, p. 21.

38. Crook, "The Commune System in Transition," p. 367.

39. Susan Shirk, AEST Report, p. 26.

40. Cf. Konstantin Simes, "The Gorbachev Generation," *Foreign Policy*, no. 59, summer 1985, pp. 3–21.

41. Domenico Mario Nuti, "Poland: Current Development and Prospects of Economic Reform," presented at NATO Colloquium: The Economies of Eastern Europe and their Foreign Economic Relations, April 1986.

# 28

## Mainland China and Hungary: To Market, to Market . . .

### Jan S. Prybyla

*[In China] we are developing a socialist commodity [market] economy which is fundamentally different from the capitalist commodity economy.*

—Tian Jiyun

*[In Hungary] we have moved in the direction of the market but the economy has not yet completely arrived there. . . . I am confident that more influence of the market on economic decisions would improve the Hungarian economy even more.*

—János Kornai

Hungary since 1968 and mainland China since 1978 have been experimenting with their economic structures, both of which had originally been adopted from the Soviet Stalinist model of central administrative command planning and comprehensive socialization of property rights in assets. The reason for this experimentation is that the model of command planning and socialized, highly centralized property is probably the world's second most inefficient way of economic decision making, the first being the model's radicalized variant known as Maoism. In Hungary the model reached the point of degenerative collapse in the revolution of 1956. It took the Hungarians another eleven years to get rid of much of it, but even now it keeps pounding at the door and occasionally, as in the years 1972–1979, breaks down the door and makes a fine mess of things. In the People's Republic of China (PRC), the decision to dump the model (together with its Maoist outgrowth) took only two years, but then the Chinese did not have to worry about what the Soviets thought, nor were they hampered in their resolve by membership in the Council of Mutual Economic Assistance (CMEA), the Warsaw Pact, and other Moscow-sponsored impedimenta. What the Chinese have most to fear is themselves. As in Hungary, but without the external (Soviet) constraint, sections of the ruling party and of society are not fully convinced of the nefariousness and alleged bankruptcy of the old model, although—visibly at least—there is not much support these days for the model's Maoist variant of barefoot industrialization and development by paroxysms. In certain well-placed quarters there is a good deal of nostalgia for the (as they now recall them) dynamic, spiritual-pollution-free times of the neo-Stalinist First Five-Year Plan (1953–1957). Born-again hardliners like Chen Yün believe that with a little twiddling of policy knobs on the rusty machine, the old model could be made to work again in a reincarnated form of enlightened Stalinism.

## Some Theoretical Questions

A few conceptual hurdles must be cleared at this time. There is, first of all, the question of comparability. Hungary is small, resource deficient, short of labor, heavily dependent on foreign trade, saddled wth a large hard currency debt, and handicapped by an exiguous domestic market. China is none of these. There is a big difference between the two in level of development, about as big as between the mainland and Taiwan. While these and other differences are real, they are also essentially "technical," that is, nonsystemic. What we are interested in are systemic arrangements for the generation, conveyance, and processing of information about costs and utilities in the economy, the coordinating mechanisms, the motivational subsystems, and the nature of property rights with respect to assets. On this level of economic organization, comparisons between national entities are legitimate and instructive no matter how great the technical differences. In their attempt to rid themselves of economic decision-making models inherited from the past, mainland China and Hungary have much to learn from each other.

This happens to be even more so because the direction of economic experimentation in Hungary and mainland China is similar. Despite ideological disclaimers, the fact is that, as of now, the economic structures of China and Hungary are moving in the direction of the market. Inevitably, the marketization of information, coordination, and motivation in both economies has been accompanied by an expansion of rights vested in the actual users of assets in regard to the assets they use. Another name for it is privatization or property rights to the level of the firm.

It will be helpful at this time to clarify the operative terms. By "central administrative command planning," or "plan" (the system of economic organization invented by Stalin and adopted by Hungary and mainland China in the late 1940s and early 1950s), is meant the setting by government officials of mandatory general and specific goals regarding production, exchange, and distribution and procedures for attaining those goals, the goals and procedures being expressed in physical/technical and financial terms and enforced primarily by administrative means. All significant means of production and distribution are government owned—directly (nationalization) or indirectly (collectivization).

The term "market" is taken to mean voluntary, contractual, competitive, horizontal transactions carried out by individual autonomous property-owning buying and selling units for utility or profit-maximizing purposes, by reference to spontaneously generated price signals, through the disbursement of money votes.

To accomplish their purpose of apportioning relatively limited resources to competing alternative uses, both plan and market make use of institutional arrangements for the generation, transmission, and analysis of *information* about the changing relationship of resources and objectives (costs-utilities, supplies-demands); the *coordination* of such information into a coherent pattern of production, exchange, and distribution; the *motivation* of the principal economic agents; and the extent and distribution of *property* rights with respect to assets.

I propose to handle the Hungary–mainland China comparison by looking first at the role played by the price system in performing the information and coordination functions in the post-1967 Hungarian New Economic Mechanism (NEM) and the post-1978 mainland Chinese economy. Next, I shall take up the changes made in the motivational (incentive) arrangements in both economies, that is, look at reward mechanisms directed at peasants, workers, and managers. Next to be examined will be property rights in assets, their privatization and increasing diversity; then the peculiar case and place of the so-called "second economy" in the new scheme will be looked at. Finally I shall try to draw some hopefully useful conclusions.

## Price System: Information and Coordination

### Importance of the Price System

There can be no real reform of administrative central command planning without a profound qualitative change in the nature and role of the economy's price system. Changes that do not touch the vitals of the price system are adjustments of the existing economic system—repair jobs and replacements of worn-out parts that do not address themselves to the core of the economic engine's efficiency problems.

In the command economy, information about what is to be done and coordination of decisions take the form of quantitative orders issued by the planners, cast in physical-technical terms, backed by administratively determined accounting prices, and sent to specific recipients. These addressee-specific, unconditional commands are coordinated at the center and lower levels of the administrative hierarchy through a process of bureaucratic iteration known as the method of material and financial balances. The whole process is vertically structured and involves substantial transactions costs.

A word about the "prices" that supplement the system's *Tonnenideologie*: The two sets of prices backing up physical-technical commands are prices at which the state buys agricultural produce from the (nationalized, collectivized) peasantry under compulsory physical delivery quotas (quota agricultural procurement prices) and industrial wholesale prices, that is, prices at which state firms transfer goods among themselves. Both categories of prices are set by the state, usually on a cost of production plus profit margin basis, with little or no regard to supply and demand. Since the allocation of quota farm produce and industrial producer goods is determined by physical rationing, the prices attaching to these goods are merely accounting devices, intended to be allocatively neutral (which, in practice, they are not). They are allocatively irrational, divorced from the scarcity relationship (supplies-demands, costs-utilities) prevalent in the economy.

There are other categories of prices in a command system that take some account of supply and demand forces, mainly to make less burdensome the planners' job of physical rationing. Retail prices are of this kind. They are usually set at levels that hopefully clear the market, and are moved up and down by the planners—often with considerable lag—in response to planner-perceived changes in the relationship of demand and supply in particular commodity markets. Wages of labor (in most command economies, except mainland China for many years) are also partly, but very imperfectly, cognizant of supply and demand in the labor market, but they too are altered by the planners at infrequent intervals.

A conservative change in the command system—or "intrasystemic adjustment"—the kind that has been implemented by the Soviet Union and most East European countries since a little after Stalin's death, consists of two parallel movements. First, there is a movement away from physical-technical norms to price indicators. Second, there is a movement away from mandatory planning by direct orders to "guidance" through price and price-related indicators. It should be noted that the obsession with tonnage and the compulsion to dictate in minute detail are reduced but not done away with. Firms are now instructed to fulfill profit, profitability, and sales targets, and to pay more attention to costs. The instructions are less openly administrative and commandist, more indirect and clothed in generalized price expressions. There is, in other words, marginally less economic physics and *Diktat*. Some relative prices are adjusted up, some down, the methodology of cost accounting is slightly improved, and profit margins are altered. The systemically crucial point, however, is that while individual prices are changed and the importance attached to prices and price-related phenomena (e.g., profit) as indicators of the firms' success is increased, the price *system* remains unchanged. It continues to be unrepresentative of the cost and utility relationships in the economy. It remains allocatively irrational. Since it does not reflect the opportunity costs of the economy, it cannot be used as a guide to allocatively meaningful (rational, optimal, efficient) decisions by economic agents. But it is, in fact, expected to do just that. The profits that firms are urged to make, deriving as they do from a constellation of daft prices, are not a synthetic mathematical expression of the reconciliation of the micro interests of the firm and the macro interests of society. In terms of efficiency of resource use they mean nothing. There is, under the circumstances, substitution of new allocative distortions for old, as well as some addition.

If improvement of allocative efficiency is to be achieved, the movement away from physical indicators to price indicators and from mandate to guidance must be accompanied by a movement away from administratively set accounting prices to market-determined, workably competitive, opportunity-cost prices. In other words, the price system must be liberated; that is, people must be freed so they can make their own decisions in accordance with their own maximizing calculus. As carriers of information, prices must emerge from untrammeled, lateral, buyer-seller transactions voluntarily and competitively entered into. For the price system to act as a coordinating mechanism, the volume and structure of production must respond to the profitability signals emanating from the system. Price fluctuations—price flexibility—must be recognized as a necessary condition of market coordination, and there must be constant, spontaneous adaptation to price changes by buyers and sellers. This is something many socialist economists (never mind the professional *apparatchiki*) have trouble understanding. They have by now grasped the need for relative price changes carried out once in a while (in a "planned manner") to bring prices more in line with supply-and-demand conditions. But they have yet to intellectually assimilate the need for continuous price fluctuations and ongoing automatic adaptation of the volume and structure of supply and demand to such "anarchy."

## The Price System in Hungary

*Agricultural Prices.* Agricultural prices consist of agricultural procurement (producer) prices and retail prices of agricultural products. Under the NEM there are no administratively set compulsory quota deliveries or sowing plans for collective and state farms. State trading companies are commissioned to buy some portion of the total farm output at long-term, state-fixed prices (mainly grain, animal products, and sugar beets). However, these assignments have to be carried out by means of contracts negotiated by the companies with the farms, and the purchase prices can be adjusted with an eye to general market conditions. Moreover, selling to state trading companies is only one way of disposing of farm produce. The farms can sell many agricultural products directly to state processing concerns, on the free market, or—in some cases—export their products directly to Western firms. Producer decisions in this multichannel sales system are guided by expected profitabilities based on relatively flexible, market or market-related prices. The co-ops' decision to sell to state trading companies at below-market equilibrium prices may be dictated by a desire to bring some safety into their transactions, a course of action that may concurrently contribute to greater overall agricultural price stability. The multichannel sales system is also available for marketing the produce of the 1.5 million private plots legally owned by cooperative and state farm members and of the minifarms owned by urban residents (workers, employees). It is thought that at least one quarter of the Hungarian population owns a private plot or minifarm. These account for half the total production of vegetables, fruit, and wine, and a sizable share of the total output of pork (60 percent), eggs, poultry (40 percent), and rabbit meat.[1] What we have here is clear evidence of a movement away from the regime of economic physics (physical-technical norms) and compulsion (mandatory planning). We also have a not insignificant marketization of the information and coordination functions of the agricultural price system. There is a net increase in voluntary, lateral, competitive, contractual transactions carried out through multiple sales channels, and there is a tendency for the size and composition of farm output to be affected more than before by a freer price system together with taxes, state-set wages, credits, subsidies, and other indirect, financial indicators.

It is official policy to aim for domestic self-sufficiency with respect to all foods that can be produced in the country and to have as great an exportable surplus as possible primarily for sale to hard-currency customers, but also to CMEA partners. This objective has, in fact, been achieved.[2] What is of interest from the pricing standpoint is the attempt made under the NEM to increase the role of world market prices in the calculation of domestic farm product prices, particularly for products linked to nonruble foreign trade. This has been true, for example, of those agricultural goods that are largely imported from hard (convertible) currency sources (e.g., protein feeds), of domestically produced substitutes for goods that would normally be imported from hard-currency sources (e.g., some seeds), and of goods a substantial part of which is exported to hard-currency areas. In these cases the domestic prices are adjusted to (nonruble) foreign trade prices through so-called "uniform foreign trade multipliers." The prices of agricultural products domestically consumed for the most part (e.g., early vegetables), are calculated on the basis of domestic input costs and are not directly related to the level of (nonruble) import and export prices. This attempt to partially internationalize domestic farm product prices is another manifestation of the trend toward the marketization of the agricultural price system.

However, one must not be carried away. Although efforts are made to reduce the disparity between the structure and level of agricultural producer and consumer prices through the reduction or partial removal of differential taxes and subsidies, such disparities persist, particularly for agricultural staples with inelastic demand curves, the reason being the perceived need to protect urban real incomes. Another problem is that the calculation of correct farm costs of production is hampered by the system's inability to determine the appropriate scarcity charges for land use (rent). Additionally one may ask how voluntary, lateral, contractual, and competitive is the relationship between cooperative and state farms on the one hand, and the state trading or processing companies on the other, when it comes to purchasing such "key" commodities as grain.[3] In monoparty states with significant remnants of command institutions and commandist philosophy espoused by a bureaucracy that, in János Kornai's estimation, is like a cancer (you can cut it out, but it will probably reappear elsewhere), the borderline between mandate and guidance is not well defined. One may also ask how reliable are the "uniform foreign trade multipliers" and associated exchange rates in translating world market prices into domestic prices. The answer is, not reliable.

*Industrial Prices.* With few exceptions, the setting of output targets for firms and the physical rationing (central funding) of key inputs by planners and supervisory ministries have been abolished. The latter (material-technical supply network) has been replaced by multiple-channel trade in the means of production.[4]

Industrial prices—both wholesale (producer) and retail—have been freed from central control in varying degrees. There are (1) state-fixed prices, which can be changed only by the government price office; (2) maxima prices, which are allowed to float in response to changes in market supply and demand, but only below a state-determined maximum ceiling; and (3) free-market prices (Figure 28.1).

An attempt has been made to align the structures of industrial producer and consumer prices so as to clear the information channels between buyers and sellers through the removal of various taxes and subsidies.

Because of Hungary's heavy reliance on foreign (including hard-currency) trade and the consequent need for the domestic price system to reflect worldwide scarcity values so as to arrive at a notion of comparative advantage, an effort has been made, since 1980, to align some domestic industrial producer prices with world market prices. The share of such "competitive" prices is 80 percent in machine building, 50 percent in the chemical industry, and 20 percent in food processing.[5] Firms whose prices are subject to such linkage are those exporting more than 5 percent of their output in hard-currency trade and those using a high proportion of materials imported in such trade.

As with agricultural prices, the formal steps taken to marketize the industrial price system do not tell the whole story. In actuality marketization of industrial prices has been more hesitant, partial, and characterized by a stop-go pattern. This situation has given rise to an information and coordination network that, in the words of one Hungarian economist, is neither market nor plan, or "half-market, half-bureaucratic control"—an incompatible combination.[6]

The checklist reads as follows: First, as regards the changeover from mandate to guidance, it is true that since 1968 the party-government has been (by no means consistently or unanimously) more favorably inclined toward the idea of competitive, lateral, contractual information and coordination spontaneously generated by buyer-seller transactions. But old commandist habits die hard, and the temptation to dictate remains strong. What can be said in good conscience is that the once highly visible hand of the planners has become less visible: Firms are advised rather than ordered to do certain centrally desired things, but in practice the advice is as binding as the former orders, norms, balances, and allocation certificates. In the opinion of one Hungarian economist, the firms subject themselves "almost voluntarily to patronage."[7]

Second, just as the degree of firm independence under the NEM is less than meets the eye, so also is the degree of price freedom. The ratios of free to controlled prices shown by Figure 28.1 are somewhat misleading

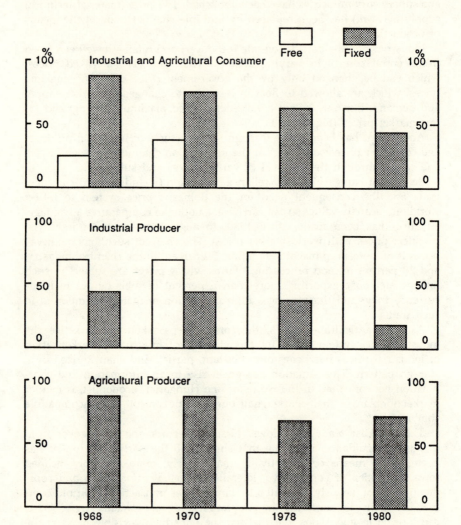

FIGURE 28.1
Price Categories in Hungary (*Source:* National Bank of Hungary, IMF.)

because they do not take into account the relative weights of free and controlled prices in the economy. Many prices of "key" commodities (e.g., fuels, raw materials, basic intermediate products) are fixed, while prices of "luxuries" are not. Then there is the problem of nominal versus effective control over prices. Calculation of the effective control over output prices should include the degree of control over the prices of inputs that go into output.[8] There is also the fact that the "free" trade in and free pricing of producer goods (the 80 percent) take place in highly imperfect, near-monopolistic markets in which buyers' free choice remains formal and the crucial ingredient of competition is missing. Finally, numerous regulations inhibit the free movement of prices in the free sphere. Perceptive Chinese observers of Hungarian pricing practices have remarked that

> on the surface, enterprises [in Hungary] seem to have a lot of decision-making power to fix prices. But actually this is not so because the floating prices, which follow the maximum limited prices, have actually become fixed. Both the floating prices and the fixed prices must be authorized by the commodity price control office. The enterprises only have some power to fix their floating prices at the lower levels. The free prices also have restrictions. While fixing the free prices, the enterprise must follow government regulations. . . . If the price of the free-price products is to go up, the factory must submit its application to the price control bureau six months in advance. Six months later the price will be raised automatically if the bureau has no objections. If the bureau has complaints about the price, then the application is shelved for future study. The government has set up a strict control system to supervise the retail prices set by commercial enterprises. When we visited a private clothing shop, the owner told us that the price of goods was a free one, which he could set by himself. But according to government stipulations, the differential rates of all clothing should be set ranging from 8 to 20 percent. When setting a price the shop should not exceed this rate. Otherwise it is an offense against the law. Punishment includes a warning, a fine, and revocation of business license.[9]

Kornai agrees:

> There are still many areas where prices are centrally fixed. Again in other areas prices are not fixed, but there are very detailed instructions issued by the price office telling the firm how to calculate the price on a "cost plus" basis and constraining the seller and the buyer in deciding on the price in a free contract. There are still many arbitrary, non-market-clearing prices. And since all prices are interdependent, the arbitrariness of some important prices has a spillover effect and leads to severe distortions in the whole price structure.[10]

The multichannel wholesaling of industrial producer goods is still obstructed by rules that limit its scope, and informal interventions by state authorities in the wholesale market are common; while they are not blanket interventions, they distort the intent and execution of market-type allocation. In sum, the right of Hungarian firms to set and vary the prices of their products (even where these prices are in the free sphere) is quite limited, restricted by many specific legal-administrative rules. In this regard the basic relationship remains, by and large, vertical—between the firm and the government price office—but the verticality is less formal than it was before. Kornai characterizes the new relationship as a "regulator game," repeated matches in a game, in which the players try to outsmart each other.[11]

Third, industrial wholesale (producer) and retail prices remain separated by a variety of taxes and subsidies—less than before 1968, but still to an extent where one cannot speak of unobstructed information flows and unhindered structural adaptation between the two.

Fourth, the alignment of domestic with convertible-currency world-trade prices in the "competitive" sphere of the economy is imperfect and frequently violated. World market prices do not act directly on domestic prices, but instead are simulated through "a rather peculiar pricing procedure."[12] Moreover, whenever the profitability of exports declines, thus obliging export firms to reduce their domestic prices accordingly, and thereby reduce their profitabilities with adverse effects on the firms' management and workers' profit-sharing salary and wage supplements (and perhaps even employment), the state steps in with tax and subsidy measures designed to compensate the firms for the adverse effects on them of foreign competition. In fact, there is no import competition to speak of (although Hungarian firms do have some latitude with regard to convertible-currency-area exports). In the absence of such import competition, there is no perceptible alignment of domestic industrial producer prices with world market prices.

## The Price System in Mainland China

*Agricultural Prices.* Until 1985 (with increasing relaxation) in the PRC, the state maintained a monopsony (first introduced in 1953) with regard to grain, oil-bearing crops, cotton, and timber. Grain, cooking oil, cotton wadding, and cotton cloth were rationed to urban consumers (the last two being rationed to both urban and rural consumers). The retail prices of these goods were below their state procurement prices, entailing a heavy burden of budgetary subsidies. In addition, there were compulsory delivery quotas for more than 100 other categories of farm and sideline products. After Mao's death and until 1985, rural production teams and households had four marketing channels for their products (two for products subject to state monopsony) and four sets of prices (two for monopsony goods). (1) Products subject to compulsory delivery quotas were sold at state-fixed quota prices. (2) Some portion of output over and above the quota was sold to state procurement agencies at higher, above-quota prices fixed by the state. Both of these were mandatory prices. (3) After fulfillment of quota and above-quota obligations, extra output could be sold to the state at negotiated prices. (4) Anything left over after that, and goods not subject to quotas, could be sold on rural markets at "free" market prices, the freedom being restricted by allowable price ranges set by the state.[13]

In what was billed as the "second stage of rural structural reform," the state monopsony and fixed-quota purchase system were to be gradually phased out. The movement was to be away from physical mandate, toward guidance and the market. Except for certain stipulated products, state quotas for the delivery of products at state fixed prices have been abolished and replaced by a system of contracts based on negotiated targets and paid for at state fixed prices. Any surplus remaining after the targets have been met can be sold on the open market at market prices. The state is to buy a stipulated 75–80 million tons of grain every year at its unified price (also known as "preferential" price). This price is a weighted average made up of 30 percent of the former quota price and 70 percent of the former above-quota price. The rest of the crop is to be regulated by market forces. However, at least in 1985–1986, when the market price "goes low" (below the old quota price) the state will purchase any surplus grain (as well as surplus cotton and oil-bearing crops) from the peasants at "protective" prices, higher than the market prices. On the other hand, when the market price "goes high," the state will sell appropriate quantities of its reserves on the market to bring the price back down.[14]

Prices of fish, poultry, eggs, vegetables, meat, and other nonstaple perishable products have been partially decontrolled, meaning that the state "gave localities the go-ahead to fluctuate prices."[15] The partial decontrol of nonstaple product prices resulted in initial sharp increases in those prices. However, by the third quarter of 1985 there were signs of price stabilization as supply began to react to demand changes communicated by the more flexible prices.

As in Hungary, what happened in mainland China by mid-1986 was a movement away from the regime of economic physics and compulsion, accompanied by significant marketization of the information and coordination functions of the agricultural price system. As in Hungary, there has been a net increase in voluntary, lateral, competitive, contractual transactions carried out through multiple trade channels, and a tendency for the size and composition of farm output to be affected more than before by a freer price system, together with taxes, credits, state subsidies, and other indicative, financial instruments. In 1984, 25–30 percent of retail and agricultural procurement trade in mainland China was transacted in a marketized and privatized context, both marketization and privatization, however, being restricted in various ways.[16]

As in Hungary, the dematerialization, decompulsion, and marketization of the agricultural price system have been far from complete. For staple commodities, direct linkage between state procurement prices and state retail prices has not been established. The agricultural tax and many more or less arbitrary, sometimes capricious local levies in China (and in Hungary the land tax, collective income tax, labor remuneration tax, personal income tax, and production taxes on nonagricultural rural production) interpose themselves between producer and consumer with distorting effects on economic calculation. In China, like Hungary, the lateralness, voluntariness, and competitiveness of the contractual relations between tenant farm households and the state procurement agencies may be questioned. Commandist habits are alive and well. Fluctuations of the decontrolled prices in response to changing supply and demand forces in China, as in Hungary, remain subject to numerous administrative restrictions.

*Industrial Prices.* Until recent years industrial wholesale (producer) prices in the PRC were set by the state along familiar Soviet-style lines. They were cost-plus prices (average planned cost of production in the given industrial branch plus a profit margin) and paid little or no heed to the underlying conditions of supply and demand. The cost was calculated according to a peculiar Marxist costing procedure (no allowance for the scarcity cost of land and capital); the profit margins were economically arbitrary, determined for the most part by the planners' sociopolitical preferences; and no account was taken of demand. The allocative usefulness of these prices was zero. In fact, as noted earlier, industrial wholesale prices were not supposed to exercise allocative influence, being simply accounting backup devices to physical apportionment through material balances. In the immediate post-Mao period an effort was made to adjust individual producer goods prices—the more blatantly distorted ones—the adjustment being limited to making individual prices reflect average branch production costs more accurately. Industrial retail prices were insulated from producer prices by commercial and industrial taxes (positive for most goods, negative for some). The taxes were adjusted up and down from time to time, thus raising or lowering retail prices for particular goods in order to ease shortages or eliminate surpluses in individual goods markets, mainly by bringing consumer demand for such goods into rough concordance with the planner-determined supply. Domestic prices were divorced from world market prices. The whole system was allocatively irrational and very wasteful of scarce resources.

The verticality of the information and coordination network varied over time but has always been dominant. The number of centrally determined material balances covering category I and II goods (widely used and specialized materials allocated by the State Planning Commission and central "branch" ministries) has been reduced from a peak of 592 in 1964 to around sixty at the present time (and there is talk of bringing these down to thirty). Concurrently there has taken place a large increase in local-government (provincial, municipal, prefectural, even township) control over physical and financial allocation of resources, which is not necessarily indicative of a significant lessening of the verticality of the information-coordination network.[17] These trends are to continue. In other words, the scope of mandatory physical planning is to be reduced and the scope of administratively decentralized financial guidance planning is to increase, as is the sphere of market transactions. However, mandatory planning will not be dispensed with altogether. It will be retained for "major products" and "major economic activities that affect the overall situation" (a catch-all caveat). Presumably major products include primary energy, key raw materials, steel, large machinery, synthetic fibers, newsprint, and some other materials and semifabricates. The right of firms to enter into lateral contractual relations with one another is to be enlarged (from very little).[18] The Hungarian experience suggests that even where mandatory planning (centrally determined material balances) is abolished for the bulk of products, the propensity persists for governmental authorities at different hierarchical levels to mandate guidance.

The blueprint for industrial sector change is contained in the "Decision of the Central Committee of the Communist Party of China on Reform of the Economic Structure" adopted by the Twelfth Central Committee at its Third Plenary Session on October 20, 1984.[19] The decision—which was put on the back burner in 1986—also envisages marketizing changes in the industrial price system. The intent is to gradually reduce "the scope of uniform prices set by the state and appropriately enlarge the scope of floating prices within certain limits, and of free prices." However, since the prices of many key inputs are to remain centrally fixed, the "Hungarian" question of the weights to be attached to the controlled versus "free" prices and the effective control over the price system through control of input prices is posed. There is, further, the question of the incompatibility of fixed, semifixed, and free prices both across products and for the same products. As matters stand now, industrial prices consist of (1) state-fixed prices, (2) floating prices, (3) negotiated prices, and (4) free-market prices.[20] Each category is supposed to apply primarily to a particular sphere of the economy. Thus the stable state-fixed prices apply mostly to goods produced and transferred within the command sphere (i.e., under the mandatory state plan), but also to some goods produced and traded outside the mandatory plan, in the guided sphere. Moreover, once the mandatory quota is fulfilled at the state-fixed price, the producing firm can apparently dispose of any surplus at either floating, negotiated, or perhaps even free-market prices.[21] One result has been dual pricing. Bergson reports that the basic state-fixed price for steel is 600 yuan per ton, but the same steel outside the plan can sell for 1,300 yuan a ton, a difference that does not make for improved economic calculation.[22] Negotiated prices and free-market prices apply primarily to goods produced and traded outside the state mandatory plan (the so-called self-disposal goods). They are mostly small goods and sideline commodities. There is some evidence that the attitude of local authorities toward the non-fixed-price sphere is at best ambivalent, that while it is generally understood that the price structure must be changed, the indispensable complementary understanding that the change must be a continuing one (temporal price flexibility) is missing. The authorities' inclination to freeze industrial prices (producer as well as consumer) when these prices move up in search of a market-clearing equilibrium level (and to accuse those engaged in the *tâtonnement* of "price gouging") is well known. It is related to the socialist (including Hungarian) politically induced imperative to prevent price increases from adversely affecting living standards. This imperative puts a dampener on the reformist quest for improvement in allocative efficiency.

The industrial system of mainland China is in a state of transition and flux. Indications are that the decision of October 20, 1984, to reconcile the rigid industrial economy with the marketization changes carried out in the agricultural economy was slowed in late 1985 and in 1986, as the size and complexity of the task came to be better understood. So far the Chinese changes in the industrial information and coordination system have been more modest and conservative than the Hungarian and more internally inconsistent. (But then, the Hungarians have been at it, on and off, for more than eighteen years.) The institutional contradictions between the Chinese industrial and agricultural price systems appear to be greater than they are in Hungary. Information and coordination in the Chinese industrial economy remain primarily vertical, that is, characterized by still considerable physical-commandist elements.

Last, where do the special economize zones (SEZs) and related experiments with liberalization fit into all this? The SEZs are controlled experiments that are expected to serve as both positive and negative role models in the search for socialist allocative efficiency—with "Chinese characteristics" and capitalist input. The zones are special, encapsulated phenomena in the learning process, and their didactic contribution to China's long march to the market may turn out to be quite marginal.

## Motivation

A serious problem of centrally planned administrative command economies has been at all times the insufficiency and perverse working of positive incentives to peasants, workers, and managers, and the considerable component of compulsion and fear (negative incentives). Next to a thorough reform of the price mechanism, reform of the motivational structure of the command system is indispensable if progress is to be made in improving the system's allocative efficiency.

### Peasant Incentives

The Hungarian NEM, apparently with success, provides incentives to farmers at several levels. Members of agricultural cooperatives and state farm workers are paid guaranteed state-set wages (which constitute a sort of safety net), bonus payments linked to farm profits (6–20 percent of members' earnings from the collective), and the social wage (social benefits). These are made credible by the (near) voluntary nature of membership in the socialized farms, the farms' relatively wide rights of decision-making (in which members are associated; not just pro forma), and the not overly demanding amount of yearly working time that has to be put into the collective by individual members. An additional incentive is the opportunity for collective and state-farm workers to set up small cooperatives of various kinds and subcontract land and specialized farm and farm-related off-farm jobs from the parent collective—even to own land and other productive assets. These subunits work strictly on the basis of profit and loss. Members share profits and losses and are not rescued by the parent collective if they experience persistent losses. Members of collective farms and state farm workers own small plots, the produce of which is sold at market prices.

Earnings from this source are believed to double, perhaps as much as quadruple, peasant income derived from collective/state-sector work. The plots can be rented out to the cooperative at fixed money payments. Thus, in the case of private plots, small cooperative farms, and big cooperative/ state farms, a direct link (strongest in the first two instances) is established through the profit motive between the volume and assortment of production and a partly marketized price system. The result is a reasonably accurate and frictionless reconciliation of the private and social interest at a fairly "low" (micro) societal level.

In general (except for occasional bureaucratic outbursts of antiplot mentality, as in 1975), the authorities have pursued a constructive policy with respect to private plots and private initiative. They have supported them with bank credits and comparatively liberal access to modern inputs (chemicals, small machinery). Last, cooperative and state farmers have availed themselves of opportunities to work in or, in fact, run a variety of local industries and businesses, some closely connected with agricultural production, others not. This has become an important source of income for many (now part-time) farmers. In short, the successful (as judged by output and productivity) motivational apparatus of Hungarian agriculture owes its success to flexibility, multiplicity of forms, voluntariness, participation in decision making by members of collectives, and the importance of market-determined profit as a guide to production.

One should, however, keep these qualities in perspective. As noted in connection with the discussion of the agricultural price system, many questions of bureaucratic interference, hostility to markets and private initiative, and distortion of economic calculation through subsidies, taxes, and strange costing methodologies remain unresolved. But, on balance, the distance traveled by the Hungarian rural economy in the direction of market reform of the motivational system has been substantial, if not always proceeding in a straight line.

In the PRC since 1980 there has been a more formal decollectivization of agriculture. The *baogan daohu* (household production responsibility) system with its fifteen-year leases of collectively owned strips of land to individual peasant families in return for contractual produce deliveries at unified or protective prices and the household payment of the agricultural tax and other levies, is in essence a system of family tenant farming operating in a still imperfect but widespread market setting.[23] The central motivation is the households' net income from sales of produce over and above the contractual part at market or near-market prices—that is, the profit motive. While profits and profitability rates are distorted by the continued presence of administrative rules, haphazardly determined levies, and dictatorial modes of thought and behavior on the part of local officials, the net incentive effect on household producers has been positive as evidenced by increased output and labor productivity. Since the peasant household's production surplus above the contracted portion goes to the household to be disposed of freely, the household will tend to increase its output until its marginal cost equals its marginal revenue at the market price, thereby maximizing its profit. The structure of farm production has undergone changes to conform to demand signals emanating from the market; the movement has been from cruder to finer grains, from grain to more profitable cash crops, from general farm production to specialized production, and from agricultural work to nonagricultural service and industrial activities, the latter mainly in the area of food processing and industrial consumer goods.

But there are also problems with the newly marketized and privatized motivational system.[24] The problems, I think, reside in the present incompleteness of the changes. Marketization has an inner logic which requires that it be carried out *in toto*. Halfway arrangements will not do. Two examples drawn from the Chinese experience will illustrate the point.

1. Collectively owned land has been leased to peasant households in narrow strips (some good land, some not so good, some with access to roads, some not) for reasons of fairness. The total size of these strips per family depends on such nonmarket criteria as the number of people or the number of able-bodied workers in the family. "Excessive" consolidation of landholdings and "excessive" hiring of farm labor by individual landholders is frowned upon as evidence of emerging landlordism. (More generally, labor mobility remains restricted.) So there is a remarkable fragmentation of landholdings that makes it difficult to take advantage of economies of scale and inhibits mechanization. In addition, "large" investment in rural infrastructures (irrigation and drainage works, roads) is reportedly neglected under the regime of miniholdings and short and narrow investment horizons, when what is already there is not altogether dismantled and put to private use. Since people are still apprehensive about the durability of the marketizing-privatizing changes, there is a tendency to go for quick production payoffs through, for example, overchemicalization of land. All this raises questions about the permanence of the output and productivity upsurge of the last several years. To remedy the situation, the market has to be allowed to determine the optimal size of holdings, and property rights in land have to be further privatized. At the same time, cooperative arrangements freely entered into by the entrepreneurial farmers could be encouraged through fiscal and credit policy to help take care of larger infrastructural investments.

2. There is evidence that income and wealth differentials in the countryside are increasing—as they tend to under the regime of the market—and that instances of jealousy and harassment of the better-off farmers by their poorer neighbors and unreconstructed cadres are on the rise. The pursuit of efficiency within the setting of markets will necessarily produce inequalities of outcomes. Tax measures can be taken to reduce some disparities (those arising from economic agents' acting in restraint of competition, or the socially and politically more intolerable ones—but here one has to be discreet in what is labeled intolerable), but they cannot be eliminated.

## Industrial Wages

Under the classical administrative command plan, the motivational system applied to industrial (or more generally, nonagricultural) workers has the following major characteristics: Wage levels are pressed down to ensure high rates of investment and keep consumption (hence inflationary pressures) in check and to elicit high labor participation ratios (Stalin's "Law of Rational Low Wages"); consumer goods are in chronic short supply and of inferior quality and assortment; occupational choice and labor mobility are administratively controlled; the use of negative incentives administratively enforced is widespread; in the Stalinist version, wide money wage disparities are permitted (in fact, encouraged under the shock-worker system), while in the Maoist variant they are compressed; much attention is given to non-material, "moral" prods, particularly in the Maoist variant; each (state sector) firm's wages fund, wage categories, and wage scales are determined at a high level of the central planning.hierarchy (i.e., firm managers have minimal discretion in setting basic wages, and only a little more when it comes to the distribution of bonuses); and hiring and (especially) firing of workers are largely out of managerial hands (full-employment constraint).

Changes in the industrial wage system under the Hungarian NEM are in the nature of an adjustment rather than reform of the old system. Stalin's "law" of rational low wages is repealed: basic (tariff) wages are raised, the raises being usually linked to increases in the firms' profits. Through an intersectoral reallocation of investment, consumer goods become more plentiful but are mostly high priced. As one Polish traveler put it, Poles have money but nothing to spend it on, while Hungarians "can look but not touch"; that is, many Hungarian goods are too expensive for the average wage earner.[25] While the quality and assortment of industrial (consumer and producer) goods are better than before, the goods are still not competitive on hard-currency world markets (though a few make a big splash on the CMEA market). Compared with the situation in Hungary before the NEM and with other centrally planned economies today, there is—whatever the reservations—a net lowering of consumption costs: less lining up, less hassle, more goods. There is more occupational choice and labor mobility, but administrative restrictions persist, some of them connected with urban housing shortages. Money wage differentials are significant, not only because of differential bonuses, but above all because of some workers' access to very remunerative registered and unregistered employment outside the official economy. Different earning possibilities when linked to consumer price increases (in the free-market and floating spheres) have resulted in the emergence of an economically deprived class composed of some 1.5 million pensioners, blue-collar workers, young people, and others living on fixed incomes, without access or with only limited access to extraofficial sources of earnings.[26] The rising income gap poses a worrisome political threat to the continuance of the NEM's marketizing and privatizing changes.

The state continues to exercise considerable control over the industrial wage system by both indirect and direct means. Indirect means include the use of taxes to determine what portion of retained firm profits is to be allocated to the firm's bonus fund and price supports/subsidies that influence the size of firm profits and, hence, basic wages. There are three kinds of direct wage controls. (1) With the relative wage level, the state limits increases in the average wage of individual firms. Increase in the average wage is linked to the growth of wages and profits per workers. (2) With the relative wage bill, the total wage bill is regulated on the basis of increases in value added, limited by the prescribed increases in average wages. (3) Centrally determined wages are based on either the average wage or the total wages bill of the firm. The most common is the regulation of the relative wage bill (55 percent of firms), followed by centrally determined wages (30 percent of firms) and relative wage level (15 percent of firms).[27]

While this regulation is important—not the least in reducing the influence of market forces in the labor market—in terms of motivation, less controlled or uncontrolled income from outside the official system is motivationally very important. In Hungary under the NEM, "Almost everyone lives partly, or—even more exactly—to a very small extent from his formal wage or salary. To a far greater extent they live from other activities, from those activities associated with the secondary, parallel, hidden, or more simply market economy."[28]

The discretion of managers with regard to hiring and—especially—the dismissal of workers has not been significantly increased.

In mainland China changes brought about so far in the industrial wage system are also adjustments, not reforms. Money wages have been raised, and overtime and bonus pay has been reintroduced after a hiatus during the Cultural Revolution. Bonus funds linked to profits have been instituted at the firm level, but there has been a concurrent tendency (deplored by the authorities) for managements to distribute bonuses in an egalitarian fashion, as across-the-board wage supplements. Attempts have been made to introduce a responsibility system, whereby basic wages and bonuses are linked to the workers' productivity performance rather than seniority. The state has intervened with various kinds of money grants to compensate urban wage earners for steep increases in nonstaple food prices and public transportation.

In 1984 there was bold talk about going beyond adjustment toward reform. The Soviet-type eight-grade tariff wage system was to be abolished in state firms, the firms were to have more control over wage determination, and total payrolls were to be allowed to float according to individual enterprise performance.[29] Such practices, however, would require the freeing of industrial labor (marketization of the labor force) so that labor could move spontaneously in response to fluctuating wage differentials. So far this alteration has not happened except at the margin (some collective-sector and free-sector labor). The greater part of the labor force continues to be assigned to their workplaces (*danwei*) by labor bureaus, and both inter- and intrafirm labor mobility is subject to mandatory administrative planning; there is fear in official quarters about the possible consequences of the "anarchic free flow" (i.e., market allocation) of labor.

Increase in money wage differentials (especially when bonuses are included) has occurred. It has been praised as necessary from an efficiency standpoint. However, in China, as in Hungary, such differentials cannot exceed—at least in the official sphere—certain rather narrowly defined limits without giving rise to political difficulties. Redistributive mechanisms (such as progressive income taxes linked to transfer payments) are not yet in place, so wage control has to be more direct. The Hungarian experience with state wage controls suggests that however "liberal" the changes may be as compared with the old plan, the state is unlikely to relinquish its hold over the industrial wage system, occupational choice, labor mobility, or all three. This determination is partly a result of fear of inflation, partly a result of the already noted concern over the ethically permissible degree of income disparity in socialist society.

So far the result has been that in terms of marketization of the motivational system the changes in the industrial economy lag behind those in agriculture, thus injecting an element of intersectoral disharmony to the system.

## Incentives to Managers

Under the old Stalinist motivational arrangement, managers of industrial and other state-sector firms were rewarded and punished primarily by reference to indicators of gross output—the infamous *val* (*valovnaya produktsiia*, or gross value of output). Under both the Hungarian and Chinese new economic regimes, the leading indicator of managerial success becomes the firm's profit (even though remnants of the *val* mentality haunt ministerial couloirs). Various schemes are devised to (1) give managers broader rights to make profits (through, for example, wider pricing rights and expanded latitude in the hiring and firing of labor), retain profits, and dispose of them (including investment); and (2) link managerial compensation to profit performance. It should be noted that such schemes are not overly innovative; they draw on Y. Liberman's ideas of the early 1960s and usually involve various firm-based funds among which the retained portion of profits is distributed, both the amount of profits and their precise interfund distribution being affected in different degrees by government fiscal actions and administrative regulations. In mainland China, before the changes, 100 percent of firm profits reverted to the state budget. Under the new policy, instead of remitting all profits, state firms pay a tax on profits (tax-for-profits scheme). This and other taxes are used by the state as "economic levers" to induce the desired firm behavior (including investments) with respect to the after-tax profits retained by the firms (which will be discussed later). In Hungary, the firm's management committee decides how much of the after-tax profit is to be put into the firm's bonus fund. Normally, out of the share going to the firm's development fund, 60 percent is taxed away, 10 percent goes into a reserve fund, and the rest (not very much) is available for autonomous investment by the firm.

The fatal flaw in this new preoccupation with profit as indicator of the efficiency of firm operations is that the profit emerges from a still very distorted industrial price system and is not, therefore, in any way a summation of socially felicitous outcomes. It is not reflective of costs and utilities in the system and does not represent a reconciliation of individual and social interests. Like its predecessor under the regime of central administrative command planning, it is just a number, and the rest is dross. The underlying price distortion arises, as we have seen, from the internally inconsistent and conflicting coexistence of state-set (cost-plus), floating, and free-market prices, and from the absence of real market competition. (This statement is particularly true of the Hungarian economy, which is noted for its highly concentrated, amalgamated, monopolistic industrial structures.)

Realizing this problem, the Chinese and the Hungarians have introduced numerous taxes intended to correct the distortions. These probably add to the confusion. The Chinese taxes include a products tax, which is applied uniformly throughout the country but is differentiated among products, its purpose being to confiscate that part of (windfall) profits on certain goods that arises from "wrong" pricing (e.g., profits on some consumer durables and cigarettes). There is also a resource tax designed to eliminate rent differentials among extractive industries and mining, and an adjustment tax the purpose of which is to remove differences among enterprises in the same industrial branch, whenever such differences arise from "undeserved" causes. A capital charge is levied on fixed and working capital. A bonus tax is in effect to help curb the "blind" and "wanton" disbursement of premiums. An eight-grade progressive income tax (long used in collective undertakings) is being applied to state firms.[30] Needless to say, what is "undeserved," "wrong," "wanton," or "blind," is answered by reference to all sorts of criteria (mainly those relating to the socialist ethical code), among which market tests of efficiency are notable by their rarity and weakness.

In Hungary the situation is similar. When firm profits and profitabilities emerged from the changed system of "competitive" prices, they were quickly annulled by differentiated taxes and subsidies, the result of which was to restore the *status quo ante*. Of a total of 1,135 industrial units, 971 (85.5 percent) reverted to the old allocatively useless profitabilities within less than two years of the introduction of the "competitive" price system. Between 1968 and 1980 more than 100 orders and legal rules were introduced to regulate the profits and profit-sharing decisions of the firms. About two-thirds of the firms' gross profits were taxed away and redistributed by the ex-planners. What kind of redistribution was involved? As in the PRC, the redistribution tended to equalize profits across firms by taxing away the profits of highly profitable firms and using them to cover the losses of unprofitable ones.

The last action is indicative of what Kornai has repeatedly denounced as the "soft budget constraint" of firms in socialist economies, whether of the old Stalinist or NEM type. Just as socialist workers do not get fired, socialist firms do not go bankrupt. They can almost always count on the state bureaucracy for a handout. Their budget line is not binding; it is expanding. This policy leads to carelessness with costs, inflated investments, and other behavioral distortions that entail inefficiencies on a grandiose scale.

We see here a vicious circle. Prices are distorted. Therefore profitability measured at the incorrect prices is not a true reflection of efficient performance. Not even in a stochastic sense do profits measured this way reflect the degree of efficiency statistically in most of the cases. Profitability does not have much prestige under such circumstances. A firm lobbying for subsidies may argue that the loss occurred not because of poor performance but because of incorrect prices. All right, it receives a subsidy, and others also get them, each of them bargaining for better treatment in the complicated network of fiscal redistribution. As a consequence, we arrive at dozens or hundreds of taxes and tax exemptions, highly differentiated, sometimes almost tailor-made tax and subsidy rules. And that inevitably leads to price distortions. The soft budget constraint is both a cause and a consequence of the price distortions.[31]

## Property

By "property" is meant a socially enforced bundle of economically valuable rights to the acquisition, use, and disposal of assets. Privatization involves the enlargement of these rights with respect to the actual user of the assets (the operator of the farm, the manager of an industrial firm, the worker with regard to his labor). Property rights are important in the overall scheme of economic organization because of their effects on the motivation of economic agents, the distribution of income and wealth within the system, and the distribution of power.

### Agriculture

Characteristic of both the Hungarian and Chinese economic changes is the de facto privatization of property and the proliferation of property forms.

Privatization of property has taken the form of enlarging the use rights of the operator of assets, including the right to distribute the income generated by the assets. In Chinese agriculture this is manifested by the extension of land leases from the former one to three years to the present fifteen years (thirty years for grasslands and woodlands) and the vesting of those leases in the family. Subject to payment of the quasi rent (contractual deliveries of produce at state-set prices), the agricultural tax, and some collective levies, the family is free to decide on its production pattern and schedule, disposal of its produce, and distribution of its income. Although land parcels cannot be bought or sold by the family tenant farmers (there is no free, rent-bidding, market for land), the contracts can be transferred and land strips consolidated with the permission of the collective; instances of individual contracts involving 750 mu of land (more than 100 acres) have been reported. This privatization has been accompanied by the individual tenant's right to hire a limited number of workers: at first it was six to eight people, then any number so long as they were family members, now—apparently—unlimited numbers, family or not.[32] Acquisition and legal ownership of productive equipment (tractors, machinery, trucks, processing equipment, draft animals) is permitted and widespread. Many formerly collectively owned and operated assets have been leased to the highest bidder, either an individual, a family, or a group of individuals or families (voluntary association). These assets include not only ponds, pastures, forest, commune and brigade (now township and village) industries, transportation, and many services (including trading), but also dispensaries, clinics, and even schools. Although restrictions on labor migration to the larger cities are in effect (with some evidence of decreasing effectiveness), the right of the individual peasant to his own labor has been expanded in the sense of greater mobility being granted to those who wish to leave farm work and seek employment in rural industry and the newly bourgeoning services sector in rural towns. (The slogan is "leave farming but not the countryside.") Since 1980 roughly 100 million peasants have abandoned farm work—roughly one-third of the agricultural labor force. Many of them have found employment in industrial and service establishments in rural towns.

In Chinese agriculture, privatization has been unabashedly to the level of the private family unit with, so far, relatively little development of mixed property forms (voluntary cooperative arrangements). Legal social ownership of land has been maintained. As suggested earlier, for infrastructural investment reasons, either these de facto private farms will have to freely find their own market-dictated optimal size (including the extent of private ownership of productive assets other than land and the size of the privately hired labor force), or forms of voluntary cooperation in certain undertakings (infrastructural investment included) will have to be developed.[33] In the absence of such developments a reversal of rural structures to neo-Stalinist collectives cannot be ruled out.

Hungarian agriculture under the NEM has opted for an interesting solution. On the surface Hungarian agriculture looks highly socialized. Some 85 percent of the land is under state and cooperative farms yielding 66 percent of the gross value of agricultural output. The cooperative farms (about 1400) range in size from 50 to 60,000 acres. The socialized sector is, however, significantly privatized in terms of de facto property rights: There is a strong element of voluntariness, a relatively wide scope for decisions by the cooperative or state units, and a not unimportant degree of participation by members in the decision-making process. Members receive land rent for land which they own but which is collectively cultivated; the privately owned land can be inherited by the owner's children, but if they are not members of the cooperative they must sell the land to the cooperative. Within the state and large cooperative farms, various forms of subcontracting or outright sale of land and specialized tasks to small cooperatives have been developed. There are about 3,000 such small co-op units employing more than 200,000 workers. They do work that for one reason or another the parent cooperative/state farm finds unprofitable.

In addition, special organizations have been established to diffuse modern farm technology and agribusiness mentality within a region (Technically Operated Production Systems, or TOPS). Last but not least, the private sector consists of 1.5 million privately owned plots and minifarms. These occupy 15 percent of the land and produce 33 percent of the gross value of agricultural output. Restrictions on the sale of tools, small machinery, fodder, fertilizer, pesticides, and other production inputs to households for use on the plots have been lifted and legal restrictions on the number of animals permitted on the plots have been abolished. Credit has been made available to households for livestock purchase, acquisition of equipment, and modernization of structures. The average area (0.6 hectares per plot) can be doubled by leasing land that the collective or state farms have found unsuitable for large-scale cultivation.

The success of Hungarian agriculture in output, quality, factor productivity, and export performance is due in large measure to privatization of social property in a variety of sizes and forms. De facto privatization of state and collective farms and small cooperatives has been combined with the de jure privatization of plots and small farms. The privatization process at the state farm/large cooperative levels is far from complete and conflict-free, as we have seen (in the sections on price system and motivation). But the degree of privatization appears to be sufficient to limit the damage caused by the continued contradiction of market and plan instruments in agriculture.

## Industry

Privatization in Chinese industry is less advanced than in agriculture. The most important development so far has been the destatization of state firms and their de facto collectivization, a change that involves less direct state intervention in the affairs of these firms. The official intent is to get government bureaucracies out of the business of running industrial firms (separation of ownership and management).[34] Many industrial and service activities have been leased to private individuals or cooperatives, most of them in the consumer goods and services sector (restaurants, repair maintenance, construction). In the period 1985–1987 all firms with fixed assets of less than 1.5 million yuan ($500,000) and annual profits of under 200,000 yuan are to be contracted out or leased to individuals or cooperatives for periods of up to five years. The leased firms are required to pay rent and taxes to the state. They are granted relatively broad rights of business decision making, including decisions about the distribution of their profits. Firms operating under the leasing arrangement are allowed to avoid restrictions on the hiring of labor applicable to private sector enterprises. It is expected that by 1987 most industrial output value will be produced under the leasing cooperative arrangement. Various joint state-collective, state-private, and collective private ventures have been reported, practices reminiscent of an earlier united-front "New Democracy" (pre-1953) age. Extending the lateral ties between various firms and gradually establishing lateral associations of firms is also intended over the next several years. Unless carefully managed, this policy could lead to Hungarian-type (or for that matter Soviet-type) amalgamations and a reduction rather than increase in competition (the Hungarian experience will be discussed later on). The legal urban private sector has been much expanded from very little—more than fifteen times in terms of employment between 1978 and 1985. However, the legal private sector accounts for only a very small proportion (less than 3 percent) of total urban employment. There has also emerged a considerable but not easily quantifiable amount of semilegal and illegal business activity, including the proliferation of so-called briefcase companies set up by party and government bureaucrats with access to scarce materials and connections, but also by academics and others. Official attitude toward these shadowy formations fluctuates from tolerance to sudden violent campaigns of repression. Unlike Hungary, mainland China has not yet come to terms with the socialist black market.

In the PRC, as in Hungary, equity participation in industry by foreign investors is permitted. It takes various property forms ranging from co-production agreements, through compensation trade arrangements and joint equity ventures, to outright foreign ownership (limited in time).

As we have seen, the Hungarian firm has been significantly liberated on its input acquisition side through the commercialization of producer goods and materials supply. On the output side, too, the abolition of mandatory targets set by the planner has resulted in the expansion of firm autonomy. However, the central authorities still keep a tight grip on enterprise contractual delivery obligations ("sales" performance), so that on this side the room for maneuver by the firm is more limited. The firm has gained some rights to set prices (particularly of new products) and to make investment out of its retained profits, but these rights remain residual. Still, as compared with the past, the sphere of prices determined by direct agreements between buyer and seller has been considerably enlarged. While investment by firms remains comparatively small, investment decisions have been pluralized. Instead of being determined by a central planning board, they are now the joint responsibility of the central authorities, the state banking system, and the firms.

While many organizational forms exist, the problem is primarily one of the size distribution of state-sector industrial enterprises. Hungary has one of the highest industrial concentration ratios in the world: a very small number of very large firms.[35] This concentration is the result of policy measures pursued throughout the 1960s and 1970s for reasons of ease of control, economies of scale, and technological diffusion. In fact, the Hungarian enterprise or firm is more like a trust or a Soviet "association." One of the consequences of this high concentration is the absence of competition over wide areas of the industrial economy, which in turn reduces the possible efficiency-producing effects of marketization of information and privatization of property rights. Since 1980 attempts have been made to break up these industrial dinosaurs, but progress has been sluggish. In 1982–1983 there were 700 state-owned industrial enterprises (more than half of them with an annual output value of more than 50 million forints). Of these 700 firms, 275 produced 73 percent of the total industrial output value. In the following two years some eighty to ninety smaller firms were created by breaking up the large enterprises. Hungarian industry thus continues to suffer from the rigidities of large size, especially in light industry where flexibility is highly desirable. Less than 19 percent of all industrial workers are employed in enterprises with a total work force of fewer than 100 each; in Sweden the equivalent ratio is 45 percent.

Small and medium-sized firms can be created in Hungary not only through the breakup of large firms, but by the establishment of new ones from the top down or—more interestingly—from the bottom up. In 1982 regulations were issued (there always have to be regulations) allowing ministries, local councils, and state-owned enterprises to set up affiliate firms. These are of two kinds: "enterprise business work partnerships" (EBWP), and "business work partnerships" (BWP), or simply "small cooperatives." The EBWPs come in several variants. One of the more imaginative involves the new affiliate unit's subcontracting a part of the parent enterprise's operations, including use of the enterprise's fixed assets, and paying a fee for it, but keeping its own profits. These profits may be distributed as bonuses among the affiliate's workers. However, the affiliate workers' basic (tariff) wages are paid by the parent enterprise. The BWPs or small cooperatives can be set up by ministries, local councils, large enterprises, or individuals. There are fewer administrative and other restrictions on them than on the larger firms, as is the case with cooperatives generally, but at the same time they cannot ask for help from the founding authority in the event of financial difficulty. In 1980 with 3 percent of the industrial capital stock, they employed 14 percent of the industrial labor force, accounting for 6 percent of gross industrial output and a much larger share of net output. Small co-ops formed by individuals are common. They range in employment size from two to thirty people (two-man co-ops?!) and are primarily concentrated in the service trades, including professional services (e.g., management consulting, writing computer software). The partners who supply the bulk of the capital—earned, no doubt in the underground economy—are legally liable for all debts incurred by the co-op. Despite very progressive taxes imposed on the co-ops' profits, the lack of infrastructural facilities for small business in a land of giant enterprises, and bureaucratic foot-dragging, the productivity of these private co-ops is high: The per capita income of small private cooperatives is four times that of the orthodox ones. Unlike the typical traditional service cooperatives, the BWPs provide badly needed services (e.g., plumbing, auto repairs) when they are needed, not two or three years later. Another novel organizational and property form (from the bottom up) consists of "new operational systems" (NOS). The NOSes involve the awarding to individuals through auction of the right to lease small businesses of all kinds (restaurants, food stores, barbershops, tourist lodgings). The lease typically runs for five years, but it can be renewed. With rare exceptions, each entrepreneur is limited to operating only one business unit; there are no chain stores here. The NOSes are given considerable latitude in obtaining inputs and setting prices, and they are fully responsible for their profits and losses. They do very well, their services being responsive to demand through the market. In early 1984 the NOS arrangement counted 22,000 people.

TABLE 28.1
Combinations of Public Ownership and Private Entrepreneurial Activities

| Owner of the Means of Production | User of the Means of Production | Arrangement for Use of Capital Equipment | Typical Branches |
|---|---|---|---|
| State enterprise or cooperative | Private person or group of private persons (In some cases the lessee is chosen through auction) (NOS) | Leasing fixed capital for a definite rent[a] | Catering, trade |
| State enterprise or public institution | "Economic team" formed from the employees (EBWP; some BWPs) | The team works, under the protection of the employer, and uses part of the fixed assets for which it pays rent | Maintenance, repair, fitting (as yet preliminarily planned) |
| Partly state enterprise or public institution, partly the user | Workers of the enterprise or institution in question | Illegal informal work done during regular working hours, perhaps with the use of employer's equipment | Construction, maintenance work, repairs, trucking |

Source: János Kornai, "Comments on the Present State and the Prospects of the Hungarian Economic Reform," Journal of Comparative Economics, vol. 7, no. 3, September 1983, Table 6, p. 239.

[a]A related form is the so-called "contractual" operation; in this form the owner enterprise or cooperative also procures a portion of the materials.

The public-private property enterprise combinations are shown in Table 28.1.

## Co-opting the Second Economy:
## The Nationalized Black Market

Perhaps the most interesting characteristic of the Hungarian economic experiment is the co-opting by the half-plan, half-market official economy of the shadowy "nonplanned sphere" (or the "second economy") where legal public and private enterprise imperceptibly merges with manifold money-making pursuits of various degrees of illegality and moral shadings. Altogether 1.2 million man-years are believed to be expended in the legal private economy by an economically active population of 5.2 million people. Many more million man-years are spent in extralegal and semipublic, semiprivate, and private activities. The Hungarians say that they earn 4,000 forints a month, spend 7,000, and bank the rest. Much of the success of the Hungarian NEM in regard to consumer material welfare through reduction of consumer aggravations is due to the official toleration, indeed, integration of the shadow economy in the official one on the principle that "if you can't beat them, join them." In official phraseology this is known as the "extension of the state sphere." The state settles for its citizens' wheeling and dealing even—perhaps mainly—on government time and with the aid of discreetly appropriated (stolen) government assets. The Hungarian party and state have come to terms with this condition to a greater extent than their Chinese counterparts. The Hungarians were really the first to quietly practice Deng's dictum that it doesn't matter whether a cat is black or white so long as it catches mice. The result is an unstable mixture of pretend socialism and pretend capitalism that nevertheless generates much more income than is revealed by the statistics.

## Conclusions

The mixture of half plan, half market; neither plan, nor market; pretend socialism, pretend capitalism, with ill-defined borders between legality and illegality; socialist moral codes and principles of market efficiency; neither this nor that; half this, half that; in short a condition of "market socialism," the NEM, or "socialism with Chinese characteristics," is an unstable condition—economically and ethically. Sooner or later (probably sooner) either plan and centralized social property or market and private property must prevail and dominate the system. There has to be further movement in the direction of marketization and privatization, or there will be retrogression to one or other variant of the central administrative command plan.

This conclusion is true despite the achievements of the Hungarian and Chinese experiments on this or that front: mainly on the front of consumer welfare—the reduction in consumer costs that are not easily quantifiable (shorter lines or no lines outside stores, less of a sellers' market, plentiful food, more and better quality consumer durables, and so on).[36] Hungary's achievements under the NEM in terms of the more orthodox measures of success have been questioned. Murrell, for example, argues that although the visitor to Hungary "sees bustling restaurants, . . . direct observation cannot provide an accurate picture of economic performance." Compared with other East European countries by measures such as per capita gross national product and its growth rate in the 1970s and 1980s, per capita net debt to Western commercial banks, and the rate of this debt's reduction, Hungary does not come out well, all of which, Murrell concludes, "will certainly convince other East European leaders that market-oriented reforms are not the route to economic success and independence."[37]

Although Murrell's argument is flawed in that it appears to ignore the composition of per capita national income in Hungary and other East European countries and omits the sizable contribution (not revealed in national income statistics) of the co-opted Hungarian shadow economy, there is an (unintended perhaps) element of truth to it. The Hungarians, like the Chinese, have not gone far enough on the road to market; not by a long stretch. Kornai is right that:

the main cause of [the Hungarian] slowdown is not in too much but in too little decentralization—that is, in too little confidence in and reliance on the market. We didn't adjust quickly enough to the changing world situation. I think many of the market economies responded better to the changing world trade situation than Hungary did, with its half-market, half-bureaucratic control.

In my judgment, we could advance still further toward a shift in the combination of vertical interaction in the planning bureaucracy with horizontal coordination through the market system, in favor of the latter, to bring greater economic benefits, more efficiency, and better productivity.[38]

And because marketization has not moved far enough, the economy remains in a state of systemic disequilibrium. This disequilibrium has two main causes.

First, market institutions of information, coordination, and motivation and private property rights in assets are incompatible with the institutions of central administrative command planning and centralized public property rights. Each set has its own internal logic that requires it to be dominant within the system. One has to accept, if not the whole package, at least enough of it for its contents to determine the structure of the economy. Otherwise one runs the risk of getting the worst of both worlds.[39] In this analytical sense "market socialism," which I take to denote a compromise of market-plan and private-public property fairly evenly balanced, is not a viable remedy for the command economy's efficiency troubles. The construct is prone to contradictory pulls in market and command directions.

Second, there is a contradiction between the dictates of economic efficiency and what has come to be known as the "socialist ethical code." The code is one part of a neofeudal social contract that communist authorities (at least since Stalin's death) enter into with their subjects. Kornai lists the principles that make up the code: (1) socialist wage setting—to each according to his work and equal pay for equal work; (2) solidarity—help the weak to rise rather than punish them through "blind" competition; (3) security— full employment guaranteed by society and immortality of socialist firms guaranteed by state budgetary bailouts; and (4) priority of the social interest as interpreted by the state over "partial" (individual) interest.[40] These principles are inserted by the party-state into the *contrat social féodal* in return for the citizens' acceptance of very modest rates of increase in their standard of living, tolerance of daily frustrations associated with a permanent sellers' market and retail void, restrictions on personal mobility, and, above all, strict limitations placed on freedom of expression and organization. The dictates of economic efficiency, on the other hand, read as follows: (1) an incentive mechanism designed to stimulate better performance from all individuals participating in production; (2) careful calculation of costs and benefits and termination of nonefficient production activities; (3) fast and flexible adjustment to the current situation and external conditions (spontaneity); (4) entrepreneurship, implying freedom of individual initiative; and (5) personal responsibility.[41] Only in the academic imagination of Oskar Lange is the contradiction between the values of economic efficiency and the ethical values of socialism resolved in the context of a "decentralized market economy along Walrasian lines, which functions efficiently and at the same time fits without difficulty into a system built on socialist ethical principles of justice." However, "in light of our experience in the real world, there are conflicts when we have to make choices."[42] Soon after markets and privatized property rights make themselves felt in the cause of efficiency within an economic structure that still contains powerful elements of central administrative command planning and centralized public (state and quasi-state, that is, collective) property, cries of anguish are heard from a variety of adversely affected interests. Before the efficiency results have a chance to materialize in more and more productively produced goods, the four socialist guarantees are likely to be broken and with them the social contract. The long march toward the market is stalled for "digesting" purposes, and there is some or much regression benefiting central command: home again, home again, jiggedy jog.

In addition to systemic disequilibrium of the economy, there is a moral instability that afflicts society, a sense of alienation, void, and purposelessness, a "live for the day" mentality, a feeling of deception and malaise. There is deep cynicism about society, the leadership, and much else fed by the knowledge that things are not what they appear or what officially they are said to be. The moral malaise of the half-and-half solution is shared by Hungary and mainland China. So far the tangible economic benefits have obscured the moral crisis from Western eyes, with a few exceptions.[43] One hesitates to end on this depressing note.[44] It is, however, appropriate, for it reinforces the overall conclusion that market-type changes applied to a centrally planned administrative command system cannot stop halfway; that they have to proceed to their logical outcome of systemic transformation or else they run the risk—through the inherent instability of halfway solutions—of being pushed back to some form of modernized Stalinism.

## Notes

1. Csaba Csaki, "Economic Management and Organization of Hungarian Agriculture," *Journal of Comparative Economics*, vol. 7, no. 3 (September 1983):321–322.

2. On the success of Hungarian agriculture: Michael Marrese, "Agricultural Policy and Performance in Hungary," *Journal of Comparative Economics*, vol. 7, no. 3 (September 1983):329–345; "Hungary: The Quiet Revolution," *The Economist* (London), September 20, 1980, p. 68; and R. W. Apple, Jr., "Hungary Reaps Harvest of Its Showplace Farms," *New York Times*, October 18, 1982, p. A2.

3. "Since 1956, when compulsory deliveries to the state were abolished, government control of agricultural producer cooperatives [in Hungary] has been indirect, rather than direct, yet its influence remains considerable. The state maintains control of prices of outputs and inputs; and while cooperatives aim at profit maximization and can use internally-generated funds for expansion, large investment projects require credit which, again, is subject to state control. By not cooperating with the government and ignoring its requests, the cooperative might lose its 'creditworthiness' and therefore be unable to acquire the chronically scarce capital goods its needs." A. L. Muller, "The Hungarian Socialist Market Economy (Review Note)," [Review of P. G. Hare,

H. K. Radice, and N. Swain, *Hungary: A Decade of Economic Reform* (London: Allen & Unwin, 1981)], *South African Journal of Economics*, vol. 50, no. 3 (1982):274.

4. Támás Bauer, "The Hungarian Alternative to Soviet-Type Planning," *Journal of Comparative Economics*, vol. 7, no. 3 (September 1983):305.

5. Bela Balassa, *Reforming the New Economic Mechanism in Hungary* (Washington, D.C.: World Bank, Staff Working Papers No. 534, 1982), pp. 1–11; Laszlo Racy, "On the New Price System," *East European Economics*, vol. 12, no. 1 (Fall 1981):49–69.

6. János Kornai, "Hungary's Reform: Halfway to the Market," *Challenge*, May–June 1985, p. 31; Bauer, "The Hungarian Alternative," p. 312.

7. János Kornai, "The Dilemmas of a Socialist Economy: The Hungarian Experience," *Cambridge Journal of Economics*, vol. 4, no. 2 (June 1980):151. Kornai describes the new coordinating mechanism in the following terms: "There is not one central planning authority, but many subcenters—one for prices, another for foreign trade, a third for banking, one for customs—and their decisions are often mutually inconsistent, and even contradictory. The bureaucratic bargaining that goes on now is not about physical targets and quantitative inputs; it is bargaining about subsidies, or tax exemptions or the price to be set for administratively priced goods, or customs and tariffs. There are hundreds of specific import licenses or export promotions. There are hundreds of small affairs where you as a producer are more interested in getting support from the bureaucracy than from the buyer in the marketplace. This excessive vertical intervention diverts the attention of producers from the market" (Kornai, "Hungary's Reform," p. 26). Quotations from "Hungary's Reform" reprinted with permission of the publisher, M. E. Sharpe, Inc., 80 Business Park Drive, Armonk, New York 10504 USA, from the May/June 1985 issue of *Challenge*.

8. These points are made by James Mulick, "The New Economic Mechanism in Hungary: A True Reform?" M.A. paper in economics, Pennsylvania State University, 1984, pp. 11–12.

9. Zhang Hiachi and Chen Jianfa, "The Decisionmaking Power of Enterprises and Free Prices—Eyewitness Account of Hungary's Economic Reform," *Renmin Ribao* April 4, 1983, p. 6, in *Foreign Broadcast Information Service* (*FBIS-CHI*), April 7, 1983, p. H4.

10. János Kornai, "Hungary's Reform," p. 20.

11. János Kornai, "Comments on the Present State and the Prospects of the Hungarian Economic Reform," *Journal of Comparative Economics*, vol. 7, no. 3 (September 1983):231.

12. Bauer, "The Hungarian Alternative," p. 314.

13. Frederick W. Crook, "The *Baogan Daohu* Incentive System: Translation and Analysis of a Model Contract," *China Quarterly*, no. 102 (June 1985):295. In 1984–85, 30 percent of grain was bought by the state at the quota price and 70 percent at the higher above-quota price; Zhao Ziyang, "Why Relax Agricultural Price Controls?" *Beijing Review*, February 18, 1985, p. 17. Quota and above-quota procurement prices were increased by nearly 48 percent between 1979 and 1983 (or more than 8 percent per annum); Nicholas R. Lardy, "Consumption and Living Standards in China, 1978–83," *China Quarterly*, no. 100 (December 1984):861. Since urban retail prices of staples were kept unchanged, the agricultural subsidy in 1984 was estimated at 20,000 million yuan; ibid., p. 905.

14. Zhao, "Why Relax Agricultural Price Controls?" p. 17; Zhao Ziyang, "Market to Replace the Quota System," *Beijing Review*, January 14, 1985, pp. 7–8.

15. Tian Jiyun (vice-premier), "On the Present Economic Situation and Restructuring the Economy," *Beijing Review*, February 10, 1986, p. IX.

16. Jan S. Prybyla, "The Chinese Economy: Adjustment of the System or Systemic Reform?" *Asian Survey*, vol. 15, no. 5 (May 1985):565.

17. Christine Wong, "Material Allocation and Decentralization: Impact of the Local Sector on Industrial Reform," in Elizabeth J. Perry and Christine Wong (Eds.), *The Political Economy of Reform in Post-Mao China* (Cambridge, Mass.: Harvard University Press, 1985); Prybyla, "The Chinese Economy," pp. 568–569.

18. Zhao Ziyang, "Report on the Seventh Five-Year Plan" (delivered at the Fourth session of the Sixth National People's Congress, March 25, 1986), April 21, 1986, p. XII.

19. *Beijing Review*, October 29, 1984, pp. I–XVI.

20. On the various industrial price categories: "Questions and Answers on Prices," *Zhong Quo Fazhibao*, November 11, 1985, in *Inside China Mainland* (Taipei), March 1986, pp. 16–17. The problem of the spillover effect of irrational prices on the price structure as a whole is similar to that experienced in Hungary.

21. "As for the more important means of production, such as raw and semifinished materials and steel, the price for that amount required for planned distribution remains basically unchanged, while the remaining portion can be sold at market prices"; Tian, "On the Present Economic Situation," p. IX. On emerging markets for the means of production in mainland China, see William Byrd, "The Shanghai Market for the Means of Production: A Case Study of Reform in China's Material Supply System," *Comparative Economic Studies*, vol. 27, no. 4 (winter 1985):1–29.

22. Abram Bergson, "A Visit to China's Economic Reforms," *Comparative Economic Studies*, vol. 27, no. 2 (summer 1985):79.

23. "More than 80% of the population functions in a private enterprise environment. And the sphere of private enterprise is growing rapidly and vigorously"; William Hinton, "Which Way China? December 1985 Observations," *Far East Reporter*, March 1986, p. 31. Hinton is not sympathetic to the marketizing changes.

24. E.g., William Hinton, "Responsibility and Enterprise: A New Leap or A New Elite," *Far East Reporter*, March 1986, pp. 3–9; William Hinton, "An Analysis of the Responsibility System: Where Will the New Polarization Lead?" *Far East Reporter*, March 1986, pp. 10–17.

25. Victoria Pope, "Hungary Braces for Austerity Plan," *Wall Street Journal*, July 2, 1983, p. 27.

26. Frederick Kempe, "Budapest's Economic Changes Prompt Concern of Hungarian, Soviet Officials," *Wall Street Journal*, April 1, 1985, p. 26.

27. Bela Balassa, "Reforming the New Economic Mechanism in Hungary," *Journal of Comparative Economics*, vol. 7, no. 3 (September 1983):264–267. Mulick, "The New Economic Mechanism in Hungary," p. 23.

28. Istvan Kemeny, "The Unregistered Economy in Hungary," *Soviet Studies*, vol. 34, no. 3 (July 1982):349–366.

29. "State Council Provisional Regulations on Greater Decision-Making Powers of State-Owned Industrial Enterprises," *Beijing Review*, June 18, 1984, pp. 10–11; Zhao Ziyang's speech to the National Committee of the Chinese People's Political Consultative Conference, January 1, 1985, *Beijing Review*, January 7, 1985, p. 15.

30. On the various taxes in mainland China, see Christine Wong, "The Second Phase of Economic Reform in China," *Current History*, September 1985, pp. 260–262; Barry Naughton, "False Starts and Second Wind: Financial Reform in China's Industrial System," in Perry and Wong, *The Political Economy of Reform in Post-Mao China*.

31. Kornai, "Hungary's Reform," pp. 27–28. A fuller statement of the soft budget constraint problem may be found in his *Economics of Shortage* (Amsterdam: New Holland, 1980).

32. Hinton, "An Analysis of the Responsibility System."

33. Such developments would presuppose the emergence of democratically constituted village or township councils—an unlikely event in the present political temper of mainland China.

34. This separation is to be accompanied by a far-reaching delegation of supervisory-advisory functions from the central to local governments. James P. Sterba, "Central Control Subdued Under Peking's Plan," *Wall Street Journal*, April 15, 1986, p. 37.

35. József Macsáry, "Centralization of the Hungarian Enterprise System and Its Impact on the Efficiency of Production Control and the Regulatory System," *Eastern European Economics*, winter 1982–1983, pp. 34–61: Márton Tardos, "The Increasing Role and Ambivalent Reception of Small Enterprises in Hungary," *Journal of Comparative Economics*, vol. 7, no. 3 (September 1983):277–287.

36. Statistical data documenting the performance of mainland Chinese and Hungarian economies under the post-1978 changes (China) and the post-1968 NEM (Hungary) may be found in a number of sources. For example, for China: *Statistical Yearbook of China*, compiled by the State Statistical Bureau of the People's Republic of China (especially from 1983 onward); Li Chengrui, "Economic Reform Brings Better Life," *Beijing Review*, July 22, 1985, pp. 15–22, which contains useful tables and a diagram comparing the situation in 1978 with 1984; Richard Critchfield, "China's Agricultural Success Story," *Wall Street Journal*, January 13, 1986, p. 25; U.S. Department of Agriculture, Economic Research Service, *China: Outlook and Situation Report* (Washington, D.C., July 1985), and *Agricultural Statistics of the People's Republic of China, 1949–82* (Washington, D.C., October 1984); U.S. Congress, Joint Economic Committee, *China: Economic Performance in 1985* (Washington, D.C., 1986). For Hungary: World Bank, *World Development Report 1985; Statistical Pocket Book of Hungary*, annual, (Budapest); and *Statisztikai evkonyv* (Statistical Yearbook), annual (Budapest).

37. Peter Murrell, "Hungary's Hidden Economic Handicaps," *Wall Street Journal*, October 22, 1984, p. 30.

38. Kornai, "Hungary's Reform," pp. 31 and 26. Compare: "The general principle is to give more power to the role of market forces while upholding the country's planned economy"; Zhao Ziyang, *Beijing Review*, January 14, 1985, p. 8.

39. On being caught between market and plan institutions, see Gertrude Schroeder, "The Soviet Economy on a Treadmill of 'Reforms,'" in U.S. Congress, Joint Economic Committee, *Soviet Economy in a Time of Change* (Washington, D.C.: U.S. Government Printing Office, 1979), pp. 312–340, and Gertrude Schroeder, "Soviet Economic 'Reform': More Steps on the Treadmill," in U.S. Congress Joint Economic Committee, *Soviet Economy in the 1980s: Problems and Prospects* (Washington, D.C.: U.S. Government Printing Office, 1982), part 1, pp. 65–88.

40. Kornai, "The Dilemmas of a Socialist Economy," p. 148.

41. Ibid., p. 148.

42. Kornai, "Hungary's Reform," p. 31.

43. One of the exceptions is Ivan Volgyes. See his "Kadar's Hungary in the Twilight Era," *Current History*, November 1984, pp. 361–364, 386, and his "Hungary: A Malaise Thinly Disguised," *Current History*, November 1985, pp. 365–368, 388. Victor Pope, "Hungarians Show Discipline and Old World Restraint," *Wall Street Journal*, March 7, 1983, p. 26. Jan S. Prybyla, "The Hundred Flowers of Discontent," *Current History*, September 1981, pp. 254–257, 274.

44. The note, however, is depressing primarily in a relative sense. Compared with the darkness of Stalinism and Maoism, the alienation of the half-plan half-market,

neither-plan-nor-market society may be seen as a development toward moral health, the beginning of the shedding of Marxist-Leninist hypocrisies among the people and segments of the party, and a rejection of ideological inanities. There is in it an element of overcompensation for past material privations, a feverish quest for money making, and an impatient desire to start living with some degree of physical comfort. There is not much inherently wrong with that, except its denial by the purist guardians of official morality.

# References

Bauer, Tamás. "The Second Economic Reform and Ownership Relations." *Eastern European Economics*, spring-summer 1984, pp. 33–87.

Berend, Ivan T., and Gyorgÿ Ránki. *The Hungarian Economy in the Twentieth Century.* New York: St. Martin's Press, 1985. Especially Chapters 6, 7, and 8.

Bornstein, Morris. "The Soviet Industrial Price Revision." In *Socialist Economy and Economic Policy: Essays in Honour of Friedrich Levcik,* ed. G. Fink, pp. 157–170. Vienna and New York: Springer-Verlag, 1985. For general understanding of Soviet-type industrial producer prices.

Crook, Frederick W. "The Reform of the Commune System and the Rise of the Township-Collective-Household System." U.S. Department of Agriculture Working Paper. Washington, D.C., 1985.

Csikós-Nagy, B. "Further Development of the Hungarian Price System." *Acta Oeconomica*, vol. 32, nos. 1–2 (1984):21–37.

Freidländer, Michael. *Die Ungarische Wirtschaftsreform.* Forschungsbericht der Wiener Institut für Internationale Wirtschaftsvergleiche, Nr. 99, October 1984 (78 pp).

Furgeri, I., and J. Betlen. "The Past, Present and Future of the East-European Economies: The Hungarian Case." *Acta Oeconomica*, vol. 31, nos. 3–4 (1983):297–326.

Hartford, Kathleen. "Hungarian Agriculture: A Model for the Socialist World?" *World Development*, January 1985, pp. 123–150.

Hsu, Kuang-t'ai. "Property Rights in Mainland China's Common Rules of Civil Law." *Issues & Studies*, vol. 22, no. 5 (May 1986):7–9.

Liu, Guoguang. "Changes in Ownership Forms: Problems and Possibilities." *Beijing Review*, May 12, 1986, pp. 17–22.

Marer, Paul. "Economic Reform in Hungary: From Central Planning to Regulated Market." In *East European Economies, Slow Growth in the 1980s,* pp. 223–297. Selected Papers, U.S. Congress, Joint Economic Committee. Washington, D.C.: U.S. Government Printing Office, 1986.

Myers, Ramon H. "Price Reforms and Property Rights in Communist China Since 1978." *Issues & Studies*, vol. 21, no. 10 (October 1985):13–33.

Prybyla, Jan S. "China's Economic Experiment: From Mao to Market." *Problems of Communism*, vol. 35, no. 1 (January-February 1986):21–38.

# 29

## Economic Reform and Foreign Economic Relations: Systemic Conflicts in a Theoretical Framework

*Yuan-li Wu*

### Introduction

The purpose of this paper is to examine the interaction of the expanding foreign economic relations of the People's Republic of China (PRC) with its economic reform, both of which it has vowed to pursue in the interest of "modernization." The paper will explore certain effects of this interaction on (1) the course economic reform might follow in the next several years and the problems one should logically expect, as well as (2) the country's external relations, especially with the West, the Soviet Union, and other countries of the Council for Mutual Economic Assistance (CMEA). The analysis will be attempted in a theoretical framework so that one can better understand how the PRC's experience is only a special case of systemic conflict that other planned systems attempting reform either have undergone or should expect to face in the future.

The expansion of foreign trade is necessary for Communist China's modernization because new technology, whether "embodied" or not, must be imported. Such imports must sooner or later be paid for with exports. Furthermore, for quite some time to come, Communist China will have to augment its domestically financed investment with foreign capital, which must then be serviced. Economic reform is necessary for the success of modernization because productivity cannot be increased, waste of resources cannot be reduced, and exports cannot be significantly expanded unless (1) a better and more effective incentive system can be established, (2) resource allocation becomes more efficient in satisfying the public's demand, and (3) exports stay competitive in an expanding market. None of these conditions can be satisifed if things stay are they are.

## The Nature of Economic Reform and Greater Orientation to the West

When the Chinese Communists began to embark upon their current reformist policy, they introduced two catchwords to describe their dual objective: adjustment and reform. A great deal has already been written on this subject.[1]

The term "adjustment" focuses attention on the need to alter the pattern of end use of resources—involving ratios between investment and personal consumption, agricultural and nonagricultural output, production in heavy industry and that of light manufacturing, and so forth. "Reform" is meant to subject the entire economy to a more fundamental change in the way economic decisions are reached and actual production and distribution are carried out. The impact of these two types of changes cannot of course be confined to the purely economic. Having played a predominant role heretofore, both the state and the Chinese Communist Party cannot avoid suffering an adjustment of their own once the methods of making and enforcing economic decisions are substantially altered.

The Chinese Communists' scheme in analyzing and solving their economic problems obviously aims at specific policy goals. A quick *adjustment* of production and aggregate expenditure patterns would alleviate the shortages of supply of many consumer goods. It is supposed to reduce rural poverty in particular. This effect is meant to be in the final instance a short-run palliative that might restore the public's confidence, which Mao Tse-tung and his policies irrevocably lost toward the end of his life. Whether this objective will extend to a longer period is not clear. Reform, on the other hand, is to be a long-run program intended to help propel the Chinese economy on a more productive path with increasing output and factor productivity. However, the need for optimal proportions in expenditure, production, and the like is just another way of describing general equilibrium; it is not something to be obtained only once in a time period that is specially designated as a period of adjustment. The objective of economic reform is to ensure that economic decisions will *always* be conducive to producing optimal results so that there will be an automatic process of *continuous adjustment* toward general equilibrium or, in the Communists' jargon, toward "correct proportions."

Partly for this reason, but partly because of an academic partiality toward methodological tidiness, I have suggested elsewhere[2] that another way, perhaps a more useful one, of looking at the current Chinese economic policy is to classify Beijing's economic changes into two categories: micro- versus macroeconomic. Microeconomic reform is to substitute for the previous Chinese practice of issuing commands and instructions in terms of targets and norms for specific tasks with simpler instructions aimed at indicators of maximizing profitablity that link performance to rewards and punishments of a material kind. Microeconomic reform, therefore, involves both administrative and economic decentralization.[3] It also entails shifts in the role of the Communist Party in enterprise management. Not the least far-reaching consequence of decentralized economic decision-making, however, is the implication of freedom of making production and income distribution decisions involving property rights in means of production that could affect the ideological basis of the communist system.

On the other hand, macroeconomic reform focuses on two other related aspects: (1) the introduction of a better information system—price setting in a free market—to serve especially the decentralized sector so that resources can be allocated on the basis of the reformed microeconomic behavior; and (2) the development and use of a set of economic levels (taxes, subsidies, market interest rates and exchange rates, money and credit supplies, etc.) to replace direct commands in order to match aggregate as well as specific demand with aggregate and specific supply.

For purposes of modernization, these micro- and macroeconomic reforms must take place within an increasingly open economy. To the extent, however limited it may be in practice, to which the world economy competes with the domestic economy either as an alternative market or as an alternative source of goods, decision makers in a decentralized Chinese economy may choose to deal with, or through, the world outside at the expense of the remaining planned sector or at the expense of the domestic economy as a whole. The existence of a large world market in relation to the Chinese economy means in general that world prices will prevail in foreign trade; the Chinese buyer or seller will be a price taker. These prices will differ from administratively set prices in China—as long as prices in the PRC are not completely freed in one stroke and some are still government set. Finally, once the Chinese economy is opened to the outside world, it can no longer be insulated from the world's many unexpected economic and other shocks. By the same token, unexpected shocks originating in mainland China can also produce reverberations outside. In short, economic reform on the one hand and foreign trade and other external economic developments on the other impact upon each other and produce both domestic and external effects. How the interactions may then work out can be seen in the following illustrative cases.

## Competition for Scarce Resources Between the Centralized and the Decentralized Sectors: The General Case Versus a Special Case

Under centralized planning, scarce resources are allocated to individual producers according to a previously determined plan. Within this central plan the matching of available supplies—domestic current production plus inventory withdrawal plus imports—with the aggregate amounts of planned use constitutes the plan of "net material balance." This has been the practice in Soviet-type economies for many years and was also the system imported into the PRC during the 1950s. Restoration of the same method appears to have been attempted in the centralized state sector of the Chinese economy in the post-Mao period. The system is economically inefficient when the pattern of allocation does not correspond to the real relative scarcities of resources and the relative preferences of the users of the goods they help produce. This inefficiency is the combined outcome of the system's failure— to be more correct, inability—to account for all costs and the divergence of the central planners' preferences, which enjoy absolute priority in such a system, from the ordinary users' priorities. In an economy in which scarcities and preferences change, which gives rise to the need of frequent corrections of production and investment plans, a centralized system of resource allocation suffers from the slow communication process linking the final decision makers on resource allotment to the grass-roots resource users who are closest to the real changing conditions of production and consumption. The time required for the transmission of commands, the collection and feedback of new information, verification of new data, and approval and retransmission of new commands adds to the original static inefficiency of the system. When the vertical chain of the centralized command system is divided into a number of subcommand levels—for instance, central ministry, industry, branch, and enterprise levels, or central, regional, provincial, and local governments—the aggregate reaction time to new developments is unavoidably multiplied. This slowness is the usual reason why, even within the bureaucratic Communist Party, there are those who advocate decentralization in the allocation of certain scarce resources.

However, once a scarce resource is no longer centrally allocated according to a fixed plan, the decentralized sector—which need not be a market sector of "privatized" enterprises at all[4]—is likely to appropriate the scarce resource required for its own use, if the demand for the products the decentralized sector can supply is strong, at the expense of the remaining centralized sector. For a time this development may very well be hidden from the view of the central authorities because of their information lags. What happens when they are belatedly awakened to the fact that the scarce resource needed for the realization of their own priority objectives is no longer available or not available on the same terms? Recentralize control? Cut back severely on the demand of the decentralized sector? Find substitute sources of supply of the scarce resource, or do away with the need for it altogether, which is a more drastic way out of the embarrassment?

As the current Chinese Communist leaders have partially decentralized and opened up the economy to the West in the interest of greater efficiency and modernization, a special case in this general category of problems has developed. This was the large, unplanned drop of a scarce resource, convertible foreign currency, in 1984 and 1985. From the planners' point of view, modernization requires the importation of Western equipment and materials. Furthermore, in order to pay for the imports, exports have to be expanded, and this expansion in turn requires imports. Besides, importation for the purpose of export expansion can by itself also be a channel of inward technology transfer. For all this to take place efficiently, the users of imports and the producers of PRC exports must be in direct contact with foreign suppliers and buyers. The customary separation of Chinese import users as well as export producers from their individual foreign trading partners by state trading companies and the centralization of sale and purchase orders in the hands of the Beijing bureaucracy thus become a serious barrier. Besides, potential foreign investors, as well as traders, have been, and still are, vociferous in their complaint about the Chinese Communists' overcentralization of control. All this accounts for the partial decentralization of decision making in importation and the reservation for their own use of a portion of the foreign exchange earnings of exports initiated by regional, provincial, and municipal governments and large state enterprises.

Two additional circumstances aggravating the impact of this decentralization should be noted. First, the decentralized sector is interested in imports not only of capital and producer goods but also of consumer goods, especially durables (e.g., television sets, refrigerators). Demand for such goods was so restricted during recent decades that, given a large cash balance and less political restraint on spending, the public, especially its privileged party elite, was quite ready to expand the purchase of imports. Therefore, decentralization has led to a large increase in imports of goods for consumption as well as investment.

A second point to be noted is that even within the centralized state sector there exist multiple systems of vertical command. Thus the disposition of foreign capital inflow as a source of convertible foreign exchange is divided among many government agencies.[5] Bilateral government loans are controlled by the bureau administering foreign capital in the Ministry of Foreign Economic Relations and Trade (MOFERT); credits from multilateral international financial agencies such as the affiliates of the World Bank are handled by the Ministry of Finance; foreign private commercial bank credits are within the domain of the Bank of China for use by various government agencies; and private foreign direct investment is the responsibility again of MOFERT. Even the Bank of China, which from time to time may actually hold more foreign exchange than the official reserve, was reportedly keeping its total foreign exchange holdings (which are much larger than and often mistakenly spoken of as reserves) in separate "pockets" for which a total accurate accounting is not necessarily instantly available.

### An Increase in Capital Account Credit Entries in the Balance of Payments: Heavy Reserve Loss (PRC) Versus Increased Indebtedness (CMEA)

Those of us who delve in international economics will recognize that the PRC's loss of foreign exchange reserves in 1984 and 1985 was but a special case of the general problem one should expect to encounter when an inefficient centralized state sector competes with a more efficient decentralized sector in the use of foreign currency. If the latter is partly privatized, or if

TABLE 29.1
Average Annual Changes in Net Hard-Currency Indebtedness (in billion U.S. dollars)

| | 1970–1976 | 1976–1980 | 1980–1981 | Value of Indebtedness Peak Through 1970 | Value of Indebtedness Peak Through 1981 |
|---|---|---|---|---|---|
| Bulgaria | 0.35 | –0.03 | –0.60 | 0.70 | 2.8 (1976) |
| Czechoslovakia | 0.13 | 0.55 | –0.10 | 0.60 | 3.6 (1980) |
| East Germany | 0.60 | 1.70 | 0.20 | 1.40 | 1.20 (1981) |
| Poland | 1.70 | 2.90 | 1.80 | 1.10 | 25.0[a] (1982) |
| Romania | 0.15 | 1.67 | 0.60 | 1.60 | 9.80 (1981) |
| Hungary | 0.35 | 1.00 | 0.20 | 0.60 | 6.90 (1981) |
| USSR | 1.50 | 0.12 | 2.90 | 1.00 | 12.40 (1981) |

*Source:* Calculated from original data in Hans-Hermann Hohmann and Christian Meier, *Wirtshaftslage, Aussenwirtschaft, und Aussenpolitik in Osteuropa: Zur Politischen Ökonomie der RGW-Gipfelkonferenz* (The Economic Condition, Foreign Economy, and Foreign Policy of Eastern Europe: The Political Economy of the CMEA Summit Conference) (Cologne, West Germany: Federal Institute of Eastern & International Studies, No. 55, 1984), p. 17.

[a]Subsequently reported at $29 billion in 1984.

an effective profit incentive enters upon the scene *indirectly*, (e.g., through the "second economy"), the impact can be even more traumatic. Such was indeed the case in the celebrated Hainan scandal. In the Chinese Communist case, the result was a heavy loss of official reserves. Had Beijing been less conservative in foreign borrowing, the result might have been a large increase in international indebtedness, which happened to some Eastern European countries that borrowed heavily in the 1970s in order to finance imports from the West—both for consumption and for modernization (see Table 29.1).

In the period between 1970 and 1981, the Soviet Union and Poland registered the same highest average annual increase in net indebtedness in hard currency, at $2.9 billion. This figure was reached during 1976–1980 in the case of Poland and, for the Soviet Union, during 1980–1981. The CMEA countries piled up during a longer period an aggregate indebtedness far larger than the amount by which the PRC drew down its official reserves during 1984–1985. The Chinese reserve loss in a single year, however, was definitely a noteworthy example of the unintended effect of decentralization (see Table 29.2). Poland appeared to offer a similar case in which individual enterprises contracted for imports without worrying about their financing. Yugoslavia, a non-CMEA member, had a comparable operative experience through decentralization in financing imports by its constituent republics.

Both Communist China and the CMEA countries experienced a sharp curtailment of imports when the sudden loss of reserves or the inability to service existing loans, respectively, became a sharp reminder of reality. Drastic measures were taken. The Chinese Communists canceled many existing import contracts. The Eastern European countries tried to buy their

TABLE 29.2
Change in PRC Foreign Exchange Holdings

|  | December 1983 | September 1984 | September 1985 |
|---|---|---|---|
| Gold (000 troy ounces) | 12,670 | 12,670 | 12,670 |
| Reserve of the State Treasury, excluding gold[a] (billion U.S. dollars) (*Kuo-chia k'u-ts'un*) | 8.901 | 12.184 | 3.377 |
| Bank of China Holdings[b] (billion U.S. dollars) (*wai-hui-chieh-tsun*) | 5.441 | 4.490 | 9.215 |

*Sources: Zhongguo Jinrong* (Beijing), no. 4, 1984, p. 21; no. 12, 1984, p. 55; and no. 12, 1985, p. 37.

[a]Includes the outstanding balance of foreign borrowing.
[b]Believed to be the outstanding balance of assets, without deducting deposits of clients and correspondents and other payables.

way out through additional borrowing to service their existing debts. The Chinese measure earned for Beijing bewilderment among many businesses trading with it, both in Hong Kong and elsewhere. The effect of the *virtual* debt moratorium on the part of some CMEA countries has instead been hard on members of the West's banking community.

### Competition and the Exchange Rate in an Open Market

We turn next to the substitution for allocation of resources by administrative fiat of allocation based on market prices as indicators, supplemented by the application of the profit incentive on the part of individual enterprises in regulating their respective activities. As students of neoclassical economics have long learned, for this process to work efficiently, prices must be allowed to vary in accordance with changing demand and supply; the resultant changes in profitability must then be allowed to guide the use of all material and human resources, both in current production and in investment. Implied in this process of continuous market adjustment, in response to change in the underlying conditions of demand and supply, is the prospect that the more daring and profitable enterprises will be able to attract resources away from the less enterprising and profitable, which are probably in this predicament because they are producing goods demanded by the government but not by the paying public. The impact of such a reallocation of resources was already discussed in the preceding section.

However, another implication of the market adjustment process is that if individual enterprises are free to buy goods where they are cheap and sell where they are dear, a perfectly competitive market will see to it that the same good will command the same price. When this principle is applied to goods traded by both the PRC and the outside world under conditions of free competition and the rule of profit maximization by individual enterprises, a single price must prevail for the same good. Thus Chinese enterprises would not be able to sell their products above world prices. Similarly, domestic Chinese products cannot compete with imports if their prices are above world prices as a result of higher costs or inappropriately large profit margins. This discrepancy can occur because at the initial opening of the Chinese economy to the outside world, relative prices in the PRC differ substantially from world prices. After the initial opening, the two sets of relative prices will continue to be different as long as the removal of rigid government control over domestic Chinese prices is incomplete. As the Chinese authorities have announced more than once,[6] caution dictates that prices be freed only for a small number of goods at a time, and the government must have countermeasures ready to combat what it regards as excessive price changes (usually price increases).

As we know, when internal commodity markets are in disequilibrium, the Soviet Union no less than some Eastern European countries[7] have frequently resorted to the manipulation of taxes and subsidies in order to nudge demand and supply toward equilibrium. Commodity taxes and subsidies are among the economic levers that advocates of the PRC's economic reform regard as superior to administrative modifications of input/output relations in the economic plan. An alternative method of adjusting relative prices in foreign trade is to change the exchange rate. If the change in the ratio between foreign and domestic prices is not to vary in the same degree from one commodity to another, multiple exchange rates are the answer. The PRC has already tried this method in promoting its sale of textiles in the United States.

What are the consequences of using the tax-subsidy mechanism or multiple-exchange-rate variations to replace the adoption of market-determined prices as a means of increasing the sale of specific exports and the reduction of specific imports that would not otherwise occur? First, the original price distortions and the consequent malallocation of resources will persist. Second, the existence of this mechanism or of multiple exchange rates will be interpreted by some countries as "unfair competition" calling for retaliation. In 1984, U.S. textile manufacturers did use the existence of an internal Yuan-dollar conversion rate for PRC textiles manufactured for export that differs from the official rate as evidence of a multiple exchange rate practice, demanding retaliation. While this particular complaint of the textile industry was staved off, it was, in a sense, a not-so-remote cause of the broadened and far more virulent form of protectionism represented by the 1985 Jenkins bill, which tried to roll back U.S. textile imports from the principal foreign suppliers.[8]

Third, use of the tax-subsidy-exchange-rate levels to manipulate market imbalances will be necessary—so the official argument will go—to correct temporary balance-of-payments disequilibrium; it will be, therefore, justified in this manner in the eyes of the IMF and GATT. However, they are in fact attempts to perpetuate an inherent systemic disinclination to allow free prices, in the final analysis, to replace government price setting perpetuated for political and ideological reasons.

Here are some of the political reasons why Zhao Ziyang, for one, is afraid to free too many prices at once. First, there is ambiguity between an upward adjustment of some relative prices when they are freed from control and individual price increases as a part of general inflation. What may be abundantly clear to economists and persons accustomed to price volatility in a free market may be less clear to both policymakers and the mainland Chinese public, which has been long secluded in a command economy of fixed prices.[9] Fear of the political impact of runaway inflation based on the experience of the late 1940s and early 1950s may have added to Zhao's concern. Besides, opponents of economic reform may make political hay of any apparent inflation. Of course, once some prices rise, speculators may step in, especially if there is expectation of inflation, which will cause additional price increases, at least in the short run. Moreover, if the prices of staple consumer products rise significantly, a problem of income distribution will arise, accentuating the class disparities that already plague the Chinese Communists, who try to play down the widely heard complaint about special privileges enjoyed by some party cadres and their families.

From the point of view of economic reform, however, another consequence of the tax-subsidy-multiple-exchange-rate level requires continuous "fine tuning" of the economic system, which in turn will require a large national and lower-level staff to administer the changing regulations. One can envisage two possible developments: a bureaucratic maze that would stagger the imagination and add to inefficiency; and, alternatively, an increase in attempts to bypass the regulations through favoritism and therefore both bribe taking and bribe giving.

Externally, one should expect more disputes with the PRC's trading partners over "unfair competition" and "dumping." In view of the avowed PRC policy to become a member of GATT and its hope thereafter to gain GSP (duty free import, up to a specific amount, for certain designated commodities under Generalized Special Preference) status in trading with the United States, the conditions of either the PRC's entry into GATT as a new signatory or its resumption of signatory status in the agreement (on the theory that the Republic of China's withdrawal from GATT only resulted in a prolonged Chinese absence) must be carefully examined in the light of other GATT signatories' experience with nonmarket economies.

## Credit Control

A third major economic impact of decentralization in the course of reform has to do with financing and monetary policy. As decisions on economic activities (production, investment, foreign trade, etc.) devolve on lower-level government agencies and enterprises, decisions on the financing of these activities tend to shift in the same direction vertically. This shift means that more credit institutions must be founded, and the authority they will have in extending credit and administering loan disbursement and repayment must be fixed. In the foreign economic area, the corresponding issue is focused on the entry of foreign banks and the scope of their permissible activities. Since one can also take for granted that foreign banks will not stand idly by, waiting for the PRC to open its doors wide,[10] their initiative may very well force the issue sooner than the PRC would like. Besides, countries like the United States that wish to include the service industry in multilateral negotiations on lowering trade barriers will wish to tear down barriers to their own financial services. Hence, foreign banks and insurance companies may very well be among the service providers demanding a more active role as Beijing expands its external contacts.

When regional and local banks engage in direct financing of foreign trade or in soliciting foreign capital, there is a double risk. There is, in the first place, the risk of overextending external commitments in hard-currency payments, leading to the kind of foreign exchange loss or international indebtedness discussed in the first section of this chapter. There is, however, the additional macroeconomic problem of overexpansion of credit and with it of aggregate demand. Availability of foreign credit does not impinge on the balance of payments alone. In order to have imported foreign equipment installed and put to use, local spending, financed either by credit or through budget appropriation, will have to be made. If foreign banks are available on the spot, local governments and enterprises will find it much easier to raise the foreign currency required to meet their needs. It will be much more difficult to exercise overall control of credit and aggregate money supply. Since a macroeconomic policy aimed at internal economic equilibrium has yet to be developed in the PRC and its fiscal monetary tools remain to be sharpened, decentralization of financing could enhance instability of money supply and the price level, thus impeding reform by undermining confidence in its success.

## Vulnerability to External Shocks

By opening up the mainland Chinese economy to the outside world, the PRC authorities have also made the country far more vulnerable than before to world demand, supply, and price changes over which it has no control and which it cannot fully anticipate. The approach toward domestic economic reform may therefore be affected in turn. Two such external developments in recent times have been the instability of energy prices and greater protectionist pressures in the West. The PRC has been doubly affected because oil (inclusive of petroleum products) and textiles are two of its principal export groups for which substitutes cannot be quickly developed. In 1985, for instance, out of $3,861 million of PRC exports to the United States, $985 million (25.5%) came from petroleum and refined products. Exports of textiles and apparel ($1,368 million) constituted 35.4% of the PRC's total exports to the United States in the same year.

There is no doubt that the sharp rise of crude oil prices in the 1970s, punctuated by the 1973–1974 and 1979–1980 quantum jumps, gave Beijing a powerful push toward the decision to invite international oil companies for offshore and, subsequently, even onshore exploration. Chinese Communist planners were probably influenced by Western and Japanese interests and publicists who reinforced Chinese hopes with their own enthusiasm, thus in the end misleading each other. Those planners and Communist Party leaders who decided equipment and technology apparently underestimated the time it might take to locate commercially worthwhile deposits or to put installations in place to start the oil flow. Together with the rest of the world, they did not foresee the sharp decline of crude oil prices as a result of increased production outside the OPEC cartel and reduced demand from conservation and recession on the part of large importing countries. In the long run, perhaps a most serious uncertainty that complicates Communist Chinese planning stems from the reduced inclination and ability of the international banking community and oil companies to finance massive and risky investments with a long payoff period even in much better circumstances of international indebtedness and at somewhat higher oil prices than the July 1986 low.

History has made the textile industry one of the most developed light manufacturing sectors in China, going far back in the pre-Communist period. This condition is aided by low Chinese wages. Hence textiles and garments have been among the PRC's core exports to the rest of the world along with mineral exports (including oil). Since textile exports are subject to quotas under the Multifiber Arrangement, Beijing, under a bilateral agreement with the United States, ships a substantial volume indirectly through Hong Kong, using the latter's quota. This practice will sooner or later create a post-1997 issue.

Given the uncertain future facing one major export like oil[11] and the barriers facing another export group whose production can be expanded, what might the planners do and how might their decisions affect economic reform? On the export side, the answers are obvious. The PRC, like any country facing similar problems, will come up with diversification into other exportable goods and services and redirection to other markets. On the import side, there will be reduction of imports through tighter trade and exchange controls and a shifting of sources of supply from hard-currency areas to countries that may wish to take Chinese exports that they cannot afford to buy in hard-currency areas. The redirection of purchases by the buyers of Chinese Communist goods would yield a net benefit to Beijing, however, only if the redirected Chinese exports are among those that the PRC cannot sell in expanded quantities in hard-currency countries.

The above points will affect the PRC's economic reform in several ways. First, tighter direct controls would work in favor of recentralization and against decentralization, which appears to remain as the present guideline for the seventh five-year plan (1986–1990). A compromise would be continued decentralization in matters except exchange control, which could be put under stricter central control. It goes without saying that such a policy orientation would greatly reduce flexibility in the financing of economic activities, militating against greater efficiency. We shall, however, focus our attention on a second point: the effect on reform of the redirection of trade.

## Redirection of Trade Toward the Soviet Union and Other CMEA Members

The PRC's interest in redirecting trade toward the Soviet Union has already been reciprocated by Moscow. On the Chinese side, a curtailment of investment is apparently now desired,[12] and this can be accomplished to a degree by replacing planned new investments with renovations and extensions of old plants built with Soviet aid during the first two five-year-plan periods. Reports on Soviet-PRC conversations in 1985 and 1986 have mentioned larger long-term projects involving technology transfers, which might involve both hydro and nuclear power. It is not clear whether the Chernobyl disaster will cast a pall on Chinese thinking regarding the reliability of Soviet nuclear power technology. On the other hand, the high cost of U.S. equipment and technology poses a real problem to Beijing, where Soviet arguments may find a sympathetic hearing on the part of some PRC like Li Peng, leaders known to be personally familiar with Soviet power technology.

On the Soviet side, Chinese textiles that the United States and the European Community will not accept can probably be bartered away, as can grain and other food items that the Chinese farmers may again be induced to produce if the government-set cereal prices are once more raised. In the recent report on the Seventh Five-Year Plan, mention has also been made on the possible export of Chinese labor.[13] Perhaps the two countries can find uses for such labor on projects of common or "parallel" interest—if not in the Soviet Union, then elsewhere.

When one adds to these economic considerations the political argument that an increase in bilateral trade at this time would be conducive to a political rapprochement, a strong case can be made that would recommend itself to both Moscow and Beijing.

Of particular interest to us in this chapter, however, is the fact that an increase in Sino-Soviet trade in this manner would increase somewhat the degree to which the PRC's planned state sector will be integrated with planned imports, thus reducing the state sector's vulnerability to further shocks from unexpected developments in the world of market economics. Since Sino-Soviet trade is currently at a very low level, even a substantial increase would not greatly alter its relative importance as a proportion of the two countries respective total commerce with the world. Hence, a significant increase in interdependence would not develop, which is probably another reason why the prospect of such a development appears quite high. In short, given certain undesired effects of economic reform on the country's external balance, the Communist Chinese response is not limited to less decentralization or less free market; closer integration with another planned economy may present a third alternative. To this author the leaders in Beijing seem to be searching for a combination of all three solutions.

A complicating situation should be noted. This is the changing relationship between the East European CMEA members and the Soviet Union, which must be considered in the light of the world's energy market and the still high indebtedness of some Eastern European countries to the West. The latter are eager to increase their exports to the West; the Soviet Union has urged them to export more quality products to it; the decline of the price of oil has further pinched the USSR's hard-currency earnings; and any renewed oil price drop is going to make the three-year average oil price used for selling Soviet oil to its Eastern European CMEA allies more than a little onerous. It is under these conflicting conditions that the developing Sino-Soviet economic relations must be evaluated. How will Soviet–Eastern European economic relations interact with Sino-Soviet economic relations? Unfortunately, we shall have to leave this issue unexplored in the present chapter.

## Other Unexamined Questions

Still other intriguing matters will have to be left undiscussed. They deserve, however, to be at least aired in passing. One issue of importance is the current PRC practice of separating the right to use farmland by individual households from the right of alienation (through sale, mortgage, or inheritance) of land assigned to a household by the state. This practice seems to be one under examination by Soviet leaders.[14] The issue of property rights may come up also if direct foreign investments develop further in the PRC. After all, property rights are tightly intertwined with the law of contract.

Another issue that deserves more thoughtful analysis is the potential complementarity between emerging Sino-Soviet economic relations and recent PRC announcements on the locational and regional aspects of the Seventh Five-Year Plan. The latter points to a return to certain regional priorities corresponding to the plans advocated by Liu Shao-ch'i and his lieutenants (including at that time Teng Hsiao-p'ing). These ideas were predicated upon cooperation with the Soviet Union, not long-term hostility.

It may be fitting to end this chapter by pointing to the "special economic zones" (SEZs) as a case in which the problems of balance of payments, partial economic liberalization, and faulty expectations are all mixed up. The SEZs of Kwangtung and Fukien have been set up essentially (1) to increase net foreign exchange earnings, (2) to induce the inflow of foreign capital, technology and management, (3) to provide a demonstration of how the market economy might work in a controlled atmosphere, and (4) to expand contact between the PRC and the outside world. Quite apart from the fact that the investors from Hong Kong and other countries interested in investing in these zones so far cannot really provide much new technology while those who might supply it do not find the infrastructure and labor supply attractive enough for them to invest, the SEZ experience has brought several issues to the front. First, the exportable products the SEZ can supply, such as textiles and apparel, are faced with the type of import barriers discussed earlier in this chapter. Other goods that the SEZ can produce unfortunately cannot be sold abroad because of poor quality. When the SEZ producers turn to the PRC domestic market, they defeat the purpose of making the SEZ a major foreign exchange earner for the country. It is not at all clear what lessons the SEZ can offer on the nature and degree of economic liberalization PRC planners would be willing to adopt for the entire country. It does appear, however, that both money and people tend to gravitate toward these economically and otherwise freer zones from the rest of mainland China.

All these issues lead us to the larger questions unanswered by the PRC—the fundamental nature of its future economic system and the country's longer-term internal as well as external political orientation.

## Notes

1. See, for instance, Jan S. Prybyla, "Economic Problems of Communism: A Case Study of China," *Asian Survey*, vol. 22, no. 12, December 1982, pp. 1217–1234; also "China's Economic Development: From Mao to Market," *Problems of Communism*, January–February, 1986, pp. 21–38. Chu-yuan Cheng, "Economic Development in Taiwan and Mainland China," *Asian Affairs: An American Review*, spring 1983, pp. 60–86. Many of Cheng's more recent writings have also appeared in Chinese.

2. See Yuan-li Wu, "The Rocky Road of Beijing's Economic Reform: Can Trial and Error Lead to Dynamic Equilibrium?" *Journal of Northeast Asian Studies*, fall 1985, vol. 4, no. 3, pp. 3–11.

3. See Paul Marer, "Economic Reform in Hungary," in Morris Bornstein (ed.), *Comparative Economic Systems*, 5th ed. (Homewood, Ill.: Richard D. Irwin, 1985), pp. 282–283.

4. All that it takes for the previously mentioned effect to be felt is for the decentralized sector to be quicker and more alert than the more ponderous centralized bureaucracy. See also Yuan-li Wu, *Planners and Entrepreneurs in the PRC: Sources of Systemic Instability and their Political Implications* (Stanford, Calif.: Hoover Institution Reprint, Series No. 47, 1981).

5. ChangTzu-chien and Sung Hsu-wen, "Lueh-lun wai-tzu t'i-chih ts'u-hsien chung-ta pien-ke chih-chi-ti tuei-ch'e" (On the Proper Policy in Utilizing Foreign Capital at a Time of Systemic Change), *Kuo-chi Mo-i Wen-t i* (International Trade Journal), no. 4, 1985, p. 9.

6. See the abstract of the Seventh Five-Year Plan (1986–1990) in *Renmin Ribao* (overseas edition), San Francisco, April 15, 1986, pp. 1–4. We abstract here from the fact that some Chinese goods are not tradable even under a hypothetical, free-trade regime.

7. See Marer, "Economic Reform in Hungary."

8. The PRC was actually required to submit to less relative reductions of its textile quota. The Thurmond-Jenkins bill was adopted by both houses but vetoed by the president. The House later (in August 1986) failed in its override attempt. The bill sought to reduce the import quotas assigned to Hong Kong, Korea, and Taiwan much more than for the PRC.

9. Wu, "The Rocky Road of Beijing's Economic Reform."

10. Bank of America reported in May 1986 that it had increased its branch banks in mainland China to three. They are located in Beijing, Canton, and Shanghai.

11. Coal export can only partially compensate for the loss of export revenue from oil.

12. See note 6.

13. Ibid.

14. Gorbachev's address at the Twenty-seventh Soviet Communist Party Congress.

# PART SIX

# Science and Technology

# 30

---

# The Soviet Union's Evolving Perceptions of China's Science and Technology

*Leo A. Orleans*

## Soviet Research and Publications on China's Science and Technology

Science and technology represent a prime motive force in the development of a nation. It is logical, therefore, that anyone interested in a nation's progress and potential will analyze and evaluate its scientific and technical base. Because the People's Republic of China (PRC) was viewed as an enemy, real or potential, in the 1950s and 1960s, its scientific and technical establishment (small as it was) was closely followed by U.S. government analysts, as well as a handful of academics, who found such research both important and a challenge to scholarly ingenuity.

Since the death of Mao Zedong in 1976, and especially since 1978, U.S. concern with Chinese science and technology has accelerated rapidly. Beijing's almost absolute reliance on science and technology as the primary force in the policy of Four Modernizations and the simultaneous sharp turn to the West for technology and know-how have stimulated the interest of U.S. commercial, industrial, governmental, and academic representatives in China's scientific and technical capabilities and potential. China's search for an appropriate science policy, its ability to absorb advanced technology, the constraints it faces owing to shortages in scientific and technical personnel, its budgetary problems, and a host of other related issues are closely followed, analyzed, and discussed at meetings and in print.

Soviet interest in Chinese science and technology, on the other hand, reflects the very different genesis of Sino-Soviet relations. When the People's Republic of China was established in 1949, Moscow saw an emerging socialist nation which, after years of war and revolution, required massive assistance for rebuilding the economy and expanding and improving the educational system. Moscow was eager to provide general support and advice to a government that was perceived to be, if not a satellite, then a close, long-term ally. Motivated by both ideological and strategic considerations, the

Soviet Union did indeed provide China with extraordinary and broad-based support during the first decade. Science and technology, as important forces in modernization, also required Soviet inputs. Soviet involvement in Chinese science was, for the most part, very direct and practical in nature. It also included the direct involvement of hundreds of Soviet specialists, who were instrumental in molding the science policy by participating intimately in drafting and reviewing scientific and engineering plans, structure, and performance. Since the Soviets viewed Chinese science and technology from the ground floor, they were not subjects for "study" in Soviet research institutes as they were in the United States. Consequently, there was no reason to write much about science and technology; the Russians and Chinese were brothers under socialism.

Not unlike U.S. science journals of the 1970s, Soviet science journals in the 1950s included trip and work reports by scientists and engineers, describing what they saw, with whom they spoke, and the state of the art in a particular field or subfield of science and technology. The differences, however, are very apparent. Although there was a tendency among some U.S. scientists to overstate the Chinese case during the scientific tourism period of the early 1970s, even so most of the trip reports strived for objectivity and presented both the pros and cons of Chinese science. But as long as China "adhered to the socialist course in scientific development," Soviet scientists could not express any critical comments even as the schism between the two countries started to develop. There was indeed scientific substance in most of the reports, but they also never failed to praise the competence of Chinese scientists, their willingness to share knowledge, and the bright future for scientific exchanges and cooperation between the two fraternal nations. Thus what was written in the 1950s was, for the most part, descriptive, rather than analytical or critical. It was so ordained.

In 1960 and 1961, however, the decline and virtual break in relations between the two countries resulted in a drastic reduction in Soviet publications throughout the rest of that decade. Books and articles that did appear were virtually devoid of substance, focusing almost entirely on unrestrained attacks on Mao's adventurism and his misuse and perversion of Marxist-Leninist theories and doctrines, and occasionally including highly polemical analyses of developments in China. Only a few sinologists were recruited to participate in these diatribes and, given the national mood, there probably was no objective research being conducted even behind closed doors. As for science and technology, with access to Chinese scientific institutions barred and acquisition of scientific and technical journals denied, Soviet scientists lost interest in China and turned their attention to their own more immediate scientific concerns. As with most U.S. scientists who visited China in the 1970s, China became an interesting interlude in their professional careers, but certainly not a lifetime concern.

By the end of the Cultural Revolution (1969), Soviet leaders had abandoned hope that common sense would finally prevail in China and that Beijing would return to the socialist camp under the benign tutelage of Moscow.

It was time to supplement the propaganda against Chinese policies with some solid analytical work. But this could not be done quickly. Surprising as it might seem, the Soviet Union had some outstanding scholars working on Chinese literature, history, language, culture, and so on, but precious few individuals, especially in the academic community, were experienced in analytical research on contemporary China. The new emphasis on China studies, proclaimed by Leonid Brezhnev in 1969, required both the training of new students in Chinese political and economic affairs and the reassignment of scholars in humanities who were fluent in the Chinese language to the study of political, economic, and social conditions in China. Progress was relatively slow. It was not only a matter of training and retraining; it also took many years to make the transition from polemics to substantive research—a gradual process that was evident throughout the 1970s. Toward the end of the decade, aside from the prescribed digs and scoffs at Beijing's false doctrines and a standard set of seeming misinterpretations, most of the Soviet writings on China showed a marked improvement in objectivity of analysis and overall scholarship.

Not receiving significant Soviet attention, especially when compared with U.S. research, were, and continue to be, the fields of science and technology. When appropriate, they are discussed in writings on various economic sectors, they may be mentioned in books and articles on education, and sometimes they are covered in connection with other topics under study. But the number of Soviets who make Chinese science and technology the central topic of their published research is small indeed.

The irony is that while we may be surprised at the comparative neglect of this important subject in the USSR, Soviet China scholars and embassy officials have wondered aloud (especially prior to normalization) why so much time and effort are devoted in the United States to China's activities in science and technology. They are aware of the political significance of scientific contacts between the United States and China, but there is a tone of sincerity in their question, What can the world's most advanced nation learn from the backward Chinese?[1] Although this same question is often asked in the United States as well, the Soviets' incredulity is clearly influenced by their own experience in China in the 1950s. Radically different from what the Chinese would say, the Soviets remind you of how little was received in return for the advanced technology and know-how they imparted to the Chinese, of their frustrations in working with Beijing, and of the unreliability of Chinese promises and friendship. Furthermore, Soviet lack of interest in Chinese science and technology is a reflection of more than twenty years of limited economic and commercial relations and, until very recently, the total absence of any firsthand contact between Soviet and Chinese scientists and engineers.

In fact, considering the Soviets' sour experience with their "ally" in the 1950s, their low esteem toward China's science and technology, and the limited direct contact between the two scientific establishments since then, a question might well arise as to why they follow Chinese scientific and technological developments at all? Soviet interest in Chinese science was first aroused when U.S. scientific delegations started to shuttle in and out of China in the mid-1970s, and continued to peak with the gradual progression from concepts and ideas, to machines and factories, to ever more sophisticated dual-purpose and technology. Consequently, while writing on Chinese science and technology per se are still rare, Soviet economists, political analysts, military specialists, and a host of other watchers of China and the United States closely monitor those U.S. commercial, professional, and military contacts and activities that involve the flow of scientific and technical goods and know-how to China. In other words, Moscow's primary concern here is the Washington connection and what it may mean in terms of an expanded Chinese military capability. Obviously, the view from Moscow is that virtually all scientific and technical research in China is related directly or indirectly to China's military needs and global ambitions and, that being the case, the lively intercourse in science and technology between China and the United States (and other countries as well) is directly supportive of Chinese military goals. The fact that so many foreign observers considered the Soviet fear of Chinese expansionism as unrealistic and that there is a touch of paranoia in Moscow's views of China's policies and intents are incidental and beyond the scope of this paper.[2] Of importance here are the sincerity and persistence of Soviet convictions.

Since the 1980s, Soviet writings on all aspects of Chinese development—including science and technology—have taken a giant qualitative leap. In fact, Western analysts studying Chinese domestic developments might be surprised to find Soviet publications to be interesting, perceptive, and not nearly as prone to ideological tampering as books and articles dealing with foreign affairs, which continue to be much more polemic. To the regret of many Soviet scholars who are usually intimately familiar with Western literature on contemporary China, their own names and works are, for the most part, unknown in the West.

The sections that follow are based almost exclusively on Soviet sources and therefore present the various aspects of Chinese science and technology from the Moscow perspective. It is balanced only through occasional commentary rather than documentation.

## The Decade of Collaboration

The Soviets' intimate collaboration with China in the 1950s and the subsequent traumatic break left an indelible scar on the psyche of the Soviet nation. Consequently, in order to understand the present attitudes of both political leaders and research analysts in the Soviet Union, it is important to understand the characteristics of the collaboration that existed between the Soviet Union and China in science and technology, and how that period is now evaluated by the Soviets. Only such a review can fully explain why the Soviets are still unable to overcome the hurt, dismay, and disappointment they experienced in China and why they continue to lament Mao's ingratitude in cutting off the hand that "fed" China and, even worse, how he not only belittled their efforts but flatly denied that the Soviet Union played any significant role in China's economic development.

There is no doubt that in the case of China, the Soviet Union took Lenin's principle of fraternal mutual assistance literally. Indeed, they acted on the precept that scientific and technical cooperation between socialist countries "convincingly and fully show the brotherly, selfless character of relations between these countries," and that, thanks to this cooperation, "national achievements and experience of individual countries in the field of scientific knowledge and technical progress become the practical achievements of all socialist nations."[3] What follows is an overview of how the Soviets describe their assistance to China in science and technology.[4]

Although China was not a member of the Council for Mutual Economic Assistance (CMEA), the Soviet Union based its economic relations with China on the principles adopted by the socialist countries within the CMEA framework and applied to China all the favorable terms and privileges ensuing from those principles. The Soviets claim that "it is probably impossible to name a field of science and technology in which the Soviet Union did not share with China, free or at very favorable conditions, its advanced achievements and rich experience"—even long before the first agreement on cooperation in science and technology, which was not signed until October 12, 1954. Two other agreements followed: one signed on January 18, 1958, and the other on June 19, 1961—much later than anyone familiar with Sino-Soviet relations at the time might have imagined. In addition to these broad intergovernmental agreements negotiated within the framework of the Soviet-Chinese Commission for Scientific and Technological Cooperation, about twenty Soviet ministries and government departments and approximately 160 research and development organizations maintained independent contacts with some ninety research and development organizations in China. It is not clear whether these figures include the institutes of the academies of sciences, which also negotiated numerous agreements. In many instances even individual factories, laboratories, and other organizations of the two countries established direct contacts. To those who have followed the evolution of scientific and technical contacts between China and the United States as of the late 1970s, the pattern must appear all too familiar.

There is no reason to doubt the impressive statistics published by the Soviets with regard to the specifics of these intergovernment agreements in science and technology, and, although in themselves these figures would be of little interest to most readers, without them the range and magnitude of Soviet assistance to China could not be fully appreciated.

As part of the agreements, which encompassed some 15,000 topics, the Soviet Union turned over to China 14,915 sets (more than 150,000 titles) of scientific and technical documentation, including 1,408 sets of designs for capital construction, 5,513 sets of blueprints for machines and equipment, 1,536 sets of technical documents, 4,933 sets of departmental technical documents, and 1,525 sets of documents from research institutes. In addition,

102 expert evaluations were made of research projects carried out at Chinese scientific institutions, and 4,261 sets of curricula of Soviet educational establishments were passed on to China, as well as 375 samples of scientific instruments and apparatuses and 4,602 "state standards" of the Soviet Union. Finally, the USSR Academy of Sciences transferred to the Chinese Academy of Sciences documentation for several thousand scientific and technical topics—mostly free of charge.

Soviet assistance in the construction of industrial projects extended well beyond the schism between the two countries. From 1950 to 1966 a total of 256 industrial projects were built or reconstructed with Soviet assistance. In connection with these projects the Soviet Union turned over, free of charge, licenses, blueprints of machinery and equipment of the latest types, descriptions of technological processes, and instructions and rules for the operation of machinery and equipment to China's technical libraries, which also received hundreds of thousands of books from the USSR. Among the major projects completed with Soviet participation was China's first atomic reactor and cyclotron. The agreement for this project was signed in April 1955, the reactor was completed in September 1957, and, according to the Soviets, it is this nuclear plant that started China's extensive research in nuclear physics. And it was in connection with this project that Chinese scientists—for several years numbering 140—trained and worked at the Atomic Energy Institute in Dubna.[5] The Soviets regard their assistance in the nuclear field to be the most eloquent testimony of their good will toward China.

A parallel phenomenon was the movement of large numbers of scientific and technical personnel between the two countries. There are some variations in figures, but it safe to say that some 8,000 to 10,000 Soviet specialists were sent to China between 1950 and 1960. East European countries sent another 1,200 specialists to train and to relate their experience to the Chinese.[6] More precise figures are given for the high-level personnel. Under the intergovernmental agreements, between 1950 and 1962 the Soviet Union sent 868 prominent Soviet scientists, including world-renowned members of the Academy of Sciences, to work on major scientific and technical problems and projects, to help introduce the latest achievements, to pass on advanced methods, and to act as consultants and lecturers. The USSR Academy of Sciences sent 722 scientists to China to work on joint scientific problems, to participate in research and scientific expeditions, to help draw up research programs and plans for individual scientific institutes, and, most important, to help China in the drafting of the Twelve-Year Plan for Science and Technology. Other thousands of Soviet specialists were sent to China under agreements between ministries, institutions, and enterprises.

There is no reason to doubt the number of scientists sent to China, but apparently it is inappropriate to lump them all in the "prominent" category, as the Soviets are prone to do. According to M. A. Klochko, a Russian chemist who defected to Canada in 1961 after two assignments in China, the Soviet authorities viewed the state of science in China as similar to that in some of the countries of Central Africa, and therefore they were reluctant to send top scientists to China unless they were requested by name. Nevertheless, Chinese scientists and technicians had great expectations of Soviet specialists, and every Soviet specialist was expected "to be a sort of magician, capable of giving them the one current answer to all sorts of complex problems in pure and applied science in a few minutes."[7]

From 1952 to April 15, 1963, 522 Chinese specialists underwent training in the research institutes of the Soviet Academy of Sciences, and of the 318 who were enrolled in formal postgraduate programs, 206 completed all the requirements and received graduate degrees.

Even more impressive—albeit confusing—are the numbers of students, scholars, and other specialists who went to the Soviet Union. Between 1950 and 1960 more than 38,000 Chinese "students and trainees" were accepted by leading Soviet industrial enterprises, research centers, and institutions of higher education. Between 1949 and 1966 (once again, note the date of termination) about 10,000 Chinese engineers, technicians, and workers and more than 11,000 students—at both undergraduate and graduate levels—completed their course of study or training in the USSR. An additional 8,173 Chinese traveled to the Soviet Union for practical on-the-job training in connection with the industrial enterprises that were being built with Soviet assistance.

L. V. Filatov estimated that the cost of Soviet scientific and technical assistance (broadly defined) under special intergovernmental agreements was about US$14 billion (using the 1978 rate of exchange)—a figure that is considerably higher than any Western estimate. Whatever the value of this help, what the estimate does not fully show is the intimacy of Soviet involvement and the extent to which Soviet influence permeated the system. It is not simply that the Chinese adopted the Soviet model in organizing their scientific establishment and in structuring their production system; the influence extended still further, to such intangibles as style, attitude, and temper. And why not? Until 1958 Soviet scientists and specialists acted as advisers at every stage of remolding Chinese science, technology, and economy. They participated in organizing plants and laboratories, and made significant inputs into major national documents, such as the First Five-Year Plan (1953–1957) and the Twelve-Year Plan for the Development of Science and Technology (1956–1967).

In the case of the Twelve-Year Plan, Chinese scientists worked together with their Soviet counterparts. After approval by the Chinese Communist Party, the plans were sent to the Soviet Union in the fall of 1957 where they were examined, evaluated, and discussed with Chinese scientists. It was then decided that almost 100 problems could be handled jointly by the scientists of both countries.[8] But after hundreds of Soviet scientists spent tens of thousands of hours on the plan, scientific activities started to slow down in 1957 and, as the Great Leap Forward overwhelmed China, they "came to a complete standstill in 1959." However, Soviet efforts in relation to the Twelve-Year Plan were not altogether wasted. In the mid-1970s the

Soviets noted that the Ten-Year Plan for Science and Technology, which was introduced in 1963 and interrupted by the Cultural Revolution, incorporated many parts of the original plan; and in the 1980s they wrote that even the 1978–1985 plan for the development of science and technology (announced in March 1978) contained many of the recommendations included in the original plan drawn up with so much Soviet assistance.[9] The claim does not seem farfetched: Certainly most of the priorities remained the same and most of the long-term goals were still to be achieved. Furthermore, despite the well-known political permutations, the basic model in science, in research, and (to a lesser extent) in education that had been developed in the 1950s held through most of the 1970s—and how solidly it was implanted can be seen, in part, by the difficulties the Chinese reformers are having in the 1980s in making long-sought changes.

As already suggested, whether motivated by graciousness—a gentleman does not advertise the gifts or loans he makes to a less fortunate friend— or habitual secrecy, in the 1950s the Soviets were extremely low-key about the help they were providing. In fact, there seem to have been more "thank yous" from the Chinese than "look what we are doing" from the Soviets. The details of the aid given China did not become the dominant theme of Soviet writings until Mao spurned their advances and actually denied that the support provided during the course of the ten-year affair was at all significant. In one official letter to the Central Committee of the Communist Party, dated February 29, 1964, for example, "Peking alleged that no such thing as Soviet aid to China had ever existed—there had only been ordinary 'trade operations.'"[10] Is there any wonder that, frustrated and hurt, the spurned lover had to tell all and wistfully express the belief that the "gratitude to the Soviet people for the disinterested help they provided is ever engraved on the heart of the true Chinese patriot."[11] And curiously, even in the 1980s, a week seldom passes that the Soviet newspapers and radio commentators do not find occasion to review the generosity of Soviet assistance to their Chinese compatriots.

## Growing Tensions and Soviet Withdrawal

On the basis of materials published both in the Soviet Union and in China in the 1950s, there was little to indicate the existence of any strains between the two countries. Although it was clear that China's Great Leap policies in 1958 and 1959 ran contrary to Soviet advice, the optimists in Moscow believed that only truth could come from debates between like-minded individuals so that whatever dissatisfaction and bickering took place was not vented in public pronouncements. But given the radical nature of the Great Leap, "truth," apparently, was not forthcoming, and the pullout of Soviet scientific and technical advisers in the summer of 1960 came as a surprise even to specialists who watched Sino-Soviet relations closely.

As with the shrouded Soviet assistance to China, so too the problems and disagreements between the two countries were revealed only gradually over the course of subsequent years. The more serious strains apparently started to surface as early as 1957, when the Great Leap Forward was still a gleam in Mao's eyes, and intensified as Beijing started to implement the Leap policies. According to Moscow, when the Maoist regime embarked on its "adventurist proposals which ran counter to technological standards," Soviet specialists "were derided as bearers of 'technological backwardness' and 'conservatism' and their suggestions and recommendations were ignored." Soviet specialists were treated with mistrust and suspicion; even "their belongings were secretly searched and they were subjected to various forms of harassment." Under these circumstances, the Soviet government, on several occasions, raised the question of whether it was not time to recall the specialists. In response, the Chinese "invariably requested that the Soviet specialists be permitted to continue their work in China." Here it should be noted that the claimed mistreatment of Soviet specialists in China need not contradict the warm and friendly experiences of Soviet scientists mentioned previously. It is in the nature of the discipline that visiting scientists—especially guests of the Chinese Academy of Sciences—could establish sincere friendships with their colleagues, while an engineer, for example, responsible for helping construct or operate a factory could find a totally different, even hostile, atmosphere.

To continue with the Soviet version of the story—a version the Chinese vehemently deny—despite Chinese official insistence that the specialists remain, the situation continued to deteriorate.[12] Thus, since the Maoist leadership refused to create "normal conditions" for the working Soviet specialists, and since the latter were not permitted to argue against anti-Leninist views of the Maoists (apparently a restriction that extended to personal contacts), Moscow decided that, to prevent serious clashes, its only option was to recall all the scientists, engineers, and other specialists in China. A note to that effect was sent to Beijing on July 16, 1960. No response was forthcoming, but when the specialists started to leave, according to the Soviets, only then did Beijing formally request that they remain.

As might be expected, the sequence of events during the couple of years prior to the Soviet pullout is a major point of contention between Moscow and Beijing. The Soviets point to the period between 1958 and 1960 to prove that the Chinese did not want Soviet specialists, who had become "a source of embarrassment" to Beijing. The Chinese, on the other hand, point to the request by their Foreign Ministry that the specialists remain, to prove their contention that the USSR created long-lasting enmity by suddenly, and against Beijing's wishes, recalling their specialists. The Soviets also ask, How could we be responsible for adversely affecting China's economic plans, when even the term "economic planning" is a complete misnomer for the Great Leap period and when Soviet specialists had absolutely nothing to do with backyard furnaces, the emphasis on traditional industries, and other "half-baked ideas" introduced by the Maoists? Furthermore, even though the Soviets pulled out the specialists, they had every intention of abiding by the other commitments until the Chinese side invalidated them.

First, on October 31, 1960, China introduced a proposal revising all existing agreements and protocols on scientific and technical cooperation. And just a few months later, on February 12, 1961, the Chinese submitted the draft of a letter invalidating not only the government-signed umbrella agreements and protocols on science and technology, but all other agreements concluded between the ministries, departments, and individual institutions of the two nations. Some Soviet media are even more blunt about China's culpability, claiming that "the Chinese Government *demanded* that the Soviet Government drastically reduce all economic, scientific and technical cooperation agreements and contracts" and that "the Chinese leaders even uttered such things as 'There is no need for China to develop scientific and technical relations with the Soviet Union.'"[13]

There was another aspect of relations with the Chinese that apparently has bothered Moscow but that, for obvious reasons, was not known to outsiders at the time. And once again the scenario bears some resemblance to the postnormalization U.S. relations with the Chinese. Soviet organizations and returning scientists charged that starting in the late 1950s China expressed more and more interest in new secret accomplishments of the Soviet Union, especially in the fields of military technology and science. Not only did Chinese scholars in the Soviet Union endeavor to become involved in secret projects, but in many instances the Chinese also attempted to change the lecture topics of Soviet scientists visiting China, urging them to speak on subjects which would reveal secret information. Even after the pullout of specialists, at the meeting of the Sino-Soviet Commission in September 1961, the Chinese representatives insisted on changes in the topics to be covered under the scientific-technical cooperation agreement, attempting to include subjects concerned with the newest technology on secret scientific and technological research in nuclear and defense industries, rocket technology, space flight, and the like.[14]

All these differences did not in themselves terminate the relations in science and technology in the early 1960s, but, as the Soviets saw the situation, the word "cooperation" no longer applied. This trend became especially evident in a variety of cooperative research projects. The Chinese initiated a policy of "blanket secrecy" about everything pertaining to China, from their natural resources to their borders. Among the examples reported is China's cancellation of the planned cooperative research on the geology of Xinjiang.[15] First they prevented Soviet scientists from continuing their paleontological expedition to Western Gansu, and later they closed off all access to this area, which had the most promising digs. Furthermore, China forbade Soviet scientists to publish joint research if it included the reproduction of maps—a restriction the Soviets blame on China's desire to change the national borders between the two countries.[16]

After so many years of virtually free access, as of August 24, 1961, Soviet citizens were no longer able to visit Chinese factories, research institutes, and other organizations where scientific and technical work was carried on. This drastic turnaround extended to the acquisition of publications. In the early 1960s there was an overall reduction in the number of titles published in China, and many of the journals in print were withdrawn from public sale. These restrictions applied to the Soviet Union as well, and its embassy in Beijing could neither purchase nor otherwise acquire these publications. Furthermore, the Chinese made it clear that they were not interested in exchanging information about research under way in academic or industrial facilities. The Soviets suggest two reasons for China's secrecy in science and technology: first, the Chinese were not doing anything of any significance, and second (a related reason), the Chinese scientists were afraid of criticism.

But although the situation continued to deteriorate and by the end of 1962 trade between the two countries dropped to 5 percent of what it was in 1959, the Soviets claim that they never ceased their efforts to improve relations. The Chinese, however, rejected virtually all advances. For example, they rejected most of the research themes proposed by the Soviet Union under the auspices of the Soviet-Chinese Commission for Scientific and Technological Cooperation, which was never disbanded. In 1963 the Chinese accepted only eight of twenty-three invitations from the Soviet Academy of Sciences to participate in scientific conferences and symposia; at the same time, no Soviet scientist was invited to any conference in China.[17] In May 1964, the Chinese embassy in Moscow sent an official communication to the Ministry of Foreign Affairs slandering Soviet universities and professors, questioning the need for Chinese students still in Moscow to attend classes and pass examinations, and, in effect, attempting to annul a 1952 agreement stipulating that Chinese students would have to abide by all the rules applicable to their Soviet counterparts.[18] And in April 1965, China did not even respond to an invitation to participate with other socialist countries in space exploration.[19] If all this is true, as it appears to be, it is not easy to argue with Moscow's conclusion that the Chinese leaders sacrificed progress in science and technology in order to pursue their anti-Soviet goals.

Such conditions of course precluded objective research in general, and developments in science and technology during the 1960s are hardly ever mentioned in Soviet writings. One of the very few (if not the only) exception is a chapter on the subject by V. I. Akimov.[20] He correctly points out that although Chinese sciences were greatly weakened by the end of the Great Leap, with the assistance of know-how from capitalist countries, signs of recovery were becoming evident between 1962 and 1965. While the main emphasis was on science for industrial development, military priorities were uppermost in the minds of Mao and his colleagues during those years. In mentioning the Ten-Year Plan for the Development of Science and Technology, which was promulgated in 1963, Akimov does not refer to its wide-ranging goals, but states flatly that it was directed at the production of intercontinental ballistic missiles with nuclear warheads by 1972. Expenditures on scientific research between 1962 and 1964 were said to equal more than US$2 billion, of which "no less than three-fourths went to the nuclear/rocket programs." To add credibility to these figures, Akimov cites "foreign experts"—surely more impressive to Soviet readers, who have no way of knowing how broad is the range of all foreign estimates on China, especially for the mysterious 1960s. And when Beijing started to push self-sufficiency and urged the country to "break the chains of foreign science and develop its own Chinese road to science and technology," Akimov was very skeptical, concluding, "In this clearly nationalistic call, it is possible to see a tacit admission of the fact that Chinese science and technology depend on foreign achievements and have few of their own which are original and not borrowed."

Having focused almost exclusively on the growing disruptions in science and technology, it is well to remind ourselves of the obvious: that these disputes—as with the border issues later in the decade—were but symptoms of more basic problems beginning to emerge between the two countries. Some of the main issues were deep-rooted in history, while the more apparent ones sprung from ideological and political differences relating to world revolution, coexistence, the leadership of the communist world—all of which were periodically accentuated by such events as the Cuban missile crisis, the Soviet invasion of Czechoslovakia, the Cultural Revolution, and so forth. The intensity of the 1960s controversy was, at the time, difficult for many people in the West to believe, and it was not uncommon to read statements by both politicians and scholars to the effect that the border clashes "were premeditated," or that "the statements issued by Moscow and Peking are in reality a carefully contrived means to further their common international victory."

## Backing into Concern over China's Science and Technology

The most militant and vociferous years of the Cultural Revolution waned as the 1960s ended, but by then the Soviets had to accept the unhappy fact that the "good old days" of the 1950s in Sino-Soviet relations were gone and China would not return to the fold, as they had hoped for so many years. To make matters worse, what had started out as seemingly innocent Ping-Pong diplomacy gradually progressed to an ever more complex relationship between Washington and Beijing.

Obviously, the improvement of relations between their two adversaries did not please the Soviet leadership, but to the world, the oft-repeated official line was that the Soviet government has "always favored Sino-U.S. normalization so long as it takes place on the basis of peaceful coexistence principles and so helps to create favorable conditions for socialist construction of China."[21] Contrary to this expressed position, the Soviet Union never believed that the goals of rapprochement were compatible with peaceful coexistence, and they were delighted to find in Henry Kissinger's memoirs (and elsewhere) a most authoritative source for their apprehension. Kissinger "repeatedly points out," they say, "that negotiations between Washington and Beijing were directed against the Soviet Union, reflecting the geopolitical reality stemming from concerns about growing Soviet power." They then conclude that in the process of pursuing rapprochement, the United States is using economic relations and cooperation in science and technology "to bring China closer to the system of international capitalism . . . which will further deform the socialist foundations of China."[22] As for the Chinese, rapprochement with the United States provides them with the "trappings of globalism and the status of a 'superpower.'"

## Motive Forces Behind the U.S.-China Policy

In interpreting the role science and technology have played in the evolution of relations between the United States and China, Soviet analysts tend to turn to U.S. sources. But although there is much factual data in their descriptions, by the time they pass the information through an ideological centrifuge built into the anatomy of every Soviet observer, sprinkle it with the prescribed jargon, and place it into a specious context, even interpretations that approach validity are difficult to swallow and digest.

The forces that have caused a shift in American policies toward China are carefully analyzed by many Soviet authors, but one of the most fascinating discussions of the politics behind these policies is presented in a book by Ye. P. Bazhanov, a foreign service official who spent many years in the San Francisco consulate of the Soviet Union.[23] He details the role of Congress and its individual members in both opposing and supporting closer ties with China, pointing out that the more conservative members who came in with the election of President Ronald Reagan were much more likely to "use China against peaceful socialism." He discusses the strong pro- and anti-Beijing positions taken by bureaucrats in Washington's foreign policy establishment, the differences between the Defense and State departments, and how the final decision was made to "play the China card." He also candidly admits that the Soviet invasion of Afghanistan provided a significant push to improving U.S.-China relations. Bazhanov assesses the role of the media, concluding that it cooperated with the military-industrial complex corporations and thereby brainwashed the American public. He does not explain, however, how the "liberal media" found itself in bed with the capitalists. Bazhanov also concludes that China scholars had a significant influence on U.S. policy. He points out that in the 1960s there was an explosion in the training of highly qualified China specialists in the United States. In the 1970s and 1980s they became bureaucrats, consultants, testifiers at congressional hearings, writers of articles, and employees of large corporations, and in these capacities sinologists played a key role in molding U.S. policies in favor of rapprochement.

Since our focus here is science and technology, it is appropriate to consider in somewhat more detail Bazhanov's contention that it is U.S. big business that has played and continues to play the most prominent role in U.S.-China relations—a unanimous view of Soviet observers. Although some corporations resisted any changes toward the People's Republic because of close ties with Taiwan, such resistance was not well organized, and by the late 1960s an ever-growing number of financial and industrial groups were pushing Washington to change its strategy toward Beijing. Once President

Richard Nixon took the initiative and established relations with China, he opened the floodgates of support, and even the most reactionary elements of the military-industrial complex decided to rely on his "political sense" in relation to the China question. Progress was rapid. The White House initiated the establishment of the U.S.-China Trade Council, Washington-based bureaucrats traveled around the country lecturing businessmen interested in pursuing trade with China, and soon tremendous competition developed among thousands of large, medium-size, and small companies, each striving to beat the other to the Chinese market.

At the same time, the Chinese wined and dined top business leaders and congressmen, dangling before them long lists of potential purchases: aircraft, ships, factories, agricultural machinery, communications equipment, and more. Beijing also "threw in bits of information" about vast, newly discovered oil deposits on the continental shelf and in Xinjiang. These were mentioned not only to lure U.S. capital to China, but also to neutralize the interests of Americans in investing in the development of oil and gas resources in the eastern regions of the USSR. The "Chinese propagandists" also attempted to convince small and medium-size firms that the Soviet Union is very negligent toward "little fish" and, unlike China, cannot meet the special requirements of small enterprises.

By 1974 the initial spurt of enthusiasm on the part of U.S. businessmen was dampened by obstacles placed by the State Department, the Atomic Energy Commission, the Pentagon (which insisted on a complete embargo on all technology which could have "military application"), and COCOM (NATO's informal coordinating committee for the licensing of exports to communist nations). A variety of contractual problems created by the Chinese further strained relations. Because of disillusionment with China—which in the mid-1970s seemed to be saying to the businessmen, "Don't call us, we'll call you"—much of the capital went to Taiwan.

The slowdown in the process of rapprochement, which gave the Soviets reason to breathe a sigh of relief, was only temporary. Many conservative and reactionary elements of the business world, connected to the military-industrial complex, started to look to China not so much as a potential commercial partner, but rather as an extremely important military-strategic partner. The top echelons of the monopolists were also concerned about losing out to other capitalist competitors on military technology sales. In pressuring the White House to permit the export of dual-purpose technology, the military-industrial monopolists argued that such sales would not be disadvantageous to the United States: China will buy obsolete technology, and the gap between the two countries will only increase. The arguments were successful. First President Gerald R. Ford and then President Jimmy Carter gave in to monopolists, but the momentum of the rapprochement was really resumed only after National Security Adviser Zbigniew Brzezinski's China trip in May 1978. Even though by 1979 more than 1,000 U.S. corporations from virtually every economic field had succeeded in making contacts with China, continued pressures by commercial, industrial, and financial circles on the executive branch and on Congress caused President Carter and, later, President Reagan to further liberalize trade with China.

Despite problems and disillusionment on both sides of the Pacific the ties between China and the United States strengthened. The conservative and anti-Soviet military-industrial corporations have not only provided China with ever more sophisticated military technology, but also created a climate in which the American public has come to accept as completely logical the notion that China is a potential military ally of the West—an idea that would have been inconceivable just a half dozen years earlier. But since the Soviets believe that the United States backed into its China policy under pressure from big business, they also visualize the possibility that if the commercial appetite of corporations is not satisfied and if big business finds China relations unprofitable, the same corporations that got the United States into China will get it out of China.

*Science and Technology:*
*The Mortar of Rapprochement*

The Soviets believe that in establishing scientific and technical relations with China, the United States has been using a well-defined pattern.[24] Washington clearly understands what a revolution in science and technology means to a developing country and is aware of the close interrelationship that exists between the development of science, technology, and education and the country's military-economic potential. The Soviets say that in return for permitting these countries to use the fruits of American inventions, the United States expects economic and political concessions that gradually tie these nations to the U.S. sphere of influence. This is exactly the pattern that was followed in establishing ties with China. Although there were no official relations between Beijing and Washington in the early 1970s, "on the initiative of nongovernmental organizations, but with the silent approval and support of both governments," relations in science and technology served, first, as an instrument in normalizing diplomatic relations and, second, as a means of applying pressure on the Soviet Union. But although the use of science and technology as a tool of U.S. diplomacy was spelled out from the start in the Shanghai Communiqué, because of the low level of China's science and technology (especially right after the Cultural Revolution), Washington had to stimulate the interest of the American scientific community artificially in those early years.

The Soviets were, of course, essentially correct in their low evaluation of Chinese science in the first half of the 1970s. Although some U.S. observers managed to find merit in the policies that were followed even then—seeing them as more appropriate to China's specific needs and level of development—for the most part, Soviet and U.S. criticism of Chinese science and technology tended to coincide. The opinions diverged on cause. Scholars in the West usually look into China's history and culture to explain the country's scientific backwardness, pointing to bureaucratic, institutional, linguistic, and other traditional factors that have repressed scientific innovation and creativity.

The Soviet explanation is much more simplistic. Early scientific backwardness was due to "exploitation by feudal lords and imperialists," while more recent lack of scientific progress was due almost entirely to the priorities given to the military and China's financial inability to support many scientific and technical fields that were not related to the military.[25]

After Mao's death, of course, and especially since 1978, China's interests in advanced technology and scientific achievements increased dramatically. Furthermore, the new leadership decided that the most expeditious way to acquire such expertise was to borrow it from the United States and other Western countries and adapt it to Chinese needs. In this connection, A. A. Nagornyy and A. B. Parkanskiy observe that China very skillfully utilized "the contradictions and the special interests of all its partners" in acquiring new scientific and technological knowledge and equipment. China's principal partner in foreign trade is Japan; Western Europe is the main supplier of military technology and techniques; and the United States is the main source of all types of information, technology, and scientific-technical experience that cannot be obtained from the other partners (space technology, basic research, offshore oil technology, hydro energy, etc.). But despite Soviet concerns, most Soviet observers believe that China's economy cannot develop on the basis of foreign science and technology.

The actual reviews of the chronology of developments in science and technology are generally factual and detailed, especially when covering the period following the signing of the Agreements of Cooperation in Science and Technology (during the January 1979 visit of Deng Xiaoping to the United States) and the creation of the Joint Science and Technology Commission to review and administer the government-to-government program. But despite the numerous governmental protocols and institutional agreements in science and technology, the Soviets stress that these are nothing more than skeletons that have to be covered with flesh through substantive negotiations—a process which has produced more problems than either side anticipated.

One author, who repeated the often-heard Soviet belief that scientific and cultural exchanges contradicted the attitudes of the American public, listed the following characteristics of scientific exchanges in the first half of the 1970s. First, most of the delegations consisted of natural scientists, especially physicists and medical doctors. Second, since Beijing rejected any formal agreements so long as there were no diplomatic relations between the two countries, the scientific exchanges were "uneven"—meaning that they were basically ad hoc without any concrete goals. Third, they were one-sided, in that many more U.S. scientists visited China than the other way around. And fourth, U.S. delegations included many scientists of Chinese extraction, who were welcomed by Beijing in the hope that "great-Han chauvinism would conquer the 'ideals' of American democracy" and inspire them to undertake roles similar to those played by Chinese-American scientists who returned in the 1950s and who were so instrumental in militarizing China.[26] The imbalance of the exchanges was also cited by B. Zanegin in the mid-1970s, when he wrote that "there is nothing equitable about these exchanges: it is the Chinese who decide which Americans will be invited to the PRC and which Chinese are to be sent over to the United States."[27] Although exaggerated, the accusation was not unfamiliar in the United States during those years. He also expressed his concern that no matter what their specialties, American visitors to China are subjected to intensive and brazen anti-Soviet conditioning not only in China, but also by exposure to anti-Soviet literature sold in various branches of the U.S.-based China Book Store, which is "connected with leftist groupings." And yet, the U.S. administration "has done nothing about Peking and pro-Peking propaganda in the United States that affects Soviet interests."[28] In general, the Soviets consider exchanges with China as a form of U.S. patronage over Chinese universities and research institutions, but although these exchanges are significant in upgrading China's science and technology, the Soviets think that the United States lags behind its European partners, who take whole institutions under their wing for long periods of time.

The Soviets follow all areas of cooperation in science and technology, but since they are convinced that China's primary interests lie in the modernization of its armed forces, there is a tendency to focus on energy (especially nuclear), on space research and communications satellites (which are used to "conduct military espionage"), and on other fields that could have military applications. Their concern naturally peaked after Secretary of Defense Harold Brown visited China in January 1980. As the Soviets see it, that visit laid the groundwork for the establishment of direct military ties between the two countries and resulted in an agreement between Washington and Beijing to "coordinate their military-political actions in the world arena." After the trip, the United States and other Western nations "started viewing China as something like a sixteenth member of NATO," and it "became clear" to the Soviets that repeated U.S. statements that the United States does not intend to supply arms to China "were but a fig leaf covering up Washington's true intentions and actions."[29]

Nagornyy and Parkanskiy[30] describe a rather chummy relationship between the United States and China in science and technology, but they end this discussion by pointing to the "considerable differences and contradictions" that continue to exist. The problem mentioned most often by all Soviet analysts is the uneven development of science and technology in the two countries. There is little that the United States can learn from the Chinese, and cooperation in the sciences will continue to require "artificial stimulation" of the American scientific community. The Soviets seem to delight in picking up all statements by U.S. observers that stress the weaknesses of China's science and that country's inability to absorb advanced technology. Referring to statements by U.S. sinologists, the Soviets point to several problems relating to the uneven development of the two countries. First, China will continue to demand as much information as possible on natural sciences and technology, while Americans will be more interested in research in the humanities and in the analysis of China's sociopolitical situation. Second, Beijing's chauvinism and ethnocentricity will deny U.S. scientists the kind of access to China and its institutions that the Americans desire, which will "automatically cause unhappiness." Third, Beijing will be completely satisfied with cooperation in science and technology only when the United States accepts the People's Republic as a full military-political partner. The United States, on the other hand, looks at China as a "friendly developing nation" and places restrictions on the scientific and technical information that Beijing wants the most—that with military significance. And finally, according to the authors, Americans are willing to cooperate with the Chinese in science and technology only so long as China is not a serious rival or competitor. As China will continue to develop, U.S. interest in providing extensive assistance in science and technology will greatly diminish.

It is difficult to say whether some of these conclusions are wishful thinking, a desire to calm the concerns of the Soviet reader, or a genuine conviction that contradictions between China and the United States are too basic to result in any close, long-term relationship.

Another Soviet specialist also discusses a series of problems between the two countries, but then comes to a somewhat different conclusion. In his list of difficulties between Washington and Beijing, V. Petukhov includes China's inability to absorb modern military technology and the country's xenophobia.[31] In addition to these obstacles, he mentions that closer relations are bound to create adverse reactions on the part of Taiwan, other Asian allies, and the Soviet Union. As long-run contradictions, he points to the Soviet contentions that since "aggressive expansionism" is characteristic of both the United States and China, the relationship is bound to lead to intense rivalry; that the Chinese people have not forgotten or forgiven the United States for isolating the PRC—especially as U.S. policy continues to waver in relation to Taiwan; and, finally, that the contradictions represented by the differences in socioeconomic systems and ideology are too severe to overcome the ever-present concern of the United States that China and the Soviet Union might settle their differences. But after listing all these obstacles and recognizing Washington's caution in selling China military technology and China's constraints in purchasing and absorbing it, Petukhov's conclusion may come as a surprise. At least for the time being, all these problems become unimportant because of the parallel strategic interest shared by Washington and Beijing and because this relationship is in line with the interest of Western arms manufacturers.

Even disregarding ideological differences, it is easy to see how the Soviets would consider close scientific and technological ties between the world's most technically advanced country and the largest developing country to be "unnatural," as they say. But most Soviet observers would agree with a few basic conclusions: Although the building blocks of Sino-U.S. cooperation may be made of geopolitical reality, the mortar consists of military hardware and science and technology; in the long run (and no one attempts to estimate the duration) serious snags are bound to develop in the relations between

China and the United States; but in the short term, mutual interests and practical considerations tend to overcome the contradictions. And it is because of these mutual interests that "both sides are not averse to overevaluating China's potential in science and technology."

## The Role of Science and Technology
## in the New Push for Dialogue and Cooperation

There is little doubt that in recent years the Soviets have raised their evaluation of China's capabilities in science and technology. It is also clear, however, that so far, at least, they still view scientific and technical contacts between the two nations as just one of many bridges to normalization and Chinese science and technology as being of only limited value to the USSR.

Although most observers would consider the 1950s to be an aberration and the years that followed to be more consistent with the historical tensions between the two neighbors, Soviet leaders from Brezhnev to Gorbachev have been wooing Beijing by stressing that "we have never considered normal the state of hostility between our countries."

The obstacles that the two nations must overcome are formidable indeed. Throughout most of the 1970s negotiations were concerned with the relatively insignificant border issues. According to the Soviets, if the Chinese were serious in their desire to make the boundaries more precise, there was enough time during the ten years of negotiations "to survey every meter of the border and dispose of the problem on the basis of existing documents." China, they say, was not interested in such a settlement; it was merely using the border issue for political reasons.[32] After the Soviet invasion of Afghanistan, the border issue took a back seat to the problems that separated the two countries. The last round of discussions on the border issues took place in 1978, and since then, although wary about all Soviet policies around the world, Beijing has listed the now familiar three basic conditions if talks are to resume: the pullback of Soviet troops from Afghanistan, the termination of Soviet support for Vietnamese troops in Cambodia, and the removal of Soviet troops from the Chinese borders—the one issue of the three that the Soviets consider to be appropriate for bilateral negotiations. The Soviets, on the other hand, are convinced that were it not for the U.S. imperialists, none of these problems would stand in the way of accommodations, stressing that the United States "makes no secret of its jubilation" when relations between China and the Soviet Union sour. And their frustration is reflected in the press, which inevitably overreacts to news that suggests either progress or strains in Chinese relations with the United States. Just as a visit by a high-level U.S. delegation becomes a conspiracy, minor irritants also become prominent headlines, such as "Reagan Humiliates Deng on the Hu Na Case"—the incident of the defector tennis player.

When the daily polemics in the Soviet and Chinese press are taken into consideration, it is difficult to imagine that the Soviet proposals to renew dialogue "on the basis of equality and in the spirit of mutual understanding" could make any headway. The official Soviet press—the *Pravdas* and the *Izvestias*—tend to be somewhat more circumspect in their attacks, but the Soviet "commentators" and "news analysts," and especially the broadcasts in Chinese that are beamed at China, have been anything but cautious in their persistent assaults on China's policies. Never attacking the Chinese leadership per se, the blame continues to be placed on the faceless "Maoists," thus implying that the problems are created by some small faction—no matter that the actual policies now followed by Beijing would be anathema to Mao.

Public opinion is, of course, immaterial in the shaping of Soviet foreign policy, but the anti-Chinese bias of the Russian people is also fed by details of China's anti-Soviet propaganda, which "daily crams its readers with a thick collection of fabrications about the situation in Afghanistan," accuses the Soviet Union of "hegemonism," and stresses the Soviets' responsibility for "the exacerbation of international tension and the intensification of the arms race." Curiously none of these denunciations in the Chinese press prevent the Soviet press from immediately coming to the defense of China when they can identify a U.S. policy to be "an insult to the People's Republic of China" or one that "disregards PRC interests."

Polemics in the state-controlled media do not necessarily interfere with the broader objectives of either China or the Soviet Union. Just as public abuse of the United States in the Chinese media did not interfere with rapprochement between the two countries, the name-calling by the Soviet press and radio does not seem to interfere with its official drive to improve relations with China. But whatever progress has been realized as a result of both official efforts and unofficial initiatives, the improvement in relations usually shows little evidence of overt enthusiasm on the part of the Chinese. According to Moscow Radio, the Chinese response to Brezhnev's Tashkent plan was typical. China was not against a relaxation of tensions, but since Beijing's conditions "demanded a fundamental change in the entire foreign policy of the USSR," the Soviets concluded that "any sovereign state with self-respect would not accept such an arrogant demand."[33]

Negative reactions notwithstanding, practical considerations obviously superseded the lack of overt enthusiasm: In October 1982, after a three-year interruption, and some seven months after Brezhnev's Tashkent speech, discussions between Moscow and Beijing resumed. These practical considerations—stemming as they do from China's determined drive for economic development and modernization—include a broad range of closely related strategic and economic factors, which fall outside the purview of this chapter. In general, however, by reducing tensions along its borders, the Soviet Union maintains that China would be able to devote a larger proportion of its scarce resources to modernization; it would derive obvious benefits in closer economic ties and the growth in bilateral trade; despite ideological differences, better government-to-government relations would, on the one hand, prove China's independence from the West and, on the other hand, diversify its contacts with foreign nations—a standing Chinese goal since the 1950s; and finally, should the requirement surface, improved relations with the Soviet Union would provide a degree of leverage on the United States.

As for scientific and technical cooperation, in December 1981 the Soviet Foreign Ministry offered to renew contacts between the two countries and, as a first step, to exchange one or two groups of specialists in order to familiarize each side with the achievements of the other. Specifically, the Soviets offered exchanges on the following topics: technology of silk fabric production, production technology of porcelain, production of mineral fertilizers (including raw material), and production of pesticides. They were also willing to consider any other problem or subjects the Chinese might propose. Although "there was no response to this proposal" from the Chinese,[34] during 1981 China sent seventeen groups of scientists to the Soviet Union, and four Soviet delegations visited China. The Soviet complaint about these exchanges does not refer to the obvious numerical imbalance but rather to the familiar complaint that while the Chinese visitors are "granted wide opportunities to learn about the Soviet Union," individual Soviet scientists and specialists can visit China only as guests of the Soviet embassy—albeit more recently they have been given some assistance in visiting certain enterprises and scientific and educational institutions.

Some initial steps have also been made in the exchange of students. In February 1981 the USSR Ministry of Higher and Secondary Specialized Education proposed an annual exchange of students and teachers. The proposal suggested only ten students from each country to spend up to ten months in the other country.[35] Apparently the actual exchange did not occur until 1983, when ten students were sent by each country for language study. This exchange was deemed to be successful, and after the signing of the April 1984 protocol both sides "agreed to send 70 students to each other's country and exchange two educational groups during the 1984–85 academic year."[36] By 1986 it was reported that some 200 Chinese students were studying in the Soviet Union, with a similar number of Soviet students in China.[37] By way of contrast, it should be pointed out that from 1979 to 1986 almost 50,000 Chinese students and scholars entered the United States for periods of several weeks to several years and that an estimated 20,000 are still in the country.[38]

So far, it appears that the scientific and technical content of the rapidly increasing trade between China and the Soviet Union has been minimal. Under the existing agreements, "China exports mineral products, frozen and canned meats, soybeans, vegetable oil, silk fabrics, cotton, knitwear and garments, light industrial goods, tea and animal byproducts to the Soviet Union," which in turn exports "pig iron, nonferrous metals, timber, chemical fertilizers, cement, plate glass, chemicals, vehicles and machinery to China."[39] The Soviets also entice the Chinese by hinting that since in the past they "purchased from China large quantities of products that could find no market elsewhere in the world," they would do it again.[40] They also stress that as a highly advanced industrial country it can "ensure for China supplies of modern industrial plant and technology which the Chinese people need so badly to modernize their economy."[41] In this connection, after some lengthy negotiations the Soviet Union finally signed a protocol not only to modernize seventeen industrial plants in northeast China, which were built with Soviet assistance in the 1950s, but take part in building seven new ones.[42] This will bring Soviet experts back to China for the first time in more than twenty-five years.

Western involvement in China's nuclear energy is not deterring the Soviets from competing in this field, as they remind Beijing of their early involvement in planning and building China's first atomic reactor and cyclotron. But while for a number of years now "reliable sources" have been suggesting that the Soviets are close to selling China nuclear-power-generation equipment and possibly cooperating in uranium development and peaceful use of isotopes, so far negotiations have not produced an agreement. Even before the Chernobyl nuclear accident, Vice-Premier Li Peng said that technical cooperation with the Soviet Union in the nuclear power field "has not yet been placed on the agenda" and decisions will be made only after a Chinese delegation visits the Soviet Union "for a purely technical study of Soviet nuclear power stations."[43] After Chernobyl, agreement may be even further away.

\*    \*    \*

Those who follow Sino-Soviet relations are unanimous in their opinion that the two countries cannot return to the loquacious harmony of the 1950s, but there is also a tendency to believe that despite ideological differences that have restricted party-to-party contacts, barring some unforeseen developments, scientific and economic contacts should gradually improve the overall relations between the two governments. In the past, by overreacting to pronouncements of real or assumed cooperation between Beijing and Washington, Moscow has, on a number of occasions, undercut its own objectives and retarded progress in rapprochement with Beijing. Now, based on some of Gorbachev's recent pronouncements, the Soviet Union seems to accept the fact that improved diplomatic and trade relations with China will have to take place within the current competitive environment. The Soviets are also gradually learning to accept more graciously China's drastic economic reforms, which for years have been considered to be a shocking perversion of the socialist system and "a monstrous hybrid of planned and market economies." In fact, although they are not likely to admit it, the Soviets have been observing China's "voluntarist experimentation" with more than academic curiosity, and it may not be too farfetched to suggest that some of Gorbachev's own reforms were partly inspired by some of China's economic successes.

Since both the Soviet Union and the People's Republic of China attach great importance to improving relations, it is safe to predict that economic, trade, and scientific and technical cooperation and contacts will continue to grow, but the most important impediment to political harmony and international collaboration will not disappear. All problems between the two countries are so magnified by fear, hatred, prejudice, and suspicion, which are so deeply ingrained in the psyche of the leaders and the people on both sides of the border, that rapprochement between China and the Soviet Union will "never" evolve into a trusting and lasting cooperative relationship.

## Notes

1. Soviet humor regarding all aspects of relations with China is highly developed. In the late 1950s, China's technical immaturity was ridiculed with this witticism: "Have you heard that the Chinese finally launched a Sputnik of their own? True, it took six million coolies to pull the slingshot, but they did it." (Albert Parry, "Russia Cracks Jokes About China," *New York Times Magazine*, June 26, 1966, p. 38.)

2. See, for example, Leo A. Orleans, "The 'Chinese Threat' and Soviet Emotions," *Russia*, no. 1, 1981, pp. 46–50.

3. A. N. Bykov, *Nauchno-tekhnicheskiye svyazi stran sotsializma* (Scientific-Technical Cooperation of Socialist Countries) (Moscow: Mysl' Publishers, 1970), p. 3.

4. Unless otherwise indicated, the information in this section is generally based on L. V. Filatov, *Ekonomicheskaya otsenka nauchno-tekhnicheskoy pomoshchi Sovetskogo Soyuza Kitayu, 1949–1966* (Economic Estimate of Scientific-Technical Assistance by the Soviet Union to China, 1949–1966) (Moscow: Nauka Publishers, 1980). This source contains the most complete textual and statistical documentation on the voluminous assistance provided to China.

5. Moscow in Mandarin, February 1, 1981; Foreign Broadcast Information Service (hereafter FBIS), Daily Report, Soviet Union, February 4, 1981, p. B2.

6. Z. A. Muromtseva, *Problemy industrializatsii Kitayskoy Narodnoy Respubliki* (Problems of Industrialization of the People's Republic of China) (Moscow: Nauka Publishers, 1971), p. 121.

7. Mikhail A. Klochko, trans. Andrew MacAndrew *Soviet Scientist in Red China* (New York: Praeger, 1964), pp. 22–23.

8. Ibid., p. 6.

9. A. A. Antipovskiy, "Nauka" (Science), in A. A. Antipovskiy, N. E. Borevskaya, and N. V. Franchuk, *Politika v oblasti nauki i obrazovaniya v KNR* (Politics in the Fields of Science and Education in the PRC) (Moscow: Nauka Publishers, 1980), pp. 194–195.

10. O. Ivanov, *The Truth Will Out* (Moscow: Novosti Press, 1971), p. 16.

11. M. S. Kapitsa, "Debunking Falsifiers of Chinese History," *Far Eastern Affairs* (Moscow), no. 2, 1978, p. 154.

12. This discussion is based primarily on Oleg Ivanov, *Soviet Chinese Relations* (Moscow: Novosti Press, 1979), pp. 24–79.

13. In Mandarin to China, July 22, 1981; FBIS, July 24, 1981.

14. Filitov, *Ekonomicheskaya otsenka*, p. 74.

15. We can only wonder if the closing of Xinjiang was a direct reaction to the fact that "the Soviet Union unilaterally requested the expansion of the prospecting area of the Sino-Soviet petroleum company in Xinjiang," while declining to increase its investment, provide additional new equipment for the oil field, or compensate China for the extra land. (*Beijing Review*, no. 47, November 21, 1983, p. 21.)

16. Filatov, *Ekonomicheskaya otsenka*, p. 75.

17. O. B. Borisov and B. T. Koloskov, *Sovetsko-Kitayskiye otnosheniya, 1945–1977* (Soviet-Chinese Relations, 1945–1977) (Moscow: Mysl' Publishers, 1977), pp. 294–295.

18. Ibid., p. 343.

19. Ibid., p. 298.

20. V. I. Akimov, "Yestestvennyye i tecknicheskiye nauki" (Natural and Technical Sciences), in *Kitayskaya Narodnaya Respublika* (Chinese People's Republic) (Moscow: Nauka Publishers, 1975), pp. 354–355.

21. B. Zanegin, "Sino-U.S. Rapprochement: What It Is and Why," *Far Eastern Affairs* (Moscow), no. 1, 1975, p. 69. Ironically, only a few words need be changed to express precisely the public position of Washington toward the current negotiations between Moscow and Beijing.

22. S. K. Merkulov, *Amerikano-Kitayskoye sblizheniye* (American-Chinese Rapprochement) (Moscow: Nauka Publishers, 1980), p. 60.

23. Ye. P. Bazhanov, *Dvizhushchiye sily politiki SShA v otnoshenii Kitaya* (Motive Forces of U.S. China Policy) (Moscow: Nauka Press, 1982). Unless otherwise indicated, the material in this section is from this book.

24. One of the best and, at the same time, most typical Soviet expositions of scientific and technical cooperation between the United States and China is in A. A. Nagornyy and A. B. Parkanskiy, *SShA i Kitay: Ekonomicheskiye i Nauchno-Tekhnicheskiye Aspekty Kitayskoy Politiki Vashingtona* (USA and China: Economic and Scientific-Technical Aspects of Washington's China Policies) (Moscow: Nauka Publishers, 1982). Unless otherwise indicated, the information here is from Chapter 3 of this book, "Ostonovnyye aspekty naucho-tekhnicheskogo sotruduichestva SShA s KNR" (Basic Aspects of Scientific-Technical Cooperation Between the USA and the PRC), pp. 112–151.

25. One somewhat facetious reason for China's backwardness was given by Soviet specialists in the 1950s: The Chinese could "catch up with us and overtake us as soon as they start working in their characteristic Chinese style, and give up those idiotic conferences." (Klochko, *Soviet Scientist in Red China*, p. 103.)

26. See, for example, V. B. Vorontsov, *Kitay i SShA: 60-70-ye Gody* (China and the USA: The 1960s and 1970s) (Moscow: Nauka Publishers, 1979), p. 97.

27. Zanegin, "Sino-U.S. Rapprochement," p. 74.

28. Ibid., p. 75.

29. V. Petukhov, "PRC-USA: A Threat to Peace and Security," *Far Eastern Affairs* (Moscow), no. 3, 1980, p. 59. Some perspective on the Soviet view that China's primary concern is with building up the country's military capabilities can be gained from the following Defense Intelligence Agency estimate, which reflects the predominant U.S. viewpoint: "An example of the military's low priority has been the moderate level of weapons production during the last five years. . . . The Chinese are caught in the difficult position of being reluctant on the one hand to continue massive procurement of old unsophisticated systems, while at the same time having both economic and technical constraints against adopting the more desirable modern weapons." ("Allocation of Resources in the Soviet Union and China, 1982," Hearings before the Joint Economic Committee, Congress of the United States, June 29 and December 1, 1982, Washington, D.C., 1983, p. 55–56.)

30. See note 24.

31. See note 29.

32. M. S. Ukraintsev, "Sovetsko-Kitayskiye otnosheniya problemy i perspektivy" (Soviet-Chinese Relations: Problems and Prospects), *Problemy Dal'nego Vostoka* (Problems of the Far East), no. 2, April–June 1982, p. 18.

33. Moscow Radio, March 30, 1982; FBIS, April 2, 1982, p. B2.

34. Ukraintsev, "Soviet-Chinese Relations," p. 22.

35. Ibid.

36. Moscow in Mandarin to China, April 17, 1984; FBIS, April 18, 1984, p. B3.

37. Tokyo, Kyodo in English, March 24, 1986; FBIS, March 24, 1986, p. B1.

38. From a forthcoming study prepared by Leo A. Orleans for the Committee on Scholarly Communications with the People's Republic of China, National Academy of Sciences.

39. *Beijing Review*, no. 21, May 21, 1984, p. 12.

40. Moscow in Mandarin to Southeast Asia, January 28, 1983; FBIS, February 1, 1983, p. B2.

41. Moscow World Service in English, August 30, 1983; FBIS, September 1, 1983.

42. Moscow in Mandarin, March 14, 1986; FBIS, March 17, 1986.

43. Beijing in Russian, April 4, 1986; FBIS, April 7, 1986, p. C1.

# 31

## Nuclear Power in China, 1978–1986

*James Reardon-Anderson*

In the mid-1980s, as most of the world grows wary and weary of nuclear power, its dangers, and its cost overruns, the People's Republic of China is taking its first steps into this field. If current trends continue, by the early 1990s the PRC will have at least two nuclear power plants in operation: a large twin-reactor unit built by French engineers in the Shenzhen Special Economic Zone opposite Hong Kong, and a smaller reactor of China's own design and construction near Shanghai. This chapter describes Beijing's decision to adopt nuclear energy, the reasons for this decision, the debate over what kind of nuclear power plants China should have, and recent developments that indicate a shift in China's nuclear power program.

### The Decision

China, like all other nuclear weapons states, was first drawn to the atom for strategic purposes and turned to peaceful applications later, as a spinoff of its established nuclear capability. In 1970, when Beijing's weapons program was in place and a nuclear power industry was blossoming in the West, Zhou Enlai issued the first directive approving development by a research team in Shanghai of a relatively small, 300-megawatt (MW) power reactor. Study of the problem dragged on until 1978, when Beijing made its first solid commitment to a nuclear energy program. In December, the Third Plenum of the Eleventh Central Committee announced the decision to shift a portion of China's existing nuclear industry from military to civilian use. At the same time, a trade agreement was signed with France, which included terms for the French to sell to China two 900-MW nuclear power plants.[1]

Interest in the nuclear option cooled, however, in 1979. First, the economic readjustment, which followed Beijing's realization that it had become overextended in its commitments for foreign purchases, led to cutbacks in several nonessential areas. Then, in March, came news of the accident at Three Mile Island, which raised doubts in China about the safety of nuclear power and gave further impetus to what was by then a global trend away from this option. In May, Beijing canceled the order for French plants, and its nuclear program stalled.[2]

Interest picked up again in 1980. Statements by Chinese officials and articles in the press indicated a growing consensus that China should proceed with nuclear power, although the exact shape of that program was still in dispute. Talks with French and German suppliers resumed in the spring, focusing on a proposed site at Daya Bay, in the Shenzhen Special Economic Zone of Guangdong Province, opposite Hong Kong. In October, French President Valéry Giscard d'Estaing during his visit to Beijing reached an understanding with Premier Zhao Ziyang on terms for the sale of a complete plant to be built at this site. Since then, Daya Bay has remained at the forefront of negotiations for complete nuclear power plant imports, with the French firm Framatome considered to have the inside track on supply of the nuclear island.[3]

Finally, questions about the degree and nature of Beijing's nuclear energy program were resolved in the latter half of 1982, when approval was given to both domestic production of a small plant and a larger project that would rely on foreign imports. In August it was announced that China would build the first plant, a 300-MW reactor on the model developed during the 1970s, near Shanghai. (It was later revealed that the site of this project would be Qinshan.) At the same time, Communist Party Secretary-General Hu Yaobang told foreign reporters that China would produce more than 10,000 MW of nuclear power during the next ten to twenty years, a goal that has been reaffirmed several times since then. In November the State Council confirmed the inclusion of two 900-MW nuclear power sections for the Daya Bay plant in the Sixth Five-Year Plan (1980–1985). Later, in April 1984, the same body announced further plans to build two 900-MW sections each in southern Jiangsu (Sunan) and Liaoning provinces under the Seventh Five-Year Plan (1986–1990). These larger plants were to be built with foreign assistance.[4]

Whatever doubts may have lingered in the minds of some Chinese, public statements by leading officials in following years have demonstrated a firm, one might even say blind, commitment to nuclear energy. Jiang Shengjie, president of the Chinese Nuclear Society, has called nuclear power "the most promising new energy source," a view that he and others assert is shared by the international community at large—with no mention of signs to the contrary. Jiang, like other Chinese nuclear advocates, also stresses the safety and low environmental impact of this technology, citing, ironically, the lesson of Three Mile Island: "Experience of the past 30 years has shown that people so far have not suffered serious harm from radioactivity from nuclear power stations. No one has died of radiation leakages, and even during the 1979 Three Mile Island accident in the United States, which was caused by human error, no one in or outside the power station died."[5]

Comments of this type are not unknown among proponents of nuclear power outside of China. It is striking, however, that Jiang was later named director general of China's Nuclear Safety Administration, and other officials in charge of regulating nuclear development and monitoring environmental impact have made equally bullish statements on nuclear energy—even before examining their own studies of this problem. It is evident from an authoritative report that appeared in March 1985, for example, that by this date the Chinese had not yet conducted hydrological and geological surveys or formulated any of the standards, codes, or regulations that are required for the safe operation of nuclear power plants and the disposal of nuclear wastes. In a separate article published at the same time, Qu Geping, director of the Office of Environment Protection of the State Council, agreed that "up till present, no country in the world has yet successfully devised a final disposal method for . . . spent fuel elements," and that procedures for dealing with these problems in China were still in draft form. Yet Qu voiced confidence that the problem of waste disposal would be solved and dismissed arguments that nuclear power plants pose a significant safety hazard:

> Accidents of "reactor core melt-down" may do serious harm to human beings and the environment. But the occurrence rate of such accidents is very low. According to foreign statistics, such an accident may occur only once in about 17,000 reactor-years. . . . Investigations of [the Three Mile Island] accident showed that the effect the incident had on the inhabitants in the neighbourhood of the plant was almost negligible. . . . In fact, the Three Mile Island incident has testified [to] the safety of generating electricity by nuclear energy.

In the wake of the April 1986 accident at the Chernobyl nuclear power plant in the Soviet Union, the Chinese have confirmed the decision to proceed with development of nuclear energy and pointed out that Chinese pressurized water plants will have several features—triple shield, auxiliary cooling systems, and strict controls—that will make them, like Three Mile Island, safer than Soviet graphite reactors.[6]

These assertions about the global trend toward nuclear power and its safety demonstrate a confidence in this technology that is no longer widespread outside of China. On one hand, Chinese policymakers are not ignorant of nor indifferent to issues of nuclear safety. Almost all have publicly stated their awareness of and concern for safety. Standards and regulations, although not now in place, are in the pipeline and could be ready by the time they are needed. The design of the Qinshan plant includes both additional cooling systems and reactor containment, which increase the cost but reduce the possibility of serious accident. Foreign suppliers are sure to insist on and help the Chinese understand the importance of international safety standards. On the other hand, despite questioning of the environmental impact by domestic fishing interests, China is still without an organized watch-guard or antinuclear movement. The background of regulatory officials like Jiang Shengjie, who served as chief engineer at China's largest nuclear power plant and oversaw construction of China's largest reactor, and their apparent enthusiasm for nuclear power leave questions as to how much pressure can be mounted for effective enforcement of regulations, in whatever form they finally appear.[7]

By the end of 1985, plans set in motion three years earlier had begun to bear fruit. Preparation of the Qinshan site was complete, and construction of the main buildings well under way. Contracts for the importation of key components were signed in 1984 with several foreign suppliers. Recent reports place the program on its announced schedule, under which the plant should begin operation in 1989. In January 1985, the Guangdong Power Company and the China Light and Power Company of Hong Kong agreed to establish the Guangdong Nuclear Power Joint Venture Company, which will build and operate the Daya Bay plant. By the end of the year, construction of a road, reservoir, transmission line, and breakwater was complete. Sites had also been selected for the next two large imported plants, in Jiangsu and Liaoning, and feasibility studies were in process. Contracts were reportedly near with French and British firms for construction of the Daya Bay facility, and Beijing had begun talks with German and French manufacturers for the nuclear island at Jiangsu. Both development of a small indigenous reactor and importation of larger whole nuclear power plants were well under way.[8]

## The Reasons

The decision to develop a nuclear power industry in China has been made after considerable debate, and opponents remain, though they lack public prominence. The opposition has raised questions about cost, safety, technical feasibility, and the desirability of entering a new, unknown field when China's traditional energy resources have not been fully exploited. Yet it is the arguments of Chinese proponents of nuclear power that have thus far carried the day: the tremendous demand for energy, the problems with alternative sources, the availability of an existing, untapped nuclear industry, and the sense that exploitation of this sector fits with the reforms now under way in the economy as a whole.

### The Need

By 1983, China's total production of electricity had reached 351 billion kilowatt hours (kWh), but remained 40–50 billion kWh below demand, causing a reduction of more than 20 percent in industrial productivity. During 1983–1985, China's industrial growth accelerated from 10 to 18 percent per year. Thanks to energy conservation and the shift from heavy to light industry, these increases were achieved with approximately half the rise in energy production, which advanced only 5–9 percent per year during the same period. But savings of this type produce diminishing returns, and there is little prospect for achieving the stated goal of quadrupling GNP by the year 2000 without substantial increases in energy output.[9]

### The Alternatives

Beijing has little choice but to persist with its current priorities on thermal (coal and oil) and hydro power, which will remain the most important sources of Chinese energy for the foreseeable future. The decision to add a relatively small nuclear component—projected to be 10 billion of a total 1,200 billion kWh by the year 2000—derives in part from the intractable problems with traditional alternatives. Coal, by far the largest source of energy in China, is abundant, but it is located primarily in north China, far from the site of greatest demand in the south. At present, 43–47 percent of the already weak and overburdened rail and water transport systems are devoted to coal. Similar transport problems limit the attraction of oil, most of which comes from the northeast and northwest. While China has virtually limitless coal, proven oil reserves are being used up faster than new ones are found. If current trends continue, China will become a net importer of petroleum by the end of the century. Foreign explorers failed to locate offshore sources during the decade of high oil prices; given the drop in prices, it is doubtful that they will risk further investment in pursuit of this elusive goal. China has relatively little natural gas, most of which is located and consumed in Sichuan. Burning of fossil fuels contributes to the already serious pollution in China's industrial centers, where the demand for energy is highest. The most attractive clean and renewable source of energy is hydro power, which now accounts for about 20 percent of China's electricity and could be substantially increased by tapping the estimated 380 billion kilowatts of exploitable falling water. Most of this potential, however, is in the remote southwest, and China lacks the long-distance transmission lines required to bring power generated in the mountains to consumers on the coast. The construction of dams is expensive, floods out existing agricultural land and other resources, requires resettling of people and livestock, raises potential environmental hazards, and threatens downstream areas with the disaster of flood.[10]

Despite these problems, China will continue to rely primarily on coal, oil, and hydro power for the production of energy and will continue to expand these industries as much as resources and logic permit. But the pressing need for energy and the problems associated with alternative sources make a nuclear supplement attractive. Nuclear power plants place little burden on transportation or transmission networks, they can be located near to consumers without contributing to air pollution, and, in the current view of Chinese decision makers, they are safe. Regional interests representing such areas as Guangdong and Liaoning, which have their own uranium, also see the nuclear option as a way to reduce dependency on outside bureaucracies that control fuel and transportation.[11]

*The Available Industry*

It is less likely that Beijing would have opted for nuclear power if it were not for the fact that an industry already erected to build nuclear warheads could be adapted to this new use. By the early 1980s, China had a large and diverse network of nuclear research institutes and more than ten experimental and production reactors, uranium enrichment plants, and other facilities that had enjoyed three decades of successful experience.

Employment in this sector has been estimated at between 100,000 and 150,000 persons. The Chinese Nuclear Society (CNS) is said to have more than 20,000 members. China operates a complete, independent nuclear fuel cycle, and according to official estimates has proven uranium reserves sufficient to supply 15,000 MW(e) of installed capacity for more than thirty years, which is substantially more than current plans require. Outsiders see this industry as a ripe fruit that can help feed China's civilian sector; insiders form a lobby that would like to expand into new and profitable areas.[12]

## The Reform

The proposal to transform a portion of the established military industry to a new civilian purpose has attracted adherents, both inside and outside the military, because it fits with the current program of economic and organizational reform. Vice-Minister Li Peng, Minister of Nuclear Industry Hiang Xinxiong, Minister of Defense Zhang Aiping, and other top officials have called on this industry to shift its orientation from command to market mechanisms, open up to foreign sources of capital and technology, implement incentive programs for managers and ordinary workers, and adopt measures that will enable the enormous investment in plant and people to produce attractive and useful products for a more competitive market-place. According to one analysis, this policy offers the military, which previously enjoyed relatively generous cost-plus contracts from the state, the best means of surviving in the current environment of tight budgets: "Developing nuclear technology for military purposes requires fairly large funds and the state's appropriations for military expenditures are rather limited. But, developing diversified operations can open up new financial sources and this can subsidize part of the expenditures for studying and making new nuclear weapons and equipment and maintain the capacity for producing nuclear weapons." In an age of reform, making something useful is increasingly the measure of success and in extreme cases the price of staying in business at all. "If the nuclear industry wishes to survive and develop," one study observes, "it must be brave enough to compete and be good in competition."[13]

Notable by its absence from this debate has been a compelling argument that nuclear power is cheaper than the alternatives. According to one source, during the 1970s "certain leading cadres" blocked the development of nuclear power plants on the grounds that they were not economically competitive against coal-fired plants of a similar size. But an authoritative study done in 1980 by a group of scientists and engineers under the State Scientific and Technological Commission found that (1) the investment required to build a nuclear power station in southeast China was about the same as that needed for a thermal power station of a similar scale, and (2) the cost of electricity generated by nuclear power would be about 10 percent lower than by coal-fired power in Guangdong and 5 percent lower in east China. Still, most Chinese analysts of nuclear power have been hard-pressed to demonstrate the superior economics of this technology. One pronuclear author, writing in the journal Nuclear Power Engineering in December 1983, pointed out that the cost of nuclear power had gone up since 1980, so that in the current environment it would "possibly" be lower than coal-fired plants, provided that the prices of Chinese coal and transportation are adjusted upward and the techniques of constructing large (1,000 MW) imported nuclear power plants are mastered. Even this rather marginal vote for nuclear power was countered by a reply in *World Economy*, in September 1984, which presented data supplied by the U.S. antinuclear organization Worldwatch Institute to explain the economic reasons for which most other countries were turning away from nuclear: namely, the high costs of capital, operations, decommissioning, and waste disposal.[14]

Since their own research does not indicate a clear advantage for nuclear on the basis of cost, Chinese officials who have made the strongest case for this option do not cite this as a reason. Jiang Shengjie, a leading advocate of nuclear power, cites energy need, problems with alternative sources, and availability of a nuclear infrastructure, but *not* cost, as justifications for this stance. Vice-Premier Li Peng has said that the cost of nuclear-generated electricity in China will drop below that of thermal power only *after* China has produced key equipment that can displace the expensive imports required for constructing the first nuclear plants. Finally, Peng Shilu, vice-minister of electric power and a leading figure in the negotiations over Daya Bay, warned in an article that appeared in June 1985 of the danger of cost overruns resulting from delays in construction and shutdowns resulting from malfunctions.[15]

### The Means

Overlaying discussions of whether or not to develop nuclear power has been a second debate over means, pitting proponents of self-reliance against those who favor the importation of large whole plants. This debate was first spelled out by Wang Ganchang, one of China's most senior nuclear scientists, in a speech to the American Nuclear Society in November 1980:

> We might seek technical help from a friendly country well-advanced in nuclear power and undertake with her an all-out cooperative program, like that between Brazil and the Federal Republic of Germany, so as to realize technical transfer in the shortest time, leading to a capacity of designing, building, and operating a commercial nuclear power plant by ourselves in the 1990's.
>
> As an alternative, we might also choose to rely mainly on self-reliance with a limited amount of technical help from abroad. In this alternative, demonstration nuclear power plants of smaller capacity are to be built and operated as a first step before full-sized commercial plants are constructed.[16]

Wang has been a proponent of the internationalist school, but, on the other hand, some favor self-reliance. Hopes of this group have fastened on the 300-MW reactor mentioned previously. This unit, a pressurized water reactor of standard two-loop design, was selected in a study conducted by the Second Ministry of Machine Building in the mid-1970s as the best candidate to be China's first home-grown nuclear power plant. Since then, this ministry, renamed the Ministry of Nuclear Industry (MNI) in 1982, has taken responsibility for developing the prototype, now under construction at Qinshan.

There are good arguments for the proposition that China should build its own plants. Self-reliance makes maximum use of existing Chinese resources, minimizes the drain on foreign reserves, enhances the capability of native research and development, and has a desirable ripple effect on those industries called upon to supply component parts and services. On purely technical grounds, it has been pointed out that the 300-MW reactor of the type China can build itself will fit within the limited capacity of existing electrical grids, while larger (1,000 MW) imported reactors will not. Finally, the native model appeals to those who take pride in symbols of China's scientific and technical competence, a sentiment richly rewarded by previous successes of the Chinese nuclear program.[17]

For all these reasons, MNI was given the green light, in 1982, to build the Qinshan plant, which is now much further advanced than other Chinese nuclear power projects. It became clear, early in this process, however, that one of the principal arguments in favor of the small model—namely, that it could be built by the Chinese themselves—was not entirely valid. At the outset, the Chinese had indicated that they would import some key components, such as reactor coolant pumps, the neutron flux-mapping system, and complex castings and forgings. MNI told at least one foreign company that the State Council had allocated $100 million in foreign exchange for this purpose. On the other hand, a 1983 report in the Chinese press indicated that Shanghai factories were being geared up to supply Qinshan and would build fourteen of the fifteen pieces of major equipment, including the reactor pressure shield, steam generator, and structural elements of the reactor. Chinese planners impressed foreign suppliers with their determination to limit foreign assistance to technical seminars and studies of individual design problems, while remaining in control of the engineering and design. By the middle of 1984, however, they had come to recognize the need for broader foreign assistance and signed contracts for the purchase of the reactor vessel (Japan), reactor coolant and injection pumps (West Germany), steam generator tubes (Sweden), and in-core instrumentation and training for its installation and use (France). While buying the pieces, MNI retains the role of architect and general contractor.[18]

This experience has lent credibility to those Chinese who argue for the importation of larger, more advanced reactors. The centerpiece of this program, also approved in 1982, is the Daya Bay plant, which is to house two 1,000-MW pressurized water reactors of foreign design and construction. Negotiations with French, German, and British suppliers have focused not only on price and terms of credit, but also on the forms of technology transfer, which will give China eventual manufacturing capability. The target date for start-up of this plant is 1992. Sites have been selected for second (Jiangsu) and third (Liaoning) plants to follow the Daya Bay model.[19]

Several influential figures in the Chinese nuclear field—including Wang Ganchang, Jiang Shengjie, and Peng Shilu—have all indicated a preference for the foreign import strategy. Selection of Daya Bay as the first site gives weight to the argument that the import of whole plants provides a quick fix, which can be turned around to earn back hard currency. In this case, much of the capital for construction is to be borrowed abroad, and 70 percent of Daya Bay's electricity is to be sold in Hong Kong. While defenders of the Qinshan plant argue that Chinese must learn new techniques by doing things themselves, proponents of the import model point out that this approach means working on yesterday's technology, while the state of the art recedes farther from reach. Discussions with Framatome have included proposals for the French to build the first four reactors, while the Chinese would learn from the process and construct the fifth reactor on their own. Several observers have noted that a key consideration for the Chinese in selecting foreign partners has been the determination to acquire not only the hardware but also the manufacturing capability. Beijing's pursuit of a nuclear exchange agreement with the United States, for example, has been due in large part to the knowledge that while the Europeans have similar hardware, the Americans have experience in transferring the technology to others. Finally, those who favor imported plants have argued that only at this large scale does nuclear energy become economically competitive against thermal power.[20]

This debate has been conducted in part on the merits of the case: a reading of the Chinese press reveals that serious efforts have been made to understand the economic and technological choices. At the same time, there is evidence that the issue involves a struggle over control of this industry, which pits the Ministry of Nuclear Industry against the Ministry of Water Resources and Electrical Power (MWREP). This conflict surfaced in 1982, when, according to some foreign businessmen, sponsors of the two projects were not on the friendliest of terms. MNI has a well-established and recognized responsibility over the nuclear fuel cycle, which gives it a claim to this field and explains why it (more precisely its predecessor, the Second Ministry of Machine Building) was charged with developing a new technology that evolved into the Qinshan reactor. Production of electricity, on the other hand, belongs to MWREP, so it was natural that construction of a new power plant should be referred to this ministry. Peng Shilu, vice-minister of electric power, who conducted the negotiations over the Daya Bay facility, explained in an article written in late 1984, that his ministry "has been authorized to take charge of the country's nuclear power projects and will be responsible for siting, inviting bids, construction, operation and so on." As an indication of this policy, in early 1985, MWREP established a subsidiary to manage construction of the second large imported plant, planned for southern Jiangsu.[21]

## The Denouement

By the end of 1985, it appeared that whatever its internal divisions, China was committed to a wide-ranging program of nuclear development that would include one plant of local design and construction and several larger whole-plant imports, over the next two decades. Events of early 1986, however, indicated a shift in priorities. Beijing has reduced the overall position of nuclear in China's energy future, while placing greater reliance on local efforts to meet these more limited goals.

One sign that seemed, at first, to point in the opposite direction was the signing, on March 12, of a letter of intent for the Guangdong joint venture company in charge of Daya Bay to purchase two 980-MW nuclear islands from the French firm Framatome. The French had pursued this agreement for eight years, at an unrecoverable cost of 150 million francs and with the intervention of two presidents. As the talks dragged on and China pressed for better terms, Framatome dropped the price to a level so low that, according to its chief executive officer, Jean-Claude Leny, "either we will just break even, or we will lose money," while the French government agreed to guarantee a 100 percent loan (85 percent loan plus the 15 percent down payment) at a special low rate (8.8 percent), which had been grand-fathered out of the 1984 OECD "nuclear consensus," which sets a lower limit on the financial terms that sellers can offer for nuclear exports to China. What the French got in return was the first nuclear plant export agreement since 1980 (the last was a Korean purchase, also from Framatome) and a foot in the door to what they hope will be an important new market.[22]

The significance of this agreement lies in the financing: The Chinese have bought a plant that will be paid for by loans raised and guaranteed abroad and whose cost to China can be recouped by the sale of electricity to Hong Kong. It is this foreign-investment/buy-back arrangement, rather than a commitment to China's own energy needs, that persuaded Beijing to take this long-delayed step. Viewed in this light, approval of the Daya Bay scheme, which must still be ratified by the State Council, is consistent with a seemingly contrary decision, also reached in early March, to defer construction of the next large-scale plant, planned for southern Jiangsu (Sunan). In this case, as in the economic readjustment of 1979, a sharp increase in the PRC trade deficit ($14.9 billion in 1985) persuaded the fiscally conservative Chinese to cut back on imports. At the same time, Beijing may be adjusting its anticipated power demands downward, while counting on traditional sources to fill this need: The Seventh Five-Year Plan, which was put in final shape in March 1986, calls for 25,000 MW of coal-fired capacity and 7,400 MW of hydro power.[23]

Li Peng in a press conference held in Beijing on April 3, 1986, explained the decision to delay construction at Sunan:

After comparing the sites in Qinshan and in southern Jiangsu, we found that the Qinshan site has more favorable conditions for future expansion. At the same time, our investigations also show that China possesses the necessary abilities to build nuclear power stations with a generating capacity of 300,000 to 600,000 kilowatts on its own. Therefore, we will mainly rely on our own strength in the construction of nuclear power stations, while seeking technical support and cooperation from other countries, and will change the method of purchasing whole plants from abroad.

This statement sets forth the three essential features of China's revised nuclear strategy. First, there has been an overall reduction in the place Beijing now accords to nuclear in China's energy future. According to the *South China Morning Post*, Li said flatly, "I don't think there will be an ambitious plan for the construction of nuclear plants," and called the goal of 10,000 nuclear megawatts by the year 2000, which had been restated by Chinese officials on several occasions since 1982, "just something that had cropped up in discussions, there had never been a policy decision." Second, the deferral of Sunan and the decision to limit foreign participation to "technical support and cooperation," rather than construction of whole plants, further reduces the place foreign suppliers will have in an already shrinking Chinese nuclear pie. Finally, the assertion that China "possesses the necessary abilities" to expand the Qinshan plant from its current goal of 300 megawatts to 600 megawatts is a major statement of faith in the principle of self-reliance and in those Chinese who have favored this line. These decisions have not been shaken by recent events. On May 4, 1986, after a week of silence during which Beijing studied news of the Chernobyl disaster, Jiang Shengjie told the press, "The Soviet Chernobyl nuclear plant accident will not affect the progress of nuclear power development that China has started."[24]

The shift from whole-plant imports to the strategy of relying on China's own resources is underlined by organizational changes that have accompanied these decisions. As noted above, the Ministry of Nuclear Industry has had charge of the native Qinshan project, while the Ministry of Water Resources and Electrical Power has handled negotiations for foreign imports. In part because these two parties had to compete for limited resources and control over common turf, this arrangement never worked out. Initially, the solution was to empower Vice-Minister Li Peng to serve as arbiter in the nuclear field. According to one report, Li worked through the Nuclear Power Leadership Group, located under the State Economic Commission and composed of representatives of MNI, MWREP, and the Ministry of Machine Industry. In an article published in January 1985, he explained that the MWREP would be responsible "for the construction of large-scale nuclear power stations," while MNI would undertake "the construction of the nuclear island of the power stations." But this arrangement, which places different parts of the same plant under different supervisors, did not survive. In the case of Daya Bay, the Guangdong Nuclear Power Company may have been set up precisely to bypass MWREP and give Li more direct control. More recently, in April 1986, it was announced that MNI will take charge of the Daya Bay project. According to one report, MWREP, recognizing that the economics of nuclear energy no longer appear favorable, has chosen to concentrate on thermal and hydro power and willingly abandoned its long battle with MNI for control of the nuclear sector. Peng Shilu, formerly vice-minister of MWREP, will be transferred to a "responsible position" in the Ministry of Nuclear Industry, which is now in control of all Chinese nuclear power activities.[25]

* * *

In sum, the Chinese, after vacillating on nuclear energy for more than a decade, seem to have arrived at a middle ground. They will proceed with development of their own small prototype reactor and import one large plant, primarily for the export market. This modest undertaking suggests that for the moment, Beijing wants to develop a capability for, but not make a full-scale commitment to, a potentially important, yet controversial, energy technology.

## Notes

1. Trade agreement: Kevin Fountain, "On the Back Burner: Nuclear Power in China," *China Business Review*, November–December 1979, p. 39. Third Plenum: *Foreign Broadcast Information Service (FBIS)*, April 18, 1985, p. K16. Other details: Gerard Gourievidis, "Nuclear Power in China," *Joint Publication Research Service (JPRS)*, CST-85-005, February 20, 1985, pp. 107–109.

2. Cancel French order: Fountain, "On the Back Burner," p. 39. Chinese doubts: *FBIS*, April 30, 1986, p. A1.

3. Dori Jones, "Nuclear Power: Back on the Agenda," *China Business Review*, January–February 1981, pp. 32–35. Gourievidis, "Nuclear Power in China," pp. 111, 121–122.

4. 300 MW and Hu Yaobang: *FBIS*, August 24, 1982, pp. K10–11. Daya Bay, Jiangsu, Liaoning: Gourievidis, "Nuclear Power in China," pp. 121–122. Consensus develops: Jiang Shengjie, "Developing Nuclear Energy . . .," *JPRS*, CEA-84-070, August 24, 1984, p. 142.

5. Jiang on future of nuclear: *JPRS*, CEA-84-070, August 24, 1984, p. 138. Jiang on safety: Jiang Shengjie, "Developing China's Nuclear Power Industry," *Beijing Review*, June 18, 1984, p. 2. Other sources showing commitment to nuclear: see articles by He Mingxing and Zuo Hu, *JPRS*, CEA-84-070, August 24, 1984, pp. 158–161.

6. Jiang as director general: *JPRS*, CEA-85-069, August 1, 1985, p. 68. March 1985 article: Luo Shenggeng and Yu Chengze, in *Chinese Journal of Nuclear Science and Engineering*, *JPRS*, CST-85-032, September 19, 1985, pp. 55–61. Qu Geping: Qu Geping, "Nuclear Industry and Environmental Protection," *Industrial Equipment and Materials Quarterly (IEMO)*, vol. 6, no. 4 (Winter 1984), *Nuclear Industry Special Edition*, pp. 34–36. Chernobyl: *FBIS*, May 8, 1986, pp. C1–4; May 22, 1986, pp. K13–15; May 27, 1986, pp. K14–16.

7. Qinshan design: Martin Weil, "The First Nuclear Power Projects," *China Business Review*, September–October 1982, p. 42. Fishing interest: ibid., pp. 40–42. Jiang Shengjie: *FBIS*, May 5, 1986, p. C2.

8. Construction of Qinshan: *JPRS*, CEA-86-012, February 3, 1986, p. 136. Qinshan contracts: *Nucleonics Week*, December 13, 1984, pp. 2–3; *FBIS*, January 30, 1985, p. K15. Joint venture: *Nucleonics Week*, December 13, 1984, p. 3. Daya Bay construction: *JPRS*, CEA-86-012, February 3, 1986, p. 137. Sunan bids: *Nucleonics Week*, April 4, 1985, p. 1.

9. Electricity, 1983: Jiang Shengjie, *Beijing Review*, June 18, 1984, p. 17; Jiang Shengjie, "Developing Nuclear Energy . . .," *JPRS*, CEA-84-070, August 24, 1984, pp. 139–140. Industrial growth, 1983–1985: "China: Economic Performance in 1985," a report to the Joint Economic Committee by the Central Intelligence Agency (Washington, D.C., March 17, 1986), p. 3. Energy figures, 1983–1985: "Energy

Technology Transfer to China: A Technical Memorandum," Congress of the United States, Office of Technology Assessment (Washington, D.C., September 1985), pp. 19–20.

10. Projections in 2000: Jiang Shengjie, *Beijing Review*, June 18, 1984, p. 17. Other details: "Energy Technology Transfer to China," pp. 19–22.

11. Jiang Shengjie, *Beijing Review*, June 18, 1984, pp. 18–20. Regional interests: Weil, "The First Nuclear Power Projects," p. 41.

12. Employment and CNS membership: "Energy Technology Transfer to China," p. 33. Uranium: Jiang Shengjie, *Beijing Review*, June 18, 1984, p. 18.

13. Li Peng: *FBIS*, January 10, 1985, p. K14; January 30, 1985, p. K13. Jiang Xinxiong: *FBIS*, February 4, 1985, p. K9. Zhang Aiping: *FBIS*, April 12, 1984, p. K1. Quotations: Li Yingxiang and Guan Zhihong, in *Jingji guanli*, July 1985, *JPRS*, CEA-85-087, September 27, 1985, pp. 82, 85.

14. 1980 study: "A Proposal to Construct Nuclear Power Plants in Southeast China," *Beijing Ribao*, October 1, 1980, p. 4. This report is discussed in Luo Anren, "An Economic Comparison Between Nuclear and Coal Power Plants in Southeast China," *Nuclear Power and Engineering*, December 1983, *JPRS*, CEA-84-070, August 24, 1984, p. 143; and Jones, "Nuclear Power," pp. 33–34. December 1983 article: Luo, "An Economic Comparison," p. 156. September 1984 article: Yang Haigun, "On the Decline of the World Nuclear Energy Industry," *Shijie jingji*, September 1984, *JPRS*, CEA-85-010, January 29, 1985, pp. 17–20.

15. Jiang Shengjie: *Beijing Review*, June 18, 1984, pp. 17–18. Li Peng: *FBIS*, January 30, 1985, p. K14. Peng Shilu: Peng Shilu, "The Role of Nuclear Power in China's Power Structure," *Nuclear Power Engineering*, June 1985, *JPRS*, CEA-85-111, December 9, 1985, pp. 133–137.

16. Jones, "Nuclear Power," p. 35.

17. Arguments for self-reliance: Cui Lunyuan, *Nuclear Power Engineering*, December 1984, *JPRS*, CEA-85-023, March 6, 1985, p. 82. Grids: ibid., p. 81; Yang Haiqun, *JPRS*, CEA-85-010, January 29, 1985, p. 20. Nationalism: Gourievidis, "Nuclear Power in China," pp. 108–110.

18. Early MNI plans: Weil, "The First Nuclear Power Projects," p. 41. Shanghai factories: *FBIS*, February 16, 1983, p. K18. Chinese planners: Weil, "The First Nuclear Power Projects," p. 42. 1984 imports: *Nucleonics Week*, December 13, 1984, pp. 2–3.

19. Daya Bay: Peng Shilu, "Prospects for Nuclear Power and Development in China," *IEMQ*, vol. 6, no. 4 (Winter, 1984), pp. 17–19; Gourievidis, "Nuclear Power in China," pp. 111, 121–122.

20. Wang Ganchang: Jones, "Nuclear Power," pp. 32, 35. Jiang Shengjie: *JPRS*, CEA-84-070, August 24, 1984, p. 141. Peng Shilu: "Prospects for Nuclear Power," p. 19. Framatome plan: Gourievidis, "Nuclear Power in China," pp. 121–122. Large scale: Luo Anren, *JPRS*, August 24, 1984, pp. 143–157.

21. 1982 conflict: Weil, "The First Nuclear Power Projects," pp. 41–43. Peng Shilu: "Prospects for Nuclear Power," p. 19. WMREP subsidiary: *FBIS*, February 4, 1985, p. K11.

22. Guangdong-Framatome agreement: *Nucleonics Week*, March 20, 1986, pp. 1–3.

23. State Council ratification: "China Puts Nuclear on Backburner," *Nuclear Engineering*, May 1986. Sunan deferred: *Nucleonics Week*, March 6, 1986, p. 1. Trade deficit: "China: Economic Performance in 1985," p. 4. Seventh Five-Year Plan: *Nucleonics Week*, March 13, 1986, p. 2.

24. Li quotation: *FBIS*, April 4, 1986, p. W3. *South China Morning Post: FBIS*, April 9, 1986, p. W4. Jiang Shengjie: *FBIS*, May 5, 1986, p. C2.

25. Li Peng as arbiter: Gourievidis, "Nuclear Power in China," p. 115. Li Peng article: *FBIS*, January 30, 1985, p. K14. Control of Daya Bay: Gourievidis, "Nuclear Power in China," pp. 121–122; *FBIS*, April 15, 1985, pp. W6–7. MWREP shift: "China Puts Nuclear on Backburner," *Nuclear Engineering*, May 1986. Peng Shilu: *FBIS*, April 15, 1986, p. W10.

# 32

## The Evolving Role of Reform in China's S&T System: A Critical Assessment

*Denis Fred Simon*

*Whether or not the numerous problems confronting our economic construction can be effectively resolved depends on whether or not major breakthroughs can be achieved in scientific and technological areas. Similarly whether or not our economic development can keep forging ahead also depends on the most profound source of stamina, namely scientific and technological development.*

—Premier Zhao Ziyang[1]

### Introduction

Faced with the reality of a backward and generally inefficient domestic science and technology (S&T) system, leaders in the People's Republic of China (PRC) have been engaged in an all-out effort to restructure their research sector and to modernize indigenous S&T capabilities. This effort, which actually has its roots in the 1956 Twelve-Year Science and Technology Plan formulated under the direction of former Premier Zhou Enlai and Marshall Nie Rongzhen, has undergone a number of significant changes in focus and direction since its resurgence in early 1978. Nonetheless, a number of themes have remained constant, the most outstanding one being the drive to improve the links between research and production. The Chinese leadership recognizes that without significant contributions by the S&T sector to industry, agriculture, and national defense, it will be hard to sustain the long-term momentum of their modernization program and difficult to attain their goal of quadrupling the gross value of industrial and agricultural output by the year 2000.

In contrast to the regime's initial efforts to promote scientific and technological advance in the aftermath of the March 1978 National Science Conference, however, the current drive is characterized by the strong emphasis being given to organizational reform and structural change in the research and development (R&D) system. So far, the reforms proposed in science and technology have been extensive. The degree to which the leadership is prepared to initiate fundamental change is personified by the March 1985 Central Committee Decision on Reforms in Science and Technology. The document spells out a broad array of modifications regarding the funding of science and technology activities as well as the treatment of technical know-how and the procedures for managing scientists and technicians, among others. Most important, the document represents an attempt to make explicit the role and responsibilities of government actors (central and local), research institutes, and production enterprises regarding science and technology work. By helping to clarify the various roles of these respective actors, the PRC leadership is hoping to break down the bureaucratic boundaries and related obstacles that have long worked against the effective and efficient use of S&T resources.

China's efforts to reform its S&T system must be viewed against the backdrop of the ongoing efforts in both the industrialized nations and the Third World to find a more successful formula to promote technological innovation and advance. In the majority of cases ranging from Japan to Brazil, the role of government has assumed importance, whether through direct intervention—that is, national funding programs and national research laboratories—or through "indirect" means, the bulk of which have stressed encouraging innovation through changes in the economic and S&T environment.[2] In fact, the critical role of government policy has become a central theme in the literature on technological innovation—in spite of the fact that a good deal of the writings on the subject have emphasized the decisive importance of so-called "demand-pull" factors.[3] As Mowery and Rosenberg have suggested, "The role of demand has been overextended and misrepresented, with serious possible consequences for our understanding the innovation process and the appropriate government policy alternatives to foster innovation."[4]

China's policy of introducing so-called market forces as a tool for managing its economy and stimulating technological advance, while at the same time still relying on centrally directed control over research in key areas, stands out as one attempt to sort out the most appropriate role for government in the research sector. In many respects, the Chinese, in their efforts to utilize a "two-pronged" strategy for bringing about fundamental improvements in their science and technology system, are engaged in a unique experiment. There are numerous historical examples in both the East and West that suggest the presence of inherently contradictory elements in such a strategy. Nonetheless, Chinese leaders appear committed to the simultaneous use of what Lindblom has called "authority structures" and "exchange mechanisms" to promote national scientific and technological modernization.[5]

Underlying China's emerging science and technology strategy is a two-edged definition of reform. On the one hand, one dimension of S&T reform has focused on initiating improvements in the operation of the existing centrally oriented S&T structure. The desire to maintain the central tasking mechanism in place reflects two factors. First, the leadership continues to look back fondly on some of its previous successes in science and technology, foremost among them being the development of the country's atomic weapons and ICBMs. These achievements were made by the military through a top-down process, with the national defense S&T and production organs working together to mobilize and target the country's limited S&T capabilities on a high-priority project. The decision to appoint Song Jian, formerly affiliated with China's Ministry of Space Industry, as head of the State Science and Technology Commission in 1983 seems to reflect a determination to maintain some aspects of the "command" system in science and technology affairs.

And second, the leadership refuses to allow the vagaries of the market to determine the outcome of future priority endeavors—favoring instead to reserve a number of key technology areas, such as large-scale integrated circuits, for nurturing by centrally directed organizations. Accordingly, a special leading group for electronics development was created under the State Council in 1983 to coordinate and manage *national* development of capabilities in this important field.

On the other hand, the complementary side of the S&T reform movement has been focused on the introduction of essentially new operating principles and institutions into the research system.[6] The PRC leadership recognizes that the key to the postwar development of U.S. technological capabilities and vitality is to be found in a combination of entrepreneurial talent and market stimuli. Dorfman, for example, in her analysis of the emergence of Route 128 in Massachusetts suggests that the "electronics boom occurred basically without the benefit of concerted efforts to make it happen by academic institutions, government bodies, or other interest groups."[7] In this context, an explicit attempt has been made to link the economic reforms with the reform of the S&T system. As Deng Xiaoping has noted, "The new economic structure must be favorable to science and technology advancement, and the new R&D system should, in turn, be conducive to economic growth. The two systems should go hand in hand, and the long drawn out problem of mismatch between the two may be resolved satisfactorily."[8] Changes in the operating mode and management of the production enterprise are designed to encourage factory directors to pay more attention to the potential value of adopting new technologies—both in terms of process and production innovation.

This chapter examines the role of recent reforms in China's S&T system, specifying the types of changes the Chinese have introduced and the objectives they hope to achieve. The chapter also identifies the limits to reform, some of which remain in the realm of politics and others that are inherent in the nature of China's economic system. The chapter concludes with a comparative section that not only poses questions about China's reform in comparison with the Soviet Union, but, more broadly, in the context of other Third World efforts. It will be argued that Chinese reforms are on the right track in terms of their primary thrust and direction, but also that the entire effort still lacks an adequate degree of institutional support at the level where it matters the most, that is, at the enterprise and institute level. Accordingly, obstructionism remains a serious problem—particularly in terms of the treatment of scientific and technical personnel—one that will require further political reforms if the changes introduced by the leadership are to achieve their desired results.

## The Essence of S&T Reform

Beijing's drive to reform its S&T system has been a building-block effort. The March 1985 Central Committee document represented, in many respects, the formalization of a process of organizational change and institutional refinement that had begun as early as 1981. On a number of occasions, experimental sites were chosen in order to introduce and test new policies and programs. Given the problems left over from the Cultural Revolution and the historical legacy of tension between the Communist Party and the scientific community, the leadership recognized that a broad base of support would have to be established in order to carry its intended reform program forward on a broad scale. The process of building coalitions, however, has not been limited to securing support in the party; a number of other constituencies, such as the economic planners, have been skeptical of the merits of investing large sums of financial resources in research and giving the S&T community greater political influence and power.

Much has already been written about the rebuilding of the S&T system in the aftermath of the demise of the Gang of Four.[9] This literature, in terms of both Chinese and Western perspectives, stresses the bottlenecks faced by the leadership in its efforts to construct a system that had been left in shambles by the political turmoil of the ten previous years. The most visible manifestation of the new attitude toward science and technology was the National Science Conference held in March 1978. The meeting, which was held one month after the formal announcement of the Four Modernizations program, was characterized by a high degree of optimism—with many of the participants apparently believing that China could "catch up" with the advanced industrialized nations and close the prevailing technological gap with the West and Japan in a relatively short span of time.

In most respects, the program for S&T development announced at the meeting was overambitious and did not reflect the true extent to which China's infrastructure for research had been damaged. In addition, China's period of S&T stagnation occurred precisely at the time when the industrialized West was making rapid strides in such key technologies as electronics and computers. Most critical, however, was the shortage of scientific and technical personnel that had developed as a result of the closing of research institutes, universities, and so on. Moreover, Chinese organizations lacked the necessary equipment and instrumentation to undertake and complete much of the research work that needed to be done. In effect, Chinese leaders had hoped to overcome this dismal state of affairs without considering major structural changes in the operation of the S&T system. As one Chinese scientist has remarked, "We had to get the patient well before we could begin to operate."

Between 1978 and 1980, the S&T modernization drive basically stalled. Many individuals merely paid lip service to the calls for S&T advance, while in other cases, efforts to thwart the enhanced status of S&T work were more explicit. The leadership also ran up against serious resources constraints and limitations—many of which derived from the turmoil of the Cultural Revolution.[10] Fundamentally, a disjunction had emerged between what the central leadership was saying in terms of the importance of science and technology to the Four Modernizations program *and* what local leaders interpreted as their obligation and responsibility. Implementation problems were widespread as the central government found it more and more difficult to ensure close adherence to the policies and pronouncements that were being made by organizations such as the State Science and Technology Commission (SSTC). Moreover, even when research activities did progress, there was very little incentive on the part of the institutes or potential end users to link together, even when internal transfers from research to production had been arranged from above.[11]

## The Onset of S&T Reform

Restructuring the S&T system in order to close the prevailing technological gap has taken on a sense of urgency among Chinese leaders. As one leading scholar has remarked:

> We must realize . . . that a new technological revolution has been developing rapidly in the world today and that an increasingly large number of countries are focusing their attention on developing science and technology. Under such circumstances, if we fail to adopt correct policies for taking advantage of this opportunity to confront the challenge, the gap between us and the developed countries will not be narrowed, but it will be further widened instead, and the task of catching up with developed countries economically and technologically will become increasingly more difficult.[12]

The major impetus to S&T reform actually occurred in early 1981 when a number of preliminary changes were introduced into the research sector. First, an election at the Chinese Academy of Sciences (CAS) led to the reemergence of the 400-member Scientific Council as the governing body of that institution. The fact that scientists were put in charge of scientists was an important step forward in the effort to give the scientific community confidence in the staying power of the Four Modernizations. Second, along with the changes at the CAS, an increasing number of individuals with scientific and technical credentials were being placed in positions of authority not only within institutes but also within government offices at the provincial and municipal level. And third, stronger attention was paid to the links between research and production. Scientists, engineers, and technical personnel were admonished to ensure that research served the needs of the economy. While a concerted effort was made to accomplish this last and perhaps most important goal, however, the fact remains that aside from the encouragement at the top, very few, if any, mechanisms existed to facilitate the development of these types of linkages.

Strategically, the clearest evidence that the leadership was dissatisfied with the pace of S&T advance was the speech made by Zhao Ziyang at the October 1982 national science awards meeting in Beijing.[13] Zhao's speech attacked those who had been obstructing the efforts of the central government to launch a concerted drive to develop the country's S&T base. Interestingly, a few months later, the creation of a special leading group for science and technology under the State Council headed by Premier Zhao Ziyang signified the extent to which Zhao's speech reflected a source of deep concern among the upper echelon of the leadership about the need to speed up S&T modernization.[14]

The role of the leading group cannot be underestimated, for it has helped to spearhead the reform movement within the S&T arena. In this regard, the decision to create such a group at such a high level can be attributed to several factors. First, the SSTC had revealed itself unable to carry through on a number of the S&T-related policy initiatives directed by the top leadership. For example, the SSTC was essentially unable to mend its relationship with the CAS. Ever since the creation of the SSTC in the late 1950s, this relationship had been strained. Second, the need to ensure closer integration between research and the economy meant that greater coordination at the highest levels would be necessary, as well as desirable. More specifically, the State Planning, State Economic, and State Science and Technology commissions would all have to work together on a more sustained basis. The leading group was viewed as a means to accomplish this goal. And third, creating a leading group with Zhao Ziyang in charge was a way to place the imprimatur of the office of the premier on the drive to modernize science and technology. Without such visible evidence of high-level support, it would have been difficult for the S&T modernization effort to gain sufficient momentum.

The mandate of the leading group included the following five tasks: (1) long-range science and technology planning; (2) formulation of national policy for key S&T areas; (3) coordination of national level S&T efforts as well as central-local S&T relations; (4) the effective allocation of S&T resources; and (5) reform of the S&T system. According to one member of the office of the leading group, "If the SSTC cannot do something, then we step in." For example, a number of S&T organizations have wanted to publish an S&T newspaper, including the SSTC, the CAS, and the Ministry of Education. The leading group stepped in and decided that the SSTC would have the sole responsibility for producing this newspaper, hereafter called the *Keji Bao*.

The organization of the leading group is rather interesting. Under Zhao Ziyang sit three deputies: Fang Yi, an adviser to the State Council who also formerly was minister in charge of the SSTC and president of the CAS; Song Ping, minister in charge of the State Planning Commission; and Song Jian, minister in charge of the State Science and Technology Commission. There is a second decision-making tier under these three individuals with representatives from the Chinese Academy of Sciences (Yan Dongsheng); the State Education Commission (He Dongchang); the State Economic Commission (Lu Dong); the National Defense Science, Technology, and Industries Commission (Ding Henggao); and the Ministry of Labor and Personnel (Zhao Shouyi). These individuals are responsible for making sure that their home institutions incorporate S&T considerations into their overall activities.

The "office" of the S&T leading group is directed by Song Jian, who has two deputies, Guo Shuyuan of the SSTC and Qian Zhenmeng of the Beijing Heavy Electric Motor Corporation. The office is divided into five functional divisions: (1) management systems, which is responsible for funding mechanisms and oversight of the science foundation (4–5 persons); (2) policy research, which examines broad policy issues (4–5 persons); (3) coordination, which ensures that each of the commissions and the ministries is working together on S&T issues (4–5 persons); (4) S&T cadres, which focuses on the treatment of scientific and technical personnel as well as issues such as labor mobility (4–5 persons); and (5) comprehensive affairs, which is the administrative arm of the leading group (6–7 persons). All together, there are about thirty persons attached to the leading-group office.

The power of the leading group comes from the influence it exerts through the various commissions. It does not have a budget for project allocation. Yet, through the State Planning Commission it can ensure that sufficient funds are made available for specific projects and priorities. The leading group for S&T is somewhat different, for example, from its counterpart at the State Council—the leading group for revitalization of the electronics industry. Even though in principle the two groups share the common goal of improving coordination and bringing greater coherence to key national policy-making areas, the latter group is much more oriented toward substantive issues. The electronics leading group, through a number of formal advisory bodies, helps set electronics and computer policy, whereas the S&T leading group is much more administratively oriented.[15]

Acknowledging this administrative emphasis, however, members of the office of the leading group were intimately involved in the drafting of the March 1985 S&T reform document—which in many ways represents the institutionalization of a new approach to managing S&T affairs. In this context, its principle role was ensuring that the substantive recommendations made by various advisers and formal participants were viable from the perspective of the key government bodies. Only in this fashion, for example, could the reforms have any credibility. Moreover, without the leading group, chances are that the catalyst to bring about fundamental reform in science and technology would have been lacking.

## The March 1985 Reforms

As mentioned, the main impetus to the reform of the science and technology system has been a growing belief that managerial deficiencies and organizational bottlenecks—even more than physical inadequacies—were constraining S&T advance. Wu Mingyu, former vice-minister of the SSTC, has summed up what most proponents of reform believe are the three major shortcomings of China's pre-reform S&T research system.[16] First, the system relied too heavily on administrative measures and neglected the role of economic levers in managing S&T activities. Second, there has been a tendency to overdevelop "independent research institutes" while neglecting S&T activities within production enterprises. For example, China now has more than 9,300 research institutes, the majority of which are not directly connected with enterprises (5,700); more than 90 percent of Japan's R&D units are directly linked to companies. And third, there has been excessive rigidity in management of S&T personnel. Very little room exists for mobility of personnel, as individuals tend to spend their entire careers in one organization.

The formulation of the reform document apparently involved some rather intense political negotiation and compromise.[17] According to one report, the document was amended eleven times! Moreover, it was reviewed personally by Zhao Ziyang and Hu Yaobang on several occasions. In addition, twenty-five Chinese-American scientists were asked to review the document and render their opinions. As will be discussed later on, the issue that stimulated the most controversy was the question of S&T personnel and labor mobility.

The reform document, which is divided into nine sections, actually focuses on four major issues: reform of the funding system; the establishment of technology markets; the strengthening of enterprise capabilities to absorb and explore for new technologies; and the training and career patterns of young and middle-aged scientific and technical personnel.[18] The most wide-ranging aspect of the S&T reforms deals with the funding question. Essentially, the central government hopes to alter the past practice of supplying almost 99 percent of the funding for research activities in the form of grants. Under the guidelines provided in the reform statement, each year the state will reduce the amount of funds it provides institutes for operating expenses. And, an appreciable percentage of the projects sponsored by the central and local government will be issued on the basis of competitive tenders and bids. Moreover, research managers and personnel will be encouraged to seek out research projects themselves in enterprises and the market.

The fact that the central government is actually decreasing the amount of funds it will directly make available to research units does not mean that investment in S&T activities will decline.[19] In reality, during the Seventh Five-Year Plan, the leadership has committed itself to increasing the funds available for S&T activities at a faster rate than the growth in general financial expenditures. Major national projects as well as the construction of key laboratories and experimental sites will still be funded by the central or local government. For example, the development of large-scale integrated circuits is considered one of the country's top S&T priorities. As such, development efforts will receive substantial support from the central government—though some will come in the form of competitive tenders and bids. The same can be said about China's efforts to build a so-called silicon valley in both the Beijing and Shanghai/Wuxi areas.

In addition, a national science foundation is also being established. This fund builds on a number of more modest funding efforts begun over the last three years in the CAS and the State Seismology Bureau. Institutes engaged in basic and some applied research will be able to draw their project funds from the foundation. The only research entities that will be exempt from these rules will be the ones engaged in research activities in the following fields: public health, basic technological services, standardization, metrology, monitoring and surveying, and information gathering.[20]

Institutes under the Chinese Academy of Sciences also fall within the guidelines of the reform document. Under the previous mode of operation, the CAS allocated equal amounts of research funds to each affiliated research unit in accordance with the existing functional divisions. Each institute, in turn, distributed these funds to their respective research groups without distinguishing their capabilities or performance. In many instances, problems emerged, including duplication, extensive delays in dispersement, and insufficient funding. As a result, the CAS has introduced a contract system that will bind each institute to a certain performance level and schedule. In addition, in 1985, the CAS withheld 17 percent of the operating budget of a number of successful research institutes. These funds were then used to provide support to research units engaged primarily in theoretical research.[21]

These changes in the modes and mechanisms for funding research could not have been introduced without the second element of the reforms, namely, the introduction of so-called technology markets. The decision to treat technology as a commercial commodity represents an abrupt departure from previous thinking, which treated the product of mental labor as a public good that could not be privatized. With the growing support for a national patent law (which was issued in April 1985) and the realization that technology does have commercial value, the Chinese have tried to stimulate the diffusion of technology through profit-type incentives. Chinese leaders see technology markets playing a variety of roles: (1) stimulating production-oriented research and development; (2) speeding up the development time for new products; (3) helping to delineate research priorities; (4) breaking down administrative barriers; (5) rewarding hard work; (6) encouraging S&T labor mobility; and (7) improving the status of experts.[22]

Technology markets are viewed as an effective means to help convert research results into production. One manifestation of the drive to create technology markets was the holding of the first national S&T fair in Beijing in 1985 (240 local fairs were held in 1984 and 1985). A total of 4,180 actual transactions were made at the fair with an assessed value of more than 2.1

billion yuan. In addition, a large number of letters of intent were also signed. A similar result—though on a smaller scale—occurred in Tianjin, where close to 500 agreements worth 3.5 million yuan were signed in the span of just over one week. In order to further popularize S&T achievements, the central government under the SSTC has also created the National Market Development Center, which will aid in diffusing technology-related information to potential end users throughout the country.

The interesting feature of China's technology market is that the concept is being treated in a highly flexible manner. Relationships between research institutes and production enterprises can include joint development efforts, long-term cooperation agreements, joint bidding, foreign as well as domestic partners, and multiple players in any one of the previous ventures. Payments can be made on a royalty basis, flat fee, and some combination of the two. In addition, a series of legal regulations are being devised to provide the support structures to make the technology markets work. The leadership has even gone so far as to approve the creation of a "venture capital" company called China Venturetech Investment Company.[23] The company will invest mainly in developing new technology for data processing, biotechnology, electronics, and new materials.[24]

To accomplish its purpose of facilitating technology transfer, however, the technology market must depend on a rational price structure. Yet price reform remains the Achilles' heel of the working of the technology market in China.[25] Chinese enterprise managers as well as research directors are frequently perplexed when it comes to the question of pricing, especially concerning the introduction of new products and components. Some of the more sophisticated attempts at price determination have tried to distinguish between (1) actual value, the net income from the sale of a product using the technology; (2) secondary value, the additional value of the product gained by applying the technology; and (3) latent value, which refers to the potential number and types of applications for the technology. Yet, in spite of these efforts, pricing remains a serious problem—one that has already served to inhibit the effectiveness of this mechanism on a number of occasions.

A number of other factors have also plagued the technology market. First, many suppliers of technology, unable to determine an appropriate price for their technology, have been reluctant to offer their technology in the market for fear of creating a competitor. This continues to be the case in spite of the implementation of the national patent law in April 1985. Second, on a number of occasions, research units have offered "unproven" technologies, and when the purchaser's expectations were not met, he or she held the developer directly responsible. Third, some units have intentionally engaged in fraud and deceit in order to make a profit, while others have plagiarized the research results of geographically distant research institutes and offered them for sale on the open market.[26]

The third element of the reforms deals with the absorption capabilities of enterprises.[27] In many respects, this problem is intimately associated with the issue of technical renovation—which involves a concerted effort by the State Economic Commission to modernize both plant and equipment within Chinese industry as well as to improve management techniques and related aspects on the software side of production.[28] The goal of Chinese leaders is to transform the thinking of the typical factory manager and to encourage him or her to think about technology as part of the competitive arsenal. Heretofore, most factory managers have been insensitive to the potential role of technology on both the process and product dimensions of manufacturing. The current program to strengthen the buyers capacity to utilize acquired technology is designed to provide the factory manager with a set of better tools for responding to the new economic environment in China— all of which was spelled out in the October 1984 CCP Central Committee Decision on Reform of the Economic System.

Funds for technical transformation are to come from the central or local government in the form of both loans and grants. These funds, however, are only a means to help enterprises absorb some of the start-up costs for taking advantage of emerging market opportunities. In some respects, just as the changes in the funding situation are designed to encourage research institutes to seek out potential buyers of their technology, the program of technical renovation is aimed at motivating enterprises to look for potential partners in the R&D community who can help them solve existing manufacturing problems, develop a new product, or improve the quality of an existing item.[29] Moreover, by changing the nature of enterprise behavior, the leadership hopes to create the essence of a demand-pull effect, thus improving the links between research and production.

The last element in the reform program concerns the treatment of S&T personnel. This problem has been the most difficult to resolve because of its broader political implications.[30] The reform document principally talks about the lack of mobility among S&T workers as a major defect in China's S&T modernization program. The problem affects students and scholars who have recently been sent abroad as well as individuals who have not left the PRC for overseas training.[31] According to Zhou Guangzhao of the CAS, this lack of mobility stifles creativity and inhibits the diffusion of technology and know-how within the society.[32] One major cause of the low mobility is the practice of inbreeding, whereby a university or research unit seeks to retain those individuals who are trained by the unit. The aim of the reform is to provide a mechanism for talented S&T personnel to move to those places where their skills and expertise can be more fully and appropriately utilized.

Relatedly, the reforms regarding S&T personnel also aim to free up scientific and technical labor so that individuals with a certain type of expertise can serve as consultants or advisers to government offices, enterprises, and the like. Once an individual completes his or her assigned duties, the person is free to engage in off-duty consulting. Not only does such activity help provide income supplements to these persons, but it also facilitates the application of technical knowledge to problem-solving activities in the area of policy formulation and manufacturing.

Resistance to this element of the reform program has been widespread because political cadres see themselves as being displaced by scientific and technical personnel. Party officials have felt insecure in granting these individuals more authority and independence, especially since they threaten the party's own claims to be the main purveyor of truth and knowledge in society. In addition, there is the problem of jealousy that has emerged as some individuals could use and have used their expertise to earn added income. In some cases, these individuals have been accused of extortion and blackmail by jealous individuals who have not had such opportunities available to themselves.[33] There is also a concern that individuals will use existing resources and know-how to benefit themselves and ignore the larger needs of their unit or community. As a result of these continuing bottlenecks, the effort to alter the status and opportunities available to S&T personnel has encountered substantial problems. And finally, along with the prospects of greater mobility have emerged fears about "personnel raiding." Institute directors, particularly those in remote areas, are concerned about losing their best talent to "recruiters" from the coastal areas who may try to entice key individuals to change jobs.

The reform document also touches on a number of other areas, some of which are outside the scope of this chapter. Two additional issues, however, do deserve our attention. First is the question of foreign technology imports. Generally speaking, the Chinese remain committed to the use of foreign technology and know-how. They have decided to deemphasize the acquisition of whole plants and equipment and focus their attention on the software side of technology imports. The desire to draw from the global bank of technology, however, must be examined from the perspective of a growing debate within China between those who have immediate needs for equipment and therefore want to import such items as foreign-made computers and machinery and those who seek to strengthen indigenous S&T capabilities and therefore are willing to forgo large numbers of final-product purchases from abroad. In the area of microcomputers and television sets, for example, steps have already been taken to introduce protectionist methods to deter large-scale imports—suggesting that supporters of the latter position may have won the first round of this debate.

In the context of this analysis, the issue of foreign borrowing also holds some special importance because the current reform effort is modeled, in many ways, on that of the United States. The extent to which the idea of "copying" institutions from the West is being criticized is reflected in an article in the January 1985 issue of *Keyan Guanli*. In this article, the author, who is from the Ministry of Machine Building, sharply attacks the notion of "hiving off' research institutes to Chinese factories just because it is done that way in the West.[34] More specifically, the author suggests that while this approach may help stimulate new product development, it will necessarily lead these research institutes to ignore the economic plan as well as their larger social and national responsibilities.

More broadly, there has emerged growing concern that an excessive tendency to rely on foreign technology has developed. A recent article by

Zhang Aiping, minister of defense, in the December 16, 1985 issue of *Hongqi* (Red Flag) raised the following issue:

> A tendency has emerged in the course of breaking away from national seclusion. In some comrade's opinion, it seems that everything foreign is good. They only think of reaping without sowing and of immediate interests regardless of national interests. They introduce foreign technology without serious consideration. As a result, foreign equipment which we can manufacture through our efforts after studying it is also imported, causing serious losses to the state and having a bad influence in the world.

More significant, however, is what Zhang goes on to say:

> What merits particular attention is that some comrades turn a deaf ear to the repeated instructions of the CPC Central Committee. A similar situation can be found in our propaganda work. Comrades in charge of propaganda work have laid too much emphasis on imported equipment and production lines. They have not paid enough attention to the propagating of good products we have manufactured through our own efforts.[35]

Zhang's comments reflect China's continued commitment to achieving enhanced self-reliance in most technology areas. In effect, he is referring to previously mentioned problems of ineffective assimilation that continue to plague China.[36] An article that appeared in *Guangming Ribao* during the summer of 1985 summed up China's desired approach: "Let us change as soon as possible the formula of 'the first machine being imported, the second machine being imported, and the third machine also being imported' into one of 'the first machine being imported, the second being made in China, and the third machine being exported.'"[37] These concerns about the proper approach to foreign-technology acquisition as well as its use suggest that there remain a number of unresolved policy issues regarding the "real" meaning of the open door.

The second issue deals with the effort to promote closer ties between the military and civilian sectors. Up until the early 1980s, the relationship between PRC military and civilian R&D sectors had been highly compartmental. And, while CAS institutes and several key universities had frequently been tasked to participate in defense-related projects, the same could not be said for military R&D institutes with respect to most large civilian projects.[38] The key to the successful performance of certain elements of the defense sector, such as strategic weapons programs, lies in the ability of a centralized agency at the top to create a team made up of a critical mass of individuals and give them the necessary funds, equipment, and support to achieve their stated goal. Under the reforms, military units have been instructed to use their superior resources and more extensive experience in dealing with technology to help solve civilian problems.

This is not to suggest that the military has been without innovation problems. For example, up until the 1982 bureaucratic reform, two separate offices existed for overseeing military R&D (National Defense S&T Commission) and production (National Defense Industries Office). In 1982 these two units were combined into the National Defense Science, Technology, and Industries Commission. In some respects, this change made the military R&D-production nexus a powerful force in the bureaucracy—though at the time the effort to streamline military spending and close down obsolete production lines did offset some of this new acquired clout. More important, the NDSTIC retained much of its tasking authority. This decision, combined with the fact that defense S&T and production leaders see great potential benefit in helping to strengthen the civilian S&T base suggests that the commitment to better civilian-military linkages will serve as a mechanism for broader defense involvement in all facets of the S&T modernization program—with the implication that in critical fields a strong central government role will continue to be present.

## Prospects and Conclusions

So far, this chapter has presented a number of the key elements of China's S&T reform program, identifying the introduction of new market forces as well as continued reliance on centralized controls for bringing about S&T advance and closer links between research and production. Chinese leaders recognize that they cannot relinquish total control over S&T activities, especially since resources are limited and funding is in short supply. Concerns have already emerged that some research units are focusing on short-term goals and projects because of their immediate financial payoffs rather than concentrating on long-term issues and technological possibilities.[39] Thus we are likely to see a continued effort to maintain an amalgam of authority and exchange structures to promote S&T modernization.

One of the most interesting developments from the perspective of this two-pronged strategy is the emergence of what have come to be called research-production alliances (*lianheti*). In some cases, they involve the coming together of research units, design units, and production enterprises into a single working entity. The gap between research and production is bridged as new product or design possibilities are addressed in a coordinated fashion. On several occasions, these alliances have involved organizations from different ministerial or administrative jurisdictions, suggesting that the *lianheti* may be a means to breakdown the bureaucratic barriers that heretofore have plagued China's S&T efforts.

The idea of the *lianheti* has recently been carried one step further by officials in China's Ministry of Electronics Industry. According to a report in the *China Daily*, MEI officials hope to establish ten large research-production complexes throughout China by the 1990s. These complexes will include a number of research and production organizations from MEI as well as other ministries and localities. Their purpose is to facilitate links between research and production, while at the same time providing enhanced potential to respond to market opportunities for new components, final products, and so on. Ideally, these complexes are to act in fashion similar to U.S. corporations rather than administrative entities. The notion is that they will compete with each other rather than specialize—though there will be some internal specialization. Whether or not they will behave as "economic actors" depends, to a great extent, on how far China's overall economic reforms proceed in the coming years and the extent to which authority structures give way to exchange mechanisms as the principal form of organization.

As China enters the post–Deng Xiaoping era, its strategy for S&T modernization will increasingly reflect the attempt to combine elements of state and market. State-led S&T policies—many of which will be a product of the leading group for S&T—will be aimed at developing an adequate infrastructure for promoting indigenous development and absorbing foreign technology, while the market will be used to ensure that enterprise and research managers are concerning themselves with innovation opportunities. This strategy, in many respects, is one that is converging with many of the Asian newly industrialized nations. In such places as India, Taiwan, and South Korea, for example, a mixture of state and market are being used to establish a base for high-technology industries such as VLSI production or computer development.

The fact that China's reforms may be moving it more in the direction of other successful nations bodes well for the Chinese modernization effort. China's leaders understand the nature of their country's problems and have already been modestly successful in offering a range of acceptable solutions to these problems. The role they have assigned to government is different from the stultifying role it played in the past. At the same time, however, there are strict limits to how far S&T reform can proceed in the future unless further political and economic reforms are introduced. In the political realm, these reforms will have to include a further diminished role for the Communist Party in the research sector as well as improvements in the status and treatment of S&T intellectuals. Some of this has begun with the recent housecleaning that has taken place at the level of China's municipal and provincial S&T commissions. In most large cities and provinces, new, technically competent individuals have been appointed to direct local S&T activities. In addition, many of these localities have also established their own "leading groups" for science and technology—a move that reinforces the continued role of government in S&T affairs. In Shanghai, for example, the local S&T leading group has been responsible for clarifying the S&T priorities of the municipality and mobilizing resources in such areas as microelectronics and biotechnology.

In the economic realm, further price reform is essential. Until there is substantial price reform, the technology market will not function effectively, and the issue of price will limit the number of persons who will turn to this type of mechanism to sell or acquire technical know-how. Moreover, management training is another essential element. All too often, factory managers still consider technological innovation to be more of a bother than a benefit; they are afraid to accept the risk of employing a new product or component when they feel secure with their existing technology. These managers need to better understand the role of technology in the firm and how to use technology to their advantage. Much work remains to be done.

These same types of problems exist within the research community as well. After "eating out of the big pot" for so long, many institutes are finding it difficult to escape from the ideology of the three depends: dependence on the state for funding, dependence on upper level to designate research projects for the lower levels, and dependence on others regarding the application of research results. In addition, apprehension about making mistakes is also widespread. Moreover, institute personnel, uncertain of the full meaning of the reforms or fearful of their consequences, have tried to emphasize the "uniqueness" of their research charter in an effort to block the reforms from taking hold at their institutions. It will take time to overcome these problems and build forward momentum for the reforms at the working level.

As indicated by Premier Zhao Ziyang's comments at the Fourth Session of the Sixth National People's Congress, the drive to reform and modernize science and technology has taken on added importance as Chinese leaders have sought to respond to what Toffler and others have claimed is the onset of a new global technological revolution. This new revolution is characterized by the significant role of four key technologies: microelectronics, computers, new materials, and biotechnology. China's leadership has decided to accept the challenge posed by this so-called technological revolution.

While the notion of a global technological revolution is indeed attractive, it should not force the Chinese to lose sight of the fact that history has shown that incremental progress in science and technology rather than quantum leaps has characterized the success stories in the development process. Even in the case of Japan, whose rapid growth has been held up as a potential model in China, progress was accomplished on the basis of taking existing technologies and improving on their performance through modest innovations. While government did not play a huge role, it did play a significant role. The Japanese case shows that it is not the quantity of government intervention that counts but rather the quality and nature of that intervention.

Most important, the effort to attain substantial levels of growth and technological advance can be accomplished only after a workable S&T infrastructure has been put in place. Policies for science and technology are part of an entire package, involving all sorts of inputs ranging from finance to marketing. Starting in 1985, China took some bold steps to reaffirm the importance of S&T and to stimulate forward momentum. The success of this effort will not come from adhering in a rigid fashion to catchy themes or by pursuing strategies that are based on the political fear of fallling behind. Rather, the long-term viability of China's present "mixed strategy" will be allowing the strategy to evolve in conjunction with the further changes that are needed in the economic system. Government policy can only have its desired impact when the economic signals being sent to the various actors in the system are, on balance, logical and internally consistent. In this regard, Deng Xiaoping appears correct; what is needed is a Chinese type of modernization. Out of this search for a Chinese style of modernization may come a model for combining state-led initiatives with market forces in a more effective way than either most developing nations or most socialist countries have been able to achieve.

## Notes

1. "Zhao Ziyang Delivers Work Report at NPC Opening" (Fourth Session of the Sixth National People's Congress, March 25, 1986) *Foreign Broadcast Information Service (FBIS) PRC*, March 28, 1986, pp. K1–28.

2. For a discussion of some of these issues in the context of the United States, see Christopher Hill and James Utterback, eds., *Technological Innovation for a Dynamic Economy* (New York: Pergamon, 1979). See also William Abernathy, Kim Clark, and Alan Kantrow, *Industrial Renaissance: Producing a Competitive Future for America* (New York: Basic Books, 1983). For a discussion of these issues in the context of the Third World see Martin Fransman and Kenneth King, eds., *Technological Capability in the Third World* (New York: St. Martin's, 1984).

3. C. A. Tisdell, *Science and Technology Policy: Priorities of Governments* (London: Chapman and Hall, 1981).

4. David Mowery and Nathan Rosenberg, "The Influence of Market Demand upon Innovation: A Critical Review of Some Recent Studies," *Research Policy*, April 1979, pp. 103–153.

5. Charles E. Lindblom, *Politics and Markets* (New York: Basic Books, 1977).

6. Denis Fred Simon, "Rethinking R&D," *China Business Review*, July–August 1983, pp. 25–31.

7. Nancy Dorfman, "Route 128: The Development of a Regional High Technology Economy," *Research Policy*, December 1983, pp. 299–316.

8. Song Jian quoting Deng Xiaoping in "Science Reforms Vital," *Science*, August 9, 1985, p. 526.

9. R. P. Suttmeier, *Science, Technology and China's Drive for Modernization* (Stanford, Calif.: Hoover Institution Press, 1980). Leo Orleans, ed., *Science in Contemporary China* (Stanford, Calif.: Stanford University Press, 1981).

10. In many respects, the leadership initially underestimated the damage that had been done to the S&T system as a result of the Cultural Revolution. The manpower constraint, created in large part by the closing of China's education institutions, was perhaps the clearest example of the consequences of the Great Proletarian Cultural Revolution.

11. See Joint Publications Research Service, ed., *China Examines Science Policy*, vol. 1 (January 1982) and vol. 2 (JPRS 83240, April 12, 1983), Springfield, Va.: Foreign Broadcast Information Service.

12. *FBIS-PRC*, March 28, 1986, p. K11.

13. *Beijing Review*, November 15, 1982, pp. 13–20.

14. *FBIS-PRC*, January 31, 1983, p. K8.

15. See Denis Simon and Detlef Rehn, "Innovation in China's Semiconductor Industry: The Case of Shanghai," *Research Policy*, forthcoming.

16. Ma Lili, "The Concept of China's Scientific Research Reform: A Visit to Wu Mingyu, Vice-Minister of the State Science and Technology Commission," *Huashengbao*, April 10, 1985, p. 31, translated in *JPRS-CST-85-028*, August 27, 1985, p. 1.

17. Dai Yaping, "Running Water Flows into the Scientific and Technological Circles in China," *Zhongguo Xinwen She*, March 20, 1985, translated in *FBIS-PRC*, March 26, 1985, p. K10.

18. "CPC Central Committee's 13 March 1985 Decision on the Reform of the Science and Technology Management System," *Xinhua*, March 19, 1985, translated in *FBIS-PRC*, March 21, 1985, pp. K1–9.

19. According to Chinese estimates, the PRC spends about 0.6 percent of its national income on R&D while the industrialized countries spend between 2.0 and 3.0 percent.

20. *FBIS-PRC*, March 21, 1985, pp. K2–3.

21. *China Daily*, January 8, 1985, p. 1.

22. "The Technical Market Must Serve Economic Construction: An Interview with Guo Shuyuan, Vice Minister of the State Science and Technology Commission," in *Liaowang*, May 27, 1985, pp. 38–39, translated in *JPRS-CST-85-038*, November 5, 1985, p. 3.

23. "New Ideas to Get Funds Despite Risk," *China Daily*, January 13, 1986, p. 2.

24. Ironically, 40 percent of the capital for the 40 million yuan company has come from the State Science and Technology Commission, raising questions about how "market-driven" decisions on investments might ultimately be.

25. Xu Yi, Chen Baosen, and Liang Wuxia, *Shehuizhuyi Jiage Wenti* (Beijing: Chinese Finance and Economics Press, 1982), translated in *JPRS-CEA-85-019*, February 20, 1985, esp. pp. 75–80.

26. R. P. Suttmeier, "New Conflicts in the Research Environment," *Bulletin of the Atomic Scientists*, October 1984, pp. 7S–11S.

27. See Li Boxi et al., *Zhongguo Jishu Gaizao Wenti Yanjiu* (Analysis of the Problems Regarding China's Technical Transformation), vols. 1–2 (Shanxi: People's Publishing House, 1984).

28. "Technical Renovation Is the Catchword," *Intertrade*, October 1985, pp. 9–13.

29. *Hongqi* (Red Flag), August 16, 1985, pp. 28–33, translated in *JPRS-CRF-85-021*, October 15, 1985, p. 57.

30. See Denis Fred Simon, "China's S&T Intellectuals in the Post-Mao Era: A Retrospective and Prospective Glimpse," *Journal of Northeast Asian Studies*, Summer 1985, pp. 57–82.

31. "Returned Students Feeling Stifled," *China Daily*, August 31, 1984, p. 4.

32. *Guangming Ribao*, December 21, 1984, p. 1, translated in *JPRS-CST-85-010*, June 12, 1985, pp. 22–24.

33. "Guanxi Reports on Persecution of Engineer," translated in *FBIS-PRC*, July 20, 1984, p. P3.

34. Zhang Xicheng, "An Outline of the Reforms in the Scientific Research System of the Machine-Building Industry," *Keyan Guanli* (Scientific Research Management), January 1985, pp. 26–28.

35. Zhang Aiping, "Strengthen Leadership and Do a Better Job in Importing Technology," *Hongqi*, no. 24, December 16, 1985, pp. 4–9.

36. "Strive for Self-Development," *Tianjin Ribao*, October 18, 1985, p. 1.

37. *Guangming Ribao*, July 4, 1985, p. 1.

38. One piece of evidence that this situation has begun to change deals with the active involvement of many of the scientists formerly involved in China's nuclear weapons program in the country's nuclear energy program.

39. Two party cadres from the Yantai S&T Commission in Shandong recently received disciplinary warnings for using scientific research funds and equipment to make business deals. They used the Scientific Equipment Company affiliated with the commission to sell equipment under the guise of scientific exchange. *China Daily,* September 19, 1985.

# 33

## The United States, the PRC, and Japan: Military Technology Transfer Policies and Strategic Collaboration

### William T. Tow

One of the most striking aspects of Asian-Pacific security politics during the 1980s has been the maturing in geopolitical relations conducted between the United States, Communist China, and Japan. Deng Xiaoping's continued determination to acquire high technology from foreign sources in order to stimulate the PRC's economic growth as well as to enhance its strategic power against the Soviet Union has led Beijing to cultivate a gradual but steady growth of quasi-military ties with Washington and, to some extent, with Tokyo. The pace and scope of such ties, moreover, has continued to increase steadily despite intermittent Sino-American tension over the Ronald Reagan administration's sensitivity about the Republic of China's continued security and over Communist China's own determination not to become too closely affiliated with either superpower. It also seems evident that the premises underlying common PRC-Western security interests will not be disrupted by the Soviet Union's latest diplomatic overtures extended to Communist China, notwithstanding the relative sophistication with which these initiatives have been presented by the Mikhail Gorbachev regime.[1]

Japan's emergence as an important politico-strategic actor in the East Asian region as well as selected global security issues was inevitable, given Tokyo's worldwide trading interests and the growing size of its industrial-technological infrastructure. Indeed, Japan's obvious economic prowess constituted the very basis for increased pressures extended by the United States and by other industrial democracies for Tokyo to assume a greater proportion of the West's overall defense-burden-sharing role. As significant over the long term, however, could be a developing convergence of Sino-Japanese security interests within the general framework of global power politics: ensuring that future European arms control agreements focusing on Soviet SS-20 deployments in Western Russia will not compromise the East Asian region's prospects for achieving the same levels of SS-20 reductions, developing eventual political stabilization for the Korean Peninsula, or responding effectively to the burgeoning nuclear-free-zone movement now capturing the imagination of many Asian-Pacific populations and states. Even more fundamentally, both Communist China and Japan now view economic strength and technological progress as ultimately the best means for guaranteeing their own security as well as their region's future stability.

In any context of U.S.-PRC-Japanese triangular geopolitics that may now be evolving, therefore, the increased compatibility of Communist China's and Japan's strategic outlooks as it might affect American security calculations needs to be assessed. It is contended in this paper that military or military-related technology transfers between the three states in question provide one of the best measurements for examining such U.S. calculations. In particular, two major patterns will be assessed here: the impact of U.S. military technology transfers to the PRC and the implications for pending "reverse military technology flows" from Japanese industries to the U.S. Department of Defense, which represent the first instance in postwar history where the United States has specifically pursued an ongoing high-military-technology relationship with itself as the beneficiary. These two issue-areas will be assessed because they seem to represent a common triangular response (at the national-actor level) to a threat deemed so serious as to represent a potential disruption to the entire Asian-Pacific power balance—the growing strength and mobility of Soviet forces deployed throughout Northeast Asia and, increasingly, throughout other Asian-Pacific littorals.

Initially, military technology transfer politics would appear to represent a readily available as well as a rational division of strategic labor for Washington, Beijing, and Tokyo to undertake in response to Soviet military challenge now emerging in the Pacific. Yet, other regional security actors, most notably the members of the Association of Southeast Asian Nations (ASEAN), continue to be wary of either Communist China becoming a first-rate military power or of Japan becoming too independent militarily from the U.S. forces in Northeast Asia. Military technology transfer politics, then, must be addressed with the following question in mind: Is the United States really prepared to orchestrate the diverse policy options available for projecting the military technology politics it institutes with either Communist China or Japan as an instrument for realizing its own, concretely defined regional security objectives for this region? Or, conversely, have the Americans been lured into military technology transfer politics especially by the PRC leadership but also by various Japanese industrial interests based on short-term commercial incentives and on bureaucratic inertia alone?

## Communist China's Strategic Needs and the U.S. Military Technology Tie

Communist China's present regime is implementing historic shifts in its traditional strategic doctrine. The PRC's Central Military Commission has mandated that the defense sector will no longer enjoy privileged status but will be compelled to integrate with the other production sectors of Chinese society. At an early 1986 meeting of the PRC's Ministries of Aeronautics and Ordnance Industry, Premier Zhao Ziyang warned defense industry officials that not enough had yet been done in merging the efforts of defense and civilian personnel to overcome technological deficiencies in the nation's military system:

> The defense industry should equip itself with a crack contingent of scientific and technical personnel to tackle difficult assignments. . . . More enterprises, workers and staff members, and scientific and technical personnel from the defense industry front should gear to the needs of the modernization drive. . . . Only when the defense industry is geared to serve the overall modernization drive is it possible to facilitate the modernization of our national defense. To further tap the production potentials of defense industry enterprises, it is necessary to transform them into enterprises producing civilian goods use.[2]

Zhao's tough rhetoric has been substantiated by the Communist Chinese government's actual behavior. A 25 percent reduction of People's Liberation Army (PLA) manpower (from 4 million to 3 million personnel) has been combined with the recent streamlining of the PRC's regional military commands. Beijing desires to attain greater centralization of Communist China's overall defense structure by reinforcing tightened command and control over the PLA, integral toward instituting an "active defense" strategy within Communist China. Mao Zedong's traditional glorification of protracted warfare, with ideology and morale portrayed as invariably stronger assets than an enemy's technological superiority in weapons and firepower, has now been refuted as inappropriate for preparing the PRC to face Soviet military power in the north or the Vietnamese war machine in the south.

Communist China's defense science and technology infrastructure, however, has far to go before it even begins to meet the requirements of credible active defense now endorsed by its leadership. U.S. Department of Defense spokesmen estimate that while Chinese units in the northern military regions have enjoyed some improvement in mechanization and firepower since the 1969 Sino-Soviet border skirmishes, the PRC's air support and comparative theater nuclear weapons capabilities in this area of operations remain drastically inferior. Indeed, these analysts assert, the gap between overall Chinese and Soviet military power has continued to widen in Moscow's favor over the years with the Russians' addition of mobilized firepower and more combat support units.[3] Communist China's present tactical/theater nuclear weapons (T-TNW) inventory is neither diverse nor sophisticated enough to slow a concentrated Soviet axis of advance and combined arms operations in any future Sino-Soviet conflict, and little hope exists for the Chinese to achieve the type of sequential nuclear targeting needed to block a systematic Soviet offensive spearheaded by its own sophisticated T-TNW arsenal. The PRC needs advanced antitank and antiaircraft weapons systems to complement its own rudimentary armored and nuclear forces, and such technology is only procured or developed with greater funds than Communist China's austerity defense budget can presently support.

At the strategic conflict level, Chinese abilities to engage in discriminate targeting during wartime are more impressive. In September 1985, for example, the PRC tested a CSS-4 intercontinental ballistic missile outfitted with what Western intelligence experts believe may have been a multiple independent reentry vehicle (MIRV) nuclear delivery system.[4] Even more recent Chinese press reports (January 1986) point to a "successful range-increasing test of a certain underwater missile . . . [which] has markedly improved the capability of this missile, increased the number of targets it can hit, expanded the coverage area of the control target, and increased the flexibility of its firepower application."[5] Western visitors to Chinese booster rocket production centers have reported sighting prototypes of advanced American and European computer systems in operation there. Foreign military technology is obviously vital to most PRC strategic operations now under development within Communist China.

While U.S. technology transfer regulations applicable to the PRC's military requirements have been liberalized significantly in recent years, even the most accommodating technology transfer criteria could well be hindered by the apparent current lack of reciprocity for such U.S. generosity in terms of both accountability and marketing considerations. The PRC continues to insist, for example, that sales of military end items be as limited as possible and always subject to indigenous Chinese replication and production of the weapons system in question. Increasingly, Chinese defense plants are becoming integrated with their civilian production counterparts so that future technology transfers from abroad can be applied to both military and civilian goods production.[6] To what extent the PRC will really be able to compensate for its reluctance in purchasing finished American or allied defense items and achieve sufficient interplay between its military doctrinal objectives and technological proficiency remains unclear. But Communist China's present skills for combining the dynamics of changing technology into its overall national infrastructure still seem to be impeded by a determination even on the part of Communist China's current "pragmatic" leadership that the principle of self-sufficiency in defense shall reign within the PRC at all costs. This is the case notwithstanding the reality that any such path of "self-reliance" delays indefinitely Communist China's entry into the select club of nations capable of waging modern war comprehensively—a club which the PRC desperately seeks to join.

Several key aspects of science and technology (S&T) directly relate to Communist China's long-term aspirations of becoming a first-class military power. Electronics research, for example, is directly applicable to strengthening Chinese command, control, communications, and intelligence (C[3]I) proficiency as time-critical data processing and advanced electronics instrumentation become more crucial in modern weapon systems' production and operation. While the PRC's performance in the metallurgical industry has been somewhat more impressive—the PRC can now, for instance, recover titanium, vanadium, and other rare-earth metals with fairly efficient techniques if judged by Western standards, and these materials directly relate to its ability to build modern weapons systems—the quantity and quality of metallurgical end products in China still fall short of both military and civilian needs. Domestically produced axle bearings, for example, last only a quarter of the distance of those produced in the West, and the PRC's high-speed drill bits cannot begin to match the durability of those made abroad.[7] Telecommunications equipment is also a premium item within PLA inventories, as the lack of adequate high-frequency radio communications during the Sino-Vietnamese border war fought during early 1979 graphically illustrated. The PRC's military satellite communications needs will also become more important as Beijing moves to enhance its overall military modernization over time.

The basic constraints related to Communist China's overall military S&T development can be summarized as follows:

*Finance*

Foreign exchange reserves, while comparably strong for a third world nation, could be exhausted rapidly with major purchases of nuclear power plants or finished defense end products from abroad. The U.S. Office of Technology Assessment has estimated that only 10 percent of the foreign exchange produced by Communist Chinese oil and coal exports can then be reallocated to the foreign procurement designed to reinforce the PRC's overall energy sector.[8]

*Manpower*

The PRC still faces a shortage of technologically proficient personnel needed to create interplay between defense and civilian production sectors. Part of the problem stems from an immobility in the labor pool of what technocrats *are* available (i.e. directors of military research institutes are seldom willing to lose people whose skills might better be applied elsewhere because of their fear in losing political clout or economic prerogatives within a centrally planned economic system). Other drawbacks include uneven distribution of resources among subsystems, institutional barriers to incentive systems and to increasing wages, limited promotion opportunities, and "non-professional" (i.e. political) demands on researchers' time.[9]

*Bureaucratic Decision Making*

"Departmentalism" within Chinese S&T infrastructures still abounds with little inter-organizational communication really taking place. From a defense perspective, potential S&T suppliers become justifiably frustrated over how to perceive the influence of, say, the Commission on Science, Technology and Industry for National Defense (NDSTIC)—allegedly the coordinating center for PLA weapons procurement, research, and testing—in relation to that of the Chinese Communist Party's Military Affairs Commission (MAC), thought to be the most powerful decisionmaking component on military affairs in Communist China. There seems to be little, if any, lateral transfer of authority or function from one entity to another on a basis readily understood by Western defense contractors. Under such circumstances, the extent to which the renegotiated 1985 Sino-American Protocol for Science and Technology—supposedly allowing greater U.S. access and understanding on how Chinese S&T, in general, functions—is really useful remains questionable. As U.S. Commerce Undersecretary for International Trade Lionel Olmer recently testified before Congress: " . . . It depends on what it is the Chinese want. There have not been . . . the kind of detailed specifications as to what Chinese objectives are and what it is we are being asked to transfer."[10]

Despite these barriers both to understanding the nature of Chinese S&T and to the strengthening of what S&T functions *are* identifiable, particularly in Communist China's defense sector, the U.S. role in Chinese military technology planning and organization has increased steadily throughout the 1980s. Although the groundwork for such cooperation was laid initially with Secretary of Defense Harold Brown's visit to Communist China in 1980 (shortly after the Soviet Union's invasion of Afghanistan), the two most important high-level military exchanges between the United States and the PRC took place under the Reagan administration, with Secretary of Commerce Malcolm Baldrige's journey to Beijing in August 1983 and Defense Secretary Caspar Weinberger's visit a month later.[11] Baldrige was instrumental in pushing through the liberalization of U.S. "dual use" exports (applicable to both civilian and military purposes), and Weinberger established procedures and programs for the subsequent exchange of the military services' senior leaders and technocrats, as well as setting into motion a U.S. interagency review process for incoming Chinese requests relating to U.S. weapons technology and end systems.[12] Subsequently, Communist China's Defense Minister Zhang Aiping and PLA Naval Commander Liu Huaqing visited the U.S. (June 1984 and November 1985) while Secretary of the Navy John Lehman (August 1984), Chairman of the U.S. Joint Chiefs of Staff General John W. Vessey, Jr. (January 1985), and Chief of Staff of the U.S. Air Force General Charles A. Gabriel (October 1985) reciprocated with trips to the PRC.

U.S. military technology sales to the PRC have also accelerated. Such transactions are channeled through either the Department of Commerce's Commodity Controls List (CCL) or the Department of State's International Munitions List (IML). The U.S. Department of Defense (USDOD) and the National Security Council, however, still exercise the right of review and veto over all military-related sales to Beijing, and intrabureaucratic conflict often does occur between the responsible U.S. government agencies over what can and cannot be sold. Testifying before the U.S. Congress in support of a comprehensive telecommunications protocol between Communist China and the United States, for example, Olmer noted:

It is our understanding that the hangup is with DOD. Not only have they not signed off, but they haven't been very specific about what they want. . . .
    . . . I don't want to prejudge whatever their concerns might be with the protocol, but it would seem, minimally, we ought to be able to expect them to respond in some fashion so that whatever problems there may be, to the extent they can be legitimately ironed out, we can move ahead.[13]

Similar issues related to bureaucratic clearance occur in COCOM (Coordinating Committee for Export Controls to Communist Nations) with the European NATO members and in Japan's monitoring of proposed U.S. technology sales to Communist China clearly designed to neutralize American commercial advantages vis-à-vis similar commercial endeavors involving their own high-technology firms with sales to Beijing.[14]

The major question for U.S. security planners who favor continued momentum in technology transfer relations with the PRC is how that nation will actually exercise its military and economic capabilities as they grow over time. Some Western observers have warned that as the Chinese Communists drive toward strategic parity with Moscow and Washington, they will be more prone to disrupt the Asian power balance.[15] The majority of U.S. officials and independent strategic observers, however, contend that qualified U.S. military and technology assistance programs extended to the PRC would actually stabilize the Asian-Pacific region in the long term. Following his return from the PRC as part of President Reagan's visiting entourage in April 1984, Assistant Secretary of State for East Asian and Pacific Affairs Paul Wolfowitz related in congressional testimony that the major American geopolitical rationale behind forging a strategic relationship with Beijing is "to put U.S.-China relations on a more stable and increasingly comprehensive basis—one that avoids the extremes of hostility and suspicion without succumbing to the opposite extreme of euphoria and sentimentality."[16] Department of Defense spokesmen, perhaps attempting to explain their past reticence for approving high-technology transfers to the PRC "carte blanche" in response to pressures by the Department of Commerce or by other trade-oriented bureaucracies, have supplemented Wolfowitz's characterization of U.S. policy interest:

> Our goal is to have an enduring defense relationship which will move in measured steps. [Communist] China has made it clear to us that it seeks no alliance. Rather [U.S.-PRC] defense relations must mirror the slow but steady growth of the U.S.-[Communist] China political and economic relationships. . . .
>
> Our position is that, first of all, the mission areas to which the technology applies would have to be evaluated. And then the items requested, themselves, would have to be considered for approval on a case-by-case basis.[17]
>
> The willingness of the United States to develop a military relationship with the PRC is founded on the assessment that the United States and the PRC share important parallel interests, both globally and regionally. Foremost among these is a common security concern—the growing threat of the Soviet Union. Thus, an objective of U.S. policy is to build an enduring military relationship with the PRC which would support [Communist] China's national development and maintain [Communist] China as a force for peace and stability in the Asia-Pacific region and the world. We believe a more secure, modernizing and friendly [Communist] China—with an independent foreign policy and economic system more compatible with the West—can make a significant contribution to peace and stability.[18]

During late 1984, U.S. defense technology-related sales to the PRC accelerated following President Reagan's comments offered in June that such transactions would "strengthen the security of the United States and promote world peace."[19] By mid-1986, Washington had approved several military end items for sale to Beijing: advanced gas turbine engines to enhance the PLA's naval modernization (August 1984), prototypes of selected explosives as the first component of a planned US$98 million artillery munitions factory complex to be built in the PRC for manufacturing antitank and artillery shells (September 1985), and advanced jet fighter avionics and navigation equipment (early 1986).[20] Such military technology transfers have been approved mostly on the assumption now prevalent in Washington that the nature of the Soviet threat in the Asian-Pacific *region* justifies military relations with the PRC as part of America's overall *global* strategy.

Other U.S. calculations, however, also play a role in the continued U.S. pursuit of military relations with Beijing. A Communist China "secure" from Soviet or Vietnamese military threats would, it is thought by U.S. defense planners, continue to pursue Western economic development models along similar lines to those successfully adopted by the so-called "little gang of four" (South Korea, the Republic of China, Hong Kong, and Taiwan) and perhaps somewhat less successfully by other ASEAN states. In this context, the PRC would eventually, along with Japan, form the eventual groundwork for a Pacific Basin of unparalleled wealth and stability during the next century. A militarily formidable PRC would also provide the strategic basis for a "two-front" global deterrent, along with NATO Europe, for checking further Soviet expansion. Continued U.S.-PRC military technology ties would also assure Washington that it could extract various "quid pro quos" from Beijing in its strategic behavior, such as continued access to PRC tracking stations in Xinjiang for monitoring Soviet missile tests or even gradual access to Communist Chinese ports during future Soviet-U.S. confrontations in the Asian-Pacific theater—an especially appealing prospect if continued instability in the Philippines, for example, were to compromise American basing operations there or if the Soviets were to continue expanding their own basing activities at Cam Ranh Bay and at Danang in Vietnam.[21]

Admittedly, counterarguments to all of the above projections justifying U.S.-PRC military cooperation are readily available (for example, the extent to which Beijing would involve itself in an East-West conflict originating in central Europe seems highly tenuous, at best). The extent to which U.S.-PRC relations would develop around a much wider stategic framework than mutual animosity directed toward Moscow therefore remains unclear. In this sense the hope often expressed by U.S. officials that Communist China's economic system will ultimately become "Western" may be overly optimistic, given the historical obsession by Chinese leaderships for retaining sovereign control over their own nation's political destiny and cultural identity. China's traditional xenophobia is certainly a basic concern of Washington's allies in East and Southeast Asia. As one careful analyst of Communist Chinese strategy has stated, the United States has yet to demonstrate convincingly that "its evolving relations with [Beijing] are not based upon naive predictions for the future—that the long-term interests of the United States in Asia are intimately entwined with those of its [more traditional] friends."[22]

## U.S.-Japan Military Technology Transfer:
## Impact on the U.S.-Japan-PRC Strategic Triangle

Japan has developed its economy in the postwar era to such an extent that it now stands as the prime candidate for matching the United States over the near term in producing both civilian and military-related technology outside the Soviet bloc. The Japanese have spent more of their GNP in percentage terms on high-technology research and developmoent (R&D) than any other state since the mid-1960s, and they have been especially impressive in developing artificial intelligence capacity, fifth-generation computer technology, and related "knowledge management" capabilities such as fiber optics, high-speed information processing, microcircuitry, and biotechnotics.[23] By the early 1980s, it had become increasingly obvious to Washington that Japanese R&D was becoming increasingly convergent with the research and deployment of American high-technology military systems such as the Strategic Defense Initiative (SDI). In November 1983, an "Exchange of Notes" was negotiated between the United States and Japan, clearing the way for Japanese firms to sell military-related technology in selected areas directly to the U.S. Department of Defense (USDOD). In December 1985, even more extensive "Procedures for Transfers," building upon the 1983 accord, were announced. Japan now seems to have assumed a direct role in the conceptualizing and structuring of future American deterrence forces and has relinquished, in part, its "strict constructionist" approach to "self-defense" clauses found in its national constitution. Tokyo's past reliance on the American umbrella of strategic deterrence to ensure its own security allowed the Japanese to minimize the development of their own national defense infrastructure and to prohibit the transfer of arms or weapons technology to third parties, which usually is a primary means to finance any such infrastructure. Currently, therefore, U.S. defense burden-sharing pressures appear to have overridden strong Japanese resistance to ever becoming more than a very limited defense actor in Japan's own immediate region. The sovereign defense identity problem now confronted by the Japanese and stemming from their new military technology transfer understandings with Washington can be viewed at least in somewhat parallel terms to those factors driving China toward military technology cooperation with the United States. Will Beijing eventually accept the need to compromise at least some sovereign control over its own defense R&D with American or external suppliers of modern defense technology in ways similar to those in which the U.S. has encouraged Japan to participate directly into USDOD production channels?

The PRC has been somewhat ambivalent in its attitudes toward Japan's growing technological involvement in defense-related projects and its reading of future Japanese military power. Beijing still entertains its old fears that "Japanese militarism" could develop to levels well beyond the "solid, independent self-defense force" for Japan that the PRC, in general principle, supports.[24] At the same time, the Chinese Communists have been eager to solicit various Japanese firms for selected high technology that may be applicable to their own military needs. Specifically, the PRC has solicited Tokyo for high-technology access to computers, space technology, advanced instrumentation, and jet engine metallurgy.[25] Most recently (January 1986) *Kyodo Press* reported that Japan would extend Y2.36 billion in grant assistance for improving Communist China's industrial measuring instruments, a transaction certainly applicable to defense as well as civilian industry.[26] Other high-technology projects applicable to the PRC's military programs have also been carried out with low-key—but unmistakable—Japanese involvement, including the transfer of casting technology needed for jet engine housings, aircraft wings, brakes, bearings, and turbine blades; the retrofitting of electronics systems applicable to $C^3I$ in naval escorts and tactical battlefield communications; and assistance in spent nuclear fuel verification techniques as part of ongoing Sino-Japanese nuclear reactor cooperation agreements.[27]

Perhaps the most significant future dimension of the PRC's high-technology relations with Japan, however, relates what—if any—restraints Beijing may be able to level over Tokyo's possible research contributions to the United States' SDI project. If the PRC is actually about to deploy at least rudimentary MIRVing capabilities on its nuclear ballistic missiles, SDI—if successfully developed—would certainly affect the credibility of any middle nuclear power such as the PRC or France to maintain assured second-strike nuclear targeting capabilities. In the absence of strong Communist Chinese dissent or other factors discouraging its participation, Japan could move ahead with research in SDI technology, rationalizing its need to sustain a national competitiveness for reaching the cutting edge in future technological breakthroughs, applicable to defense as well as to the commercial/industrial sector. In any case, the Japanese would most likely stay in character by gauging their SDI participation in ways consistent with COCOM standards but intermittently and subtly transfer related technology to Soviet, Chinese, and other prospective technology customers at times when Washington softens its own rhetoric and pursues increased commerical ties with communist states. Prospects that SDI-related technology would drive a wedge between Communist Chinese and Japanese strategic collaboration over the long term are therefore probably remote. By contrast, continued problems with the U.S. space program could well lead to greater collaboration between the PRC and Japan in this area of technological pursuit. Such cooperation would have obvious implications for military-related research in both countries if for no other reason than that both the PRC and Japan are accelerating their funding and energies into the type of space research that has direct applicability to communications, systems/redundancy, and other areas of traditional military concern.[28]

Military exchange visits between PLA and Japan Defense Agency (JDA) officials also continue to take place. In July 1984, Communist Chinese

Defense Minister Zhang Aiping journeyed to Tokyo, and this tour was reciprocated by JDA Vice-Minister Haruo Natsume's visit to the PRC in May 1985. During the latter's trip, PLA-JDA guidelines for continued exchanges were revealed, with consultations over Soviet SS-20 deployments as well as over joint military education projects announced as ongoing features of Sino-Japanese defense collaboration (although specific information concerning the exact nature of PLA and Japan Self-Defense Force exercises would not be exchanged on a regular basis). After his trip to the PRC, Natsume summarized the overall process as contributing to "friendly ties between the two countries . . . help(ing) lead to peace and stability in Asia and the rest of the world."[29]

To what extent a steady increase in PRC-Japanese military collaboration—even at low levels—would affect U.S. security calculations over time remains uncertain at present. The growth of Sino-Japanese military consultations *was* listed as a "major topic" for discussion between JDA chief Kochi Kato and U.S. Defense Secretary Weinberger at a June 1985 meeting, but what was specifically discussed in such a context remains largely classified.[30] It seems reasonable to conclude, however, that the following considerations were at least raised:

- Implications of remarks made by Chinese Communist Party head Hu Yaobang when visiting Tokyo in November 1983 to the effect that the PRC and Japan shared an interest over the "enduring stability" of the Korean Peninsula. Japan has now committed its direct logistical support to U.S. forces in any future military contingency involving South Korea, and it may well be that China's interest in achieving a diplomatic settlement of the Korean Peninsula's overall political status—so as to avoid increased Soviet influence over North Korea close to or following North Korean leader Kim Il Sung's death—could make overt Japanese military support of any such U.S. defense more palatable in the context of Japan's own "self-defense" politics.
- What type of "military balance" in Northeast Asia the PRC will endorse in relation to Washington's and Tokyo's own security interests pertaining to the area: that is, can Japan's defense buildup of offshore (air and naval) power be calibrated to prevent the PRC from worrying that combined U.S.-Japanese military power would outweigh Soviet assets to the extent that a Sino-Soviet rapprochement might be in Beijing's best strategic interests?
- To what degree can the "Nixon Doctrine"—calling for the U.S. to fight 1½ wars simultaneously around the globe—remain credible if it is assumed that U.S. and Japanese forces can remain uninvolved in any Northeast Asian conflict where Chinese military power is deemed sufficient to deter the USSR from directly attacking China or Japan? Can China, over time, come to play a decisive role in preventing Soviet-Vietnamese incursions into peninsular Southeast Asia (ASEAN), thereby supplementing U.S./Japanese efforts in this regard? Can the "China

factor" lead to a tacit security coalition with Washington and Tokyo at least to the extent that the United States could then implement future "swing strategies" in the European (NATO) or Middle Eastern theaters by shifting part of the Pacific Command (PACOM) to these other areas and confidently relying upon the PRC and Japan to make up at least part of the power differential resulting in the Far East?

The U.S. Pacific Fleet, of course, is already obligated to defend Japan in the event of a Soviet attack against that country. Varying scenarios could arise, however, leading either to broader U.S.-Soviet confrontations in the Pacific or to Washington shifting part of its forces to the Gulf, the Caribbean, Europe, or other possible crisis points. Resulting U.S. force deficiencies in Northeast Asia could, in turn, lead to Soviet intimidation of Communist China, Japan, the ROC, South Korea, and even the ASEAN states, with this prospect becoming more likely in the absence of the PRC's participation in an Asian-Pacific regional coalition against future Soviet offshore power projections in the region. As one USDOD official—testifying independently from his DOD affiliation—related to the U.S. Senate Foreign Relations Committee in January 1982:

> U.S. agreement to broaden [its] defense obligation [to Japan] to include at least some portion of the maritime defense of [Communist] China would seem a likely ingredient in any form of "de jure" Sino–United States coalition. That would seem to depend upon whether the U.S. Pacific Fleet is free from any necessity to redeploy from the Pacific in event of hostilities with the Soviet Union without having first disposed of the Soviet Pacific Fleet. Defeating the Soviet Navy in the Pacific would, moreover, require that the U.S. Pacific Fleet be armed and maintained in sufficient strength to take the offensive promptly, eliminating or neutralizing the Soviet Pacific Fleet before it could develop its full potential to menace Japan or China.[31]

From Japan's perspective, however, any PRC-U.S. maritime operations as overt and interregionally comprehensive as those outlined above could well be viewed as unacceptably detracting from USPACOM commitments to the U.S.-Japan Mutual Security Treaty (MST). They may also undermine the Japanese public's traditional postwar support for Tokyo's unconditional membership in the Western alliance system, traditionally seen as a necessary price for allowing an otherwise pacifist society to pursue unparalleled economic success without fear of external invasions. Although maturing as a politico-strategic force in the West, Japan still tends to emphasize its economic and social preoccupations within an overall "comprehensive diplomacy" approach toward the outside world in which the Japanese claim to "have no enemies." This uniquely Japanese security perspective varies— at times, significantly—with American frameworks of analysis substantiating the development and use of military technology in an inherently hostile international environment. Under such circumstances, Japanese preferences for implementing the 1983/1985 military technology transfer arrangements with the United States must be implemented delicately, in sequence with the proper timing and regional security environment needed for securing Japanese public support of a higher national defense profile. Portraying Beijing as a justifiable catalyst for either spurring increased U.S.-Japan high-technology relations or for Tokyo to undertake greater defense burden-sharing responsibilities would appear to be too crude and provocative under such circumstances. It would also be less than a positive inducement for Moscow to discard what "grand designs" it may wish to implement throughout the Asian-Pacific region.

## Conclusion

The United States seems to lack a coherent, long-range "game plan" for interrelating its own assimilation of military-related technology from Japan into a geopolitical blueprint designed to enhance its own security objectives or to support effectively those which may be held by its various Asian-Pacific allies. The PRC's present willingness to tolerate greater assimilation of external technology into its own society, moreover, reflects a policy compromise evolving from internal political disparities and rivalries. It has little to do with either understanding or complying with the geopolitical imperatives of either Washington or Tokyo. The future course of Communist China's own S&T modernization and how effectively the West can participate in it, therefore, will most likely rest upon Chinese societal factors having little to do with an external actor's influence as opposed to the development of Communist China's *own* set of strategic prerogatives within the international system. It is clear, however, that Beijing will most often insist that any military technology relationships it sustains with the United States or with Japan be carried out on Chinese—rather than on the supplier's—terms. To what extent this insistence, derived from cultural and historical factors almost entirely separate from the ongoing process of technological change itself, will be too high a price for the Americans or Japanese to pay cannot yet be predicted.

The critical determinants of success or failure in Asian-Pacific military transfer politics, therefore, may well rest more on the West's ability to establish consistency or firmness within what technology relations it does opt to pursue with Communist China than on Beijing's ability to adapt to changing technology or the state of Sino-Soviet relations at any given time. If such is the case, the policy instruments of export transfers or export controls can be crafted gradually, meticulously, and in ways designed to achieve a more enlightened strategic understanding between the PRC and the West. Only by adopting such a course, can Washington, Beijing, and Tokyo hope to move toward war avoidance and regional stability. It is such aspirations that successive American presidents have most likely had in mind when they have declared it to be in the United States' best interest to help build a "strong and modern China."

## Notes

1. John F. Burns, "Chinese Rebuffing Soviet on Parley," *New York Times*, April 17, 1986, p. 6, notes that the PRC rejected a suggestion by Moscow that the USSR and PRC hold a summit meeting, calling the proposal "unrealistic." Also see analysis by Richard Baum, "China in 1985: The Greening of the Revolution," *Asian Survey* 26, No. 1 (January 1986), pp. 46–48, and "Li Peng on China's Foreign, Domestic Policies," Foreign Broadcast Information Service (hereafter cited as FBIS), *China (Daily Report)*, May 1, 1986, p. A-1, where the vice-premier of the State Council noted during an interview with Hong Kong's *Liaowang* news daily that while Gorbachev has "spoken of his desire to improve relations with China," the PRC "thinks the important thing is deeds rather than words. . . . China and the Soviet Union will not become allies as they did in the 1950's."

2. *Xinhua*, January 24, 1986, reprinted in FBIS, *China (Daily Report)*, January 27, 1986, p. K-2.

3. Estimates offered by James A. Kelly, Deputy Assistant Secretary of Defense for East Asia and Pacific Affairs in Hearings before the Committee on Foreign Affairs, House of Representatives, *United States–China Relations* 98th Cong., 2nd Sess. June 5, 1984, pp. 197–198.

4. Report in *Aviation Week and Space Technology* (February 17, 1986), p. 28. For a recent and comprehensive background report on Chinese strategic force capabilities, consult G. Jacobs, "China's Strategic Forces," *Asian Defense Journal* (November 1985), pp. 34–43.

5. *Remin Ribao* report, in FBIS *China (Daily Report)*, January 27, 1986, p. 1.

6. See especially observations of Denis Fred Simon, "Technology for China: Too Much Too Fast?" *Technology Review* 87, No. 7 (October 1984), pp. 38–48. Also consult Richard E. Gillespie, "Marketing to the PLA," *The China Business Review* 11, No. 4 (July/August 1984), especially pp. 38–39.

7. See K. C. Yeh, *Industrial Innovation in China with Special Reference to the Metallurgical Industry*, N–2307 (Santa Monica, Calif.: RAND, May 1985), pp. xiv and 61, as well as Jonathan Pollack, *The R&D Process and Technological Innovation in the Chinese Industrial System*, RAND/R3284 (Santa Monica, Calif.: RAND, May 1985), p. 10.

8. Office of Technology Assessment, U.S. Congress, *Energy Technology Transfer to China* (Washington, D.C.: OTA, September 1985), p. 25.

9. Yeh, *Industrial Innovation*, pp. 35–53.

10. Hearing before the Special Subcommittee on U.S. Trade with China of the Committee on Energy and Commerce, House of Representatives, *Telecommunications Trade with China*, 98th Cong., 2nd Sess., August 8, 1984, p. 44.

11. Baldwin described the liberalization of technology transfers to China negotiated during his trip in a hearing before the Special Subcommittee on U.S. Trade with China of the Committee on Energy and Commerce, House of Representatives, *U.S. Technology Transfer to China*, 98th Cong., 1st Sess., September 27, 1983. Weinberger's visit has been described in most detail by Edward Ross, Assistant for China, Office of the Assistant Secretary of Defense, International Security Affairs, "U.S.-China Military Relations," unpublished paper presented to the Heritage Foundation, Washington, D.C., January 28, 1986, especially p. 3, and by Kelly, *United States–China Relations*, p. 193.

12. U.S. governmental interagency review is thoroughly discussed by William T. Archey, Acting Secretary for Trade Administration, Department of Commerce, and by Donald M. Anderson, Acting Deputy Assistant Secretary for East Asian and

Pacific Affairs, Department of State, in hearings before the Subcommittee on International Policy and Trade of the Committee on Foreign Affairs, House of Representatives, *Controls on Exports to the People's Republic of China*, 98th Cong., 1st Sess., November 17, 1983.

13. *Telecommunications Trade with China*, pp. 38–39.

14. COCOM is discussed in *Telecommunications Trade with China*, pp. 5–6, on an in-depth basis.

15. For example, see Thomas Robinson, "Boosting China's Military: Lessons for Washington," *Far Eastern Economic Review* 129, No. 23 (June 13, 1985), pp. 28–29. Also see Ray Cline, "China's Conversion Is Cause for Caution," *The World and I* (January 1986), pp. 95–99.

16. *United States–China Relations*, p. 190.

17. Ibid., pp. 196, 147.

18. Ross, "U.S.-China Military Relations," p. 12.

19. Cited by David B. Ottaway, "Arms Sales to China Near," *Washington Post*, September 19, 1985, p. 33.

20. Ibid.; Kerry B. Dumbaugh and Richard F. Grimmett, *U.S. Arms Sales to China*, CRS Report No. 85–138 F (Washington D.C.: Congressional Research Service, July 8, 1985), especially pp. 16–22; Nayan Chanda, "Hi-Tech Diplomacy," *Far Eastern Economic Review*, February 20, 1986, pp. 36–37; and Jim Mann, "U.S. Weapons Sale to China Reported Near," *Los Angeles Times*, January 24, 1986, p. 1.

21. Three recent statements of the PRC's propensity to follow "united front" or security coalition politics include the optimistic assessment of Captain James J. Patton, former head of the War Plans and Policy, U.S. Pacific Fleet, and Executive Director, Chief of Naval Operations, Executive Panel, in testimony before the Senate Foreign Relations Committee, *The Implications of U.S.-China Military Cooperation*, 97th Cong., 1st Sess., October 28, 1981, pp. 84–90, and more sober assessments by Henry B. Gass, *Sino-American Security Relations* (Washington D.C.: National Defense University, 1984), especially pp. 23–29, and Jonathan Pollack, *The Lessons of Coalition Politics: Sino-American Security Relations*, RAND–3133–AF (Santa Monica, Calif.: RAND, February 1984), especially pp. 125–132.

22. Paul Godwin, "The United States and China's Defense Modernization: Some Reflections on Technology, Politics, and Policy," unpublished paper presented to Asian Studies Association, Chicago, March 1986, p. 12. Permission to quote the author has been granted.

23. For background, see "Abe, Mansfield Sign Technology Accord," Kyodo press report reprinted in FBIS, *Asia & Pacific (Daily Report)*, November 8, 1983, pp. C–2 through C–3. A copy of the Memorandum of Understanding (MOU) accompanying the 1983 agreement as well as guidelines for the 1985 "Procedures" is found in Office of the Under Secretary of Defense for Research and Engineering (International Programs and Technology), *Japanese Military Technology: Procedures for Transfer to the United States* (Washington, D.C.: U.S. Government Printing Office, February 1986). For background studies on the U.S.-Japan military technology transfer policies, see William T. Tow, "U.S.-Japan Military Technology Transfers: Collaboration or Conflict?" *Journal of Northeast Asian Studies* 2, No. 4 (December 1983), pp. 3–23, and Tow, "Japan, China, and the U.S.: Strategic Concepts And High Technology," Wilson Center East Asian Studies Paper No. 27 (forthcoming).

24. See, for example, Di Ershi, "Japan's Security and Development Strategy," *Guoji Wenti Yanjiu*, No. 1 (January 1982), reprinted in *Beijing Review*, No. 18 (May 3, 1982), pp. 22, 23–24, as cited in Pollack, *op. cit.*, p. 99 for a typical PRC statement of concern regarding Japanese military modernization.

25. For background, see William T. Tow, "Sino-Japanese Security Cooperation: Evolution and Prospects," *Pacific Affairs* 56, No. 1 (Spring 1983), pp. 51–83.

26. As reported in FBIS, *Asia & Pacific (Daily Report)*, January 15, 1986, p. C–5.

27. For background, see David Shambaugh, "China's Defense Industries: Indigenous and Foreign Procurement," in Paul Godwin (ed.), *The Chinese Defense Establishment* (Boulder, Colo.: Westview, 1983), pp. 43–88, and Lee Collins, "Standoff over Safeguards," *China Trade Report* 22, No. 1 (January 1984), p. 11.

28. For reports on Japanese space programs, see *Japan Times*, May 10, 1985, p. 3, and *New York Times*, May 10, 1985, p. 14. On China's recent space efforts, see Bradley Hahn, "China in Space," *China Business Review* 11, No. 4 (July/August 1984), pp. 12–24, and *Aviation Week and Space Technology* (July 8, 1985), pp. 11, 16–21.

29. "Defense Vice Minister Leaving Today for Beijing," *Japan Times*, May 9, 1985, p. 3; "Defense Official Visits China," *Japan Times Weekly*, May 25, 1985, p. 2; "Vice Defense Minister Comments on PRC Visit," FBIS *Asia & Pacific (Daily Report)*, May 16, 1984, p. C–5; and G. Jacobs, "Japan Sets Guidelines for Exchanges with China," *Jane's Defense Weekly* 3, No. 8 (March 23, 1985), p. 292.

30. "Kato, Weinberger to Mull Japan-China Military Ties," *Japan Times*, June 9, 1985, p. 1.

31. Patton, *The Implications of Cooperation*, p. 90.

# PART SEVEN

# Society

# 34

## Religion and Modernization in the People's Republic of China Today: The Christian Experience

*P. Richard Bohr*

### Introduction

One of the most dramatic signs of change in the People's Republic of China (PRC) since the death of Mao Tse-tung has been the resurgence of public worship since 1979. Nowhere has this been more remarkable than among China's Christians. By the time of the Communist victory in 1949, more than 3 million Chinese Catholics and 750,000 Chinese Protestants were worshipping in public—the result of long years of missionary effort that absorbed more personnel and money than any other mission field in the world.

When Mao Tse-tung died in 1976, there was virtually no public expression of religion in China. Now, ten years later, Teng Hsiao-p'ing has set China on a new course of economic reform and an "open door" to the outside world. He has welcomed the initiatives of China's Christians to assist in achieving the goal of quadrupling the country's agricultural and industrial output by the year 2000.

Today, about the same number of Catholics worship openly as in 1949. But the number of Protestants in open churches has quadrupled. In October 1981, a delegation of Chinese Christian leaders attended their first international ecumenical conference since 1949 and announced to the world that after three decades of isolation from the universal church, Chinese Christians wanted to reestablish spiritual contact with foreign Christians—but only on terms of equality and mutual respect. The PRC's fourth constitution, promulgated the following year, guaranteed "toleration" of religious belief. In 1985, Chinese Christians began to create the mechanisms through which to channel international Christian educational and social service resources into China.

The rapid reemergence of Christianity in China is only the latest phase of a stormy history. Of all China's religious traditions, Christianity has been the most problematic. It was not only considered the most "foreign" of religions in China, but it was the religion most closely linked with the colonial powers that dominated China. At times Christianity has been tolerated by the state; at other times harshly repressed.

This pendulum pattern brings into focus four issues about relations between Christianity and the state during this present liberal phase. This chapter will analyze (1) the history of relations between Christianity and the state in China; (2) the current policy of religious toleration; (3) the role of Christianity in China's current modernization program; and (4) Christianity's future prospects in the PRC.

## State and Religion in China Before Communism

The PRC's religious policy represents a continuity of the uneasy relationship between state and religion during imperial times.[1] Since the Han dynasty, when the Confucian Three Bonds and Five Relationships were linked with the centrality of the imperial institution, the religion of the people was to embody this orthodoxy. Religion was, at all costs, to be subordinate to and serve the needs of the state.[2]

Yet as new religious strains were introduced into China, the religious mix grew increasingly volatile. Except for Confucianism and Taoism, China's religious traditions were imported from the second century A.D. on. These included Buddhism, Islam, Judaism, and Christianity. The government was constantly watchful of religion. True, these religions—except for Christianity—were becoming sinicized, and most religious communities lived in harmony with the state. Yet religion contained potentially heterodox ideas— egalitarianism and distributive justice, for example—that ran counter to Confucian social ethics and could inspire dissidence and even rebellion. In addition to ideas, religion was an organizational vehicle, because it included such elements as an integrated system of leadership, a mass following, and a congregational structure.

Recent studies[3] show that from the Yellow Turban and Five Pecks of Rice uprisings in the second century A.D. to the White Lotus Rebellion in the nineteenth, traditional religious ideals were often the dynamic that sparked rebellions against the throne. Moral ideals, messianic leadership, egalitarian practices, dissident ritual, and millennial visions on occasion fused with ethnic conflict, natural calamity, landlord exploitation, and government corruption to inspire efforts to overthrow a ruling dynasty perceived to be corrupt and replace it with a more virtuous ruling house. In response to this situation, the throne became increasingly strict in its definition of religious orthodoxy and tightened its control of religious practice by monitoring congregational gatherings, temple construction, and licensing of priests. At times, the government eradicated "heterodox" sects altogether.

While suspicious of religion generally, the emperors saw Christianity, with its connection to a monotheistic God superseding loyalty to the emperor and its belief in the sanctity of the individual, as potentially the most subversive of all religions in China. They saw the Christian message not only as an attack on Chinese culture but also as a profound threat to social relations and the authoritarian, hierarchical, and communal values that underlay them. Aside from its goal to bring spiritual salvation, Christianity's social activism brought the missionary into conflict with the gentry's status as moral teacher and benefactor.

The Jesuits introduced Roman Catholicism by "accommodating" Christian doctrine to Chinese culture.[4] In response to the pope's rejection of the accommodation policy, the Yung-cheng Emperor (1723–1736) revoked the 1692 edict of Christian toleration. Since then, many Chinese intellectuals have spent a good deal of time and energy vilifying Christianity's "heterodox" nature. At the same time, ironically, the court often employed missionaries and their Chinese converts as technical advisers because of their knowledge of Western science and technology.[5]

The explosive effect of Christian ideals with Chinese society was most dramatically demonstrated by the Taiping Revolution of 1851–1864. The Taipings forged a compelling synthesis of Biblical monotheism, morality, and millennialism with traditional Chinese religious ideals, theocratic organization, and utopian goals. The Taipings' ideological mix and organizational effectiveness not only offered the greatest threat yet to the Confucian orthodoxy but in fact nearly eliminated the imperial system altogether.[6]

Christianity's apparent link with Western material power and colonial penetration was even more alarming than its heterodox nature. After 1842 the "Unequal Treaties," backed by extraterritoriality and the foreign gunboats, safeguarded the missionaries and their Chinese converts. The missionary could bring his converts under the protection of Western law. (Hence the adage about conversion in China: "One more Christian, one less Chinese.") This situation gave rise to decades of sporadic anti-Christian rioting.[7]

Despite this atmosphere of hostility, however, some Chinese intellectuals were receptive to Christianity and the Western culture it embodied. In their effort to modernize China along Western lines beginning in the late nineteenth century, they looked to Christian civilization as the key to the West's dynamic philosophy and material power. They therefore welcomed the missionaries' efforts to administer famine relief; publish books and periodicals; build schools, colleges, hospitals, YMCAs, and YWCAs; undertake rural reconstruction; and promote Western science and technology, women's rights, and democratic institutions. They were convinced that Christian ideals could serve as the basis of social and institutional reform needed to create a strong new China.

Some were also receptive to Christianity's spiritual message.[8] Most Chinese Christians were organized along denominational lines of their missionary mentors. Yet from the beginning of the twentieth century, some Chinese Christians became independent of the missionaries as they established such autonomous, indigenous communities as the "Little Flock" and "True Jesus Church."

Although Christians numbered less than 1 percent of China's population, they were enormously influential in the country's modern development.

During the forty years following the 1911 Revolution, Christianity—primarily in its Protestant form—and modernization became closely linked. Much of China's leadership was the product of missionary institutions and enjoyed foreign Christian support.[9]

By 1949 there were an estimated 750,000 Chinese Protestants scattered among 130 denominations under the tutelage of some 8,000 missionaries. Most of them were concentrated in urban areas and educated in 240 Protestant secondary schools, thirteen universities, and forty-four theological seminaries. There were some 3,275,000 Chinese Catholics, whose strength was in the rural areas, under the guidance of 2,090 foreign and 2,968 Chinese priests and trained in 2,071 primary schools, 189 secondary schools, and three universities.[10]

## Christianity Under Mao, 1949–1976

When he proclaimed the creation of the PRC on October 1, 1949, Mao Tse-tung declared that China had "stood up" against the "imperialist" domination of the West and China's "feudal" past. To the Communists, religion was one of the "four thick ropes" from which the people needed to be unbound. Taoism, Buddhism, and the many forms of popular religion that fused elements of both were "superstitions" that kept the people subservient to the landlord-official ruling class. Christianity was denounced for keeping Chinese converts dependent on the foreigners.[11]

Although Communists disparaged religion, they were willing to tolerate its observance, at least initially. They subscribed to the Marxist dictum that religion would eventually dissipate as material conditions improved under socialism and as scientific education was disseminated.[12] In the interest of creating a "united front" to consolidate control of the country and expand the people's productivity, the Common Program of the early 1950s did not prohibit the expression of religious faith. The PRC's first constitution of 1954 stipulated that China's citizens "enjoy the freedom of religious belief."[13]

However, this provision was extended to Chinese Christians only if they cut their ties to foreign Christians and became self-reliant and patriotic. Moreover, they must confine themselves to pastoral work only. Since social conditions were to improve under Marxism, the Communists insisted, Christians need not concern themselves with social ministries. Until the ideal society was achieved, they reasoned, the government would provide for education and social welfare.

By the end of 1951, foreign missionaries, accused of being agents of imperialism, had either been expelled or imprisoned. The government nationalized all church-owned property. Although some Christians opposed any accommodation with the new government, many were willing to work within a Marxist structure and were eager to demonstrate that Chinese Christians, too, had "stood up."

During the first decade under communism, Christians tried to preserve their existence as a worshipping community by developing a modus vivendi with the government and by disentangling Christianity from its Western, colonial, missionary forms. The Protestants established the Three-Self Patriotic Movement (TSPM), and the Catholics the Chinese Catholic Patriotic Association (CCPA). These national church structures were responsible for fostering the "Three-Self" principle of self-governance, self-support, and self-propagation.[14] (This formula had actually been developed a century earlier, and through the years many missionaries had used it as a rationale for creating an autonomous Chinese church.)[15]

Chinese Christians worked with the Religious Affairs Bureau (RAB), an arm of both the government's State Council and the Communist Party's United Front Work Department. Chinese Christians stressed that love of country was integral to love of church and defined the proper activities of the church as worship, nurture, witness, and compassion. By 1961, the twelve Protestant seminaries extant before 1949 were merged into Chinling Union Theological Seminary at Nanking. There clergy were trained solely for the pastoral ministry. The state insisted that, in order to maintain control of the Christian communities, the many Protestant denominations must be merged into an interdemoninational framework. This process went on through the 1950s. The Christians derived self-support from rental income on church property, member contributions, and church-operated small industries and farms.[16]

Beginning in 1957, the CCPA made Chinese Christianity's most dramatic demonstration of ecclesiastical independence from the West by consecrating bishops without Vatican approval and claiming that these bishops were in the direct line of apostolic succession.[17]

By the late 1950s church-state relations became increasingly tense as Christians came under ideological attack in the Anti-Rightist campaign after 1957 and the "socialist education" movement of the early 1960s. Mao's mobilization of the entire population for a "Great Leap" into economic development beginning in 1958 left Christians with little time for corporate worship.

Church-state relations were completely destroyed during the Cultural Revolution, which began in 1966. In a burst of iconoclastic fury, thousands of youthful Red Guards sought to eradicate religion by disbanding the RAB and attacking all religious groups except the Muslims (whose status as a minority religion was protected by the state), turning temples, monasteries, and churches into factories and other secular uses and subjecting members of religious orders to physical labor, prison, torture, and death.

Christianity was particularly hard-hit, as these radicals charged that it was still a foreign faith. They also accused it of enslaving Chinese Christians to backward, "bourgeois" attitudes which opposed "class struggle." Beginning in 1966 the Red Guards dismantled the RAB, burned Bibles, and destroyed religious art. They prohibited public worship and theological education, and they tortured, imprisoned, and killed clergy and laity. As never before, the Christians were driven into clandestine worship in a myriad of small, informal congregational units.[18]

## Christianity and China's Second Revolution

The unprecedented persecution of China's Christians during the Cultural Revolution did not ebb until after Mao's death and the arrest of the Gang of Four in 1976. Since then, Teng Hsiao-p'ing has replaced class struggle with economic development and proclaimed the ambitious goal of making China a modern socialist state by the year 2000. To implement what Teng calls China's Second Revolution, his regime has reactivated a "united front" of all Chinese to work for China's modernization.

In order to include religious devotees in the united front, Teng has reinstated the policy of religious toleration. He realizes that tens of millions of China's religious and ethnic minority people will participate in the modernization campaign only if they are allowed to pursue their religious inclinations. Hence, in Teng's words, "If people work hard, the government doesn't care which religions they practice."[19] The officially sanctioned religious communities are those of the Taoists, Buddhists, Muslims, Catholics, and Protestants.[20]

The Communist Party's Central Committee directive of March 1982, the so-called Document 19, clarifies the party's post-Mao position on religion:

> Since we cannot free ourselves from various hardships brought on by serious natural and man-made disasters within a short period of time; since class struggle continues to exist within certain limits; and given the complex international environment, the long-term influence of religion among a part of the people in a socialist society cannot be avoided. Religion will eventually disappear from human history. But it will disappear naturally, only through the long term development of socialism and communism, when all objective requirements are met.[21]

While the document reaffirms the party's traditional view of religion and the need for the state to strictly control it, it nevertheless calls for a more pragmatic policy toward religion. The document prohibits the preaching of religion outside facilities approved for religious use, condemns the exploitation of religion for personal monetary gain (faith healing, for instance), and enjoins cadres from becoming believers and taking part in religious activities. At the same time, it denounces the "leftist excesses" that victimized religious people during the Cultural Revolution, warns against abolishing legitimate religious pursuits by administrative decree, and orders bureaucrats to protect "legitimate" religious rights.

Within months of the issuance of Document 19, religious rights had a constitutional guarantee. China's second and third constitutions, adopted in 1975 and 1978, respectively, stipulated that "citizens enjoy the freedom to believe in religion . . . [and] to believe in atheism."[22] While these constitutions accorded the right "to propagate atheism," they did not provide the same right to propagate religion. However, Article 36 of China's fourth and latest constitution, adopted in December 1982, drops the clause permitting the propagation of atheism and states: "No state organ, public organization, or individual may compel citizens to believe in, or not believe in, any religion; nor may they discriminate against citizens who believe in, or do not believe in any religion."[23]

Beginning in 1978, the government began to repair the institutional framework by reorganizing the religious associations of the five major faiths. In 1979 it revived the RAB, which has since helped to secure the return of religious property confiscated during the Cultural Revolution. The enforcement of these new policies at the local level has been uneven. But reports indicate that the government has removed several obstructionist local officials.[24]

The government has begun to sponsor the academic study of religion. In addition to institutes for the study of Buddhism and Islam, the Center for Religious Studies was created at Nanking University in 1980. The government also recently set up the Institute for the Study of World Religions at the Chinese Academy of Social Sciences in Beijing. Here, researchers study Taoism, Buddhism, Confucianism, Islam, Christianity, Lamaism, folk religion, and the theory of religions. In addition, a National Conference on Religion was held in Beijing in December 1985.

Recently, some Marxist scholars of religion have gone so far as to privately acknowledge religion's positive role in society.[25] By 1985, the atmosphere was so open that Chao Fu-san, deputy director of the Chinese Academy of Social Sciences and a Protestant, could publicly challenge the prevailing orthodox view of religion in a speech, entitled "Religion, Spiritual Culture, and National Unity," before a session of the Chinese People's Political Consultative Conference (CPPCC) in Peking:

> We need to emphasize that religion is a part of the historical culture of every nation. In classridden societies, religion has been used as a tool of government by the exploiting classes, so that it has had the effect of dulling the sense of revolution in the labouring classes. In a socialist society, where class has been abolished, this negative effect has been greatly weakened, so that we should be all the more willing to regard religion as a part of the cultural history of every people. In this way it can be an aid towards internal cohesion and in bringing about the Four Modernizations.[26]

Chao further noted that there should be a more scientific analysis of religion. He went on to urge that the "indiscriminate opposition to religious values is unnecessary and even harmful. If religious people are subjected to criticism (for their faith), then they would only follow the socialist road halfheartedly."[27] The speech received a standing ovation. It was published in the overseas edition of the *People's Daily* and has sparked a great deal of comment in academic and party circles.[28]

## The Making of a Chinese Christianity

The scope and speed of religion's comeback have indeed been astonishing. To cite one example, during the Cultural Revolution the Red Guards attempted to obliterate Buddhism from Tibet. But today, Tibetan Buddhism is stronger than at any time since China's occupation of the country. The party has made major concessions to Tibetan identity by allowing the restoration of the annual "Grand Religious Vow-Making" ceremonies in which 100,000 Tibetan monks recently expressed devotion to the Buddha and the Dalai Lama, whom Beijing is trying to entice to return.[29]

As for religion among the Han Chinese, Taoists and Buddhists, once denounced by the Red Guards as "parasites," have made a strong comeback. Since 1979 the Buddhists have restored temples to public worship, revived theological studies, and ordained monks and nuns to holy orders.[30]

Christianity, too, is showing its greatest strength since before 1949.[31] Since 1979 tens of thousands of Christians have emerged from underground worship to profess their faith in the open. Christian conversion mushroomed amid the suppression of the Cultural Revolution. TSPM leaders estimate that about 3 million Protestants are publicly worshipping in the PRC today in some 3,600 churches returned to their original owners with back rent. Rural Christians are pooling their savings to build new churches on private plots. About a third of the worshippers are new believers, and another third are young people.

Clergy and lay leaders have been returned from factories, labor camps, and prison cells to resume such pastoral duties as preaching, conducting worship, officiating at weddings and funerals, teaching Bible classes, and visiting the sick and elderly. Youth work enjoys a high priority. Both YMCA and YWCA organizations have been revived in several big cities.

Publication of catechisms, devotional tracts, and hymnals has also been resumed. More than 1,700,000 copies of the Bible have been published since 1981 in Chinese, Korean, and other minority languages. Six hundred thousand copies of a new Protestant hymnal have been published. It contains 300 Western tunes and 100 new hymns in Chinese language and melody. The Protestants have also resumed publication of their bimonthly magazine, *T'ien Feng* (Heavenly Wind). It contains sermons, Bible studies, devotionals, religious essays, and church news.

Of special concern to the Protestants, whose youngest clergy are in their mid-fifties, is the urgency of theological education. In February 1981 the Nanking Seminary reopened with forty-seven students (including eighteen women) chosen from among a thousand applicants from twenty-two provinces. Supported by home congregations or seminary scholarships, these future pastors and professors have pursued a four-year course that includes Bible study, systematic theology, church history and doctrine, pastoral care, classical Chinese, Greek, Hebrew, and English. They must also take political courses. Nanking's graduates earn the equivalent of an M.Div. degree. Since 1982, eight "satellite" seminaries have been set up in strategic locations around the country. Here, students can earn a bachelor's degree. All told, there are an estimated 400 Protestant seminarians in China today.

In addition to full-time study, theological training includes correspondence courses for about 36,000 Protestants and short-term training courses, lasting from a few days to a few months, in Bible study, church history, doctrine, evangelism, and the Three-Self principle. They are administered by provincial Three-Self committees during slack times in the agricultural year. The "pastoral workers" who graduate from these courses are particularly active in ministering to the estimated 10,000 "meeting points" that are loyal to the TSPM. The members of these small groups are waiting for churches to be reopened or built. They also work with small Christian groups who are not yet within the TSPM structure.

Many Protestants believe they have achieved psychological independence from missionary Christianity. TSPM leaders lament the lack of theological creativity before 1949 because, they charge, the missionaries were reluctant to "indigenize" Christianity in China. They rejoice that socialism has eradicated the injustices of the old order and improved the people's livelihood. They "identify" with the people, and in so doing find a "spiritual liberation" from the shackles of foreign ideas and forms. They see China as a "laboratory" for theological experimentation and have developed new interpretations of some classic Christian concepts that are radically different from what they learned from the missionaries.

In the Incarnation, for instance, they see Jesus Christ identifying with all the Chinese people, not just the Christians. Hence, Chinese Christians feel the need to identify with their non-Christian countrymen. In the Trinity, they find the community of all Chinese people striving for human dignity. Prior to 1949, they claim, their primary concern was for Christian conversion. Now, the question of belief and nonbelief—which divided Chinese against Chinese—has given way to a preoccupation with reconciliation among all Chinese. Finally, the Protestants say, they have come to understand suffering, primarily as the result of the Cultural Revolution. They believe that this experience gives them profound insights into New Testament Christianity prior to .its westernization. These and other views are summarized in a catechism published in 1982.[32]

The number of China's Catholics worshipping in public today remains at the 3 million estimate of 1949. Nevertheless, the pilgrimages in the suburbs of Shanghai, increasing numbers of Catholics requesting church marriages, and the sale of religious objects are signs of Catholic revival.

About 600 Catholic churches and 1,000 shrines have been restored to religious use. A thousand priests—bypassed by Vatican II because of their isolation from Rome—still say the Tridentine mass in Latin. Seven Catholic seminaries turn out 100 ordinands a year. In addition, Chinese women are becoming nuns.

The CCPA journal, *The Chinese Catholic Church*, has also resumed publication. The journal has been emphasizing the importance of "indigenizing" Chinese Catholicism. This means making the church independent, autonomous, and self-administering, putting its resources to use in socialist construction, and creating a Chinese Catholic theology that harmonizes with the Chinese people and their culture.[33]

Two parallel church structures—with offices at national, provincial, and local levels—guide the resurgence of public worship to assure that Chinese

Christianity is both Chinese and Christian. On the Protestant side, the TSPM is responsible for church-state relations. The China Christian Council oversees congregational ministry, pastoral and leadership training, doctrinal and liturgical issues, and the management of church properties. K. H. Ting is head of both organizations, which meet jointly. The Catholics have a similar dual structure: the CCPA is responsible for political matters, and the Catholic National Administrative Commission handles pastoral concerns. Protestant and Catholic structures are under the jurisdiction of the RAB.

Despite the increase in Christian numbers since 1949, the number of religious believers relative to the total population is indeed small. Yet the cumulative effect of these changes in state policy and Christian response is one of the most striking developments in post-Mao China.

By facilitating the reemergence of public worship, Teng Hsiao-p'ing's government is permitting a form of private cultural expression that runs counter to the traditional government suspicion of religion as well as to the antitraditional and antiforeign impulses of the communist movement. By allowing the creation of two pastoral organizations—the China Christian Council and the Catholic National Administrative Commission—the government has gone beyond the pre–Cultural Revolution status quo and, in the process, given up some of its previously held monopoly over the country's institutional life. This liberalization has occurred in the face of foot-dragging, covert and otherwise, by lower-level officials responsible for ideological orthodoxy and public order. Overcoming this resistance has made the implementation of the policy of toleration more difficult than its formulation. But that fact has not negated the lengths to which the government has gone to garner public support and the vigor and confidence with which Christians have seized this opportunity to profess their beliefs publicly, to sinicize their Christianity, and to participate in nation building.

## China's Open Door and the Revival of
## Christian Activism

Even more remarkable than the state's willingness to tolerate Christian public worship is its receptivity—only ten years following Mao's death—to the resumption of Christian social activism. Lately, the Teng regime has been placing increasing emphasis on improving China's education and the quality of life of its citizens, especially the handicapped. For the first time since 1949, it is receptive to the desire of Chinese Christians to become involved in these areas once again.

The government is making strenuous efforts to improve education, which it claims is the foundation of China's economic development. During the past year, the state has increased spending for education by 70 percent. It has also mandated nine years of compulsory education, has raised the status of teachers, and is reforming the curriculum to serve the needs of technical training. In addition, it intends to expand university enrollment from 1.4 million to 2.6 million.[34]

The government is also paying increasing attention to the needs of China's estimated 20 million handicapped by establishing factories to employ disabled workers, admitting more handicapped students to schools and universities, and increasing the number of teachers in special education.[35]

Because the demand for the state's resources in these areas has outstripped its ability to supply, it is turning to private sources to contribute to educational and social service concerns. These include Chinese Christians, who are quickly becoming involved in education and social service to a degree unimagined even a few years ago. Chao Fu-san recently said about his fellow Christians: "Now we feel that we should continue to move into society. The church should not stay behind in a ghetto in a rapidly changing society which China is."[36]

Chinese Christians have been contributing money to build schools. During the past few months, for instance, Protestants in Lung-kuan County, Chekiang Province, have raised funds to establish a middle school.[37] Catholics in Beijing have pledged to teach English and other foreign languages to assist the cause of economic development.[38]

Christians are also becoming increasingly involved in helping the handicapped. Last December, Christians joined forces with Buddhists, Taoists, and Muslims to donate proceeds from the sale of religious art in Beijing to the China Welfare Fund for the Handicapped, China's leading advocacy agency for the disabled, run by Teng P'u-fang, Teng Hsiao-p'ing's wheelchair-bound son.[39] Christians in Wen-ling County, Chekiang Province, have raised enough money to build a workshop to employ thirteen blind, deaf, and lame people to produce knitwear and rubber accessories.[40] Christians have also developed projects in the areas of nutrition, mental health research, and care of mentally and physically handicapped children.[41]

Even more dramatic than the state's recognition that Chinese Christians have a central role to play in China's modernization—and their implied recognition that Marxism has not yet been able to solve China's social problems—is the party's sanction of the Chinese Christians' outreach to Christians outside China for assistance in social services—*but not evangelism*—in China.

In October 1981, ten Chinese Protestant and Catholic representatives declared at the historic international ecumenical conference, "God's Call to a New Beginning," held in Montreal that they wanted to reestablish dialogue on spiritual matters with the international Christian community. Yet this could be possible only if the Chinese church was treated according to the principle of mutual respect as a fully mature church.[42] This principle of mutuality was more fully articulated the following year by Bishop Ting's famous formula of the "Fourteen Points" for the Chinese church's international relationships. This policy enjoins Chinese Christians to deal internationally only with Christians who believe in mutuality.[43]

By 1985, Chinese Christians had gone from dialogue with foreign Christians to actually inviting them to become socially active in China. Chao Fu-san gave voice to the rationale for this policy in his speech by claiming that religion "can also be of benefit in the development of friendly and peaceful relations with other nations, and in bringing about an international environment favourable to the Four Modernizations in our country."[44]

Recent shifts in the academic view of China's missionary past are enhancing the more positive atmosphere for this development. This transition can be traced best in the work of Ku Ch'ang-sheng, professor of modern history at East China Normal University in Shanghai. In 1981, Professor Ku published a book called *Ch'üan-chiao shih yü Chin-tai Chung-kuo* (Missionaries and Modern China), which condemned outright the missionaries as proponents of Western imperialism.[45] His revised edition of 1983 removed this blanket indictment from some of the missionaries. However, in his book *Ts'ung Ma-li-sun tau Ssu-t'u Lei-teng* (From Morrison to Stuart), published in 1985, Professor Ku went so far as to insist that not all missionaries were imperialists, that imperialism and Christianity were not necessarily intertwined, that the Western learning which the missionaries promoted had a beneficial influence on China's modern development, and that some missionaries did indeed support China's modernization efforts and advocated independence for the Chinese church.[46]

Coterminous with this more favorable academic evaluation of the Christian role in the development of modern China is the growth of international linkages between Chinese Christians and their international colleagues in social service areas. These are facilitated by the Love Social Service Center in Canton and the Amity Foundation, headquartered in Nanking. The latter was established in April 1985 as a private organization not formally connected to the TSPM, although its chairman is K. H. Ting. It includes Christians and non-Christians on its board.

The Amity Foundation's objectives are threefold: (1) to contribute to China's social betterment and economic modernization by channeling international resources through existing institutions in China; (2) to make Christian involvement and participation more widely known to the Chinese people; and (3) to serve as a channel for sharing international ecumenical resources.

The foundation insists that its acceptance of international Christian support does not violate the Three-Self principle. K. H. Ting and Han Wen-tsao, general secretary of the Foundation, wrote early in 1985: "We Chinese Christians welcome these contributions in the form of funds, material, and personnel from overseas providing that they are given with due regard to Chinese national sovereignty so as to strengthen our people's efforts at the modernization of the country. We say this both as Chinese citizens and Chinese Christians. We believe that Christians have a duty to work for the social betterment of all people."[47]

The Amity Foundation has begun to attract considerable foreign funds and expertise. Within the past year, it has recruited some seventy teachers from church-related organizations in North America and West Germany to teach English in universities in Kiangsu Province. It has arranged for a North American study tour of Chinese theological students. In addition, it is soliciting foreign funds for such activities in Kiangsu as supporting projects at the Nanking Children's Mental Health Research Center, an artificial limb factory, a nutrition project, special education for the retarded, and the reeducation of delinquents. The foundation has also signed a contract with the American Bible Society and the United Bible Society to build a $6.5 million computerized Christian printing press in Nanking.[48]

The international response to the Amity Foundation and other Chinese Christian iniatives has been impressive. The Hong Kong Christian Council, for example, is cooperating with health officials in Canton on a rural health-care project.[49] The Mennonites' China Educational Exchange has twenty-eight teachers, agricultural advisers, nurses, and doctors stationed in three provinces. It has also created an exchange program in mental health and nursing education. Moreover, a European Christian organization has raised $1.6 million to build orphanages in Tientsin and Yen-t'ai.[50] Perhaps the most surprising development is the invitation by Kwangtung officials for the Mission Covenant Church of Norway to build and administer, for thirty years, a major university for 12,000 students. Chinese Christians will serve on the faculty, and a chapel will be built on the campus.[51]

## Christianity's Future in a Marxist Setting

Continued church growth in China depends on the maintenance of the current toleration policy. This is the appropriate point to ask, What factors will affect the future of relations between Christians and the state in the PRC?

The first and most obvious is a shift in the political line. By all appearances in the wake of the Chinese Communist Party Conference held in September 1985, Teng has consolidated his power to a considerable degree. Yet the permanence of the Teng regime remains to be seen. The Teng leadership continues to be attacked by orthodox elements trying to find issues—"spiritual pollution" and the increasing inequality of income distribution, for instance—with which to chip away at Teng's reform package. Teng and his colleagues have taken back some of the freedoms—in literary expression, for instance—they granted in order to preserve their power and the integrity of their economic program. Could such changes also be made in the religious policy?

Even if the current toleration policy remains in force, Christians are vulnerable in three contingencies, any one of which might narrow the parameters of the toleration policy.

### Reconciling Church Divisions

Since 1949 there has been divided opinion within both Chinese Protestant and Catholic communities over how best to preserve Christian existence in the Marxist state. TSPM and CCPA leaders have tried to preserve church-state harmony by cooperating with state power. But there are many Christians who oppose accommodationism. They denounce the leaders of the "patriotic" organizations as insincere Christians and point to the Cultural Revolution as proof of the folly of collaboration.[52]

While some Chinese Christians denounce the Communists as godless, others see the creation of the People's Republic as an opportunity for Chinese Christians to become independent of missionary Christianity. In 1983, Chao Fu-san said that Chinese Christians are no longer regarded as "secondary foreign devils" by their fellow Chinese.[53] Church leaders like Bishop Ting are imbued with the Social Gospel ideals propagated in the more liberal mission schools and in the YMCA, where he received his spiritual nurture. They praise the Communists' social and economic achievements on behalf of the Chinese people. While reviving Christian activism in recent months, Ting and his TSPM colleagues are showing Christians in China and around the world that while Chinese Christians reject Marxist atheism they can cooperate with the government in social ministries. In this way, they can be patriotic Chinese and loyal Christians at the same time.

The TSPM has offered the hand of reconciliation to their more anti-Communist brethren and seek to bring them into the "patriotic" church fold. This effort has met with some success. Many Christians who went underground during the persecution of the Cultural Revolution are returning to public worship as fast as churches can be restored to them. In this process they are proclaiming their support for the Three-Self principle. Many Christians still worship in small groups—as they had done for decades before 1949—because churches are still not available to them, and they welcome the TSPM pastors who are trying to link these groups with TSPM congregations.

At the same time, however, many Christians still do not want to join the TSPM. This makes both the TSPM and the state nervous. If the TSPM leaders cannot eventually speak for all Protestants, the state may once again feel compelled to tighten its control.

Complicating the reconciliation efforts between church and state and within the church itself is the thorny issue of perceived foreign interference. During the five years after the Montreal Conference, Chinese Protestant delegations paid official visits to South and Southeast Asia, Africa, Europe, and North America. In addition, a number of Western Christian leaders have visited China, among them the archbishop of Canterbury and Mother Teresa.[54]

The Protestant contacts have been primarily with the mainline, liberal denominations. Recently, however, TSPM leaders have stepped up interchange with evangelical groups in the effort to become more broadly ecumenical and to show that the TSPM is Christ-centered and not a superficial veneer of liberal Christianity. In 1985, for example, evangelicals from around the world held a major international conference in Nanking called "Bearing Witness to Christ in China." While Chinese Christians had no official role in this conference, some representatives were nevertheless present. And Han Wen-tsao, who is also associate general secretary of the China Christian Council, was an unofficial observer at the fifteenth Baptist World Congress in Los Angeles in July of 1985. The Baptists have declared their intention to cooperate with the Amity Foundation and other foundations. Recently it was announced that Billy Graham has been invited to lecture on Christianity in China.[55]

Increasing Chinese Christian international contact is consonant with the open policy characteristic of Teng's China today. At the same time, Article 36 of the 1982 constitution warns that "religious bodies and religious affairs are not subject to any foreign domination."[56] Is there a point at which foreign cooperation could appear to become "foreign domination"?

During May 1986 international Christian representatives met in Nanking for a conference sponsored by North Americans on the sharing of international Christian resources. Some discussion was held on how to contribute international resources to Chinese Christians without engendering the specter of old-fashioned missionary paternalism. While many in the international community are sensitive to this issue, will all foreigners be willing to play by the rules established by the state and the TSPM and CCPA?

In the early 1980s foreign agencies smuggled Bibles into China, eliciting the wrath of the government and severely embarrassing TSPM leaders. The recent expansion of Christian publishing in China has considerably decreased the need and opportunity for Bible smuggling. However, outside Christians continue to interfere in internal Chinese church affairs in other ways. Some charge that the TSPM Christians are not "true" Christians because of their "collaboration" with the Marxist state. By extention, these foreigners automatically see Christians in "house fellowships" as a monolithic group—anti-Three-Self, antiparty, and antigovernment—and therefore as "genuine" Christians. They claim that there are as many as 50 million Christians worshipping in these fellowships. Referring to them as "house churches," to distinguish them from the "official" TSPM churches, they insist they are covert in order to avoid "persecution" by the TSPM. They do not acknowledge that many Christians worship in small groups because there is a long history of this form of worship and because in many cases there are no churches for them.[57]

This effort to divide the Chinese into "true" and "false" Christians is dangerous at a time when China's Protestants are still trying to create a united church out of widely different doctrinal and liturgical backgrounds and also when they are still trying to become accepted by their non-Christian neighbors.

There are additional hazards of the expanding international relationships. Foreign Christians are going to China in increasing numbers to take part in the country's modernization drive. The Chinese government has assured them that they can "witness" Chinese Christians in private, but they cannot openly proselytize. But some foreign guests have overstepped the boundaries and preached in public. This is a constant temptation for some, since Christianity is by its very nature an evangelistic religion. Unless foreign Christians who do service work in China exercise self-restraint, adhere to the Three-Self principle, and refrain from openly exploiting church divisions, the TSPM could be perceived as ineffectual and lose credibility with the state.

The Chinese Catholics' international relationships are far more problematic. The fundamental dilemma confronting them is the question of who controls the Catholic Church in China. The CCPA insists that the Chinese Catholic church is completely autonomous and fully legitimate. The Vatican condemns the consecration of Chinese bishops without its approval and has never renounced its authority over the Chinese church, especially where it concerns consecration and ordination. Chinese Catholics continue to condemn Rome's "injustices," past and present—from the refusal to train a Chinese ecclesiastical leadership (in 1949 only thirty bishops out of 145 were Chinese, for example) to maintaining diplomatic ties with Taiwan.[58]

There are many Catholics in China who continue to publicly proclaim their allegiance to Rome and do not approve of the close relationship between the CCPA and the Marxist government. They accuse the CCPA of being "schismatic." Many of them worship in house fellowships, and others attend CCPA services only because they provide the benefit of sacraments.[59]

Hopes for an end to this stalemate were raised in February 1981, when Pope John Paul II issued a greeting to PRC Catholics and affirmed their right to be both Catholic and Chinese. Five months later, the pontiff tried to accelerate the pace of reconciliation by appointing Bishop Teng Yi-ming to be archbishop of Kwangtung Province. Initially, Teng seemed to be the ideal bridge between China and the Vatican. For a variety of reasons, he was recognized by important elements in the Chinese Catholic church and the Vatican. Yet the hopes were soon dashed. Shortly after Teng's appointment, on July 15, 1981, the CCPA condemned the pope's action, declaring: "Chinese bishops should be elected and ordained by Chinese clergy and congregations. The Vatican ignored this sacred right of the Chinese church by appointing Deng Yiming as Archbishop, and thus rudely interfered in China's internal affairs, encroaching on the sovereignty of the Chinese church, and violated the traditional spirit of Jesus Christ's establishment of the church and apostolic propagation of the Gospels."[60] The anger of CCPA leaders flared again in March 1982 with the pope's call for Catholics throughout the world to "pray for persecuted Catholics in China."[61] Lately, the pope's rhetoric has cooled, but he continues to call for reconciliation between Chinese Catholics and Rome. In November 1985 he encouraged Taiwan bishops to bring their "brothers" in China back to the Vatican fold.[62]

One sensitive issue at stake is the divergence of moral views between Chinese and Roman Catholics regarding birth control and abortion—practices that are officially condemned by Rome and condoned by the CCPA bishops. At an ecclesiological level is the agonizing question, Is the Chinese Catholic church indeed "Catholic"? Since it does not acknowledge the leadership of Rome, does it possess the channel of grace necessary to provide the Chinese faithful with the salvation they seek? Chinese Catholics face a unique challenge in working out these questions.

The fundamental question facing the CCPA is this: Does the Chinese Catholic church require so much independence that it must necessarily sever spiritual ties with the universal church? There are signs that the CCPA is trying to work toward some sort of dialogue between its demand for total independence and Rome's insistence on allegiance to the pope while at the same time granting legitimate autonomy to a local church.

During the summer of 1984, Shanghai's Auxiliary Bishop Chin Lu-hsien led a delegation of fellow Shanghai Catholics to Hong Kong for two weeks of discussions. In November 1985 a delegation of Beijing and Mongolian Catholics visited the University of Louvain in Belgium. And Philippines Cardinal Jaime Sin and Hong Kong Bishop John Baptist Wu visited China.[63]

It is too early to determine whether or not international Catholic assistance in educational and social action efforts is under discussion in these encounters. It is unlikely, though, that this kind of cooperation will be forthcoming until the dialogue is broadened. The most important indication that the CCPA may be willing to enlarge discussions with Vatican representatives was the release last summer of Bishop Gong Pinmei, former bishop of Shanghai, who was imprisoned in the early 1950s for his unwillingness to renounce loyalty to Rome.

## Determining the Limits of Social Activism

Relations between the state and Christianity face a test over the church's increasing role in Chinese society and politics. The question is this: Can the church remain simply a mechanism for promoting unity and activism on behalf of modernization without incurring political risks as the church-in-society issues intensify? The church's remarkable degree of social involvement must be seen within the context of K. H. Ting's admonition of 1981: "Our patriotism is not without a prophetic and critical character. It does not mean blind praise for everything in our motherland."[64]

As early as 1980, Ting and others began to object to the article in the 1978 constitution that protected the right to propagate atheism. Pressure brought to bear by religious leaders at all levels in the CPPCC contributed toward changing that provision.

Perhaps it was this success that emboldened Christians to go even further to insist that the government delineate its religious policy in a civil code that goes beyond Article 147 of the 1980 Criminal Code. (This provision mandates two years' imprisonment for anyone who deprives others of their religious rights.) In addition, Christians pledge that they will insist on strict local enforcement of the national policy on religion.

The Christians' very success at influencing legislative change raises a difficult question: At what point will the delicate equilibrium with the regime that freed Christians from their oppression be upset if the church, driven by its "prophetic and critical character," challenges the state on such political issues as demanding a greater Christian voice in national decision making, or such ethical issues as the growing inequities of Teng's economic reforms, or such human rights issues as the recent jailings of clergy for alleged political offenses?

The church also offers the state a challenge of another sort. On the one hand, the 1982 constitution guarantees the right to religious faith and practice. This provision is an effort to avoid the "leftist" excesses that wrought such widespread suffering during the Cultural Revolution. On the other hand, the government has made it clear, in the words of Article 36, that "the state protects normal religious activities. No one may make use of religion to engage in activities that disrupt public order, impair the health of citizens or interfere with the educational system of the state."[65]

Recent articles in the government and party press indicate that the official definition of "normal religious activities" is narrowing. The press has expressed outrage over such "superstitious" practices as shamanism and other forms of faith healing and fortune-telling. For obvious reasons, the Christian press, too, has echoed these criticisms and denounced such practices an incompatible with Christianity. Lately, TSPM leaders have also become concerned about the reported development of syncretistic practices in rural areas where these "heterodox" elements have combined with Christianity.[66] If the TSPM cannot maintain religious orthodoxy, local officials may tighten the reins once again.

## Ideological Control

Perhaps the greatest danger of all is Christianity's potential appeal to China's youth, who make up half of China's 1.2 billion people. The very regime that is allowing the churches to play a greater role in society has undone much of the Marxist orthodoxy in order to legitimate reform. Nor has it developed a new orthodoxy. Not only are many Chinese youth cut loose from these traditional Marxist moorings, but many young people claim to be searching for "spiritual fulfillment" which they do not find in Marxism. As many as a million young Chinese are taking part in public Christian worship. They claim to be motivated by curiosity about Western culture, disillusionment with Marxism, admiration for Christian character, and the need to find life's spiritual dimension.[67]

Government and party organs have acknowledged youthful resentment of the system. At the same time, they remind youth that the minimal requirement for good citizenship is dedication to the four fundamentals of adherence to (1) socialism, (2) the dictatorship of the proletariat, (3) the party's leadership, and (4) the supremacy of Marxism–Leninism–Mao Tse-tung thought. As for youth interested in Christianity, one YWCA official recently observed, "Patriotism and a pure religious belief are what we try to foster among young Christians."[68]

The swelling of church ranks by China's young people offers the church a rare opportunity for expansion. At the same time, it poses the greatest potential danger to the church's relations with the state. For in its efforts to meet the spiritual needs of these questing youth, the church may appear to encroach on the state's traditional prerogative of ideological control.

\*    \*    \*

To sum up, the current pendulum swing toward toleration reminds us of past times when the state allowed religion to operate within certain well-defined boundaries. Such toleration was granted when religious communities supported the state and offered something useful to it. Although it was tied to the consul and the gunboat, Christianity assisted in nation-building efforts. Many Christians in fact became ardent patriots long before 1949.

Chinese Christians now believe they have disentangled the gospel from colonial domination of the past. TSPM and CCPA spokespersons claim allegiance to the Marxist government, while not subscribing to Marxist ideology. They intend to play an important role in the latest chapter of China's long history of modernization efforts. Relations with the state may remain stable if religious leaders can invite international cooperation while maintaining their independence, achieve a united church based on a Chinese Christianity, and not shift the ideological concerns of the young too far from Marxism.

## Notes

1. This chapter represents my most recent analysis of church-state relations in the PRC. For my earlier views see P. Richard Bohr, *Religion in the People's Republic of China: The Limits of Toleration* (Washington, D.C.: China Council, 1982), and P. Richard Bohr, "State and Religion in China Today: Christianity's Future in a Marxist Setting," *Missiology*, 11.3:321–341 (July 1983).

2. For a history of church-state relations in imperial times see C. K. Yang, *Religion in Chinese Society* (Berkeley: University of California Press, 1967).

3. See, for example, Daniel Overmyer, *Folk Buddhist Religion: Dissenting Sects in Late Traditional China* (Cambridge, Mass.: Harvard University Press, 1976), and Susan Naquin, *Millenarian Rebellion in China: The Eight Trigrams Uprising of 1813* (New Haven, Conn.: Yale University Press, 1976).

4. For an outstanding recent study of the Jesuits in China see John D. Young, *Confucianism and Christianity: The First Encounter* (Hong Kong: Hong Kong University Press, 1983).

5. See Jacques Gernet, *China and the Christian Impact*, trans. Janet Lloyd (Cambridge: Cambridge University Press, 1982), 112–140. See also Paul A. Cohen, *China and Christianity: The Missionary Movement and the Growth of Chinese Antiforeignism, 1860–1870* (Cambridge, Mass.: Harvard University Press, 1963).

6. For a study of the syncretic basis of Taiping ideology and organization see P. Richard Bohr, "The Heavenly Kingdom in China: Religion and the Taiping Revolution, 1837–1853," *Fides et Historia*, 17.2:38–52 (spring–summer 1985).

7. Lu Shih-ch'iang, *Chung-kuo kuan-shen fan-chiao chi yuan-yin* (The Reasons for Gentry-Official Opposition to Christianity) (Taipei: Academia Sinica, 1966).

8. Among the many studies of particular aspects of China's "response" to Christian missionary activity see, for example, Paul Richard Bohr, *Famine in China and the Missionary: Timothy Richard as Relief Administrator and Advocate of National Reform* (Cambridge, Mass.: Harvard University Press, 1972); Jonathan Spence, *To Change China: Western Advisers in China, 1620–1960* (New York: Penguin, 1969); Adrian Arthur Bennett, *John Fryer: The Introduction of Western Science and Technology into Nineteenth-Century China* (Cambridge, Mass.: Harvard University Press, 1967); Adrian A. Bennett, *Missionary Journalist in China: Young J. Allen and His Magazines, 1860–1883* (Athens:

University of Georgia Press, 1983); Ralph Covell, *W.A.P. Martin: Pioneer of Progress in China* (Washington, D.C.: Christian College Consortium, 1978); Jessie Gregory Lutz, *China and the Christian Colleges, 1850–1950* (Ithaca, N.Y.: Cornell University Press, 1971); Shirley Garrett, *Social Reformers in Urban China: The Chinese Y.M.C.A., 1895–1926* (Cambridge, Mass.: Harvard University Press, 1970); P. Richard Bohr, "Liang Fa's Quest for Moral Power," in Suzanne Wilson Barnett and John King Fairbank, eds., *Christianity in China: Early Protestant Missionary Writings* (Cambridge, Mass.: Harvard University Press, 1985), 35–46; Adrian A. Bennett and Kwang-Ching Liu, "Christianity in the Chinese Idiom: Young J. Allen and the Early *Chiao-hui hsin-pao*," in John F. Fairbank, ed., *The Missionary Enterprise in China and America* (Cambridge, Mass.: Harvard University Press, 1974), 159–196; and Yu-ming Shaw, "The Reaction of Chinese Intellectuals Toward Religion and Christianity in the Early Twentieth Century," in James D. Whitehead, Yu-ming Shaw, and N. J. Girardot, eds., *China and Christianity* (Notre Dame, Ind.: Center for Pastoral and Social Ministry, University of Notre Dame, 1979), 154–182.

9. See James C. Thomson, Jr., *While China Faced West: American Reformers in Nationalist China, 1928–1937* (Cambridge, Mass.: Harvard University Press, 1969).

10. G. Thompson Brown, *Christianity in the People's Republic of China* (Atlanta: John Knox Press, 1983), 78–79.

11. For a Chinese Marxist assessment of the legacy of Christian missions see Ku Ch'ang-sheng, *Ch'üan-chiao-shih yü Chin-tai Chung-kuo* (Missionaries and Modern China) (Shanghai: People's Publishing Company, 1981).

12. For an analysis of the Chinese Marxist view of religion, see Donald E. MacInnis, ed., *Religious Policy and Practice in Communist China* (New York: Macmillan, 1967), 117–131.

13. Ibid., 21.

14. For an overview of the Three-Self principle see Francis P. Jones, ed., *Documents of the Three-Self Movement* (New York: National Council of the Churches of Christ in the U.S.A., 1963).

15. Kenneth Scott Latourette, *A History of Christian Missions in China* (London: Society for Promoting Christian Knowledge, 1929), chap. 26.

16. Brown, *Christianity in the People's Republic of China*, chap. 5.

17. For recent research on Catholicism in the PRC, see especially Eric O. Hanson, *Catholic Politics in China and Korea* (Maryknoll, N.Y.: Orbis Books, 1980), chaps. 5 and 6, and Angelo S. Lazzarotto, *The Catholic Church in Post-Mao China* (Hong Kong: Holy Spirit Study Centre, 1982).

18. For a case study history of "house fellowships" see Raymond Fung, comp. and trans., *Households of God on China's Soil* (Geneva: World Council of Churches, 1982).

19. Quoted in Joseph J. Spae, *Church and China: Towards Reconciliation?* (Chicago: Chicago Institute of Theology and Culture, 1980), 53.

20. Note that the PRC still regards Catholicism and Protestantism as two separate religions. This is the result of semantic confusion created during imperial times, when Catholics were referred to as the followers of the "Heavenly Lord" and Protestants as the followers of Jesus Christ. Note, too, that Judaism is not mentioned as an extant institutionalized religion because the Chinese Jewish community of earlier times has apparently died out.

21. Central Committee of the Communist Party of China, "The Basic Viewpoint and Policy on the Religious Question During Our Country's Socialist Period" (March 1982), trans. Janice Wickeri, Tao Fung Shan Ecumenical Center (Hong Kong), 2. See

also "Our Party's Basic Policy on Religious Questions During the Period of Socialism," *Red Flag* (Beijing), June 16, 1982, 2–8.

22. Ibid. For the text and analysis of the 1982 Constitution see *Beijing Review*, 26.52:10–29 (December 27, 1982).

23. Ibid. For further analysis see P. Richard Bohr, "Christianity in the People's Republic of China: Reflections from a Recent Visit," *China Spectrum*, 1.1:2–16 (winter/spring 1981), 6.

24. *Christianity Today* (Carol Stream, Ill.), 29.15:73 (October 18, 1985).

25. For a review of recent Marxist scholarship on religion see *The China Study Project Journal* (Tunbridge Wells, England), 1.1:32–33 (April 1986).

26. Chao Fu-san, "Religion, Spiritual Culture and National Unity," *The China Study Project Bulletin* (Tunbridge Wells, England), 28:15 (November 1985).

27. Ibid.

28. See *The China Study Project Journal*, 1.1:32 (April 1986).

29. *The China Letter*, 172:6 (February 1976).

30. For post-Mao developments in Chinese religions, see K. H. Ting et al., *Chinese Christians Speak Out: Addresses and Sermons* (Beijing: New World Press, 1984) and the China Study Project, ed., *Religion in the People's Republic of China: Documentation* (Tunbridge Wells, England), nos. 2–3 (July 1980) through no. 19 (December 1985). See also Robert G. Orr, *Religion in China* (New York: Friendship Press, 1980).

31. The most comprehensive history of Chinese Christianity since Mao is Brown, *Christianity in the People's Republic of China*, chaps. 5–10. See also P. Richard Bohr, *Protestant Christianity in China: Introduction, Source Materials, and a Bibliography* (St. Paul: Midwest China Center Occasional Papers, no. 2, 1983).

32. *Yau-tao Wen-ta: 100 Questions and Answers on the Christian Faith* (Tunbridge Wells, England: China Study Project, 1984). For an analysis of recent Chinese Protestant theological development see Ralph R. Covell, *Confucius, the Buddha, and Christ: A History of the Gospel in China* (Maryknoll, N.Y.: Orbis Books, 1986), chaps. 11–12.

33. See issues of *The Chinese Catholic Church* (Beijing), New Series, no. 1 (November 1980) through no. 13 (October 1985).

34. For an overview of educational reform efforts in the PRC see John Bryan Starr, "Reforming China's Schools," *China Update* (New Haven, Conn.), 5.3:1–5 (fall 1985).

35. *China Daily*, October 25, 1985.

36. Quoted in *China Notes*, 23.2–3:348 (spring–summer 1985).

37. *The China Study Project Journal*, 1.1:55 (April 1986).

38. *China News and Church Report*, 99 (April 4, 1985) and 107 (May 31, 1985).

39. *China Daily*, December 6, 1985.

40. *The China Study Project Journal*, 1.1:55 (April 1986).

41. *Bridge* (Hong Kong), 17:2 (May–June 1986).

42. See the papers presented by the Chinese delegates in Theresa Chu and Christopher Lind, eds., *A New Beginning* (Toronto: Canada China Programme, 1983). For an analysis of the issues raised at Montreal see P. Richard Bohr, "A New Beginning in Montreal: The Churches in China and Us" (St. Paul: Midwest China Center Occasional Papers, no. 1, 1983).

43. See K. H. Ting, "A Call for Clarity: Fourteen Points from Christians in the People's Republic of China to Christians Abroad," *China Notes*, 9.1:145–149 (winter 1980–1981).

44. Chao, "Religion, Spiritual Culture and National Unity," 15. The Chinese have already begun to host international religious conferences beyond those that are strictly Christian. During June 25–30, 1986, the five Chinese religious associations hosted

more than 100 religious leaders of all living faiths from thirty countries at a conference organized by the International Council of the World Conference on Religion and Peace, "Peace Through Work and Prayer," in Beijing. Some thirty representatives of the five Chinese religious associations also attended.

45. Ku, *Ch'üan-chiao-shih yü Chin-tai Chung-kuo*.

46. Ku Ch'ang-sheng, *Ts'ung Ma-li-sun tao Ssu-t'u Lei-teng* (From Morrison to Stuart) (Shanghai: People's Publishing Company, 1985).

47. Quoted in *The China Study Project Bulletin*, 27:14–15 (April 1985).

48. *Amity Newsletter* (Nanking), no. 1 (fall 1985) and no. 2 (spring 1986).

49. *Bridge*, 17:3 (May-June 1986).

50. Transcript of "Christian Social Action in China: A Midwest Response," a conference organized by the Midwest China Center, April 3–5, 1986.

51. Ibid.

52. See, for example, David H. Adeney, *China: The Church's Long March* (Ventura, Calif.: Regal Books, 1985), 145.

53. Quoted in *The China Project Study Bulletin*, 20:8 (December 1982).

54. See recent issues of *The China Study Project Bulletin*.

55. *Baptist Press* (Nashville), July 30, 1945.

56. For an analysis see Angelo S. Lazzarotto, "Religious Believers and the 'Socialist Spiritual Civilization,'" *Tripod (Ting)*, 12:64–78 (1983).

57. See, for example, Leslie Lyall, *God Reigns in China* (London: Hodder and Stoughton, 1985), chaps. 16–18, and Carl Lawrence, *The Church in China* (Minneapolis: Bethany House Publishers, 1985), chap. 5.

58. See *China's Christian Community: No Longer a Dot on a Missionary Map* (Beijing: Beijing Review Publications, n.d.).

59. Edmund Tang, *The Church in China—After Two Revolutions* (Brussels: Pro Mundi Vita: Dossiers, 1982), 14–21.

60. Quoted in Bohr, *Religion in the People's Republic of China*, 17.

61. *The Catholic Church in China* (Beijing), 5:42 (September 1982).

62. *Religious News Service*, November 11, 1985.

63. See accounts in contemporary issues of *Religion in the People's Republic of China: Documentation*.

64. Ting, "A Call for Clarity," 146.

65. See Lazzarotto, "Religious Believers," 65.

66. See recent issues of *Religion in the People's Republic of China: Documentation*.

67. Paul P. Pang, "Youth and Religious Revival in China," *CECC Newsletter* (Belgium), 13:42–45 (October 1982).

68. Quoted in *China Daily*, March 30, 1985.

# 35

## From Old to Young: The Retirement Life of Chinese Communist Cadres and Its Political Implications

*Wen-hui Tsai*

### Introduction

On the eve of the national Communist Party conference held in Beijing on September 18, 1985, 131 older Chinese officials were asked to resign and retire from the Central Committee, the Central Advisory Commission, and the Central Disciplinary Inspection Commission to make way for younger people. Commenting on this action, the political editor of the *Beijing Review*, An Zhiquo, hailed it as "both a major policy decision and a concrete step toward abolishing life-long tenure in leading posts. It will be of great significance in ensuring the continuity of China's current policies and promoting reform of the cadre system."[1]

The retirement of the elderly party and government officials in the People's Republic of China (PRC) had long been anticipated, and thus the announcement came as no surprise to China watchers in both Taiwan and the United States. The movement of power transformation from old to young has been steadily pushed since the Third Plenary Session of the Eleventh Communist Party Central Committee held in late 1978. In the process, approximately 1.08 million veteran cadres have retired and more than 200,000 younger leaders have been promoted to top posts at or above the county level. On the national level, according to one account, 100 middle-aged and younger people were promoted in 1984 to the posts of ministers and vice-ministers as well as the other senior positions under the State Council.[2] The average age of the major leaders of eighty-one departments under the State Council is now 56.6 years, and the proportion of the leaders under 55 years of age has increased to 30 percent.

The current Communist Chinese youth movement has gained worldwide attention and generally received positive acceptance from leaders of the non-Communist nations.[3] This chapter will explore the life after retirement for these elderly party and political leaders of Communist China and its impacts on future Chinese politics. We will first present a demographic account of the growth of the Chinese elderly population. Then we will examine the current Chinese retirement welfare system for the elderly in both private and public sectors, with special reference to the retired cadres. Finally, we will discuss the political implications of such a youth movement through an analysis of the interactions between the two groups of young and old political leaders.

## The Demography of the Elderly

*Population Growth*

China now has a population of more than one billion. The 1983 population census shows a total of 1,024,950,000 persons living in China. This figure reflects an increase of 483,280,000 persons, or nearly 90 percent, from the population of 1949, which was the year the People's Republic of China was inaugurated. Such a tremendous increase is the result of the combined effects of a higher birth rate and a lower death rate over a period of thirty-five years. As we can see in Table 35.1, with the exception of the two years 1960 and 1961, the crude birth rate had been exceedingly high prior to the mid-1970s, while at the same time the crude death rate had shown a steady decline during the same period. Events in contemporary China are often dictated by shifts in political and ideological currents, and population policy is no exception. Until his death in 1976, Mao Zedong was the ruler and his thought was the unchallenged sociopolitical ideology of that time. For many years, for instance, *Quotations from Chairman Mao*, or the "Little Red Book" as it is called, was the equivalent to the Bible in the Christian world. In regard to population, Mao Zedong believed that the more population China had, the stronger China would be, and that it was necessary for China to have more people if it was to successfully resist Western capitalist expansion. Mao took a supply-side view and saw population as "human hands" providing working labor, and not as "human mouths" demanding sustenance. In Mao's mind, population was never a problem and, as a result, China's population increased dramatically under his leadership.[4]

During Mao's era, the Chinese Communist Party rejected outright any attempt to control population growth. The incident of Ma Yinchu, as described in Richard Bernstein's *From the Center of the Earth*, reflected the difficulty of proposing a policy contrary to Mao's thinking: "In 1957, one of China's leading economists, Ma Yinchu, at the time president of Peking University, proposed at the Fourth Session of the First National People's Congress that a birth-control campaign become part of the mass-education curriculum. Ma, for his pains, was branded a "rightist." He was disgraced and driven from the university and remained for twenty years as an object of official contempt."[5]

Mao's legacy started to fade away, however, in the 1970s, and with his death in 1976, so did his pronatalistic view. Population problems finally

TABLE 35.1
Population Growth in China, 1949–1982

| Year | Total (000 omitted) | Birth Rates | Death Rates | Growth Rates |
|------|---------------------|-------------|-------------|--------------|
| 1949 | 541,670 | 36.0 | 20.0 | 16.0 |
| 1950 | 551,960 | 37.0 | 18.0 | 19.0 |
| 1951 | 563,000 | 37.8 | 17.8 | 20.0 |
| 1952 | 574,820 | 37.0 | 17.0 | 20.0 |
| 1953 | 587,960 | 37.0 | 14.0 | 23.0 |
| 1954 | 602,660 | 38.0 | 13.2 | 24.8 |
| 1955 | 614,650 | 32.6 | 12.3 | 20.3 |
| 1956 | 628,280 | 31.9 | 11.4 | 20.5 |
| 1957 | 646,530 | 34.0 | 10.8 | 23.2 |
| 1958 | 659,940 | 29.2 | 12.0 | 17.2 |
| 1959 | 672,070 | 24.8 | 14.6 | 10.2 |
| 1960 | 662,070 | 20.9 | 25.4 | -4.5 |
| 1961 | 658,590 | 18.0 | 14.2 | 3.8 |
| 1962 | 672,950 | 37.0 | 10.0 | 27.0 |
| 1963 | 691,720 | 43.4 | 10.0 | 33.4 |
| 1964 | 704,990 | 39.1 | 11.5 | 27.6 |
| 1965 | 725,380 | 37.9 | 9.5 | 28.4 |
| 1966 | 745,420 | 35.1 | 8.8 | 26.3 |
| 1967 | 763,680 | 34.0 | 8.4 | 25.6 |
| 1968 | 785,340 | 35.6 | 8.2 | 27.4 |
| 1969 | 806,710 | 34.1 | 8.0 | 26.1 |
| 1970 | 829,920 | 33.4 | 7.6 | 25.8 |
| 1971 | 852,290 | 30.7 | 7.3 | 23.4 |
| 1972 | 871,770 | 29.8 | 7.6 | 22.2 |
| 1973 | 892,110 | 27.9 | 7.0 | 20.9 |
| 1974 | 908,590 | 24.8 | 7.3 | 17.5 |
| 1975 | 924,200 | 23.0 | 7.3 | 15.7 |
| 1976 | 937,170 | 19.9 | 7.3 | 12.6 |
| 1977 | 949,740 | 18.9 | 6.9 | 12.0 |
| 1978 | 962,590 | 18.3 | 6.3 | 12.0 |
| 1979 | 975,420 | 17.9 | 6.2 | 11.7 |
| 1980 | 987,050 | 17.0 | 6.3 | 10.7 |
| 1981 | 1,000,720 | 20.9 | 6.4 | 14.5 |
| 1982 | 1,015,410 | 21.1 | 6.6 | 14.5 |
| 1983 | 1,024,950 | 18.6 | 7.1 | 11.5 |
| 1984 | 1,029,200 | 19.0 | 7.0 | 12.0 |

Sources: Bureau of Statistics, PRC, Statistical Yearbook of China, 1983 (Hong Kong: Economic Information & Agency, 1983), pp. 103–105; World Bank, World Development Report, 1987 (New York: Oxford University Press, 1987), Tables 1 & 28, pp. 202 and 258.

TABLE 35.3
China's Pension System for Retired Workers and Staff Members

| Requirements | Pension as a Percentage of Former Wages[a] |
|---|---|
| Those who started work after the founding of new China (October 1, 1949): | |
| 1. Worked consecutively for 10 to 14 years | 60 |
| 2. Worked consecutively for 15 to 19 years | 70 |
| 3. Worked consecutively for twenty years or more | 75 |
| Those who joined revolution during the period of the Liberation War (on or prior to September 30, 1949) | 80 |
| Those who joined revolution during the period of the anti-Japanese war (on or prior to September 2, 1945)[b] | 90 |

*Source:* Beijing Review, ed., *From Youth to Retirement* (Beijing: Beijing Review, 1982), Table 1, p. 84.

[a]Those who have been honored as National Model Workers, Labor Heroes, or Combat Heroes and those who have made special contributions can receive a pension 5 percent to 15 percent higher than the given figures.
[b]Cadres who began revolutionary work before July 7, 1937, receive a pension equal to their wages.

We can easily conclude that the life of a retired elderly person in urban China is indeed quite comfortable. But one can not ignore the fact that 80 percent of the Chinese today are still living in rural areas. The rural elderly are not covered by the retirement pension system. The great majority of the rural elderly are living with their children. In Communist China today, the traditional custom of filial care has been made into law, and maltreatment of elderly parents is punishable by law.[9] The Communist Chinese government now sees filial care provided by the family members as the best solution to the problems of aging in China for the future and, thus, encourages its citizens to maintain a reciprocal relation between elderly parents and adult children. As one Chinese youth says in a government publication, "Today we enjoy the fruits of the hard labor of our elders. Tomorrow, it is our children's turn."[10] The government wants to advocate filial care for the elderly because it will reduce the economic burden of the government; Chinese individuals welcome it, for it provides both tangible and intangible returns for them.

In addition to the previously mentioned state-supported elderly welfare programs and filial care from family members, there are other regional and local welfare programs available to the elderly. One of these programs is the senior citizen homes, which are often run by work units and communes. In general, all residents of a senior citizen home are guaranteed the freedom to enter and leave the home, to move about, to work, and to drink liquor.

TABLE 35.2
Selected Demographic Characteristics Related to the Chinese Elderly, 1960–2050[a]

|  | 1960 | 1980 | 2000 | 2025 | 2050 |
|---|---|---|---|---|---|
| Total elderly population (in thousands) | 37,678 | 72,815 | 127,389 | 234,036 | 270,469 |
| Percentage of the elderly in total population[b] | 5.6 | 7.3 | 10.1 | 16.4 | 18.5 |
| Median age | 21.0 | 21.7 | 30.2 | 37.7 | 38.4 |
| Number of the elderly per 100 workers | 10 | 13 | 15 | 25 | 29 |

*Sources:* United Nations Department of International Economic and Social Affairs, *Periodical on Aging*, vol. 1, no. 1 (1984). *Chinese Statistical Yearbook*, 1983, p. 104.

[a]The elderly population refers to the population aged sixty or older.
[b]The proportion of the population aged sixty-five or older listed in the three nationwide census was 4.4 percent in 1953, 3.5 percent in 1964, and 4.9 percent in 1982. It is also projected to reach 7.0 percent in the year 2000.

adopted in 1982 declared that the elderly have the right to receive material assistance from the society and the government, and that the nation has an obligation to provide such assistance through the implementation of such programs as social insurance, social relief, and health care systems.

In urban areas, according to the State Bureau of Labor, approximately 8 million retired workers and staff members collect pensions today. Male workers and staff members retire at age sixty, female workers at fifty, and female staff members at fifty-five. Mine workers and those who work high above the ground or in extreme heat retire five years earlier. Pensions are based on a percentge of salary that is calculated by length of time on the job, work performance, and service to the country. In addition, all retirees receive free medical care. Table 35.3 is a summary of China's current pension system.

As a socialist state, the PRC bases the wages of workers on the seniority system; that is, the longer a worker has worked, the higher his or her wage will be. Therefore, by the time a worker is ready to retire, he or she has reached a higher wage on the pay scale. It is, therefore, not surprising that the pension an urban retired worker receives is not only sufficient to provide a comfortable living, but is also very likely to be higher than the wage his or her adult children receive. A 1983 study on the income of the elderly in Beijing found that the averge income of the elderly from pensions in the city was higher than the income of their children. The retired cadres receive a monthly pension of 86 People's dollars, in comparison to their children's monthly income of 50.7 People's dollars. The retired cadre's pensions are 70 percent more than the adult children's family income. Higher pensions are also seen in other occupations.[8]

TABLE 35.3
China's Pension System for Retired Workers and Staff Members

| Requirements | Pension as a Percentage of Former Wages[a] |
|---|---|
| Those who started work after the founding of new China (October 1, 1949): | |
| 1. Worked consecutively for 10 to 14 years | 60 |
| 2. Worked consecutively for 15 to 19 years | 70 |
| 3. Worked consecutively for twenty years or more | 75 |
| Those who joined revolution during the period of the Liberation War (on or prior to September 30, 1949) | 80 |
| Those who joined revolution during the period of the anti-Japanese war (on or prior to September 2, 1945)[b] | 90 |

*Source:* Beijing Review, ed., *From Youth to Retirement* (Beijing: Beijing Review, 1982), Table 1, p. 84.

[a]Those who have been honored as National Model Workers, Labor Heroes, or Combat Heroes and those who have made special contributions can receive a pension 5 percent to 15 percent higher than the given figures.
[b]Cadres who began revolutionary work before July 7, 1937, receive a pension equal to their wages.

We can easily conclude that the life of a retired elderly person in urban China is indeed quite comfortable. But one can not ignore the fact that 80 percent of the Chinese today are still living in rural areas. The rural elderly are not covered by the retirement pension system. The great majority of the rural elderly are living with their children. In Communist China today, the traditional custom of filial care has been made into law, and maltreatment of elderly parents is punishable by law.[9] The Communist Chinese government now sees filial care provided by the family members as the best solution to the problems of aging in China for the future and, thus, encourages its citizens to maintain a reciprocal relation between elderly parents and adult children. As one Chinese youth says in a government publication, "Today we enjoy the fruits of the hard labor of our elders. Tomorrow, it is our children's turn."[10] The government wants to advocate filial care for the elderly because it will reduce the economic burden of the government; Chinese individuals welcome it, for it provides both tangible and intangible returns for them.

In addition to the previously mentioned state-supported elderly welfare programs and filial care from family members, there are other regional and local welfare programs available to the elderly. One of these programs is the senior citizen homes, which are often run by work units and communes. In general, all residents of a senior citizen home are guaranteed the freedom to enter and leave the home, to move about, to work, and to drink liquor.

TABLE 35.1
Population Growth in China, 1949–1982

| Year | Total (000 omitted) | Birth Rates | Death Rates | Growth Rates |
|------|---------------------|-------------|-------------|--------------|
| 1949 | 541,670 | 36.0 | 20.0 | 16.0 |
| 1950 | 551,960 | 37.0 | 18.0 | 19.0 |
| 1951 | 563,000 | 37.8 | 17.8 | 20.0 |
| 1952 | 574,820 | 37.0 | 17.0 | 20.0 |
| 1953 | 587,960 | 37.0 | 14.0 | 23.0 |
| 1954 | 602,660 | 38.0 | 13.2 | 24.8 |
| 1955 | 614,650 | 32.6 | 12.3 | 20.3 |
| 1956 | 628,280 | 31.9 | 11.4 | 20.5 |
| 1957 | 646,530 | 34.0 | 10.8 | 23.2 |
| 1958 | 659,940 | 29.2 | 12.0 | 17.2 |
| 1959 | 672,070 | 24.8 | 14.6 | 10.2 |
| 1960 | 662,070 | 20.9 | 25.4 | -4.5 |
| 1961 | 658,590 | 18.0 | 14.2 | 3.8 |
| 1962 | 672,950 | 37.0 | 10.0 | 27.0 |
| 1963 | 691,720 | 43.4 | 10.0 | 33.4 |
| 1964 | 704,990 | 39.1 | 11.5 | 27.6 |
| 1965 | 725,380 | 37.9 | 9.5 | 28.4 |
| 1966 | 745,420 | 35.1 | 8.8 | 26.3 |
| 1967 | 763,680 | 34.0 | 8.4 | 25.6 |
| 1968 | 785,340 | 35.6 | 8.2 | 27.4 |
| 1969 | 806,710 | 34.1 | 8.0 | 26.1 |
| 1970 | 829,920 | 33.4 | 7.6 | 25.8 |
| 1971 | 852,290 | 30.7 | 7.3 | 23.4 |
| 1972 | 871,770 | 29.8 | 7.6 | 22.2 |
| 1973 | 892,110 | 27.9 | 7.0 | 20.9 |
| 1974 | 908,590 | 24.8 | 7.3 | 17.5 |
| 1975 | 924,200 | 23.0 | 7.3 | 15.7 |
| 1976 | 937,170 | 19.9 | 7.3 | 12.6 |
| 1977 | 949,740 | 18.9 | 6.9 | 12.0 |
| 1978 | 962,590 | 18.3 | 6.3 | 12.0 |
| 1979 | 975,420 | 17.9 | 6.2 | 11.7 |
| 1980 | 987,050 | 17.0 | 6.3 | 10.7 |
| 1981 | 1,000,720 | 20.9 | 6.4 | 14.5 |
| 1982 | 1,015,410 | 21.1 | 6.6 | 14.5 |
| 1983 | 1,024,950 | 18.6 | 7.1 | 11.5 |
| 1984 | 1,029,200 | 19.0 | 7.0 | 12.0 |

Sources: Bureau of Statistics, PRC, Statistical Yearbook of China, 1983 (Hong Kong: Economic Information & Agency, 1983), pp. 103–105; World Bank, World Development Report, 1987 (New York: Oxford University Press, 1987), Tables 1 & 28, pp. 202 and 258.

received greater attention from the government. Communist China's new leaders have decided that the only solution to the problem of poverty and underdevelopment is to step up production and, simultaneously, make population control a state policy. A birth planning program was launched in the early 1970s to slow down China's population growth. This program is generally known as "Wan-Xi-Shao," meaning the postponement of marriage and birth (Wan), the spacing of birth (Xi), and the smaller number of children (Shao). A tougher birth control program was implemented in 1980 by the new leadership under Deng Xiaoping. With this program, each family will be permitted to have only one child. Punishments are imposed on those who have more than one child.[6] The steady decline of crude birth rates and of natural growth rates shown in Table 35.1 reflect the impact of these birth control programs. The Communist Chinese government hopes that with the help of these programs the Chinese population will not exceed 1.2 billion by the year 2000.

## The Elderly Population

Along with the increase of China's total population, the elderly population has also shown increases, both in number and in proportion to the total population. The elderly population aged sixty and over was reported to be approximately 37,678,000 in 1960, and it increased to 72,815,000 in 1980. In comparison to the total population, the elderly population's share was 5.6 percent in 1960 and 7.3 percent in 1980. With the expected decline in crude birth rates and improved health services, the elderly population will reach 270,469,000 by the year 2050, and it will account for 18.5 percent of the total population. A recent report made by the Bureau of Statistics showed that 8 percent of China's population in 1985 was aged sixty-five and over. It also predicted that by the year 2040 this aged population would reach 33 percent of the total population.[7]

The increase of the elderly population in China will have at least two significant consequences. First, it will undoubtedly hasten the aging process of the Chinese population. The median age of the Chinese population was 21.0 in 1960; it increased to 21.7 in 1980; and it is expected to be 38.4 by the year 2050. In other words, nearly half of the Chinese population in 2050 will be nearing forty years of age. Second, it will also create a tremendous burden on economically productive age groups. The United Nations estimate shows that the number of the elderly per 100 workers in China in 1960 was 10 and that the number will increase to 29 in 2050. In other words, by the year 2050 every three Chinese workers will have to support one elderly person. Table 35.2 presents a summary of the selected demographic indicators of the Chinese elderly between 1960 and 2050.

## Social Welfare for the Elderly

The increase of the elderly population has prompted the PRC government to pay attention to the potential problems facing the elderly. The constitution

Another program for the retired elderly is the organization of associations for the retirees, as well as helping them with personal or financial problems. Sometimes these associations serve as a think tank for work units and production teams through discussion sessions between workers and retirees. A program to establish universities for the elderly is currently under study in Beijing to provide an environment not only for learning, but for leisure activities as well.[11]

Until now, the Communist Chinese model of elderly welfare, characterized by a combination of filial care and state assistance programs, seems to work well. It provides the elderly with financial security and continuous contact with family members. However, the future success of this model will be dependent upon the willingness and ability of the family to support filial care for the elderly, the availability of housing space allocated to urban workers, a much-improved national economy, and a continuous observation of traditional respect to the elderly parents both in the family and in the larger society. The government has recently admitted that the current pension system is a heavy burden on the national economy. *China Daily* reported at the end of 1985 that between 1980 and 1984, the number of the retirees in Communist China increased by 80 percent, and pension payments increased by 78.7 percent. In Shanghai, for example, pension payments have doubled since 1978; and the expenditures for pension payments and elderly medical care are now one-fourth of the city's total budget expenditures.[12]

## The Elderly and Political Power

In 1983, Parris H. Chang made the following observation on Communist China's aging leadership. "When the Chinese Communists siezed power in China in 1949, the new regime was then headed by a relatively young leadership nucleus which consisted of approximately 800 leaders. . . . The passage of time and constant political conflict over the past three decades have taken a heavy toll of this elite group, and only about half of these 800 revolutionary leaders have survived. Nonetheless these veterans still retain firm control over China's ship of state today."[13]

Chang's remark was made in 1983 prior to the mass retirement of the elderly cadres in September 1985. Although Deng's vigorous youthful campaign had already started, it continued receiving resistance from the older group. Numerous older leaders were able to stay on in the party's top policymaking bodies. The event of September 18, 1985, is seen by many China specialists in the West as the great triumph of Deng Xiaoping in pushing toward a youthful new leadership in Communist China. As a result, the event has received worldwide attention and is praised as one of the Chinese Communists' great accomplishments in comparison to the aging leadership of the other Communist nations.

However, our analysis of the age composition of the three leading policymaking bodies in Communist China's political structure after the recent reorganization shows that the average age for members of the Standing

TABLE 35.4
Age Distribution of Three Decision-Making Bodies After the Reorganization of September 1985

| Age | Standing Committee of the Politburo | Politburo | Central Secretariat |
|---|---|---|---|
| 80+ | 2 | 4 | 0 |
| 70–79 | 1 | 5 | 3 |
| 60–69 | 2 | 6 | 3 |
| 50–59 | 0 | 5 | 4 |
| 40–49 | 0 | 0 | 1 |
| Total membership | 5 | 20 | 11 |
| Average age | 75.2 years | 69.3 years | 61.2 years |

Sources: "Changing Power in Communist China," World Daily, September 28 and 29, 1985, p. 22. Fang Hsueh-ch'un, "Personnel Changes in the CCP's Central Leadership," Chung-kuo ta-lu yen-chiu (Mainland China Studies), vol. 28, no. 4 (October 1985), p. 14.

Committee of the Politburo is 75.2 years, and for the entire Politburo membership 69.3 years, as shown in Table 35.4. Only the Central Secretariat office shows a younger average age, 61.2 years, and it has traditionally been the youngest among the three policymaking bodies.[14]

It is clear then that the youth movement seems to be taking place primarily in the administrative branches of the government, including the party's Central Secretariat office, the departments under the State Council, and various regional and local offices. Power in the decision-making bodies is still controlled by the elderly leaders. In reference to the 131 officials who retired from higher office, it was reported that they were promised to be able to keep their cars, houses, and same salary, and to guarantee positions for their children.[15] At the retirement banquet that Deng Xiaoping held in honor of the retired high-ranking cadres on the day of the national Communist Party conference on September 23, 1985, an eighty-five-year-old retired cadre told Deng Xiaoping and other participants, "Our Party wants to abolish the lifelong system of leadership, I totally support this policy. We need to start with us here to establish the rule and to set up a good example for others to follow. . . . This is our wish and historical responsibilty. It is also from our inner heart."[16] He then drank with Hu Yaobang, Li Xiannian, and Deng Xiaoping, wishing them success in managing the country.

With the promise from Deng Xiaoping of a good life after retirement and a willingness of the older cadres to retire, it seems this group of elderly leadership will fade away and lose their influence on power. We have already mentioned that the top decision-making bodies are still in the control of a few older leaders. But those who accepted retirement will not be totally isolated from politics or, thus, from power either. The following institu-tionalized factors will be in effect to make the retired cadres continuously influential and powerful.

1. Age in China has always played an important role in human interactions. From traditional times to modern China, the aged have always received respect from the society and enjoyed a high status in society. Thus their voice will be not only heard but also respected. Through this respect, the retired cadres will exercise a certain influence on younger leaders in the decision-making process.

2. Power and authority in China have always been given to the individual who occupies the office, not to the office itself. This is even more true in Communist China today, as Deng Xiaoping continues to have the final say in all major decisions, even though he holds only a minor, insignificant administrative office. As a result, power and authority go with the individual whether he holds office or not. The retirement of the elderly cadres, therefore, does not necessarily mean the loss of power; they still could exercise power and influence from behind the scene.

3. As political power and authority are not built upon institutionalized means, Chinese politics, from traditional to contemporary China, have always operated around a system of teacher-pupil relationships. The pupil owes his political entrance and advancement to his teacher, and, in return, he listens to the teacher and accepts the latter's advice and orders. Through his young pupil who is now holding office, an elderly retired cadre could continue to enjoy power.

4. In his bargaining with the elderly cadres for their retirement, Deng has promised to recruit their children into administration. A careful examination of the new appointees at both national and regional levels of office will show indeed that many of these children are holding important offices in all branches of the government throughout China.[17]

5. Communist China is still a totalitarian state in which politics are controlled by a single party. The recruitment of its party members in such a system is likely to emphasize party loyalty. However, the development as well as the evaluation of the member's party loyalty cannot be done in a short period of time. The newly recruited cadres will not be easily trusted by the old-timers. As we have seen in Communist China today, Deng Xiaoping may have recruited a large number of younger cadres into the leadership, but the center of power still is held in his hands and the hands of a few trusted old guards.

6. The great majority of those who were forced to retire are those who fought the war against Chiang Kai-shek and made a great contribution in establishing the Communist regime in 1949. They will not be pushed aside and yield their power to a group of juniors who did not play any role in the Liberation Revolution of 1949. They may not hold office any more, but they will certainly want to continue to enjoy the fruits of their earlier struggle.

7. Even though Communist China has gained improvements economically in recent years under the new economic policy, China is still a poor country. As in many poor Third World nations, money and other

earthly luxuries the elderly cadres have enjoyed in the past all came from the power they held. Without power, all these will be gone. The promise from Deng Xiaoping to allow the retired cadres to continue to keep their houses and cars will gradually disappear once they lose power. The longer they hold power, either formally or informally, the longer they will be able to enjoy their luxurious life-styles.

8. The three criteria in Deng's current recruitment campaign are youth, education, and knowledge. But none of these three characteristics will guarantee that the newly recruited cadres can make decisions without first checking with the retired cadres whose influence is still evident. As a matter of fact, for these young, educated, and knowledgeable new leaders to be able to exercise their power, to which they are supposedly entitled, they must find alliances among the retired cadres, which then extend the latter's control even further.

As these factors come into play, the retired cadres will not likely be totally isolated from politics; they will continue to exercise certain influence in the decision-making process, either formally or informally. As uncertain and unstable as Communist China's politics are, no one really knows whether the younger new leaders will be able to replace the elderly cadres and just be themselves in their management of China. For now, however, we cannot underestimate the manipulation by the elderly from behind the scenes.

## Concluding Remarks

China is now pushing toward modernization. Deng Xiaoping has called for a campaign of Four Modernizations, which include the modernizations of industry, agriculture, the military, and science and technology. The Four Modernizations program represents a significant shift from Maoism, which had called for a total dedication to the state, to a more pragmatic approach with a mixture of socialism and capitalism.

Perhaps the most crucial factor in Communist China's efforts toward modernization lies in the effectiveness of its political leadership. Communist China represents a classical example of a modernization from the top; that is, modernization is initiated by the leadership at the top of the social hierarchy, not by the mass at the bottom.[18] The political style of the leader will, therefore, affect not only the type and function of political structure, but also the tempo and destination of the society's economic and social transformation. Modernization in Communist China, like all other modernizing societies, involves to some extent the transfer of political power from old hands to new. Thus a major problem facing Deng Xiaoping and his modernizing group is the transition from a political leadership wedded to the status quo to one that favors thorough modernization. The elderly cadres, as symbolic leaders of the traditional way of life and the status quo, present a threat to Deng's efforts toward modernization and thus must be replaced. The recent youth movement in the Communist Chinese power hierarchy is clear evidence of such an attempt.

As we have argued in this chapter, although Deng has been relatively successful in recruiting younger leaders into his administration, the elderly cadres by no means are completely withdrawn from power. Through various formal and informal channels, the elderly and now retired cadres can be expected to have some continuous influence in Communist China's decisionmaking process. The success of Communist China's modernization efforts in general and the stability of its political power structure in particular will be dependent upon the ability of this newly recruited younger leadership to be independent from the older group and to be able to make policy decisions by themselves without serious interference from the old. The sooner the younger group achieves this independence, the better the chance for Communist China to move ahead toward a whole modernization.

To a certain degree, the youth movement currently underway in Communist China can also be seen as a process of routinization of charismatic authority. As the legitimacy of Communist China is built upon a charismatic leader, whether he be Mao Zedong or Deng Xiaoping, there is always inherited instability with constant power struggle and policy inconsistency. It therefore becomes necessary for the current leadership of Communist China to shift its authority from the individual charismatic quality to a more rational institutionalized norm. The newly recruited leaders are younger, more educated, and technologically competent; they could provide stability and continuity in future Chinese politics if they were given power and were independent from the old guards.

Yet, the breakaway of young from old cadres in the political decisionmaking process also presents a potential threat to the existence of the Communist system in mainland China. Martin Lipset once used legitimacy and effectiveness as measures of political stability in a society. Legitimacy is the degree to which people accept the form of the government, while effectiveness refers to the degree to which government is capable of implementing its policy decisions. Lipset suggested that nations in the Communist bloc are without legitimacy or, at best, have only a lower degree of legitimacy, and thus their existence is dependent upon effectiveness through a strong commitment to Communist ideology and party loyalty and a tight military control over their citizens.[19] Lipset's concern over the lack of legitimacy in Communist nations is shared by Alan Liu in his study of Communist Chinese politics. "Socialism as the only way for China had been accepted by Chinese Communist leaders as a matter of faith ever since their late adolescence, when the Communist party was organized. The hard road to power that the CPC traversed further strengthened the emotional nature of the Chinese Communists' commitment to socialism. . . . Under this circumstance no rational discussion of the suitability of socialism for China was possible."[20] The existence of the Communist Chinese regime and its ability to govern have been built upon a high degree of effectiveness through the two folds of tight control: a strong commitment to party ideology and power structure, and a military means of organizational control over its citizens. Until now, Communist China has been able to achieve stability as a result of the lifelong commitment of its elderly cadres, whose devotion to communism and Maoism is without question. The current movement toward youth in the power transformation, however, is likely to undermine the ideological cohesiveness in Communist China's new leadership, for the younger group never took part in the Chinese Communists' struggle against the Nationalists prior to 1949 that created a sense of identity and togetherness for the older cadres. The commitment from this younger group to communism and to the established norms set up by the old cadres will likely be minimal. Chaos and normlessness can be anticipated during this phase of power transformation, as evidenced by a rapid increase of corruption and crimes in mainland China in recent times.

The history of Communist China is a history of trial and error. It is hoped that the current trial of youthful leadership will work, and with a minimum of error and human cost.

## Notes

A different version of this discussion, entitled "Life After Retirement: Elderly Welfare in China," appeared in *Asian Survey*, vol. 27, no. 5 (May 1987), pp. 566–576. The research in this study was partially funded by two grants: a field study grant from International Study Programs at Indiana University and a research grant from the Association of Chinese Social Scientists in North America.

1. An Zhiguo, "Reshuffle and Policy Continuity," *Beijing Review*, vol. 28, no. 38 (September 23, 1985), p. 4.

2. "Conference Puts Future into Younger Hands," *Beijing Review*, vol. 28, no. 39 (September 30, 1985), pp. 6–8.

3. "The Second Revolution: Deng's Reforms Are Taking China on a Courageous if Uncharted Course," *Time*, September 23, 1985, pp. 42–56. Also "Golden Handshakes in Peking," *Time*, September 30, 1985, p. 52.

4. Li Wen-lang, "Population and Prospects of Social Change in People's Republic of China." Paper read at the Thirteenth Sino-American Conference on Mainland China held in Taipei, Taiwan, June 12–15, 1984.

5. Richard Bernstein, *From the Center of the Earth* (Boston: Little, Brown, 1982), pp. 50–51.

6. Qian Xinzhong, "China's Population Policy: Theory and Methods," *Studies in Family Planning*, no. 14 (1984), pp. 295–310.

7. Demographic Department of the State Statistical Bureau, "Forecasts on the Aging Population," *Beijing Review*, vol. 29, no. 30 (March 10, 1985), pp. 25, 34.

8. Lin Lolung and Di Kun, "A Study on the Retired Workers and Staffs," *Social Sciences Frontlines*, no. 3 (1983), p. 105.

9. Chiang Cheng-chang, "Essay on Problems of Aging in Mainland China," *Issues & Studies*, vol. 37, no. 6 (1984), pp. 71–80.

10. Beijing Review, ed., *From Youth to Retirement* (Beijing: Beijing Review, 1982), p. 100.

11. This was mentioned to me during a discussion session I had in Beijing with members of the Beijing Sociological Association and the Beijing Demography Society in June 1985.

12. Quoted from a news report in *International Daily News*, March 5, 1986, p. 9.

13. Parris H. Chang, *Elite Conflict in the Post-Mao China* (Baltimore: University of Maryland, 1983), p. 37.

14. Wen-hui Tsai, "Life After Retirement: Elderly Welfare in China," *Asian Survey*, vol. 27, no. 5 (May 1987), pp. 566–576.

15. "Golden Handshakes in Peking."

16. Quoted from a news report in *International Daily News*, October 15, 1985, p. 7.

17. The recent crackdown on the crimes committed by children of the retired cadres can be seen as a warning to the younger generation that they must be independent from their parents and that their parents are no longer capable of protecting them from the consequences of wrongdoing or misbehavior.

18. Wen-hui Tsai, *From Tradition to Modernity*, Occasional Papers/Reprints Series in Contemporary Asian Studies No. 1 (Baltimore: University of Maryland, 1986).

19. Martin Lipset, *The First New Nation* (Garden City, N.Y.: Doubleday, 1964).

20. Alan P. Liu, *How China Is Ruled* (Englewood Cliffs, N.J.: Prentice-Hall, 1986), p. 338.

# 36

## Changing Concepts of Corruption in Communist China: Early 1950s Versus Early 1980s

*Lynn T. White III*

*Unto a stranger thou mayst lend upon usury; but unto thy brother thou shalt not lend upon usury.*
— Deuteronomy 23:20

*The great achievement of the ethical religions, above all of the ethical and aesceticist sects of Protestantism, was to shatter the fetters of the kinship group.*
— Max Weber, in *The Religion of China*[1]

How much corruption plagues China? A question that takes precedence, if only because of measurement problems, seems simpler: What is corruption? Since Deuteronomy was written, ideas about rectitude have altered. Lending at interest no longer presents a problem, because morals have modernized. Some ethics mesh well with modern economic and bureaucratic organization; others mesh less well. Corruption changes. Popular attitudes toward the relation between private and public interests shift over time, apparently in an alternating pattern.[2] For example, Chinese ideas of public cleanliness in the antilibertine period of "Liberation," after 1949, can be compared with those in the more pragmatic post-Mao era, especially since 1980. The contrast of trends at these two times provides a way to test the flow and ebb of China's revolution.

Political scientists have done more to define corruption than to show how it evolves. They have surprising consensus on the proper definition. To cite some of the writers: James Scott relies on Joseph Nye's particular words; Nye relies on Edward Banfield's. In this usual view, corruption is *"behavior which deviates from the formal duties of a public role because of private-regarding (personal, close family, private clique) pecuniary or status gains, or violates rules against the exercise of certain types of private-regarding influence "*[3] (emphasis added).

316

The advantage of this definition is that it helps calculate the costs or benefits of explicitly political corruption, in terms of specified norms. It also implies a procedure for research: The public "rules" can be explained; normative "roles" and "duties" can be described on the basis of attitude surveys or value statements from the culture being studied. Once norms are set, it is possible to show the results of their violation and to see whether corruption, defined in this way, helps or harms the stability of the system.

Such a method tells what corruption does, but not how it changes. Two of its traits underlie its handiness for judging corruption's effects: First, the focus is usually limited to politics in a narrow sense, as if authority could be exercised only in government organizations, or only by formally higher offices over lower ones. But the actual scope of corruption is broader. The government elites of some countries so thoroughly dominate the sources of our data on public norms (which should in theory be induced from society as a whole) that research from any other starting point is difficult. A study of corruption in such a highly politicized case, where practically all organizations become governmental, may help stress the unrealism of any implicit assumption that politics, the public sphere, is an aspect of society easy to separate from the rest.

Second, the usual method refers to duties that are stable over time. This method similarly aids in making a firm basis to fulfill the purpose of the definition, which is to judge the efficiency of corruption in political systems. But it involves another loss of realism, because it is unable adequately to weigh the fact that concepts of corruption change, sometimes rather quickly. The literature's definition cannot be called ethnocentric or unrelative; it carefully avoids specifying the content of formal duties or rules anywhere. But it has no dynamic aspect. It cannot tell us how norms evolve, or why particular acts (usury is the classic case) are considered corrupt in certain periods and places, but not in others. Some authors, who have used the main definition of corruption for its intended and legitimate purpose, nonetheless hint they are not totally satisfied with it.[4] They do not go on to suggest a general reason: It is static and cannot deal with problems of development and cultural change.

What, then, should supplement this unipurpose definition of corruption? Rather than proposing some rival words, this essay begins with the previous definition but expands its coverage. In this discussion, "duties" and "rules" become less formal; and "public" becomes more social. *Readers are forewarned that previous criteria of relevance for data concerning corruption may thus be challenged here.* If political corruption is inseparable from broad perceived public uncleanliness in many social spheres, then garbage on the streets and disloyalty to the government may become classified together as corrupt. Such data are more relevant to a study of corruption and change than they would be to a study of corruption and system. And other data, previously thought necessary for such topics, may become dispensable. For example, if we are studying the alterations of rules rather than comparing behavior under stable rules, then the usual attempt to make an exhaustive search for corruption's supporting or nonsupporting norms is less relevant than an effort to show that norms in many sectors of society alter together, at the same time. Corruption comes like asparagus, in seasons and in bunches.

Weber and the brilliant sociologists who wrote Deuteronomy suggest that morals do not exist in isolation from groups. Ideas, including concepts of corruption, inhere in specific communities. They cannot be understood separate from the identifications of the people who think them. The most obvious way to relate ideas to groups is to show their simultaneous changes. Benjamin Nelson, who studied the history of usury, found he could not describe his subject without reference to communities. He associated rules against this corruption with the existence of a "tribal brotherhood" under moral rules. He said the rise of the new capitalism in Reformation Europe correlated with a new ethic of "universal otherhood." Moral communities expanded in size, and old bonds were weakened.[5] New types of behavior became legitimate. Notions of cleanliness in the political, economic, religious, and even physical fields changed together. This chapter explores many kinds of corruption and quasi corruption—and links them more tightly than is usual—in order to show the strength of correlation of the timing of such change.

Values, by definition, cannot be measured; but this chapter can compare ideas of corruption at two times, 1949–1952 and 1980–1986, to show contrasting trends in these two periods. It may not fully describe corruption in the People's Republic of China (PRC), but its purpose is to talk about changing perceptions of different kinds of uncleanliness, and to show opposite trends of change in the two time periods.[6] Most of the data comes from Shanghai, which is surely a promising place for such study.[7] The operative concepts of corruption vary in different parts of this essay, because they varied in Shanghai. What unifies them is a metaphor:[8] Dirt, *anything* seen as unclean in public, may help us understand people's notions of community propriety.[9]

Five attempts to clean up the city, each only partly successful, will be considered in order in this chapter: (1) Communist moves to ostracize disloyal Kuomintang nationalists from political life, (2) projects to cleanse the city physically, (3) efforts to purify it of foreign influences, (4) campaigns to make businessmen and bureaucrats serve the interests of the state, and (5) official pressures to encourage citizens' greater identification with China as a whole, rather than mainly with family groups.

## 1. The Attack on Political Independence as Corrupt

Disloyalty to governments was a long-standing tradition in Shanghai,[10] and this was particularly evident in the final days of Kuomintang (KMT) rule. When the last truck of Nationalist soldiers pulled away from the center of Shanghai in May 1949, a white flag appeared above the municipal police headquarters. Three cars soon drove up, and out of the first stepped a lieutenant colonel of the People's Liberation Army. He was smartly saluted by a large group of policemen from the old regime, who lined up outside the station's entrance to welcome him.[11] His way had been well prepared before the KMT departed. Members of the new Communist government, even at the moment of victory, could reasonably have wondered how much effort it would take to unify public attitudes in this city.

When the Communists arrived in Shanghai, they inherited more than 49,000 city officials from the Kuomintang government—and nearly a million workers.[12] The task of judging the loyalty and efficiency of so many was far beyond the personnel resources of the new regime. It therefore kept them at work as "retained cadres" (*liuyung kanpu*), even when the institutions where they worked were sharply reorganized. For example, the Nationalists' system for police and residence control had been denounced by the Chinese Communist Party (CCP) before 1949. This "*paochia*" system was declared out of existence as soon as the Red Army marched into the city. But the new government also ordered that ex-*paochia* officials should not be criticized just because they had been part of the old regime's apparatus. In one section of the city, the thirty-eight *pao* and 957 *chia* were restructured by July 1949, to become ten "administrative offices."[13] These were predecessors of the later Communist street offices. No organization so serviceable could be called unclean.

But disloyalty came under more penetrating attack by 1949 than ever before in China. The political education of functionaries held over from the old government was an immediate priority. As early as June 11, special courses were announced for all who wished to remain in government jobs. The lessons were more effective toward changing behavior patterns than instruction usually is. All new applicants for the civil service had to write long curricula vitae since age 12. They were supposed to give full information about their past friends and politics.[14]

The harshest police campaign ever conducted in Chinese cities, the Movement to Suppress Counterrevolutionaries (*su fan*), began in late summer and fall of 1950. This movement was a phase of the civil war.[15] A "Winter Defense Campaign," beginning November 1950, involved the execution of many "armed bandits and secret agents," before the main suppression started. In January of the next year, Yang Fan was appointed People's Procurator in Shanghai. His inaugural address emphasized that the "strict suppression of reactionary activities would form the primary task at the present juncture."[16] Everyone with any previous formal connection to the KMT was required to register through work units. State factories, many confiscated from fleeing KMT owners, were first to organize the registration procedures (*tengchi shouhsü*). The number of suspects was large; forty-two plants listed 1,500 employees who claimed to have been "spy elements" (*t'ehwu fentzu*). Assessing such data from all sources took party cadres the better part of a year, from the fall of 1950 to the spring of 1951. Persons who registered were told that this process was a bureaucratic necessity.

Some anti-Communist organizations could not be made to register, and both KMT and independent groups were among them. During the campaign, and on a continuing basis in later times, the party applied similar measures to KMT organizations and to bands of ordinary robbers, whose interests were mainly economic, not political. A guerrilla leader named Lü Wei-hsing, who may have had Nationalist sympathies, established himself in parts of Kiangsu close to Shanghai for some time before he was caught in 1951.[17] On the other hand, a group of boatmen-thieves called the "Water and Fire Clique" (Shui Huo P'ai) after 1949 were apparently innocent of any broad politics. They robbed for a living on Soochow Creek and the Whangpoo River. By 1953 internal dissension within their organization allowed the Shanghai police to arrest many of them.[18] In all earlier regimes, a degree of anarchic independence had been taken as matter of course; but in New China, the government moved decisively to stamp out this kind of perceived corruption.

On April 23, Deputy Mayor P'an Han-nien addressed a session of the Shanghai Political Consultative Conference and advocated "mobilizing the broad masses" to use the registration lists to hunt counterrevolutionaries. The conference established a prestigious subcommittee (with P'an, Yang, Pa Chin, Shen Han, Chou Yü-t'ung, and others) to lend dignity to this task. On May Day, Party First Secretary Jao Shu-shih held a radio forum on it. He cited anonymous complaints that the government was being too lenient with counterrevolutionaries, and he said he must bow to this justified indignation. He gave assurances that the Military Administration Committee would now begin to enforce the people's will "strictly."[19]

On the same day, 293 counterrevolutionaries in Shanghai were executed.[20] Three days later, an account from a single district of the city reported that 700 counterrevolutionaries were denounced. The era of "boundless magnanimity" was said to be ended.[21] Among the first sentenced or executed were people who had attempted to escape the registration. In Ch'ingp'u County near Shanghai (later incorporated into the municipality), some bandits had been marauding the Shanghai-Nanking and Shanghai-Hangchow railways since March 1949. It is unclear whether this group contained any KMT people, but several of its members were caught and put to death.[22] In the city itself, the last day of May was celebrated with the executions of 205 urban "counterrevolutionary tyrants" (*fankoming ohpa*).[23]

Almost every day, the newspapers now contained exemplary publicity about the fates of people who were suspected of disloyalty. An article of mid-June reported the death or imprisonment of 432 counterrevolutionaries. Among this group, 70 percent were executed immediately, 25 percent were jailed for life, and 3 percent were imprisoned for correctional terms.[24] These penalties "killed chickens to scare monkeys." It showed an effective official intolerance for diversity that was without recent precedent, but it affected more people indirectly than it harmed directly.

By August the number of trials apparently rose, but the severity of punishments decreased, as lesser disloyalists were ferreted out. On August 6, five hundred counterrevolutionaries were sentenced, but only to terms of labor reform for fifteen years or less.[25] *Liberation Daily* reported, at the end of the month, that 38,000 counterrevolutionary cases had been tried in Shanghai from April 27 to August 27. Although only a few of these received capital punishment, the six officially established execution grounds in Shanghai were kept busy enough to make a public impact.[26]

During this movement, the party used many methods to involve ordinary citizens. Official standards for denunciation were announced. It was said that "any person shall have the right to expose counterrevolutionaries" and denouncers should be rewarded.[27] But minor criminals were often sent from Shanghai to "Tungt'ai Village for New Men," a reformatory run by Shanghai in northern Kiangsu.[28] Others were trusted, "placed under mass control," and released on bail in Shanghai.[29] Neighborhood committee members and policemen served as their probation officers.

This emphatic suppression of disloyalists did not end in 1952, when the formal movement ended.[30] As the official campaign ebbed, institutions supporting the new standard of unity were regularized at low levels, where they could have more persistent and long-run effects on public morals. "Security committees" of three to eleven members were established in every school and work unit by mid-1952. These groups oversaw persons recently suppressed, and they kept a watchful eye on political rectitude in general.

Small incidents could become occasions for propaganda at local levels. When the Fuk'ang Rice Company had the bad luck to deposit in its bank account a currency bill on which a reactionary slogan had been scribbled, party officials of T'ilanch'iao District called many meetings to make sure everyone understood why this type of disloyalty must not occur.[31] After the formal anti-KMT movement had peaked, eminent Shanghai citizens like novelist Chou Erh-fu, bourgeois journalist Chin Chung-hua, party factotum Hsü Chien-kuo, and others were enlisted on committees for the continuing movement to suppress counterrevolutionaries—a Durkheimian gesture.[32] A low standard of tolerance for dissent had been set. The suppression could thus remain effective, even without its early harsh measures.

*Three decades later, by the 1980s,* disillusionment with the Anti-Rightist Movement, the post-1958 famine, and the Cultural Revolution had changed the party—and had weakened its claim against dissent. Four times as many party members per capita were ordained by the 1980s as in the early 1950s.[33] They had become a more diverse lot, and distinctions between them and nonmembers had become a bit less important politically. Everyone was supposed to follow the "Four Basic Principles" (socialism, the proletarian dictatorship, leadership by the Communist Party, and Marxism–Leninism–Mao Tse-tung thought),[34] but these are vague enough to cover a host of sins. "Rightists" and other dissidents had been amnestied in 1979. Some had been liberalized by their oppressions—but were still in the party.[35] As one scholar has written, "The Party apparently cannot enforce discipline by permanently contracting its membership."[36] But also, it cannot move to modernization without recruiting more expert members, who are likely to have minds of their own.

"Discipline inspection committees" were revived in the late 1970s.[37] But after the Cultural Revolution, these organs could not fully stop the tide of

political diversity.[38] Political discontent was obvious in 1984 Chinese performances of Jean-Paul Sartre's play Dirty Hands, concerning Communist
officials in Eastern Europe who carried out murders to increase their own
power.[39] In another recent drama, a girl leaving her country to marry overseas
cynically bids, "Farewell to China! Household registration, farewell! Rations,
farewell! What is the motherland? An employment agency?"[40] A high official,
making a speech against such "spiritual pollution," said he thought these
remarks were even worse than screenwriter Pai Hua's earlier taunt, "You
love the motherland, but does the motherland love you?" Purists in the
party now have more trouble enforcing loyalty. In 1985, Judith Shapiro and
Liang Heng claimed China was "at it freest since before 1949."[41]

Conspicuous examples of somewhat increased political diversity have
involved writers. In August 1984, Pa Chin, prominent novelist and victim
of the Cultural Revolution, was removed as head of the Shanghai Federation
of Literary and Art Circles.[42] Journalist Wang Jo-wang and playwright Sha
Yeh-hsin objected, at first to no avail. But five months later, the Chinese
Writers' Association elected Pa Chin its chair, the major antibureaucratic
writer Liu Pin-yen its vice-chair, and Pai Hua (not on the official roster of
candidates) a member of its council. Hsiao Cheng-nung, Pa Chin's replacement
as head of the Shanghai Federation, was on the official roster for the Writers'
Association council—but was not elected. China's democratic centralism is
less centralist than it was in the 1950s.

In its political effects, the Spiritual Pollution Campaign was unlike the
Suppression of Counterrevolutionaries, even though both movements aimed
at political uniformity. These were the most hard-line urban campaigns in
their eras. The 1980s event did not involve major official direct violence
against dissidents; memories of the Cultural Revolution made that difficult
for ideologues to achieve. Also, the 1950s campaign ended only after achieving
its aims and leaving a legacy of neighborhood committees to maintain them.
But the Spiritual Pollution Campaign was abandoned partly because of
political pressure from its intended victims.

By the fall of 1985, Politburo member Hu Ch'i-li said, "Sometimes you
have to steer to the right, sometimes to the left; but the important thing
is that you stick to the course."[43] Purist sermons for Mao's thought, which
punctuated the Spiritual Pollution Campaign in 1983 and 1984,[44] had given
way to an admission in the People's Daily that Marxism was "not necessarily
very appropriate to China's problems."[45] By spring 1986, the party's paper
allowed elliptical critiques of all taboos to be published, questioning customs
of loyalty that had developed in Chinese history from as far back as the
Sung.[46] Conformity was now being questioned more often, not less often.
Late in a revolution, bureaucrats enjoy only weak legitimacy.[47] The trend
toward somewhat greater political diversity in the 1980s contrasts with the
emphasis on loyalty in the 1950s. The degree and sureness of the new
trend can easily be overstated, but they indicate that the party does not
control as much as it once did in China.

## 2. Assorted Plain Cases for the Broom

Many of the early campaigns to clean up Shanghai were literal. Soon after the Red Army moved in, soldiers and unemployed people reportedly took 11,000 tons of garbage from the streets. By the end of 1949 the total had risen to 18,000 tons.[48] In June 1952 the movement to clear rubbish "assumed a mass character." Newspapers reported that 26,344 tons of ordinary junk were moved to fill 8,400 stagnant ditches. The official harvest of mosquitoes that July was carefully weighed at 653 catties. The Health Bureau said such information was incomplete, but the data that month for 66,843 caught rats and 1,377 catties of swatted flies were published.[49]

Visible accomplishments in Shanghai created public pride for the new city government. The pond at the Temple of the City God was dredged, and the flow of water was increased to reduce stagnancy. The Bund park (where once stood an imperialist sign excluding Chinese and dogs) was replanted and repaved.[50] In 1951 and 1952, the Shanghai Race Course at the center of town was converted into a people's square. It ultimately included a swimming pool, a concert hall, two playgrounds, a library, and an artificial lake.[51] The site of the first Chinese Communist Party congress was renovated, along with its bordering streets and a room where Mao Tse-tung had slept.[52]

In less monumental moves toward cleanliness, the ordinary crime rate was reduced after liberation. Small rings of pickpockets, whose adroitness had been a public marvel in pre-1949 times, were gradually incarcerated or reformed. In June 1949, the police reported 173 major robberies; but they claimed the monthly rate was down to 56 by December of that year, and to 31 by April 1950.[53] Another indicator of social pollution is disease. Smallpox was one of the first maladies whose control was stressed by the Communist government. In March and April 1951, the Health Bureau claimed it had vaccinated a truly spectacular 5,880,000 people in Shanghai.[54] In late July, the total elimination of this disease was reported. By the end of the year travelers were supposed to show vaccination certificates before they could buy long-distance tickets.[55]

An attack on venereal disease was launched through efforts to reduce prostitution (see Table 36.1). The last of Shanghai's brothels was not officially closed until late November 1951. This surprising leniency can be attributed to the fact that prostitution was not, after all, a serious political crime.[56] Brothel owners and procurers were given much harsher treatment than ordinary streetwalkers. The latter were sent, in well-registered batches, to a Women's Education and Care House (Funü Chiaoyang So).

Salacious advertising—or commercial enticement that the cadres felt was improper—also became the object of directives in 1949. On December 18, advertising agents were ordered to register. Rules of taste were tightened only in September 1951, when industrial units of the city government began to censor advertising copy.[57] A glance at later newspapers suggests that the regulatory offices were not strict at first. The Ling Bamboo Garden no longer publicized itself as "the one and only tropical-like night spot in town" with

TABLE 36.1
The Closure of Shanghai Brothels, 1949–1951

| | Number of Brothels | Number of Prostitutes | Average Number of Prostitutes per Brothel | Average Monthly Decrease in Prostitutes (%) |
|---|---|---|---|---|
| January 1949 | 800 + | 4,000 + | 5.0 | — |
| May 1949 | 518 | 2,000 | 3.9 | 13 |
| November 1949 | 264 | 1,300 | 4.9 | 8 |
| November 1951 | 72 | 180 | 2.5 | 13 |

*Source:* The absolute figures are tabulated from a narrative article in *Chiehfang jihpao* (Liberation Daily), Shanghai, November 25, 1951. Both of the last two columns have been computed, and the base of the percentage is the average number in each period noted. These figures should be treated with caution; such enterprise is secret.

a "most cozy atmosphere,"[58] but in December the First Avenue Cosmetic Store still advertised "Toni Wave Sets." A stationer, in good Shanghai tradition, touted "Discounts for all Purchasers."[59]

A search for new standards of strictness was evident in many fields; the cadres created many new quasi corruptions. For a while in 1952, the Transport Bureau "served the people" by approving late-night bus and tram schedules; but apparently for puritan as well as economic reasons, these were soon canceled.[60] The reeducation of "hoboes" was a well-publicized aim of the new government. "Petty thieves, pickpockets, bag snatchers, loafers, and criminals" were "taken off the streets and housed in camps." "After a short period of education, they were offered an opportunity to live in a new way. . . . Those who chose to go were sent by reclamation authorities to North Kiangsu, to reclaim 600 hectares of barren land."[61] No less than 7,000 were in the initial group that went forth under this plan; and only 1,000 left the camp after the first year. Bentham would have been thrilled.

Some reeducated persons had high social status. Huang Chin-jung, former chief inspector of the French Concession Police and a distinguished secret society ex-leader, became in old age a supporter of New China. His personal background was impeccably proletarian. His first job had been as apprentice at a relative's picture-framing stall in the Temple of the City God. His political savvy, and his work with the French police, led to such a high position in the Mutual Advance Society (Kung Chin Hui) that even when he broke with that group, he retained a large number of personal followers. In retirement after liberation, he "found the Communist Party good in all respects." He claimed he repented his previous sins and was "most thankful for the generosity shown him by the People's Government."[62]

Secret societies and Taoist cults are two further huge topics that loosely relate to postliberation notions of corruption, though for reasons of space these can only be mentioned here.[63] Strong secret societies, made up mostly of workers in transport industries, were repressed by party policies of cooption and purge. The techniques of the takeover are interesting; but the public propaganda about it would have been more extensive if these organizations had been less proletarian.

Taoist cults tended to be politically weak. Repression of them was implemented by the standard processes of registration, public persuasion, separation of leaders from followers, and large-scale amnesties. Relatively mild tactics were effective, because they made the moral legitimacy of the Taoist organizations seem outdated, banal, culturally unnecessary, politically moribund—in general, more corrupt than dangerous. The registration requirement for Taoist cults in Shanghai was not handed down until June 5, 1953.[64] Deputy Mayor Hsü Chien-kuo announced two days later that some leaders had been arrested, particularly from the large Yi Kuan Tao cult. He averred that burning joss sticks and eating vegetarian food were passé. He said the cult leaders' collaboration with Japanese occupation forces had been unpatriotic. The extravagance of some high priests (defined by specific levels in the religious hierarchy) had to be punished; but "minor leaders" would not be hurt if they cooperated with the government.[65] Trials of major clerics were in full swing by mid-June. A few death sentences were ordered at seven military tribunals set up for this purpose in Shanghai. The executions were attended by 91,500 people. But the "masses of members" of Taoist organizations were told that they could "save themselves from the pit of fire by withdrawing from the reactionary cults and severing all relations with them."[66] Jonathan Edwards would not have put it differently; he too was an advocate of new community by means of spiritual purification.[67]

*Three decades later, by the 1980s,* some kinds of ordinary cleanliness had improved, but some were worse. Epidemic and venereal diseases could be controlled by collectivist campaigns; but Shanghai's cancer rate had doubled—in part because of contamination by heavy metals in water.[68] Four million cubic meters of unprocessed sewage were annually being dumped in the Whangpoo Basin by 1980. During a particularly dry season of 1981, the municipal discharge equaled the volume of downstream flow, so that a large portion of the city's drinking water was chlorinated sewage.[69] Water pollution had become a widespread and expensive problem by the mid-1980s. A small paper factory put waste water into the sea and killed crustaceans. Although the factory's profit was only 10,000 yuan a year, the cost in lost shellfish was 4 million yuan.[70] Air pollution was a concomitant of the Four Modernizations, and investment funds were seldom used to control it. In Ho-t'ien, Chapei District, fifty-five factories involving thirteen industrial bureaus were responsible for a smog that included sulfur dioxide, hydrogen sulfide, and hydrochloric acid. In this area, more than 90 percent of the residents suffered inflammation of the nose and difficulty breathing. The army selected few recruits from this area, because most youths among the 100,000 population failed health tests. At Ho-t'ien Middle School, the windows of the classes had to be kept closed in 1986; the glass became opaque because of chemical erosion on the outside. Heart disease and cancer rates were abnormally high. Ho-t'ien was described as archtypical of about seventy badly polluted areas in Shanghai.[71]

Campaigns against animal nuisances had been sharply reduced by the 1980s. These began in Mao's time, to oppose the "five pests" (*wu hai*): rats, mosquitoes, fleas, flies, and sparrows. But after the sparrow purge reduced their numbers, the insects they ate became more troublesome; so "Mao liberated the sparrows."[72] Movements against the remaining "four pests" (*szu hai*) failed to suppress the three insects among them; so swatting was decollectivized, and it became an individual responsibility. By 1985 only the rats were left; and a vice-mayor led a campaign for three citywide applications of rat poison in as many months.[73] But the targeted kinds of beasts were fewer than they had been in the 1950s, the local committees provided less reliable infrastructure for such campaigns, and newspapers lacked data—or enthusiasm—to report how many rats were caught.

Urban crowding had become an obvious physical difficulty in Shanghai by the 1980s. At rush hour, sidewalks in the center of the city had an average of only 2 square meters per pedestrian.[74] A calculation of the crunch on Shanghai buses revealed that twelve persons stood on each square meter. A "foreign expert" was reported to call this a "world miracle"—indeed, it seemed so, because twenty-four pairs of shoes were found not to fit on 1 square meter. The answer to the conundrum was simple: Many Shanghai bus passengers stand like cranes on one foot, slightly raising the other.[75]

The press was free enough, by 1985, to lambaste many physical quasi corruptions that arose from thirty years' neglect of infrastructural investment. Traffic and communications problems, the low number of telephones per capita (still less than a 1950s peak), insufficient and unreliable electricity supply, lack of garbage and sewage service, lack of capacity in railways, airports, small docks, and harbor facilities—the list was long.[76] The three decades' decrease in housing per capita was not even mentioned in most catch-all articles; so big a topic produced a muckraking literature all its own.[77]

These difficulties were made worse by a rise in immigration to cities. Economic prosperity reduced the ability of the household system to limit rations, and rural decollectivization loosened ties that had kept peasants on their land.[78] Gone were the days when the government could easily load any large portion of the "hoboes" on trucks and ship them out to the countryside. The "floating population" of cities rose by several times in the 1980s.[79] The immigrants did odd jobs, including itinerant carpentry, bottle collection, construction work, and illegal trade. One dealer, who specialized in selling copper and aluminum products on consignment for workers who had stolen them from their factories, charged a 25 percent commission. He claimed, "The police are cracking down. When they catch someone, they confiscate the goods and fine him double their value."[80] But he was not banished to rural areas or sent to jail. Residence laws are strict on the books, but enforcement during the past few years has often been lax.

The expanded "informal economy" traded new as well as old goods; and some of these, such as pornographic videotapes, raise moral problems. Ch'en Yün, head of the Discipline Inspection Commission, said children of

CCP members were involved in trades like smuggling and prostitution.[81] Sexual mores were loosened in the 1980s, partly because so many nonregistered, irregularly employed youths were back in cities after rural experiences during the Cultural Revolution. Previous puritanism about sexual topics created a culture in which young people knew too little, causing medical and social scandals. By the spring of 1986, previously taboo topics were broached; a new book entitled *Sexual Medicine* was advertised,[82] and sex education was introduced for some Shanghai high school students.[83]

Another kind of straightforward social problem that received publicity by the 1980s was apolitical, factual lying. Chad Hansen has speculated that "truth" in China depends less on the link of a proposition to empirical or logical reality than on its relation to pragmatic uses in communities.[84] Whatever the applicability of his notion may be, China's 1980s publications show more worry about factual lying than 1950s newspapers did. In a sample of clients at Shanghai marriage introduction agencies, only a fifth of those with psychological records admitted as much, and only 4 percent of those with jail records replied truthfully to a direct question about that. Because height is thought desirable for marriage, some of the applicants claimed to be 1.7 meters tall, but none actually measured that height.[85] Newspapers detailed all this, and they suggested less lying.

Concern for factual truth may not be carried far enough in any society, but this interest is associated with undogmatic social toleration for many propositions. "Rights of hypothesis" have been asserted by Chinese academics in the Deng era with varying degrees of success.[86] A good test of these rights in a whole political system may be the degree of toleration for traditional religions. The CCP discouraged Buddhist and Taoist cults as straightforward superstitions during the 1950s, but popular resurgence of these religions has not been successfully restrained during the 1980s.[87] Party doctrine may decree such habits to be moribund or unclean, but many Chinese obviously disagree—and they can often act by their own lights.

### 3. Patriotism as a Value to Order the Rest

All the Shanghai ills that have been described thus far were at least Chinese. Western things became more suspect after 1949. The information services of the United States and Great Britain were ordered to close at Shanghai on July 15, 1949.[88] The most effective propagandists of foreign ideas in the city before liberation, however, had been religious, not governmental. During 1949 a French missionary doctor was brought into a people's court on charges that his medicine had caused the death of a child.[89] The Holy Mother Institute had a seventy-year history in Shanghai; but the Communists closed it, alleging that its orphans' handicraft factory hired workers who were not orphans, that the salaries were exploitively low, and that much of the output (embroideries for the church) was useless.[90] Communist allegations of Roman Catholic quasi corruption in Shanghai ranged from matters as serious as spying and private militia building to matters as minor as the government's preference for cremation rather than burial.[91]

Protestants were generally accused of less serious mistakes. Three-quarters of the Protestant community in China was rural rather than urban, and the party's methods for dealing with most of it were like those used for Taoist cults. More than 2,000 of Shanghai's Seventh Day Adventists gathered, on October 14, 1951, for a revival to accuse Hsü Hua (president of their China Council) and three of his lieutenants of having concealed funds worth US$400,000 and being "running dogs of American imperialism."[92] One of these ministers was further indicted for having "distorted the Bible," saying he had received divine power. When this and other Protestant groups were provided by the government with new leaderships and secure places in the "Three-Independence Movement" (Santzu Yüntung), their patriotism was officially certified—so long as they stayed within the new, narrower range of official tolerance for the corruption inherent in foreign religions.

Foreign jazz was not banned from Shanghai's ballrooms and cafés until early 1952. Then a "grand rally for the reform of music and songs," not a bit like Woodstock, was held to provide a forum for entertainers' testimonials. They promised to be better patriots, more progressive public figures.[93] Later that year, foreign-language trademarks were prohibited for all goods made at Shanghai.[94] The U.S.-owned *Shanghai Evening Post and Mercury* published its last issue on June 25, 1949. The *North China Daily News*, owned by an Englishman, continued until his death on September 21, 1951.[95] Foreign things had to be phased out, because alien political and aesthetic values were seen by the new government as different strains of the same germ. A general quarantine was established against them, at this time. Soviet styles became more modish at this time because of the PRC's "lean to one side," but they were scarcely a replacement for the cosmopolitanism that central Shanghai inherited from its days as the "International Settlement."

The registration of Western residents took place in November 1950. Four days after it ended, these aliens were again asked to present themselves at police stations for further questioning.[96] A few months later, they once again were all summoned to apply for residence permits. Early in 1952, these documents came due for renewal, in still another process.[97] The red tape required of foreigners was considerable; but once they wished to move abroad and obtained exit permits, their way was expedited.[98]

Foreign business firms were seen as unhealthy and corrupting influences. But the party prevented obvious confiscation in most cases. Not until December 30, 1950, five weeks after the first mass actions by Chinese soldiers in Korea, did the Shanghai government summon the heads of eighty local U.S. firms to a meeting. They were told to sell none of their property, to submit various reports, and to continue business as usual.[99] Soon thereafter, investigations and charges were leveled at many Western enterprises. Bribery, waste, embezzlement, excessive profits, exploitive labor policies, substandard production, concealment of assets, and every other commercial sin were discovered in these alien businesses.[100] Also, Chinese naturally replaced English as the language in many firms.[101]

During mid-1951, all foreign companies' major transactions and personnel transfers became subject to the approval of the Shanghai Bureau of Industry and Commerce.[102] Batches of Merck streptomycin and Kirby penicillin were banned from use in Shanghai, because of their reportedly impure quality.[103] Some firms published formal apologies in newspapers when they took actions without authorization from the government.[104] The alien businesses were not confiscated, but special interpretations of their debts made many bankrupt. Funds had to be sent from abroad before foreign personnel could be transferred out of China. Western Electric and Singer Sewing Machines, for example, did not close their Shanghai branches until early 1954.[105]

The Korean War became a litmus test for patriotism among Westernized Chinese in Shanghai. Most of them did not need much acid to change color. On November 28, 1950 (only four days after a U.S. general near the Chongchon River was surprised that "lo and behold, the whole mountainside turned out to be Chinese"),[106] more than 2,000 representatives from 272 Shanghai industries went to the first large meeting for "resisting the U.S. and aiding Korea." They passed a Five-Point Patriotic Pledge, to be observed by all citizens.[107] Mayor Ch'en Yi, in a later speech, said candidly that the purpose of the campaign was as much to encourage loyalty for China as aid for Korea.[108]

Businessmen were rallied to protest the alleged rearmament of Japan,[109] and workers were urged to set up labor efficiency campaigns and competitions.[110] Voluntary groups were asked to subscribe to the "Shanghai People's Patriotic Compact," adopted by the municipal All-Circles' Conference.[111] Shanghai's "Patriotic Donation Movement" netted pledges of 210 billion yuan by National Day, 1951.[112] Shanghai's contribution to arms production was one-third of the national total.[113] Chinese private enterprises were given more independence in return for promises to produce and pay more taxes.[114] Students not only contributed money for guns and planes, they also joined military cadre schools in greater numbers, and they obeyed the "unified distribution" (*t'ungyi fenp'ei*) of job assignments more readily.[115] Institutions too large and many for direct control were reoriented by this wartime emphasis on national community. Savings rates were raised, and talented people were recruited into control functions, for use some rainy day when loyalty might not come so easily.

Political standards began to influence aesthetic ones more strongly. Attempts in 1950 to persuade movie theaters to show Soviet and Chinese films—and not to show American ones—had failed for lack of supply and variety among the approved reels. Official effort was then directed to keeping the theaters in use for dramatic productions, rather than for movies of any sort.[116] But by the end of the year, Chinese soldiers were in Korea, censorship was tighter, and new films such as *Chennault, the Flying Tiger Bandit* and *The Yankees in Shanghai* were shown. A new drama, *Sketches of American Atrocities*, opened December 3. It starred a Roman Catholic priest in the pay of the U.S. Embassy, heading a school for Chinese girls "in which the American way of life was introduced."[117] An art gallery featured paintings of Chinese volunteers in Korea, with woodcuts of women there crowding to serve them tea.[118]

The Nationalists on Taiwan contributed to this patriotic climate by sending planes to bomb the main Shanghai electric plant. They sent more on March 27, 1951, and one was shot down in Chiangwan.[119] A Civil Air Defense Committee was formed, and another incursion in Nanhui on August 25 gave pith to warnings that "the people must realize the importance of air defense work."[120] In the following month, air raid sirens were introduced. Then the owners and occupants of all buildings more than four stories high were registered for watch service.[121] The political effect of these precautions was more important than their military value.

In an atmosphere like this, the intellectual nationalization of schools was not difficult to engineer. The party's educational cadres had earlier lacked a public basis to install intensively political schooling. In 1949 some Shanghai children had been taught to read from the New China Agency's commentary on the U.S. White Paper about China,[122] but the Shanghai educational system at liberation was largely private. Schools, like businesses and hospitals, had merged and declined in number during the early months. By the second half of 1950, the number of Shanghai's universities had gone down sharply. In June of that year the city had forty-three university-level institutions (about 20 percent of the Chinese total); but at the end of the year the number had dropped to twenty-nine.[123]

When Chinese troops entered Korea, St. John's University and other bastions of "foreign cultural aggression" explored their histories.[124] On January 18, all foreign-subsidized cultural and religious bodies had to register with the city government.[125] Of 660 that did, 62 percent were Protestant, 28 percent were Catholic, and 10 percent were Jewish or nondenominational.[126] The Communists wanted these organizations to reform their performances, not close their doors. To this end, their leaders were convened in meetings "to restore educational sovereignty to the nation." Curriculum and admissions policies were supposed to serve the needs of China's masses.[127] Organizations like Aurora and Shanghai universities were placed under direct supervision by the Military Administration Committee.[128]

Shanghai's cultural institutions had talents to prove their patriotism. Even before their religious names were changed to modern numbers, St. John's University and St. Elizabeth's and St. Luke's hospitals formed a joint volunteer medical team that went to Korea. Another consortium of Shanghai universities formed a "language work corps," going to propagandize U.S. prisoners of war; so even the city's expertise in alien English found some national use.[129] When Japan set up a "national Police Reserve" of 70,000 infantry troops, the memories of past war in Shanghai enabled the party to hold a large conference of missionary schools, which quickly "submitted, and became the people's own schools."[130] The former U.S. consulate-general building in Shanghai was converted to be a headquarters for the "East China Committee Against American Aggression," whose task was to arouse patriotism in Shanghai schools.[131]

This purification of the city's education system had specific curricular effects. During 1951 at the Shanghai College of Finance (Shanghai Ts'aiching Hsüehyüan), the number of students increased from 600 to 2,250. About 30 percent of the new faculty was created by using cadres seconded on a part-time basis from finance organs. Elective subjects were eliminated. The four-year academic curriculum was shortened, and practical work became required for graduation. The teaching of English was stopped, and Russian was initiated. Books and lectures were in Chinese. Forums for the study of Chairman Mao's thought were established. Teachers were directed to write their syllabi collectively, not as individuals. Students set up a "representative system" (*taipiao chihtu*), and "they gave up their ideas of going abroad to study, and hold that they have to work for their own country."[132] Such changes were enough, in 1951, to redeem most high-level schools in the eyes of the party. At Shanghai University, such changes were so significant that the institution celebrated its "new birth." This would be more glorious in retrospect, had the university not been abolished several months later, in August 1952.[133]

The Korean War created the Shanghai party's base of support for major mergers among universities, because in war the strengthening of political control was an accepted goal. The Shanghai College of Law and Economics was founded (ostensibly as a private institution) by amalgamating the Shanghai College of Law and Political Science, the jurisprudence department of the Shanghai Law School, Kuanghsia Commercial College, New China Law and Commerce College, and New China College. East China Teachers' University was set up at this time, by joining the staffs, students, and properties of the history and journalism departments from St. John's, all of Kuanghua and Tahsia universities, the agriculture and economics departments from Foochow University, and other components from Nanking and elsewhere. Shanghai Medical College was reorganized under its new president Kung Nai-ch'uan (who was not a doctor), and it assimilated components from the old Red Cross, the missionary Women's and Children's Hospital, the Jewish Hospital, and other previous medical establishments.[134]

A showpiece for this kind of change was the joining of the McTyeire School for Girls (Mme. Chiang Kai-shek's alma mater) with another similar bastion of women's learning called St. Mary's Hall. The new amalgamate was given a number for a name, and it was integrated with the regular city school system. With relish, the party's educational cadres arranged that 70 percent of new admissions to this particular school would be children of workers and peasants, even though it was necessary to "waive many restrictions to facilitate their enrollment." It is unclear how these proletarian students felt in their new surroundings, since the McTyeire school buildings are stony castles in colonial Anglo-Gothic style.[135]

The Thought Reform Campaign of mid-1952 was an extension into schools of the purification movement at the same time in business and bureaucratic circles. Especially during the summer vacation of that year, teachers in many Shanghai universities and middle schools were required to attend courses in political training. They and their students were sent in great numbers to rural areas for work experience.[136] Some institutions, such as St. John's and Shanghai universities, were abolished that summer; and some others (including the excellent East China Chemical Engineering College, and the East China Aquatic Products College) were newly established.[137] The "unified distribution" of jobs was taken more seriously for graduates than ever before, and the Shanghai Education Bureau advised all junior and senior middle school students wishing to continue their schooling to take courses "geared to immediate practical requirements."[138] By the time the Thought Reform Campaign was "concluded" in October, the movement to purge foreign influences from Shanghai schools had become a means to realign the interests of young people toward a larger, domestic political community.

*Three decades later, by the 1980s,* Chinese patriots still decry "worship of foreign things" (*ch'ungyang miwai*)—but on a more selective basis than before. When Shanghai novelist Chou Erh-fu visited Japan in late 1985 and went as a tourist to the Yasukuni Shrine, he was dismissed from the party and lost his vice-chairmanship of the Committee for Friendship with Foreign Countries.[139] But Chou's faux pas came near the time of a similar flap about a visit there by Premier Yasuhiro Nakasone; and because of war memories, Japan is not just any foreign country. Far more typical is an interviewee's statement, "Today in Shanghai, almost anything foreign is good."

Foreign war rages in Korea no longer, and many PRC citizens' curiosity about the outside world has been pent up for a long time. The problem now, according to some, is not the adoption of foreign models but the adoption of bad rather than good ones. In music, Maestro Li Teh-lun of the Central Philharmonic bemoans that interest in rock and roll displaces popular appreciation for Western classical music, which flourished in the immediate aftermath of the Cultural Revolution.[140]

The most attractive of all overseas things is economic prosperity. Foreign trade figures dramatize how much Shanghai has lost under the PRC: In 1958, Shanghai still exported 20 percent more than Hong Kong, twice as much as Taiwan, and thirty-four times as much as South Korea. By 1981, however, the city's foreign exports were about one-quarter the level of any of these places—and local journals published the scandal this change implies.[141] The Shanghai Economic Zone, created in 1983, is too large a topic for full discussion here;[142] but from 1983 through mid-1986, Shanghai contracted to absorb a future US$1.2 billion, although it actually received only $300 million.[143] Many considered this kind of progress too slow. Even though the State Council had designated Shanghai a "city open to the outside" (*tuiwai k'aifang ch'engshih*), some argued it should be a "free port" (*tzuyu kang*), like the world's three greatest financial centers, New York, London, and Hong Kong—the last of which is envied most because it is Chinese.[144]

Lack of infrastructural investment in Shanghai for three decades explains why the inflow of capital has been slow. Businessmen from overseas, either Chinese or foreign, generally want quicker profits than highways, water facilities, housing projects, or schools can provide—though some Shanghai economists suggest borrowing money for these neglected fields from foreign countries.[145] No longer is there embarrassment about linking Shanghai's loss of foreign resources and markets to its loss of domestic production for PRC consumers, which has also been much less than officials hoped.[146]

Some new companies established in the 1980s had new corporate names: in Chinese, but foreign-sounding. For example, when the Ministry of Electric Industry established a new firm, it chose the name Jui-ta (using a *jui* that suggests Sweden, Switzerland, or Hong Kong's Shui Hing Department Store, along with a *ta* that resembles words for radar or Rado-brand watches).[147]

Such cultural uncertainties even led to doubts about personal motives that were thought common in China. Debate raged about "Oriental jealousy" (*tungfang shih tuchi*), which allegedly animates Chinese individuals to hope for their rivals' downfalls. This motive is supposed to contrast with Westerners' habit of trying to surpass each others' performances.[148] "Oriental jealousy" is a moot notion; but the fact that the idea provoked public debate in Shanghai shows a self-doubt, which contrasts with the Chinese pride of the early Communist period. Another example of this trend may be a recent published observation that, in Mao's era, Chinese who spoke frankly with foreigners often asked the outsiders not to publish such conversations abroad. But now, they often want foreign publicity about Chinese problems, since they believe that only after issues appear in the foreign or Hong Kong press will Chinese officials take these matters seriously and try to find solutions.[149] Shanghai journals reported *Time*'s article about Teng as "man of the year"— and for their headlines, they quoted it to the effect that Shanghai's industry grows more slowly than Chungking's, Canton's, or Peking's.[150]

A healthier trend of contemporary thought compares Chinese and Western habits but takes full account of Chinese traditional virtues. In 1986, K'uang Ya-ming (Head of the Confucius Foundation, K'ungtzu Chichin Hui) defended the enduring values of the Chinese sage: "Confucius can't be struck down! Of the world's three most famous people—Jesus, Buddha, and Confucius— two have already become gods. But Confucius remains human, struggling for humanity all his life. I think Confucius is the best of these!"[151] Prominent articles now praise mainstream traditional Chinese philosophy, and these are often written by "four teachers" ( *szu taoshih*) who are informally seen as representing China's intellectuals.[152] Old styles find new uses, and similar informal recognition has been extended by Shanghai students to a younger, modernizing group of "four gentlemen" (*szu chüntzu*).[153] Appreciation for Chinese ways no longer necessarily leads to general disdain for things foreign.

## 4. Businessmen as Secular Moralists

The most obvious economic corruption in May 1949 was rampant inflation. Three successive Nationalist currencies had collapsed. U.S. and Mexican dollars had become legal tender. The Shanghai government outlawed private transactions in foreign currencies on June 9, 1949, and in gold and silver on June 11. The next day, police raided the Shanghai Stock Exchange and arrested "speculators." On June 13, food prices went down slightly.[154] The underlying causes of the inflation were, however, still present. The Communists' complex and classic solutions to this problem included a unified currency, restoration of railways to put more goods alongside money, tax incentives to agricultural production, free trade in rural areas, monopoly trading companies for control of prices in some markets, direct price control in others, centralization of reserves in a new People's Bank, selling victory bonds to soak up money, wages based on price indices, and more balance in the government budget. These measures were not local to Shanghai, but they affected economic morale and morals widely.

The most important effort to change long-range habits of action in Shanghai's business community began only after the inflation was under control, and even after negotiations for a Korean armistice had started.[155] Here we need only mention a few points on the "Five-Anti" Campaign (*wufan yüntung*), to extract the aspects of that movement which are most relevant to moral habits.[156] A municipal organization administering this campaign was publicly unveiled four days before the end of 1951 by the Shanghai Federation of Industry and Commerce. In the first week of January 1952, its suborgan the Austerity Inspection Committee put "accusation boxes" (*chienchü hsiang*) all over the city, to collect charges against miscreant businessmen.[157] An officer of the Hsinhua Bank confessed he had received presents from "illegal merchants." He repented his sins and apparently was not punished.[158] The main goal of the movement, especially at first, was to change habits of economic conduct, not to catch past economic criminals.

On January 15, a large meeting was called at the Takuangming Theater in the center of Shanghai, to initiate a "Four-Anti" movement (*szufan yüntung*) against bribery, cheating, quick profits, and tax evasion.[159] The Four-Anti Movement Committee on January 21 invited anyone who knew about economic wrongdoing to send a complaint to the Post Office, Box 628. A Control Committee (Chiench'a Weiyüanhui) was to read these complaints and set up a reception room (*chiehtai shih*), in which people could be interviewed.[160] When the East China Military Administration Committee summoned merchants to a meeting, twelve of them confessed "on the spot."[161] Official economic agencies were mobilized to survey—and scare—large parts of Shanghai's business community at the same time.

Regulations governing branches of the Four-Anti Movement Committee were published on January 22. Subcommittees had been set up in all districts of the city, so that the campaign would be uniform everywhere. Activists from trade unions and local "Resist America, Aid Korea" committees served on local Four-Anti teams.[162] "Confession and investigation congresses" were held in each district as early as January 25.[163] Several days later, very distinguished industrialists such as Jung Yi-jen (who later became a deputy mayor) were confessing their commercial sins in large meetings.[164] Many district and local sessions, involving less powerful bourgeois businessmen than Jung, were more probing and less formal than the city-level meetings.

An example can give the flavor of small-time business corruption as it was uncovered in these local meetings. The Laohohsing Foreign and Chinese Goods Store of Huangp'u District kept two complete sets of accounts—one for the owners and one for the tax cadres. In this enterprise, a father and son cooperated to hide their inventories and conduct a secret business, parallel to their legal trade. All went well for them until the district tax bureau became suspicious and sent investigators, who found the real ledger concealed in a rice bin.[165]

By the beginning of February, many top party leaders felt the Shanghai Federation of Industry and Commerce, running the Four-Anti Campaign, had been too lenient. The federation therefore conducted "top to bottom self-criticism," because its work was "feeble and lacking in determination," so that "only a small number of merchants and industrialists had taken the first step of declaring their attitude in this movement." On February 6 it was announced that the municipal government would take over direction of the committees that had already been established, and the movement's name would become "Five-Anti."[166] High officials like T'an Chen-lin, Ch'en Yi, and P'an Han-nien made speeches to declare that Shanghai "still lags far behind other cities" and should "map out new operational plans" to declare "total war" against corrupt businessmen.[167] The party hierarchy sent down list after list of procedures, rules, and prescribed techniques to scrub clean the stains of economic corruption. Once the government determined to use most of its cadres in this campaign, their license to search everywhere was important in changing economic habits for a long time.[168]

By late April the cadres apparently found less criminality than they expected. Of the 41,000 medium and small Shanghai firms they processed, 68 percent were declared to be "law-abiding." Only 2 percent were seriously compromised by discoveries during the campaign.[169] These figures may not reflect any particular virtue on the part of small Shanghai firms; they may only indicate the difficulty of detecting many kinds of illegal maneuvers in which such firms can engage. It is easy to emphasize the powers of organization among the cadre "tiger hunters," and to list all the methods they attempted to use. But in behavioral terms, power was exercised from the bottom whenever these procedures were evaded. Nonetheless, the ethics of future economic behavior in Shanghai were long affected by the inquiries that took place. In late May, after the peak of the movement had passed, a series of meetings was held to summarize the new ethical consensus.[170]

*Three decades later, by the early 1980s,* the most obvious economic sins of Shanghai were no longer inequality and disorganization, but inefficiency, lack of incentive, and poverty. Quasi corruptions like unemployment and inflation were still seen as undesirable in Teng's time, but slow growth and excess demand were now recognized as causes of these faults. By the 1980s, it was also obvious that some socialist institutions could make these ills worse.

Decentralizing reforms that give lower managers control of resources but provide no sanctions against efficiency failures may lead to allocative change

of the wrong sorts—overly enthusiastic expansion plans for capital, over-
generous wage increases to spur labor, and a "free-for-all spread to lavish
gifts, 16-course banquets, and even graver forms of malfeasance."[171] In the
last quarter of 1984, bank lending for all purposes rose 46 percent, and the
People's Bank of China raised the currency in circulation by a value of
US$2.8 billion. In this same time, the government deficit was $1.8 billion.
No longer was inflation seen as the cardinal economic sin. Some of the
new policies allowed structural readjustments that reduced excess demands,
but their net effect was sharply inflationary. By mid-1985, retail sales prices
were 10 percent over levels in the middle of the previous year.[172]

Managers' new notions of proper entrepreneurial styles are now deeply
influenced by examples overseas—as are consumers' perceptions of proper
living standards. These notional changes are hard to measure, but they
translate into large quantities of new economic demand. In the late 1970s,
urban consumers mainly wanted the "four things that go around" (bicycles,
electric fans, wristwatches, and sewing machines). Now they hope for the
"eight big things" (color television sets, cameras, cassette tape players,
motorcycles, air conditioners, washing machines, refrigerators, and VCRs;
the *"pa ta chien"*). These things are now on the market for high prices,
especially in cities recently opened for more trade. But they are known to
be even more available in "special economic zones" like Shenchen, and to
be usual in those much-envied southern places, Hong Kong and Taiwan.

Now that poverty is seen as the main corruption, new economic patterns
are acceptable to some high cadres but not to others. Po Yi-po in 1985
railed against Shenchen's "rampant economic crimes,"[173] and by old criteria
he was right. Shanghai wits quipped that the old Maoist motto "look to
the future" (*hsiang ch'ien k'an*) had become "look to money" (*hsiang ch'ien
k'an*, with a different *ch'ien*). "Leather bag" holding companies (*p'ipao kungszu*),
on paper only, have been generally approved under the reforms, because
they can reduce red tape and allow more efficient trading.[174] But this policy
for efficiency also allows for enterprising swindlers. In mid-1985, the Shanghai
police arrested Huang K'uei-yüan, a Hong Kong citizen who for half a year
traveled through many provinces impersonating a representative of foreign
companies and signing more than forty contracts, for future trade of $7.55
billion (plus 1.63 billion yuan). Before he was caught, Huang received only
1 billion yuan in credit, including 200,000 yuan in cash.[175] His exploits
show the eagerness of Chinese managers to export, a motive that made
them gullible.

The PRC joined Interpol to fight white-collar crime of this sort.[176] From
January to November 1985, the Shanghai police found 402 "serious economic
criminal cases"—but arrested only 260 people in them.[177] Throughout China
during 1985, only 15,500 people were sued for all economic crimes, and
the state recovered just 286 million yuan.[178] Considering the size of the
country, these figures are trivial. Much wrongdoing was unpunished.

Some economic activities that had previously been illegal were now
positively encouraged. Stock ownership had been fixed since 1956, when
capitalists in "joint state-private" companies received shares that soon became

important stigmas, not just assets. But in January 1985, the Shanghai Yenchung Plastics Company sold 100,000 shares for 5 million yuan, and a year later it reported profits of 490,000 yuan, of which 610,000 yuan were the first dividends paid by a Shanghai company under the reforms.[179] In some parts of China, stock exchanges have been reestablished.[180] But the theoretical need for a return on capital has received more attention than has the practical need to compensate entrepreneurs whose economic guesswork turns productive. This aspect of modern economics strongly resembles gambling, and the CCP's puritan streak works against it as an old Chinese tradition, not just as a market practice.

Gambling has spread rapidly in recent years, even though the Shanghai police try to stop it. In 1985 the police closed forty-five illegal casinos and designated 110,000 players for "emphatic education" against gambling.[181] It held 400 propaganda meetings on this topic, and 600,000 people attended. State norms on risk taking are still ambiguous, but social habits do not conform to them. A letter to the editor asked whether a gambling debt IOU should be enforceable.[182] The official reply was negative; but the IOU would not have been written or received if it had no social meaning.

Private firms, called "individual households" (*kot'i hu*), avoided depositing funds in state banks, lest they be caught by differences between loosening social norms and stricter official norms.[183] They reportedly had "three fears" (*san p'a*): that changes in bank policy would restrict use of their money, that their accounts would be audited, and that banks do not provide enough service.[184] A sample of these firms showed that they had an average in the bank of only 1,300 yuan; and an extrapolation from the sample suggested to bank officials that 120 million yuan of deposits in Shanghai alone were lost because of the "three fears." There were 110,000 such firms in the city. A great many more unlicensed and illegal companies [185] could have contributed more but had no accounts.[186] Even well-established, official firms complained against the extent of commercial regulation. As a manager in the industrial suburb of Minhang said, "If we want to cash a 1,000 yuan check, we have to run over 30 kilometers to get it to the Bank of China."[187] He reported that business was good, but that problems with materials, transport, and bureaucracy had become excessive.

The new economic corruption is slow development. Mayor Chiang Tse-min, in a 1986 speech, said that Shanghai's task over the next five years would be to strengthen infrastructure, attract foreign capital, and speed scientific research.[188] But these reforms would be insufficient without attention to the bureaucracy that fetters "productive forces slumbering in the lap of social labor."[189] Because economic development is a project of growth as well as equity, use of the modern commodity market has in many countries made for alternating elites and concepts of corruption.[190]

## 5. Discipline Within the Official Tribe

Bureaucratic corruption is, in many accounts, the main or only kind. During early 1952 the Three-Anti Movement among bureaucrats was aimed at Shanghai's new official community, and it influenced public morals by a demonstration effect. This was not the first purge in the party, nor was it the first time the CCP had clamped down on nonparty cadres working for the revolutionary cause. But its timing was apt: It followed the quick recruitments to posts after 1949, and it was simultaneous with the Five-Anti Movement that tried to impose new moral standards on businessmen.

The East China Military Administration Committee published its "Five-Point Disciplinary Code" against corruption and bureaucracy on December 27, 1951—the very day on which the first citywide committee to inspect economic transactions was also created.[191] Chairman Jao Shu-shih set up a letter box to receive complaints against officials; and three days later, he spoke to 2,000 cadres on investigations of bureaucratic corruption that had already been found. He said 615 bad officials had been dealt with—76 percent in financial and economic departments, 15 percent in political and legal offices, 5 percent in culture and education, and 4 percent in "people's" and other organizations. When classified by backgrounds, 42 percent were nonparty "retained personnel" from the previous government, 22 percent were newly recruited officials, and apparently 37 percent were party members.[192] Two days later, Mayor Ch'en Yi made a speech urging purification of work style among East China Army units.[193]

The first week of January saw propaganda for virtue among bureaucrats. Youth League members were called into conference by Lu Kuang, one of their leaders in Shanghai, and were exhorted to be active in the campaign to criticize bad officials.[194] Even the Public Security Bureau vowed to "study seriously all Three-Anti documents" and to "criticize errors that may exist." Newspapers reported the case of a policeman who took bribes, admitted his sins—and had been forgiven.[195] Six specific grades of punishment were laid down for bureaucratic wrongdoers, and death sentences figured among them.[196] In timing, this movement was like the Five-Anti Campaign; but in style, it more closely resembled the Suppression of Counterrevolutionaries. The people it concerned had greater power.

There is an old tradition of collective responsibility in China. When an embezzler was discovered in a state food company, the innocent manager of the unit received almost as much criticism as the criminal himself.[197] Tax personnel at the Hsüehchiapin Slaughterhouse in Tungchiatu, Yangszu District, were accused of "collective corruption" (*chit'i t'anwu*), to the tune of 230 million yuan, but there was scant attempt to distinguish the major wrongdoers from their accomplices.[198] So much corruption was found at the Chouchiatu Police Station that its vice-head—not charged with criminality himself—was dismissed from his job and from the party too.[199]

Jao Shu-shih vowed in mid-January to "lead the movement" for eradication of the three evils of corruption, waste, and bureaucracy. He again invited accusation letters against any cadre, now to be sent to his personal box at the post office.[200] In all units, party cadres were supposed to confess before their nonparty colleagues had to do so.[201] In some offices, such as the Shanghai Railroad Bureau, the movement was particularly severe, and many were sent off to labor reform.[202] In others, such as the East China Textiles Administration, high officials only made "self-examinations."[203]

From the end of January through early March, some actions against party members were serious. Ts'ai Hui, director of the General Office of the East China Finance Committee, was accused of making dubious loans and receiving illegal remittances from Hong Kong; so he had to leave his post. Li Yü, secretary-general of the Party's Shanghai Municipal Committee (who had only held that post since January 20—and who may have been the victim of a drama to impress businessmen in the Five-Anti Campaign) was removed from all his jobs. Two members of the party's Economic and Finance Subcommittee, a member of the party group in the Shanghai General Federation of Trade Unions, a former secretary of the party group in the Shanghai People's Government, a member of the party committee in the Shanghai Power Company, and a former chief of the control department of the Shanghai Public Security Bureau were all expelled from the party and punished.[204] The reasons for these sentences are in many cases unclear, but Shanghai citizens outside the party could not claim, after this, that there was no scrubbing of stains on the inside, too.

*Three decades later, by the mid-1980s,* the CCP had conducted many campaigns against bureaucratic corruption, but with mixed success.[205] In Teng's era, the Chinese press has published antibureaucratic muckraking, anticadre satire, and railing against "under-the-table relationships."[206] In Shanghai the most spectacular recent corruption in official families involved Ch'en Hsiao-meng (son of the CCP propaganda chief, Ch'en Ch'i-wu) and Hu Hsiao-yang (son of the chair of Shanghai's Political Consultative Conference, Hu Li-ch'iao), who were found to have raped six women and molested forty-two others. For these sexual offenses, they were executed. Newspapers published articles saying that "all are equal under the law."[207]

The national scene is rife with allegations of commercial or criminal wrongdoing by "crown princes" (*t'ai tzu*) related to top cadres. The sons of Hu Yao-pang, Chao Tzu-yang, and Po Yi-po, the son and grandson of Yeh Chien-ying, and even the paraplegic son of Teng Hsiao-p'ing have all been implicated in various irregularities, at least by rumor.[208] Most cases involve the use of parental connections for commercial purposes, and many have not been tried or proven. In any case, similar patterns are common through many levels of China's highly politicized economy. Minor bribery is so much a matter of course that a kind of cigarette is known as "machine gun brand" and a kind of liquor as "hand grenade brand" because these have weapon-like powers for demolishing red tape.[209]

The most egregious case has been from January 1984 to March 1985 on Hainan Island, where the Discipline Inspection Commission found a "web of corruption spreading across China and involving some Central departments." Hainan officials imported 89,000 vehicles, 2.8 million television sets, 252,000 video recorders, and 122,000 motorcycles—but the two top state officials on the island only lost their jobs, and only "serious warnings" were given to the two top party leaders. "They were not seeking personal gain."[210]

When a commercial branch of the Ministry of Aviation needed to show
a profit, it got loans from a provincial branch of the Bank of China to
import 180,000 French color television sets (on an outdated import license,
issued to another office). A former minister and a current vice-minister were
held responsible—but not arrested. A former head of the party in the
ministry was "suspended" from the CCP while he was "put under sur-
veillance" for two years.[211] A survey of 785 economic crimes showed that
66 percent involved cadres taking advantage of their positions, and 60
percent benefited collectives, not just individuals or families.[212] Many economic crimes mixed individual with collective motives. One enterprising
cadre, for example, cheated eighty-eight work units in seventeen provinces
of 20 million yuan, but he kept only one million for himself, distributing
the rest to followers.[213] Shanghai interviewees joke that the old Maoist
slogan "Serve the People" (*wei jenmin fuwu*) is now replaced by a new
ethic for small collectives: "Corruption for the People" (*Wei jenmin t'anwu*).

Hu Yao-pang said in late 1985, "Since cracking down on economic and
other crimes, 20,000 or 30,000 party members have been dealt with by
criminal laws and party discipline."[214] But Hu Ch'i-li of the Politburo reported
in 1986 that there were 44 million party members, and that each year
beginning in 1981 0.2 or 0.3 percent of them have been "disciplined and
punished,"[215] implying that about 500,000 party members were thus affected.
These two reports, both from high officials, are difficult to reconcile, since
Hu Ch'i-li's estimate is about twenty times Hu Yao-pang's. The total number
of crimes by bureaucrats is, in any case, almost surely far above the number
caught and punished.

At the beginning of 1986, Hu Yao-pang and Chao Tzu-yang spoke to a
major meeting of 8,000 top cadres, urging yet a new set of anticorruption
rules.[216] First, party and state cadres were forbidden to start firms. Second,
cadres could not take positions in private companies on retirement, and
should resign these if they already had them; nor were current cadres to
take such posts, even if they stopped their salaries (*t'ing hsin*). Third, private
cadres could work in industries unconnected with their former units—but
only after a two-year waiting period, and only by forgoing their pensions
and other benefits. Fourth, disregard of these rules was supposed to mean
punishment. Fifth, cadres' dependents with official jobs were also forbidden
to do private business. But as many rumors suggest, these rules are skirted
even by family members of the top politicians who propound them. Such
rules describe what is going on more than they effectively prohibit it.

As China's top economic managers become aware of past losses from
inefficiencies, they need to give old cadres a stake in the reform system.
Doing so involves buying off old officials for the sake of political stability
at a time of economic change. Montesquieu, after arguing in *Esprit des lois*
that good government depends on a fairly equal distribution of wealth,
makes an exception for states with growing markets: "The spirit of commerce
brings with it the spirit of frugality, of economy, of moderation, of work,
of wisdom, of tranquility, of order, and of regularity. In this manner, as

long as this spirit prevails, the riches it creates do not have any bad effect." Adam Smith also made this argument; and another Scot, Sir James Steuart, put it most concisely: "A modern economy, therefore, is the most effective bridle ever invented against the folly of despotism."[217] In China, it is slowly being realized that even a market which commoditizes land, money, and labor has moral virtues, not just moral faults. Such a market can be the most powerful and permanent counter to bureaucratic corruption.[218]

## Conclusion: Communities and Corruptions

What does all this tell us about corruption? First, perceptions of it have ebbs and flows, and these changes in concepts of cleanness sweep far beyond politics. Purist governments in Shanghai came with cleaner gutters. More libertine officials mixed with dirtier air (and more economic growth). The link is a correlation, not a cause-effect sequence, and not just in politics. Morals changed together with attitudes toward loyalty, toward cleanliness, toward foreigners, toward commerce, and toward official work. We will do best with an idea of corruption that can handle change in all these realms.

Second, it should be evident that such a definition will be strongest if it depends on groups of people, rather than on the formal traits of acts. Bribery, nepotism, simony, barratry, graft, usury—not a single one has been always corrupt. Corruption implies at least two different groups, with different norms. Traditional kinship loyalties conflicted squarely with the Communists' sharp call for devotion to state purposes. Some high virtues of China's old order were corrupt in terms of new goals after 1949. A member of the 1952 Youth League in Sungshan District helped the Shanghai Public Security Bureau to arrest his own nephew, who had refused to confess after evading taxes.[219] Even among Communists, personal relations of trust—the essence of success in urban underground work before liberation—were dubious to the party after its suzerainty was established. Li Chien-hua, a Communist agent, infiltrated the KMT government so well that he became deputy director of Chiang Kai-shek's Bureau of Social Affairs in Shanghai; but in 1952 he was expelled from the Communist Party (which he had joined in 1934) because he protected his landlord brother, tried to protect his father, and "promoted cadres on the basis of personal relations."[220] League activist Hsü Yü-ying urged her father to confess economic irregularities in his Shanghai tubing factory; and when he did so, she was declared a "model student." But her sister in filial rage "beat and wounded her," so that she had to be taken to hospital. After the Public Security Bureau came to investigate, Hsü Yün-ying averred that she would not press legal charges, if her father and sister repented and if both asked for leniency.[221]

No single campaign could possibly have engineered this change, which was in any case incomplete—as the trends of the early 1980s clearly show. Benjamin Nelson's notions "tribal brotherhood" and "universal otherhood" are good for suggesting questions about groups and ethical standards. Families at low levels and "tribes" at high ones are just two points along a spectrum of sizes of groups, with which people may identify and on which they base actions.

Family harmony is now a concern in the Chinese press, after years of campaign appeals based on larger communities, especially during the Cultural Revolution. In Shanghai an old man used all his savings to buy a sewing machine, a television set, and a tape recorder for his four sons and two daughters—but he reportedly starved to death because they failed to support him.[222] An old lady, living in a Shanghai apartment, adopted a young couple without urban household registrations; she even switched to an apartment elsewhere in the city, where the police could be fooled into thinking they were her children—but the youths abandoned her as soon as they registered the new place in their names, obtaining urban status.[223] By the 1980s such breakdowns of proper intergeneration ties were infamous scandals, even though propaganda in previous decades had positively glorified such breaks. Nuclear families, too, now receive press attention. A philandering husband of a faithful wife had his sins detailed in the *Wenhui pao*.[224] Married couples were urged to share household chores.[225] Urban grooms' average expenditures on marriages reportedly rose from 2,000 to 3,300 yuan from 1980 to 1985.[226] Families, both extended and nuclear, are of great and increasing public interest in the 1980s.

So are individuals. A recent writer claims: "Our ideal person not only creates [for society] but also enjoys life."[227] Another writer argues against too much government effort to organize individuals' interests, presenting the discussion in terms of old debates between the Han thinkers Szu-ma Ch'ien and Tung Chung-shu. Tung felt that the tendency of people to follow their own interests was as natural as water running down a hill—so education was necessary to dam this flow. Szu-ma disagreed, urging less state interference and describing options of decreasing desirability: best, to let interests follow their own flow; or second, to channel them; or third, to force them through instruction; or fourth, to curtail them; or in the worst case, to have the state control them.[228] As Szu-ma implies, "individual responsibility" is not mainly a state policy; it is a fact. Explicit arguments for the rights of individuals were not evident in the 1950s, but they appear sometimes in the 1980s.[229]

Individual, family, work group, region/city, nation, world—each may now be assigned some emphasis.[230] The campaigns starting in the early 1950s did not destroy any of these, as evidence from the 1980s abundantly shows. How permanent the current trends are, no one knows. It would be naive to claim that hardliners in the party will never again have success defining corruption narrowly, for the interests of just a few of these sizes of groups— and for the sake of augmenting their own power. There is no need either to overstate or to ignore the recent trend, which results from an interaction of powerful social motives that will continue in conflict and frequent flux.

At Shanghai from 1949 to 1952, new public ethics and communities were sponsored under government auspices, with much coercion. The effect of campaigns on individuals' identities was real, but also temporary and partial.

In modern development, the goals of individuals and many sizes of groups often alter, and resources shift to meet them. But in the long run, each size of human organization retains its own quantum of sovereignty. Political morals relate to communities and change with them. The corrupt view of corruption may be any which neglects the human groups that naturally occur.

## Notes

This chapter began in a very different draft long ago, and the author extends thanks to many who have helped with it, though he is guilty of all the corruptions that remain. Special gratitude goes to Mr. Feng Shengping, who helped with research on the post-Mao period.

1. Reinhard Bendix's translation, *Max Weber: An Intellectual Portrait* (Garden City, N.Y.: Doubleday, 1960), p. 139, is used rather than Hans Gerth, *The Religion of China: Confucianism and Taoism* (New York: Macmillan, 1964), p. 237.

2. See at least three books by Albert O. Hirschman, *The Passions and the Interests: Political Arguments for Capitalism Before Its Triumph* (Princeton, N.J.: Princeton University Press, 1977); *Shifting Involvements: Private Interest and Public Action* (Princeton, N.J.: Princeton University Press, 1982); and an effort to unify politics and economics by showing the conditions under which individual decisions can be effective in public, *Exit, Voice, and Loyalty: Responses to Decline in Firms, Organizations, and States* (Cambridge, Mass.: Harvard University Press, 1970).

3. James C. Scott, *Comparative Political Corruption* (Englewood Cliffs, N.J.: Prentice-Hall, 1972), p. 4, cites J. S. Nye's justly famous "Corruption and Political Development: A Cost-Benefit Analysis," *American Political Science Review*, June 1967, pp. 417–427, also reprinted in Norman T. Uphoff and Warren F. Ilchman, eds., *The Political Economy of Development* (Berkeley: University of California Press, 1972), pp. 463–475. See also Edward C. Banfield, *Political Influence* (New York: Free Press, 1961), p. 315. Other important statements include Ronald Wraith and Edgar Simkins, *Corruption in Developing Countries* (London: Allen and Unwin, 1963), and Colin Leys, "What Is the Trouble About Corruption?" *Journal of Modern African Studies* 3:2 (1965), pp. 215–230. The purely administrative view of the problem is expressed concisely in Robert C. Wood, "Ethics in Government as a Problem in Executive Management," *Public Administration Review* 15 (winter 1955), pp. 1–7. The text here uses Nye's words, rather than the slight misquote in Scott's major book.

4. Scott, in *Comparative Political Corruption*, comes out for a consciously legalistic criterion for defining corruption, as against any vague "public interest" or "public opinion" criterion. But he does so only for an epistemological reason: Illegalities and their effects can be distinguished more clearly than violations of extralegal norms. Nye, in "Corruption and Political Development," concedes, "Definitions pose a problem. Indeed if we define political development as 'rational, modern, honest government,' then it cannot coexist with corruption in the same time period. And if corruption is endemic in government, a politically developed society cannot exist." The best example of Banfield's difficulty is his book *The Moral Basis of a Backward Society* (New York: Free Press, 1958). He criticizes Carlo Levi's *Christ Stopped at Eboli*, trans. Frances Frenaye (New York: Noonday, 1969). On pp. 35–37 Banfield concedes that "there is an element of truth" in each of Levi's cultural explanations of private-regarding amoral familism. But Banfield, p. 83, rejects these explanations because they are not "predictive." By this, he means they are not simple and replicable;

they predict (better than amoral familism does) the corporate, antiregime, often messianic movements of Italian peasants described by Levi, Vittorio Lanternari in *Religions of the Oppressed* (New York: Borzoi, 1964), and Eric Hobsbawm in *Primitive Rebels* (Manchester, England: Manchester University Press, 1959), pp. 30–73, 90–107. Corruption is a difficult topic for strictly positive science, since there is no way to define it without considering what people think, as well as their behavior.

5. Benjamin N. Nelson, *The Idea of Usury: From Tribal Brotherhood to Universal Otherhood*, History of Ideas Series, No. 3 (Princeton, N.J.: Princeton University Press, 1953). Nelson's categories are similar to *Gemeinschaft* and *Gesellschaft*, but they are preferred here because of their specific reference to a kind of corruption.

6. For more, see Lynn T. White III, "Modernization, Deviance, Rations and Household Registration in Urban China," in Sydney Greenblatt, Amy Wilson, and Richard H. Wilson, eds., *Deviance and Social Control in China* (New York: Praeger, 1977), pp. 151–172.

7. Even before 1949, Shanghai presented a real smorgasbord of corruption, in the eyes of practically all observers. Confucian traditionalists never liked Shanghai's mixed and cosmopolitan atmosphere; Soochow was their main center of official propriety in East China. Europeans found that Shanghai was a city for adventurers, where ordinary rules of social interaction were often suspended. In the guerrilla Communist view, many of Shanghai's people not only had low levels of political consciousness; they had consciences of positively the wrong kind. Nearly everyone agreed the place was corrupt, though there were differing reasons to explain how.

8. Clifford Geertz, "Notes on the Balinese Cockfight," in *Interpretation of Culture* (New York: Basic Books, 1973), chap. 15. Because the symbol here is "dirt," surely the analysis may be claimed as substructural.

9. This procedure may be objected to because it classes immoralities with mere problems, "sins" with "mistakes." Maybe an aspect of political development is the increase in debate that avoids such aspersions. But some unintended mistakes (in China, the post-1958 famine is an example) assume a moral character. For purposes here, there is evidence that Shanghai publics have mixed these categories often; and the essay will follow them, without making excessive claims for the procedure.

10. For more on this tradition, see Lynn T. White III, "Non-Governmentalism in the Historical Development of Modern Shanghai," in L.J.C. Ma and E. W. Hanten, eds., *Urban Development in Modern China* (Boulder, Colo.: Westview, 1981), pp. 19–57.

11. Margaret W.W. Chang, "Chinese Communist Takeover and Control of an Urban Center . . . Shanghai" (unpublished, Columbia University, 1967), p. 12.

12. Cf. Ch'en Yi, "Two Months' Work in Shanghai," *China Digest*, vol. 6 (September 21, 1949), pp. 8–9, and Yinmaw Kau, "Government Bureaucracy and Cadres in Urban China Under Communist Rule, 1949–1965" (Ph.D. dissertation, Cornell University, 1968), p. 84.

13. *Chiehfang jihpao* (Liberation Daily), Shanghai (hereafter CFJP), July 21, 1949.

14. Many articles could be cited about these retraining programs, especially in economic units; for a summary, cf. Chang, "Chinese Communist Takeover," p. 32.

15. For example, cf. Ezra Vogel, *Canton Under Communism: Programs and Politics in a Provincial Capital, 1949–1968* (Cambridge, Mass.: Harvard University Press, 1969), pp. 62–65.

16. *Takung pao* (L'Impartial) (hereafter TKP), Hong Kong, November 17, 1950, reproducing New China News Agency (hereafter NCNA) cables from Shanghai of November 15 and 16. Cf. also *Shanghai News* (hereafter SN), Shanghai, January 25, 1951. Yang Fan is the only known person to have toppled with P'an Han-nien in

a local mid-1950s purge. On the suppression procedures in factories, see *Laotung pao* (Labor News) (hereafter LTP), Shanghai, February 3, 1951.

17. *Hsinwen jihpao* (News Daily) (hereafter HWJP), Shanghai, March 18, 1951. Six culprits were executed in Nanhui County, which later came under Shanghai's jurisdiction. Cf. CFJP, March 27, 1951, on the executions of reported former collaborators of Chiang Kai-shek and Wang Ching-wei.

18. *Wenhui pao* (Wenhui News) (hereafter HWJP), Shanghai, April 27, 1953.

19. SN, May 1, 1951.

20. HWJP, May 1, 1951, and CFJP, May 1, 1951.

21. CFJP, May 4, 1951.

22. CFJP, May 17, 1951.

23. LTP, June 1, 1951.

24. The percentages were calculated from absolute figures in LTP, June 16, 1951. Of the convicts, two (0 percent) were released on bail.

25. CFJP, August 7, 1951.

26. CFJP, August 29, 1951.

27. CFJP, May 11, 1951.

28. SN, July 14, 1951. This village was under the city's Civil Affairs Bureau, and the inmates were "former drug dealers and petty thieves" rather than politicians. They shouted "Long Live Chairman Mao!" as they passed through the streets to a wharf in Shanghai, where they were "seen off by a group of cadres."

29. CFJP, July 13, 1951.

30. To see just one example, cf. CFJP, July 3, 1952, about a credible KMT spy on Shanghai's antiaircraft installations. Cf. also the less clear evidence against a former Nationalist military judge in rural Shanghai, CFJP, April 25, 1953. Still another example: CFJP, April 26, 1954.

31. *Shanghai kungshang tzuliao* (Materials on Shanghai Industry and Commerce) (hereafter SHKSTL), Shanghai, 2:46 (June 9, 1951), p. 1635.

32. WHP, April 26, 1953.

33. Calculated from figures in Ramon Myers and Lynn White, "Political Structure," in Gilbert Rozman, ed., *The Modernization of China* (New York: Free Press, 1981), p. 275.

34. See Lowell Dittmer, "Party Rectification in Post-Mao China," and Lynn White, "Chinese Intellectuals and Party Policy," in Yu-ming Shaw, ed., *Mainland China: Politics, Economics, and Reform* (Boulder, Colo.: Westview, 1986), pp. 103–120 and 205–255.

35. A clear example is Yue Daiyun, author with Carolyn Wakeman of *To the Storm: Odyssey of a Revolutionary Chinese Woman* (Berkeley: University of California Press, 1985). The political diversity of Chinese Communist Party members who are students or researchers at U.S. universities is obvious, though they are not a random sample of the party.

36. Roberta Martin, *Party Recruitment in China: Patterns and Prospects* (New York: Columbia East Asian Institute, 1981), p. 82.

37. *Jilü chiencha weiyüanhui.* See the important articles by Alan P.L. Liu, "The Politics of Corruption in the People's Republic of China," *American Political Science Review* 77:3 (September 1983), pp. 602–623, and Graham Young, "Control and Style: Discipline Inspection Commissions since the Eleventh Congress," *China Quarterly* 97 (March 1984), pp. 24–52.

38. See David S.G. Goodman, *Beijing Street Voices* (London: Boyars, 1981), and Liang Heng and Judith Shapiro, *Intellectual Freedom in China after Mao* (New York: Fund for Free Expression, 1984), and many other works. Robert A. Dahl, *Polyarchy:*

*Participation and Opposition* (New Haven, Conn.: Yale University Press, 1971), suggests that such diversity or "contestation" is one aspect of democracy, which may be considered separately from its other main aspect, "inclusiveness." Even the PRC develops, though slowly.

39. Speech of Chu Mu-chih, *Wenyi bao* (Literature and Art), Shanghai, no. 1 (January), 1984, reprinted in *Hsinhua yüehpao* (New China Monthly), Beijing (hereafter HHYP), no. 1 (January, 1984), pp. 166–170. Dissidence even more surely exists in the countryside, which is less subject to central control: Elizabeth J. Perry, "Rural Collective Violence: The Fruits of Recent Reforms," in Perry and Christine Wong, eds., *The Political Economy of Post-Mao China* (Cambridge, Mass.: Harvard University Press, 1985), pp. 175–192.

40. Perry, "Rural Collective Violence," p. 168.

41. Judith Shapiro and Liang Heng, *Intellectual Freedom in China: An Update* (New York: Fund for Free Expression, 1985), p. 2. Note the contrast with their earlier book.

42. See Merle Goldman, "Culture," in Steven M. Goldstein, ed., *China Briefing, 1984* (Boulder, Colo.: Westview, 1985), p. 30. Pa Chin's wife died during the Cultural Revolution; see his *Random Thoughts*, trans. Geremie Barmé (Hong Kong: Joint Publishing Company, 1984). Also see Anne Thurston, *Enemies of the People* (New York: Knopf, 1987), which has more on Pa Chin and others whose experiences reduced political doctrinairism in Deng's era.

43. Julian Baum, "China's Anniversary: Festivity and Debate," *Christian Science Monitor* (hereafter CSM), October 1, 1985.

44. Teng Li'ch'ün, "Pay Attention to Studying Real Problems," *Hsinhua wenchai* (New China Digest), Beijing (hereafter HHWC), no. 3 (March 1984), p. 32.

45. *Jenmin jihpao* (People's Daily), Beijing (hereafter JMJP), December 7, 1984.

46. *Jenmin jihpao haiwaipan* (People's Daily, Overseas Edition), Beijing (hereafter JMJPHWP), April 1, 1986, contains a fascinating critique of taboos in general, emphasizing that the prohibition against widows' remarriage dates only from the Sung. Such customs were deemed unnecessary, and the article implied that people should think through all their habits.

47. Some scholars, such as A. A. Rogow and H. D. Lasswell, note that this may be a natural trend in the life cycle of a political movement. See Liu, "The Politics of Corruption," p. 616.

48. TKP, Hong Kong, November 3, 1951.

49. SN, July 11, 1952.

50. Part of this area was a "reserve garden." Cf. an old picture of the English language sign on plate 10 in Hsiang Hua (pseudonym), ed., *Shanghai shihhua* (Talks on Shanghai History), (Hong Kong: Muwen Shuchü, 1971).

51. Cf. NCNA, Shanghai, August 29, 1951, and November 4, 1952.

52. TKP, Shanghai, September 28, 1951.

53. HWJP, August 27, 1951. This article attributes minor variations in the robbery rate to foreign-related incidents like the February 6, 1950, bombing at Shanghai and the approach of U.S. soldiers to China's northeast border in October of that year. The longer trend, not influenced from abroad, seems more important. Sophia Knight, *Window on Shanghai* (London: André Deutsch, 1967), p. 173, reports that the Chapei railway station, wharves, and certain entertainment spots had been the centers of minor crime in earlier years.

54. SN, October 14, 1951. The 5.88 million inoculated people included some transients through Shanghai.

55. SN, November 8, 1951. Cf. also CFJP, March 27, 1952, on the creation of the Shanghai Spring Epidemic Prevention Committee, chaired by Ch'en Yi.

56. LTP, November 27, 1951. For a Cantonese comparison, cf. Vogel, *Canton Under Communism*, p. 65. It is also possible that high party leaders wanted to test their own cadres in Shanghai by keeping some brothels open for a while.

57. SHKSTL, 2:71 (September 5, 1951), p. 2537. This 1951 change coincided with greater controls over credit and contracts, by banks and by the East China Transport Bureau.

58. SN, September 15, 1951—before the new regulations.

59. SN, December 15 and 16, 1951—after the regulations. The flavor of these English-language examples is easiest to set down in an English article. The Chinese press was comparable.

60. SN, March 21, 1951.

61. NCNA, in English, Shanghai, April 18, 1951.

62. TKP, Shanghai, May 20, 1951.

63. Vogel, *Canton Under Communism*, pp. 64–65, shows the relationship between the attack on secret societies and the Democratic Reform Campaign. Kenneth Lieberthal has done research in Tientsin sources for this subject. These are topics for books, not for sections of articles.

64. CFJP, June 5, 1953.

65. CFJP, June 8, 1953.

66. CFJP, June 13, 1953.

67. This paragraph neglects Buddhism because that religion was politically inert and very majoritarian. It was reformed more slowly than Christianity and Taoism. The great abbot T'ai-hsü (1889–1946) attempted to create a viable Buddhist social organization, but he ultimately failed. Cf. Stanford University China Project, *East China* (New Haven, Conn.: Human Relations Area Files, 1956), pp. 343–344; also, the works of Professor Holmes Welch. Monks of the Fatsang Temple in Shanghai were sent to work on nearby farms after liberation. Shanghai's Islam had just the opposite characteristics; it was very minoritarian and within its group very strong. A similarly gradual reform policy was applied by the government. The Committee to Promote the Manufacture of Leather with Pig's Skin (Chup'i Chihko T'uihsing Weiyüanhui) was established for reasons of economic rationality, and it was arranged so as not to offend the Muslims. HWJP, January 8, 1952.

68. This statement is based on more specific statements in Vaclav Smil, *The Bad Earth: Environmental Degradation in China* (Armonk, N.Y.: Sharpe, 1984), p. 165.

69. Ibid., p. 104. This issue is complex, because at least some of the water is from the Yangtze, pushed up the Whangpoo by the tidal bores.

70. HHWC, January 8, 1984.

71. *Shihchieh chingchi taopao* (World Economic Herald), Shanghai (hereafter SCCCTP), January 27, 1986.

72. Interview with a former resident of Shanghai.

73. JMJPHWP, November 15, 1985.

74. SCCCTP, September 30, 1985.

75. SCCCTP, October 21, 1985.

76. SCCCTP, September 30, 1985.

77. There is no hope of covering this problem of residential space here; but the latest major statement is R.J.R. Kirkby, *Urbanization in China* (New York: Columbia University Press, 1985), chap. 6.

78. See Lynn White, *Careers in Shanghai* (Berkeley: University of California Press, 1978), and William Parish and Martin Whyte, *Village and Family in Contemporary China* (Chicago: University of Chicago Press, 1978).

79. Precise data are unavailable, but an informal Wuhan estimate suggests a fourfold increase in recent years. The next few sentences are based on an article by a Princeton graduate student, Marlowe Hood, "Freer Economy in China Causing Increase in Illegal Urban Residents," *Wall Street Journal*, February 1, 1986.

80. Ibid. The site here was Peking.

81. CSM, October 1, 1985.

82. *Hsing yi-hsüeh*. JMJPHYP, April 1, 1986.

83. Interview with former resident of Shanghai.

84. See Chad Hansen's provocative "Chinese Language, Chinese Philosophy, and 'Truth,'" *Journal of Asian Studies* 44:3 (May 1985), pp. 491–519. Karl Mannheim, *Ideology and Utopia* (London: Routledge, 1936), would broaden this to all cultures.

85. *Hunyin chiehshao so*. WHP, December 14, 1985.

86. *Chiashuo ch'üan*. See Ying Kuo-ch'ing and Hsiao Wan-ch'üan, *Shanghai k'o-hsüeh* (Shanghai Science), Shanghai (hereafter SHKH), no. 6 (June 1980).

87. The author witnessed a traditional Buddhist funeral, complete with the burning of paper models of objects to be used by the deceased, at the Yüfo Temple, Shanghai, in the summer of 1983. See also Paul Richard Bohr, "Religion in the People's Republic of China: The Limits of Toleration," in Richard C. Bush, ed., *China Briefing, 1982* (Boulder, Colo.: Westview, 1983), p. 69. But apparently a full treatment of Chinese religions' resurgence during the 1980s is still to be written.

88. *China Weekly Review*, Shanghai, July 27, 1949.

89. Otto van der Sprenkel, with Robert Gullain and (Lord) Michael Lindsay, *New China: Three Views* (New York: John Day, 1951), p. 105.

90. *Yi pao* (Further news), Shanghai, January 12, 1962.

91. Cf. Stanford University China Project, *East China*; JMJP, October 21, 1952; and many works published by clerics. Roman Catholics forbid cremation under an exegesis of the Doctrine of the Resurrection; the Communists ostensibly were trying to save space in a crowded city.

92. TKP, Shanghai, October 17, 1951.

93. TKP, Shanghai, January 25, 1952.

94. SN, May 11, 1952.

95. Chang, "Chinese Communist Takeover," p. 15. After liberation, Shanghai's *Takung pao* and *Hsinmin pao* were reorganized. *Wenhui pao* was reinstated after suppression by the Nationalists in 1947. *Chiehfang jihpao* began publication in Shanghai on May 28, 1949. Papers containing local news, which had mostly stopped publication when the Communists arrived, were at first greatly reduced in number; but by the end of 1949 eleven of them had been reorganized and revived.

96. SN, November 28 and December 2, 1950.

97. SN, May 1, 1951, and April 13, 1952.

98. One shipping company advertised that household goods could be sent by rail to Hong Kong with only one customs examination (in Shanghai), and with most of the charges payable in Chinese yuan. SN, December 21, 1952. Those who received permission to leave were not delayed at all.

99. TKP, Hong Kong, January 1, 1951.

100. SN, January 4, 1951.

101. For example, NCNA, Shanghai, February 11, 1951.

102. SN, August 25, 1951.

103. SN, September 9 and November 7, 1951.

104. For an example, SN, January 18, 1952.

105. CFJP, January 9 and February 11, 1954.

106. David Rees, *Korea: The Limited War* (Baltimore: Penguin, 1964), p. 155.

107. NCNA, Shanghai, November 28, 1950.

108. SN, January 10, 1951.

109. NCNA, Shanghai, February 26, 1951.

110. NCNA, Shanghai, March 24, 1951.

111. SN, July 17, 1951.

112. SHKSTL 2:18 (October 6, 1951), p. 2903. Here "patriotic donation" is *aikuo hsienk'uan;* but in the September 29, 1951, issue of the same journal, p. 2833, it is *aikuo sunk'uan.*

113. NCNA, Beijing, October 31, 1951. Chang, "Chinese Communist Takeover," p. 28, gives a lower figure of 15 percent over a different category and time period. Cf. also NCNA, Beijing, November 3, 1951.

114. Cf. P'an Han-nien's important speech in SN, April 29, 1951.

115. *Chinpu ch'ingnien* (Progressive Youth), Shanghai, 2:38 (August 1951), p. 44.

116. Cf. Hsia Yen's report reprinted in SN, October 16, 1950.

117. SN, December 5, 1950. The epilogue combined Western ballet with Chinese dancing in a way that presaged Cultural Revolution styles.

118. NCNA, in English, May 7, 1951.

119. SN, March 29, 1951.

120. CFJP, June 10, 1951, and TKP, Shanghai, August 26, 1951.

121. SN, September 27 and October 18, 1951.

122. Van der Sprenkel, *New China,* p. 107.

123. Cf. report of Minister of Education Ma Hsü-lun in *Jenmin jihpao* (People's Daily), Beijing, June 14, 1950. By 1955, Shanghai had fourteen such institutions, *Kuangming jihpao* (Bright Daily), Beijing, June 19, 1955. According to Chi Wang, *Mainland China Organizations of Higher Learning in Science and Technology and Their Publications* (Washington, D.C.: Library of Congress, 1961), by 1961 the number was down to eleven.

124. SN, December 7, 1950. T. V. Soong, V.K. Wellington Koo, and other KMT notables were alumni of St. John's University.

125. SN, January 19, 1951.

126. NCNA, Shanghai, March 27, 1951.

127. Two such conferences for private middle schools are reported in *Shanghai kungshang* (Shanghai Industry and Commerce) 2:1 (November 1, 1960), p. 21, and SN, February 20, 1951.

128. SN, February 17, 1951, and TKP, Hong Kong, February 17, 1951. The dean of Aurora University, Yang Shih-ta, and its president, Hu Wen-yao, became prominent in the nationalization of China's Roman Catholic Church.

129. NCNA, Shanghai, February 15, 1951, and SN, February 22, 1951.

130. SN, March 13, 1951. Cf. Richard Storry, *A History of Modern Japan* (Harmondsworth, England: Penguin, 1960), p. 244. U.S. officials had earlier written Article 9 of the Japanese Constitution, which prohibited that country from belligerency. Korea changed the Americans' minds.

131. HWJP, May 28, 1951.

132. CFJP, December 31, 1951.

133. SN, December 8, 1951, and CFJP, August 6, 1952.

134. On these amalgamations: HWJP, July 14, 1951; TKP, Shanghai, July 13, 1951 and January 1, 1952; and TKP, Hong Kong, July 20, 1951.

135. SN, July 6, 1952. Knight, *Window on Shanghai,* mentioned the incongruence of these McTyeire buildings as late as the Cultural Revolution.

136. See CFJP, July 3, 1952, on reform classes for primary middle school teachers, and TKP, Shanghai, September 18, 1952, on faculty and student *hsiafang* from Futan University.

137. CFJP, August 6, 1952.

138. CFJP and SN, both August 9, 1952.

139. JMJPHWP, March 4, 1986.

140. JMJPHWP, February 20, 1986, reprinted from *Hsian wanpao* (Sian Evening News) of January 30.

141. SHKH, No. 2 (February), 1983, pp. 27–8.

142. See Lynn White, "Bureaucrats and Economic Strategy in the Shanghai Zone," in a forthcoming volume edited by Robert Dernberger.

143. JMJPHWP, February 16, 1986.

144. SCCCTP, September 23, 1985.

145. SCCCTP, February 17, 1986.

146. See White, "Bureaucrats and Economic Strategy."

147. JMJPHWP, February 7, 1986.

148. Interview with a recent resident of Shanghai, discussing an article that used this strange phrase "Oriental jealousy."

149. JMJPHWP, April 1, 1986, contains an article on such "feedback."

150. SCCCTP, February 17, 1986.

151. JMJPHWP, February 19, 1986.

152. An example is JMJPHWP, February 23, 1986, an article by Li Tse-hou, one of these "four teachers," who are not officially designated but are informally recognized by students as such. This kind of recognition is like that accorded to the "six gentlemen" (*liu chüntzu*) of 1898, including the martyr T'an Szu-t'ung—or like another "seven gentlemen" (*ch'i chüntzu*) of the 1930s and 1940s.

153. These "four [young] gentlemen" include an editor now visiting in Michigan named Chu Chia-ming and a professor named Wen Yuan-k'ai who is vice-president of the Chinese University of Science and Technology.

154. TKP, Shanghai, June 9, 11 and 14, 1949.

155. Cf. Rees, *Korea*, p. 289, on the meeting at Kaesong Teahouse of July 8, 1951, which began a two-year negotiation prior to the armistice.

156. The reader should consult John Gardner, "The *Wu-fan* Campaign in Shanghai: A Study in the Consolidation of Urban Control," Doak Barnett, ed., *Chinese Communist Politics in Action* (Seattle: University of Washington Press, 1969), pp. 477–539.

157. *Yi pao*, January 5, 1952; and SHKSTL 3:6 (January 23, 1952), p. 3402.

158. HWJP, January 17, 1952.

159. *Fan hsinghui, fan ch'icha, fan paoli, fan t'oulo.* HWJP, January 15, 1952; cf. also the issue of January 18.

160. *Yi pao*, January 22 and 24, 1952.

161. HWJP, January 19, 1952.

162. HWJP, January 22, 1952, is an absolute gold mine.

163. *T'anpai chiench'a tahui. Yi pao*, January 24, 1952.

164. NCNA, Shanghai, January 28, 1952. Jung's "Sing Sung Cotton Textile Company" was more than a year late in delivering a state order of yardage.

165. HWJP, January 22, 1952. The article mentioned that these capitalists, Han Pao-fu and his son Han Pin-k'un, also broke the law in an additional way: "They conspired with other merchants in the same business by the method '*feikuo hai*'" (literally, "flying across the sea"). This was manipulation of unreported orders and inventories.

166. CFJP, February 7, 1952. The Five-Anti Campaign opposed bribery, tax evasion, theft of state property, fraud, and theft of state economic secrets.

167. NCNA, Shanghai, February 24, 1952.

168. NCNA, Shanghai, February 18 and March 26, 1952; and CFJP, April 3, 1952.

169. CFJP, April 24, 1952.

170. CFJP, May 20, 1952, on the lifting of restrictions on travel by managers of private Shanghai enterprises. Also NCNA, Shanghai, May 27, 1952, on conferences mentioned in the text.

171. John Burns, "Some Take Liberties in China's Free Market," *New York Times*, March 31, 1985.

172. *China Macroeconomic Newsletter*, Rock Creek Research (Washington, D.C.), 2:2 (January 27, 1986), Table 2. See also Julian Baum, "Watershed Year for Deng's Reforms," CMS, March 4, 1986, which makes an estimate of 9 percent.

173. CMS, August 1, 1985.

174. An article approving these companies is in SCCCTP, July 22, 1985.

175. JMJPHWK, January 15, 1986.

176. *C.J.* [Criminal Justice] *International* 2:1 (January–February 1986), p. 9.

177. WHP, December 15, 1986.

178. JMJPHWP, March 13, 1986.

179. JMJPHWP, February 25, 1986.

180. An informal report indicates a small stock exchange in Wuhan as early as 1981.

181. *Chungtien chiaoyü* (this term means no more than stern lecturing). WHP, December 22, 1985.

182. WHP, December 18, 1985.

183. SCCCTP, November 18, 1985.

184. SCCCTP, November 18, 1985.

185. See Ch'en Ya-ni, "Shanghai Bans Unlicensed Businesses and Illegal Trading," in John Burns and Stanley Rosen, eds., *Policy Conflicts in Post-Mao China* (Armonk, N.Y.: Sharpe, 1986), document 59, trans. JMJP, July 6, 1983.

186. Lynn White, "Low Power: Small Enterprises in Shanghai," *China Quarterly* 73 (March 1978), pp. 45–76, and Wojtek Zafanolli, "A Brief Outline of China's Second Economy," *Asian Survey* 15:7 (July 1985), pp. 715–736, contain information about the twilight economy, which is large and increasing.

187. SCCCTP, February 17, 1986. There was no way to speed bank procedures by telephone.

188. JMJPHWP, April 1, 1986.

189. The phrase is from Karl Marx and Friedrich Engels, *Manifesto of the Communist Party* (Beijing: Foreign Languages Press, 1970), p. 37.

190. This relies on Karl Polanyi, *The Great Transformation* (New York: Rinehart, 1944), and E. E. Schattschneider, *The Semi-Sovereign People* (New York: Dryden Press, 1960).

191. NCNA, Shanghai, December 27, 1951.

192. CFJP, December 30, 1951. The percentages were calculated from absolute figures; the number of party members was residual after the other two categories had been deducted.

193. CFJP, January 1, 1952.

194. HWJP, January 4, 1952.

195. HWJP, January 5, 1952.

196. HWJP, January 6, 1952. The six punishments (and calculated percentages of a group of 332 persons to whom they were applied on January 5) were as follows: death sentence to be carried out immediately, 6 percent (*szuhsing lichi chihhsing*); death sentence to be carried out later, 6 percent (*szuhsing huanch'i chihhsing*); imprisonment for life, 10 percent (*wuch'i tuhsing*); imprisonment for a fixed period,

57 percent (*yuch'i t'uhsing*); restriction, 14 percent (*kuanchih*); and, finally, release on bail, 7 percent (*paoshih*).

197. HWJP, January 5, 1952.

198. HWJP, January 6, 1952. Appropriately enough, these tax cadres were accused by the slaughterhouse butchers.

199. Ibid. The organ that expelled Ch'ü from the party was the Discipline and Inspection Committee (Chilü Chiench'a Weiyüanhui) of the Shanghai Party Committee's Suburban Work Committee (Shih Wei Chiaoch'ü Kungtso Weiyüanhui). In other words, the suburban districts were lumped together for the discipline function in the party's organization at this time.

200. HWJP, January 8 and 15, 1952.

201. CFJP, January 11, 1952.

202. HWJP, January 20, 1952.

203. JMJP, January 12, 1952.

204. CFJP, January 31 and especially March 2, 1952. Cf. also HWJP, January 20, 1952. Less important cases of party corruption—usually involving a simple taste for luxuries—are not emphasized here because of their minor public effect; but for two examples, cf. CFJP, January 10 and March 13, 1952. The Huang Yi-feng case was of national importance but had few public effects until early 1953.

205. Alan P.L. Liu, *How China Is Ruled* (Englewood Cliffs, N.J.: Prentice-Hall, 1986), p. 175, notes the Three Antis, as well as the Four Cleans of 1963–1966, as predecessors to the current campaign. Another kind of precedent would include the Streamlining Administration Movement of late 1957, as well as the Cultural Revolution—despite the long-term ineffectiveness of these campaigns for their ostensible goals.

206. *Kuanhsihu*. See Burns and Rosen, *Policy Conflicts in Post-Mao China*, an August 6, 1981, Central Discipline Inspection Commission report, a satiric dialogue about bureaucracy (trans. Tom Gold), and muckraking reports by Liu Pin-yen, documents 34–37.

207. JMJPHWP, February 20, 1986.

208. *Chengming*, Hong Kong, February 1986, contains a long gossip article summarizing these reports.

209. Liu, "The Politics of Corruption," p. 617. A large Beijing example reports twenty-two government officials receiving bribes that totalled 1 million yuan over eighteen months; JMJPHWP, December 17, 1985.

210. JMJPHWP, August 6, 1985.

211. JMJPHWP, February 7, 1986.

212. *Kuangming jihpao* (Bright Daily), Beijing, July 12, 1982.

213. JMJPHWK, December 21, 1985.

214. Lu K'en, *Hu Yao-pang fangwen ji* (Interview with Hu Yao-pang) (Hong Kong: Paihsing Monthly, 1985), p. 32.

215. *Huayü k'uaipao* (Sino Daily Express), New York, April 14, 1986.

216. JMJPHWP, February 6, 1986, and CSM, July 13, 1986.

217. The Montesquieu and Steuart quotations are from Hirschman, *The Passions and the Interests*, pp. 71 and 85.

218. See Polanyi, *The Great Transformation*. A rural application of this idea is in Nicholas R. Lardy, *Agriculture in China's Modern Economic Development* (Cambridge: Cambridge University Press, 1983), p. xi.

219. CFJP, February 1, 1952.

220. CFJP, March 11, 1952.

221. HWJP, May 17, 1952.

222. WHP, November 2, 1985.

223. WHP, December 18, 1985.

224. WHP, December 18, 1985, another article.

225. JMJPHWP, two articles on March 16 and 18, 1986.

226. JMJPHWP, February 3, 1986; this is from a Tientsin sample.

227. HHWC, no. 2 (February 1984), p. 138.

228. JMJP, December 10, 1984.

229. Related issues are addressed in John F. Copper, Franz Michael, and Yuan-li Wu, *Human Rights in Post-Mao China* (Boulder, Colo.: Westview, 1985), and in Andrew Nathan, *Chinese Democracy* (New York: Knopf, 1985).

230. At base, this is an epistomological problem that applies to any analysis or synthesis. See Stephen C. Pepper, *World Hypotheses: A Study in Evidence* (Berkeley: University of California Press, 1970).

# PART EIGHT

# Literature and Education

# 37

## Change and Continuity in Communist Chinese Policy on Literature and Art

*Chou Yu-sun*

Communist Chinese policy on literature and art is mainly grounded in Mao Tse-tung's "Talks at the Yenan Forum on Literature and Art" in 1942. The purpose of the forum was to castigate outspoken writers such as Wang Shih-wei and silence other dissenting voices. This kind of critical background has resulted in Beijing's art and literature policy being irrevocably bound up with political rectification. In May 1982, in commemoration of the fortieth anniversry of the publication of Mao's "Talks," Beijing launched two slogans that called for Mao's ideas on literature and art to be both "upheld" and "developed." "Upholding" signals "no change," whereas "developing" denotes changes. For a clear view of Beijing's stand, as well as its rationalization, it is necessary to probe into the present situation while at the same time examining Mao's policy.

### Mao's Policy on Literature and Art

Notwithstanding his occasional versifying endeavors, Mao Tse-tung was by no means an adherent of the Chinese poetic tradition; nor did he have a theory of literature and art of his own. The theory of party-mindedness in proletarian literature was actually first set out by Marx and then developed by Lenin and Stalin.

As far back as 1845, Marx and Engels stressed party-mindedness in literature and art, and said that it should take the form of class struggle in order to defend the interests of the Communist Party. In their debate with Heinzen, they derided the belief that the interest of the whole of humanity could be above that of one's class. The task of a party press, Engels pointed out, is "to debate, first and foremost, to explain, to expound, to defend the party's demands, to rebut and refute the claims and assertions of the opposing party."[1] These words were later echoed by Mao. However, while Marx and

Engels, as theorists, opposed official censorship and defended freedom of speech, Mao seized power over the party, the government, and the military and used literary censorship to consolidate his regime. The differences between Marx and Mao mirror those existing between the theorists and those in power.

As Lenin, the professional revolutionary, became the most prominent interpreter of Marxism, he tended to stress the practical application of literature and art in advancing revolution.[2] After the general political strike of October 1905, Lenin published "Party Organization and Party Literature," which asserted that literature must "become part of the common cause of the proletariat, 'a cog and a screw' of one single great Social-Democratic mechanism." Thus he shouted, "Down with non-partisan writers! Down with literary supermen!" In the article, he admitted that "literature is least of all subject to mechanical adjustment or levelling, to the rule of the majority over the minority," and that "in this field greater scope must undoubtedly be allowed for personal initiative, individual inclination, thought and fantasy, form and content." Yet he insisted that writers "must become members of party organizations," and that "newspapers must become the organs of the various party organizations, and publishing and distributing centers, bookshops and reading-rooms, libraries and similar establishments—must all be under party control."[3] Hence, there is the concept of "party literature" which covers not only literary works, but any publications. Lenin's regimentation of literature and art was later continued and increased by Stalin and Mao Tse-tung.

In short, from Lenin to Mao, in addition to a general interaction with politics, the political function of the arts was assumed to work through the political party.[4] This assumption also became the basis of the Chinese Communists' insistence on their leadership over literature and art. However, owing to Lenin's death soon after seizing power, it was left to Stalin to launch the darkest period in the history of Russian literature. In October 1932, Stalin first used the term "socialist realism." In October 1934, the first congress of the Union of Soviet Writers agreed to the pact drafted by Stalin's right-hand man A. A. Zhdanov that established "socialist realism" as the basic guide for works of literature and criticism and called for the ideological remaking and reeducating of workers in the spirit of socialism and the cultivation of new writers from the ranks of factory workers, peasants on collective farms, and soldiers of the Red Army.[5] In addition, Zhdanov stressed that the main and model characters in Soviet literature were laborers, peasants, party members, staff workers in economics, engineers, and youth and children's league members.[6] All this was borrowed by Mao Tse-tung in Yenan when he advocated worker-peasant-soldier literature. He consolidated his power by means of "socialist realism," just as Stalin used it as the sole standard in literature and criticism to castigate all dissenters.

In May 1942, at the Yenan Forum on Literature and Art, Mao Tse-tung declared that literature and art should "fit well into the whole revolutionary machine as a component part," and "operate as powerful weapons for uniting and educating the people and for attacking and destroying the enemy." To achieve this objective, he said, the following five points must be attended to. First, the class stand must be that of the proletariat and the masses. For members of the Communist Party, this means adhering to the stand, the spirit, and the policy of the party. Second, it was the task of revolutionary writers and artists to expose and defeat the enemy, while an attitude of alliance and criticism should be adopted with allies. Writers should always praise the masses. Third, the audience for works of literature and art should consist of workers, peasants, soldiers, and revolutionary cadres. Fourth, writers and artists should first remold their thoughts and feelings so that they can understand workers, peasants, and soldiers and be accepted by them. Finally, writers and artists should study Marxism-Leninism and society.[7]

From then on, Mao began to assign various tasks for his "cultural army" and set out taboos for writers. Literature and art have always been used by the Chinese Communists as weapons for political struggle. In the 1930s, after setting up his headquarters in Yenan, Mao put great emphasis on these things in order to ensure the Communists' survival and expansion. Now, with this further step toward dogmatization and politicization, he ended an era of free writing. Mao himself declared that the view that "this is still the period of the satirical essay, and Lu Hsün's style of writing is still needed"[8] was not applicable within the Communist-held areas. Thus he established the Lu Hsün Academy of Literature and Arts, but made Chou Yang, Lu Hsün's enemy, its president. While mouthing praise for Lu Hsün, he was trying to suffocate his followers' spirit of opposition.

Mao's "Talks" reveal another scheme characteristic of the Chinese Communists; namely, they pin labels on people and then turn to the strategy of alliance and struggle, following the principle of "using contradictions to win over the majority, to oppose the minority and then defeat them individually." Because 90 percent of the total population of China at that time were either workers, peasants, soldiers, or urban petty bourgeoisie, Mao, ignoring Marx's criticism and exclusion of the peasants, followed Stalin in advocating that literature and art should serve these four kinds of people. The writers of the 1930s who searched for individualism and freedom and whom Mao made great efforts to attract to Yenan were members of the urban petty bourgeoisie. It was at these people's complaints that the threats and cajolery in his "Talks" were directed.

Repeating Lenin's words, Mao asserted that literature and art are "a cog and a screw" in the machine of the proletariat, that they have a definite and assigned position and therefore are without freedom. They should be subordinate to politics and should create contradictions and struggle. "There is," he said, "in fact no such thing as art for art's sake, art that stands above classes or art that is detached from or independent of politics."[9] Thus to do battle against these things, which according to him did not exist, Mao initiated numerous political campaigns at the cost of thousands of lives, to say nothing of the suffocation of numberless talents.

By publishing these "Talks" Mao hoped to get his writers to close ranks and open fire on his opponents. The main target at the Yenan Forum; Wang Shih-wei, who had translated about 2 million words of Marxist-Leninist writings into Chinese, was soon thrown into jail for his well-intentioned criticism. On January 31, 1962, at the Enlarged Work Conference of the Central Committee of the Chinese Communist Party (CCP), Mao himself revealed that Wang had been killed, "There was also Wang Shih-wei, a hidden spy of the Kuomintang, who published the article entitled 'The Wild Lily' to attack revolution and degrade communism. Later we put him in jail and executed him."[10] When he was attacked, Wang requested that he be allowed to withdraw from the party, as he himself put it, "There is hardly any way out of the conflict between the party and myself,"[11] a statement which indeed was a protest against Mao's utilitarian view of literature and art at the forum.

For a score of years thereafter, the Chinese Communists adhered to Mao's instructions at the Yenan Forum, and drew up various regulations to ensure the full loyalty of writers. As Hu Feng complained, "This rigid rule over literature means that even a cough from us will be recorded and checked."[12] His friend Chang Chung-hsiao also openly voiced his criticisms, "The 'Talks' might have worked for the Yenan period. Now, I don't think they would. In the current situation, they would only bring about a slaughter. No wonder some literary hacks worship them as a totem."[13] Such criticism provoked Mao himself to lead a campaign against Hu Feng's group. Hu Feng's tragedy was brought about by his freedom of thought and Chou Yang's personal vindictiveness. Of course, the latter owed his long period in power to his skill in catering to Mao's tastes. Nevertheless, despite his obedience, even he could not survive the Cultural Revolution. Mao was apparently more at ease with Chiang Ch'ing, Chang Ch'un-ch'iao, and Yao Wen-yüan. Since the Cultural Revolution was intended to destroy all ideas opposed to those of Mao, Chiang Ch'ing's line on literature and art naturally met his requirements.

It has been reasoned that Mao was not to blame for the catastrophe, but that in his dotage, he was used by the "Gang of Four." But his talks at Yenan in fact contained a foreboding of the inevitability of the campaign. Inasmuch as Mao Tse-tung set limits on literature and art according to the Soviet model, he naturally would regard ideas different from his own as poisonous weeds. What stood in opposition to Mao's thinking was the conglomeration of bourgeois and modern revisionist ideas on literature and art, as well as the literature and art of the 1930s. These views are represented by theories such as those of "truthful writing," "the wide path of realism," "the deepening of realism," "middle characters," "compounding the spirit of the age," and of opposition to "subject matter as the decisive factor," opposition to "what smells of gunpowder," and "rebelling against orthodox teachings," as well as of "literature and art of the whole people," and "freedom of creation." In addition, there were Yang Han-sheng's "ten ropes" and Hu Feng's "five daggers," which all voiced opposition to the uniformity represented by the Yenan "Talks." Faced with a policy such as Mao's, and full of complaints, no wonder the writers tried to throw off the shackles.

### Teng Hsiao-p'ing's "Upholding" and "Developing" of Mao Tse-tung's Policy on Literature and Art

One month after Mao's death in September 1976, the arrest of the Gang of Four by Hua Kuo-feng symbolized the end of the Cultural Revolution. In August 1977, the Eleventh National Congress of the Chinese Communist Party (CCP) formally declared it over and started the criticism of the Gang of Four. Mao's death and Chiang Ch'ing's fall brought in the Teng Hsiao-p'ing era starting in December 1978, with the opening of the Third Plenary Session of the Eleventh Central Committee of the CCP.

In order to encourage people to attack the evils of the Cultural Revolution, the Beijing regime allowed the appearance of "Democracy Wall" and encouraged "scar literature." But when this movement got out of control, no longer limiting itself to accusing the Gang of Four but rather beginning to expose the shortcomings of the communist system as a whole, the regime was worried, reneged on its promises, and began a counterattack. At the Fourth Congress of Chinese Writers and Artists in October 1979, parts of Teng's speech bore a remarkable similarity to what the Gang of Four had said, "We must adhere to the principle put foward by Comrade Mao Tse-tung—that literature and art should serve the broadest masses and, first of all, the workers, peasants and soldiers."[14] At the same congress, Chou Yang also expressed his disapproval of the naturalistic, detailed depiction of the dark side of communist society lest it should arouse negative thoughts and emotions. Obviously, the regime had no intention of endorsing "scar literature"; its approval of it was merely a temporary adaptation to the mood of the time.

Thus, as expected, Sha Yeh-hsin's film script *Chia-ju wo shih chen-te* (What If I Really Were?) was banned right after Hu Yao-pang, Teng's protégé, had reiterated at a February 1980 forum on script writing that literature and art should reflect Marxism-Leninism and Mao's thought and criticized the script. February and March 1982 saw the issuance of Central Committee documents No. 7 and No. 8. The former instructed writers, under the guidance of Marxism-Leninism and Mao's thought, to criticize works that advocate erroneous ideas. In the meantime, they should follow the leadership of the party, unconditionally uphold political uniformity, and not publish anything that runs counter to the Central Committee's line, principles, and policies. The latter empowered high-ranking cadres to arrest advocates of democracy and ban underground publications, and instructed them not to be softhearted toward people who oppose the party and socialism. These documents marked the end of "scar literature."

Starting from April 1981, Pai Hua's script *K'u lien* (Unrequited Love) was the target of a series of attacks, first from the *Liberation Army Daily*, later joined by the *People's Daily, Beijing Daily*, Shanghai's *Liberation Daily*, and the Central Committee organ, *Red Flag*. On July 17, Teng Hsiao-p'ing himself gave the indictment: "I have seen the movie 'Sun and Man,' which follows the script of 'Unrequited Love.' Whatever the author's motives, the movie gives the impression that the Communist Party and the socialist system are bad. It vilifies the latter to such an extent that one wonders what had happened to the author's Party spirit."[15] Finally, on August 3, at an ideological forum, Hu Yao-pang gave Pai Hua the signal that he should undertake self-criticism by echoing the *Liberation Army Daily*'s opinion that *Unrequited Love* was not an isolated case, that many works deviated from the socialist track and from the Communist leadership and engaged in bourgeois liberalization, and that "there should be a serious criticism of this erroneous tendency before it spreads."[16] Consequently, in September, Pai Hua presented a written self-criticism, which, however, did not gain official approval. In October, after Teng Hsiao-p'ing had ordered an article criticizing the script to be published in *Wen-i Pao* (Literary Gazette) and then reprinted in the *People's Daily*, he at last admitted his faults openly and expressed his gratitude for the criticism. This incident reminds us of the Movement of Handing in Hearts directed by Mao Tse-tung in the 1950s—an example of the Communists' method of "destroying the spirit instead of killing the man."

Furthermore, in May 1982, when the regime was advocating "upholding and developing" Mao's thought on the fortieth anniversary of the Yenan "Talks," it asked writers to hold to the "Four Cardinal Principles," guard against the tendency toward bourgeois liberalization in literature and art, bravely sing the praises of new persons, new things, and new ideas, and go deep into the struggles of the masses. In June, the second plenary session of the Fourth National Committee of the China Federation of Literary and Art Circles passed the "Literary and Art Workers' Pact" in which writers were asked to study Marxism-Leninism and Mao's thought. Even after Mao's death, writers in mainland China have not enjoyed real liberty.

With regard to "upholding," emphasis is placed on Mao's idea, expressed in the "Talks" and other writings, of literature and art serving primarily workers, peasants and soldiers. This principle has always served and will always serve as the guiding light for Chinese Communist policy on literature and art. On the other hand, "serving the people and socialism" is a "development" of this idea. Chou Yang, although now admitting the erroneousness of regarding literature as subordinate to politics, still asserts that there is a relationship between them and denies that they can be detached from each other:

> Since the Third Plenary Session of the CCP's 11th Central Committee, the mainstream of literature and art has been good and should be affirmed; nevertheless, there are mistakes and some other tendencies. The one that should not be neglected is the tendency toward bourgeois liberalization on the ideological front as a result of the policy of opening up to the outside world and revitalizing the national economy. As far as literature and art serving socialism is concerned, this tendency ought to be opposed.[17]

Chou Yang, handcuffed and held in solitary confinement for nine years during the Cultural Revolution, is now, since his rehabilitation, regarded as a mouthpiece of the current regime.

It is clear that Teng Hsiao-p'ing's intention in developing Mao's ideas on literature and art is not to free them from their political shackles. It is important to remember that for the Communists, the terms "people" and "socialism" bear different definitions from those usually accepted in the noncommunist world. For instance, in the "Common Program of the Chinese People's Political Consultative Conference" "the people" refers to the "working class, the peasantry, the petty bourgeoisie, the national bourgeoisie, and certain patriotic democratic elements of the reactionary class who have repented their mistake."[18] Here, their definition of "the people" is broadened by the demands of the "united front," but it still does not include all citizens. As for socialism, it is regarded as a necessary stage on the road to communism. The two terms originally had important legal and economic meanings. Now, to serve their own ends, the Chinese Communists have transferred them into politics. In other words, when they insist that "literature and art are serving the people and socialism," they mean that they are "serving the party." The Chinese Communists should admit this, and by so doing explain why asking writers to stick to the "Four Cardinal Principles" does not contradict the principle of "serve the people." The core of the Four Cardinal Principles is insistence on the leadership of the Communist Party.

So, when the Chinese Communists began a new rectification movement in 1983, it came as no surprise. In October, at the Second Plenary Session of the CCP's Twelfth Central Committee, Teng Hsiao-p'ing raised the issue of eliminating spiritual pollution on the ideological and cultural front and formally started a rectification of the fields of theory and literature and art. In the process, two factors have been singled out to shoulder the blame for the ideological pollution of recent years: remnant feudal influences and the corrosion of capitalism. The latter is especially feared, and this fear betrays the ineffectiveness of previous warnings to writers and exposes the extent of outside influence on mainland China's writers. During the campaign, as a manifestation of their support for the regime, its loyal literary officers have one by one joined the parade of criticism and self-criticism. Hence, Pai Hua's *Wu wang chin-ko Yüeh wang chien* (The Story of King Kou-chien) and Hsü Ching-ya's *Chüeh-ch'i te shih-ch'ün* (Poems of the Uprising) both encountered attacks. Pai Hua's historical script was accused of running counter to the spirit of socialism. At the same time, his *Unrequited Love* was again attacked for its depiction of human alienation and the Communists' suppression and destruction of human nature, and, like Chang Hsiao-t'ien's *Li-li yuan-shang-ts'ao* (The Thriving Grasses on the Prairie), its vilification of the socialist system. Given that *Unrequited Love* started the wave of alienation in mainland China's literature, and that its insinuation that Mao was the cause of the tragedy contradicted Teng Hsiao-p'ing's reiteration that "Mao Tse-tung's merits were primary and his mistakes secondary," Pai Hua was an obvious target in the campaign.

Be that as it may, Teng Hsiao-p'ing is facing a dilemma in that the Four Modernizations drive needs the support of intellectuals if it is to succeed, so there is a danger that the campaign against spiritual pollution might have a detrimental effect on development and even discourage the influx of foreign capital and manpower. Consequently, in mid-August 1984, *Red Flag* was stressing that, in literature and art criticism, "watering flowers" and "hoeing up weeds" should go hand in hand, since in the struggle between them, as one falls, the other rises.[19] *Red Flag* also said that it was necessary to follow the "principle of the three nots"—not pinning on labels, not beating with clubs, and not grabbing by the pigtails. However, this principle and that of "letting a hundred flowers bloom and a hundred schools of thought contend"—are both identified with Mao Tse-tung and stir up unpleasant memories. By digging up these slogans again in an effort to deceive its writers, the Beijing regime betrays the meagerness of the content of its theoretical journal and arouses suspicion as to its sincerity.

Speculation had been aroused by the absence of Hu Ch'iao-mu and Teng Li-ch'ün from the Fourth Congress of the Chinese Writers' Association, held from December 29, 1984 to January 5, 1985. It is true that there were some speeches at the opening session on freedom in literary creation, and at the closing session such phrases as "fully observing the objective laws governing art and literature, carrying forward democracy in them, and assuring freedom of creation" were included in the association's new constitution, which did indeed rekindle hope among writers. But written words alone cannot guarantee anything. In his speech to the Fourth Congress of Chinese Writers and Artists, Teng Hsiao-p'ing had adopted a similar turn of phrase:

> In the production of literature and arts, which involves complex mental labour, it is essential that writers and artists follow their own creative spirit. What subjects they should choose for their creative work and how they should deal with those subjects are questions that writers and artists themselves must examine and gradually resolve through practice. There should be no arbitrary meddling in this process.[20]

While these words were still echoing in our ears, however, Teng began the criticism of *Unrequited Love* and started calling for the elimination of "spiritual pollution." The applause of the assembled writers was soon to be betrayed by Teng; and this time the applause again proved to be premature.

On the first day of the Fourth Congress of the Chinese Writers' Association, the *People's Daily* published a commentary which, besides reasserting the principle of the "three nots," again mentioned the necessity of "resisting corrosion by decadent bourgeois ideology and the evil legacy of feudalist thought,"[21] phrases used in the campaign to eliminate spiritual pollution. At the congress, Hu Ch'i-li quoted Stalin's words, "Writers are engineers of the souls of the human race." This was not so much a compliment as an instruction to writers. Communists believe that in order to remold the world, the human mind should be remodeled first. Since writers are to be given this task, they should be the first to be brainwashed. To appease the writers, Hu Ch'i-li admitted the shortcomings in the party's leadership over literature and art:

> First of all, the Party was affected by "leftist" tendencies in exercising its leadership over literary and art work. For a long time, there had been too much interference, the practice of pinning labels on writers and administrative orders. Second, some cadres the Party sent to the literary and art departments and units did not quite understand the profession . . . ; and this affected the Party's relationship with writers and literary and art workers. Third, the relationships among literary and art workers, among writers, including Party members and non-members, and between different regions are abnormal. They are oversensitive, argumentative, and overcriticial of each other.

Yet Hu's solution to the problem was that the "Party's leadership over literary work must be improved and strengthened,"[22] which indicates that the Beijing regime has no intention of relaxing its grip on the literary profession, nor of paying any heed to the old actor Chao Tan's warning, "With too much interference, the arts have no hope." Hu Ch'i-li was actually contradicting himself when he, on the one hand, conceded the shortcomings of too much interference and on the other demanded that the party's leadership be strengthened.

Hu Ch'i-li's assertion that "on the whole, our Party's leadership over literary and artwork has been good" and his quote from Lenin that socialist literature is "a really free literature" were also contradictions of historical fact. From Wang Shih-wei's execution to Pai Hua's forced self-criticism, the sufferings and nightmares of the mainland's writers all prove that the Chinese Communist Party's leadership over literature and art has, on the whole, been pretty bad. It is Leninism that should take the blame for this. But Hu Ch'i-li's prescription for leading writers on to genuine creative freedom is a rejection of "the pernicious influence of decadent capitalist thinking and feudalism." This kind of official instruction is by no means promising. Moreover, the newly adopted constitution still calls for the party's leadership and the guidance of Marxism-Leninism and Mao's thought. The appearance of this in the same article with words like "guaranteeing freedom of creation" once more exposes the regime's contradictions and traps. Is this the so-called really free literature? On what else can the mainland's writers pin their hopes?

At the Writers' Association work meeting, held from October 31 to November 4, 1985, Wang Meng, now Teng Hsiao-p'ing's blue-eyed boy, added a footnote to Hu Ch'i-li's speech at the Fourth Congress by pointing out that the "creative freedom" granted by the regime is accompanied by several "demands": "Writers should study Marxist theory, foster a scientific, progressive, and revolutionary world outlook, live a life of arduous struggle, and understand the fundamental interests of the Party's cause,"[23] and so on. It was in accordance with these demands that Liu Pin-yen's *Ti-erh-chung chung-ch'eng* (The Second Kind of Loyalty) and *Wo-te jih-chi* (My Diary) and the film *WM*, scripted by Wang P'ei-kung and directed by Wang

Kuei, were subsequently banned. Evidently, under the Teng regime, writers and artists are still not free from fear, and those who are unwilling to comply with the regime face no other choice but to lay down their pens.

## Conclusion

More than ten years have passed since Mao's death, but his shadow still hangs over the Beijing regime's policy on literature and art and has its effect on writers.

There is no doubt about the fact that Mao Tse-tung takes the role of the Chinese Communists' Lenin and Stalin, and it is for this reason that they cannot discard Mao entirely as their Soviet counterparts did with Stalin. Praise for Mao and his ideas appeared several times in Teng's speech to the Fourth Congress of Chinese Writers and Artists, which is now regarded as having laid down the guidelines for literature and art in mainland China. In Teng's *Selected Works*, published in July 1983, Mao's name is mentioned as many as 521 times,[24] mostly in order to praise him. Teng's utterances and measures concerning literature and art prove that he himself cannot get rid of Mao's shadow.

In fact, Teng has never had the least intention of freeing himself totally from the shackles of Maoism. Communism is an ideology, and the attractive part of ideology is literature and art. Napoleon even went into battle with a copy of Goethe's *Sorrows of Young Werther*. Even before the Chinese Communists established their base in Yenan, they had gained the whip hand in the field of literature and art. Mao was indebted to the writers of the 1930s for their help in communizing mainland China, and Teng follows in his footsteps when he resorts to threats and cajolery. Today, just as in the Mao era, writers have to pass through a series of examinations before their works are published. As the Chinese saying goes, "Freedom of creation produces inspiration whereas its absence produces a block." It is wishful thinking to expect inspiration with a socialist freedom of creation that hinges on the Four Cardinal Principles.

Politics is an art that emphasizes the middle way. But to the Communists, art is a part of politics and hence there is a policy for it. As far back as the eve of the 1930s, Liang Shih-ch'iu, in his debate with Lu Hsün, drew attention to the absurdity of pinning a policy on literature and art. Behind the Soviets' policy, he reasoned, lay only two petty intentions: One is autocracy, to strip writers of their freedom of thought through political means; the other is stupidity, to make literature and art uniform through political means.[25] This conclusion holds for both the Soviets and the Chinese Communists, since the latter adopted their policy on literature and art from the former. There is a Chinese saying that a bird is startled by the mere twang of a bowstring. Mainland China's writers are trying to get rid of the "bowstring," which is the regime's policy on literature and art. For a long period of time it has been held taut by the Chinese Communist leaders and their literary cadres, who although they may sometimes relax their grip would never lay down the bow. The people who pin their hopes for literature and art or even politics on Teng Hsiao-p'ing are doomed to be disillusioned; they forget one thing: Teng is a Communist in power.

We should remember, however, that Teng Hsiao-p'ing himself suffered during the Cultural Revolution. With this painful experience in mind, he is unlikely to start a similar movement, nor is he likely to encourage a situation where, in the words of Hu Feng, "heads roll with every breath of wind." Besides, any such wind would definitely be detrimental to the Four Modernizations. Thus Teng has not gone as far as executing writers, as Mao did. Still, the demand that art and literature should serve the party and that writers should be kept under control, as well as the empty promise of creative freedom, are the unchanging elements of Chinese Communist policy on literature and art. Therefore, despite Teng's reassertion of Mao's promise, it is hard to imagine that a garden in which a hundred flowers bloom with flourish on the mainland in the near future.

## Notes

1. F. Engels, "The Communists and Karl Heinzen," in Karl Marx and Frederick Engels, *Collected Works*, vol. 6 (Moscow: Progress Publishers, 1976), 294.

2. Ch'en Kuan-chung, "Reevaluation of Marxist Theory on Literature," *Ming-pao yueh-k'an* (Ming Pao Monthly) (Hong Kong), no. 173 (May 1980): 39.

3. V. I. Lenin, "Party Organization and Party Literature," in *Collected Works*, vol. 10 (Moscow: Foreign Languages Publishing House, 1962), 45–46.

4. Huang Chi-ch'ih, "A General Review of Mao Tse-tung's Thoughts on Literature and Art," *Ming-pao yueh-k'an*, no. 180 (December 1980): 38.

5. Ts'ao Pao-hua, ed., *Ma-k'e-ssu, en-ke-ssu, shih-ta-lin lun wen-i* (Marx, Engels, Lenin and Stalin on Literature and Art) (Beijing: People's Literature Press, 1953), 247.

6. Pao Ch'üan and Liang Hsiang, trans., *Lun wen-hsüeh, i-shu yü che-hsüeh chu wen-t'i* (On several problems concerning literature, art and philosophy) by A. A. Zhdanov (Shanghai: Shanghai Times Publishing House, 1949), 24.

7. Mao Tse-tung, "Talks at the Yenan Forum on Literature and Art," in *Selected Works*, vol. 3 (Beijing: Foreign Languages Press, 1965), 70–73.

8. Ibid., 92.

9. Ibid., 86.

10. Mao Tse-tung, "Talk at the Enlarged Work Conference of the CCP Central Committee," in *Mao Tse-tung ssu-hsiang wan-sui* (Long live Mao Tse-tung thought), vol. 1 (n.p., 1969; reprint, Taipei: Institute of International Relations, 1974), 421.

11. Chao Ts'ung, *Hsin wen-hsüeh tso-chia lieh-chuan* (The lives of new literature writers) (Taipei: Sunday Times Publishing Company, 1970), 30.

12. Hu Feng to Lu Ling, January 12, 1950, "The Second Collection of Material on the Hu Feng Antiparty Clique," *People's Daily*, May 24, 1955.

13. Chang Chung-hsiao to Hu Feng, August 22, 1951, "The Third Collection of Material on the Hu Feng Antiparty Clique," *People's Daily*, June 10, 1955.

14. Teng Hsiao-p'ing, "Speech Greeting the Fourth Congress of Chinese Writers and Artists," in *Selected Works (1975–1982)* (Beijing: Foreign Languages Press, 1984), 203.

15. "Concerning Problems on the Ideological Front," in *Selected Works (1975–1982)* (Beijing: Foreign Languages Press, 1984), 368.

16. Hu Yao-pang, "Speech at the Forum on Problems Concerning the Ideological Front," in *San-chung ch'üan-hui i-lai chung-yao wen-hsien hsüan-pien* (Selection of important documents since the Third Plenary Session of the Eleventh CCP Central Committee), vol. 2 (Beijing: People's Press, 1982), 898.

17. Chou Yang, "First, Upholding and Second, Development," *People's Daily*, June 23, 1982.

18. See *Tseng-ting chung-kung shu-yü hui-chieh* (Collections of Chinese Communist Terminology), 3rd ed. (Taipei: China Publishing Company, 1977), 22.

19. Kao Chan-hsiang, "Initiate a New Style of Literature and Art Criticism," *Red Flag*, 1984, no. 16: 15.

20. Teng, "Speech Greeting the Fourth Congress of Chinese Writers and Artists," 206.

21. Commentator, "Great Drive, Great Unity, Great Prosperity—Hailing the Convening of the Fourth Congress of the Chinese Writers' Association," *People's Daily*, December 29, 1984.

22. Hu Ch'i-li, "The Congratulatory Speech at the Fourth Congress of the Chinese Writers' Association," *People's Daily*, December 30, 1984.

23. "At the China Writers' Association Work Meeting Wang Meng Said It Is Imperative to Stress Writers' Social Responsibility While Upholding Freedom of Creation," *People's Daily*, November 6, 1985.

24. Hsing Kuo-ch'iang, "On the *Selected Works of Teng Hsiao-p'ing*," *Fei-ch'ing yüeh-pao* (Chinese Communist Affairs Monthly) (Taipei), 26, no. 2 (August 1983): 7.

25. Liang Shih-ch'iu, "The People for the So-called Policy on Literature and Art" in *P'ien-chien chi* (The Collections on Prejudice) (Taipei: Ta-lin Bookstore, 1969), 57.

# 38

## Liu Pin-yen: The Politics of Reportage Literature in Mainland China

*Jenny Tu-li Teng*

Liu Pin-yen is the most daring, the most penetrating, and also one of the most celebrated writers in mainland China today. He has created a tremendous stir both at home and overseas. There has been great concern for his well-being among people interested in modern mainland literature because it reflects the literary "climate" in mainland China.

Liu is the author of two important works of reportage literature, "People or Monsters," which depicts corrupt practices, and "Another Kind of Allegiance," which describes the misfortunes of two young men who admonish Chairman Mao. In addition to about forty works of reportage literature, he has also written in other genres such as fiction and the essay form.

Liu inherited the Confucian pragmatic and ideological attitude that aims to indoctrinate and intimidate both the ruler and the masses through literature. Though Western writers generally do not want to preach, moralize, or convey a message, Chinese literature has certainly outstripped this point of view as may be observed in the works of many prominent writers of the past as well as those of contemporary writers such as Liu Pin-yen. On the other hand, the ruling authorities in China, being the target of such criticism, have always been very sensitive to literature and have often considered writers to be one of the most problematic groups to exercise control over.

During the four decades of Communist rule in mainland China, this tension between the government and writers has increased because of Communist China's tight control over the literati. A writer who depicts his or her real feelings toward society in a subjective way will be criticized as bourgeois and rightist, while in the West such an attitude is an inseparable part of what is considered literature.[1] Therefore, the contribution that Chinese writers offer to our understanding of contemporary China has, on the whole, been ignored by writers and therefore missed by the readers as well. Thus a study of the following three examples of reportage from successive periods should reveal not only Liu's contribution to modern Chinese literature but also the continuities and changes in Chinese literature between the early and the contemporary periods.

This chapter examines the politics of reportage literature in mainland China by analyzing three representative works of Liu Pin-yen, each of which appears at a different stage of his life, by pointing out his motives in writing these works, by touching the great sensation they caused, by indicating the social abuses he exposes, and by commenting on the literary technique he uses. As critics have agreed, literature in contemporary China should be read in its historical context.[2] Therefore, a study of Liu can be seen as an exploration of the context in which works are written. Hopefully, through the study of his works, the literary atmosphere and the current and future stance of China's writers will be better understood. Since Communist China has never clearly defined the boundaries of freedom for its writers, Liu's experience can be employed to test them.

These three particular works were chosen for discussion not only because they created a great sensation for their forthright exposure of social problems, but also because they represent three major stages both in the life of their author and in the history of China since 1949. The first work, "Our Paper's Inside Story" (henceforth abbreviated as "The Inside Story"), was written in 1956, less than ten years after the Communist takeover of mainland China and a year before the Anti-Rightist Campaign. The author is highly visible, though disguised, as the central character. This semiautobiographical work clearly illustrates Liu's character as a rebel and an independent thinker. The second work discussed here was written in 1979, three years after the death of Mao Tse-tung and two years after Liu returned from more than twenty years of internal exile. The third, which was written in 1985 and has since caused quite a sensation, can be looked at as representing his latest work.

Most of the works Liu has written are classified as reportage literature, as are the three works discussed here. Chinese reportage literature is effectively employed to reproduce the social macrocosm rather than to explore the human microcosm. The genre emerged around the era of the May Fourth Movement (1919). Later it was advocated by members of the "Left League" who intended to use it to promote a communist revolution.[3] Mao Tse-tung's "Yenan Talks" further stimulated the development of reportage literature by claiming that writers ought to eulogize the masses of workers, farmers, and soldiers and reflect their way of life. Famous poets, dramatists, and journalists responded to Mao's call and wrote works of reportage literature.[4] In Yenan, writers were sometimes organized to write such works collectively.[5] They were often published in wall-poster form or in tabloid newspapers. Though the literary technique and the thoughts involved often varied, the themes were always the same: praise for the victory of the Communists, criticism of the Nationalist government, and hatred for the savage Japanese invaders.

According to Liu's definition, reportage falls between news reporting and pure literature.[6] Events and characters are real, not imagined, though names are usually changed except for a few major characters. The sources can be the author's own experience, as in "The Inside Story," news stories, as in "People or Monsters," or materials given directly to the author, as in "Another Kind of Allegiance." The three works chosen here happen to represent these three different sources of reportage literature. As for the subjects of reportage, according to Liu there are two: renowned people of achievement and social conflicts.[7] The former are praised for their struggle to succeed; there is no social conflict involved in this. The second kind of reportage dissects the social conflicts involved in certain events involving certain people. Obviously Liu's writings mostly deal with the second kind of subject, which seems to be what readers expect from reportage.

The flourishing of reportage in recent years can be attributed to the lack of an effective legal system in mainland China. The masses have turned to reportage authors for help in the hope that the power of public opinion can pressure the government to respond to their grievances. In his "Yenan Talks" Mao said, "Defects in society are not to be pointed out by intellectuals but are to be handled by the party alone."[8] Nevertheless, Liu contends that literature should aim to move society forward and to help solve social problems.[9] Liu's view of the writer's task is influenced both by the traditional conventions of the Chinese intelligentsia, and also by Russian authors. Liu once mentioned that his favorite author, Ivan Sergeevich Turgenev (1818–1883), often wrote on the social problems of his time. His book *Father and Son* depicted the events of 1859 and was published the same year.[10] Since the major function of reportage literature is to reflect society, content is more important than literary technique. The criteria for a good writer of reportage are, first, keen perception, second, a mission to create a better society, and last of all, technique.[11] Therefore, the major criterion is not technique, but the courage to expose social problems.[12] Thus the works of Liu Pin-yen, a writer of integrity and artistry, deserve a thorough analysis.

In the following section, the author will examine the literary "climate" which prevailed before and during the period when these works were written, the writing of the works, and finally the effects they produced, in order to give a better understanding of the context in which the works were written, the author's motives, and their consequences.

## The Context and Effect of "The Inside Story"

After the Wu Hsün (1838–1896) film incident of 1951, literary policies became more rigid and were aimed at discrediting certain writers and their supporters.[13] In 1954–1955, a year or two before Liu's "The Inside Story" was published, literary policies were tightened again, and this time the target of denunciation was Hu Feng (1903–1985), who maintained that judging literature by political standards would eventually suffocate literary creativity.[14] Nevertheless, in the spring of 1956 Mao launched the Hundred Flowers campaign, the most dramatic development since 1949. In May, a month before "The Inside Story" was published, Lu Ting-i (1904–   ), then the head of the Chinese Communist Party (CCP) Central Committee's Propaganda Department, argued that free discussion and independent thinking were necessary to avoid academic stagnation, and he also remarked that the imposition of narrow, doctrinaire restrictions on intellectual life was the "bitter enemy" of true Marxism-Leninism.[15] It is possible that "The Inside Story" was published as a response to Lu's declaration. However, only a year later in 1957, after criticism of the party had gone well beyond mere suggestions for improvement, there was a severe crackdown on intellectuals in the Anti-Rightist Campaign. Approximately 500,000 intellectuals, including Liu Pin-yen, were persecuted.[16]

According to Liu, after a sequel to "The Inside Story" was published in July or August 1957, he was criticized for his forthright exposure of social problems.[17] In January 1958, the *China Youth News* held a meeting in which Liu's works were discussed. Before the meeting, copies of Wang Shih-wei's work "Wild Lily" were distributed among the participants. Wang had been executed for his writings, and according to Liu, this meeting put enormous pressure on Liu himself. Right after he returned to Beijing in June, Liu was suspected of being antirevolutionary, and he was one of the first group within the party to be labeled as a rightist in early July. He was proscribed publicly in the newspaper, and was denounced as an ultrarightist. An article rebuking him in the *China Youth News* was several pages long. Liu was expelled from the party, and his salary droped from 150 yuan a month plus the fees he received for his published works to 20 yuan a month. The next year Liu was dispatched to work in the countryside. During these years of internal exile, he dared not make contact with anybody, fearing that they would suffer for being associated with him. Thus he suffered both psychologically and physically.

In March 1966 Liu Pin-yen was exonerated, but in May of that year he was jailed for a second time until 1977, when Teng Hsiao-p'ing was restored to his posts and the radical Gang of Four was expelled permanently from the party. One possible explanation for his abrupt release and rearrest might lie in the events of that time. In February 1966, a month before Liu was exonerated, an outline report drawn up by P'eng Chen was approved by the Politburo in Mao's absence. This report attempted to confine the debate to the academic sphere and to disassociate it from politics. This might have been the reason for Liu's exoneration. Later the same year the Central Committee issued the "May 16 Circular," drawn up by Mao, which clearly shifted the movement out of the academic sphere and into that of politics. The appearance of this circular coincided with Liu's rearrest and might have had some connection with it. Liu certainly paid in short the high price of more than twenty years of his life for "The Inside Story." Although the torture inflicted on him was certainly severe, Liu claims that it benefited him by giving him a better understanding of life in the rural areas that he would not have been able to obtain otherwise. These experiences are apparent in the second of his works discussed here.

## The Context and Effect of "People or Monsters"

"People or Monsters" reveals the corruption of society as exemplified by a fuel company manager and secretary of the party branch, Wang Shou-hsin, from Pin Hsien in Heilungkiang Province. The work was published in September 1979 in the journal *People's Literature*. "People or Monsters" caused a great sensation in literary circles as well as in society as a whole, not only because Wang stole such an enormous amount of money (500,770 yuan—equal to US$156,490), but also because of the author's courage in exploring the dark side of society. The Chinese Communist authorities considered it the most "poisonous weed" that had appeared since 1949, yet the public were very interested and enthusiastic about the work.

Liu revealed that none of the top-level party committees nor the social affairs department had ever sent people to investigate society and the party organization in Pin Hsien after the notorious corruption case. This failure to investigate had inspired Liu to explore the reasons behind the affair. His responsibilities as a writer had made him use his sharp and candid pen to expose social abuse. Liu's motive in writing this reportage can only be understood from the quotation from a big-character poster written by one of the characters in the work: "To dissect her and analyze her will urge the development of human society and social studies." Liu considers Wang's case as a social problem whose cause ought to be located so that society can be improved. He has admitted that the whole development of Wang's case reveals to us the symptom of contemporary China's malaise.[18]

This work was completed in less than one month, and the actual writing took only ten days.[19] Except for the protagonist, Wang Shou-hsin, and the second-most-important character Yang, most of the names have been changed.

For almost three decades, until a year after the death of Mao in 1976, writers wrote only of the "bright side" of Chinese socialism. Yet after the death of Mao, Teng Hsiao-p'ing's leadership sought to win the cooperation of the intellectuals by encouraging them to speak against the Gang of Four and the Cultural Revolution. In addition, economic development was emphasized rather than politics; hence, greater freedom has been accorded to the literati. During the post-Mao literary thaw of 1978–1981, the dark side of society was depicted relentlessly.[20] And in 1979, after the Beijing-Washington normalization, this relaxation of control over intellectuals reached a peak. Liu's "People or Monsters" was published in September of that year. At the Fourth National Congress of Writers and Artists convened in Beijing in October, Chou Yang, the president of the China Federation of Literary and Art Circles, encouraged artists to liberate their thinking. He also praised Liu's "People or Monsters" in his speech.[21] Teng Hsiao-p'ing also maintained that the party ought to lead art instead of controlling it, yet he did not forget to remind writers to produce works with a benign social impact. "People or Monsters" was named as one of the five best reportages in a 1979–1980 literary competition held in Beijing.[22] The September issue of *People's Literature* sold for 3 yuan a copy on the black market. The work was reprinted in seven other newspapers and was broadcast on three radio stations.[23] The University of Heilungkiang requested the *Heilungkiang Daily* to reprint the article, but the request was refused. The university then printed 20,000 copies itself. This controversial work soon attracted the attention of overseas Chinese as well as foreigners interested in contemporary Chinese literature and the situation in mainland China. The work was reprinted in Taiwan's *Central Daily News,* and an English translation of "People or Monsters" and other reportages by Liu Pin-yen was edited by UCLA Professor Perry Link and published in 1983 by Indiana University Press.

Although Liu was criticized by the few, he was praised by the many. *People's Literature* received thousands of letters after "People or Monsters" was published.[24] Liu himself received ten to fifteen letters every day after publication.[25] People even called him Liu Ch'ing-t'ien after Pao Ch'ing-t'ien (999–1063), an upright official known for his upholding of the law and appeals to reverse miscarriages of justice. Apparently this was a time of increased literary freedom. Nevertheless, after two years, in April 1981, the *Liberation Army Daily* denounced Pai Hua's screenplay *Unrequited Love,* which effectively put an end to the short literary thaw. Journals like *Shantung Literature* and the *Heilungkiang Daily* started to print articles attacking Liu Pin-yen and claiming that Liu's work had had an adverse effect on society. The CCP Central Committee's Document No. 7 proscribed a number of leading figures in the "protest literature" movement, and Liu was certainly on that list.[26] Liu's response to the sensation caused by the work is apparent in an appendix written a month after "People or Monsters" was published. The appendix appeared, together with the main text, in *Selections of Liu Pin-yen's Reportage Literature,* published in February 1981. Liu admitted that the sensation caused by the publication of "People or Monsters" had outstripped his expectations. He felt grateful for the support shown by his readers, and he believed that this gratitude and happiness would compensate for the price he had paid and would pay. He apologized for his lack of literary technique resulting from his more than twenty years of absence from normal life. He regretted also not being able to publish the sequel to "People or Monsters." Freedeom to publish is certainly more difficult to obtain than freedom to write. He also admitted that he had received some criticism. In another article, Liu revealed that the Heilungkiang Provincial Party Committee had made serious accusations against him.[27] At the end of the appendix, he stated that if he had a chance later to revise the article, he would praise the hundreds of cadres who contributed tremendously in investigating the Pin Hsien corruption case.

One can see from the foregoing that Liu is an upright man. He is not only willing to sacrifice himself for the sake of his integrity, but he is also very conscious of his literary technique. These are the reasons why his works are often more readable than other examples of reportage in terms of content and form.

## The Context and Effect of "Another Kind of Allegiance"

Liu's most recent important work, "Another Kind of Allegiance," was printed in March 1985 in the first issue of the bimonthly journal *Pioneer*, published in Beijing. Again, it caused a great stir in mainland China. Not only was the work's sequel not allowed to be published, but the publishing house itself was closed down after the first two issues.[28]

The protagonists are Ch'en Shih-chung, who had criticized Mao, and Ni Yü-hsien, who had denounced Chang Ch'un-ch'iao, who was then the vice-premier. The work depicts their courage in daring to criticize their high-ranking superiors and their subsequent sufferings. The author attempts to emphasize their loyalty in risking their lives to denounce their superiors. However, this kind of loyalty is usually not appreciated, and one may even have to give up one's freedom or one's life for it.

Over time party policy toward the literati has fluctuated between *shou* (restrictiveness) and *fang* (tolerance). In fact the party has not been able to exercise effective control over the literati since the original 1978–1981 thaw.[29] Even the action against Pai Hua remained what critics of contemporary Chinese literature consider a "pseudocampaign." Controls were relaxed again during the first half of 1985.[30] Liu's "Another Kind of Allegiance" was published in March of that year, so he was able to avoid too severe a bout of criticism. Though the work created a great sensation, as "People or Monsters" had done, the authorities did not criticize him in the papers, except for a few articles in *Wen-hsüeh pao* (Literary Gazette) and the *People's Daily*.[31] Liu had become a celebrity both at home and overseas after he published the rather daring "People or Monsters." The Chinese Communists certainly did not want to overreact without regard for the consequences. Nevertheless, Liu's freedom of expression was actually curtailed.

When "Another Kind of Allegiance" was published, the Shanghai *Wen-hui yüeh-k'an* had been carrying installments of another work by Liu, "My Diary." The editor of the journal was forced to cease publication of this work and explain that this break was a temporary consequence of Liu's going abroad. However, Liu's planned visit to West Germany was canceled six days before he was due to leave. Nonetheless, the reaction of the party toward "Another Kind of Allegiance" increased sales of the journals that carried it. The *San-wen pao* (Prose Gazette), printed in Sian, published the work on the front page and sold more than a million issues. The newspaper was later ordered to close down by the local government.[32]

It was reported that Liu had said he would give up literature. He did state that not only was he disappointed, but he actually felt hopeless. It was said that Teng Hsiao-p'ing himself had criticized Liu Pin-yen, and there was also an "internal document" ordering that he be punished in such a way as not to provoke a great movement against him.[33] Liu, however, denied that Teng had criticized him and maintained that the pressure was not from the party Central Committee. He proclaimed that officials from the central authorities had never told him formally that there were any mistakes in his work.[34] However, one wonders if there might not have been some informal accusations. Again this reportage attracted great interest overseas. Many articles on Liu Pin-yen have been published in Hong Kong, and a few in Taiwan as well. In January, one of the protagonists in "Another Kind of Allegiance," Ni Yü-hsien, went to the United States and denounced the Communist Party publicly. It seems that the sequel to "Another Kind of Allegiance" is now publicly available.

## The Reflection of Social Problems

Liu Pin-yen tries to convey his moral and political message through his description of problems that have arisen in mainland China. Therefore, before we can discuss the literary technique or the form of Liu's works, we must examine their content. Then we will have a better understanding of Liu's message as a journalist, a writer, and a sociologist, for his ultimate concern is social problems. The socialist system in mainland China has produced a bloated and overly rigid bureaucracy that is the source of various problems. In Liu's careful description of these problems one can find flashes of insight that illuminate the society of modern China more vividly than one might have expected.

### Social Problems Reflected in "The Inside Story"

The major social problems reflected in "The Inside Story" include problems in the newspaper office, problems with party members, and problems with manpower.

*Problems in the Newspaper Office.* Few reports are allowed to be published. Any articles that criticize the provincial factories or superiors are considered partial and therefore inappropriate for publication in the paper. Nonetheless, they are urged to print long and boring inside reports originally supposed to be read by a few people in a paper aimed at general readers. Government orders and propaganda are published, but interesting reports written by the journalists and the masses are left out or given limited distribution separately.

Newspapers often discuss production, yet pay little attention to social issues. They only publish articles about topics that have been discussed and decided by the central authorities. Readers' letters that reveal social evils never have a chance to be published. There is undue interference by superiors, who rigidly control the paper's content and what topics are to be written about. Liu compares this situation to that of a box that is safe and sound inside, yet is separated from the sunshine.

*Problems with Party Members.* Sectarianism was being vigorously criticized in 1956, the year in which this work was written.[35] Nonparty intellectuals were usually looked down upon by sectarian party cadres, and in a January 1956 report Chou En-lai criticized this attitude. What troubles the protagonist of "The Inside Story" most of all is the fact that she is not a party member, and this fact causes her a lot of frustration when she is covering news stories. Besides, one has to be a party member in order to attend meetings, and so have an opportunity to raise problems and have them solved. Yet recruitment is so selective that those who are really concerned with the interests of the party are usually excluded.[36] In January 1956, Chou En-lai laid down an official policy calling for easier admission to the party.[37]

Liu often complains in his reportages of the incompetence of party members resulting from this recruitment policy. Because Liu himself is a party member, he is always very much aware of the qualities of other members. According to Liu, some of the characteristics of Communists are obedience, diligence, responsibility, discipline, and apathy; yet they are unsympathetic to the suffering of the masses, and they are not concerned about the nation's future. They have lost one vital characteristic of a Communist—enthusiasm. Liu writes: "It seems that right after liberation, people lost their strong feelings of happiness, anger, sadness and gladness" (p. 73).

*Problems with Manpower.* People are not allowed to choose their own jobs; they are assigned work by the Labor Bureau. Thus a chemist has to work in a mine, and a miner has to work in a chemical factory. Again in January 1956, Chou En-lai called for more effective and suitable employment for people with specialized skills. In addition, too frequent political meetings in factories result in a waste of manpower. In the factory the protagonist goes to visit, the employees have to get up at 2 o'clock in the morning, walk a long way to the factory, and attend two meetings before they start work at 6 o'clock; they get off at 3 P.M., attend another meeting until 6 or 7 o'clock, and then walk back home. When they get home, it is past 9 o'clock. Altogether they get only four hours sleep. Yet according to the employees, they would rather work than attend the meetings, because everybody who attended meetings was forced to speak. The Communists call this the "mass line," which the party needs in order to communicate with the masses. This frequency of meetings is reflected in a popular and cynical phrase, "Documents [as high as] a mountain, meetings [as endless as] the ocean" (*wen-shan hui-hai*).

## Social Problems Reflected in "People or Monsters"

In "People or Monsters," Liu attempts to explore the social problems behind corruption. He claims at the end of this work that even though Wang was arrested, the social conditions which gave rise to her corruption have not been changed. The major areas of social injustice and abuses depicted in this work are analyzed as follows:

*Competence of Party Members.* Competence is something about which Liu, as a party member himself, is very concerned. Again in this work he criticizes the injustice shown in admitting people to the party. People who aim to improve society are usually refused admittance and therefore have no chance of getting into any position where they can put their ideas into practice. Yet less competent people are usually accepted into the Communist Party. With special permission from the official, Yang, Wang Shou-hsin joins the party, and membership further allows her to obtain other important positions and power. Liu exclaims that the ten people who were jailed for their involvement in the corruption case were all Communists.

*Graft.* Graft becomes a habit. Liu attributes the cause of Wang's corruption to a general decline in society's moral standards. The masses gradually come to accept illegal activities as if they were legal. For example, bribery is employed so frequently that it becomes a habit. People have therefore become used to it and are unaware that it is illegal. Liu cynically describes the scale of and the demands for bribes which eventually lead Wang to construct fish ponds, pigsties, and vegetable fields in order to provide her superiors with food that is not adequately supplied in the market. In addition, she establishes a center for "educated youths" to accommodate her superiors' children, thus solving the problems which concern them most—their children's education and employment.[38] As the demands for bribes increase, she begins to conspire with the accountant in the coal company to steal money from the company, which finally costs her her life.

*Gap between Rich and Poor.* Liu writes: "Farmers feed on substitute food made from flour sifted from the scraps of *tso*[39] leaves, corn leaves, and corn cobs, while the children of the secretary of the district committee play by throwing steamed dumplings made with white flour at a dog. So the discrepancy between rich and poor is certainly not confined to capitalist countries; it is found in socialist countries as well."

*Yes-men.* Meek officials are afraid to offend other people. Some of the officials realize that Wang is corrupt, yet they are too polite to accuse her. Liu exclaims that officials are afraid to offend some people, but are nevertheless not afraid to offend the "people"—the "masters" of the "People's Republic of China."

## Social Problems Reflected in "Another Kind of Allegiance"

1. *Humanism is ignored; human life is treated like grass:* The protagonist tells the author about a case of injustice he experienced in prison. A criminal who walked across a boundary by mistake was shot and left to die. The author then exclaims: "In those ten years [of the Cultural Revolution] the death of a single human being hardly meant anything at all."
2. *Flaws in the cadre system:* The cadre system is based on lifelong tenure. Once appointed, a cadre can stay in his position until he retires or dies. For this reason, many talented cadres are deprived of opportunities for promotion and of fulfilling their ambitions. This problem is experienced and delineated by Ch'en, another protagonist in this work.
3. *Worship of superiors:* Dissidence is not allowed. People who dare to criticize the government suffer severe penalties. As a consequence, officials who want to improve society by admonishing the government become estranged and alienated. Therefore, the author calls for people of "Another Kind of Allegiance," people who will risk their lives to

admonish their superiors in order to weed out mismanagement, corruption, and poverty.

Ch'en has studied in the Soviet Union and graduated with honors. Yet when he comes back to China and observes the destruction brought about by "leftist" policies, he is so disappointed that he writes a letter to Chairman Mao in May 1963. Two months later he is jailed for breaking into the Soviet embassy. In jail, he writes another letter to Chairman Mao entitled "Admonishing the Party." In this letter he points out that the most dangerous and horrible thing about the central government is that they still do not realize what a serious mistake they have committed—that is, because of their deification of and blind belief in Chairman Mao. Mao does not allow any dissidence; sooner or later, leaders such as Liu Shao-ch'i, Chou En-lai, Teng Hsiao-p'ing, Chu Te, and Lin Piao will all be castigated as antiparty and antirevolutionary.[40] According to Ch'en, Mao is mistaken in demanding that the masses follow Lei Feng, whose famous slogan was "Whatever Chairman Mao says, I will do exactly that."[41] Ch'en accuses Mao of asking the masses to believe blindly. He implores, "Dearest Chairman Mao, please repent before it is too late." He further states, "After you finish reading this letter, in fury, there is great possibility that you will order my execution. In the forty-two-year history of the Chinese Communist Party, examples of this kind have certainly not been few." Ch'en is sentenced to eight years.

Ni Yü-hsien, another protagonist, joins the army after high school and saves up to buy a whole collection of works by Marx, Lenin, Stalin, and Mao. He finds that their principles conflict with the facts of Chinese society. He has personally seen the destruction of agriculture through the implementation of ultraleftist policies. At the age of 18, he writes a letter to Chairman Mao in which he maintains that it was man rather than natural disasters that caused the destruction, and he goes on to suggest many agricultural reforms. The letter is returned to the Shanghai garrison three months later, and Ni is discharged from military service. He later enters the pelagic department of the Shanghai College of Marine Transportation. During the Cultural Revolution, he puts up posters attacking Chang Ch'un-ch'iao and Yao Wen-yuan who suppressed the student movement. He even publishes privately 10,000 copies of Lenin's lectures so that people can see how they contrast with those of Chairman Mao. As a consequence, Ni is expelled from the college. Yet he still keeps on putting up his posters against the government. He even suggests that Teng Hsiao-p'ing should return to power. In September 1977, a month after Teng was restored to his posts following the fall of the Gang of Four, Ni is sentenced to death. A last-minute letter of appeal to Yeh Chien-ying written when he is on death row leads to a postponement of his execution. He is released in January 1979.

Liu's narrative techniques have rarely been studied, although his mastery of the written word and reportage literature has often been praised. Analysis of the narrative elements of Liu's works, however, reveals their basic artistic principles and structural unity.

## Literary Technique of "The Inside Story"

"The Inside Story" is narrated in the realist style; therefore, an analysis of its technique should lead to a better understanding of the story's auto-biographical elements and to a more substantial formulation of its ideological message. In this work, Liu does not pay much attention to technique. Instead, he emphasizes sincerity and florid emotionalism. The language used is plain and candid, yet not very acrimonious.

Instead of extolling the "bright future" of Chinese socialism and the heroic exploits of the Chinese, this work delves to the very roots of social problems. Therefore, the characters are ordinary people who can make mistakes, rather than the perfect heroes of most other literary works advocated by the Communists.

The plot is not well planned. Either the author has not paid much attention to the plot, or he does not even consider it to be essential, since the story is taken directly from real life. Once the author finished with the protagonist, he finishes the story, even though a few minor characters are introduced at the very end. Strictly speaking, "The Inside Story" is not comparable to Liu's other works written twenty years later, which are much more so-phisticated in both content and technique.[42] Nonetheless, readers can sense the sincerity of his work, which certainly makes it more objective and therefore more readable than other works written for propaganda purposes.

## Literary Technique of "People or Monsters"

The language employed in the work "People or Monsters" is lively and natural, and it has a sense of intimacy and familiarity. Slang is employed and explained in the notes. The vivid language of the dialogue complements the lively descriptions of characters, while the use of earthy and picturesque metaphors adds to the sarcastic effect. For example, Liu says, "In the soil of poverty and underdevelopment, the blossom of power blooms with extraordinary vigor; aromatic and attractive"; "Once the surge of the Cultural Revolution came, it aroused Wang's desires; the political aggressiveness which had slumbered for years suddenly raged"; "Wang Shou-hsin is an affectionate woman capable of strong feelings of both love and hatred. Ten thousand tons of coal and nine trucks; in her hand is her pen and ink, which she uses daily to compose lyrics" (p. 113).

Sometimes Liu achieves very persuasive effects by piling up words one on top of the other, such as, "She pats you, pulls you, drags you, and hauls you viciously without an end" (p. 116). Contrast is used in key phrases of philosophical perception, such as, "The Communist Party regulated every-thing, but did not regulate the Communist Party" (p. 124); "In Pin Hsien, nice people suffer indignities, while an evil person enjoys dignity" (p. 130); "The line between the legal and the illegal is rather vague" (p. 128). Liu's artistic consciousness is apparent in his application of metaphors in ironic expressions.

Liu's characterization certainly cannot compare with that of contemporary Taiwan writers, such as Pai Hsien-yung and Chang Ai-ling, who are concerned (perhaps too much) with literary technique. Nevertheless, Liu's straightforward technique (or style) is quite impressive in its own way. Though he may overlook some details, his unique style seems to fit his themes quite well, which are more socially oriented than style oriented. His characterization is simple yet persuasive. He depicts Wang as follows: "Her hair is short, just covering her ears, and it is shining black. Though she puts less powder on her face now than before liberation, with her fair complexion she looks beaming and good-looking, not like a woman of forty-five." "No matter how high the officials are, she is relaxed and easy with them at the first meeting. She has a charm which is rare in a woman of fifty."

Other characters besides the protagonist are not so carefully depicted. One disadvantage of such scant characterization is that if the same character appears later in the work, one can recall little about him or her.[43] Liu's characterization is different from that traditionally practiced in novels, perhaps because an author of reportage has less control over plot and characters, and therefore would hardly presume to depict in detail real characters with whom he is not familiar. Characters are more often described in a terse abbreviated sketch that provokes the reader to use his imagination.

The structure of this work could have been tighter if the author had had more time to polish it. For example, the author mentions another corrupt official who, however, is not involved in the case he is talking about (p. 134).[44] The author may be rather overambitious in that he attempts to include all the information he has, with the result that the continuity of certain events is interrupted. Leo Ou-fan Lee, a professor of contemporary literature at the University of Chicago, maintains that the author is concerned with the combination of materials and has neglected the harmony of the plot. This comment may be true, since in reportage that author has little control over the materials, and too much or too little material can certainly affect the plot of a work. For reportage whose subject is real events, the author may ignore material not relevant to the plot, yet he can hardly make up events to supplement it.

## Literary Technique of "Another Kind of Allegiance"

One major point is emphasized in the work "Another Kind of Allegiance"— the need to admonish one's superiors candidly for the sake of improving society. The personal experiences of two independent individuals form two story lines, linked together into one coherent plot. Unity is then achieved through a similar theme and similar organizing procedure, in this case, a description first of their disappointment with socialism, then their admonition, and finally the results.

The characters are depicted quite simply, as is the plot. The language employed in this work is not as vivid as that of "People or Monsters," which has a complicated plot and characters. Nonetheless, the language used here is the characteristic of the author—candid, forthright, and penetrating in a way that surpasses most other contemporary works.

The characters are less lively than those of "People or Monsters." However, this difference has more to do with the characters themselves than with the author's power to characterize. An evil person, such as Wang in "People or Monsters," seems to take more delineation and therefore appears more lively and persuasive than a positive character like Ni Yü-hsien in "Another Kind of Allegiance," who seems rather weak. When the attributes of reporting are emphasized over those of literary technique in a reportage, the work usually appears less lively than a reportage in which literary technique is also stressed—less lively, but more factual.

Because it has two protagonists, the structure of this work is certainly less tight than that of "People or Monsters," which has only one main protagonist. To avoid the appearance of two unrelated events occurring in one work, the author has intersected the descriptions of the development of the two events. Therefore, confusion occurs when the author starts to write about the second protagonist, interrupting his description of the first. When this kind of interruption has occurred several times, readers may tend to lose track of the story.

## Conclusion

To conclude this chapter I would like to discuss briefly the possible reason why Liu Pin-yen was not persecuted severely after he had written "reactionary" works such as "People or Monsters" and "Another Kind of Allegiance," and what conclusions can be reached about the prospects for literature in mainland China viewed from the treatment he received.

Though Liu's reportages do not have optimistic endings like most of the other literary works written in mainland China, careful readers may find that he is, all the same, eager to exonerate the central authorities. Often he holds local officials responsible for mistakes, instead of blaming the central government. Though literary policies play an important role in the fate of both works and authors, there are other factors that can be decisive as well. In Liu's case, there are a few possible reasons why he has not been jailed.

First, because of the Communists' desire to have the appearance of granting literary freedom, they perhaps have allowed Liu, so influential both in mainland China and overseas, to write without undue interference.

Second, because of Liu's influence, the Communists want to avoid being criticized further for persecuting him.

Third, Liu is especially favored by the young; therefore, the Communists either hope to reach young people through him, or they may be afraid of provoking them to start another protest movement.

Fourth, in Liu's works, one often finds that he tends to blame the executors of policies for the destruction caused instead of the high officials. For example, Liu writes: "There were occasions when subordinates made decisions recklessly. They have twisted the opinion of the Party Central" ("Another Kind of Allegiance," p. 110); "The Food Bureau had decided to supply the people with sufficient food, yet the officials of the city, the district, and the community did not execute their orders properly";[45] "The party organization had acted without following the orders of the central government."[46]

Even in interviews with the press, Liu has stressed that the central government is correct.[47] And in his most recent interview, he contended that the pressure put on him for his exploration of the evils of society did not come from the Party Central.[48]

Fifth, Liu also attempts to blame society in general rather than certain high officials. In "People or Monsters" he blames society, not socialism, for corruption (p. 191). This view of his is apparent not only in his work, but also in his public statements. In one interview he asserted that society and history should take the blame for various problems.[49] If one reads Liu's reportages carefully, one will realize that while he forthrightly exposes the evils of society, he never forgets to absolve the Communists. This may also be one reason why his works are still published. Early critics also commented on his loyalty to the party, and thus felt disappointed that he seems to have failed to recognize the truth of communism. Nevertheless, even that was "seditious" enough, because he suffered for more than twenty years for "The Inside Story." If he had pointed a finger at the central authorities, I am afraid "The Inside Story" would have been his last work.

Sixth, Liu repeatedly declares that he is loyal to the party as well as to the nation. As a matter of fact, he has always been considered a faithful party member. This might be another reason why he has not been persecuted severely in recent years.

These three works were all written during periods when controls were relaxed. The last two works discussed here are far more "reactionary" than the first one, yet, although Liu was exiled to the countryside for almost twenty years for the first, he escaped any serious punishment for the latter two. Therefore, we can conclude that, for various reasons, in recent years the conditions for the literati in mainland China have improved. As for the future prospects for literature in Communist China, one can sense from the government clampdown after the publication of Liu's works that pressure from the leftists will still cramp literary creativity. However, the party may vacillate because of internal dissension.[50] The power of the leftists should not be underestimated, although Liu himself declared that the wealth of material for writers in Communist China assured a very bright future there for literature. Nonetheless, it seems that what Liu said was incomplete, because the problem is not the amount of material, but whether writers will be permitted to write and publish the works and whether the public will be allowed to read them.[51]

## Notes

For the page numbers that follow the quotations in the text, please refer to the following sources: for "The Inside Story"—*Liu Pin-yen pao-kao wen-hsüeh hsüan*

(Selections of Lui Pin-yen's Reportage Literature) (Beijing: Beijing Press, 1981); for "People or Monsters"—*Chung-kuo hsin hsieh-shih-chu-i wen-i tso-p'in hsüan* (Selections of China's Neorealist Literature) (Hong Kong: The Seventies Press, 1980); and for "Another Kind of Allegiance"—*Chiu-shih nien-tai,* no. 189 (October 1985).

1. See Howard L. Boorman, *Literature and Politics in Contemporary China* (New York: St. John's University Press, 1960), 102.

2. See Helen Siu's review of *Stubborn Weeds,* edited by Perry Link, *Journal of Asian Studies* 44 (February 1985):377–378.

3. See the introduction to *Collections of Reportage Literature* (Changsha: Hunan People's Press, 1984), 1–7.

4. Writers such as Ting Ling, Ho Ch'i-fang, Ouyang Shan, Chou Li-po, and Mao Tun have written reportage literature.

5. They have written works such as "Twenty-five Thousand Miles," "Yenan in May," and "How I Came to Northern Shensi."

6. See Shih Li-min, "An Introduction to Liu Pin-yen," *Nan-pei-chi,* no. 151 (December 1982):80–81.

7. *Wen Wei Po* (Hong Kong), October 7, 1982.

8. See Tony Saich, *China: Politics and Government* (New York: St. Martin's Press, 1981), 176.

9. See note 7.

10. "Full text of Liu Pin-yen's Talk in Heilungkiang," *Kuang chiao ching,* no. 90 (March 1980):10–23.

11. *Ming Pao,* January 13, 1983.

12. Barbara Spielmann, "A New Trend in the Literature of the PRC Which Moves Readers in the West," paper presented at the Second Sino-European Conference at Oxford, England, in August 1985.

13. In May 1951, Mao personally initiated criticism of the movie *The Biography of Wu Hsün.* Wu Hsün is well known for having saved money he had begged to construct a school for the poor. Mao nonetheless considered Wu Hsün a reactionary because in Mao's view Wu had advocated feudal culture.

14. For details of the event, see Wang Chang-ling, *Chung-kung te wen-i cheng-feng* (The Rectification of Literature and Art in Mainland China) (Taipei: Institute of International Relations, 1967), 99–118.

15. Saich, *China,* 219.

16. See also Perry Link, *Roses and Thorns* (Los Angeles: University of California Press, 1984), 11.

17. See Li I, "Liu Pin-yen and His Time," *Ch'i-shih nien-tai,* no. 155 (December 1982):64–76.

18. See Yen Hua, "An Author Who Asks for Clemency for the People: The Search and Quest of Liu Pin-yen," *Chung Pao,* no. 30 (July 1982):59–63.

19. See note 6.

20. See Helen Siu and Zelda Stern, eds., *Mao's Harvest* (New York: Oxford University Press, 1983), iii.

21. See Howard Goldblatt, ed., *Chinese Literature for the 1980s* (New York: M. E. Sharpe, 1982), 23.

22. *Ming Pao,* May 25, 1980.

23. See Wen Hsieh, "The Writing of 'People or Monsters' by Liu Pin-yen," *Tung-hsiang,* no. 19 (April 1980):25–26.

24. *Chung Pao,* August 31, 1982.

25. Hsia Yen, "An Interview with Liu Pin-yen, the Author of 'People or Monsters,'" *Ching Pao,* no. 32 (March 1980).

26. See Hsia Pen-ch'ing, "Liu Pin-yen, One Proscribed by the Communist Party's 'Number Seven Document,'" *Ta-lu kuan-ch'a* 9, no. 9 (September 1981):42–45.

27. *Ta Kung Pao* (Hong Kong), May 2, 1983.

28. Li I, "Truth and Allegiance—Reading Liu Pin-yen's 'Another Kind of Allegiance,'" *Chiu-shih nien-tai*, no. 189 (October 1985):92–94.

29. Leo Ou-fan Lee, "Chinese Literature for the 1980s: Prospects and Problems," in *China: The '80s Era*, ed. Norton Ginsburg and Bernard Lalor (Boulder, Colo.: Westview Press, 1984), 285; and Jeffrey Kinkley, "Current Problems and Prospects for Chinese Literaure in Mainland China," *Issues & Studies* 22, no. 1 (January 1986): 113.

30. Kinkley, "Current Problems," 117–118.

31. Wang I-ling, "Liu Pin-yen Is Limited by the 'Internal Document,'" *Cheng-ming*, no. 99 (January 1986):60–61.

32. Hsin Miao, "Does Liu Pin-yen Really Feel Hopeless?" *Ching Pao*, no. 99 (October 1985):8–11.

33. See note 31.

34. Chiang Ching-k'uan, "The Inspiration of 'Another Kind of Allegiance,'" *Chiu-shih nien-tai*, no. 194 (March 1986):98–99.

35. Saich, *China*, 221.

36. Though the CCP is the largest Communist Party in the world with a membership of 38 million (1980), it is one of the most exclusive, as less than 3 percent of the population are members. Ibid., 112.

37. Ibid., 219. The recruitment policy has changed over time in accordance with the general line of the party. In general, any Chinese worker, peasant, soldier, or any other revolutionary over eighteen may become a member of the party. However, before applicants can join they must be recommended by two party members, be accepted by the next higher committee, and undergo a one-year probationary period. People who offend a member of the committee will often find it difficult to get approval from that committee, while approval is easier for people who keep on good terms with committee members to obtain. The protagonist in "The Inside Story" belongs to the first category, although the protagonist in Liu's second story is a representative of the second.

38. See Steven Mosher, *Broken Earth*, Chinese edition (Taichung: Taipao Press, 1983), 69–92, for a detailed description of bribery. He comments that in mainland China one has to bribe even for trivial things like theater tickets as well as for more important things like constructing houses.

39. A thorny evergreen tree with small leaves and fine and sturdy wood. Its scientific name is *Myroxylon racemosum*.

40. Most of the high officials Ch'en mentions here were castigated later, such as Liu, Teng, Chu, and Lin.

41. Lei, a native of Hunan, was born in 1940. During his youth, he was praised as a model for the young. In 1959 he joined the army and was again celebrated as a model soldier. He died in a car accident in 1962 at the age of 22. In the spring of 1963, a movement for "learning from comrade Le Feng" was started by the People's Liberation Army.

42. Therefore, I certainly do not agree with Li I, a critic of contemporary Chinese literature, who proclaims that Liu's later works are not as good as "The Inside Story."

43. Leo Ou-fan Lee maintains that the author does not depict clearly the history of his characters, yet Lee defends Liu by questioning whether the history of the characters can be thoroughly depicted in such a complicated society.

44. Leo Ou-fan Lee also mentions it.

45. Consult pp. 116, 138, and 141 for similar expressions.

46. *Chiu-shih nien-tai,* no. 189 (October 1985):108.

47. Ibid.

48. See note 34.

49. *Wen Wei Po,* October 8, 1982.

50. Some people believe that Teng intended to relax control over the literati, but the conservatives in the party's Central Committee pressured him to tighten up control because of the repercussions created by certain literary works. The critic Helen Siu, for instance, holds this opinion. See Siu and Stern, *Mao's Harvest,* xliv.

51. Liu has recently been retired from his position as a journalist for the *People's Daily.*

# 39

## Communist China's Educational Reforms: An Analysis

*Wang Hsueh-wen*

Since the Communists founded the People's Republic of China (PRC) on October 1, 1949, they have conducted an unceasing series of overall educational reforms. As the reforms have always been linked to class and line struggles, a comprehensive and applicable educational system has not yet been established. Originally, the Communists seemed to attach considerable importance to education. Nevertheless, under the influence of Mao Tse-tung's theory that "the philosophy of the Communist Party is the philosophy of struggle,"[1] they do not regard a school as a place simply for transmitting knowledge, but as a battlefield of class struggle.[2] They even consider, as they asserted in 1973, that "it is difficult to distinguish between the right and wrong line and between the right and wrong views in the educational sphere in which class and line struggles are very complicated."[3] Because of this, the evolution of educational reforms in mainland China is, indeed, the history of line struggles in education. During the seventeen years before the cataclysmic Great Proletarian Cultural Revolution (1966–1976), Mao's "socialist educational line" constantly collided with Liu Shao-ch'i's "revisionist educational line." During the decade-long upheaval a large-scale educational reform deprived all students of normal schooling. The situation deteriorated to such an extent that in some places, schools had no systems, teaching was not planned, teachers had no lesson plans, and students had no textbooks. After the Cultural Revolution, the Communists proposed the Four Modernizations policy with science and technology as the key and education as the basis. To realize the program, they initiated another large-scale educational reform. Their current educational reform policy was then gradually formed.

At the National Conference on Educational Work convened by Peking's Ministry of Education in January 1980, the Communists listed eight important educational tasks as follows: (1) to strengthen politico-ideological work in all kinds of schools; (2) to continue universalizing primary education; (3) to reform the structure of secondary education; (4) to operate key middle and primary schools and key secondary technical schools properly; (5) to develop higher education; (6) to promote vigorously international scientific and cultural exchanges; (7) to strengthen the educational work in border and minority regions; and (8) to develop spare-time education for adults.[4] At the National Forum on Educational Work held in December 1980, the Communists asserted that because of the many problems left over by the decade-long Cultural Revolution, educational work remained in the rehabilitation stage, and that the main tasks in this sphere were "readjusting, restructuring, consolidating and improving." They emphasized that the party's work, the work of the Communist Youth League, and the teaching of political lessons in all kinds of schools should be strengthened, and that to realize this aim, the ranks of politico-ideological workers should be consolidated, and their role in school education should be fully affirmed.[5] In short, these two conferences on education gave top priority to the politico-ideological work, though they stressed universalizing primary education and improving the level of education at the same time.

In an interview with *Ta Kung Pao* journalists from Hong Kong on April 3, 1983, Ho Tung-ch'ang, the Chinese Communist minister of education, explained Peking's readjustment and restructuring policy for education:

> Universalization of primary education will be basically realized before 1990. Secondary education will be restructured so that in 1990 half or more than half of all secondary schools will be technical, professional, or vocational schools. As to higher education, leadership groups will be readjusted on the basis of rejuvenation and professionalization, and institutions of higher learning will be given more decision-making power to improve the quantity and quality of higher education, to raise the level of scientific research, and to increase efficiency.[6]

Obviously, the Communists hope to train more capable people to meet the needs of the modernization drive by reforming education at all levels, especially higher education.

At the National Conference on Educational Work jointly held by the Central Committee of the Chinese Communist Party (CCP) and the State Council in May 1985, which was hailed by the Chinese Communists as a "magnificent meeting unprecedented in China's educational history,"[7] a "Decision on Reform of the Educational System" was submitted for discussion. This decision, the third programmatic document on reform of systems issued by the CCP's Central Committee,[8] indicated that the Communists were trying to solve some serious problems in the educational sphere because they realized the serious consequences caused by the contempt for knowledge in previous educational reforms.

The conferences on educational work and Ho Tung-ch'ang's explanation of Peking's educational policy envisaged the prospects of education in the PRC. Nevertheless, the implementation of the new reform policy in recent years encountered many obstacles. The Communists have so far made little progress toward their aims.

## Ideas About the Educational Reform

The Chinese Communists have come up with some new ideas about their educational reform plan, which are discussed in the following sections.

### Objectives

In September 1983, Teng Hsiao-p'ing urged that "education should be oriented to modernization, the world, and the future." He did so in an inscription for the Chingshan School in Peking.[9] To realize this objective, the Communists instituted some new systems to universalize primary education, restructure secondary education, and readjust higher education. In a speech at the opening on May 15, 1985, of the National Conference on Educational Work, Hu Ch'i-li asserted:

> Economic construction, social development, and scientific and technological progress all depend on talented personnel, and the key to solving the problem lies in education. Doing a good job in reforming the educational structure to allow educational undertakings to develop vigorously on the basis of the needs of the Four Modernizations is truly an urgent and fundamental strategic task. In order to respect knowledge and talented personnel, it is first of all necessary to respect education.[10]

The Decision on Reform of the Educational System issued on May 27, 1985, by the CCP's Central Committee said that the fundamental goal of the ongoing educational reform was to "improve the quality of the whole people and train a large number of capable people." To strengthen leadership for the educational reform, a State Education Commission was established. Judging from the foregoing, the current educational reform in mainland China is aimed at training capable people for the promotion of the Four Modernizations.

### The Strategy for Educational Development

The Technical Economic Research Center under the State Council (renamed the Economic, Technical, and Social Development Research Center), together with the State Planning Commission, the State Economic Commission, the State Scientific and Technological Commission, and the Academy of Social Sciences of China, organized in 1983 more than 400 experts from more than 100 units to conduct research on "China in the year 2000." Two years later, in November 1985, they produced twelve specific reports (on population and employment, economy, consumption of the people, science and technology, education, natural resources, energy, environment, agriculture, transport and communications, the international situation, and a comprehensive quantitative analysis of mainland China in the year 2000) and a general report, and on the basis of these reports, proposed a "General Strategy for Advancing Toward the Year 2000."[11] Their efforts were aimed at (1) exploring a "socialist road with Chinese characteristics" and (2) striving for gigantic achievements in the fifteen years before 2000.

The foregoing "General Strategy" advocated orienting educational development toward the Four Modernizations, the world and the future. It asserted:

> The world economic competition is in reality a competition in the quality of various peoples. Faced with future stern challenges, we must first do a good job in promoting basic education, including primary and secondary education. We must reform traditional views on education, renew teaching contents, and introduce new educational methods so as to train sufficient specialists in accordance with the needs of economic and social development. To have capable people who are creative, specialized in one field but with knowledge in other fields, and determined to carry out reforms, we must enlarge the scope of knowledge for all students and develop their exploration and creative ability. At the same time, we must pay special attention to establishing a lifetime educational system for the whole people.

A research paper entitled "China's Education in the Year 2000"[12] published in November 1985 explained the key points of the strategy for reforming the educational system in the PRC as follows: (1) The "strategic key points" of education should lie in primary and secondary education; hence, it is necessary to carry out the nine-year compulsory education program in a systematic and down-to-earth manner. (2) Strenuous efforts should be made to develop various forms of vocational and technical education, prejob or on-the-job, regular or irregular (short-term training classes), and divorced from or linked with production (courses for personnel released from production or on production duties). (3) Prejob higher education should be run mainly at full-time educational institutions, and on-the-job higher education should mostly be conducted in evening colleges and universities, as well as in colleges and universities that give lessons through correspondence, broadcasting, and television.

In fact, the Chinese Communists have to improve their educational work quickly to meet the requirements of their Four Modernizations program.

## The Future Prospects of Education

Some scholars and specialists have in recent years conducted research on mainland China's potential educational development in the year 2000. Here are some of their expectations and suggestions:

1. Primary education will be basically universalized in the 1980s. From 1990 to 2000, junior high school education should be basically universalized throughout the mainland; senior high school education should be universalized in big cities; about 10 percent of all college graduates should receive postgraduate education; and efforts to train healthy and able specialists who are both red and expert will continue.[13]

2. Mainland China's educational development will have the following characteristics: (a) the extension of one's educational period to a lifetime; (b) the change of the role of education from passing on knowledge to developing the ability of students to acquire it; (c) the transformation of education from a "close, unidirectional, and inactive" type to an "open, multidirectional, and active" type; (d) the substitution of the system of individual education for the system of collective education; and (e) the tendency to provide basic education to all people.[14]

3. Mainland China's education will evolve toward lifetime education and the socialization of education; hence it is necessary to build up a clear-cut lifetime educational system, such as a system for employees to pursue further study while receiving their normal pay. At the same time, efforts should be made to encourage the establishment of privately run short-term universities and universities for training staffers and workers. Educational institutions should be encouraged to set up various kinds of social service centers.[15]

4. It will be appropriate as a first step to operate four universities, in the American, Soviet, Japanese, and West German styles, respectively, and then operate a "comprehensive university in the Chinese style" on the basis of the experience gained from running the four different universities. Expansion of existing key universities has been proposed as a way to achieve this aim. For instance, the Harbin Industrial University, where courses have been taught in Russian since 1949, may be expanded into a comprehensive university oriented toward the Soviet Union. The Dairen Engineering Institute, Tsinghua University, and Tungchi University may be expanded into comprehensive universities oriented toward Japan, the United States, and West Germany, respectively. Peking University, the China Science and Technology University, and the China People's University may serve as the basis for the establishment of a comprehensive university that will combine the strong points of both the East and West to become an "institution of higher learning and a research center of Chinese schools of thoughts."[16] However, since the levels of mainland China's key universities lag far behind the first-rate universities in the United States, Japan, the Soviet Union, and West Germany, the establishment of these universities remains only an idea.

Judging from the foregoing suggestions, the Chinese Communists may possibly introduce another large-scale educational reform. However, in 1985 they frankly admitted the following: "Our target of economic development for the year 2000 is to increase the per capita national income to US$1,000 per year, approximately corresponding to the level of Japan and the Soviet Union in the 1950s. Our target of technological development in 2000 is to reach the level of industrialized countries in the late 1970s. Our intellectual development in 2000, therefore, should at least catch up with the level of Japan and the Soviet Union in the 1960s."[17] In other words, even if the Communists carry out their reforms successfully, their educational level in the year 2000 will still lag behind that of Japan and the Soviet Union by more than thirty or fifty years, because the educational level of other countries will continue to improve year after year.

## The Present Reform Policy

The Decision on Reform of the Educational System (hereafter referred to as the Decision) issued by the CCP's Central Committee on May 28, 1985, contains the following main guidelines for the present educational reform on the mainland.

### Training Qualified People

Qualified people should be trained at all levels and in all spheres. The Decision asserts that the fundamental purpose of reform of the educational system is to improve the quality of the nation and to produce more capable people, that able people hold the important key to the success of socialist modernization, and that to solve the problem of able people, education must be significantly developed on the basis of economic development. At the National Conference on Educational Work, Vice-Premier Wan Li stated: "The current practice of scrambling for available capable personnel, including school teachers at various levels, is tantamount to killing the hen to get the eggs. Instead of solving problems, it will aggravate the problems and make them more difficult to solve. If we really value capable personnel and want to have better educated people, we must promote education. The extreme importance of capable personnel determines the strategic role of education in the Four Modernizations."[18] However, because mainland China does not have enough qualified teachers to shoulder the task of promoting education, and because some Communist policies on the educational reform have not yet been thoroughly implemented, the objective of training various kinds of qualified people will be difficult to attain.

### Implementing Nine-Year Compulsory Education

Various localities are to be entrusted with the responsibility of developing basic education and implementing nine-year compulsory education in a systematic way. Because of the vast size of the mainland and the uneven economic and cultural development, the requirements of compulsory education should also be diverse in accordance with local conditions. The whole PRC is to be divided into three categories:

The first includes cities, economically developed areas in coastal provinces, and a small number of developed areas in the hinterland, accounting for about a quarter of the total population of the mainland. In these places, the popularization of junior high school education should be completed by about 1990.

The second category includes towns and villages with a medium level of development, accounting for about half the total population of the mainland.

In these places, the popularization of junior high school education should be completed by about 1995.

The third category includes economically backward areas, accounting for about a quarter of the total population of the mainland. In these areas, various forms will be adopted to popularize basic education at various levels, according to the levels of their economic development. No time limit has been set for completion of this plan.

Judging from the foregoing plans, basic education cannot be quickly popularized in most places in the mainland. Besides, there are two types of school system on the mainland: the "five-five" system that provides five years of primary education and five years of secondary education, and the "six-six" system that provides six years of primary education and six years of secondary education. Therefore, nine-year compulsory education can only be implemented in the limited number of "key schools practicing the six-six system." According to the third national census conducted in 1982 in the mainland, of all the people more than twelve years old, illiterates and semiliterates totaled 235,820,000, accounting for 23.5 percent of the total population. If compulsory education is not quickly popularized, the number of illiterates and semiliterates will continue to increase, leading to a further lowering of the cultural standards of the mainland.

## Developing Vocational and Technical Education

The Communists intend to readjust secondary education and energetically develop vocational and technical education, stressing the establishment of a system of vocational and technical education, ranging from primary to senior levels, with proper coordination with the related occupations, reasonable in structure, and capable of linking up with ordinary education. They are to follow the principle of "offering jobs after training has been completed," which specifies that when recruiting workers in the future, all units should first select the best from among graduates of vocational and technical schools. In fact, vocational and technical education have not received enough attention on the mainland because most cadres attach more importance to running ordinary high schools well and to increasing the rate of entrance to institutions of higher education. Supplementary schools for graduates of senior high schools are run to prepare them for entrance examinations to universities, but vocational and technical education are neglected. The Decision, as well as Wan Li's speech at the National Conference on Educational Work, frankly asserted that vocational and technical education are precisely the weakest link in mainland China's education as a whole. This weakness has seriously hindered improvement of the quality of workers and the quality and quantity of products in the PRC.

## Expanding the Decision-Making Power in Management of Institutions of Higher Learning

The Communists plan to reform the enrollment plan and graduate-assignment system of institutions of higher learning and expand their decision-making power in management. The plan calls for adoption of three practices: (1) enrollment according to the state plan, (2) enrollment at the request of employers, and (3) enrollment of a small number of self-supported students in addition to the students enrolled under the state plan. All students must pass entrance examinations administered by the state before they are enrolled by the schools. The institutions of higher learning are allowed the following powers: the power to readjust the objectives of various disciplines, formulate teaching plans and programs, and compile and select teaching materials; the power to accept projects from, or cooperate with, other social establishments for scientific and technological development, as well as establishing combines involving teaching, scientific research, and production; the power to suggest appointments and removals of vice-presidents and other staffers and professors; the power to dispose of capital construction investment and funds allocated by the state; and the power to develop international educational and academic exchanges by utilizing their funds.

In recent years, mainland China's higher education has developed rapidly in quantity, but not in quality. According to the "Circular on Relevant Questions Concerning the Establishment of New Ordinary Institutions of Higher Learning" issued by the State Education Commission in December 1985, the number of ordinary institutions of higher learning increased very quickly, from 598 in 1978 to 1,016 in 1985. Some of these new institutions provide only very poor conditions of education. Some are too small in scale. The courses they offer largely overlap. They are unable to produce much return on investment or social benefit. Therefore, the circular described the consolidation of existing colleges and universities as an urgent task and contended that the increase of institutions of higher learning should be kept under control. Consequently, in the next two or three years, no new institutions of higher learning will be established.[19] There are still many obstacles to the reform of higher education. The reform policy will be difficult to carry out.

## Strengthening Leadership for the Reform of the Educational System

The Decision urged the establishment of a State Education Commission, steps to arouse the enthusiasm of teachers, and the institution of a system under which school principals assume full administrative responsibility. At present, the Ministry of Education has been abolished and the newly established State Education Commission has become a unit of the State Council in charge of educational work and the reform of the educational system. The school principles, however, do not exercise true leadership in schools. For instance, Ch'ien Wei-ch'ang, president of the Shanghai Industrial University, compared a school to a police substation and the school principal to a director of a police substation. He asserted: "A school principal has to report everything to the leadership cadres responsible for school administration and wait for instructions."[20] In short, a system under which school principals enjoy full administrative responsibility will be difficult to implement in the near future.

## Current Situation in the Educational Sphere

In the research paper "China's Education in the Year 2000," the Chinese Communists frankly admitted that the current situation in the educational sphere could not meet the needs of the Four Modernizations. In fact, in promoting educational work, they have encountered the following difficulties:

1. Primary and middle schools have been established in cities and villages on the mainland, but there are serious shortages of qualified techers and teaching facilities; hence, the educational level remains low.
2. Vocational and technical education and secondary professional education have developed slowly, and the system of prejob training for technical personnel has not yet been initiated. The quality of staffers and workers is, therefore, relatively low.
3. Higher education has developed very quickly, but the structure is imbalanced. New institutions of higher learning are often too small in size, inefficient in performance, and irregular in quality.
4. Educational funds grow too slowly to match quick educational development.[21]

In fact, the Chinese Communists urgently need solutions to the following problems:

### Common Negligence of the Importance of Education

Cadres in the PRC do not understand the extreme importance of education. Their order of priority is (1) industry, (2) finance and trade, and (3) culture and education. Sometimes, they even forget culture and education altogether.[22] At the National Conference on Educational Work, Wan Li asserted: "Holding education in contempt is still a rather common fact. Some cadres are still totally unaware of the extreme importance of education; they think it is inessential and that they can get by without it. Some comrades are very much concerned over industrial growth and highly interested in construction of office buildings, but they pay little attention to education. Some have even used the school campuses for other purposes, dismissed good teachers, and diverted educational funds to other uses."[23] Obviously, this concept is an obstacle to educational reform.

### The Lack of Education Funds

Educational funds that are already scarce in the mainland are often deliberately reduced and appropriated for other purposes. For instance, in 1975, the per capita educational fund was US$471.40 in the United States, US$247.70 in Japan, US$18 in Egypt, and US$3.90 in India, but only US$2.70 in mainland China.[24] At present, half the schools on the mainland have no funds to pay for expenses other than the wages of the teachers. Many schools have nothing except teachers, students, and a few textbooks.[25] They depend on collecting fees to support themselves. They thus create various kinds of pretexts such as tuition fees, miscellaneous charges, and school fines. Some of them appeal to overseas Chinese for contributions. Some even solicit foreign investment. However, as some people have asserted, if the operation of universities only loses money and never produces any profit, overseas Chinese and foreign friends will find it difficult to invest more in higher education in the mainland.[26] The per capita educational fund in the mainland is the third lowest in the world. Now, the emergence of strange methods designed to collect fees will increase the resistance to popularization of education.

## Low Quality of Teachers

The Decision asserted that to reform the educational system, it is necessary to rely on teachers, and the most important thing is to arouse their enthusiasm. At the National Conference on Educational Work, Wan Li described the shortage of qualified teachers, especially in schools in rural areas, as a big problem in promoting education. He urged that those qualified teachers who have been transferred elsewhere should be transferred back and that efforts should be made to transfer back at least a number of backbone teachers. In 1982 only about one-third of all primary and higher school teachers were graduates of universities, colleges, and secondary normal schools. Many high school graduates were teaching in high schools, and many primary school graduates were teaching in primary schools. Four years later the situation had not changed for the better. It is, therefore, difficult for such unqualified teachers to train a large number of capable people.[27] As to professors and lecturers in institutions of higher learning, they are unenthusiastic about teaching, and many of them hope to leave for other occupations. For instance, in 1973 many professors and lecturers in the Chekiang University of Medical Science filed requests for transfer elsewhere. It was estimated that if the university allowed professors to leave at their will, more than 100 middle-aged intellectuals would request transfer because they are dissatisfied with the shortage of chairs, chalk, and drinking water in classrooms, and especially with the bad living conditions. These intellectuals lived in laboratories, offices, warehouses, and student dormitories, and some administrative cadres were accommodated in two apartments.[28] Professors and lecturers in other institutions of higher learning faced similar problems. Many of them could not teach or were unwilling to. This situation will surely affect the promotion of the educational reform and the Four Modernizations in the PRC.

## Inadequate Teaching Material and Methods

In the fall of 1980, primary and high schools in mainland China began to use the "General Teaching Material for Full-Time Ten-Year-System Primary and High Schools Throughout the Country." The use of this teaching material in recent years has given rise to two contradictory problems: The ordinary schools practicing the five-five system feel that the material is too difficult and overburdened, and the key schools practicing the six-six system consider that it contains insufficient content. As to the more than 1,000 kinds of teaching material that institutions of higher learning began to use in the spring of 1984, most were reprints of the material used before the Cultural Revolution. Ch'ien Wei-ch'ang, president of the Shanghai Industrial University, therefore commented that knowledge was outmoded in mainland China. In addition, schools at various levels, especially primary schools, tend to pay more attention to higher classes than to lower classes, to top students than to bad students, to difficult problems than to basic lessons. As to the politico-ideological lessons that the Chinese Communists regard as the most important, the teaching methods are inappropriate. The two old methods—that is, to take class struggle as the key link and to teach the politico-ideological lessons of the current decade with the methods used in the 1950s—have proved ineffective, but applicable new methods have not yet been found.[29] Accordingly, most students on the mainland are dissatisfied with politico-ideological education, especially lessons about "firm adherence to the Four Cardinal Principles (the socialist road, the dictatorship of the proletariat, the leadership of the Communist Party, and Marxism-Leninism and Mao Tse-tung thought)." Some college students have even complained that "those professors who teach party history tell lies, those who teach political economy exaggerate, those who teach philosophy talk emptily, and those who teach scientific socialism talk nonsense." Their criticism was not only a mockery of teachers but also a complaint against the propagandistic education on the mainland.[30] In fact, in the PRC, books on politics, especially textbooks, are still in the Soviet style. Such political teaching, divorced from reality, is certainly unacceptable to college students in mainland China.

## Conclusion

Since 1949 there have been three big changes in the educational sphere in the PRC. The first big change took place in 1958 when the Three Red Banner Policy (the General Line for Socialist Construction, the Great Leap Forward, and the People's Communes) was implemented. At that time, the whole party and the whole people participated in a movement to run schools, and part-work (farming) and part-study schools were established on a trial basis. In 1961, Lu Ting-i, head of the CCP Central Committee's Propaganda Department, asserted that this educational reform had caused "disorder, damage, and deviation." The second big educational reform began in 1966 when the Great Proletarian Cultural Revolution was launched. Educational work was nearly completely interrupted. At the National Forum on Educational Work on December 13, 1980, Chiang Nan-hsiang, minister of education, declared that educational work had suffered a disastrous decline in both quantity and quality during the Cultural Revolution. The third educational reform was decided at the National Conference on Educational Work in January 1980. Since then, measures have been adopted to universalize primary education, restructure secondary education, and develop higher education so as to train enough capable personnel needed for the Four Modernizations program. Obviously, the first two educational reforms were destructive, but the third one, the current one, is constructive.

However, the current constructive educational policy has not been implemented in a down-to-earth manner. There is still a potential educational crisis. For instance, in a speech before the National Conference on Educational Work on December 13, 1980, Chiang Nan-hsiang, former minister of education, admitted that the aftermath of the Cultural Revolution had not yet been remedied, and that if things continued in the same way, the educational work on the mainland would lag farther and farther behind the advanced world level, thus endangering the promotion of the Four Modernizations program.

In an article entitled "The Potential Crisis of China's Education" published in December 1985, Ho Po-ch'üan, a mainland intellectual, openly described the potential crisis in the educational sphere in the PRC. He made the following four points: (1) Judging by the statistic that the per capita educational fund on the mainland in 1982 was only 11.20 yuan, insufficient for buying even a desk, mainland China is one of the fourteen countries in the world whose per capita educational fund is less than US$5. (2) More than 3 million teachers, about one-third of all the teachers on the mainland, are unqualified, thereby causing a terribly vicious circle because unqualified teachers will produce unqualified students. (3) The current educational system cannot meet the changing needs of capable personnel, and the operation of vocational education for 20 million to 30 million people a year surely represents a significant challenge. (4) The biggest crisis comes from within the educational system because when society changes at a high speed, the difference between the newest knowledge, textbooks, and application in reality may be gradually enlarged. It is commonly speculated that mainland China will develop into a society emhasizing academic achievements and that the entrance examination to universities will inevitably become the orientation of senior high school education.[31]

On the other hand, mainland China's education work has constantly been influenced by politics. As admitted by the Chinese Communists themselves, education has been an appendage of politics. Whenever political movements are launched, they disrupt normal activities in schools, turning teachers and students into political instruments. As a result, priority is given to political requirements instead of to teaching and learning, and teachers and students spend most of their time in transforming their ideology. With "politics in command," it is extremely difficult for educational institutions to produce educated people who are really politically conscious and professionally competent.[32] Although the Communists are emphasizing the constructiveness of education because of the needs of the Four Modernizations, they continue to uphold the Four Cardinal Principles and strengthen politico-ideological education. The political significance of education has not yet been reduced.

In short, in carrying out the educational reform in the current decade, the Chinese Communists tend to adopt constructive concepts, policies, and measures, but the reform itself is still fundamentally linked to politics. Therefore, the contribution of educational reform to the Four Modernizations will be limited, and the Four Modernizations will be of very little help to educational reform. In fact, the quality of education remains low in the PRC, and very few qualified personnel have been trained. Such a backward situation in the educational sphere is a hindrance to promoting the Four Modernizations program.

## Notes

1. *Mao Tse-tung ssu-hsiang wan-sui* (Long Live Mao Tse-tung Thought) (1949–1968) (n.p., 1969; reprinted, Taipei: Institute of International Relations, 1974), 308.

2. The Revolutionary Committees of the Tsinghua and Peking Universities, "Consolidate and Develop the Educational Revolution in Universities," *Red Flag*, 1974, no. 1:54.

3. Chung Shih, "Carry on the Proletarian Educational Revolution to the End," *Red Flag*, 1973, no. 12:41.

4. *Ta Kung Pao* (Hong Kong), January 26, 1980.

5. New China News Agency (Peking), December 21, 1980.

6. Yeh Chung-min and Lü Te-jun, "Ho Tung-ch'ang on Prospects of China's Education," *Ta Kung Pao*, April 4, 1983.

7. *People's Daily*, May 29, 1985, 1, 3.

8. The first two documents were the Decision on Reform of the Economic Structure and the Decision on Reform of Scientific and Technological Systems.

9. *People's Daily*, September 11, 1983.

10. *People's Daily*, May 16, 1985, 1.

11. *People's Daily*, November 25, 1985, 5.

12. *Ching-chi jih-pao* (Economic Daily) (Peking), November 9, 1985, 3.

13. Chang Chien, "China's Education in the Year 2000," *Wei-lai yü fa-chan* (The Future and Development) (Beijing) (quarterly), 1984, no. 2:17.

14. Hu Chia-ching, "The Trend of Educational Development in the Future," *Wei-lai yü fa-chen*, 1985, no. 2:43.

15. Ku Hsin, "Two Tremendous Trends of Education in the Future and Our Countermeasures," *Wei-lai yü fa-chen*, 1985, no. 3:26–27.

16. T'ang Ch'iung, "Ideas About First-Rate Universities," *Ta Kung Pao*, November 17, 1985, 15; November 18, 1985, 19.

17. Shu Wen and Hu Jui-wen, "A Preliminary Probe into the Development of Our Educational Work and the Exploitation of Our Intellectual Resources," *Chiao-yü yen-chiu* (Educational Studies) (Peking), 1985, no. 5:15.

18. *People's Daily*, May 18, 1985, 1.

19. *Kwangming Daily*, December 3, 1985, 1.

20. *Kwangming Daily*, April 7, 1985, 1.

21. See note 12.

22. *People's Daily*, June 15, 1985, 1.

23. *People's Daily*, May 31, 1985, 1.

24. *Kwangming Daily*, June 15, 1980.

25. *Ta Kung Pao*, October 9, 1980.

26. Meng Ming-i, "Make Full Use of the Favorable Situation, Be Bold in Introducing Reforms to Accelerate the Development of Higher Education," *Wei-lai yü fa-chan*, 1985, no. 2:5.

27. *People's Daily*, March 16, 1982.

28. *People's Daily*, April 19, 1983.

29. *Jen-min chiao-yü* (People's Education) (Peking), 1981, no. 5:11.

30. Ma Chung-yang, "Political Readings Should Have Three Characteristics," *Tu-shu* (Bookwork) (Peking), 1980, no. 4:25.

31. *Wen Wei Po* (Hong Kong), January 8, 1986, 16.

32. Editorial, "The Fundamental Aims of China's Educational Reform," *Wen Wei Po*, May 30, 1985.

# About the Contributors

**P. Richard Bohr,** director of international trade for the state of Minnesota, is the author of *Famine in China and the Missionary* (1972) and *Religion in the People's Republic of China: The Limits of Toleration* (1982).

**David Wen-wei Chang** is a professor of political science at the University of Wisconsin, Oshkosh.

**Chu-yuan Cheng,** professor of economics at Ball State University, Indiana, is the author of more than twenty books and many articles on mainland China's economy. His most recent book is *China's Economic Development: Growth and Structural Change* (1982).

**Yu-sun Chou,** assistant research fellow at the Institute of International Relations, Taipei, is the author of several books on contemporary Chinese literature, including *A Renewed Inquiry into Literature and Art in Mainland China* (1984, in Chinese).

**Robert F. Dernberger,** professor of economics at the University of Michigan, is the author of *China Trade and U.S. Policy* (1971) and many articles on the economy of mainland China.

**John P. Hardt,** associate director for senior specialists of the Congressional Research Service, the Library of Congress, is also an adjunct professor of economics at both George Washington University and Georgetown University. He has authored and edited numerous books and articles on East-West commercial relations and the economies of Eastern Europe, the Soviet Union, and mainland China.

**Leo A. Orleans** is currently a consultant to the Committee on Scholarly Communications with mainland China, National Academy of Sciences, and the Congressional Research Service, Library of Congress.

**Jan S. Prybyla,** professor of economics at the Pennsylvania State University, is the author of many articles and books on mainland China's economy, including *Market and Plan Under Socialism: The Bird in the Cage* (1986).

**James Reardon-Anderson** is Sun Yat-sen research professor of Chinese Studies at Georgetown University, School of Foreign Service. He is the author of *Yenan and the Great Powers: The Origins of Chinese Communist Foreign Policy, 1944–1946* (1980).

**Edward K. Sah,** associate research fellow at the Institute of International Relations, Taipei, is the author of *An Introduction to Management Mathematics* (1982, in Chinese).

**Denis Fred Simon** is Ford international assistant professor of management and technology, Sloan School of Management, M.I.T. He is the author of many articles and books, including *Taiwan, Technology Transfer and Transnationalism: The Political Management of Dependency* (1987).

**Jenny Tu-li Teng,** formerly associate research fellow at the Institute of International Relations, Taipei, is now associated with the Institute of Asian Studies, St. John's University, New York.

**William T. Tow** is an assistant professor at the School of International Relations, University of Southern California. He is the author of numerous articles and books, including *U.S. Foreign Policy and Asian-Pacific Security: A Transregional Approach* (1982).

**Wen-hui Tsai** is a professor at Department of Sociology and Anthropology, Indiana University–Purdue University at Fort Wayne, Indiana. He is the author of many articles and books, including *Patterns of Political Elite Mobility in Modern China, 1912–1949* (1983).

**Hsueh-wen Wang,** research fellow at the Institute of International Relations, Taipei, is the author of many articles and books on mainland Chinese educational and cultural affairs, including *Chinese Communist Education: The Yenan Period* (1975).

**Lynn T. White III** teaches Chinese politics and development policy at Princeton University. He has headed the graduate and undergraduate programs at that university's Woodrow Wilson School, and he has published books and articles about Shanghai, the social bases of the Cultural Revoluion, and comparative modernization.

**Yuan-li Wu** is a consultant at Hoover Institution. He is the author of many books and articles on mainland China's economy.

**Teh-pei Yu** is a professor of economics at Soochow University and a research fellow at the Chung-Hua Institution for Economic Research, Taipei. She is the author of *The Economic Development in Mainland China and Its Influence on Taiwan* (1985).